KIERKEGAARD AND HIS DANISH CONTEMPORARIES

TOME I: PHILOSOPHY, POLITICS AND SOCIAL THEORY

Kierkegaard Research: Sources, Reception and Resources
Volume 7, Tome I

Kierkegaard Research: Sources, Reception and Resources
is a publication of the Søren Kierkegaard Research Centre

This volume was published with the generous financial support
of the Danish Agency for Science, Technology and Innovation

Kierkegaard and His Danish Contemporaries

Tome I: Philosophy, Politics and Social Theory

Edited by
JON STEWART

Published by

Ashgate Publishing Limited
Wey Court East
Union Road
Farnham
Surrey, GU9 7PT
England

Ashgate Publishing Company
Suite 420
101 Cherry Street
Burlington
VT 05401-4405
USA

www.ashgate.com

British Library Cataloguing in Publication Data

Kierkegaard and his Danish contemporaries.
Tome 1, Philosophy, politics and social theory. –
(Kierkegaard research : sources, reception and resources v. 7)
1. Kierkegaard, Søren, 1813–1855. 2. Kierkegaard, Søren, 1813 – 1855 – Friends and associates. 3. Philosophy, Danish – 19th century.
I. Series II. Stewart, Jon (Jon Bartley)
198.9-dc22

Library of Congress Cataloging-in-Publication Data

Kierkegaard and his Danish contemporaries / [edited by] Jon Stewart.
p. cm. — (Kierkegaard research: sources, reception, and resources ; v. 7)
Includes bibliographical references and indexes.
ISBN 978-0-7546-6872-5 (hardcover : t. 1 : alk. paper)
1. Kierkegaard, Søren, 1813–1855—Sources. 2. Denmark—Intellectual life—19th century. I. Stewart, Jon (Jon Bartley)
B4377 .K512
198'.9—dc22

2009014986

ISBN 9780754668725 (hbk)

Cover design by Katalin Nun.

Printed and bound in Great Britain by
TJ International Ltd, Padstow, Cornwall

Contents

List of Contributors

Julie K. Allen, University of Wisconsin-Madison, Dept. of Scandinavian Studies, Van Hise 1302, 1220 Linden Drive, Madison, WI 53706, USA.

Andrew J. Burgess, Philosophy Department, Humanities 533, MSC03 2140, The University of New Mexico, Albuquerque, NM 87131-0001, USA.

Finn Gredal Jensen, Society for Danish Language and Literature, Christians Brygge 1, 1219 Copenhagen K, Denmark.

Carl Henrik Koch, Department of Media, Cognition and Communication, Faculty of Humanities, University of Copenhagen, Njalsgade 80, 2300 Copenhagen S, Denmark.

Andrea Scaramuccia, University of Pisa, Dipartimento di Filosofia, Via Pasquale Paoli, 15, 56126 Pisa, Italy.

K. Brian Söderquist, Søren Kierkegaard Research Centre, Farvergade 27 D, 1463 Copenhagen K, Denmark.

Jon Stewart, Søren Kierkegaard Research Centre, Farvergade 27 D, 1463 Copenhagen K, Denmark.

J. Michael Tilley, Department of Philosophy, Georgetown College, 400 East College Street, Georgetown, KY 40324, USA.

Bjarne Troelsen, Center for Filosofi og Videnskabsteori, Aalborg Universitet, Fibigerstræde 10, 9220 Aalborg Øst, Denmark.

Preface

Kierkegaard was in a certain sense a profoundly local thinker. He was often in dialogue with his fellow Danes or, indeed, fellow Copenhageners on key issues of the day. His authorship would be unthinkable without the signal conflict with the Danish State Church or without reference to important Danish institutions such as the Royal Theater or the University of Copenhagen. Likewise, his relation to various Danish newspapers and journals, such as *The Corsair*, *Fædrelandet*, and *Kjøbenhavns flyvende Post*, played an undeniable role in shaping his thought and authorship.

But this is, of course, not to imply that Kierkegaard was a provincial thinker or can simply be reduced to his immediate context. The Danish figures that he was reading and engaged with ranked among the greatest minds of Europe at the time. The period of Kierkegaard's life corresponds to what has been dubbed by historians as "the Golden Age of Denmark," which covers roughly the first half of the nineteenth century, when Denmark's most important writers, philosophers, theologians, poets, actors and artists flourished. This was the age of Hans Christian Andersen's (1805–75) fairy tales and Hans Christian Ørsted's (1777–1851) natural scientific theories. It was a period when the Royal Theater was one of the leading playhouses in Europe. It was likewise the age of some of Denmark's most famous poets and literary critics, and when Danish sculpture and painting achieved new heights with figures such as Bertel Thorvaldsen (1768–1844), and Christoffer Wilhelm Eckersberg (1783–1853). Finally, the Golden Age produced the towering figures of Danish theology who were so important for the development of Kierkegaard's thought.

In this context Kierkegaard was thus merely one actor on a stage, which he shared with a host of other extremely gifted writers and thinkers. The rich interdisciplinary nature of the period is reflected in his authorship, which seems to defy any clear determination with regard to genre or scholarly discipline. Given this, it can come as no surprise that the single most extensive body of sources for Kierkegaard's thought comes from Denmark itself (followed closely by his German sources). Some of his best-known thoughts and ideas were born in the dialogical exchange with his Danish contemporaries.

In recent years scholars have become increasingly interested in understanding Kierkegaard as an integral figure of the Golden Age. The landmark publication in this regard is Bruce H. Kirmmse's *Kierkegaard in Golden Age Denmark*.[1] This work brought to the attention of the international reader the importance of Kierkegaard's

[1] Bruce H. Kirmmse, *Kierkegaard in Golden Age Denmark*, Bloomington and Indianapolis: Indiana University Press 1990.

Danish contemporaries for an understanding of his intellectual development. It demonstrated the value of contextualizing Kierkegaard's writing in the wider Danish intellectual milieu of the day. The anthology *Kierkegaard and His Contemporaries: The Culture of Golden Age Denmark*, followed up on Kirmmse's work, attempting to introduce key Danish figures in their relation to different aspects of Kierkegaard's thought.[2] This interest in the historical context has been further cultivated by the explanatory notes in the new Danish edition of Kierkegaard's writings, *Søren Kierkegaards Skrifter*.[3] The commentators of this edition have provided the world of Kierkegaard studies with an enormous service by, among other things, identifying in Kierkegaard's texts the various quotations and allusions that he makes to any number of Danish authors. They have demonstrated beyond any doubt the enormous significance that these figures had for him.

The Søren Kierkegaard Research Centre has in recent years launched two new series in order to address the need for more source-work research into Kierkegaard's Danish contemporaries. The first is a translation series entitled *Texts from Golden Age Denmark*. This series, which has appeared since 2005, is dedicated to English translations of classic Danish texts from the period. The volumes are accompanied by extensive introductions that present the featured authors and works in their original context. In addition, the primary texts are accompanied by detailed "point" commentaries, like those in *Søren Kierkegaards Skrifter*, that provide information about, for example, people mentioned, texts quoted or topographical references. The second series is entitled *Danish Golden Age Studies*, which began publication in 2007. This is a monograph series that features dissertations, *Habilitation* theses, anthologies, and other works dedicated to exploring some aspect of the cultural achievements of the period. The diversity and disciplinary cross-over that characterizes so much of the period is reflected in the interdisciplinary conception of both series.

The present volume features articles that employ source-work research in order to explore the individual Danish sources of Kierkegaard's thought. The volume is divided into three separate tomes in order to cover the different fields of influence.

Tome I is dedicated to exploring the sources that fall under the rubrics "Philosophy, Politics and Social Theory." With regard to philosophy, many Danish scholars of the day studied in Germany or Prussia and were profoundly shaped by German idealism. For example, one of Denmark's greatest philosophical minds, Frederik Christian Sibbern (1785–1872), was influenced by Schelling, as was Henrik Steffens (1773–1845), who was, indeed, one of Schelling's friends and closest associates. Similarly, the aforementioned Hans Christian Ørsted, although known today for his natural scientific advancements, was deeply marked by the thought of Kant. Finally, Johan Ludvig Heiberg (1791–1860) zealously dedicated himself to promoting Hegel's

---

2 *Kierkegaard and His Contemporaries: The Culture of Golden Age Denmark*, ed. by Jon Stewart, Berlin and New York: Walter de Gruyter 2003 (*Kierkegaard Studies Monograph Series*, vol. 10).

3 *Søren Kierkegaards Skrifter*, vols. 1–28, K1–K28, ed. by Niels Jørgen Cappelørn, Joakim Garff, Jette Knudsen, Johnny Kondrup, Alastair McKinnon and Finn Hauberg Mortensen, Copenhagen: Gads Forlag 1997ff.

philosophy in Denmark. Kierkegaard read the works of all of these thinkers and their German antecedents. While he was sympathetic to individual ideas, analyses, and insights offered by this tradition, he was generally keen to criticize the German model of philosophy and to propose a new paradigm for philosophical thought that was more in tune with lived existence.

Kierkegaard also experienced first-hand the dynamic period in history that saw the great upheavals throughout Europe in connection with the revolutions of 1848. While Denmark was spared the worst of the conflicts, with the king consenting to the introduction of a constitution that was ultimately established in 1849, it was nonetheless perceived by many to be an uncertain and even chaotic age, where everything that had been previously taken for granted had to be thought anew. The sense of uncertainty was further fueled by the First Schleswig War that Denmark fought with Prussia from 1848 to 1851 in order to retain the breakaway duchies of Schleswig and Holstein. Figures such as Orla Lehmann (1810–70) and Ditlev Gothard Monrad (1811–87) played key roles in these events. The Danish press, with figures like Jens Giødwad (1811–91), the editor of *Fædrelandet*, also often made heroic efforts, criticizing the government in spite of pressure from the censors. While it has often been claimed that Kierkegaard was not interested in politics, his long discussions about politics on his walks with the jurist J.L. Kolderup-Rosenvinge (1792–1850) seem to imply a quite different picture. To be sure, he cannot be regarded as a political scientist or social theorist in a straightforward sense, but he was nonetheless engaged in the issues of his day and in his works one can certainly find material that can be insightful for the fields of politics and social theory.

Tome II is dedicated to the host of Danish theologians who played a greater or lesser role in shaping Kierkegaard's thought. In his day there were a number of competing theological trends within the church and at the Faculty of Theology at the University of Copenhagen, and not least of all in the blossoming free church movements. One of the favorite targets of criticism that often united otherwise antagonistic factions was rationalism. It would probably be mistaken to designate this as a school since it is usually thought to be represented by the person of Henrik Nicolai Clausen (1793–1877), a professor of theology at the university. Clausen was attacked by N.F.S. Grundtvig (1783–1872), and although Grundtvig lost the libel case that Clausen filed against him, the event nonetheless rallied a group of people to his side, and the Grundtvigian movement was born. It is wrong to think of this movement as being just about the personality of a single man since it included a number of talented scholars such as Jacob Christian Lindberg (1797–1857), Andreas Gottlob Rudelbach (1792–1862), and Kierkegaard's elder brother Peter Christian Kierkegaard (1805–88). There were also a number of important figures within the Danish church who were significant for Kierkegaard's universe of thought. Most scholars are familiar with his problematic relation to Bishop Jakob Peter Mynster (1775–1854), but Kierkegaard was also exercised by other leading personalities in the church such as Eggert Christopher Tryde (1781–1860) and Just H.V. Paulli (1808–65). Finally, one should not forget the importance of Hegelianism for Danish theology of the day. In this context figures such as Adolph Peter Adler (1812–69) and Hans Lassen Martensen (1808–84) were the frequent objects of Kierkegaard's various attacks on what he perceived as the confusion of Christianity with objective thinking that was characteristic of the time.

Tome III is dedicated to the diverse Danish sources that fall under the rubrics "Literature, Drama and Aesthetics." The Golden Age is known as the period when Danish prose first established itself with authors such as Hans Christian Andersen, Steen Steensen Blicher (1782–1826), Meïr Goldschmidt (1819–87), and Thomasine Gyllembourg (1773–1856). This was also an age when Danish poetry flourished in any number of different genres. Accordingly, this tome contains articles on Kierkegaard's use of the great Danish poets of the period such as Jens Baggesen (1764–1826), Christian Winther (1796–1876), Carsten Hauch (1790–1872), and Adam Oehlenschläger (1779–1850), whose verses are scattered throughout Kierkegaard's writings. As is well known, Kierkegaard frequently attended dramatic performances at the Royal Theater, where he was captivated by actors such as Joachim Ludvig Phister (1807–96) and Johanne Luise Heiberg (1812–90) as well as dancers such as August Bournonville (1805–79). He comments on these figures in both his published works and his journals. Finally, Kierkegaard was also keenly interested in literary and dramatic criticism. This tome features articles that treat his use of the critics Johan Ludvig Heiberg and Peter Ludvig Møller (1814–65), who were among the polemical masters of the day.

As the main figures of the Danish Golden Age gradually become better known to the world of Kierkegaard studies, new connections and insights will doubtless emerge about Kierkegaard's often complicated use of them. It is hoped that the present volume will make an important contribution in this regard in its attempt to see Kierkegaard not as an isolated genius, but rather as a thinker continuous with his age and in constant dialogue with it, indeed, as a Golden Age figure *par excellence*.

Acknowledgements

Many people have worked long hours on this volume, and it thus represents a collective effort of many different individuals and institutions. I would like to take this opportunity to express my gratitude to the Danish Agency for Science, Technology and Innovation for sponsoring this project with a three-year grant from 2005 to 2007. During this period the Søren Kierkegaard Research Centre at the University of Copenhagen was the host institute, providing invaluable administrative support. In 2006, the Hong-Kierkegaard Library at St. Olaf College made it possible for the editors of this project to do crucial bibliographical work with the use of their outstanding collection; the enormous kindness, generosity and general support of the project by Cynthia Lund and Gordon Marino in that context were greatly appreciated.

I would also like to thank a number of individuals who have provided assistance with various aspects of this volume: István Czakó, Philip Hillyer, Poul Houe, Carl Henrik Koch, Finn Gredal Jensen, Søren Jensen, David D. Possen, Richard Purkarthofer, Joel Rasmussen, Peter Šajda, Heiko Schulz, and Brian Söderquist. I gratefully acknowledge the monumental efforts of Katalin Nun who compiled the bibliographies for the articles in this volume (as for the other ones in the "Sources" part of the series) and who has had the responsibility for the editing and formatting of these articles electronically. This series would not have been possible without her efforts.

I am profoundly grateful to all the authors who have contributed to this volume. Thanks to their joint efforts and those of many others, I am proud to be able to present this volume to the reader. It is my sincere hope that the scholarship presented here will serve at the basis for the next generation of researchers interested in exploring Kierkegaard's relation to his Golden Age contemporaries.

List of Abbreviations

Danish Abbreviations

B&A *Breve og Aktstykker vedrørende Søren Kierkegaard*, ed. by Niels Thulstrup, vols. 1–2, Copenhagen: Munksgaard 1953–54.

Bl.art. *S. Kierkegaard's Bladartikler, med Bilag samlede efter Forfatterens Død, udgivne som Supplement til hans øvrige Skrifter*, ed. by Rasmus Nielsen, Copenhagen: C.A. Reitzel 1857.

EP *Af Søren Kierkegaards Efterladte Papirer*, vols. 1–9, ed. by H.P. Barfod and Hermann Gottsched, Copenhagen: C.A. Reitzel 1869–81.

Pap. *Søren Kierkegaards Papirer*, vols. I to XI–3, ed. by Peter Andreas Heiberg, Victor Kuhr and Einer Torsting, Copenhagen: Gyldendalske Boghandel, Nordisk Forlag, 1909–48; second, expanded ed., vols. I to XI–3, by Niels Thulstrup, vols. XII to XIII supplementary volumes, ed. by Niels Thulstrup, vols. XIV to XVI index by Niels Jørgen Cappelørn, Copenhagen: Gyldendal 1968–78.

SKS *Søren Kierkegaards Skrifter*, vols. 1-28, K1-K28, ed. by Niels Jørgen Cappelørn, Joakim Garff, Jette Knudsen, Johnny Kondrup, Alastair McKinnon and Finn Hauberg Mortensen, Copenhagen: Gads Forlag 1997ff.

SV1 *Samlede Værker*, vols. I–XIV, ed. by A.B. Drachmann, Johan Ludvig Heiberg and H.O. Lange, Copenhagen: Gyldendalske Boghandels Forlag 1901–06.

English Abbreviations

AN *Armed Neutrality*, trans. by Howard V. Hong and Edna H. Hong, Princeton: Princeton University Press 1998.

AR *On Authority and Revelation, The Book on Adler,* trans. by Walter Lowrie, Princeton: Princeton University Press 1955.

ASKB *The Auctioneer's Sales Record of the Library of Søren Kierkegaard*, ed. by H. P. Rohde, Copenhagen: The Royal Library 1967.

BA *The Book on Adler*, trans. by Howard V. Hong and Edna H. Hong, Princeton: Princeton University Press 1998.

C *The Crisis and a Crisis in the Life of an Actress*, trans. by Howard V. Hong and Edna H. Hong, Princeton: Princeton University Press 1997.

CA *The Concept of Anxiety*, trans. by Reidar Thomte in collaboration with Albert B. Anderson, Princeton: Princeton University Press 1980.

CD *Christian Discourses*, trans. by Howard V. Hong and Edna H. Hong, Princeton: Princeton University Press 1997.

CI *The Concept of Irony*, trans. by Howard V. Hong and Edna H. Hong, Princeton: Princeton University Press 1989.

CIC *The Concept of Irony*, trans. with an Introduction and Notes by Lee M. Capel, London: Collins 1966.

COR *The Corsair Affair*; *Articles Related to the Writings*, trans. by Howard V. Hong and Edna H. Hong, Princeton: Princeton University Press 1982.

CUP1 *Concluding Unscientific Postscript*, vol. 1, trans. by Howard V. Hong and Edna H. Hong, Princeton: Princeton University Press 1992.

CUP2 *Concluding Unscientific Postscript*, vol. 2, trans. by Howard V. Hong and Edna H. Hong, Princeton: Princeton University Press 1992.

EO1 *Either/Or*, Part I, trans. by Howard V. Hong and Edna H. Hong, Princeton: Princeton University Press 1987.

EO2 *Either/Or*, Part II, trans. by Howard V. Hong and Edna H. Hong, Princeton: Princeton University Press 1987.

EOP *Either/Or*, trans. by Alastair Hannay, Harmondsworth: Penguin Books 1992.

EPW *Early Polemical Writings*, among others: *From the Papers of One Still Living*; *Articles from Student Days*; *The Battle Between the Old and the New Soap-Cellars*, trans. by Julia Watkin, Princeton: Princeton University Press 1990.

EUD *Eighteen Upbuilding Discourses*, trans. by Howard V. Hong and Edna H. Hong, Princeton: Princeton University Press 1990.

FSE *For Self-Examination*, trans. by Howard V. Hong and Edna H. Hong, Princeton: Princeton University Press 1990.

FT *Fear and Trembling*, trans. by Howard V. Hong and Edna H. Hong, Princeton: Princeton University Press 1983.

FTP *Fear and Trembling*, trans. by Alastair Hannay, Harmondsworth: Penguin Books 1985.

JC *Johannes Climacus, or De omnibus dubitandum est*, trans. by Howard V. Hong and Edna H. Hong, Princeton: Princeton University Press 1985.

JFY *Judge for Yourself!*, trans. by Howard V. Hong and Edna H. Hong, Princeton: Princeton University Press 1990.

JP *Søren Kierkegaard's Journals and Papers*, vols. 1–6, ed. and trans. by Howard V. Hong and Edna H. Hong, assisted by Gregor Malantschuk (vol. 7, Index and Composite Collation), Bloomington and London: Indiana University Press 1967–78.

KAC *Kierkegaard's Attack upon "Christendom," 1854–1855*, trans. by Walter Lowrie, Princeton: Princeton University Press 1944.

KJN *Kierkegaard's Journals and Notebooks*, vols. 1–11, ed. by Niels Jørgen Cappelørn, Alastair Hannay, David Kangas, Bruce H. Kirmmse, George Pattison, Vanessa Rumble, and K. Brian Söderquist, Princeton and Oxford: Princeton University Press 2007ff.

LD *Letters and Documents*, trans. by Henrik Rosenmeier, Princeton: Princeton University Press 1978.

LR *A Literary Review*, trans. by Alastair Hannay, Harmondsworth: Penguin Books 2001.

M *The Moment and Late Writings*, trans. by Howard V. Hong and Edna H. Hong, Princeton: Princeton University Press 1998.

P *Prefaces*, trans. by Todd W. Nichol, Princeton: Princeton University Press 1997.

PC *Practice in Christianity*, trans. by Howard V. Hong and Edna H. Hong, Princeton: Princeton University Press 1991.

PF *Philosophical Fragments*, trans. by Howard V. Hong and Edna H. Hong, Princeton: Princeton University Press 1985.

PJ *Papers and Journals: A Selection*, trans. by Alastair Hannay, Harmondsworth: Penguin Books 1996.

PLR *Prefaces: Light Reading for Certain Classes as the Occasion May Require*, trans. by William McDonald, Tallahassee: Florida State University Press 1989.

PLS *Concluding Unscientific Postscript*, trans. by David F. Swenson and Walter Lowrie, Princeton: Princeton University Press 1941.

PV *The Point of View* including *On My Work as an Author*, *The Point of View for My Work as an Author*, and *Armed Neutrality*, trans. by Howard V. Hong and Edna H. Hong, Princeton: Princeton University Press 1998.

PVL *The Point of View for My Work as an Author* including *On My Work as an Author*, trans. by Walter Lowrie, New York and London: Oxford University Press 1939.

R *Repetition*, trans. by Howard V. Hong and Edna H. Hong, Princeton: Princeton University Press 1983.

SBL *Notes of Schelling's Berlin Lectures*, trans. by Howard V. Hong and Edna H. Hong, Princeton: Princeton University Press 1989.

SLW *Stages on Life's Way*, trans. by Howard V. Hong and Edna H. Hong, Princeton: Princeton University Press 1988.

SUD *The Sickness unto Death*, trans. by Howard V. Hong and Edna H. Hong, Princeton: Princeton University Press 1980.

SUDP *The Sickness unto Death*, trans. by Alastair Hannay, London and New York: Penguin Books 1989.

TA *Two Ages: The Age of Revolution and the Present Age. A Literary Review*, trans. by Howard V. Hong and Edna H. Hong, Princeton: Princeton University Press 1978.

TD *Three Discourses on Imagined Occasions*, trans. by Howard V. Hong and Edna H. Hong, Princeton: Princeton University Press 1993.

UD *Upbuilding Discourses in Various Spirits*, trans. by Howard V. Hong and Edna H. Hong, Princeton: Princeton University Press 1993.

WA *Without Authority* including *The Lily in the Field and the Bird of the Air, Two Ethical-Religious Essays, Three Discourses at the Communion on Fridays, An Upbuilding Discourse, Two Discourses at the Communion on*

Fridays, trans. by Howard V. Hong and Edna H. Hong, Princeton: Princeton University Press 1997.

WL *Works of Love*, trans. by Howard V. Hong and Edna H. Hong, Princeton: Princeton University Press 1995.

WS *Writing Sampler*, trans. by Todd W. Nichol, Princeton: Princeton University Press 1997.

Andreas Frederik Beck:

A Good Dialectician and a Bad Reader

K. Brian Söderquist

Andreas Frederik Beck (1816–61) is a little-known scholar and journalist named in a handful of Danish intellectual histories, where his contributions are said to be modest. Beck is portrayed as one of the few figures in Danish intellectual life who made an attempt to introduce a version of left-Hegelian thought into theological and church circles, but like other Danish thinkers who had similar interests such as Hans Brøchner (1816–61), Christian Fenger Christens (1819–55), and Rudolph Varberg (1828–69), Beck made no inroads in either scholarly or church circles.[1]

Despite Beck's obscurity in Danish intellectual life, his name appears from time to time in Kierkegaard studies.[2] This stems not least from the fact that Beck reviewed both *The Concept of Irony* and *Philosophical Fragments*, and Kierkegaard responded sarcastically to both reviews. While Kierkegaard is almost silent with regard to Beck's left-Hegelian ideology and scholarly analyses, he unfurls some caustic critique about Beck's inability to interpret irony and indirect communication.

---

1 Carl Henrik Koch, *Den danske idealisme 1800–1880*, Copenhagen: Gyldendal 2004 (*Den danske filosofis historie*, ed. by Sten Ebbesen and Carl Henrik Koch), pp. 487–96; p. 487; S.V. Rasmussen, *Den unge Brøchner*, Copenhagen: Gyldendal 1966, pp. 186–7; Jens Holger Schjørring, *Teologi og filosofi. Nogle analyser og dokumenter vedrørende Hegelianisme i dansk teologi*, Copenhagen: C.A. Reitzel 1974, pp. 36–49; see p. 38.

2 See Paul Muench, "The Socratic Method of Kierkegaard's Pseudonym Johannes Climacus: Indirect Communication and the Art of 'Taking Away,' " in *Søren Kierkegaard and the Word(s): Essays on Hermeneutics and Communication*, ed. by Poul Houe and Gordon Marino, Copenhagen: C.A. Reitzel 2003, pp. 139–50. See also István Czakó, "Feuerbach: A Malicious Demon in the Service of Christianity," in *Kierkegaard and His German Contemporaries*, Tome I, *Philosophy*, ed. by Jon Stewart, Aldershot: Ashgate 2007 (*Kierkegaard Research: Sources, Reception and Resources*, vol. 6), pp. 25–47; see pp. 31–3; p. 37; p. 39; David James and Douglas Moggach, "Bruno Bauer: Biblical Narrative, Freedom and Anxiety," in *Kierkegaard and His German Contemporaries*, Tome II, *Theology*, ed. by Jon Stewart, Aldershot: Ashgate 2007 (*Kierkegaard Research: Sources, Reception and Resources*, vol. 6), pp. 1–21; see p. 5; Bruce H. Kirmmse, "Socrates in the Fast Lane: Kierkegaard's *The Concept of Irony* on the University's *Velocifère*," in *The Concept of Irony*, ed. by Robert L. Perkins, Macon, Georgia: Mercer University Press 2001 (*International Kierkegaard Commentary*, vol. 2), p. 78; Jon Stewart, *Kierkegaard's Relations to Hegel Reconsidered*, Cambridge: Cambridge University Press 2003, p. 11, note; p. 69; p. 140; p. 233; p. 280; pp. 336–7; p. 600.

In short, we see in Kierkegaard's relationship to Beck evidence that Kierkegaard is rather uninterested, almost neutral, with regard to left-Hegelian thinking, understood here as the tendency to argue that the biblical narratives are not literal history but rather religious myth or fiction.[3] Alternatively, the so-called right-Hegelian attempt to defend or explain Christianity intellectually receives a disproportionate amount of attention in Kierkegaard's authorship. Secondly, Kierkegaard's relationship to Beck also reveals the extent of his refusal to enter scholarly debate on academic premises and his penchant for ironically tearing down the façade of serious academic debate.

I. Beck's Life and Works

Andreas Frederik Beck was born in Skarum on the island of Mors in northern Jutland, where his father was a priest.[4] He was educated in Copenhagen, however, graduating in 1834 from preparatory school, The School of Civic Virtue, where Kierkegaard himself had graduated four years earlier. Beck continued his education at the University of Copenhagen as a resident at Borch's College and ended up completing his university studies before Kierkegaard, graduating in 1838 with a degree in theology, and then, one year later, receiving his doctorate from the University of Kiel for a dissertation on Hebrew poetry.[5]

Beck published his only major philosophical work, *The Concept of Myth or the Form of Religious Spirit*,[6] two years later, in 1842, and this work ended up defining the rest of his career. Here, Beck made explicit and extensive use of Bruno Bauer (1809–82), a left-Hegelian, at a time when Bauer's views were controversial in theological and church circles in both Germany and Denmark.

In *The Concept of Myth*, Beck aims to give an account of the "mythical character" of religious consciousness, and consistent with much of Bauer's thought, he argues that religious consciousness has mistakenly objectified truth by focusing on external history played out by historical characters. At the same time, the immediate religious consciousness also ends up attributing to historical events and characters a transcendent dimension: historical events are abstracted from lived history and become idealized. They are transformed into narratives, into myths, which then take leave of the actual world in which they originated. In his account, religious consciousness "allows supernatural forces"[7] to enter the sphere of historical actors and provide them with a truth that they seem to lack. The narratives or myths in

---

3 I use the terms "left Hegelianism" and "right Hegelianism" hesitantly. As Jon Stewart has shown, the terms are too reductionistic to do justice to the complexity of the debates about the status of religion among Hegel-inspired thinkers after Hegel's death. See Jon Stewart, *A History of Hegelianism in Golden Age Denmark*, Tome I, *The Heiberg Period: 1824–1836*, Copenhagen: C.A. Reitzel 2007 (*Danish Golden Age Studies*, vol. 3), pp. 21–7.

4 For biographical information, see *Dansk biografisk Leksikon*, vols. 1–27, ed. by Poul Engelstoft, Copenhagen: J.H. Schultz 1933–44, vol. 2, pp. 290–2.

5 Koch, *Den danske idealisme*, p. 487.

6 Andreas Frederik Beck, *Begrebet Mythus eller den religiøse Aands Form*, Copenhagen: P.G. Philipsen 1842 (*ASKB* 424).

7 Ibid., p. 14; see also Koch, *Den danske idealisme*, p. 493.

which these figures play roles become "glorified at the expense of the world."[8] The result is a divided consciousness that fails to recognize that truth is immanent to Spirit, and a consciousness that is only reconciled with itself with knowledge won through speculative philosophy.

For the theologians and academics who read Beck's monograph, the implications of this mythologizing theology were clear. As Carl Henrik Koch puts it, Beck, like Bauer, seemed to be suggesting that the gospels were works of fiction, that the Christ figure was a work of imagination without any historical reality, and that the entire account of Christ's life and works was the product of an unconscious desire among religious people for a better existence.[9]

Together with Hans Brøchner's studies on Strauss, Beck's monograph represented the emergence of so-called left Hegelianism in Danish theological circles. As Jens Holger Schjørring notes, the tension in Denmark surrounding left Hegelianism reflected the radicalization and polarization of the debate that had taken place in Germany after 1840 with writers such as Strauss, Bauer, and Feuerbach.[10] Several members of the Faculty of Theology at the University of Copenhagen were interested in Hegel, including Hans Lassen Martensen (1808–84) and Henrik Nicolai Clausen (1793–1877), but they ended up choosing a middle path, respecting the ultimate harmony of personal faith and systematic philosophy.[11] Beck, Brøchner, and a handful of younger theologians, all members of Kierkegaard's generation of students, worked for a more radical interpretation of Hegel that stressed the mythological interpretation of religious narratives.

Brøchner was not allowed to take the theological examination that would have qualified him to take a position within the church,[12] and even though Beck was awarded degrees, his left Hegelianism did not sit well with the members of the faculty, either. When a position in Old Testament studies opened in the mid 1840s, Beck was passed over even though he was one of the best-qualified candidates; the faculty simply did not want Beck's left Hegelianism to disturb the ideological balance already in place.[13] Beck met with similar opposition from the church,

---

8 Beck, *Begrebet Mythus*, p. 14; see also Koch, *Den danske idealisme*, pp. 493–4.

9 Koch, *Den danske idealisme*, p. 489.

10 Schjørring, *Teologi og filosofi*, p. 36.

11 The ideology at the faculty has been described as generally sympathetic to Schleiermacher. It championed the historical-critical method, but was also supportive of a deep subjective faith in Christ. See Leif Grane, "Det Teologiske Fakultet 1830–1925," in *Københavns Universitet 1479–1979*, vol. 5, *Det Teologiske Fakultet*, ed. by Leif Grane, Copenhagen: G.E.C. Gads Forlag 1980, pp. 325–500, see pp. 330–1.

12 According to Schjørring, Martensen, Rasmus Nielsen, and other scholars interested in "theologizing" speculative philosophy were able to outmaneuver and marginalize Beck, Brøchner, and the young left Hegelians early on. See Schjørring, *Teologi og filosofi*, pp. 36–8; Stewart, *A History Hegelianism in Golden Age Denmark*, Tome II, *The Martensen Period: 1837–1842*, Copenhagen: C.A. Reitzel 2007 (*Danish Golden Age Studies*, vol. 3), pp. 678–88.

13 Grane, "Det Teologiske Fakultet 1830–1925," p. 331.

particularly Bishop Jakob Peter Mynster (1775–1854), who became Beck's target in public debate for the next decade.[14]

After his exclusion from the university and church, Beck continued to publish essays critical of conservative theological positions, focusing in particular on the Hegel-inspired theology of Hans Lassen Martensen. In remarks reminiscent of Kierkegaard's criticism of employing speculative philosophy to defend religious faith, Beck writes in the late 1840s in an ironic tone that Martensen's form of theology "developed a surprising wisdom about transcendent things,"[15] and that, in essence, Martensen makes reason subordinate to the Christian tradition rather than allowing reason to work itself through and out of the tradition. As Beck sees it, Martensen arrogantly and tyrannically declares that mere human reason, autonomous of Christian dogma, deserves scholarly contempt. On the contrary, he retorts: it is the subordination of reason to dogma that properly deserves scholarly contempt.[16]

Because his possibilities for employment at the university and in the church were cut off, Beck worked most of his life as a journalist, employed by several different newspapers in Copenhagen. Throughout his career he became more interested in political issues, often writing anti-nationalistic political pieces, though he did return to the philosophy of religion in the late 1850s with a series of articles on the later Schelling.[17]

II. Kierkegaard's Interaction and Non-interaction with Beck

Kierkegaard mentions or alludes to Beck only a handful of times in his entire authorship, and were it not for Kierkegaard's ironic public responses to Beck's reviews of *The Concept of Irony* and *Philosophical Fragments*, it would hardly be worth mentioning their relationship at all. While Kierkegaard read Beck's reviews carefully enough to note that Beck missed his subtle wit and genius (and Kierkegaard does not think this could be a flaw in the execution of his work as witty author), there are few hints that he read anything else by Beck. Even though Kierkegaard owned a copy of Beck's *The Concept of Myth*, his direct and indirect allusions to it are so broad that it is hardly clear he studied it.

On a personal level, Kierkegaard obviously knew Beck from their days as students at the university; Beck was an *ex auditoria* opponent at Kierkegaard's dissertation defense.[18] And late in Kierkegaard's life, he also reportedly ran into Beck occasionally "on Sunday mornings at church time" at the Athenæum, a private library where intellectuals met.[19]

---

14 Koch, *Den danske idealisme*, p. 488; Grane, "Det Teologiske Fakultet 1830–1925," pp. 331–2.

15 Beck, *Theologiske Tilstande i Danmark i Aarene 1842–46*, Copenhagen: n.p. 1847, p. 2. Quoted in Koch, *Den danske idealisme*, p. 490.

16 Koch, *Den danske idealisme*, p. 490.

17 Ibid., p. 488.

18 Kirmmse, "Socrates in the Fast Lane," pp. 77–80.

19 See Bruce H. Kirmmse, *Encounters with Kierkegaard: A Life as Seen by His Contemporaries*, Princeton: Princeton University Press 1996, p. 247.

There is evidence in Kierkegaard's journals and papers that he noticed Beck's participation in the theological debates in the 1840s, but he shows little interest in Beck's arguments. For the most part, these debates become occasions for Kierkegaard to write ironically about particular local personalities. He seems to allude to Beck's political problems with Mynster, for example, in a journal entry in the *Journal NB14* written in 1849: he blasts Mynster for showing his great "concern" as bishop by "preventing a poor theological graduate from getting a job."[20] Elsewhere in his papers, Kierkegaard suggests that Beck's public animosity toward Mynster could be interpreted as an "unhappy" or "unrequited" love in the same way that all public feuds reveal an inability to just let go of a bitter relationship.[21] Finally, in an unpublished draft to a newspaper article, Kierkegaard writes a rather telling non-response to Beck's involvement in a debate with Mynster: rather than responding to the issues raised by Beck or Mynster, Kierkegaard ironizes over the contradiction that lies in Beck's pseudonym, "A Pastor," given that Beck was not a pastor and would never be a pastor.[22]

If more is to be drawn from Kierkegaard's relationship to Beck, it lies in his published works. In the *Postscript*, Beck's school of thought is briefly alluded to in Climacus' ruminations about the tension between speculative scholarship and subjective inwardness. In this context, he mentions "the modern mythical allegorizing trend"—which could well include Beck—a trend that implies that Christianity is "a myth."[23] Noteworthy here is how disinterested Climacus seems to be in engaging in debate with this kind of Hegelianism. He writes:

> The modern mythical allegorizing trend summarily declares Christianity to be a myth. Such a procedure is at least forthright behavior, and everyone can easily form a judgment about it. The friendship of speculative thought is of another kind. To be on the safe side, speculative thought opposes the ungodly mythical allegorizing trend and then goes on to say "speculative thought, on the hand, accepts the paradox, but does not stop with it."[24]

While the mythologizing trend of left Hegelianism, represented locally by Beck, is more or less given a free pass by Climacus because it is up front about interpreting religious consciousness as myth rather than transcendent truth, "speculative thought" is said to be problematic. The remainder of the chapter and much of the rest of the *Postscript* is a sarcastic diatribe against those pious thinkers who come to the defense of Christianity by "explaining" it.[25] Interestingly, Climacus juxtaposes

---

20 *SKS* 22, 382, NB14:63m. The editors of *SKS* suggest that this is an allusion to Beck. See *SKS* K22, 479.

21 *Pap*. VII–1 B 87, p. 285 / *CUP2*, Supplement, p. 125, note.

22 *Pap*. IV B 58 / *EO2*, Supplement, pp. 412–14. In keeping with his ironic distance to such debates, Kierkegaard signs his piece, "A Grocer."

23 *SKS* 7, 199 / *CUP1*, 218. In addition to Baur or Beck, this could be an allusion to Strauss, as the Hongs suggest; see *CUP2*, p. 230, note 305. See also George Pattison, "D.F. Strauss: Kierkegaard and Radical Demythologization," in *Kierkegaard and His German Contemporaries*, Tome II, *Theology*, pp. 233–57; see p. 234.

24 *SKS* 7, 199 / *CUP1*, 218.

25 *SKS* 7, 199–203 / *CUP1*, 218–23.

two kinds of Hegel-inspired thought: the "mythologizing trend," on the one hand, and "speculative thought," on the other. This suggests that at least in this context, "speculative thought" is associated with so-called right Hegelians like Martensen and Rasmus Nielsen, not left Hegelians like Beck, Brøchner, et alii. Climacus' general apathy here toward left Hegelianism reveals that the "mythologizing trend" is simply not as provocative to him as right Hegelianism; it is the philosophical defense of Christianity that elicit his ironic attacks. For Climacus, the real threat to genuine inner spiritual life is the sort of Hegelianism that attempts to defend divine transcendence by showing its rationality rather than the version of Hegelianism that implies it is ahistorical fiction.[26]

Kierkegaard's published responses to Beck's reviews of *The Concept of Irony*[27] and *Philosophical Fragments*[28] are interesting for other reasons. In both cases, Beck delivers careful and intelligent summaries of the books. And in both cases, Beck concludes the overwhelmingly favorable reviews with only minor complaints about Kierkegaard's witty writing style. Kierkegaard, in turn, responds to almost none of Beck's philosophical analyses, but chooses rather to focus on the few lines of criticism, ironizing over Beck's inability to grasp his irony.

A. Beck's Review of The Concept of Irony

For the most part, Beck's apt review of *The Concept of Irony* aims to provide a scholarly overview of the book, focusing especially on Kierkegaard's historical methodology. Particularly interesting for Beck is the way Kierkegaard mines the tension between actual historical events, on the one hand, and the texts that record those historical events on the other. Beck sees an immediate parallel with his own

---

26 Climacus' disinterest in engaging in debate about "mythologizing trends" is generally consistent with Kierkegaard's authorship in which he and his pseudonyms are less critical, sometimes even respectful, of left-Hegelian thinkers. For Kierkegaard's relationship to Feuerbach, for example, see István Czakó, "Feuerbach: A Malicious Demon in the Service of Christianity," pp. 25–47; David James and Douglas Moggach, "Bruno Bauer: Biblical Narrative, Freedom and Anxiety," pp. 1–21; Pattison, "D.F. Strauss: Kierkegaard and Radical Demythologization," pp. 233–57. Personally, Kierkegaard seems to had some respect for other local writers who espoused left-Hegelian views. Kierkegaard refrained from criticizing Brøchner, and he also spoke respectfully of Christian Fenger Christens, who was inspired by Feuerbach and whom Kierkegaard got to know in Berlin in the winter of 1841–42. Kierkegaard told Brøchner that "Christens was the brightest of all the Danes who had been in Berlin that winter." See Kirmmse, *Encounters with Kierkegaard: A Life as Seen by His Contemporaries*, p. 230. See also Rasmussen, *Den unge Brøchner*, pp. 186–7.

27 Frederik Andreas Beck, "[Review of] *Om Begrebet Ironi, med stadigt Hensyn til Socrates* af Søren Kierkegaard," *Fædrelandet*, nos. 890–7, May 29 and June 5, 1842, columns 7133–40, columns 7189–91, and column 7191.

28 Anonymous [Andreas Frederik Beck], "*Philosophische Smuler eller en Smule Philosophie* (*Philos. Brocken oder ein Bischen Philosophie*). Af S. Kierkegaard. Kiöbenhavn, Reitzel. 1844. 8°," *Neues Repertorium für die theologische Literatur und kirchliche Statistik*, vol. 2, no. 1, April 30, 1845, pp. 44–8 (reprinted in *Materialien zur Philosophie Sören Kierkegaards*, ed. by Michael Theunissen and Wilfried Greve, Frankfurt am Main: Suhrkamp 1979, pp. 127–31).

left-Hegelian interests in biblical criticism: while Kierkegaard attempts to isolate the actual historical Socrates from the ideal narratives that provide the accounts, Bauer and Strauss attempt to isolate the historical Jesus from the gospel narratives. As Beck puts it: "This treatise thus has a speculative-critical character and furnishes an interesting parallel to the critique of evangelical history that in recent years has stirred the theological world."[29] And as Beck sees it, Kierkegaard's dissertation is loyal to the Hegelian historical-critical method in a way right Hegelians like Rasmus Nielsen are not: Beck writes that, unlike Nielsen, Kierkegaard does not work with concepts "in complete abstraction from the historical element (as if we had only to deal with these concepts in their pure ideality), but instead the author sets a more concrete and determinate task for himself,"[30] namely, to show how "the actual historical phenomenon is concealed beneath another phenomenon, which is its reflection in a certain consciousness that has been unable to appropriate it in its pure objectivity."[31] In other words, Beck appreciates Kierkegaard's aim to liberate actual history from a naïve interpretation or "mythical consciousness."[32] That this methodology has implications when applied to biblical texts was obvious, and Beck notes on several occasions that one sees similar results in Bruno Bauer's interpretation of the Gospel of John.[33]

While it is not clear whether Kierkegaard initially recognized Beck's attempt to interpret his dissertation as a work consistent with the historical-critical method, based on Beck's review alone, this must have become obvious when Beck published *The Concept of Myth or the Form of Religious Spirit* in 1842.[34] Kierkegaard's responds to Beck's review later in 1842 in an ironic newspaper article entitled "Public Confession."[35] Beck's name first appears in a sarcastic and dismissive line where he is grouped together with others members of the "remarkable age" who have contributed to the amazing feats of the times. While right-Hegelian Rasmus Nielsen is ironically praised for completing 21 paragraphs of an "extremely large" encyclopedia, Beck is said to have "abolished religion in order to make room for the system."[36] Kierkegaard continues his critique of Beck in a postscript, where, in the same sarcastic tone, Kierkegaard notes that his "esteemed critic" has indeed saved his dissertation "from oblivion" with his review of it.[37] But Kierkegaard is not entirely happy about it. After chiding Beck for believing that he had understood the dissertation, he writes:

---

29 Beck, "[Review of] *Om Begrebet Ironi*," column 7133; from an unpublished translation by Paul Muench.

30 Ibid., columns 7133–4; Muench's translation.

31 Ibid.

32 Kierkegaard himself suggests that Plato's narratives have a strong mythologizing element, which attributes doctrines to Socrates that the historical Socrates never held. See *SKS* 1, 150–62 / *CI*, 96–109, especially *SKS* 1, 158 / *CI*, 104.

33 Beck, "[Review of] *Om Begrebet Ironi*," columns 7136–8.

34 Andreas Frederik Beck, *Begrebet Mythus eller den religiøse Aands Form.*

35 Kierkegaard's "Public Confession," appeared in *Fædrelandet*, vol. 3, no. 904, June 12, 1842 (reprinted in *SV1* XIII, 397–406 / *COR*, 3–12).

36 *SV1* XIII, 400–1 / *COR*, 6.

37 *SV1* XIII, 404 / *COR*, 9.

> In the book Herr Doktor recently published, I see that he has most incredibly thrust me in among the Straussians. In formation with Strauss, Feuerbach, Vatke, Bruno Bauer, I must, whether I want to or not, keep in step while Dr. B. counts, *ein, zwei, drei*....[A] person has to put up with it if he does not belong to the systematic intelligensia.... If one is simply a poor renter who cultivates his own little plot, he must come when the owner whistles and be assigned his place, now here, now there.[38]

Kierkegaard does not reveal how and to what degree the aims of his dissertation depart from those of the left Hegelians named by Beck. He is not interested in a scholarly discussion of the matter, even if he declines membership among those who abolish religion in order "make room for the system."[39]

While Kierkegaard offers little academic argumentation in his "Public Confession," he concludes by making fun of Beck's failure to read the text in the right way: it seems Beck's interest in the academic content blinds him from seeing what is going on with the irreverent form. Tellingly, Kierkegaard offers no direct criticism of Beck's summary of "the content of the book," though he adds sarcastically that he "learned nothing new from it."[40] Apparently the straightforward account of the philosophical content is not worth discussing. A complaint from Beck about Kierkegaard's writing style, on the contrary, draws a long, sarcastic response. In the last line of the review, Beck had written:

> The language of the author is flowing, light, and free from all the astringency found in school terminology. The presentation itself is permeated by a certain humor that will also make the reading of this writing charming for the cultured. On the other hand, it must be faulted for the fact that there are to be found a number of allusions and intimations in the book that probably very few will understand, and concerning which the reviewer in particular does not have the honor of following the author. The author also often seems to be less successful when he has in a more positive way wanted to shine forth with his wit; for what can be pleasing and pass muster in a chat that takes place in an alley or in one's dressing gown makes an entirely different impression through the pretension with which it appears in printed text: to be sure it can be amusing, that we do not deny, and it really has amused the reviewer, but—not to the benefit of the author.[41]

Kierkegaard's responds ironically that Beck "concludes that I deserve to be criticized because there are several allusions he does not understand."[42] He continues by offering several tongue-in-cheek reasons for thinking Beck is wrong, including the possibility

---

38 *SV1* XIII, 405 / *COR*, 10–11.

39 *SV1* XIII, 400–1 / *COR*, 6. Kierkegaard's dissertation, however, is about an ironic consciousness that aims to abolish immediacy in order to make room for something else. But that "something else" is not systematic philosophy, be it Plato's or Hegel's. If anything, irony makes room for a subjective pathway to a truth, a truth that remains indeterminate in *The Concept of Irony*, but which is consistent with the inward Christianity that Kierkegaard's authorship explores.

40 *SV1* XIII, 404 / *COR*, 9.

41 Beck, "[Review of] *Om Begrebet Ironi*," column 7191; Muench's translation.

42 *SV1* XIII, 404 / *COR*, 9.

that Kierkegaard ought to be praised because Beck does not understand him or that "Dr. B." deserves praise because his review "indicates a laudable naiveté."[43]

B. Beck's Review of Philosophical Fragments

Kierkegaard returns to Beck's inability to understand irony in Johannes Climacus' response to Beck's review of *Philosophical Fragments*.[44] In a long footnote in the *Postscript*, Climacus dismisses Beck again for similar reasons: even though Beck's summary of the philosophical content of the book is accurate, his failure to grasp the ironic form leads to the most egregious misinterpretation possible, namely, reading the work as if it were a straightforward "didactic" argument.

In Beck's unsigned review, he singles out the unique methodology as particularly important, just as he did in his review of *The Concept of Irony*: "This work by one of Denmark's most productive writers is not unworthy of a brief review on account of the peculiarity of its method."[45] That method, he says, consists in analyzing Christian presuppositions as general hypotheses without regard to their historical manifestation, that is, distinguishing between the ideal and the historical.[46] Here again, Beck is intrigued by a project that separates the sphere of historical events from the sphere of ideal content, and he seems to find an analysis of Christianity that is close to his left Hegelianism. And once again, he offers an overwhelmingly favorable review, complimenting Climacus for the clarity, acuity, and attention to detail with which he treats the concepts and problematicizes them for "our age, which levels, neutralizes and mediates everything."[47] Finally, like his first review a Kierkegaardian text, Beck finishes with a minor criticism of the style: "We keep to ourselves any contrary remark, for, as was said, our goal was to illustrate the peculiar method of the author. For the rest, we leave it to the judgment of the reader whether he wants to seek seriousness or perhaps irony in this apologetic dialectic."[48] This last line in enough for Climacus, for it is obvious to him that if Beck has to indicate that there might be some irony involved, he clearly has not understood the book at all. Climacus is the first to admit that Beck has done a fine job summarizing the methodological aspects of the book, but that is not sufficient for understanding it: "his report is accurate and on the whole, dialectically reliable; but now comes the hitch: although the report is accurate, anyone who reads only it will receive an utterly wrong impression of the book."[49] Because the review is written in a scholarly, "didactic" tone, the reader might think Climacus' book is "didactic"—which, according to Climacus, it is not:

---

43 *SV1* XIII, 404–5 / *COR*, 9–10.

44 For an in depth and insightful treatment, see Muench, "The Socratic Method of Kierkegaard's Pseudonym Johannes Climacus," pp. 139–50.

45 [Beck], [Review of] "*Philosophische Smuler eller en Smule Philosophie*," p. 44. From an unpublished translation by Jon Stewart.

46 Ibid., pp. 44–5.

47 Ibid., p. 45; Stewart's translation.

48 Ibid., p. 48; Stewart's translation.

49 *SKS* 7, 250, note 1 / *CUP1*, 275, note.

> The contrast of form, the teasing resistance of the imaginary construction of the content, the inventive audacity (which even invents Christianity), the only attempt made to go further (that is, further than the so-called speculative constructing), the indefatigable activity of irony, the parody of speculation in the entire plan, the satire in making efforts as if something *ganz Außerordentliches und zwar Neues* were to come of them, whereas what always emerges is old-fashioned orthodoxy in its rightful severity—of this the reader finds no hint in the report.[50]

In essence, Climacus chides Beck for being a blunt reader, attentive only to the philosophical content in the *Fragments*, but deaf to its indirectness, its irony, its parody of scholarly literature. In Climacus' reading of his own book, *Fragments* says nothing new; nor is it an original argument for the truth of Christian doctrine. The interesting part for Climacus is the tension between the content and form: the dialectical or logical argument and the witty, indirect presentation. Only when one is attentive to the irony is it possible to read the book correctly. Like Kierkegaard's Socrates from *The Concept of Irony*, Climacus aims not to didactically teach something new, but to ironically take something away: to show that Christianity is not what is familiar as the age thinks it is, but something less reasonable, less attractive and more risky.[51]

Unlike many of the local figures who show up in Kierkegaard's authorship, the significance of Kierkegaard's relationship to Beck is modest. It is difficult to demonstrate that Kierkegaard was influenced by Beck's views, and there is not much evidence of great personal exchange. That said, Kierkegaard's few notes on Beck suggest at least two things: first, that Kierkegaard does not seems as provoked by the left-Hegelian tendency to argue for a mythological interpretation of biblical texts as he is by the right-Hegelian tendency to "explain" Christianity and thus make it intellectually palatable. Secondly, Kierkegaard's responses to Beck's reviews show how tricky it is to deal with ironic writers: in the view of Kierkegaard and his pseudonyms, it is one thing to be able to give good philosophical or "dialectical" account of their texts, as Beck does; it is another thing to grasp them.

---

50 Ibid.

51 Muench, "The Socratic Method of Kierkegaard's Pseudonym Johannes Climacus," pp. 139–50.

Bibliography

I. Beck's Works in The Auction Catalogue *of Kierkegaard's Library*

Begrebet Mythus eller den religiøse Aands Form, Copenhagen: P.G. Philipsen 1842 (*ASKB* 424).

II. Works in The Auction Catalogue *of Kierkegaard's Library that Discuss Beck*

Brøchner, Hans, *Nogle Bemærkninger om Daaben, foranledigede ved Professor Martensens Skrift: "Den christelige Daab,"* Copenhagen: P.G. Philipsen 1843, p. 30 (*ASKB* U 27).

III. Secondary Literature on Kierkegaard's Relation to Beck

Czakó, István, "Feuerbach: A Malicious Demon in the Service of Christianity," in *Kierkegaard and His German Contemporaries*, Tome I, *Philosophy*, ed. by Jon Stewart, Aldershot: Ashgate 2007 (*Kierkegaard Research: Sources, Reception and Resources*, vol. 6), pp. 25–47; see especially pp. 31–3.

James, David and Moggach, Douglas, "Bruno Bauer: Biblical Narrative, Freedom and Anxiety," in *Kierkegaard and His German Contemporaries*, Tome II, *Theology*, ed. by Jon Stewart, Aldershot: Ashgate 2007 (*Kierkegaard Research: Sources, Reception and Resources*, vol. 6), pp. 1–21; see p. 5.

Kirmmse, Bruce, "Socrates in the Fast Lane: Kierkegaard's *The Concept of Irony* on the University's *Velocifère*," in *The Concept of Irony*, ed. by Robert L. Perkins, Macon, Georgia: Mercer University Press 2001 (*International Kierkegaard Commentary*, vol. 2) pp. 17–100, see p. 78.

Koch, Carl Henrik, *Den danske idealisme 1800–1880*, Copenhagen: Gyldendal 2004 (*Den danske Filosofis Historie*, ed. by Sten Ebbesen and Carl Henrik Koch), pp. 487–96.

Malik, Habib C., *Receiving Søren Kierkegaard. The Early Impact and Transmission of His Thought*. Washington, D.C.: Catholic University Press of America 1997, see pp. 49–50.

Muench, Paul, "The Socratic Method of Kierkegaard's Pseudonym Johannes Climacus: Indirect Communication and the Art of 'Taking Away,' " in *Søren Kierkegaard and the Word(s): Essays on Hermeneutics and Communication*, ed. by Poul Houe and Gordon Marino, Copenhagen: C.A. Reitzel 2003, pp. 139–50.

Politis, Hélène, "Kierkegaard: Documents philosophiques," in *Kierkegaard. Vingt-Cinq Etudes* (*Le Cahiers de Philosophie*, nos. 8–9), 1989, pp. 443–72.

Rasmussen, S.V., *Den unge Brøchner*, Copenhagen: Gyldendal 1966, pp. 186–7.

Schjørring, Jens Holger, *Teologi og filosofi. Nogle analyser og dokumenter vedrørende Hegelianisme i dansk teologi*, Copenhagen: C.A. Reitzel 1974, pp. 36–49.

Stewart, Jon, *A History of Hegelianism in Golden Age Denmark*, Tome I, *The Heiberg Period: 1824–1836*, Copenhagen: C.A. Reitzel 2007 (*Danish Golden Age Studies*, vol. 3), p. 62.

—— *A History Hegelianism in Golden Age Denmark*, Tome II, *The Martensen Period: 1837–1842*, Copenhagen: C.A. Reitzel 2007 (*Danish Golden Age Studies*, vol. 3), p. 417; pp. 550–1; p. 632.

—— *Kierkegaard's Relations to Hegel Reconsidered*, Cambridge and New York: Cambridge University Press 2003, p. 11, note; p. 69; p. 140; p. 233; p. 280; pp. 336–7; p. 600.

Vergote, Henri-Bernard, *Lectures philosophiques de Søren Kierkegaard. Kierkegaard chez ses contemporains danois. Textes de J.L. Heiberg, H.L. Martensen, P.M. Møller, F.C. Sibbern, F. Beck et S.A. Kierkegaard*, Paris: Presses Universitaires de France 1993 (*Philosophique D'ajourd'hui*).

Jens Finsteen Giødwad:
An Amiable Friend and a Despicable Journalist

Andrea Scaramuccia

I. Muddle in a Puddle

In a passage from his memoirs published in 1890, Vilhelm Birkedal (1809–92), pastor in a village on the island of Funen and one of the leaders of the Grundtvigian movement, recalls the uneasiness he experienced whenever he met the famous Søren Kierkegaard on the streets of Copenhagen. The peripatetic philosopher used to engage in long conversations with people he met on his way, and at the same time employed his piercing psychological insight to investigate his interlocutor's mind. Birkedal loathed the pressure, the scrutiny of inspection, which he was subjected to when encountering his theological antagonist:

> As I mentioned, when I met S.K. like this, I was afraid of becoming more deeply involved than necessary with him. I did not want to be grilled. He could cause the most ridiculous situations. One time I was walking along Østergade and suddenly heard a voice from the opposite sidewalk: "Birkedal!" It was S.K. accompanying Cand. Gjødwad by the arm. I crossed the street diagonally towards him, while he and G. did the same, and we met in the middle of the street where we found ourselves standing in a pile of dirt. "May I present messieurs to one another," said K., "Pastor B. and Cand. G." Then we immediately bade each other farewell.[1]

In this amusing scene, Danish clergy and the "mud-slinging machine"[2] of journalism—the two institutions so often the target of Kierkegaard's own mud-slinging—congregate in person, if only for a brief moment, as Kierkegaard awkwardly bows to the vanity of genteel courtesy and introduces friend to foe in a puddle of mud in the middle of a public road. The irony was that Jens Finsteen Giødwad was not only the person (perhaps the *only* person besides Emil Boesen) whom Kierkegaard could call "my personal friend,"[3] but he also represented the institution of journalism as such that Kierkegaard so vehemently despised: "God in Heaven knows that blood-thirst is alien to my soul," he wrote in a journal entry in 1849, "but yet, yet in the

---

1 *Encounters with Kierkegaard: A Life as Seen by His Contemporaries*, trans. and ed. by Bruce H. Kirmmse, Princeton: Princeton University Press 1996, p. 107 (translation slightly modified).

2 *SKS* 23, 119, NB16:35.

3 *SKS* 21, 214, NB9:28 / *JP* 1, 711.

name of God, I would take upon myself the responsibility of giving the order to open fire the very moment I had conscientiously taken the greatest pains to ascertain that not one single other person, indeed not one living being, were in the firing line except—journalists."[4] Kierkegaard himself was the first to be puzzled and amazed at this strange relationship with Giødwad, because, despite his friend's good nature and renowned integrity, he was persuaded that "a certain degree of dishonesty is inseparable from even the most honest journalist."[5]

Giødwad was never a prolific author and certainly never exercised a theoretical influence on Kierkegaard's thinking; nonetheless, his amiability and untiring helpfulness, his strong sense of duty, his idealism and unwavering dedication had—as we shall see—an important influence on Kierkegaard's authorship.

Being a generous, humble, and selfless person, Giødwad did not leave many traces of his endeavors in life: the Royal Library in Copenhagen and the Danish State Archives hold no personal archive on his legacy, and can only offer a few scattered letters and documents from his hand. Thus, his achievements in life and his historical significance can only be traced through the testimony of his more famous comrades.

II. Giødwad's Biography and Significance

Jens Finsteen Giødwad (alternatively spelled Gjødwad, Gjødvad or Giødvad) was born in Aalborg, in northern Jutland, on July 19, 1811. He was the son of Anders Giødwad, a wealthy merchant, and Dorothea Sophie Finsteen, first daughter of a tanner. She was related via her mother to the Danish merchant tycoon and philanthropist Niels Brock.[6] Giødwad attended Aalborg's Cathedral School. He graduated from upper-secondary school in 1828, and in 1832 he graduated in law from the University of Copenhagen with the highest marks.

The young student's relatively favorable economical standing allowed him to complete his studies in time without having to work to support himself, and he could also afford memberships of the sometimes costly social clubs and societies that played a very important part in the social, cultural, and political life of Golden Age Denmark. He began to make acquaintances in Copenhagen in a club called the "Ny Forening," where he played cards with many military and civil officers of the Kingdom of Denmark, and he was a prominent member of the Student Association of Copenhagen University where the academic youth would gather for study and conversation and attend evening lectures and discussions on various topics. As a law graduate, Giødwad was repeatedly elected as "senior member" of the association's executive committee (*Senioratet*) and was therefore deeply involved in the administrative life of the institution.

---

4 *SKS* 21, 283–4, NB10:53 / *JP* 6, 6354.

5 *SKS* 22, 422, NB14:136 / *JP* 2, 2164.

6 Cf. Peter Jakob Brock-Schmidt, *Legatstifteren Grosserer Niels Brocks og Hustru Lene Brock, f. Bredals Slægt. Mands- og Kvindelinien*, Copenhagen: Boghandler P.J. Schmidts Forlag 1891, p. 18.

The Athenæum literary club and the Astraea juridical society were also important formative influences in Giødwad's life. The former was founded in 1824 and became a gathering place for Copenhagen intellectuals due to its extensive library that included an almost complete collection of contemporary national and international newspaper literature. Membership of Athenæum was relatively costly, at least for the pockets of an average university student, but in the 1830s its reading room and especially the conversation study gradually became the stage of a circle of politically interested friends who availed themselves of the library resources for study and to disseminate information on historical events in Denmark and Europe. Giødwad was, indeed, a regular member of this circle.[7] Astraea, on the other hand, was a society of young law students and graduates, who would regularly convene in the private homes of its members to discuss technical questions and practice their rhetorical skills through debate.

Shortly after graduation, Giødwad embarked on a career as a trainee solicitor at the office of a High Court lawyer, but his literary and political interests were soon to lead his professional life in a totally different direction. Ever since his arrival in the capital, Giødwad had been a frequent guest at the home of Counsellor (*Kancelliraad*) Jacob Deichmann, owner of the Gyldendal bookshop, who had welcomed him as a son and introduced him to many scholars and literary figures of the time. These acquaintances gave him his first literary undertakings: he worked as a proofreader and editor for *Dansk Literatur-Tidende* from 1834 to 1836 and published under his name bibliographies of all publications printed in Denmark in the years 1833–37.[8]

It was, nonetheless, Giødwad's political passion and idealism that were to condition his future. Strongly influenced by the ideals of the French Revolution of July 1830, which he had become acquainted with at the Athenæum and the Student Association, he realized that politics was his true vocation. He soon found a brother-in-arms in the young Orla Lehmann (1810–70), who had graduated in law from Copenhagen University in 1833 and was a leading figure in academic circles due to his political engagement, winning personality, and oratorical talent. Lehmann's outstanding eloquence and flaming rhetoric, which drew its style from the Golden Age of French parliamentarianism, increasingly inspired and fascinated the otherwise reserved and sober-minded Giødwad. The two lawyers, different in character as they were, developed a close friendship and vowed to work together for two common goals: to promote greater political and social awareness among the Danes, who in their eyes had fallen into apathy, and to bring about a free constitution,

---

7 This liberal circle was dubbed "*Scandalen*" (The Scandal) by more conservative members of the club. The group was also kept under tight surveillance by Copenhagen's chief of police, whose archive contained several reports on "*Scandalen*" filed by eager and anonymous sources at Athenæum. Cf. Lise Busk-Jensen, Peter Brask, et al., *Dansk litteratur historie*, vols. 1–9, Copenhagen: Gyldendal 1983–85, vol. 5, p. 180.

8 *Fortegnelse over de i Aarene 1833 og 34 i Kiøbenhavn udkomne Bøger, samlet af J.F. Giødwad*, Copenhagen: Gyldendal 1835; *Fortegnelse over de i Aaret 1835 i Danmark udkomne Skrifter, samlet af J.F. Giødwad*, Copenhagen: Gyldendal 1836; *Fortegnelse over de i Aaret 1836 i Danmark udkomne Skrifter, samlet af J.F. Giødwad*, Copenhagen: Gyldendal 1837; *Fortegnelse over de i Aaret 1837 i Danmark udkomne Skrifter, samlet af J.F. Giødwad*, Copenhagen: Gyldendal 1838.

which was to deliver the nation from absolute monarchy. In 1835, they published a free translation of three political discourses by the French orators François Auguste Chateaubriand (1768–1848), Paul Louis Courier (1773–1825), and André-Marie Jean Jacques Dupin (1783–1865). They believed such discourses could "serve as a model for anyone, who by speech or in writing seeks to influence the people," since "Danish literature for obvious reasons only manages to deliver very few models of worldly eloquence."[9]

Giødwad and Lehmann also realized that in order to promote a wider interest in public affairs they needed a daily newspaper at their disposal. The two major liberally-oriented news channels of the time, *Dansk Ugeskrift* and the newly launched *Fædrelandet*, were only issued weekly, and due to the severe regime of press censorship upheld by the government of Frederik VI, reformist notions could only be expressed in moderate and watered-down terms. In 1835, after a year of occasional assignments with the daily newspaper *Kjøbenhavnsposten*, Giødwad and Lehmann took the initiative to reach an agreement with editor-in-chief Andreas Peter Liunge (1798–1879) to edit the political material for the paper. From the moment they assumed editorial responsibility, the newspaper evolved from being one mainly devoted to aesthetics to becoming the nation's leading oppositional paper of the 1830s. Lehmann represented a bold reformist line, which often caused great scandal within the Copenhagen establishment. The gradual politicizing of *Kjøbenhavnsposten* and its general polemical nature also made the paper far more popular among a wider audience. Subscriptions almost doubled between 1834 and 1835, rising from 550 to 1,000.[10]

Orla Lehmann's spirited writing and the radical direction adopted by *Kjøbenhavsposten* worried Liunge, who increasingly perceived the sharp-penned journalism of his two employees as a legal liability. He finally resigned as editor-in-chief in 1837 and handed the reins to Giødwad. Liunge remained publisher with no editorial responsibility, and Lehmann kept his position as leading journalist. From that moment on, Orla Lehmann's private room doubled as *Kjøbenhavnsposten*'s office, and the entire apparatus of the newspaper outside the printing room was managed by Giødwad. When he turned up with government licensed newspapers in his pocket, a news item on his lips and an idea, a tip, a seedling for an article on his forehead, then work would soon be underway. Orla Lehmann's style of writing was indisputably the most elegant and sharp, and it was, indeed, from his pen that the series of articles originated which at the time caused the general public to hold *Kjøbenhavnsposten* in such high regard. Lehmann had a habit of dictating his articles, and once Giødwad had put his colleague's thoughts on paper, then the former would run over to a society or general assembly and devote himself to his busy political agenda, while Giødwad himself hastened to the printing office and often did the proofreading while sitting on

9 *Tre franske Taler af Chateaubriand, Courier og Dupin*, trans. by J.F. Giødwad and O. Lehmann, Copenhagen: C.A. Reitzel 1835, p. I.

10 Cf. Jette D. Søllinge and Niels Thomsen, *De danske aviser 1634–1989*, vols. 1–3, Odense: Odense Universitetsforlag 1988–91, vol. 1, p. 147.

a type case.[11] This frenetic, although in its beginning almost amateurish, journalistic partnership was to contribute greatly to the liberal cause in the years to come.

In his memoirs, published posthumously in the 1870s, Orla Lehmann painted the following portrait of his slightly younger colleague:

> Gjødvad was first and foremost a person of character—a fearless and unshakable will in a quiet, modest being; a self-denying devotee of what he considered to be righteous and a question of duty. He who knows the conditions of the press at the time, and in particular *Kjøbenhavnsposten*'s reputation in aesthetic times, will know the degree of sacrifice that his decision to assume editorial responsibility entailed, despite the fact that his solid university degree and social connections furnished him with the same favorable prospects as that of anyone else. And he who recalls the long list of abuse and persecution that the press was subjected to with mounting vehemence as it gradually shaped its opposition to the establishment, he must hold in high esteem the dauntless perseverance and endurance that remained steadfast in the face of distain and contestation until the final day of victory at which point Gjødvad's actual role had reached fruition. This is what must earn Gjødvad an honorable position among the champions of freedom in Denmark, although he was not an orator and therefore did not assume a prominent position in public negotiations. And although his talent as a writer was neither considerable, nor easy or pleasant in any way, then it is, indeed, certain that the unconditional trust he had earned among friends and foes alike, and that was merited by his high principles and unselfishness has contributed greatly to continuously elevating the moral dignity of the press. And the advancement it experienced was essentially due to the unflinching perseverance with which he year after year carried the burden of editorial office without ever soliciting gratitude or reward. The legitimacy of my testimony lies in the fact that I was the principal person from whom he sought assistance. Thus we would convene daily, and he would even seek my company late in the evening on the occasion that a new letter had been forwarded by the Chancellery that demanded a prompt reply, or when a manuscript fell short. For at the time all tasks were part and parcel of the same process and volunteers scarce. And to achieve what he desired he would follow my dictation, which was nonetheless the result of mutual consultation, and wandered often late at night over to the printing office.[12]

A public newspaper that brought criticism to bear against public affairs and undertakings was not easily tolerated under the rule of absolute monarchy. Among many other repressive decrees, the Royal Ordinance of September 27, 1799 was designed to punish "bitter grumblings over the government" with punitive censorship, and the bill of November 1, 1837 decreed fines and 1–5 years of punitive censorship for showing "lack of due consideration," which was an ingeniously elastic term that courts would interpret at their discretion. There were numerous cases in this period where fines were levied and where publishing material was confiscated. All periodicals were kept under tight surveillance, aided by the notorious Councilor (*Justitsråd*) Christian Reiersen (1792–1876), who from 1834 assisted the Chief Constable of Police (*Politimester*). Reiersen had been authorized to enforce censorship such as

---

11 Cf. Christian Kirchhoff-Larsen, *Den danske presses historie*, vols. 1–3, Copenhagen: Berlingske Forlag 1942–62, vol. 3, 1962, pp. 116–17.

12 Hother Hage and Carl Ploug (eds.), *Orla Lehmanns Efterladte Skrifter*, vols. 1–4, Copenhagen: Gyldendal 1872–74, vol. 1, pp. 76–8.

confiscation prior to distribution but was restricted to publications printed using less than 24 signatures per copy. In the late 1830s and in the 1840s such confiscations of free-spirited periodicals became almost daily occurrences. Moreover, government officials and public servants were firmly required to refrain from voicing political opinions and from offering information to newspapers without royal licences.

In November 1837, Giødwad's home in Kokkegade 136 (currently Valkendorfsgade 30) was raided by sergeant Götzsche accompanied by two police constables in reaction to the publication in *Kjøbenhavnsposten* of an internal letter dated April 27, 1837 which had been posted by the Copenhagen Customs Inspection Office and subsequently leaked to Giødwad by the indiscretion of Customs Inspector Blom. The police search was promptly denounced in *Kjøbenhavnsposten* by its infuriated editor, and the subsequent court case caused great scandal in the city.[13]

Prosecution for press law infringements perpetrated by *Kjøbenhavnsposten* increased year by year. Altogether, in the years 1837–39, the Chancellery brought six cases against Giødwad to court at the first instance (*Landsover-, Hof-og Stadsretten*) and the High Court, where he was accused of having published culpable articles in *Kjøbenhavnsposten*. Of these court cases, four led to acquittal. In two cases Giødwad was sentenced to fines of 300 rix-dollars and 50 rix-dollars respectively. In one case—brought before the High Court—he was also sentenced to two years of punitive censorship. In June 1841, Giødwad was additionally fined 500 rix-dollars by the High Court and sentenced to punitive censorship for three years for having allowed the above-mentioned material to be printed.[14] The newspaper's budget was heavily burdened by ballooning legal expenses and by the loss of revenue as the result of confiscation: "Both Orla Lehmann and J.F. Giødwad struggled against bad odds. The times were tough. The economy was in a bad shape and working within publishing was very poorly paid. It was a perilous profession in which one often fell foul of the law."[15]

In 1957, Johannes Lehmann (1896–1980) wrote the following tribute to Giødwad and Orla Lehmann's literary achievement with *Kjøbenhavsposten* in the years of their editorship:

> With the purity of his character and his integrity, [Giødwad] compelled even his political adversaries to hold him in esteem.[16] To achieve his political and journalistic goals he sacrificed everything else in life. He thus always sustained merely a modest living. The

---

13 Cf. *Kjøbenhavnsposten*, no. 312, November 11, 1837, pp. 1251–9; *Kjøbenhavnsposten* no. 313, November 12, 1837, pp. 1263–4. Cf. also Harald Jørgensen, *Trykkefrihedsspørgsmaalet i Danmark 1799–1848. Et bidrag til en Karakteristisk af den danske Enevælde i Frederik VI's og Christian VIII's tid*, Copenhagen: Munksgaard 1944, p. 171; Kirchhoff-Larsen, *Den danske presses historie*, vol. 3, p. 119 and Ole Stender-Petersen, *Kjøbenhavnsposten. Organ for "det extreme Democrati" 1827–1848*, Odense: Odense Universitets Forlag 1978, p. 17; p. 104.

14 Cf. Stender-Petersen, *Kjøbenhavnsposten*, p. 104, note 13.

15 Johannes Lehmann, *Den unge Orla Lehmann*, Copenhagen: Dansk Kautionsforsikrings-Aktieselskab 1957, p. 41.

16 Giødwad used to remember with amusement the patronizing tone used in a note of a polemical piece written against him by the famous statesman and state lawyer (*Generalprokuratør*) Anders Sandøe Ørsted: "Nevertheless, he is *apparently* reputed to be

> cause was for him everything; to him his own personality was nothing. That is why he mainly kept to the sideline and revelled in the rising celebrity of his more talented co-editor; he was more than satisfied with his backstage existence and undertaking—and his reliability was proverbial. D.G. Monrad characterized him as "the housewife of the Liberal Party."[17] A sincere relationship developed between J.F. Giødwad and Orla Lehmann. These two men, who bravely faced the firing line, were the vanguard of freedom and Danishness, and gradually more and more people joined them—and finally the whole Danish people followed....Like a skillful steersman, the more level-headed Giødwad knew how to hold back when Orla Lehmann flung into a temper, which he easily did, and he skillfully navigated between the rocks and reefs onto which in times of trouble one could so easy run aground. It was not always possible to avoid incidents, but one cannot but admire how these two young people managed to keep the little old tub afloat for such a long time.[18]

On April 11, 1839, Giødwad resigned from his editorial position at *Kjøbenhavns-posten*, not due to misgivings or the frequent disappointments he experienced, nor as the result of the fierce political persecution to which he was subjected (the verdict had not yet been passed on him).[19] Rather, his decision came about due to the diagnosis of a serious chest ailment from which he was given little chance of recovery. Shortly after him, Lehmann also left the newspaper, while publisher Liunge hired Johan Peter Grüne (1805–78) as new editor-in-chief.

After having spent the spring and part of the summer at Frederik's Hospital, Giødwad decided to heed the doctor's advice and seek a more benign southern climate. Within no time, as a gesture of gratitude for the services he had provided as a journalist, he was offered a large sum of money by traders on the Copenhagen stock exchange to cover his travel expenses to Paris where he remained until the spring of 1840. Swedish journalist and writer Oskar Patrick Sturzen-Becker (1811–69)—a close friend of Giødwad, whom he affectionately nicknamed "the old one"[20]—later remarked with poignant reasoning: "Others travelled with the patronage of Kings; *he* travelled with that of the people."[21] When he returned from his stay in France he resided for a while as the guest of Balthasar Matthias Christensen (1802–82) in a property in Grøndal, outside Copenhagen. Here a milk cure helped him recover from his ailment.

---

an honest person" (my emphasis). Cf. Hans Carl August Lund, "J.F. Giødwad," *Illustreret Tidende*, vol. 32, no. 35, May 31, 1891, p. 419.

17 "In a toast to Gjødvad at a parliamentary banquet, Monrad referred to him with emphasis as the housewife of the Liberal Party, whose quiet undertaking is less conspicuous yet nonetheless the prerequisite of cohesion and progress"; Cf. Hage and Ploug (eds.), *Orla Lehmanns Efterladte Skrifter*, vol. 1, 1872, p. 78.

18 Lehmann, *Den unge Orla Lehmann*, pp. 38–40.

19 Cf. Carl Ploug, "Minderune for J.F. Giødwad," in *Danmark. Illustreret Kalender for 1892*, ed. by Copenhagen's Journalists Association, Copenhagen: G.E.C. Gad 1891, p. 53.

20 Ragnar Sturzen-Becker, *Oskar Patrick. Sturzen-Becker (Orvar Odd)*, vols. 1–2, Stockholm: Norstedt & Söners Förlag 1911–12, vol. 1, p. 118.

21 Orvar Odd [O. P. Sturzen-Becker], *Hinsidan Sundet. Danska Epistlar af Orvar Odd*, Stockholm: Bonniers Förlag 1846, p. 49.

Before leaving on his only journey abroad, Giødwad had reached agreement with four of his political friends (Christian Nathan David, Orla Lehmann, Abraham Wessely, and the aforementioned Balthasar Christensen) to transform David's periodical *Fædrelandet* into a daily newspaper, which was originally to have been launched on New Year's Day 1840. However, the death of Frederik VI on December 3, 1839 speeded up the process and the first edition of the daily newspaper was issued as early as December 7, not least due to the strenuous efforts of Orla Lehmann. This was early enough to welcome the appointment of the king's successor Christian VIII, while also encouraging him to adopt a more liberal style of rule such as he had already done during his one-year tenure as sovereign of the Norwegian realm in 1814. Giødwad was obviously not involved in the initial editorial wrangling, but his skills and expertise were deemed indispensable by his colleagues, and from March 1840 his name appeared in the colophon among the editors of *Fædrelandet*. Here he is listed as sub-editor and economical administrator to the paper.

During the first two years of the re-launched *Fædrelandet* many members of the editorial team (including the incoming D.G. Monrad) were forced to relinquish their positions due to government pressure and punitive censorship,[22] but Giødwad and Lehmann continued as firm supporters and contributors to the newspaper, even when the latter chose no longer to appear officially as editor-in-chief in order to pursue a career as a High Court lawyer. On May 11, 1841 Lehmann was replaced by writer and poet Carl Parmo Ploug (1813–94), a well-known figure in Copenhagen's student's community, who at the time worked as a modest private tutor and therefore could undertake such a risky enterprise without compromising an established position in society. After a couple of years of apprenticeship during which Giødwad undertook to develop and nurture Ploug's political understanding and advise him on how to write editorial content, Ploug became the leading pen of *Fædrelandet*, and under his editorship the newspaper became the most important organ of the liberal opposition until the fall of absolute monarchy in 1848. The newspaper gradually gained a reputation as Denmark's most influential opinion-shaping voice, at least until the defeat of the national-liberal movement in 1864.

In a tribute penned in 1891 to the memory of his slightly younger colleague, Ploug recalls Giødwad's qualities and his influence on *Fædrelandet* at the time of their editorial partnership:

> I learnt to appreciate his noble and pure character and immense amiability. He did not have a strong urge to write. He easily became agitated during a discussion and would express his point of view with great clarity and sharpness, but once he had cooled off, and especially when writing something down, he would become too heavy in his approach and would be inclined to be too brief and easily became too dry. It therefore followed with a degree of necessity, but without prior or negotiated concord, that the actual editorial work slowly shifted to me while he, on the other hand, managed the technical apparatus and the economy, negotiated with the staff, informants and contributors and—as had, indeed, become custom—would congregate with political friends, who, when the occasion occurred with either greater or lesser frequency, would convene at the office

22 Cf. Hother Ploug, *Carl Ploug. Hans Liv og Gerning*, vols. 1–2 (unfinished), Copenhagen and Kristiania: Gyldendal 1905, vol. 1, 1905, pp. 93–6.

of *Fædrelandet* during lunchtime, which in a way was a continuation, albeit on a lower level, of the Athenæum meetings. These conversations, which in moments of upheaval would serve for mutual gratification and proved very useful for the editorial team, would in more tranquil times become such a time-robber that the person in charge of meeting the editorial deadline could not always afford such wastefulness.[23]

After Ploug's appointment, then, Giødwad's importance in relation to *Fædrelandet* had less and less to do with what he wrote for it: around the mid 1850s he had practically ceased to write articles of any substantial nature.[24] His major contribution to the paper consisted of his authoritative and much-respected presence, in the impulse he gave, in the reliability with which he carried out practical editorial duties, and in the connections he nurtured. *Fædrelandet*'s office, which since October 1844 had been located in an apartment on the second floor of Store Kjøbmagergade no. 35 (currently Købmagergade 54), and which moreover was the private residence of both Giødwad and Ploug, became a gathering place for a young generation of liberals who contributed to the paper: Ditlev Gothard Monrad (1811–87), Hother Hage (1816–73) and Alfred Anton Hage (1803–72), Anton Frederik Tscherning (1795–1874), Johan Wegener (1811–83), Peter Hiort Lorenzen (1791–1845), Laurids Skau (1817–64), Hans Brøchner (1820–75), besides the aforementioned Sturzen-Becker, Lehmann, Wessely, and Christensen.

But in addition to this, the office of *Fædrelandet* became a kind of club for Giødwad's more personal circle of friends. As the eldest and most experienced, Giødwad was a sort of "housewife of the Danish press" and the real host of the office, and he was visited by many who really had no particular affiliation with the newspaper but who liked to stop by in the morning and strike up conversation with him. Among these friends were the brothers *Carl and Ernst Weis*, *Christian Winther*, and finally *Søren Kierkegaard*...[Giødwad] possessed the fine and noble nature that was so common with our Liberals in the thirties and furthermore exhibited a steadfast and reliable character and possessed the moral audacity necessary to assume such an exposed position. His entire spiritual and moral calibre is probably best measured by the fact that so many brilliant and influential men... found satisfaction with his daily company and close confidentiality. But it is obvious that in relation to his audience he, despite his qualities, was relegated to the shadow of the more talented and authoritative Ploug, who furthermore assumed more representational duties with great skill. The public was thus not to any great degree made aware of this quiet, secluded man and only in specific circles did one later hear obscure rumblings claiming that Giødwad was the one "who wrote the very worst of all."[25]

---

23 Ploug, "Minderune for J.F. Giødwad," pp. 54–5.

24 In a letter to Orla Lehmann dated "5 December 1849," Carl Ploug writes that he cannot move from Copenhagen, "because *Fædrelandet* cannot have less than one editor or writing pen if it is not to fold—Giødwad has more than enough on hand with the finances and receiving visitors; it is ages since he wrote a line, or undertook any editorial task other than minor matters that also needed attending to." Cf. Julius Clausen (ed.), *Af Orla Lehmanns Papirer. Bidrag til Danmarks Tidshistorie i det 19. Aarhundrede*, Copenhagen: Det Nordiske Forlag/Ernst Bojesen 1903, p. 139.

25 Ploug, *Carl Ploug*, pp. 110–12.

In a letter to his fiancée dated June 11, 1860, Norwegian playwright Bjørnstjerne Bjørnson (1832–1910) refers to his visit to *Fædrelandet*'s office, offering an image of the prevailing atmosphere:

> Now I have been at Ploug's place; he is a lively, calm and strong man to speak with, and who knows all the important men in the Northern countries and passes sound judgement on them all. His companion, the same-aged Gjødwad...is a peculiar, slow-speaking, profound man with a quiet and sympathetic countenance. Every morning at Gjødwad's one finds Copenhagen's political salon: here one finds Kristian Winther, Sturtzen-Becker, a Swedish politician who has always resided here, old Levin and Pande. Ploug is more shielded from visitors, and he calls Gjødwad's salon a hornet's nest. They, Gjødwad and Ploug, are two old friends who cannot stay apart for an hour.[26]

The working partnership between Giødwad and Ploug, which moreover involved cohabitation, lasted for 27 years. They managed to maintain a good harmony, since from the beginning they always fully agreed on the goals for which they were struggling, but a letter from Ploug to Mrs. Hage from the mid-1840s pays testimony to the differences in character that would sometimes prevail and lead to occasional disagreements between the two editors:

> You know how amiable the friend is whom destiny has placed by my side; and God knows that I respect and cherish him dearly, yet we are nonetheless too different to reward each other's yearnings in life. He is reserved; I am not. He finds rest where I find none, yet in all his modesty and moderation he carried an illusion, namely, that we share the work burden, but this is not the case. *Fædrelandet* is not the fruit of two men's entire effort, which the world is led to believe and must think, but rather the fruit of one man's half effort, which is why it is sometimes so shoddy.…You must remember that the work of a journalist, if it is to be of merit, must always be awash with the bubbly champagne; it should be fresh and lively to win appeal. By nature and by its effect, it is transient and carries little reward in itself—and you will appreciate that the two mainsprings (i.e., duty and necessity) are too weighty to keep the machinery running smoothly. Then consider that we live in an office, although you will find it hard to imagine what this implies. It can be summed up in a single word: turmoil from 8–9 in the morning until 9–10 in the evening, constant disruption, constant inconvenience, perpetual demands for attention regarding the many trivial and unimportant matters. And all the while work must be undertaken, and so it is, for one can become accustomed to all sorts. But now it has finally come to be, and then what? Then I cannot be swayed by senseless amusements or inconsequential conversation, nor by the card table or punch glass—but I sit home alone—*so* alone with the dark thoughts and the bright dreams, with the reckless fantasies and the bitter tears…believe me, when my skin is roughest, my soul is softest.[27]

Ploug's judgement of his colleague's contribution to *Fædrelandet* in this letter seems to be exceedingly harsh. Giødwad's knowledge, hard work, generosity, and aimiability were all essential ingredients in creating a good working environment; moreover, his cheerfulness and subtle wit were important counterbalances to

[26] Bjørnstjerne Bjørnson, *Breve til Karoline 1858–1907*, Oslo: Gyldendal Norsk Forlag 1957, p. 4.

[27] Ploug, *Carl Ploug*, pp. 288–9.

Lehmann's passionate temper and Ploug's moody and sometimes sullen and harsh character. In a letter to Ploug dated May 1855, Orla Lehmann pays due tribute to his old friend's industrious qualities: "I ask you to give my greetings to old Giødwad, the faithful housewife in the housekeeping of the Danish press, whose quiet undertaking is not the least conspicuous, but nonetheless what keeps everything together."[28] In one of his last poems written in Paris, Christian Winther (1796–1876)—a dear friend of Giødwad's since the evenings at Counsellor Deichmann's home—expresses his fond memories and gratitude for the warm welcome he always received at the office of *Fædrelandet*, which from February 1863 had relocated to a building on the corner of Højbro Plads called "Plougs Gaard." Here Winther would come every day to discuss current political events, and the rare times when he could not be present to enjoy Winther's company, Giødwad always managed to leave a cigar in a fixed place for his devoted friend.[29]

Joseph Michaelsen, who between 1846 and 1851 was employed in *Fædrelandet*'s office, gave a vivid picture of Giødwad's personality and reliability at work:

> Ploug did the editing. He, Gjødvad and I did the proofreading....When the newspaper was made ready for the print, which did not take place in the composing room, Gjødvad took hold of matters and read it through meticulously from title to place of printing [i.e., the colophon at the bottom of the final page] and he became difficult to handle when disturbed in this undertaking. I was at the time unable to see past Gjødvad's quiet being and perceive his importance since it did not transpire in the tangible results of everyday undertaking, yet I did have a hunch that *Jens Finsteen Gjødvad* commanded extensive and sound knowledge that reached far beyond the horizon of my vision. I also had the opportunity to bow to the balanced judgement and sharp Jutland eyes of this man whereas his cheerful camaraderie and heartfelt glee over a well-timed *bon mot* seemed refreshing and enlivening when Ploug's choleric temper had lowered the temperature at the office. He has, in reality, been of the greatest significance for the newspaper, both in direct terms in regards to the depth of his knowledge, but also indirectly as a counterbalance against Ploug's moodiness and disposition towards dictate. I was even unaware of the significance of Gjødvad's revision after the proofreading. I did not know, or did not give emphasis to the fact, that the insight and precision with which it was executed would deliver it from the threat and often blind light of "persecution." Gjødvad also kept the accounts and bookkeeping. I see before me again that stout man with that pale face and those screwed-up eyes behind blue glasses wearing a black robe, white scarf and black slippers with embroidery—his stately costume at the office—hop around on one leg while holding the other in his hand and voicing a low murmur as to discreetely hint at a latent reluctance towards going along with demands for advance payment for horse rides. However, I knew I would get my way when he had tired from hopping.[30]

But there was certainly not always time for pranks at the office of *Fædrelandet*. Censorship, which had hampered the press under Frederik VI, only grew worse

28 Clausen (ed.), *Af Orla Lehmanns Papirer*, p. 155.

29 Cf. Nicolai Bøgh, *Christian Winther. Et Livsbillede*, vols. 1–3, Copenhagen: G.E.C. Gads Forlag 1893–1901, vol. 2, p. 269.

30 Joseph Michaelsen, *Fra min Samtid*, vols. 1–2, Copenhagen: Brødrene Salmonsen 1890–93, vol. 1, pp. 45–6.

under his successor. Councilor Reiersen was undoubtedly the principal censorship authority in this period and was, therefore, incessantly ridiculed by the liberal press for his single-minded and often senseless censorial zeal, and even the Chancellery would often repudiate his action. The courts of law nevertheless still offered the best guarantee for justice, but sometimes even they could not be trusted. When the Chancellery decided to prosecute a publisher for press law infringement, this would entail a direct inquiry by the court, which thereafter passed council to the defendant and to the prosecution without undertaking to assess culpability. On occasion, an editor of a periodical would be fined for merely printing a couple of dashes, and no less than 60 confiscations hit *Fædrelandet* in the troubled years of 1842–45. It has been assessed that under the rule of Christian VIII, the liberal papers *Fædrelandet*, *Kjøbenhavnsposten*, *Den Frisindede*, *Morgenposten*, and *Corsaren* were fined a total of at least 17,980 rix-dollars, of which *Fædrelandet* alone paid 6,450. This was obviously an enormous amount for a publication of limited means, amounting to approximately 6–7 per cent of its annual gross income. Moreover, in 1843 alone, confiscation affected about one-tenth of all copies of *Fædrelandet*. Such a major reduction in the already meagre income of the publisher would have resulted in ruin if not for a circle of courageous people, mainly of the merchant class, who had established a foundation that would pay the fines when push came to shove.[31]

From July 1, 1844, the punitive censorship that had been levied on Giødwad since his collaboration with *Kjøbenhavnsposten* was lifted, and he could therefore be appointed editor-in-chief of *Fædrelandet*. But as early as June 28–30, 1845 three successive verdicts were passed by the High Court that levied a total of 11 years of punitive censorship on him in addition to fines amounting to approximately 1000 rix-dollars for press law infringements. He immediately had to relinquish his position as editor-in-chief and only regained his freedom of speech when censorship laws were finally lifted after 1848. The hardest year of all for Giødwad must have been 1845, when, following his hard sentence, his 67-year-old father died on July 24, and he, as the bereaved son, had to undertake a lengthy journey to Aalborg to attend the funeral.[32] He was, moreover, forced to sell his belongings, such as furnishings and books, at a public auction on September 1, 1845 to pay the high fines levied on him.[33] The following year he served a sentence of incarceration at the prison at Kastellet on bread and water.

---

31 Cf. C.E.F. Reinhardt, *Orla Lehmann og hans Samtid. Et Bidrag til Belysning af Friheds- og Nationalitets-Tankens Udvikling i Danmark*, Copenhagen: G.E.C. Gads Forlag 1871, p. 63; Ploug, *Carl Ploug*, pp. 210–11; Kirchhoff-Larsen, *Den danske presses historie*, vol. 3, pp. 237–40.

32 Cf. Povl Bagge and Povl Engelstoft, *Danske Politiske Breve fra 1830erne og 1840erne*, vols. 1–4, Copenhagen: Rosenkilde og Bagger 1945–58, vol. 3, 1949, p. 85 (letter no. 695).

33 Cf. *Fortegnelse over Bøger og Meubler, tilhørende hr. J.F. Giødwad, som sælges for Mulcter, idømte i Pressesager, ved Auctionen paa St. Kjøbmagergade nr. 54, 2den Sal, Mandag den 1ste Sept. 1845, Formiddag kl. 10*, Copenhagen: Bianco Luno Bogtrykkeri 1845. Among the 238 books, covering a wide range of fields from law to politics, art, theater, and literature, the auctioneer's sales lists records the following publications by Kierkegaard: *The Concept of Irony*, *Three Upbuilding Discourses* (1844), *Four Upbuilding Discourses* (1844), *Philosophical Fragments*, *Three Discourses on Imagined Occasions*, and *Stages on Life's Way*.

All the pain and humiliation that he suffered in his years of tribulation nonetheless had little effect on Giødwad's good-spirited nature, or his idealism and political dedication. Michaelsen recalls:

> I often wondered how this starkly conservative nature had found his way to the opposition. Now I believe that conservatism and liberalism have nothing to do with form of government but rather are an expression of temperament, which in turn is the result of modifications in the organism of blood cells, or the interlacing parts of the nervous system, which still evades the microscope and science. Was it his characteristic sense of justice that made him abhor absolutism? One thing is sure: that he took his standpoint seriously and staked his fortune and family life for the cause he had made his own. That later, when that cause had triumphed, he did not claim the winner's prize and sternly refused honors and titles, is in perfect harmony with the life he had led. *Bene vixit, qui bene latuit*, seems to have been his motto.[34]

After 1848, when the liberalist struggle for the abolition of absolute monarchy ended with a bloodless victory and the constitution of 1849, Giødwad and Ploug were unanimous in their refusal of a proposal by the March Ministry to make *Fædrelandet* the official organ of the new government, despite the great economic advantages that would entail. They preferred to maintain the freedom to express their opinion independently. Giødwad also refused the position of state auditor, which had been offered to him by the Danish Parliament, although he would have been perfectly suited for such a position due to his eminent skills as an accountant. He deeply disliked public attention and cherished his independence.

In the winter of 1868, Giødwad's failing eyesight deteriorated to a condition of total blindness. He could no longer carry out his daily editorial duty for *Fædrelandet* but maintained an authoritative presence at the editorial office: his friends would still meet him during the usual visiting hours, and at 3 o'clock in the afternoon he was always present to supervise the proofreading, always generously sharing his experience with others. In 1870, Giødwad's sister, Birgitte, who had become a widow the previous year, moved from Jutland to Copenhagen to look after her bachelor brother, and the two moved into an apartment in Kvæsthusgade No. 3, where they took care of each other until Birgitte's death in 1887.

Blindness, mourning, the changing times, and the infirmity of old age did not stop Giødwad from keeping his political passion alive. Even when he left the editorship of *Fædrelandet* in 1877, he kept up on current political and economic affairs and followed with interest reports on scientific advances, especially within the subjects in which he showed particular interest: political economy and statistics. Until his dying day he frequented the Athenæum, where many of his friends and acquaintances would read newspapers aloud to him or engage in discussions with him.

On May 11, 1891, only two months before his 80th birthday, Giødwad died of a heart ailment following several days of hospitalization. His funeral was held at Holmens Kirke, and he was interred at Assistens Kierkegaard. His grave in the G section of this famous cemetery (at the far end of the same side of the cemetery as

---

34 Michaelsen, *Fra min Samtid*, vol. 1, 1890, pp. 46–7. The Latin motto, derived from Ovid, means: "He who has lived well concealed (i.e., unnoticed), has lived well."

Kierkegaard's grave) has since been lost and thus the worldly remains and monument to life of one of the founding fathers of the first Danish constitution have been erased for eternity. As unassuming and invisible as he desired to be in life, he has managed to remain in death.

III. Friend and Foe

Kierkegaard does not explicitly mention Giødwad in his journals until 1838, but it is very likely that the young theology student would quite frequently have encountered the spirited jurist at Copenhagen University and at the Student Association where both Giødwad and Lehmann were renowned for their outspoken political activism and journalism and were repeatedly elected as "senior members" of the association's executive committee.[35] Such political dedication and zeal would, of course, never find favor with Kierkegaard, who was noted for his royalism and disdain of politics. Rather, they only fuelled his hot polemical temper.

In his paper entitled "Our Journalistic Literature," which he presented at the Student Association on November 28, 1835 as a polemical rebuttal of Johannes Andreas Ostermann's (1809–88) lecture and views on the role of the liberal press in promoting greater political awareness among the public, Kierkegaard vehemently attacked such issues as the political opportunism of *Kjøbenhavnsposten*, whose principal undertaking he characterized as a "bustling busyness" that gave rise to "disturbing activity" and "fitful fumbling."[36] He denounced what he saw as lack of consistency and the cowardice with which its contributors would hide behind pseudonyms or anonymous masks.[37]

In the series of articles published between February and March 1836 in Johan Ludvig Heiberg's journal *Kjøbenhavns flyvende Post*,[38] Kierkegaard even went one step further and unmasked the errors, blunders and staunch ideological overkill of liberal journalists and ridiculed them with razor-sharp wit for their pompous rhetoric, pure aesthetic posturing, and lack of original character: "Yes, certainly, *Kjøbenhavnsposten* is reforming, but on closer examination it is rather a parody of the reforming endeavor."[39] And although Kierkegaard in these articles never took direct issue with the substantive positions of liberalism, he clearly succeeded in demolishing his opponents by exposing their contradictions and flushing them with insolent remarks and wry innuendo. The main target of Kierkegaard's scathing attacks was, of course, his much-loathed antagonist Orla Lehmann, yet Giødwad

---

[35] In Frederik Fabricius' student comedy "*Nu gaar Ballonen*" (*Now the Balloon Rises*), for example, which was staged at the Student Association on Christmas Eve 1836, the travellers in the hot-air balloon gondola rising from the Student Association's garden do not become aware that they are airborne before they lose sight of Giødwad's collar points, which were distinguished by their exceptional proportions. Cf. Axel Sørensen, *Studenterkomedier*, Copenhagen: Lehmann & Stages Forlag 1904, p. 8.

[36] *Pap.* I B 2, p. 173 / *EPW*, 48.

[37] *Pap.* I B 2, pp. 173–7 / *EPW*, 48–52.

[38] *SV1* XIII, 9–39 / *EPW*, 6–34.

[39] *SV1* XIII, 14 / *EPW*, 11.

was not entirely untouched by the scorn the young polemicist would level at the "little dogs that always yap, and in the moment of danger creep into hiding" and the "anonymous reformers who work under the auspices of Liunge."[40] Nonetheless, Giødwad was handed an opportunity for revenge on November 22, 1836, when he and Ostermann were among the five senior members of the Student Association's *Seniorat* whose duty it was to notify Kierkegaard that he would be barred from the association premises should he fail to settle his dues and pay four months of membership fees within two weeks.[41]

Giødwad's standing with Kierkegaard remained unfavorable even when in 1837 Giødwad took Liunge's place and became editor-in-chief of *Kjøbenhavnsposten*, thus abandoning what Kierkegaard saw as an irresponsible practice of anonymous journalism in favor of executive office. On April 15, 1838, in the first journal entry in which he mentions Giødwad directly by name, Kierkegaard directs his sarcasm towards the charges brought against the editor for press law infringement: "If Gjødwad (I want to call him the licentiate, because he takes such great license) is convicted, one could call him 'former idol in the editorial offices of *Kjøbenhavnsposten*.' Incidentally, it will be easy for *Kjøbenhavnsposten* to find a new editor, since of course they appoint chance incarnations of Brahma."[42] Furthermore, it is a commonly held by many Kierkegaard scholars that the character Ole Wadt in the draft of the satirical student play *The Battle between the Old and the New Soap-Cellars* may very well have been intended as a stinging parody of Giødwad.[43]

Nevertheless, as the year passed, Giødwad's sincerity and diplomatic discretion overcame Kierkegaard's hostility and mistrust. In a testimony from 1885, historian and archivist Adolf Ditlev Jørgensen (1840–97)—a close friend of Giødwad whom he would often meet in Athenæum—wrote:

> Giødvad told me that he first made *Sören Kierkegård*'s acquaintance when the latter came to him to ask that he publish *Either/Or*. The reason for this was that Giødvad had given a firm rebuff to someone who had wanted to know who had written an anonymous article in *Fædrelandet*. The publication of *Either/Or* was rushed to such an extent that he received thirty-two pages of proofs daily; as far as G. could remember, they began on December 23, 1842.[44]

---

40 *SV1* XIII, 14 / *EPW*, 10.

41 The document is conserved in the Manuscript Department of the Royal Library in Copenhagen: *KA* D pk. 8 læg 1. Cf. Peter Tudvad, *Kierkegaards København*, Copenhagen: Politikens Forlag 2004, pp. 204–5. In 1836, the Student Association's *Seniorat* consisted of I.P. Holm, J.H. Zahrtmann, J.F. Giodwad, H.C. Sager, and J.A. Ostermann; Cf. Hans Carl August Lund, *Studenterforeningens Historie 1820–70*, vols. 1–2, Copenhagen: Gyldendal 1896–98, vol. 1, p. 399.

42 *SKS* 18, 99, FF:125 / *KJN* 2, 91.

43 Cf. *EPW*, 262, note 13; Emanuel Hirsch, *Kierkegaard-Studien*, vols. 1–2, Gütersloh: Bertelsmann 1933, vol. 2 p. 557; Niels Thulstrup, *Kierkegaard's Relation to Hegel*, trans. by George L. Stengren, Princeton, New Jersey: Princeton University Press 1980, p. 188. Hirsch in particular is persuaded that Wadt is "*selbstverständlich*" a parody of Giødwad and that Kierkegaard's satirical intention appears to be "very well accomplished," although Hirsch does not thoroughly explicate what he means by this statement.

44 *Encounters with Kierkegaard*, trans. and ed. by Bruce H. Kirmmse, p. 56.

When Kierkegaard started publishing his pseudonymous works he went to great lengths to guard the secrecy of his authorship. He soon found in Giødwad an ardent admirer of his literary enterprise, a trustworthy confident, and prudent ally with the necessary publishing know-how. The only time Kierkegaard mentions Giødwad in one of his published writings is in *The Point of View for my Work as an Author*, which was published posthumously in 1859. Here he characterizes Giødwad as a privileged witness of his own undercover literary endeavor, which aimed to awaken authentic religious sentiments among the Danish reading public:

> I am convinced that rarely has any author used as much cunning, intrigue and ingenuity to win honor and esteem in the world in order to deceive it as I have done for the opposite reason—to deceive it into an understanding of the truth. By just a single episode, for which I have the proofreader of *Either/Or*, my friend Giødwad, as a witness, I shall attempt to give an idea of the scale on which this deception was carried out. When I was reading proof pages of *Either/Or*, I was so busy that it was impossible for me to spend the usual time strolling up and down the street. I did not finish until late in the evening—and then in the evening I hurried to the theater, where I literally was present only five to ten minutes. And why did I do that? Because I was afraid that the big book would bring me too much esteem. And why did I do that? Because I knew people especially in Copenhagen; to be seen every night for five minutes by several hundred people was enough to sustain the opinion: So he doesn't do a single thing; he is nothing but a street-corner loafer.[45]

In the early years of Kierkegaard's pseudonymous authorship, *Fædrelandet*'s office, which from April 1842 to October 1844 was located at Klædeboderne 101 (today Skindergade no. 47) close to Kierkegaard's apartment at Nørregade 230 A (present-day no. 38), doubled as a second home for the young writer:

> Kierkegaard came there daily, and in the winter of 1843 [i.e., 1842–43] the proofreading of *Either/Or* took place, so to speak, in the offices of *Fædrelandet*, a situation that was partially responsible for the fact that Carl Ploug never entered into any relation of personal friendship with the famous thinker. One must imagine what it is like to have to have a newspaper ready at a definite time—and in those days it was early in the afternoon, because the police inspector had to look at the issue before it could be distributed—and to have an impractical and very self-absorbed man sitting in the office, ceaselessly lecturing and talking without the least awareness of the inconvenience he is causing.[46]

While "Giødwad reverently sat listening at the master's feet," Ploug "had to leave the room and go into his own cubicle in order to carry out his thankless daily task," and he "subsequently resented Kierkegaard because he had commandeered his colleague in such an inconsiderate fashion and had made him his audience all morning long, which cannot fail to have influenced Giødwad's interest in the routine drudgery of the office."[47] Nonetheless, this afforded Giødwad the opportunity to develop a close friendship with Kierkegaard: they would frequently be seen walking

45 *SV1* XIII, 547 / *PV*, 60–1.

46 *Encounters with Kierkegaard*, trans. and ed. by Bruce H. Kirmmse, pp. 55–6.

47 Ibid.

arm in arm in the street, and Giødwad managed to establish and nurture a long-lasting relationship between the philosopher and his newspaper. From 1842 to 1855, Kierkegaard submitted a total of 31 of his own articles to *Fædrelandet*, of which 21 were submitted during his final broadside against the Danish State Church.[48] Many of the articles were ardently solicited by Giødwad himself, as in the case of Kierkegaard's article against *The Corsair* and of his *feuilleton* entitled "The Crisis and a Crisis in the Life of an Actress."[49]

Fædrelandet was also the first newspaper to feature a short critical review of *Either/Or*, which was issued on the very day of its publication: the critic (perhaps Giødwad himself) hailed the book as "a phenomenon within Danish literature" and "one of the most interesting works we have seen published for a very long time" and praised the author's "exceptional command of the language."[50] Moreover, in a letter to Orla Lehmann dated "9 March 1843," Carl Ploug wrote: "Recently, a large philosophical-aesthetical work in two weighty volumes has been published under the title *Either/Or* by Victor Eremita (reputedly Søren Kierkegaard), which has created great sensation and is everywhere the object of conversation—which it also deserves to be, since it is very brilliant and interesting."[51]

Kierkegaard was his own publisher until 1847, which meant that he entered contracts with Bianco Luno's printing house and would subsequently distribute his books through Carl Andreas Reitzel (1789–1853) or Philip Gerson Philipsen (1812–77). Such a setup meant he carried the financial risk himself but also enjoyed the prospect of financial gain. He later abandoned this risky method of publication in favor of accepting a royalty from the publisher, who would then have to deal with all the inconveniences at the printing office. Around half the books published by Kierkegaard himself were published pseudonymously, and until 1846, when Kierkegaard finally acknowledged authorship of his works, the person entrusted to negotiate directly on his behalf with the distributor Reitzel and the printer Luno was J.F. Giødwad. Subsequently, it is Giødwad and not Kierkegaard who appears in Luno's account books, just as it was Giødwad who was paid for the pseudonymous writings and received royalties from Reitzel for the sale of books. Giødwad signed the following sworn statement on May 11, 1845:

---

48 Tudvad, *Kierkegaards København*, p. 162. Not included in this number are the letter published in *Fædrelandet*, no. 1143, February 8, 1843 (*SV1* XIII, 467–70 / *COR*, 69–72), whose authorship is doubtful, and an unpublished letter which was meant to be sent to Giødwad and published in *Fædrelandet* (*Pap.* IV B 20).

49 Cf. *SKS* 21, 21–2, NB6:24 / *JP* 6, 6209, where Kierkegaard claims that the article had been written "to humor Giødwad, who has asked for it." Cf. also *SKS* 21, 24–6, NB6:27 / *JP* 6, 6211, where Giødwad's insistence is considered a possible "hint from the divine Governance" in order to let his piece be published, since "I actually have nothing with which to counter his request except a depressive whim."

50 *Fædrelandet*, no. 1155, February 20, 1843. Another more thorough review of *Either/Or* appeared on the Sunday literary issue of *Fædrelandet*, nos. 1227–8, 1234, and 1241, respectively from May 7, 14, and 21, 1843. This review was written by the theologian Johan Frederik Hagen.

51 Clausen (ed.), *Af Orla Lehmanns Papirer*, p. 80.

> I swear on my life that Mr. Magister S.A. Kierkegaard has the right to require of me what I receive in the way of income from the sale of the writings: *Either/Or*, *Fear and Trembling*, *Repetition*, *The Concept of Anxiety*, *Prefaces*, *Stages of Life's Way*, from Mr. Reitzel, book dealer, and that in the event of my death he is obligated to pay the sum to Mr. Kierkegaard.[52]

Giødwad was also employed as a go-between when in 1849 Kierkegaard published his *Two Ethical-Religious Essays* under the pseudonym H.H. In an entry to his journal dated May 4 and 5, 1849, Kierkegaard states that he has just dispatched the printed manuscript of the book to Giødwad, who later managed to deliver it to printer Louis Klein and the Gyldendal publishing house.[53] Kierkegaard was almost obsessive in his efforts to conceal the authorship of his pseudonymous writings, which meant that Giødwad was asked to act as a go-between whenever anyone wanted to address one of Kierkegaard's pseudonymous authors: when, for example, Peter Ludvig Møller (1814–65) attempted to contact Victor Eremita by sending a letter to Kierkegaard's address in December 1845, Victor Eremita's sardonic response was delivered through Giødwad's transaction.[54]

Giødwad's connections and publishing expertise were an important source of information and an asset in Kierkegaard's authorship: Giødwad provided the writer with inspiring stories and anecdotes that could be used in his books,[55] and he would assist his friend with technical publishing matters.[56] Giødwad was also a reliable source of reference and information on issues related to the Danish newspaper literature.[57] Kierkegaard was also extremely appreciative of Giødwad's matchless proofreading skills: not only did Giødwad read the proofs of *Either/Or*, but there is

52 Cf. Garff, *Søren Kierkegaard: A Biography*, trans. by Bruce H. Kirmmse, Princeton and Oxford: Princeton University Press 2005, p. 511. The document is conserved in the Manuscript Department of the Royal Library in Copenhagen: KA, D pk. 7 læg 1. Since the pseudonymous books *Philosophical Fragments* and *Concluding Unscientific Postscript* featured Kierkegaard's name as the editor in the title page, they did not need to be included in this testimony and were delivered to the printer and to Reitzel by the philosopher himself.

53 *SKS* 22, 12, NB11:8 / *WA*, Supplement, pp. 218–19.

54 Cf. *B&A*, vol. 1, p. 136 / *LD*, Letter 121, p. 183, and in particular the relative notes in *B&A*, vol. 2, p. 67 / *LD*, p. 470.

55 Cf. *Pap.* VI B 148 / *TD*, Supplement, p. 112, where Giødwad told Kierkegaard the story of a "Mrs. Nielsen," who "remained faithful to her beloved, although he, far away in the East Indies, at first kept up a correspondence with her for two years and later married someone else." Kierkegaard considered this anecdote to be worth a mention in the *Three Discourses on Imagined Occasions*.

56 When in 1848–49 Kierkegaard considered the publication of a number of ethical-religious writings, Giødwad—"The editor of *Fædrelandet* with whom I as such entirely concur"—promised "out of personal friendship...to manage practicalities and thus made me fall further into debt in my devotion to him than already is the case." Cf. *Pap.* X–5 B 39, p. 257.

57 Cf., for example, *Pap.* X–6 B 256 and *Pap.* XI–3 B 180.

also evidence to suggest that he was asked to help with the printed manuscript of at least a couple of edifying writings.[58]

In the late 1840s, Kierkegaard wrote a draft for a dedication to Giødwad, possibly intended to be used in a dedication copy of *Upbuilding Discourses in Various Spirits*.[59] The draft is written in scattered and fragmentary form, and Israel Levin (1810–83) states that the dedication copy of the *Upbuilding Discourses* intended for Giødwad was, indeed, never forwarded, "because as ever, Søren Kierkegaard always rewrote it twenty-seven times,"[60] but the manuscript for the dedication has been edited by H.P. Barfod (1834–92), and in his composed and revised form has been published in the volume of Kierkegaard's *Letters and Documents*:

> To Mr. Cand. juris Jens Finsteen Giødwad,
> whose self-sacrificing fidelity, whose excellent business-skill, whose endearing character my pseudonymous production owes so much.
>
> Dear friend,
> Permit me by means of this dedication to give expression to my appreciation for services that would always lay claim to gratitude, but doubly lay claim to mine owing to the special nature of the relationship. What is special is that a person who is decidedly a politician, who in the purity of his heart desires only one thing, who, without seeking and without finding any reward, womanlike in everyday faithfulness and modest frugality, is a man devoted in his work to but a single cause, that he cheerfully, kindly, with the greatest possible accessibility, finds the time in his limited leisure, with the greatest possible readiness and repeated kindness, to help him who may only be said not to have the opposite political persuasion insofar as he has none whatsoever—him who, preoccupied exclusively with his own affairs, has been completely unable to return any favor at all, not even with respect to the literary aspect that is immaterial in political differences.[61]

Despite the mutual respect and devotion nurtured by Kierkegaard and Giødwad, their relationship suffered from "something unsettled,"[62] as Kierkegaard called it. Giødwad's profession had always been a source of tension, which only increased following the so-called "*Corsair* affair."

When Kierkegaard published his articles critical of Goldschmidt and Møller's periodical in Giødwad's newspaper,[63] he considered his gesture an unselfish and gallant defense of respectable Danish literature, and at the same time "the greatest service that at that given moment could be bestowed on *Fædrelandet*. Giødvad came hurrying over to me in order to get hold of the article, standing by my side

---

58 For example, the *Four Upbuilding Discourses 1844* (Cf. *B&A*, vol. 1, p. 136 / *LD*, Letter 111, pp. 172–3) and *Upbuilding Discourses in Various Spirits* (Cf. *SKS* 20, 116–17, NB:194 / *JP* 5, 5997).

59 The document is conserved in the Manuscript Department of the Royal Library: Kierkegaard Archive, D, pk. 2, læg 9.

60 *Encounters with Kierkegaard*, trans. and ed. by Bruce H. Kirmmse, p. 325.

61 *B&A*, vol. 1, p. 344 / *LD*, Dedication 17, p. 436.

62 *B&A*, vol. 1, p. 136 / *LD*, Letter 111, pp. 172–3.

63 *SV1* XIII, 422–5 / *COR*, 38–50.

while I completed it—not that there was any agreement with *Fædrelandet*, that was far from the case, and I would not have had it."[64] But when *The Corsair* replied with a scathing attack on Kierkegaard, Giødwad's newspaper bowed its head and refrained from taking a stance in favor of the philosopher, in effect abandoning him to the "journalism of rabble barbarism,"[65] an act that Kierkegaard considered to be one of sheer betrayal[66] and which led him to break with Giødwad.[67] However, the very extensive use of adversative conjunctions, such as "but," "nevertheless," "nonetheless," "and yet," "however," in many of Kierkegaard's journal entries on this matter plays witness to his ambivalence and mixed feelings towards Giødwad, his dear friend and—low and behold—editor of *Fædrelandet*:

> *Fædrelandet* has no better than others betrayed me, and *Fædrelandet* is just as cowardly and envious as the rest of them. Giødvad is my personal friend, but that is a different matter. And it is basically inconceivable that I have had a friend who was a journalist, and it is inexplicable that such a nice and splendid person can be a journalist, since it is impossible to be a journalist without each and every day benefiting falsehood and lies in some way or other.[68]

The personal friendship between the two men must, nonetheless, have survived the crisis that followed in the wake of the *Corsair* affair. There are many documents that witness regular meetings between Kierkegaard and Giødwad in the 1850s. In 1850, Kierkegaard embarked on a confrontation with Martin Hammerich (1811–81) on a religious subject at Giødwad's home,[69] and the very same year, during an evening conversation, Giødwad suggested that the emphasis Kierkegaard had given to the idealism of Christianity might have discouraged some theological student from becoming ordained as clergymen.[70] Moreover, Pastor Tycho E. Spang refers that towards the end of Kierkegaard's life "he often had powerful attacks from his ailments when he was at Giødwad's,"[71] a testimony confirmed by Israel Levin who speaks of Kierkegaard's fainting during an evening reception "at Cand. Giødwad's."[72]

During the final year of Kierkegaard's life his ambivalent friendship with Giødwad reached a new height of complexity when in the late spring of 1855, Kierkegaard in effect decided to cease collaboration with *Fædrelandet* and founded his own periodical *The Moment*, to thus demonstrate his independence from any

---

64 *Pap.* XI–3 B 12, p. 27.

65 *SKS* 23, 280, NB18:44 / *JP* 6, 6619.

66 Many journal entries deal with Giødwad's and *Fædrelandet*'s stance on the "*Corsair* affair." Cf. *Pap.* VII–1 B 71 / *COR*, 203–4. *SKS* 21, 218–19, NB9:40. *SKS* 23, 174, NB17:16–16a. *SKS* 23, 280, NB18:44b / *JP* 6, 6621. *SKS* 24, 525–6, NB25:112. *Pap.* XI–3 B 12, pp. 27–8.

67 Cf. the sorrowful draft of letter in *B&A*, vol. 1, p. 136 / *LD*, Letter 131, pp. 187–8.

68 *SKS* 21, 213–14, NB9:28. See also *SKS* 23, 280, NB18:44 / *JP* 6, 6619. *SKS* 24, 525-6, NB25:112. *Pap.* XI–3 B 12, p. 28.

69 *SKS* 23, 480–1, NB20:163 / *JP* 4, 4307.

70 *SKS* 24, 54, NB21:83 / *JP* 2, 1791.

71 *Encounters with Kierkegaard*, trans. and ed. by Bruce H. Kirmmse, p. 112.

72 Ibid., p. 210.

political grouping.[73] Moreover, Hans Brøchner wrote to Christian Molbech (1783–1857) that the day Kierkegaard was admitted to Frederik's Hospital for the ailment that would cause his death "he sent Giødwad three hundred rix-dollars so that he could pay a few small bills for him, and certainly also in order to pay for his stay at the hospital."[74] This would seem an act of benevolence and trust, but according to Emil Boesen's account of his hospital conversations with Kierkegaard, the philosopher did not want Giødwad to visit him before after his death: "He did favors for me in private and disavowed me publicly. I don't like that. You have no idea what sort of poisonous plant Mynster was. You have no idea of it; it is staggering how it has spread its corruption."[75] This must have been a hard blow for the devoted Giødwad. Nonetheless, the eloquent obituary published by *Fædrelandet* the day after Kierkegaard's death is most probably from his pen:

> Last night, after having been bed-ridden for a short time, Denmark's greatest religious author, Dr. Søren Aaby Kierkegaard, died 43 years of age. He lived for the idea and remained faithful to it until the end. He strove to awaken religious consciousness, and many will no doubt realize with gratitude that he has caused thoughts of great gravity to stir in them; thoughts that with his help have gained such power over their soul that they will always be with them.[76]

On December 2, 1855, *Fædrelandet* published a feature article "On Søren Kierkegaard's activity as a Religious Author"[77] written—"rather against my will but at the special request of Giødwad"[78]—by Brøchner and signed by the pseudonym "r." The article that accomplished what Giødwad had insistently requested of Brøchner, namely, to produce a comprehensive review of Kierkegaard's writings, was probably intended as the amiable bachelor's final tribute to the memory of his ingenious and choleric bachelor friend of high ideals.

---

73 Cf. *Pap.* XI–3 B 157, pp. 255–7. Kierkegaard, though, made clear that "as long as I wanted to use *Fædrelandet* I was treated by the editorial team with such distinguished attention, with every wish of mine being catered to, that I truly feel a desire to publicly declare my gratefulness, especially to my personal friend Giødvad." Cf. *Pap.* XI–3 B 158, p. 27.

74 *Encounters with Kierkegaard*, trans. and ed. by Bruce H. Kirmmse, p. 252.

75 Ibid., p. 125.

76 *Fædrelandet*, no. 264, November 12, 1855, p. 1108.

77 *Fædrelandet*, no. 281, December 1, 1855, pp. 1179–80.

78 *Encounters with Kierkegaard*, trans. and ed. by Bruce H. Kirmmse, p. 249.

Bibliography

I. Giødwad's Works in The Auction Catalogue *of Kierkegaard's Library*

(ed.), *Fædrelandet*, no. 77, 1836; [in addition individual numbers from the years] 1842, 1843, 1845, 1848, 1854, and 1855, ed. by C.N. David, Jens Finsteen Giødwad, and Orla Lehmann (*ASKB* U 39).

(ed.), *Kjøbenhavnsposten*, no. 96, March 31, 1836 (*ASKB* U 75).

II. Works in The Auction Catalogue *of Kierkegaard's Library that Discuss Giødwad*

None.

III. Secondary Literature on Kierkegaard's Relation to Giødwad

Garff, Joakim, *Søren Kierkegaard: A Biography*, trans. by Bruce H. Kirmmse, Princeton and Oxford: Princeton University Press 2005, p. 213; p. 286; p. 405; p. 417; p. 472; pp. 510–11; pp. 548–9; p. 660; p. 742; p. 752.

Hannay, Alastair, *Kierkegaard. A Biography*, Cambridge: Cambridge University Press 2001, pp. 180–1; p. 382; p. 395; p. 412; p. 415.

Nielsen, Svend Aage, *Kierkegaard og Regensen*, Copenhagen: Graabrødre Torv's Forlag 1965, pp. 76–92.

Tudvad, Peter, *Kierkegaards København*, Copenhagen: Politikens Forlag 2004, p. 105; p. 128; p. 132; p. 159; p. 162.

Johan Ludvig Heiberg:
Kierkegaard's Criticism of Hegel's Danish Apologist

Jon Stewart

There can be no doubt that Johan Ludvig Heiberg (1791–1860) was a very important figure for the development of Kierkegaard's thought. Heiberg's criticism dominated an entire generation of literary scholarship and was profoundly influential on the young Kierkegaard. His dramatic works and translations are also frequently referred to and quoted by Kierkegaard and his pseudonyms. These are the sides of Heiberg as critic, dramatist, and poet that are generally well known to people today.

However, Heiberg was also a philosopher, and this dimension of his authorship has until very recently been significantly neglected. Heiberg was one of the main proponents of Hegel's philosophy in Denmark in the two decades after the latter's death.[1] His philosophical profile is clearly that of a Hegelian, and, not least of all due to Kierkegaard's influence, this has led to him being unfairly dismissed and pigeonholed as an unoriginal parrot. However, Heiberg's use of Hegelian philosophy is far from a simple, mechanical repetition. Rather, he tried to apply some of the basic principles of Hegel's thought to his own agenda in the context of criticism, aesthetics, and poetry, and it is here that his originality lies.

In the present article I will confine myself for the most part to Heiberg's philosophical production, loosely understood. I will begin with a brief account of the main stations in his biography. Then, in the second section I will provide a work-by-work overview of Heiberg's main philosophical writings, drawing attention in each case to their relevance for Kierkegaard. Finally, I will attempt a general interpretation of Kierkegaard's understanding of Heiberg as a philosophical author. I wish to argue that although he is genuinely inspired by Heiberg's aesthetics and critical works, he develops an increasingly negative disposition towards Heiberg's Hegelian philosophy over the course of time. This led to his famous anti-Hegel

1 See Jon Stewart, *A History of Hegelianism in Golden Age Denmark,* Tome I, *The Heiberg Period: 1824–1836*, Copenhagen: C.A. Reitzel 2007 (*Danish Golden Age Studies*, vol. 3); Carl Henrik Koch, "Johan Ludvig Heiberg," in his *Den danske idealisme 1800–1880*, Copenhagen: Gyldendal 2004, pp. 225–48; and Robert Leslie Horn, "The Hegelianism of Johan Ludvig Heiberg," in his *Positivity and Dialectic: A Study of the Theological Method of Hans Lassen Martensen*, Copenhagen: C.A. Reitzel 2007 (*Danish Golden Age Studies*, vol. 2), pp. 97–104.

campaign, which had Heiberg as one of its main targets. The key to understanding this campaign is to be able to distinguish Kierkegaard's criticism of Hegel himself from that of Heiberg and his other Danish and German followers.[2]

I. Heiberg's Life

Johan Ludvig Heiberg was born in Copenhagen on December 14, 1791.[3] His father Peter Andreas Heiberg (1758–1841) was a writer of dramas and political satires.[4] A true child of the Enlightenment, the elder Heiberg was an avid supporter of the French Revolution and everything francophone. He was highly critical of what he regarded as the reactionary political life in Denmark. Due to his outspoken views, he was repeatedly fined and in 1800 ultimately exiled. He went to France where he lived for the rest of his life. Heiberg's mother Thomasine Buntzen, known as Fru Gyllembourg (1773–1856), fell in love with one of her husband's pro-Enlightenment friends, the Swedish Baron Carl Frederik Gyllembourg-Ehrensvärd (1767–1815), who was living in exile in Denmark. In a move unheard of at the time, she divorced her exiled husband and married the baron. This created a scandal that sent tremors through polite society in Copenhagen.

The young Johan Ludvig Heiberg was a victim of this course of events. After seeing that he could do nothing to prevent it, Heiberg's father, reluctantly agreed to the divorce, but insisted that his son be removed from the home of his mother and her new husband. This condition was granted. Thus Peter Andreas Heiberg decided to hand over his son to his entrusted friends, the literary scholar Knud Lyne Rahbek (1760–1830) and his wife Karen Margrethe Heger (1775–1829). The young Heiberg spent two years in the Rahbeks' famous literary salon, known as the Bakkehus, which was frequented by poets, writers, and scholars of any number of different fields. The young Heiberg was profoundly unhappy with the Rahbeks, and in time it was decided that he was to be sent to one of his aunts, where he spent two more

---

2 This is one of the central theses in my *Kierkegaard's Relations to Hegel Reconsidered*, Cambridge and New York: Cambridge University Press 2003.

3 For Heiberg's biography and thinking, see Arthur Aumont, *J.L. Heiberg og hans Slægt paa den danske Skueplads*, Copenhagen: Jørgensen 1891; Morten Borup, *Johan Ludvig Heiberg*, vols. 1–3, Copenhagen: Gyldendal 1947–49; Henning Fenger, *The Heibergs*, trans. by Frederick J. Marker, New York: Twayne Publishers Inc. 1971; Johanne Luise Heiberg, *Et liv genoplevet i erindringen*, vols. 1–4, 5th revised ed., Copenhagen: Gyldendal 1973; Bruce H. Kirmmse, "Johan Ludvig Heiberg," in his *Kierkegaard in Golden Age Denmark*, Bloomington and Indianapolis: Indiana University Press 1990, pp. 136–68; Paul V. Rubow, *Heiberg og hans Skole i Kritiken*, Copenhagen: Gyldendal 1953; Vibeke Schrøder, *Tankens Våben. Johan Ludvig Heiberg*, Copenhagen: Gyldendal 2001; Niels Birger Wamberg, *H.C. Andersen og Heiberg*, Copenhagen: Politikens Forlag 1971.

4 For the works of Peter Andreas Heiberg, see C.J. Ballhausen, *Peter Andreas og Johan Ludvig Heiberg. En annoteret bibliografi*, Copenhagen: Dansk Bibliofil-Klub and C.A. Reitzel 2000. For his life, see his autobiography, P.A. Heiberg, *Erindinger af min politiske, selskabelige og litterære Vandel i Frankrig*, Christiania: P.J. Hoppes Forlag 1830; see also Fenger, *The Heibergs*, pp. 23–37; Povl Ingerslev-Jensen, *P.A. Heiberg. Den danske Beaumarchais*, Herning: Poul Kristensen 1964.

years. His mother lived with her new husband on a farm near Sorø, at a safe distance from the gossip in the capital.

Heiberg was given private instruction by tutors until he entered the University of Copenhagen in 1809. At this time he was reunited with his mother, who moved back to the capital. During these years he enjoyed the company of Copenhagen's intellectual elite. The home of his mother and her new husband became a literary meeting place for all the leading scholars and writers of the day. In this context Heiberg developed his own cosmopolitan view of the world that would be one of his trademarks throughout his life. In 1812 he took a trip to Stockholm, where he met a number of Swedish nobles.[5] He ultimately graduated from the university with a doctoral degree in 1817, which he was awarded for a dissertation on Calderón and Spanish drama.[6]

In 1819 Heiberg, with a royal travel stipend, went to Paris where he was reunited with his father.[7] He enjoyed great freedom in the French capital, although his tight financial situation obliged him to take work as a journalist and a guitar teacher. Heiberg frequented the different Parisian theaters and carefully studied the latest dramaturgical techniques and trends. This knowledge kept him in good stead some years later when he introduced some of these trends into the Royal Theater in Copenhagen, creating a great stir in the process.

In 1822 he was appointed as Lecturer of Danish Language and Literature at the University of Kiel.[8] Although he was unhappy with his position there, it was during this time that he first became aware of Hegel's philosophy. In the summer of 1824, Heiberg traveled to Berlin, where he attended Hegel's lectures and met many of the latter's leading students and associates including Philipp Marheineke (1780–1846), Leopold von Henning (1791–1866), Eduard Gans (1798–1839), and Heinrich Gustav Hotho (1802–73), all of whom were later to play instrumental roles in the creation of the first collected works edition of Hegel's writings.[9] According to Heiberg's own account in the "Autobiographical Fragments," it was in Hamburg, on his way from Berlin back to Kiel, that he had a kind of revelation that showed him the key to Hegel's thought. From that moment onward he became a convinced Hegelian, making use of different elements of Hegel's thought in his own works in different fields.

---

5 See *Brevvexling fra J.L. Heibergs Reise til Sverige i Efteraaret 1812*, ed. by A.D. Jørgensen, Copenhagen: I. Cohens Bogtrykkeri 1890.

6 Johannes Ludovicus Heiberg, *De poëseos dramaticae genere hispanico, et praesertim de Petro Calderone de la Barca, principe dramaticorum*, Copenhagen: Popp 1817. (Reprinted in *Prosaiske Skrifter*, vols. 1–11, Copenhagen: C.A. Reitzel 1861–62, vol. 11, pp. 1–172.)

7 See Henning Fenger, "Jean-Louis Heiberg et son premier séjour à Paris," in *Rencontres et courants littéraires franco-scandinaves, Actes du 7e Congrès International d'Historie des Littératures Scandinaves (Paris 7–12 juillet 1968)*, Paris: Lettres Modernes Minard 1972, pp. 129–43. See also H. Schwanenflügel, *Peter Andreas Heiberg. En biografisk Studie*, Copenhagen: Schubothes 1891, pp. 566–70.

8 See Heinrich Detering, "Heibergs Kieler Glück und Elend," in his *Andersen und andere. Kleine dänisch-deutsche Kulturgeschichte Kiels*, Heide: Boyens 2005, pp. 45–59.

9 *Georg Wilhelm Friedrich Hegel's Werke. Vollständige Ausgabe*, vols. 1–18, ed. by Philipp Marheineke et al., Berlin: Duncker und Humblot 1832–45.

Heiberg returned to Copenhagen in 1825 and had remarkable success with a series of new dramatic works at the Royal Theater. This led to a permanent appointment in 1829 as official Poet and Translator of the Royal Theater. It was also during this time that he founded his famous *Kjøbenhavns flyvende Post*,[10] a widely read literary journal that featured works by many of the leading names in Golden Age culture. A number of the most important literary disputes were carried out in its pages. The *Flyvende Post* ran regularly from 1827 to 1828, and then off and on from 1830 to 1837. It was a drain on Heiberg's energies to constantly supply the journal with new material, and so in order to help her son, his mother, Thomasine Gyllembourg, decided to write some fictional stories that could be published a few pages at a time in the journal.[11] With these popular novels, she thus became one of Denmark's most celebrated female authors and one of the founders of prose fiction in Danish.

In 1830 Heiberg was appointed as a lecturer in Logic, Aesthetics and Danish Literature at the Royal Military College. In the context of this position, which lasted until 1836, he gave courses in Hegel's logic and attempted to develop an aesthetics based on Hegel's system. This appointment provided him with a stimulus to pursue his philosophical interests. Moreover, due to the rules for instructors at the College, Heiberg was obliged to write out his lectures and publish them for internal use for his students. This external pressure doubtless helped him to produce a number of his philosophical works, since otherwise he would presumably have simply taught the courses and left behind no other record or documentation of his treatment of the material.

In 1831, Heiberg married Johanne Luise, *née* Pätges (1812–90), known later as Fru Heiberg. She was a young actress who garnered the attention of generations of Copenhagen theatergoers. Her exalted career is the object of analysis in Kierkegaard's appreciative article "The Crisis and a Crisis in the Life of an Actress."[12] In 1837

---

10 See Christian Molbech, "Johan Ludvig Heiberg," in his *Dansk poetisk Anthologie*, vols. 1–4, Copenhagen: C.A. Reitzel 1830–40, vol. 4, pp. 287–9; pp. 293–4; Uffe Andreasen, "Efterskrift," in the photomechanical reproduction of Heiberg's journal, *Kjøbenhavns flyvende Post*, vols. 1–4, ed. by Uffe Andreasen, Copenhagen: Det Danske Sprog- og Litteraturselskab 1980–84, vol. 4, pp. 549–76; Peter Vinten-Johansen, "Johan Ludvig Heiberg and his Audience in Ninteenth-Century Denmark," in *Kierkegaard and His Contemporaries: The Culture of Golden Age Denmark*, ed. by Jon Stewart, Berlin and New York: Verlag Walter de Gruyter 2003 (*Kierkegaard Studies Monograph Series*, vol. 10), pp. 343–55; see also Fenger, *The Heibergs*, pp. 118–32; Borup, *Johan Ludvig Heiberg*, vol. 2, pp. 93–132; Christian Kirchhoff-Larsen, *Den danske presses historie*, vols. 1–3, Copenhagen: Berlinske Forlag 1942–62, vol. 3, pp. 5–32.

11 Thomasine Gyllembourg made her literary debut with an anonymous letter to the editor, which was continued in such a way that it told a story. This work appeared originally in *Kjøbenhavns flyvende Post*, nos. 4, 6, 9, 12–19, 42–3, 58–9, 1827 [no page numbers]. It later appeared as "Familien Polonius" in later editions of her collected writings.

12 Søren Kierkegaard, "Krisen og en Krise i en Skuespillerindes Liv, af Inter et Inter. En Artikel i Anledning af 'Romeo og Julies' Gjenoptagelse paa Repertoiret ved Nytaarstid 1847," *Fædrelandet*, vol. 9, no. 188, July 24, 1848, columns 1485–90; no. 189, July 25, 1848, columns 1493–1500; no. 190, July 26, 1848, columns 1501–6; no. 191, July 27, 1848, columns 1509–16. (In English: *The Crisis and a Crisis in the Life of an Actress*, trans. by Howard V. Hong and Edna H. Hong, Princeton: Princeton University Press 1997.)

Heiberg launched his Hegelian journal, *Perseus*, which was influential in its own way despite the fact that it only saw two issues. Heiberg continued his editorial work into the 1840s with the *Intelligensblade* (1842–44), and *Urania* (1844–46), the latter of which was dedicated to his interest in astronomy and the natural sciences. Heiberg's most celebrated poetic work appeared in 1841, a collection called simply *New Poems*,[13] which included his satirical classic "A Soul after Death."

In 1839 Heiberg took on a number of administrative duties, and in 1849 he was ultimately appointed managing director of the Royal Theater. This position, which lasted until 1856, was marred by internal disputes with writers and actors. Despite these conflicts, Heiberg was regarded, in the twilight of his career, as a major authority in the fields of criticism and drama. Indeed, the Norwegian playwright Henrik Ibsen (1828–1906) came to Copenhagen in 1852 to learn from Heiberg about directing and theater management.

Heiberg died on August 25, 1860, and after his death his wife helped to put together the most extensive collected works edition of his writings, divided into three parts: prose writings, poetic writings, and letters.[14] Since then a number of Heiberg's individual works or collections of his poetry have been reprinted, but to date there has been no new collected works edition that compares with this one. Only the more recent edition of Heiberg's letters has surpassed the work done in this edition.[15]

By the time Heiberg died, he was a major cultural figure on the Danish landscape, although it is probably fair to say that he outlived the period of his greatest influence, which was from the mid-1820s to the 1840s. In Danish literary history he is known for founding his own school of criticism and for his brilliant polemics against some of the greatest literary figures of the age. He was clearly Denmark's most dominant literary critic during the so-called Golden Age. In the history of Danish theater he is also a major figure, regarded as an eclectic and an innovator, who introduced foreign elements, such as French vaudeville, to the Danish stage and with the resulting synthesis helped to create, somewhat paradoxically, a national theater. Heiberg's success in so many different fields during such a rich cultural period is truly remarkable.

His reputation as a Hegelian philosopher has never reached the heights of his reputation in these other fields. However, his philosophical writings should not be underestimated. He penned both monograph-length works and a number of articles that treat a manifold of different philosophical themes, including works on most all the major philosophical subdisciplines: metaphysics, epistemology, aesthetics, philosophy of history, philosophy of nature, philosophy of education, and philosophy of language. His treatises on Hegelian philosophy were among the earliest and the most extensive in the Danish language.

---

13 Johan Ludvig Heiberg, *Nye Digte*, Copenhagen: C.A. Reitzel 1841 (*ASKB* 1562). For a partial translation of "A Soul after Death," see Johan Ludvig Heiberg, *A Soul After Death*, trans. by Henry Meyer, Seattle: Mermaid Press 1991.

14 *Samlede Skrifter* (edited by Johanne Luise Heiberg and Andreas Frederik Krieger), consisting of *Poetiske Skrifter*, vols. 1–11, Copenhagen: C.A. Reitzel 1862; *Prosaiske Skrifter*, vols. 1–11, Copenhagen: C.A. Reitzel 1861–62; *Breve fra og til J.L. Heiberg*, ed. by Andreas Frederik Krieger and Carl Christopher Georg Andræ, Copenhagen: C.A. Reitzel 1862.

15 *Breve og Aktstykker vedrørende Johan Ludvig Heiberg*, vols. 1–5, ed. by Morten Borup, Copenhagen: Gyldendal 1946–50.

II. Heiberg's Philosophical Works

In what follows I will give a brief overview of Heiberg's philosophical works with an eye towards their influence on Kierkegaard. I will confine myself to his main monographs and treatises, thus omitting a number of essays, reviews and shorter works, which also in some cases contain substantial philosophical content. I will also include in this account some of Heiberg's poetic works when they are relevant for understanding his philosophy.

A. On Human Freedom *and* Der Zufall *(1824–25)*

Heiberg's first philosophical works begin to appear very shortly after his first-hand encounter with Hegel in Berlin. Immediately after his return to Kiel, Heiberg set to work on a treatise entitled *On Human Freedom: On Occasion of the Latest Disputes about this Issue*,[16] which was published in December 1824, that is, only a few short months after he returned from Berlin. Heiberg himself emphasizes the speed with which he appropriated Hegel's philosophy:

> When one considers that this work [sc. *On Human Freedom*] appeared in December 1824 and that in the month of May of the same year I had hardly known that there was a philosopher by the name of Hegel, then the fact that in such a short time I could achieve so much which this admittedly imperfect work contains, will best be able to show with what voracity I had devoured the new wisdom.[17]

This is the work that most interpreters point to as the introduction of Hegel's philosophy in Denmark. This claim must, however, be regarded with some caution since many Danish scholars were quite familiar with Hegel prior to this and a number of them had also attended his lectures in Berlin prior to Heiberg.[18] *On Human Freedom* attempts to give a Hegelian interpretation to the then current debate about free will surrounding the provocative claims made for a form of materialist determinism by Heiberg's friend Frantz Gotthard Howitz (1789–1826).[19] This was an important interdisciplinary debate that involved important figures such as the philosopher Frederik Christian Sibbern (1785–1872), the jurist Anders Sandøe

---

16 Dr. J.L. Heiberg, *Om den menneskelige Frihed. I Anledning af de nyeste Stridigheder over denne Gjenstand*, Kiel: Universitets-Boghandlingen 1824. (Reprinted in *Prosaiske Skrifter*, vol. 1, pp. 1–110.)

17 Johan Ludvig Heiberg, "Autobiographiske Fragmenter," in *Prosaiske Skrifter*, vol. 11, p. 501. (In English in *Heiberg's On the Significance of Philosophy for the Present Age and Other Texts*, ed. and trans. by Jon Stewart, Copenhagen: C.A. Reitzel 2005 (*Texts from Golden Age Denmark*, vol. 1), p. 66.)

18 See Stewart, *A History of Hegelianism in Golden Age Denmark,* Tome I, *The Heiberg Period: 1824–1836*, Chapter 1, pp. 69–114.

19 See Oluf Thomsen, *F.G. Howitz og hans Strid om Villiens Frihed*, Copenhagen: Levin & Munksgaards Forlag 1924; O. Waage, "Strid om den menneskelige Villies Frihed og Sædelærens Grundlag," in his *J.P. Mynster og de philosophiske Bevægelser paa hans Tid i Danmark*, Copenhagen: C.A. Reitzel 1867, pp. 39–104; Koch, "A.S. Ørsted og striden om viljens frihed," in his *Den danske idealisme 1800–1880*, pp. 177–208.

Ørsted (1778–1860), and the theologian Jakob Peter Mynster (1775–1854). In his treatise Heiberg attempts to mediate the different positions in a Hegelian manner by demonstrating how freedom and necessity are not distinct but rather constitute two sides of the same concept. While some attempts have been made to find a connection, there is no unambiguous documentation that Kierkegaard read this work by Heiberg.[20] When this discussion was taking place in 1824–25 Kierkegaard was still very young, and it is extremely unlikely that he would have followed the debate at this time. The open question is whether it came to be of interest to him at some later point when the debate proper was over.

Heiberg returned to Copenhagen in April 1825. At this time he set about publishing a short work that he had written in German while he was in Kiel: *Der Zufall, aus dem Gesichtspunkte der Logik betrachtet. Als Einleitung zu einer Theorie des Zufalls*.[21] In this work Heiberg attempts to apply a Hegelian dialectical analysis to the concepts of contingency, necessity, and freedom. Although *Der Zufall* is only a 30-page pamphlet that is somewhat superficial, Heiberg goes on to develop his ideas on this topic in later works.[22] Although Kierkegaard took an interest in these categories in texts such as *Philosophical Fragments*, there is no clear evidence or documentation that he read this work.

B. Outline of the Philosophy of Philosophy or Speculative Logic *(1832)*

During the second half of the 1820s Heiberg was primarily occupied with writing works for the theater and with the cumbersome job of editing his journal, *Kjøbenhavns flyvende Post*. For this reason his philosophical interests were to a certain extent put aside during this period. This changed when he received the aforementioned appointment at the Royal Military College, which provided him with a new forum in which he could develop his Hegelian philosophy. The first fruit of this position was a work on Hegel's speculative logic that appeared in 1832 under the title *Outline of the*

---

[20] See Isak Winkel Holm, "Angst og utilregnelighed. Kierkegaard og Howitz-fejden: angstbegrebet mellem lægevidenskab og idealisme," *Spring*, vol. 8, 1995, pp. 100–16.

[21] Dr. J.L. Heiberg, *Der Zufall, aus dem Gesichtspunkte der Logik betrachtet. Als Einleitung zu einer Theorie des Zufalls*, Copenhagen: C.A. Reitzel 1825. (Reprinted in *Prosaiske Skrifter*, vol. 11, pp. 325–359.) (In English in *Heiberg's Contingency Regarded from the Point of View of Logic and Other Texts*, ed. and trans. by Jon Stewart, Copenhagen: Museum Tusculanum Press 2008 (*Texts from Golden Age Denmark*, vol. 4), pp. 53–75.)

[22] See Johan Ludvig Heiberg, "Nemesis. Et populair-philosophisk Forsøg," *Kjøbenhavns flyvende Post*, I, no. 41, May 21, 1827; II, no. 43, May 28, 1827; III, no. 44, June 1, 1827; IV, no. 45, June 4, 1827 [no page numbers]. (In English in *Heiberg's Contingency Regarded from the Point of View of Logic and Other Texts*, pp. 101–25.) See also *Grundtræk til Philosophiens Philosophie eller den speculative Logik. Som Ledetraad ved Forelæsninger paa den kongelige militaire Høiskole*, Copenhagen: Andreas Seidelin 1832; see § 103, § 107, and § 111. (In English in *Heiberg's Speculative Logic and Other Texts*, ed. and trans. by Jon Stewart, Copenhagen: C.A. Reitzel 2006 (*Texts from Golden Age Denmark*, vol. 2), pp. 116–19; pp. 123–8; pp. 130–5.)

Philosophy of Philosophy or Speculative Logic.[23] This work was originally written as a compendium for his students and was intended to be used to supplement his lectures that took place at the College in 1831–32. It was then subsequently printed in a limited number of copies so that it could be made available to a wider audience. It can be said in fairness that this is not an original work but rather a paraphrase of Hegel's masterpiece in the field, that is, *The Science of Logic.*[24] Heiberg's effort is, however, a quite substantial work in its own right and, relatively speaking, a quite early one that paved the way for later works on Hegel's logic by Danish authors.

Heiberg's *Speculative Logic* addresses itself to a number of issues that were of profound interest to Kierkegaard. One of these is the question of the beginning of philosophy. At the outset of the work, Heiberg makes the case for the primacy of philosophy as the first, most fundamental discipline of all the sciences. His argument is that while the other scholarly disciplines presuppose certain of their objects uncritically, philosophy explores the most basic building blocks of thought itself. For this reason, philosophy can take absolutely nothing for granted.[25] Heiberg explains, "Philosophy then can almost be regarded as the *science without presuppositions*. It must thus begin with *nothing*."[26] This explains the infelicitous title of the work: *Outline of the Philosophy of Philosophy*. If one takes "philosophy" in the older sense of the general pursuit of knowledge in any given field, then logic is understood as a metalevel discipline that explores the basic forms of thought common to all of them. Thus, logic is a discipline that necessarily precedes all the others, critically examining the human faculty of thought or critical examination used in all the other fields: "Since thought is the common root of nature and spirit…logic is not only *the first part of philosophy*, but it is also *philosophy itself* in its deepest root and most abstract presentation. It is *the philosophy of philosophy*."[27]

---

23 Johan Ludvig Heiberg, *Grundtræk til Philosophiens Philosophie eller den speculative Logik. Som Ledetraad ved Forelæsninger paa den kongelige militaire Høiskole*, Copenhagen: Andreas Seidelin 1832. (Reprinted as *Ledetraad ved Forlæsninger over Philosophiens Philosophie eller den speculative Logik ved den kongelige militaire Høiskole in Prosaiske Skrifter*, vol. 1, pp. 111–380.) (In English in *Heiberg's Speculative Logic and Other Texts*, pp. 39–213.)

24 G.W.F. Hegel, *Wissenschaft der Logik. Erster Band. Die objective Logik*, Nürnberg: Johann Leonard Schrag 1812; *Wissenschaft der Logik. Erster Band. Die objective Logik. Zweytes Buch. Die Lehre vom Wesen*, Nürnberg: Johann Leonard Schrag 1813; *Wissenschaft der Logik. Zweiter Band. Die subjective Logik oder Lehre vom Begriff*, Nürnberg: Johann Leonard Schrag 1816.

25 Cf. G.W.F. Hegel, *The Encyclopaedia Logic. Part One of the Encyclopaedia of the Philosophical Sciences*, trans. by T.F. Gerats, W.A. Suchting, H.S. Harris, Indianapolis: Hackett 1991, § 1; *Sämtliche Werke. Jubiläumsausgabe in 20 Bänden*, ed. by Hermann Glockner, Stuttgart: Friedrich Frommann Verlag 1928–41, vol. 8, pp. 41–2.

26 Heiberg, *Grundtræk til Philosophiens Philosophie eller den speculative Logik*, § 5. (*Heiberg's Speculative Logic and Other Texts*, p. 47.)

27 Heiberg, *Grundtræk til Philosophiens Philosophie eller den speculative Logik*, § 11. (*Heiberg's Speculative Logic and Other Texts*, p. 49.) See also § 193. (*Heiberg's Speculative Logic and Other Texts*, pp. 212–13.)

In order to make a beginning with this field, one must abstract from all determination and start from the most abstract categorical structure, the category of pure being. The claim that philosophy begins with nothing or without presuppositions is one that Kierkegaard frequently returns to. For example, at the beginning of his first book, *From the Papers of One Still Living*, from 1838, he refers to "Hegel's great attempt to begin with nothing," which

> must both impress and please us; impress us, in view of the moral strength with which the idea is conceived, the intellectual energy and virtuosity with which it is carried out; please us, because the whole negation is still only a movement inside the system's own limits, undertaken precisely in the interest of retrieving the pure abundance of existence.[28]

This is not in itself unambiguous evidence, but this strikingly positive formulation does recall that found in Heiberg's treatise. This connection becomes even more compelling when one considers that Kierkegaard originally wrote this work with the intention of publishing it as a review article in Heiberg's journal *Perseus*,[29] and thus had every reason to cast the piece in a way that reflected a positive disposition towards specific aspects of Hegel's thought.

As noted, the key to beginning without presuppositions lies in the category of pure being, which is regarded as the most abstract idea that can be thought. Following Hegel, Heiberg argues for this as follows:

> If one abstracts from every determination in *everything*—which is necessary in order to exclude all presuppositions, for here it is a matter of reaching a *beginning* which is abstract immediacy—then only one thing remains from which one cannot abstract further because it is itself without presupposition and is consequently the abstract immediacy or beginning. This one thing is *being* in general or abstract or absolute being, the utmost abstraction from everything.[30]

Once the category of being is established, the dialectical analysis can get started. Being can only be thought with its opposite, nothing. If there were no nothing, there would be no being. The two are necessarily related. Heiberg writes, "To abstract further from being would be to remove the utmost (last) abstraction and consequently leave nothing. But since one *cannot* abstract from being....the utmost abstraction has already been effected to arrive at it, and *being* is thus the same as *nothing*."[31] At times Heiberg enjoys playing on words by referring to this as philosophy's beginning with nothing in the double sense of beginning with the category of nothingness and beginning with no presuppositions.

---

28 *SKS* 1, 17 / *EPW*, 61.

29 See Johnny Kondrup, "Tekstredegørelse" to *Af en endnu Levendes Papirer*, in *SKS* K1, 68–72.

30 Heiberg, *Grundtræk til Philosophiens Philosophie eller den speculative Logik*, § 26. (*Heiberg's Speculative Logic and Other Texts*, p. 55.)

31 Heiberg, *Grundtræk til Philosophiens Philosophie eller den speculative Logik*, § 27. (*Heiberg's Speculative Logic and Other Texts*, p. 55.)

Kierkegaard is also attentive to this point. In the *Concluding Unscientific Postscript*, for example, he has his pseudonym write, "Hegelian logicians...define the immediate, with which logic begins, as follows: the most abstract remainder after an exhaustive abstraction."[32] Similarly in his papers one reads the following: "An abstract beginning is neither something nor nothing, for, if it were nothing, then it would not have begun, and if it were something, it would be more than a beginning."[33] There were other works on Hegel's logic in both Danish and German where Kierkegaard might have read about this.[34] But in any case Heiberg's *Speculative Logic* is certainly a good candidate for the source of these kinds of passages.

Following Hegel, Heiberg spends a fair amount of time in his treatise elucidating the different forms of judgment. In this context he refers to negative judgments as follows:

> The negative judgments are therefore positive. This is the case with respect to so-called "infinite judgments," where subject and predicate belong to mutually exclusive spheres, and therefore no subsumption or judgment can take place but only a proposition, and a meaningless one at that (for example, the proposition mentioned in connection with the law of contradiction: "An elephant is not a cube root").[35]

In his papers Kierkegaard refers to this passage when he writes, "Every negation implies an affirmation, since otherwise it would itself be completely meaningless—this is what Heiberg calls infinite judgments."[36] This is the only unambiguous proof identified so far that Kierkegaard read this work by Heiberg. Nowhere else in his *corpus* does Heiberg refer to or define "infinite judgment," and thus it can only be from this text that Kierkegaard knows it.

Heiberg also discusses other issues that are of interest to Kierkegaard such as the notion of mediation, the sublation of the law of excluded middle, and the relation of philosophy to religion, but Kierkegaard's scattered comments on these issues seem to refer to later works by Heiberg. On the whole it is probably fair to say that *Outline of the Philosophy of Philosophy or Speculative Logic* was important more with respect to the many issues in later discussions that it anticipated than it was as a source in and of itself for Kierkegaard's thought.

---

32 *SKS*, 7, 110 / *CUP1*, 114.

33 *Pap.* II C 37 / *JP* 1, 193.

34 In German there were, for example, Karl Werder, *Logik. Als Commentar und Ergänzung zu Hegels Wissenschaft der Logik*, Berlin: Verlag von Veit und Comp. 1841 (*ASKB* 867); Johan Eduard Erdmann, *Grundriß der Logik und Metaphysik*, Halle: Johann Friedrich Lippert 1841 (*ASKB* 483); Christian Hermann Weiße, *Grundzüge der Metaphysik*, Hamburg: Friedrich Perthes 1835. In Danish there were Adolph Peter Adler, *Populaire Foredrag over Hegels objective Logik*, Copenhagen: C.A. Reitzel 1842 (*ASKB* 383); Rasmus Nielsen, *Den speculative Logik i dens Grundtræk*, Copenhagen: n.p. 1841–44. Peter Michael Stilling, *Philosophiske Betragtninger over den speculative Logiks Betydning for Videnskaben*, Copenhagen: C.A. Reitzel 1842; Rasmus Nielsen, *Den propædeutiske Logik*, Copenhagen: P.G. Philipsen 1845 (*ASKB* 699).

35 Heiberg, *Grundtræk til Philosophiens Philosophie eller den speculative Logik*, § 144, Remark 3, α. (*Heiberg's Speculative Logic and Other Texts*, p. 165.)

36 *Pap.* II C 37 / *JP* 1, 193.

C. On the Significance of Philosophy for the Present Age *(1833)*

Perhaps Heiberg's most read philosophical work was his treatise *On the Significance of Philosophy for the Present Age*, published in 1833.[37] While Heiberg's philosophical works up until this time were more or less ignored by Danish scholars, this one created a controversy due to its provocative claims about the status of religion. In this text Heiberg presents his view of the crisis that the present age finds itself in. He believes people have become alienated from their own culture. They have ceased to believe in the traditional values and institutions that were once taken for granted. As a result, art is no longer thought of as the vessel of beauty but is rather regarded as a light diversion or pastime. Similarly, educated people no longer take religion seriously; they have either ceased believing in God altogether or have ended up believing that God is a wholly mysterious entity that cannot be known. Finally, people in the present age have lost faith in philosophy and have become relativists or nihilists, denying that there is any final truth or meaning.

Heiberg attempts, with this work, to show his contemporaries the way out of the crisis. His thesis is that people must embrace philosophy, that is, Hegel's philosophy, which will put beauty, God and truth back in their proper place. Thus, philosophy is urgently needed if the present age is to stop the process of alienation that is becoming ever more acute. Hegel's idealist philosophy can serve this function since it has the ability to see through the manifold of conflicting appearances and discern the deeper truth lying within them. Once this truth is identified, it can be used to shore up the breaks in the modern world-view. People working in any given field can thus apply a philosophical methodology to restore truth to their currently disoriented and confused endeavors. However, at the same time this clearly implies that philosophy is in some significant way elevated above the other fields, for example, art and religion.

Heiberg's claim that philosophy is higher than religion or theology was the central point in the ensuing debates. This work was met by highly critical responses and reviews from Frederik Ludvig Zeuthen (1805–74),[38] Eggert Christopher Tryde (1781–1860),[39] and Mynster.[40] Uncomfortable with the idea that religion was just a

---

[37] Johan Ludvig Heiberg, *Om Philosophiens Betydning for den nuværende Tid*, Copenhagen: C.A. Reitzel 1833 (*ASKB* 568). (English translation in *Heiberg's On the Significance of Philosophy for the Present Age and Other Texts*, pp. 85–119.)

[38] Frederik Ludvig Zeuthen, "Oplysninger til Prof. J.L. Heibergs Skrift: *Om Philosophiens Betydning for den nærværende Tid*," *Kjøbenhavnsposten*, vol. 7, no. 76, April 18, 1833, pp. 301–2; no. 77, April 19, 1833, pp. 305–6. (English translation in *Heiberg's On the Significance of Philosophy for the Present Age and Other Texts*, pp. 121–30.)

[39] Anonymous [Eggert Christopher Tryde], "Om Philosophiens Betydning for den nuværende Tid. Et Indbydelses-Skrift til en Række af philosophiske Forelæsninger. Af *Johan Ludvig Heiberg*. Kbhavn. 54 S. 8°," *Dansk Litteratur-Tidende* for 1833, no. 41, pp. 649–60; no. 42, pp. 681–92; no. 43, pp. 697–704. (English translation in *Heiberg's On the Significance of Philosophy for the Present Age and Other Texts*, pp. 167–90.)

[40] Kts. [Jakob Peter Mynster], "Om den religiøse Overbeviisning," *Dansk Ugeskrift*, vol. 3, nos. 76–7, 1833, pp. 241–58. (Reprinted in Mynster's *Blandede Skrivter*, vols. 1–6, Copenhagen: Gyldendal 1852–57, vol. 2, pp. 73–94.) (English translation in *Heiberg's On the Significance of Philosophy for the Present Age and Other Texts*, pp. 139–59.)

part of the philosophical system or the Idea, they disputed the claim that philosophy was needed to come to the aid of religion. The critics invariably tried to carve out some special space for religion or theology that was separate from philosophy.

Although Kierkegaard owned a copy of *On the Significance of Philosophy for the Present Age*,[41] it is not so easy to identify unambiguous references to it in his writings. One possibility in this regard is Heiberg's attempt to refute the relativist view of philosophy, where he writes,

> But, one objects, "there are so many philosophies; the one system contradicts and negates the other; in which of these can one find the truth?" To this one can answer that the different philosophical systems—assuming that they really are philosophical, i.e., that they are penetrated by the speculative Idea, for otherwise they cannot be considered—all contain the same philosophy, only seen from different levels of culture in the development of humanity.[42]

Here Heiberg echoes Hegel's claim that philosophy represents a single, developing system and not isolated, episodic units. In *Johannes Climacus, or De Omnibus dubitandum est* Kierkegaard refers to this view as follows:

> *modern philosophy must become conscious of itself as an element in a prior philosophy, which in turn must become conscious of itself as an element in the historical unfolding of the eternal philosophy*. Thus the philosopher's consciousness must encompass the most dizzying contrasts: his own personality, his little amendment—the philosophy of the whole world as the unfolding of the eternal philosophy.[43]

Along these same lines, he writes that Johannes Climacus "one day heard one of the philosophers apropos of that thesis, say 'This thesis does not belong to any particular philosopher; it is a thesis from the eternal philosophy, which anyone who wishes to give himself to philosophy must embrace.' "[44] These statements seem clearly to be based on the same thought found in Heiberg if not the same text.

Towards the end of his treatise, Heiberg explains that this work is an invitation to a series of lectures on philosophy that interested parties can sign up for. In this context, he makes the, at the time unconventional, move of inviting women to participate as well. He explains that he "dares to believe that cultured *ladies* will also be able to participate in the lecture's serious investigations."[45] Kierkegaard seems to refer to this in an article that he wrote for Heiberg's *Kjøbenhavns flyvende Post*, under the title "Another Defense of Woman's Great Abilities."[46] Here he writes ironically, apparently in reference to Heiberg, "Thanks, therefore, to you great men, who help

---

41 See *ASKB* 568.

42 Heiberg, *Om Philosophiens Betydning for den nuværende Tid*, p. 6. (*Heiberg's On the Significance of Philosophy for the Present Age and Other Texts*, pp. 88–9.)

43 *Pap.* IV B 1, p. 123 / *JC*, 140.

44 *Pap.* IV B 1, p. 129 / *JC*, 147.

45 Heiberg, *Om Philosophiens Betydning for den nuværende Tid*, p. 53. (*Heiberg's On the Significance of Philosophy for the Present Age and Other Texts*, p. 118.)

46 "Ogsaa et Forsvar for Qvindens høie Anlæg," *Kjøbenhavns flyvende Post, Interimsblad*, no. 34, December 17, 1834, see *SV1* XIII, 5–8 / *EPW*, 3–5.

them [sc. women] up to the peaks of knowledge but nevertheless do not forget the other sex. Therefore, it is so lovely to see that the man who *especially* wishes to have an effect upon the ladies does not, however, forget *the men* and finally extends his philanthropic enthusiasm to *all*."[47] This jab does not, however, have anything to do with the substantive issues of Heiberg's treatise. While *On the Significance of Philosophy* was an important work in its day, its influence on Kierkegaard remains to be determined.

D. Introductory Lecture to the Logic Course *(1835)*

Heiberg continued his argument for the importance of philosophy in his short work, the *Introductory Lecture to the Logic Course that Began in November 1834 at the Royal Military College*.[48] As is clear from the title, this work arose in the context of Heiberg's instruction for the young officers. It was published in 1835. Although Kierkegaard did not own a copy of this text, it is clear that he has read it and was at least to some degree exercised by it.

In this most sophisticated of all of Heiberg's philosophical works, he makes the argument for the truth of idealism based on the priority of the categories for all thinking. Since the course that he was going to teach was on logic, Heiberg explains that this field is concerned with examining the fundamental structures of thought. These are the categories: that is, being and nothing, cause and effect, force and expression, etc. We must examine these basic constitutive elements of thought to understand how things appear to us in experience since every idea or impression that we receive is full of categorical determinations. Thus there is nothing more fundamental than the categories. Even religious concepts such as God, reconciliation, and heaven all ultimately contain the categories of thinking; otherwise, we could not think them. Therefore, argues Heiberg, religion, which has as its subject matter things such as this, is something secondary since it necessarily relies on the categories, which are the subject matter of philosophy or specifically logic. Logic is therefore the most primary of all the fields of study since it examines the most fundamental forms of thought, which are simply presupposed in all the other fields.

In daily life we are confronted with a confused array of impressions and experiences that seem to be arbitrary and to have no deeper meaning. This conception is a mistake that comes from a fixation on the empirical. Heiberg claims that we must learn how to recognize the truth of the Idea in the empirical phenomena. Towards the end of his treatise, he addresses his students and encourages them to pursue their different vocations with an eye towards bringing to light the ideal structure of reality. He writes:

---

47 "Ogsaa et Forsvar for Qvindens høie Anlæg," *Kjøbenhavns flyvende Post*, *Interimsblad*, no. 34, December 17, 1834, see *SV1* XIII, 7 / *EPW*, 4.

48 Johan Ludvig Heiberg, *Indlednings-Foredrag til det i November 1834 begyndte logiske Cursus paa den kongelige militaire Høiskole*, Copenhagen: J.H. Schubothes Boghandling 1835. (Reprinted in *Prosaiske Skrifter*, vol. 1, pp. 461–516. (In English in *Heiberg's Introductory Lecture to the Logic Course and Other Texts*, ed. and trans. by Jon Stewart, Copenhagen: C.A. Reitzel 2007 (*Texts from Golden Age Denmark*, vol. 3), pp. 41–72.)

> Thus, the demand of the age calls to all but doubly to the chosen, whose destiny it is to hasten ahead of the masses, each in his individual circle of activity, and plant the flag of culture in a heretofore untrodden soil. To say more as a recommendation for philosophical knowing I take to be unnecessary at least in this group. Though I thus now invite you, gentlemen, to follow me to the separate domain, in which abstract thought, set at a distance from the world's movements and the bustle of the moment, makes its invisible dominion secure, I do not forget that my honored listeners are destined to participate in these movements and bustle, to step out into life and actuality, and to give these their best abilities and powers.[49]

Heiberg's claim that it was the demand of the age to pursue philosophy in this way quickly became one of Kierkegaard's favorite hobbyhorses.

For example, in *Prefaces*, his most polemical work against Heiberg, he writes "To take a single example, is it not again and again proclaimed by the priests of philosophy 'that in our age it is a necessity for the theologian to be a philosopher in order to be able to satisfy the demand of the times?' "[50] This presumably refers to Heiberg's claims that for religion to be understood correctly, it must be given a philosophical analysis. Theologians must thus become speculative philosophers in order to grasp the true essence of their field. Also in *Prefaces* we read the following:

> If a person wants to publish a book, he should next make sure it will be of benefit. To that end he asks a publisher or a philosophical fellow or his barber or a passerby what it is the age demands. Lacking this, he himself comes up with something, about which he does not forget to say that it is what the age demands. Not everyone, of course, is given the mental capacity to understand the demand of the age, so much the less when to the doubtful it may seem that the age's demand is multifarious and that the age, although one, can have…several voices.[51]

Here Kierkegaard takes aim at Heiberg's claim that the vocation of philosophy is only for a few; in his address to his students as "honored listeners," Heiberg flatters his audience by giving them the impression that they are among the select few who have a calling to promote philosophy in the present age. Kierkegaard seems to find this a form of objectionable elitism. The other objection seems to be against the idea that there is a single demand of the age; the idea is that the age is complex and that there are thus several different demands that need to be addressed and not just the one that Heiberg is interested in.

In *The Point of View*, Kierkegaard refers to the statement about the demand of the times explicitly in connection with Heiberg's Hegelian campaign. He refers to Heiberg's two great heroes—Goethe and Hegel:

> I have not with the smallest fraction of the capacities granted me striven to express…that the world is good, loves the true, wills the good, that the demand of the times is the truth,

---

49 Heiberg, *Indlednings-Foredrag til det i November 1834 begyndte logiske Cursus paa den kongelige militaire Høiskole*, p. 35. (*Heiberg's Introductory Lecture to the Logic Course and Other Texts*, p. 66.)

50 *SKS* 4, 510–11 / *P*, 50.

51 *SKS* 4, 477–8 / *P*, 13. (Translation slightly modified.)

> that the human race is the true or presumably even God, and therefore the task (Goethean and Hegelian) is to satisfy the age. On the contrary, I have tried to express that the world, if it is not evil, is mediocre, that "the demand of the times" is always foolishness and fatuousness.[52]

What is interesting about this passage is the way in which Kierkegaard seems to portray his own mission as in direction opposition to that of Heiberg. Kierkegaard's concern is with the single individual and not with the race or the generation as a whole. He seems, moreover, to find it pretentious of Heiberg to try to take it upon his own shoulders to provide the solution to the problem of the age and thus answer the demand of the times.

This motif comes up several times in *Stages on Life's Way*. In " 'Guilty'/ 'Not Guilty' " reference is made to the Latin saying *Mundus vult decipi*, that is, "The world wants to be deceived." Then one reads, "In fact, I believe that in a wider sense it is the best that has been said about the world. Thus, speculators should not cudgel their brains trying to fathom what the times demand, for it has been essentially the same since time immemorial."[53] It is fruitless to try to figure out what the age demands since it is already clear: people do not want the truth but rather to live in deception. The "demand of the age" is also a recurring motif in Kierkegaard's review of Thomasine Gyllembourg's *Two Ages*.[54] In short, references to this motif can thus be found scattered throughout Kierkegaard's *corpus*.[55] What seems to be consistent

---

52 *SV1* XIII, 572, note / *PV*, 88, note. See also: "I see that all these real people furnish an essential appurtenance, a chorus, a priceless market-town chorus, which took its stand on what it understood, his trousers, which became 'the demand of the times,' or even more precious, a chorus that wanted to ironize—the ironist" (*SV1* XIII, 581 / *PV*, 96).

53 *SKS* 6, 316 / *SLW*, 340. See also: "Incapable as I am of understanding such tasks as the future of all mankind or what it is that the times demand, I have concentrated entirely on myself" (*SKS* 6, 322 / *SLW*, 346). "Someone who pins his hope on speculative drama serves poetry only insofar as he serves the comic. If a witch or a wizard succeeds in bringing about such a thing, if by means of a speculative thaumaturgist (for a dramaturgist would not suffice) it would satisfy the demand of the age as a poetic work, this event would certainly be a good motif for a comedy, even though it would achieve the comic effect through so many presuppositions that it could not become popular" (*SKS* 6, 382 / *SLW*, 412). *SKS* 6, 97 / *SLW*, 101: "What do the times demand? For me it is of importance only to dare to use these words, τελειος and τελεια, about married people; I leave Jupiter and Juno out of this, not wishing to make a fool of myself by wanting to solve the historical-philological problem." (Translation slightly modified.)

54 *SKS* 8, 13 / *TA*, 9. *SKS*, 8, 24–5 / *TA*, 21–2.

55 *SKS* 1, 251 / *CI*, 207. *SKS* 1, 285 / *CI*, 246. *Pap.* IV B 101 / *R*, Supplement, p. 281. *Pap.* IV B 127, p. 317 / *P*, Supplement, pp. 101–2. *Pap.* IV B 135, p. 321 / *P*, Supplement, p. 105. *SKS* 2, 141 / *EO1*, 140. *SKS* 6, 19 / *SLW*, 11. *SKS* 6, 454 / *SLW*, 493. *Pap.* V B 148.2 / *SLW*, Supplement, p. 625. *Pap.* VII–1 B 55, p. 228 / *COR*, Supplement, p. 181. *Pap.* VII–1 B 55, p. 236 / *COR*, Supplement, p. 188. *SKS* 10, 177 / *CD*, 165. *SKS*, 11, 85 / *WA*, 81. *SV1*, vol. XIII, p. 590 / *PV*, 104. *Pap.* VII–2 B 235, p. 8 / *BA*, 9. *Pap.* VII–2 B 235, p. 23 / *BA*, 24. *Pap.* VII–2 B 235, p. 24 / *BA*, 25. *Pap.* VII–2 B 235, p. 45 / *BA*, 153. *Pap.* IX B 10, p. 308 / *BA*, Supplement, p. 229. *Pap.* VII–2 B 235, p. 27 / *BA*, Supplement, p. 237. *Pap.* VII–2 B 235, p. 56 / *BA*, Supplement, p. 245.

in all of these passages is a satirical tone that mocks Heiberg's enthusiasm and zeal. Kierkegaard apparently finds objectionable what he perceives to be the arrogance behind Heiberg's philosophical prescription for the present age in order to help it to progress further. More interpretive work needs to be done to determine if there is a reasoned philosophical objection to Heiberg's position in the midst of this satire.

In the *Introductory Lecture*, Heiberg also sketches his aesthetic system, establishing a hierarchy of different forms of poetry. He presents the scheme of lyric, epic, and dramatic, that he had originally set out in his review of Oehlenschläger.[56] In his journals Kierkegaard notes this taxonomy as follows:

> I now perceive also that when Heiberg transferred Hegelianism to aesthetics and believed that he had found the triad: lyric—epic—lyric—epic (dramatic), he was right; but it is doubtful that this can be carried through on a far greater scale: classical—romantic—absolute beauty, and in such a way that precisely the Heiberg-triad becomes meaningful, since the classical, as well as the romantic and absolute beauty, has its lyrical—its epic—its dramatic. To what extent, for that matter, is it right to begin with the lyrical; the history of poetry seems to indicate a beginning with epic.[57]

Although it is unclear whether or not Kierkegaard has his information from this text and not another one from Heiberg's hand, there can be no doubt that he was interested in this dimension of Heiberg's aesthetics. Morever, the young Kierkegaard does not seem to object to Heiberg's attempt to systematize aesthetics in a Hegelian fashion.

E. The First Volume of Perseus: Journal for the Speculative Idea *(1837)*

In 1837 Heiberg published the first volume of his Hegelian journal, *Perseus: Journal for the Speculative Idea*.[58] This journal only appeared in two issues, one in 1837 and the other the following year. Kierkegaard owned a copy of this work[59] and seems at least for a time to have been positively inclined towards it. What is significant about this journal is its clear pro-Hegelian line. The first issue is inaugurated with a statement "To the Readers," in which Heiberg describes the context and profile of the new journal. He explains that the current age is being swept away by a bad empiricism that needs to be resisted. He then declares it to be the goal of his new

---

56 Johan Ludvig Heiberg, "Svar paa Hr. Oehlenschlägers Skrift: 'Om Kritiken i *Kjøbenhavns flyvende Post*, over Væringerne i Miklagard,'" *Kjøbenhavns flyvende Post*, 1828 (I, no. 7, January 25; II, no. 8, January 28; III, no. 10, February 4; IV, no. 11, February 8; V, no. 12, February 11; VI, no. 13, February 15; VII, no. 14, February 18; VIII, no. 15, February 22; IX, no. 16, February 25, [no page numbers]). (Reprinted in *Prosaiske Skrifter*, vol. 3, pp. 194–284.)

57 *Pap.* I A 225 / *JP* 2, 1565. Cf. also *SKS*, vol. 17, 113, BB:23 / *KJN* 1, 107. *Pap.* I A 212. *SKS* 1, 26–7 / *EPW*, 70.

58 *Perseus, Journal for den speculative Idee*, ed. by Johan Ludvig Heiberg, no. 1, 1837, Copenhagen: C.A. Reitzel 1837.

59 See *ASKB* 569. Kierkegaard's name appears on the list of subscribers that appears in the second issue of the journal. "Fortegnelse over Subscribenterne paa *Perseus*," *Perseus, Journal for den speculative Idee*, no. 2, Copenhagen: C.A. Reitzel 1838, p. vii.

journal to battle this tendency and secure the truth of idealist philosophy. The image that he uses is that of the Greek god Perseus who battles the Medusa (sc. empiricism) in order to free Andromeda (the speculative truth). He invites interested readers to contribute articles to this journal in any given discipline, with the condition that they attempt to make clear the Idea in their field of inquiry.

Kierkegaard was one of Heiberg's readers who harkened to the call. As noted above, he apparently submitted his review of Hans Christian Andersen's *Only a Fiddler* to Heiberg as a candidate for publication in the second issue in 1838. Evidence for this comes, among other things, from a statement by Kierkegaard's friend, Emil Boesen (1812–81), who writes on July 20, 1838: "Søren Kierkegaard… has recently written a piece on Andersen which will go into Heiberg's *Perseus*; it is written in a rather heavy style, but otherwise it is quite good."[60] This is clear indication that Kierkegaard intended to publish his review there and perhaps that by this time he had already submitted it to Heiberg's judgment. Kierkegaard's intent is confirmed by an extant letter that he addressed to Heiberg on July 28, 1838, where he writes:

> Honored Professor,
>
> I received your letter last night. Only one point in it troubles me somewhat. I am afraid that it may seem in some way as if I almost tried to get around that warning contained in your first letter by employing those same ordinary and imprecise phrases in which you orally stated your stylistic requirements. On this occasion, I cannot refrain from asking you, sir, to remember, as far as you are able to do so, those remarks I then made, which I think contained an Amen that was modified in several ways.—Unless, that is, I have been so unfortunate as to have expressed myself incomprehensibly, just as I see from your letter that I must have misunderstood you.
>
> As for my essay and its fate, I will, sir, take the liberty of visiting you in this connection very soon.[61]

This is clearly a part of an ongoing conversation that Kierkegaard was having with Heiberg about the infelicitous style of the piece. While there are certainly some gaps in our knowledge, it seems safe to conclude that Heiberg rejected the review for publication (presumably due to stylistic concerns), and Kierkegaard then decided to publish the work on his own as an independent monograph under the title, *From the Papers of One Still Living*. What is striking about this episode is that it indicates that Kierkegaard in 1838 had no objections of principle to publishing his work in a Hegelian journal. At this early stage he seems not to have had any particular problem with Hegel or with Heiberg's Hegelianism.

The first article in the journal is Heiberg's book review of Valdemar Henrik Rothe's (1777–1857) *Doctrine of the Trinity and Reconciliation*.[62] This review is important because it takes up a number of issues that had been raised against

---

60 Carl Weltzer, "Stemninger og Tilstande i Emil Boesens Ungdomsaar," *Kirkehistoriske Samlinger*, seventh series, vol. 1, 1951–53, pp. 408–14.

61 *B&A*, vol. 1, p. 43 / *LD*, Letter 9, pp. 54–5.

62 Johan Ludvig Heiberg, "Recension over Hr. Dr. Rothes *Treenigheds- og Forsoningslære*," *Perseus, Journal for den speculative Idee*, no. 1, 1837, pp. 1–89. (Reprinted in Heiberg's *Prosaiske Skrifter*, vol. 2, pp. 1–112.)

Hegel's philosophy by Hans Lassen Martensen (1808–84) in his review of Heiberg's *Introductory Lecture to the Logic Course*.[63] In this context Heiberg returns to a number of the points mentioned above, including the presuppositionless beginning. Here he argues:

> As is known, the Hegelian system moves through nothing but triads. In every one, the first moment is immediate...the second is the mediation or development of the first, and finally the third is the new and synthetic unity, which is no longer immediate, but rather produced by mediation. But every first or immediate moment is *given* by the last previous triad, whose result or not immediate unity it was. If in this way we now go further and further back, then we come to the very first moment, to the immediacy which is no longer relative but rather absolute, which is itself the system's absolute beginning.[64]

Kierkegaard seems to refer to this passage in the *Postscript*, where he writes, "The system begins with the immediate and therefore without presuppositions and therefore absolutely, that is, the beginning of the system is the absolute beginning."[65] There is another reference to the absolute beginning in *De Omnibus*: "The *absolute* beginning is that concept which is also the end of the system, the concept of absolute spirit."[66]

Heiberg continues his explanation of the beginning of philosophy in Hegel's system. He argues that the first triad, which is presupposed by the subsequent ones, is the most fundamental and thus has itself no presuppositions. He reasons as follows:

> Should we now say of this first unit, being = nothing, that it is given or not given, that it is a presupposition or not? Admittedly, it is not given in the same manner as all of those following the first moment in every triad, for these have come from a previous cycle, and prior to the first cycle there is no previous one, and therefore there is nothing that can be surpassed. The most obvious answer is that the absolute first moment is not given. One must necessarily admit this; one must recognize that the system really delivers what it promises: a presuppositionless beginning.[67]

The key term here is the expression "presuppositionless beginning," which comes to be one of the focal points of Kierkegaard's criticism of Hegelian logic. For example, in *The Concept of Anxiety*, he has his pseudonym write:

---

63 Hans Lassen Martensen, "Indlednings-Foredrag til det i November 1834 begyndte logiske Cursus paa den kongelige militaire Høiskole. Af J.L. Heiberg, Lærer i Logik og Æsthetik ved den kgl. militaire Høiskole," *Maanedsskrift for Litteratur*, vol. 16, 1836, pp. 515–28. (In English in *Heiberg's Introductory Lecture to the Logic Course and Other Texts*, pp. 75–86.)

64 Heiberg, "Recension over Hr. Dr. Rothes Treenigheds- og Forsoningslære," *Perseus*, no. 1, 1837, pp. 35–6. (*Prosaiske Skrifter*, vol. 2, p. 45.) (*Heiberg's Introductory Lecture to the Logic Course and Other Texts*, p. 92.)

65 *SKS* 7, 108 / *CUP1*, 111.

66 *Pap.* IV B 1, p. 131 / *JC*, p. 149.

67 Heiberg, "Recension over Hr. Dr. Rothes Treenigheds- og Forsoningslære," *Perseus*, no. 1, 1837, p. 36. (*Prosaiske Skrifter*, vol. 2, pp. 45–6.) (*Heiberg's Introductory Lecture to the Logic Course and Other Texts*, p. 92.)

> The term [transition] is freely used without any ado, and while Hegel and the Hegelian school startled the world with the great insight of the presuppositionless beginning of philosophy, or the thought that before philosophy there must be nothing but the most complete absence of presuppositions, there is no embarrassment at all over the use in Hegelian thought of the terms "transition," "negation," and "mediation," i.e., the principles of motion, in such a way that they do not find their place in the systematic progression. If this is not a presupposition, I do not know what a presupposition is.[68]

The objection here is clear: the methodology of Hegel's speculative philosophy contains within itself a number of unacknowledged presuppositions, while ostensibly claiming to begin with no presuppositions.

There is an extended discussion of this issue in the *Postscript*, where Johannes Climacus considers the relation between the conscious decision on the part of the person thinking and the movement of thought itself. He writes, "But if a resolution is required, presuppositionlessness is abandoned. The beginning can occur only when reflection is stopped, and reflection can be stopped only by something else, and this something else is something altogether different from the logical, since it is a resolution."[69] Here he points out that a conscious resolution or decision is always required to make the beginning, but this decision can be based on any number of things, all of which amount to presuppositions in one form or another. The difficulty of beginning without presuppositions is also satirized in *Works of Love*.[70]

In an insightful passage from a loose paper, Kierkegaard anticipates much of later philosophy of language by pointing to the fundamental nature of language as the presupposition of thought and reasoning. He writes:

> If it were the case that philosophers are presuppositionless, an account would still have to be made of language and its entire importance and relation to speculation, for here speculation does indeed have a medium which it has not provided itself, and what the eternal secret of consciousness is for speculation as a union of a qualification of nature and a qualification of freedom, so also language is [for speculation] partly an original given and partly something freely developing.[71]

In so far as speculative philosophers make use of language to articulate the beginning of philosophy, they have presupposed something for which they have given no account. In the *Journal JJ* he writes:

> Danish philosophy—should there ever be talk of such a thing—will differ from German philosophy in that in no wise will it begin with nothing or without any presuppositions, or

---

68 *SKS* 4, 384 / *CA*, 81.

69 *SKS* 7, 110 / *CUP1*, 113.

70 *SKS* 9, 220–1 / *WL*, 218: "If it is usually difficult to begin without presuppositions, it is truly most difficult of all to begin to build up with the presupposition that love is present and to end with the same presupposition—in that case one's entire work is made into almost nothing beforehand, inasmuch as the presupposition first and last is self-denial, or the builder is concealed and is as nothing."

71 *Pap.* III A 11 / *JP* 3, 3281.

> explain everything by mediating, since it begins, on the contrary, with the proposition that there are many things between heaven and earth which no philosophy has explained.[72]

There can be no doubt that this was one of Kierkegaard's favorite criticisms. Although there are some satirical elements in these passages, he does seem to have a reasoned philosophical objection to the position that Heiberg is arguing for. Kierkegaard seems to be keen to point out that the idea of a presuppositionless beginning in thought is absurd since it always presupposes a more fundamental sphere of existence that it fails to acknowledge. Thus, he spills much ink articulating that sphere in order to contrast it to what he regards as the purely cognitive enterprise of modern philosophy.

There is clear evidence that Kierkegaard was also familiar with the second article in *Perseus*, namely, Martensen's "Observations on the Idea of Faust with Reference to Lenau's *Faust*."[73] As is known, the young Kierkegaard was profoundly interested in the figure of Faust and even planned to write something on this topic.[74] This is seen most clearly from his section in the *Journal BB* entitled "Literature on Faust."[75] Here Kierkegaard collected his notes and bibliographical information on the works about Faust that he was reading. He laments as follows when he sees Martensen has written on the same topic in *Perseus*: "Oh, how unlucky I am—Martensen has written a treatment of Lenau's *Faust*!"[76] In his journals he writes satirically about Martensen often appealing to some motif in the Faust story.[77]

---

72 *SKS* 18, 217, JJ:239 / *KJN* 2, 199.

73 Hans Lassen Martensen, "Betragtninger over Ideen af Faust med Hensyn paa Lenaus *Faust*," *Perseus, Journal for den speculative Idee*, no. 1, 1837, pp. 91–164.

74 See *SKS* 17, 19, AA:11 / *KJN* 1, 13. *Pap.* I A 88. *Pap.* I A 104. *Pap.* I A 122. *Pap.* I A 150. *Pap.* I A 154. *Pap.* I A 274. *Pap.* I A 292. *Pap.* I A 333. *Pap.* I C 46. *Pap.* I C 47. *Pap.* I C 48. *Pap.* I C 49. *SKS*, vol. 19, p. 94, Not2:7. *SKS* 19, 94f., Not2:10. *Pap.* I C 61. *Pap.* I C 102. *Pap.* I C 114. See Carl Roos, "Kierkegaard og Faust," in his *Kierkegaard og Goethe*, Copenhagen: G.E.C. Gads Forlag 1955, pp. 56–157; Knud Jensenius, *Nogle Kierkegaardstudier*, Copenhagen: Nyt Nordisk Forlag, Arnold Busck 1932, pp. 36–63; Sejer Kühle, *Søren Kierkegaards Barndom og Ungdom*, Copenhagen: Aschehoug 1950, pp. 113ff. Henning Fenger, *Kierkegaard: The Myths and Their Origins*, trans. by George C. Schoolfield, New Haven and London: Yale University Press 1980, pp. 84–6; Alastair Hannay, "A Faustian Phase," in his *Kierkegaard. A Biography*, Cambridge and New York: Cambridge University Press 2001, pp. 58–87.

75 *SKS* 17, 92–106, BB:12–15 / *KJN* 1, 85–99.

76 *Pap.* II A 587. See also *Pap.* II A 588.

77 *SKS*, vol. 17, p. 49, AA:38 / *KJN* 1, 43: "In connection with a little essay by Johannes M......(Martensen) on Lenau's *Faust*, in which it is told that the piece ends with Faust killing himself and Mephistopheles' giving an epilogue, I began to ponder to what extent, after all, it is appropriate to let a work of this kind end in such a way. And here I believe that Goethe was right in ending Part One with Mephistopheles' "Heinrich! Heinrich!" A suicide would make too much of a character out of the idea: it should be the counter-weight of the whole world that crushes him, as with D. Juan.—Or end in despair (the Wandering Jew). Despair is romantic—not punishment, as it was in the case of Prometheus." *SKS*, vol. 18, p. 83, FF:38 / *KJN* 2, 76: "The Don Juanian life is truly musical, and that is why it is so fitting that in his *Faust* Lenau has Mephistopheles strike up a tune at the moment that Faust is to portray Don Juan. Marthensen has not seen the deeper significance of this situation."

F. The Second Volume of Perseus: Journal for the Speculative Idea *(1838)*

There is also strong evidence that Kierkegaard was familiar with the second issue of *Perseus* from 1838. The most important article in this issue was Heiberg's essay, "The System of Logic."[78] Here he continues his work in speculative logic. The essay presents the first 23 paragraphs of a system of logic, and thus overlaps with his previous treatise, *Outline of the Philosophy of Philosophy or Speculative Logic*. The point of repeating this material in a new treatise is to respond to critics of Hegel's claims to make an absolute beginning with the concept of pure being. This had been criticized by Sibbern in his extended review of the first issue of *Perseus*, where he took his point of departure in Heiberg's book review of Rothe's work.[79] In this context Heiberg refers to the familiar terms that he used before, such as "the absolute beginning"[80] or the abstract beginning with no determinate content.[81]

In his introduction Heiberg explains his motivation for the present piece and gives the reader reason to expect that further installments will follow:

> The author allows himself to present herewith the first contribution to the working out of a long cherished plan, namely, to expound the system of logic...Furthermore, he has the goal with the present exposition and its continuation to clear the way for an aesthetics, which he has wished to write for a long time, but which he cannot send out into the world without first having given it the support in logic upon which it can rest.[82]

The reader is thus given the impression that this will be the beginning of an elaborate system that extends into other fields as well. Kierkegaard was attentive to this and refers to it critically in a couple of places. For example, in a draft to *The Concept of Anxiety*, one reads:

> In his "The System of Logic," which despite all movement, does not come further than to § 23...and despite its proud title, was not able to emancipate itself from a very subordinate existence in a periodical, Professor Heiberg nevertheless succeeded in making everything move—except the system, which comes to a halt at § 23, although one might have believed that the system would have moved by itself through an immanent movement, and the more so because the author indicated in the "Preface" the

---

78 Johan Ludvig Heiberg, "Det logiske System," *Perseus, Journal for den speculative Idee*, no. 2, 1838, pp. 1–45. (Reprinted in *Prosaiske Skrifter*, vol. 2, pp. 113–66.)

79 Heiberg, "Recension over Hr. Dr. Rothes Treenigheds- og Forsoningslære," *Perseus*, no. 1, 1837, p. 36. (Reprinted in *Prosaiske Skrifter*, vol. 2, p. 46.) Heiberg's *Introductory Lecture to the Logic Course and Other Texts*, p. 92: "one must recognize that the system really delivers what it promises: a presuppositionless beginning."

80 Heiberg, "Det logiske System," *Perseus*, no. 2, 1838, § 3, p. 10. (*Prosaiske Skrifter*, vol. 2, p. 124.)

81 Heiberg, "Det logiske System," *Perseus*, no. 2, 1838, § 2, p. 9. (*Prosaiske Skrifter*, vol. 2, pp. 122–3.)

82 Heiberg, "Det logiske System," *Perseus*, no. 2, 1838, p. 3. (*Prosaiske Skrifter*, vol. 2, pp 115–16.)

> course of development, namely, that the published essay was "the first contribution to a long-cherished plan to expound the system of logic."[83]

The point of this satire seems to be that, despite Heiberg's grand plans, he never managed to build the monument of thought that he had intended. In fact, he never even managed to get past § 23 in what was intended to be a system of logic, let alone to develop the system into other fields, such as aesthetics. This criticism is, of course, not entirely fair since Kierkegaard knew full well that Heiberg had written a complete work on logic previously and that he had also authored quite extensive works on aesthetics in different contexts. The other point of the satire is clearly that of movement in logic, which is a feature of Hegel's speculative logic that Kierkegaard rejects with the claim that movement is a characteristic of existence and not of thought in the sense of logical forms.

Along the same lines Kierkegaard has his pseudonymous author write the following in *Prefaces*: "Therefore I vow: as soon as possible to realize a plan envisaged for thirty years, to publish a system of logic, and as soon as possible to fulfill my promise, made ten years ago of a system of aesthetics; furthermore, I promise a system of ethics and dogmatics, and finally *the* system."[84] Finally, in a draft to *Repetition*, we read, "Of late [Heiberg] has turned his gaze to the far-flung yonder, where, staring prophetically ahead like a brooding genius, he beheld the system, the realization of long contemplated plans."[85] The upshot of these two passages seems to be that Heiberg is pretentious in stating his plans to create a complete system of philosophy in this way. Unlike the passage above, these tend more in the direction of the *ad hominem* than the philosophical.

Also in his introduction Heiberg explains that his method will involve a rigorous, step-by-step demonstration of the dialectical relation of the categories such that there will be no gaps in the reasoning or the categorical system. He writes:

> Moreover, every point in logic will not be treated with equal elaborateness. After a judicious choice, the more interesting points should have preference; but the light which these throw on the surroundings should show the whole in uninterrupted continuity, so that no leap will take place.[86]

What is intriguing here is Heiberg's use of the term "leap." Kierkegaard seems to make a note to himself with regard to precisely this passage when he jots down the following, somewhat cryptic line in his papers: "Heiberg's *Perseus* cf. a pencil mark in the margin to the first §§ of the logic."[87]

---

83 *Pap*. V B 49:5 / *CA*, Supplement, p. 180. (Translation slightly modified.) See also *SKS* 4, 478 / *P*, 14.

84 *SKS* 4, 478 / *P*, 14. (Translation slightly modified.)

85 *Pap*. IV B 116, p. 278 / *R*, Supplement, p. 299.

86 Heiberg, "Det logiske System," *Perseus*, no. 2, 1838, p. 7. (*Prosaiske Skrifter*, vol. 2, p. 120.)

87 *Pap*. V C 4. See Koch's discussion of this passage: Carl Henrik Koch, *En flue på Hegels udødelige næse eller om Adolph Peter Adler og om Søren Kierkegaards forhold til ham*, Copenhagen: C.A. Reitzel 1990, pp. 190ff.

In the second to last paragraph of the treatise Heiberg tries to explain the transition from quality, which he has just treated, to quantity, which he intends to treat. He writes:

> Therefore, it would not be sufficient to define quantity by being in general which lacks qualities, but it must, as happened in the foregoing, be defined expressly in terms of *sublated* quality, that is, quantity is not the first, presuppositionless being, but it is the being, which, after having presupposed and then sublated quality, returns to the same indeterminacy.[88]

Heiberg discusses the movement of the initial triads of logic. While the system begins with the most abstract concept, pure being, it works towards concretion as the categories gradually develop. In a draft to *The Concept of Anxiety*, Kierkegaard refers explicitly to this passage as follows:

> Just an example: the Professor explains to us that in order to form the transition from quality to quantity "it is not sufficient to define quantity as being in general which lacks qualities; it is the *sublated* quality; that is, quantity is not the first presuppositionless being, but it is the being which, after having presupposed and then sublated the quality, returns to the same indeterminacy." Now this may be quite correct, but the difficulty lies in the fact that both being and quality are treated as identical. But being is no quality; logically speaking, it is rather the empty, the contentless, whereas even according to Hegel's definition, quantity is *einfache Bestimmtheit*, and therefore it is not essentially being but essentially determinateness. Thus when one proceeds from being and annuls this in order to return to it again, one will never arrive at quality, and much less a new quality.[89]

Kierkegaard is clearly skeptical of this transition in the system. He points out that the first three triads, which are initiated with the category of being, all fall under the general rubric of quality. The transition to be made is then to the next set of three triads that fall under quantity. Kierkegaard's point is that pure being is supposed to be without any form of further determination, and thus it cannot be properly characterized as "quality." Ultimately this can be understood as in continuation with Kierkegaard's objections to the presuppositionless beginning since he clearly wants to question the status of the category of being as lacking all determination.

Heiberg's "The System of Logic" seems to have been the inspiration for the section "A System of Logic Can be Given" in the *Concluding Unscientific Postscript*.[90] Johannes Climacus takes up a number of the issues discussed here—the beginning of philosophy, movement in logic, mediation—in this analysis and a parallel one entitled, "A System of Existence Cannot be Given."[91] Much of Climacus' discussion aims to distinguish the sphere of objective thinking from that of the subjective and individual existence. He thus incorporates Heiberg's analysis in order to help to

---

88 Heiberg, "Det logiske System," *Perseus*, no. 2, 1838, § 22, p. 43. (*Prosaiske Skrifter*, vol. 2, pp. 164–5.)

89 *Pap.* V B 49:5 / *CA*, Supplement, pp. 180–1. (Translation slightly modified.)

90 *SKS* 7, 106–14 / *CUP1*, 109–18. (Translation slightly modified.)

91 *SKS* 7, 114–20 / *CUP1*, 118–25. (Translation slightly modified.)

develop his own views and primarily the distinction that he finds too often blurred, namely, that between subjective and objective thinking.

G. Fata Morgana *(1838)*

Although it is not a philosophical treatise, Heiberg's drama *Fata Morgana* from 1838 is also worthy of mention in this context, not least of all due to the fact that Kierkegaard owned a copy of it.[92] Heiberg was commissioned to write this work for a special birthday celebration for the Danish King Frederik VI (1768–1839). The comedy had its premier on January 29, 1838 with the king present. With this work Heiberg attempts to develop a new genre, the so-called "speculative comedy"; or, put differently, he attempts to give some elements of Hegel's philosophy a dramatic expression. Although the performance was an utter failure, the work does contain some intriguing elements that are relevant for Heiberg's understanding of philosophy.

The main theme in the work is that of sense illusion and truth. The title of the piece comes from a meteorological phenomenon known in Sicily, which appears in the form of a fog and creates mirages. Local legend attributes this to the work of minor deities. Heiberg thus presents the deity Fata Morgana as the goddess of illusion whose main goal is to deceive humans. The allegorical dimension of the story involves the gradual coming to awareness of these illusions. Once this has become clear, the people make a violent revolt against the goddess and, with the help of poetry, liberate humanity, which, then free from all illusion, can gaze upon the truth in its own form. This can be regarded as continuous with Heiberg's previous attempts to combat what he regards as the bad empiricism with the truth of idealism. The key is to educate the mind to see the truth in the appearances and not to imagine that it has been exiled somewhere beyond them in a sphere that is unattainable by human cognition. Heiberg is convinced that his contemporaries suffer from a myopic fixation on empirical particulars that transfix the mind momentarily; but these are only transient, and while one is fixated on them, one fails to see the deeper truth.

The main character Clotaldo is initially fixated by the illusory beauty of the pearl of Fata Morgana. But when he sees his beloved princess, he realizes that its beauty is only an illusion: "He who sees the true object, / No longer praises the image."[93] This experience leads him to free his mind from the illusions that he formerly dwelt in. Clotaldo declares, "I feel my mind liberated, / When I sacrifice the image of the illusion / for the true appearance."[94] In this way Heiberg makes a Hegelian case for the truth of the Idea, not as something otherworldly, but as present among the world of appearances.

---

92 Heiberg, *Fata Morgana, Eventyr-Comedie*, Copenhagen: Schubothe 1838 (*ASKB* 1561). (Reprinted in *Poetiske Skrifter*, vols. 1–11, Copenhagen: C.A. Reitzel 1862, vol. 2, pp. 93–226.)

93 Heiberg, *Fata Morgana*, p. 44. (*Poetiske Skrifter*, vol. 2, p. 140.) "*Hvo den sande Gjendstand seer, / Hylder Billedet ei meer.*"

94 Heiberg, *Fata Morgana*, p. 45. (*Poetiske Skrifter*, vol. 2, p. 141.) "*Frigjort føler jeg mit Sind, / Naar jeg offrer Illusionens / Blendværk for det sande Skin.*"

H. Heiberg's Article on the Law of Excluded Middle (1839)

Another piece worthy of mention is Heiberg's article in the context of the debate about mediation that took place in 1839. This debate had its origin in an enthusiastic review of Martensen's dissertation, *On the Autonomy of Human Self-Consciousness*,[95] that was written by one of his friends, Johan Alfred Bornemann (1813–90).[96] This review was anxious to acknowledge Martensen's great merits for introducing Hegel and speculative theology to the University of Copenhagen. Bornemann apparently took it for granted that "In theology both rationalism and supernaturalism are antiquated standpoints which belong to an age which has disappeared."[97] By this Bornemann meant that finite standpoints of this kind have been demonstrated to be one-sided and thereby false by Hegel's speculative philosophy, which sees the conceptual truth of opposites.

Mynster found this remark too much to countenance, and so he responded with an article shortly thereafter entitled, "Rationalism, Supernaturalism."[98] Mynster was particularly incensed by the fact that Bornemann seemed to take it for granted that Hegel's speculative logic had established that all finite standpoints are in this way *aufgehoben*. He then tries to make a case for the law of excluded middle from classical logic in order to show that opposing positions cannot logically be conceived as a single position with contradicting properties. In this way Mynster in effect launches an attack on Hegel's doctrine of speculative mediation.

Heiberg's article, entitled "A Remark on Logic in Reference to the Right Reverend Bishop Mynster's Treatise on Rationalism and Supernaturalism," then addresses itself to Mynster's objections.[99] Heiberg feels called upon to defend Hegel's position on this point against the attacks made on it by both Sibbern (in his review of the first issue of *Perseus*)[100] and Mynster in his article. He sees these critics as denying the

---

95 Hans Lassen Martensen, *De autonomia conscientiae sui humanae in theologiam dogmaticam nostri temporis introducta*, Copenhagen: I.D. Quist 1837 (*ASKB* 648). (Danish translation: *Den menneskelige Selvbevidstheds Autonomie*, trans. by L.V. Petersen, Copenhagen: C.A. Reitzel 1841 (*ASKB* 651). English translation: *The Autonomy of Human Self-Consciousness in Modern Dogmatic Theology*, in *Between Hegel and Kierkegaard: Hans L. Martensen's Philosophy of Religion*, trans. by Curtis L. Thompson and David J. Kangas, Atlanta: Scholars Press 1997, pp. 73–147.)

96 Johan Alfred Bornemann, "Af Martensen: *de autonomia conscientiae. Sui humanae*," *Tidsskrift for Litteratur og Kritik*, vol. 1, no. 1, 1839, pp. 1–40.

97 Ibid. p. 3.

98 Jakob Peter Mynster, "Rationalisme, Supranaturalisme," *Tidsskrift for Litteratur og Kritik*, vol. 1, no. 4, 1839, pp. 249–68. (Reprinted in Jakob Peter Mynster, *Blandede Skrivter*, vols. 1–6, ed. by J.H. Paulli, Copenhagen: Gyldendal 1852–57, vol. 2, pp. 95–115.) (English translation: "Mynster's 'Rationalism, Supernaturalism,' " trans. and introduced by Jon Stewart, *Kierkegaard Studies Yearbook*, 2004, pp. 565–82.)

99 Johan Ludvig Heiberg, "En logisk Bemærkning i Anledning af H. H. Hr. Biskop Dr. Mynsters Afhandling om Rationalisme og Supranaturalisme i forrige Hefte af dette Tidsskrift," *Tidsskrift for Litteratur og Kritik*, vol. 1, no. 5, 1839, pp. 441–56. (Reprinted in *Prosaiske Skrifter*, vol. 2, pp. 167–90.)

100 Frederik Christian Sibbern, "Om den Maade, hvorpaa Contradictionsprincipet behandles i den hegelske Skole, med Mere, som henhører til de logiske Grundbetragtninger,"

rightful advance of Hegel's philosophy in science generally, and he claims to want to set the record straight by clearing up what he takes to be obvious and straightforward points of scholarly progress in Hegel's refutation of the laws of contradiction and excluded middle.

Heiberg attempts to explain Hegel's view by demonstrating that in Hegel's system the laws of logic apply at certain levels but not at others. For example, in the "Doctrine of Essence" from the *Science of Logic* things are conceived as dualistic, with categories such as essence and accident, cause and effect, substance and property, etc.: "Examples of where the *principium exclusi medii* finds application, may be found in this sphere."[101] By contrast, at the third level, "The Doctrine of the Concept," speculative thought enters and unites the opposites into a higher unity: "In the same fashion the *principium exclusi medii* is sublated everywhere, where one takes up the standpoint of the Concept and the Idea, for this standpoint's entire activity aims at mediating opposites."[102] Thus, argues Heiberg, the misunderstandings arise when these spheres are confused.

What was perhaps most provocative about Heiberg's article was his claim that key Christian doctrines are based on mediation. He argues:

> But if the *principium exclusi medii* were itself not excluded from the Idea, then man, as a unity of soul and body, would be impossible; the state could not be a unity of opposing forces; Christ would be *exclusus* as *medium* between God and man; no religion, art, poetry or philosophy could exist, for everywhere it would be apparent that the *principium exclusi medii* was the *principium exclusi Dei*.[103]

Heiberg thus argues that the incarnation or the person of Christ requires that there be no law of excluded middle since it states that Christ is both human and God at the same time. If the law of excluded middle were to be valid in this case, then one would have to deny either that Christ is human or that he is divine.

This debate continued with an article by Martensen[104] and a rejoinder by Mynster in the form of a book review.[105] Kierkegaard apparently read the main articles in this

---

Maanedsskrift for Litteratur, vol. 19, no. 5, 1838, pp. 424–37. Corresponds to Sibbern's *Bemærkninger og Undersøgelser fornemmelig betræffende Hegels Philosophie, betragtet i Forhold til vor Tid*, Copenhagen: C.A. Reitzel 1838 (*ASKB* 778), pp. 79–92.

101 Heiberg, "En logisk Bemærkning," *Tidsskrift for Litteratur og Kritik*, p. 444. (*Prosaiske Skrifter*, vol. 2, pp. 172–3.)

102 Heiberg, "En logisk Bemærkning," p. 445. (*Prosaiske Skrifter*, vol. 2, p. 175.)

103 Heiberg, "En logisk Bemærkning," pp. 445–6. (*Prosaiske Skrifter*, vol. 2, p. 175.)

104 Hans Lassen Martensen, "Rationalisme, Supranaturalisme og *principium exclusi medii* i Anledning af H. H. Biskop Mynsters Afhandling herom i dette Tidsskrifts forrige Hefte," *Tidsskrift for Litteratur og Kritik*, vol. 1, no. 5, 1839, pp. 456–73. (English translation: "Martensen's 'Rationalism, Supernaturalism and the *principium exclusi medii*,' " trans. by Jon Stewart, *Kierkegaard Studies Yearbook*, 2004, pp. 583–98.)

105 Jakob Peter Mynster, "*De principio logico exclusi medii inter contradictoria non negligendo commentatio, qua ad audiendam orationem.invitat. Jo. Fr. Herbart. Gottingae 1833. 29 S. 8°, De principiorum contradictionis, identitatis, exclusi tertii in logicis dignitate et ordine commentatio*. Scripsit I.H. Fichte. Bonnae 1840. 31 S. 8°," *Tidsskrift for Litteratur*

debate in 1839 as is evidenced by an entry in his *Journal JJ*.[106] In the *Postscript* he also refers to it, when he writes:

> As is well known, Hegelian philosophy has canceled the law of contradiction, and Hegel himself has more than once emphatically held judgment day on the kind of thinkers who remained in the sphere of understanding and reflection and who have therefore insisted that there is an either/or. Since that time, it has become a popular game, so that as soon as someone hints at an *aut/aut*, a Hegelian comes riding trip-trap-trap on a horse like... and wins a victory and rides home again. Among us, too, the Hegelians have several times been on the move, especially against Bishop Mynster, in order to win speculative thought's brilliant victory.[107]

In drafts of this passage Kierkegaard had initially written the names of Heiberg and Martensen in this passage but then he later omitted them, replacing them with "the Hegelians."[108] Thus, there can be no doubt that Kierkegaard was familiar with this debate. Moreover, this question of mediation can be said to be one of the central issues in Hegel's philosophy (largely via Heiberg) that exercised him.

Kierkegaard takes up this discussion explicitly in a couple of places in his mature authorship. Most obviously, *Either/Or* seems to be profoundly inspired by this discussion. The title of the work itself is a shorthand version of the law of excluded middle.[109] The work sets out two conflicting world-views, the aesthetic and the ethical. The reader is left to choose between these; they represent a dichotomy that precludes any mediation. (This was not lost on Heiberg, who refers to this in his review of *Either/Or*.[110]) There is a play on the form of the law of excluded middle in the "Diapsalmata," where the aesthete writes, "Marry, and you will regret it. Do not marry and you will also regret it. Marry or do not marry, you will regret it either

---

og Kritik, vol. 7, 1842, pp. 325–52. (Reprinted as "Om de logiske Principer," in Mynster's *Blandede Skrivter*, vol. 2, pp. 116–44.)

106 *SKS* 18, 34–5, EE:93 / *KJN* 2, 30: "In truth, we didn't need Hegel to tell us that relative contradiction can be mediated, since it is found in the ancients that they can be distinguished; personality will for all eternity protest against the idea that absolute contradictions are susceptible of mediation (and this protest is incommensurable with what mediation asserts) and it will for all eternity repeat its *immortal* dilemma: to be or not to be, that is the question (Hamlet)."

107 *SKS* 7, 277 / *CUP1*, 304–5.

108 See *Pap.* IV B 54.4 / *CUP2*, Supplement, p. 72. *Pap.* IV B 98.58 / *CUP2*, Supplement, p. 72.

109 *B&A*, vol. 1, p. 107 / *LD*, Letter 68, p. 138: "Either/Or is indeed an excellent title. It is piquant and at the same time also has a speculative meaning." Cf. also *SKS* 7, 229 / *CUP1*, 252: "*Either/Or*, the title of which is in itself indicative, has the existence-relation between the esthetic and the ethical materialize into existence in the existing individuality. This to me is the book's indirect polemic against speculative thought which is indifferent to existence."

110 Johan Ludvig Heiberg, "Litterær Vintersæd," *Intelligensblade*, vol. 2, no. 24, March 1, 1843, p. 292: "But what does the title of the book mean? The second volume is absolute, here there can be no question of an Either/Or, and the book, far from refuting the proposition that the law of contradiction is sublated (p. 176), only the contrary is a proof more for its correctness."

way."[111] This kind of dichotomy or disjunctive pair is intended to represent the opposite of mediation. The aesthete continues, "It is not merely in isolated moments that I, as Spinoza says, view everything *aeterno modo*, but I am continually *aeterno modo*. Many believe they, too, are this when after doing one thing or another they unite or mediate these opposites. But this is a misunderstanding, for the true eternity does not lie behind either/or but before it."[112] The aesthete's suggestion seems to be that the true eternity appears when one is confronted with choices, that is, when one stands opposite conflicting possibilities and is obliged to make a decision. The Hegelians, by contrast, find eternity in the circular movement of uniting opposites and thus overcoming dualisms and dichotomies. In any case, the principle of the either/or is clearly juxtaposed to that of mediation.

There is a more extended discussion of the issue of Hegelian mediation in Part Two, in the chapter "The Balance Between the Esthetic and the Ethical."[113] Here the Judge ascribes to the aesthete a Hegelian view: "You mediate opposites in a higher madness, philosophy mediates them in a higher unity...you say, 'I can either do this or that, but whichever of the two I do is equally mad, ergo I don't do anything at all.' "[114] Despite the aesthete's own apparent advocacy of the either/or, the Judge sees him as subscribing to a form of mediation. His point is that the decisions that the aesthete points out are ultimately indifferent to him. Due to his indifference, lack of commitment or aestheticism, he resembles the Hegelians who regard things, as it were, from the outside and observe the different instances of mediation in an indifferent manner.

The Judge proposes a solution to the problem of mediation that resembles that set forth by Heiberg, namely, to distinguish different spheres and then assign the law of contradiction to one of them and mediation to another. Specifically, the Judge distinguishes between "the sphere of thought" and "the sphere of freedom."[115] He claims that there can certainly be mediation in the sphere of thought, which is abstract and divorced from empirical actuality. This is the sphere of pure contemplation and abstraction. By contrast, there can be no mediation in the sphere of freedom; here the either/or and the laws of contradiction and excluded middle have their validity. The sphere of freedom is the empirical realm, where one is obliged to make choices and act in the real world. Here there can be no mediation. While speculative thought is characterized by necessity, actuality is characterized by freedom.

This discussion from *Either/Or* anticipates a couple of different treatments of this issue in the *Concluding Unscientific Postscript*. One appears in the chapter "Actual Subjectivity, Ethical Subjectivity; the Subjective Thinker,"[116] and the other in the chapter "The Issue in *Fragments*."[117] Here Kierkegaard under a different pseudonym seems to confirm many of the conclusions that were reached in *Either/Or*. The key

---

111 *SKS* 2, 47 / *EO1*, 38. Cf. also *SKS* 3, 156–7 / *EO2*, 158–9.

112 *SKS* 2, 48 / *EO1*, 39.

113 *SKS* 3, 166–72 / *EO2*, 170–6.

114 *SKS* 3, 166–7 / *EO2*, 170. (Translation slightly modified.)

115 *SKS* 3, 169 / *EO2*, 173.

116 *SKS* 7, 277–82 / *CUP1*, 304–10.

117 *SKS* 7, 363–84 / *CUP1*, 399–422.

to the solution of the problem is to distinguish between different spheres and then to assign mediation to its proper place. Johannes Climacus explains:

> Hegel is completely and absolutely correct in the claim that, seen eternally, *sub specie aeterni*, in the language of abstraction, in pure thought and in pure being, there is no *aut/aut*; where in the hell would it be since abstraction precisely takes away contradiction? Thus, Hegel and the Hegelians should rather take the trouble of explaining what is meant by the shadowboxing of bringing contradiction, movement, transition, etc. into logic. The defenders of the *aut/aut* are wrong, if they push their way into the realm of pure thought and want to battle for their cause there....On the other hand, Hegel is just as wrong, when he, forgetting the abstraction, crashes down from it into existence with violence and force in order to sublate the double *aut*. This is to do something that is an impossibility in existence, for he then also sublates existence.[118]

The problem thus lies not in the principle of mediation or in the principle of the either/or but rather in the misguided attempts to transfer the one principle into the sphere of the other. One should keep these spheres radically separate and thus appreciate the validity of each principle in its own context, recognizing its own strengths and limitations.

In this context, Climacus takes up the implications of this account for Christianity. He underscores that Christianity clearly operates in the sphere of actuality, and for this reason it is characterized by the principle of either/or: "It probably is due to this that Christianity has proclaimed eternity as the future because it was proclaimed to existing people, and therefore it also assumes an absolute *aut/aut*."[119] Christianity is a religion that is about personal choice and commitment, things which are absent in mediation. Here Climacus argues against Heiberg's (and Martensen's) claim that mediation is the principle of Christianity, and that dogmas such as the Incarnation and the Trinity cannot be made sense of without it. Climacus' central plea is to avoid confusing the two spheres and attempting to apply the principle of mediation to the sphere of actuality or Christian faith.

While the three most extended discussions of mediation appear in *Either/Or* and the *Postscript*, scattered references to it appear throughout Kierkegaard's authorship. There is clear evidence that, for example, his concept of repetition is intended as a criticism of Hegelian mediation.[120] Similarly his conception of the divine as something absolutely other or different from the human can also be interpreted as an affirmation of the principle of the either/or.[121] There can be no doubt that Heiberg's article along with the others in the debate played a central role in the development of Kierkegaard's position on this issue.

118 *SKS* 7, 277–8 / *CUP1*, 305.

119 *SKS* 7, 280 / *CUP1*, 307.

120 See *SKS* 4, 25 / *R*, 148–9. *Pap.* IV B 117, pp. 288–9 / *R*, Supplement, p. 308.

121 *SKS* 4, 249 / *PF*, 44–5.

I. "Autobiographical Fragments" (1840)

Heiberg's so-called "Autobiographical Fragments" do not belong to his philosophical texts, strictly speaking; however, this is an important text for Kierkegaard's understanding of Heiberg's philosophical disposition. Most people today know this text from its printed version in Heiberg's collected prose writings from 1861–62.[122] Kierkegaard, however, was familiar with it in a somewhat different form. In 1839 the Danish literary scholar Christian Molbech (1783–1857) requested some biographical information from Heiberg that he could use in a work he was writing on Danish poets. Heiberg complied with the request, and Molbech then made use of the short text that he received by interspersing it in his own narrative in the chapter dedicated to Heiberg.[123] The fourth volume of Molbech's work, where this chapter appears, was published in 1840, and this is where Kierkegaard read it.

Heiberg's text is significant since here he gives his firsthand account of his encounter with Hegel's philosophy. He tells the story about how he came to learn of it from his colleagues in Kiel and how he embarked on a trip to Berlin in 1824 in order to meet Hegel and to learn more about his philosophical system. Most striking is his enthusiastic description of how, after much struggle, he came to understand Hegel's difficult thought. He writes:

> While resting on the way home in Hamburg, where I stayed six weeks before returning to Kiel, and during that time was constantly pondering what was still obscure to me, it happened one day that, sitting in my room in the König von England with Hegel on my table and in my thoughts, and listening at the same time to the beautiful hymns which sounded almost unceasingly from the chimes of St. Peter's Church, suddenly, in a way which I have experienced neither before nor since, I was gripped by a momentary inner vision, as if a flash of lightning had illuminated the whole region for me and awakened in me the theretofore hidden central thought. From this moment the system in its broad outline was clear to me, and I was completely convinced that I had grasped it in its innermost core, regardless of however much there might be in the details which I still had not made my own and perhaps never will.[124]

The tone of this passage has reminded some readers of a religious conversion scene.[125] Heiberg goes on to explain retrospectively the importance of this experience for his life and later work: "It is certain that the new light which dawned on me has had a

---

122 Heiberg, "Autobiographiske Fragmenter," *Prosaiske Skrifter*, vol. 11, pp. 485–504. (*Heiberg's On the Significance of Philosophy for the Present Age and Other Texts*, pp. 55–68.)

123 Molbech, *Dansk poetisk Anthologie*, vol. 4, pp. 243–300.

124 Heiberg, "Autobiographiske Fragmenter," in *Prosaiske Skrifter*, vol. 11, pp. 500–1. (*Heiberg's On the Significance of Philosophy for the Present Age and Other Texts*, p. 65.)

125 See Fenger, *The Heibergs*, p. 73; Niels Thulstrup, *Kierkegaard's Relation to Hegel*, trans. by George L. Stengren, Princeton: Princeton University Press 1980, pp. 14–17; Grete Børsand Heyerdahl, "Den filosofiske omvendelse, eller: Hvordan blir man hegelianer, eller: Idéhistorie i praxis," in her *Idéhistoriske smuler*, Oslo: Gyldendal Norsk Forlag 1979, pp. 116–33.

definite influence on all my subsequent undertakings, even those where one would not suspect a connection."[126]

Kierkegaard was attentive to this passage and returns to it satirically in a number of different contexts both in his journals and in his published writings. In one passage he writes, "Heiberg himself is a diplomat, before that miracle in Hamburg, where through a miracle he gained an understanding of and became an adherent of a philosophy that (remarkably enough) does not accept miracles."[127] Similarly, he writes, "Who has forgotten the beautiful Easter morning when Prof. Heiberg arose to understand Hegelian philosophy, as he himself has so edifyingly explained it—was this not a leap? Or did someone dream it?"[128]

In the published writings a vague reference to this appears in *The Concept of Anxiety*, where he has his pseudonym write, "The system is supposed to have such marvelous transparency and inner vision that in the manner of the *omphalopsychoi* [navel souls] it would gaze immovably at the central nothing until at last everything would explain itself and its whole content would come into being by itself. Such introverted openness to the public was to characterize the system."[129] The most famous reference appears in the *Concluding Unscientific Postscript*, where Kierkegaard has Johannes Climacus write, "But I have no miracle to appeal to; ah, that was Dr. Hjortespring's happy fate! According to his own very well-written report, he became an adherent of Hegelian philosophy through a miracle at Streit Hotel in Hamburg on Easter morning...an adherent of the philosophy that assumes that there are no miracles. Marvelous sign of the times!"[130] In the original draft Kierkegaard first wrote Heiberg's name and then subsequently replaced it with the comic name "Dr. Hjortespring."[131] While, to be sure, most of this criticism is more of a personal than a philosophical nature, it does seem clear that Kierkegaard wishes to point out the incongruity of this kind of overly zealous conversion with respect to a sober philosophical system like that of Hegel.

J. New Poems *(1841)*

Heiberg's most successful work was the collection *New Poems* from 1841.[132] Although this is a literary and not a philosophical text, it incorporates many Hegelian elements in a way not unlike *Fata Morgana*. The new collection consists of a series of four poetic works, but clearly the most popular was the piece entitled "A Soul after

126 Heiberg, "Autobiographiske Fragmenter," in *Prosaiske Skrifter*, vol. 11, p. 501. (*Heiberg's On the Significance of Philosophy for the Present Age and Other Texts*, p. 66.)

127 *Pap.* IV B 124, in *Pap.* XIII, p. 364 / *FT*, Supplement, p. 324.

128 *Pap.* V C 3 / *JP* 3, 2347.

129 *SKS* 4, 384 / *CA*, 81.

130 *SKS* 7, 169 / *CUP1*, 184.

131 *Pap.* VI B 98.38 / *CUP2*, 44.

132 Heiberg, *Nye Digte*, Copenhagen: C.A. Reitzel 1841 (*ASKB* 1562). (Reprinted in *Poetiske Skrifter*, vol. 10, pp. 163–324.)

Death: An Apocalyptic Comedy."[133] Kierkegaard owned a copy of this collection and refers explicitly to it.

In this work Heiberg again criticizes what he regards as the cultural crisis of the age. It is the story of a respected resident of Copenhagen who has died and tries to find his way in the afterlife. He is rejected by St. Peter at the gates of heaven because he is utterly ignorant of Christianity, although he believes he is a Christian. So also he is driven away from the entrance to Elysium by Aristophanes because he is equally ignorant of classical culture, art or the humanities. As in his previous works, Heiberg highlights the contemporary crisis of art and religion by showing, this time in a humorous manner, that people have become alienated and subsequently ignorant of what were traditionally fixed points in culture.

Finally, the soul makes his way to hell, where he is convinced by Mephistopheles to enter. The souls in hell symbolically labor endlessly to fill with water a basin that has a hole in the bottom. Thus, try though they may, they do not manage to get anywhere with their efforts. The soul, the representative of Copenhagen of the age, is a victim of the bad empiricism. He is focused solely on the empirical and the individual entities. As a result he cannot see anything deeper or more meaningful beyond them. Like his contemporaries, he is under the spell of the bad infinity of finite particulars. Copenhagen thus dwells in triviality and meaningless finite pursuits. Again Heiberg's message is that one needs to break out from under this spell and see the truth of the speculative Idea. The humorous element arises from the soul's repeated failure to see that there is something beyond the trivialities that constitute his life. While this work has a poetic form, it also has a clearly intended philosophical message that is in line with Heiberg's general program to reform his contemporary age by means of Hegel's philosophy.

In the context of a brief discussion about immortality, Kierkegaard makes reference to "A Soul after Death" in the *Concluding Unscientific Postscript*.[134] From his brief comments there it is, however, difficult to determine if he is appreciative or critical of Heiberg's work.

K. Heiberg's Discussions of Either/Or *and* Repetition *(1843–44)*

An important episode in Heiberg's relation to Kierkegaard was the former's dismissive review of *Either/Or* that was published on March 1, 1843.[135] There Heiberg uses one of Kierkegaard's favorite tools—sarcasm. He imagines a reader who, after being left cold by the first part of the work, "closes the book and says, 'Enough! I've had enough of *Either*, and I'll have no *Or*.' "[136] Kierkegaard never forgave Heiberg for this. The immediate response was his polemical article "A Word of Thanks to

133 Heiberg, "En Sjæl efter Døden," in *Nye Digte*, pp. 29–158. (Reprinted in *Poetiske Skrifter*, vol. 10, pp. 183–263.) (A partial English translation appears in *A Soul after Death*, trans. by Henry Meyer, ed. by Sven H. Rossel, Seattle: Mermaid Press 1991.)

134 *SKS* 7, 159 / *CUP1*, 171–2.

135 Heiberg "Litteræр Vintersæd," *Intelligensblade*, vol. 2, no. 24, March 1, 1843, pp. 285–92 (*ASKB* U 56).

136 Ibid., pp. 290–1.

Professor Heiberg."[137] There are also satirical references to it in *Prefaces*.[138] There is, however, nothing of philosophical relevance in Heiberg's criticism of *Either/Or*.

Heiberg published an article in the first issue of his journal *Urania* (the number for 1844) entitled, "The Astronomical Year."[139] In this article he comes to discuss another of Kierkegaard's pseudonymous works: *Repetition*. The subject matter of Heiberg's journal *Urania* is the natural sciences and especially astronomy. The article "The Astronomical Year," treats the different regularities and repetitions in the heavens and in the natural world generally. Heiberg tries to place the individual in the context of these changes and understand their meaning for the modern context. His observation is that modern life has blinded us to these regular changes in the natural world, and he argues that we should attempt to get more in touch with them. In this context he mentions Kierkegaard's work for the obvious reason that it too treats the concept of repetition, albeit not exactly in Heiberg's sense:

> In a recently published work, which even has the word "repetition" as its title, something very beautiful and fitting is said about this concept, but the author has not distinguished between the essentially different meanings which repetition has in the sphere of nature and in the sphere of spirit. Thereby he has come into the error that repetition should play the same role in a future philosophy as "that which one by an error has called *mediation* plays in the present one."[140]

The last line is, of course, a quotation from *Repetition* itself.[141] Since Heiberg, as a Hegelian, is invested in the notion of mediation, he is critical of Constantin Constantius' suggestion that the concept of repetition will replace it.

Heiberg focuses on a single critical point. He believes that Kierkegaard's work has confused the spheres in which repetition is operative. He explains:

> Indeed, one can say of nature that it is itself mediated by lawful repetitions, but in the sphere of spirit mediation also encompasses something more than simple repetition, something which has already been sufficiently noted in the above remarks. The fact that the author really, in the renown he attributes to repetition, primarily has had in mind the categories of nature and perhaps, without knowing it, has extended the validity of the concept outside its rightful limits, seems to be obvious in part by the fact that he precisely has applied it to a concept of philosophy of nature, namely *movement*, in that he means that the concept of repetition would be able to provide a reconciliation between the Eleatics and Heraclitus, that is, between the two opposed philosophical schools, of which the one denied all movement, and the other by contrast saw everything in movement.[142]

---

137 Victor Eremita, "Taksigelse til Hr. Professor Heiberg," *Fædrelandet*, vol. 4, no. 1168, March 5, 1843, columns 9373–6, see *SV1* XIII, 411–15 / *COR*, 17–21.

138 *SKS* 4, 486–7 / *P*, 23–4. See also *Pap.* IV B 51.

139 Heiberg "Det astronomiske Aar," *Urania*, 1844, pp. 77–160 (*ASKB* U 57). (Reprinted in Heiberg's *Prosaiske Skrifter*, vol. 9, pp. 51–130.)

140 Heiberg "Det astronomiske Aar," p. 97. (*Prosaiske Skrifter*, vol. 9, p. 70.)

141 *SKS* 4, 25 / *R*, 148.

142 Heiberg "Det astronomiske Aar," pp. 97–8. (*Prosaiske Skrifter*, vol. 9, pp. 70–1.)

Heiberg clearly wishes to distinguish Hegelian mediation from the mechanical repetition of nature. He has the impression that the kind of repetition that Constantin Constantius discusses belongs to the realm of nature; however, Constantius mistakenly attempts to understand it to the sphere of spirit, where Hegelian mediation is the operative concept.

Predictably, Kierkegaard was angered by Heiberg's brief discussion of his book. Among his papers one finds drafts of a couple of different critical responses, one entitled "Open Letter to Professor Heiberg, Knight of Dannebrog from Constantin Constantius,"[143] and one entitled "A Little Contribution by Constantin Constantius, Author of *Repetition*."[144] Neither of these, however, was ever published. Instead Kierkegaard seems to have opted to criticize Heiberg with his short work *Prefaces*. This work, however, is more satirical than philosophical, and for this reason it is difficult to gleam genuinely philosophical discussions and criticisms from it.

III. Heiberg and Kierkegaard: A General Assessment

There can be no doubt that Kierkegaard was familiar to a greater or a lesser degree with many of Heiberg's philosophical works. However, to evaluate his views on Heiberg as a philosopher is not a straightforward matter. Although there is no shortage of passages in both the published and the unpublished writings that refer to this part of Heiberg's authorship, most of these are clouded by the soured personal relation between the two men, and many of Kierkegaard's comments are not philosophically interesting since they go in the direction of the *ad hominem*.

This interpretive difficulty is further increased by the fact that Kierkegaard's view towards Heiberg's philosophical efforts changed over time and his assessment was significantly influenced by the deterioration of their personal relationship. In his early work, *From the Papers of One Still Living*, Kierkegaard seems quite positively disposed towards Heiberg's Hegelian campaign, explicitly referring to Hegel's beginning of philosophy in a positive manner. Similarly, the young Kierkegaard seems to have no objections to Heiberg's attempts to construct a system of aesthetics along Hegelian lines, by setting up hierarchies and taxonomies of the different arts or forms of poetry. These positive views clearly change in the subsequent years, and what was once an object of praise later becomes an object of satire. Despite this, one can nonetheless draw some general conclusions about Kierkegaard's relation to Heiberg, the philosopher.

(1) One clear issue from Heiberg's Hegelian philosophy that comes up again and again in Kierkegaard's authorship is that of the beginning of philosophy. Although this was a topic of general philosophical discussion at the time, there is substantial evidence that Kierkegaard's allusions to the terms "absolute beginning" or "presuppositionless beginning" are references to Heiberg's repeated attempts to treat this issue and to defend Hegel's position.

---

143 *Pap*. IV B 110–11, pp. 258–74 / *R*, Supplement, pp. 283–98.

144 *Pap*. IV B 116–17, pp. 278–300 / *R*, Supplement, pp. 299–319.

(2) Another clearly influential issue was that of mediation, which was an important inspiration for Kierkegaard's *Either/Or*, for the concept of repetition, and for some important analyses in the *Postscript*. Although Heiberg likewise cannot be given all the credit for this since his statements on this topic appear in the context of larger discussions and not least of all are inspired by Hegel himself, nonetheless there can be no doubt that Heiberg is one of Kierkegaard's most important sources on this issue. From this one can conclude that it was Heiberg as a speculative logician who played the most significant role for Kierkegaard's development, since it was the key points in Heiberg's speculative logic that caught Kierkegaard's eye and that he returned to again and again.

(3) Finally, Kierkegaard seems profoundly critical of Heiberg's zealous attempt to promote Hegel's philosophy in Denmark. This comes out clearly in *Prefaces*, which can be seen as Kierkegaard's crowning achievement in anti-Heiberg polemics. With Kierkegaard having been thoroughly alienated by Heiberg's negative discussions of *Either/Or* and *Repetition*, this work pokes fun at many different aspects of Heiberg's activities and not just his Hegelian philosophy. The final Preface can be regarded as a satire on Heiberg's attempt to establish a Hegelian journal.[145] Here Nicolaus Notabene explains his plans to launch a new philosophical journal in order to promote the study of philosophy in Denmark. This statement seems to echo Heiberg's repeated statements about the need to make philosophy popular. Notabene explicitly compares his journal with that of Heiberg's *Perseus*. The satirical point lies in his statement that while Heiberg's journal set out to teach his readers about Hegelian philosophy, Nicolaus Notabene's journal will, by contrast, explicitly state its ignorance and solicit its readers to explain philosophy to him. Thus Notabene assumes a Socratic stance and asks his readers for instruction, while claiming to know nothing himself.[146] He requests specifically that his readers explain Hegel's philosophy to him:

> There is one thing that I do desire of my contemporaries: it is an explanation. Consequently I do not deny that Hegel has explained everything; I leave that to the powerful minds who will also explain what is missing. I keep my feet on the ground and say: I have not understood Hegel's explanation. From this, in turn, I draw no other conclusion than that I have not understood him. I leave further conclusions to the powers that be who find authorization for this in their personalities.[147]

This is clearly a jab at Heiberg's self-appointed Hegelian campaign. Nicolaus Notabene refers to Heiberg's address to his students in the *Introductory Lecture to the Logic Course* where the latter states that only a few are called to philosophy and encourages his students to pursue the speculative Idea in their different realms of

---

145 *SKS* 4, 508–26 / *P*, 47–67.

146 *SKS* 4, 512 / *P*, 51: "Is this not a good purpose, and is it not one different from the purpose of those who previously have attempted to publish a philosophical journal, even though in it there is agreement with their purpose: to want to serve philosophy. Yet the services are different: the one serves it through his wisdom, the other through his obtuseness."

147 *SKS* 4, 516–17 / *P*, 56.

activity.[148] Nicolaus Notabene then satirically plays the role of one who is not among the chosen, and who therefore is excluded from understanding philosophy.

Another significant point of criticism is Nicolaus Notabene's claims that the Hegelian philosophers are unoriginal and that they attempt to win fame by parroting what Hegel has written. He writes:

> I have read philosophical treatises in which nearly every thought, almost every expression, was from Hegel. After having read through them, I have thought: Who, now, actually is the author? Hegel, I have then said to myself, is the author; the one who has written the treatise is his reporter and as such he is dependable and accurate. This I could understand. But look! This was not the way it was; the author was a man who had gone beyond Hegel.[149]

In this context it seems clear that Nicolaus Notabene has Heiberg specifically in mind. He alludes to Heiberg's article, "The System of Logic," where Heiberg believes that he has discovered an error in Hegel's reasoning and proposes a solution that modifies the categorical analysis that he has been following. Heiberg writes:

> By way of excursus it can still be noted (for those who are interested), to what degree the exposition given heretofore is different from that of Hegel. (1) For Hegel absolute being is expounded with the categories: a) being, b) nothing, c) becoming. But this order must be seen as a slight oversight, for it is in conflict with the rest of the system's entire structure.[150]

Heiberg then modifies this first triad by combining the first two categories into a single one: being and nothing, becoming, determinate being.

Nicolaus Notabene finds this absurd since Heiberg, in this essay and in his *Outline of the Philosophy of Philosophy or Speculative Logic*, has followed Hegel's analysis almost slavishly; but now he claims originality by modifying a single point. Notabene writes:

> Hegel knew how to formulate the whole of modern philosophy in such a way that it looks as if he brought everything to an end and everything previous tended toward him. Someone else now makes a similar presentation, a presentation that to a hair is inseparable from Hegel's, that consequently is pervaded at every point by this final thought, and to this is added a concluding paragraph in which one testifies that one has gone beyond Hegel.[151]

The criticism is clearly of the attempt to claim originality in this rather inauthentic manner. From criticisms such as these it is clear that much of what has previously been seen as a part of Kierkegaard's criticism of Hegel in fact lands more on Heiberg than on Hegel himself. While he may, to be sure, have some problems with specific

---

148 Heiberg, *Indlednings-Foredrag til det i November 1834 begyndte logiske Cursus paa den kongelige militaire Høiskole*, p. 35. (*Heiberg's Introductory Lecture to the Logic Course and Other Texts*, pp. 66–7; quoted in full above.)

149 *SKS* 4, 517 / *P*, p. 57. (Translation slightly modified.)

150 Heiberg, "Det logiske System," § 23, p. 44. (*Prosaiske Skrifter*, vol. 2, p. 165.)

151 *SKS* 4, 517–18 / *P*, 57.

aspect of Hegel's philosophy, much of the polemics is not about this but rather about Heiberg's efforts to promote it in Denmark.

It is difficult to evaluate the actual philosophical merits of *Prefaces*, which is, after all, designated as "light reading." Heiberg has often been identified as a character in Kierkegaard's unpublished satirical works, *The Battle between the Old and the New Soap-Cellars* and the satirical *Johannes Climacus, or De Omnibus dubitandum est*. Thus it seems safe to conclude that Kierkegaard believed that the best way to combat Heiberg's Hegelianism was not with straightforward counterargument but rather with humor and satire.

In any case there can be little doubt that what irritated Kierkegaard the most was Heiberg's repeated zealous attempts to make Hegel's philosophy popular in Denmark. While Kierkegaard still maintained some degree of respect for Hegel himself, Heiberg, as Hegel's apologist, is subject to the most energetic satire and sarcasm.

Bibliography

I. Heiberg's Works in The Auction Catalogue *of Kierkegaard's Library*

Om Philosophiens Betydning for den nuværende Tid. Et Indbydelses-Skrift til en Række af philosophiske Forelæsninger, Copenhagen: C.A. Reitzel 1833 (*ASKB* 568).

"Recension over Hr. Dr. Rothes Treenigheds- og Forsoningslære," in *Perseus*, vols. 1–2, ed. by Johan Ludvig Heiberg, Copenhagen: C.A. Reitzel 1837–38, vol. 1, pp. 1–90 (*ASKB* 569).

"Om den romantiske Tragedie af Hertz: *Svend Dyrings Huus*. I Forbindelse med en æsthetisk Betragtning af de danske Kæmpeviser," in *Perseus*, vols. 1–2, ed. by Johan Ludvig Heiberg, Copenhagen: C.A. Reitzel 1837–38, vol. 1, pp. 165–264 (*ASKB* 569).

"Det logiske System," in *Perseus*, vols. 1–2, ed. by Johan Ludvig Heiberg, Copenhagen: C.A. Reitzel 1837–38, vol. 2, pp. 1–45 (*ASKB* 569).

"Om Malerkunsten i dens Forhold til de andre skjønne Kunster," in *Perseus*, vols. 1–2, ed. by Johan Ludvig Heiberg, Copenhagen: C.A. Reitzel 1837–38, vol. 2, pp. 101–81 (*ASKB* 569).

Digte og Fortællinger, vols. 1–2, Copenhagen: J.H. Schubothes Boghandling 1834–35 (part of *Johan Ludvig Heiberg's Samlede Skrifter*, consisting of *Skuespil*, vols. 1–7, Copenhagen: J.H. Schubothe 1833–41; *Digte og Fortællinger*, vols. 1–2, Copenhagen: J.H. Schubothe 1834–35; and *Prosaiske Skrifter*, vols. 1–3, Copenhagen: J.H. Schubothe 1841–43) (*ASKB* 1551–1552).

Skuespil, vols. 1–7, Copenhagen: J.H. Schubothes Boghandling 1833–41 (Part of *Johan Ludvig Heiberg's Samlede Skrifter*, consisting of *Skuespil*, vols. 1–7, Copenhagen: J.H. Schubothe 1833–41; *Digte og Fortællinger*, vols. 1–2, Copenhagen: J.H. Schubothe 1834–35; and *Prosaiske Skrifter*, vols. 1–3, Copenhagen: J.H. Schubothe 1841–43) (*ASKB* 1553–1559).

Prosaiske Skrifter, vol. 3, Copenhagen: J.H. Schubothe 1843 (vol. 3, in Johan Ludvig Heiberg, *Prosaiske Skrifter*, vols. 1–3, Copenhagen: J.H. Schubothe 1841–18 which is part of *Johan Ludvig Heiberg's Samlede Skrifter* consisting of *Skuespil*, vols. 1–7, Copenhagen: J.H. Schubothe 1833–41; *Digte og Fortællinger*, vols. 1–2, Copenhagen: J.H. Schubothe 1834–35; and *Prosaiske Skrifter*) (*ASKB* 1560).

Fata Morgana. Eventyr-Comedie, Copenhagen: J.H. Schubothe 1838 (*ASKB* 1561).

Nye Digte, Copenhagen: C.A. Reitzel 1841 (*ASKB* 1562).

" 'Dagens' Anmeldelse af 'Guldkorset,' " *Kjøbenhavns Flyvende Post. Interimsblade*, ed. by Johan Ludvig Heiberg , Copenhagen: J.D. Quist no. 83, 1836 (*ASKB* U 55).

"Forhandlinger med Redactionen af *Maandeskrift for Litteratur*," *Kjøbenhavns Flyvende Post. Interimsblade*, ed. by Johan Ludvig Heiberg, Copenhagen: J.D. Quist no. 113, 1837 (*ASKB* U 55).

"Tillæg til Anmeldelsen af *Ørkenens Sön*," *Intelligensblade* (ed. by Johan Ludvig Heiberg), vol. 2, no. 24, 1843, pp. 269–84 (*ASKB* U 56).

"Litteraer Vintersæd," *Intelligensblade* (ed. by Johan Ludvig Heiberg), vol. 2, no. 24, 1843, pp. 285–92 (*ASKB* U 56).

"Lyrisk Poesie," *Intelligensblade* (ed. by Johan Ludvig Heiberg), vol. 3, nos. 25–6, 1843, pp. 25–72 (*ASKB* U 56).

"Stjerne-Calender for 1845, til Orientering i Himmellegemernes Bevægelser og Stillinger," in *Urania. Aarbog for 1845*, ed. by Johan Ludvig Heiberg, Copenhagen: H.I. Bing & Söns Forlag 1844, pp. 1–88 (*ASKB* U 58).

Ulla skal paa Bal. En bellmansk Situation, Copenhagen: J.H. Schubothe 1845 (*ASKB* U 59).

Valgerda. Lystspil i to Acter, Copenhagen: J.H. Schubothe 1847 (*ASKB* U 60).

(ed.), *Kjöbenhavns flyvende Post, Interimsblade*, nos. 1–100, Copenhagen: J.D. Quist 1834–36 (*ASKB* 1607).

(ed.), *Kjøbenhavns Flyvende Post. Interimsblade*, no. 76; nos. 82–3; no. 87 and nos. 101–35, Copenhagen: J.D. Quist 1836–37 (*ASKB* U 55).

(ed.), *Intelligensblade*, no. 24 and nos. 26–7, 1843, ed. by Johan Ludvig Heiberg, Copenhagen: C.A. Reitzel 1843 (in *Intelligensblade*, vols. 1–4, nos. 1–48, ed. by Johan Ludvig Heiberg, Copenhagen: C.A. Reitzel 1842–44, vol. 2, pp. 269–92 and vol. 3, pp. 25–72, respectively) (*ASKB* U 56).

(ed.), *Urania. Aarbog for 1844*, Copenhagen: H.I. Bing & Sön 1843 (*ASKB* U 57).

(ed.), *Urania. Aarbog for 1845*, Copenhagen: H.I. Bing & Sön 1844 (*ASKB* U 58).

(trans.), Eugène Scribe, *Den förste Kjærlighed. Lystspil i een Act*, trans. by Johan Ludvig Heiberg, Copenhagen: Jens Hostrup Schultz 1832 (no. 45 in The Royal Danish Theatre's Repertoire, Part 7) (*ASKB* U 98).

II. Works in The Auction Catalogue *of Kierkegaard's Library that Discuss Heiberg*

Adler, Adolph Peter, *Populaire Foredrag over Hegels objective Logik*, Copenhagen: C.A. Reitzel 1842, p. 4; p. 12, note; p. 16; p. 78, note; p. 81; p. 165, note (*ASKB* 383).

Andersen, Hans Christian, *En Comedie i det Grønne, Vaudeville i een Akt efter det gamle Lystspil: "Skuespilleren imod sin Villie,"* Copenhagen: J.H. Schubothe 1840 (*ASKB* U 14).

Hagen, Johan Frederik, *Ægteskabet. Betragtet fra et ethisk-historiskt Standpunct*, Copenhagen: Wahlske Boghandels Forlag 1845, p. 7, note (*ASKB* 534).

Hebbel, Friedrich, *Mein Wort über das Drama! Eine Erwiderung an Professor Heiberg in Copenhagen*, Hamburg: Bei Hoffmann und Campe 1843 (*ASKB* U 54).

Martensen, Hans Lassen, "Kirke-Aaret," in *Urania. Aarbog for 1844*, ed. by Johan Ludvig Heiberg, Copenhagen: H.I. Bing & Sön 1843, pp. 161–88 (*ASKB* U 57).

—— *Den danske Folkekirkes Forfatningsspørgsmaal*, Copenhagen: C.A. Reitzel 1851, p. 33 (*ASKB* 655).

[Møller, Poul Martin], *Efterladte Skrifter af Poul M. Møller*, vols. 1–3, ed. by Christian Winther, F.C. Olsen, and Christen Thaarup, Copenhagen: C.A. Reitzel 1839–43, vol. 3, p. 268 (*ASKB* 1574–1576).

Mynster, Jakob Peter, *Blandede Skrivter*, vols. 1–3, Copenhagen: Gyldendal 1852–53 (vols. 4–6, Copenhagen: Gyldendal 1855–57), vol. 1, p. 257; vol. 2, pp. 73–94; p. 116; p. 127; p. 130; p. 385 (*ASKB* 358–363).

Nielsen, Rasmus, *Den propædeutiske Logik*, Copenhagen: P.G. Philipsen 1845, p. 15; p. 88; p. 261 (*ASKB* 699).

Paludan-Müller, “Abels Död,” *Urania. Aarbog for 1845*, ed. by Johan Ludvig Heiberg, Copenhagen: H.I. Bing & Sön 1844, pp. 113–42 (*ASKB* U 58).

Thortsen, Carl Adolph, *Historisk Udsigt over den danske Litteratur indtil Aar 1814*, Copenhagen: C.A. Reitzel 1839, p. 160 (*ASKB* 970).

Sibbern, Frederik Christian, *Bemærkninger og Undersøgelser, fornemmelig betreffende Hegels Philosophie, betragtet i Forhold til vor Tid*, Copenhagen: C.A. Reitzel 1838 (*ASKB* 778).

—— *Dikaiosyne eller Bidrag til Politik og politisk Jurisprudents for Danske, i statsretlig, kirkelig og historisk Henseende*, vol. 1, Copenhagen 1843, p. 22; p. 24 (*ASKB* U 105).

III. Secondary Literature on Kierkegaard's Relation to Heiberg

Andersen, Vilhelm, “Søren Kierkegaard,” in his *Tider og Typer af dansk Aands Historie*, vols. 1–4, Copenhagen: Gyldendal 1907–16, vol. 4, pp. 65–108.

Brandt, Frithiof, “Kierkegaard og Heiberg-kredsen,” in his *Den unge Søren Kierkegaard. En Række nye Bidrag*, Copenhagen: Levin & Munksgaard 1929, pp. 126–9.

Bukdahl, Jørgen, “The Coteries of the Cultivated,” in his *Søren Kierkegaard and the Common Man*, trans. and ed. by Bruce H. Kirmmse, Cambridge: Eerdmans 2001, pp. 55–69. (Originally “Dannelsen og dens koterier,” in his *Søren Kierkegaard og den menige mand*, Copenhagen: Munksgaard 1961, pp. 52–64.)

Caron, Jacques, “J.L. Heiberg,” in his *Angoisse et Communication chez S. Kierkegaard*, Odense: Odense University Press 1992, pp. 39–46.

Fenger, Henning, *Kierkegaard, the Myths and Their Origins. Studies in the Kierkegaardian Papers and Letters*, trans. by George C. Schoolfield, New Haven and London: Yale University Press 1980, p. ix; pp. 3–5; p. 11; pp. 17–18; pp. 28–9; p. 32; p. 42; p. 65; pp. 70–1; p. 79; pp. 81–91; p. 116; p. 123; pp. 127–9; pp. 135–43; pp. 146–9; p. 169; p. 175; p. 177; p. 180; p. 215; p. 218; p. 220. (Originally *Kierkegaard-Myter og Kierkegaard-Kilder. 9 kildekritiske studier i de Kierkegaardske papirer, breve og aktstykker*, Odense: Odense Universitetsforlag 1976.)

—— “Kierkegaard—A Literary Approach,” in *Kierkegaard and His Contemporaries: The Culture of Golden Age Denmark*, ed. by Jon Stewart. Berlin and New York: Walter de Gruyter 2003, pp. 301–18.

Fenves, Peter, *"Chatter." Language and History in Kierkegaard*, Stanford, California: University of California Press 1993, pp. 191–5; pp. 208–9; p. 217.

Høffding, Harald, *Søren Kierkegaard som filosof*, Copenhagen, P.G. Philipsen 1892, see pp. 16–17.

Kjældgaard, Lasse Horne, "Den hvilende handling. Heibergs billedkunstneriske ideal," in his *Mellemhverandre. Tableau og fortælling i Søren Kierkegaards pseudonyme skrifter*, Hellerup: Forlaget Spring 2001, pp. 48–57.

—— "Kierkegaards tableau og Heibergs store fortælling," in his *Mellemhverandre. Tableau og fortælling i Søren Kierkegaards pseudonyme skrifter*, Hellerup: Forlaget Spring 2001, pp. 131–3.

Kühle, Sejer, *Søren Kierkegaards Barndom og Ungdom*, Copenhagen: Aschehoug Dansk Forlag 1950, see p. 92; p. 96; pp. 101ff.; pp. 110ff.; p. 113; pp. 123–7; p. 134; p. 150; p. 152; p. 196; p. 203; p. 207.

Pattison, George, "Søren Kierkegaard: A Theater Critic of the Heiberg School," *The British Journal of Aesthetics*, no. 23, 1983, pp. 25–33. (Reprinted in *Kierkegaard and His Contemporaries: The Culture of Golden Age Denmark*, ed. by Jon Stewart. Berlin and New York: Walter de Gruyter 2003 (*Kierkegaard Studies Monograph Series*, vol. 10), pp. 319–29.)

—— "The Initial Reception of *Either/Or*," in *Either/Or Part II*, ed. by Robert L. Perkins, Macon, Georgia: Mercer University Press 1995 (*International Kierkegaard Commentary*, vol. 4), pp. 291–305.

Politis, Hélène, "Kierkegaard: Documents philosophiques," in *Kierkegaard. Vingt-Cinq Etudes*, 1989 (*Le Cahiers de Philsophie*, nos. 8–9), pp. 443–72.

Rasmussen, Pin and Inge Lise, "Ros som modstand. Det spændte forhold imellem Søren Kierkegaard og Johan Ludvig Heiberg," in *Literature as Resistance and Counter-Culture: Papers of the 19th Study Conference of the International Association for Scandinavian Studies*, ed. by András Masát and Péter Mádl, Budapest: Hungarian Association for Scandinavian Studies 1993, pp. 104–9.

Reuter, Hans, *S. Kierkegaards religionsphilosophische Gedanken im Verhältnis zu Hegels religionsphilosophischem Systems*, Leipzig: Quelle & Meyer 1914 (*Abhandlungen zur Philosophie und ihrer Geschichte*, no. 23), see pp. 68–74.

Rubow, Paul V., *Kierkegaard og hans Samtidige*, Copenhagen: Gyldendal 1950, p. 12; p. 59.

Scopetea, Sophia, *Kierkegaard og græciteten. En kamp med ironi*, Copenhagen: C.A. Reitzel 1995, p. 15; p. 32, note 20; p. 52; p. 82, notes 12–13; p. 92; p. 166; p. 169; pp. 235–8; pp. 240–7; p. 256, note 70; p. 371; p. 413, note 27; p. 446, note 113; p. 467.

Söderquist, K. Brian, "Kierkegaard's Contribution to the Danish Discussion of 'Irony,' " in *Kierkegaard and His Contemporaries: The Culture of Golden Age Denmark*, ed. by Jon Stewart, Berlin and New York: Walter de Gruyter 2003 (*Kierkegaard Studies Monograph Series*, vol. 10). pp. 78–105.

Stewart, Jon, "*Perzeusz* Heiberga a *Z papierów jeszcze zyjacego* Kierkegaarda" ["Heiberg's *Perseus* and Kierkegaard's *From the Papers of One Still Living*"], trans. by Bronislaw Swiderski, in *Tozsamosci Kierkegaarda*, in *Principia*, Tome 23, 1999, pp. 25–42.

—— "Kierkegaard and Hegelianism in Golden Age Denmark," in *Kierkegaard and His Contemporaries: The Culture of Golden Age Denmark*, ed. by Jon Stewart, Berlin and New York: Walter de Gruyter 2003 (*Kierkegaard Studies Monograph Series*, vol. 10), pp. 106–45.

—— *Kierkegaard's Relations to Hegel Reconsidered*, Cambridge and New York: Cambridge University Press 2003.

Thulstrup, Niels, *Kierkegaard's Relation to Hegel*, trans. by George L. Stengren, Princeton, New Jersey: Princeton University Press 1980. (Originally *Kierkegaards Forhold til Hegel*, Copenhagen: Gyldendal 1967.)

—— *Commentary on Kierkegaard's Concluding Unscientific Postscript*, trans. by Robert J. Widenmann, Princeton, New Jersey: Princeton University Press 1984. (Originally *Søren Kierkegaard. Afsluttende uvidenskabelige Efterskrift udgivet med Indledning og Kommentar af Niels Thulstrup*, vols. 1–2, Copenhagen: Gyldendal 1962.)

Tjønneland, Eivind, *Ironie als Symptom. Eine kritische Auseinandersetzung mit Søren Kierkegaards Über den Begriff der Ironie*, Frankfurt am Main: Peter Lang 2004 (*Texte und Untersuchungen zur Germanistik und Skandinavistik*, vol. 54), see pp. 114–17.

Troelsen, Bjarne, "Biedermeier—Kierkegaard, H.C. Andersen og Heiberg," in *Denne slyngelagtige eftertid. Tekster om Søren Kierkegaard*, vols. 1–3, ed. by Finn Frandsen and Ole Morsing, Århus: Slagmark 1995, vol. 3, pp. 431–49.

—— "Hegel og Heiberg" and "Heiberg og 'Det interessante,' " in his *Manden på Flydebroen. En fortælling om Søren Kierkegaard og det moderne menneskes tilblivelse*, Frederiksberg: Forlaget ANIS 1997, pp. 52–7; pp. 78–82.

Vergote, Henri-Bernard, *Lectures philosophiques de Søren Kierkegaard. Kierkegaard chez ses contemporains danois. Textes de J.L. Heiberg, H.L. Martensen, P.M. Møller, F.C. Sibbern, F. Beck et S.A. Kierkegaard*, Paris: Presses Universitaires de France 1993 (*Philosophique D'ajourd'hui*).

J.L.A. Kolderup-Rosenvinge:
Kierkegaard on Walking Away From Politics

J. Michael Tilley

Kierkegaard often expresses ambivalence toward the political concerns of his day. He regularly expresses both his ignorance of political issues in general and his disdain for religious and political reformers, but he will also offer sophisticated defenses of his purported apolitical views while at the same time offering a critique of the theoretical assumptions that justify a particular political movement. This ambivalence is illustrated in a series of letters exchanged between Kierkegaard and the law professor J.L.A. Kolderup-Rosenvinge. These letters address two topics—the idea of movement or walking and the domain and nature of the political. Each topic is initially addressed rather playfully and progressively becomes more serious in subsequent letters. In this article, I will begin by giving a brief overview of Kolderup-Rosenvinge's life and work since he is a rather obscure nineteenth-century Danish figure. I will also provide a complete account of Kierkegaard's references to and correspondence with Kolderup-Rosenvinge. Finally, I will address Kierkegaard's "theory of motion" which is described in a letter to Kolderup-Rosenvinge as it pertains to Kierkegaard's approach to political questions.

I. Overview of Kolderup-Rosenvinge's Life and Works

Janus Lauritz Andreas Kolderup-Rosenvinge was born on May 10, 1792 and died August 5, 1850 (buried in Assistens Cemetry).[1] He was a member of a prominent family in Copenhagen; his father was a Postmaster, and he married Barbara Abigael Lange—the daughter of the Postmaster General—on August 7, 1814. He began his university studies in 1809 and later passed his subject exam covering theoretical law and its practical applications. He earned the University Gold Medallion for his study on the history of Danish law in 1813, graduated with his candidate jurist degree in 1815, and was licensed as a lawyer shortly thereafter. During this time period, he also provided private legal instruction to Anders Sandøe Ørsted (1778–1860), who

---

[1] Biographical and historical information contained in the first section, unless otherwise indicated, is from Frantz Dahl's entry "Kolderup-Rosenvinge, Janus Lauritz Andreas," in *Dansk Biografisk Leksikon*, vols. 1–27, ed. by C.F. Bricka, 2nd ed., Copenhagen: J.H. Schultz 1933–44, vol. 13 (1938), pp. 113–15 and H. Matzen's "Kolderup-Rosenvinge, Janus Lauritz Andreas," in *Dansk biografisk Lexikon*, vols. 1–19, ed. by C.F. Bricka, 1st ed., Copenhagen: Gyldendal 1887–1905, vol. 9 (1895), pp. 349–54.

would later hold prominent positions in the government both prior to and subsequent to the adoption of the Danish Constitution in 1849.

In 1814 just prior to earning his candidate jurist degree, Kolderup-Rosenvinge began his career as a notary of the Faculty of Law. He quickly worked his way up the ranks of the law faculty becoming an assistant professor in 1815 and three years later becoming a full professor. As a professor of law, he published a number of academic works on Danish law, its history, and Danish church law. He also served in numerous committees concerning law and church policy and in 1848, he was given the honorific title Conference Counselor [*Konferensraad*]—which Kierkegaard uses in the salutation of his letters.

As is evident in some of his letters to Kierkegaard, Kolderup-Rosenvinge was a well-known religious, social, and political conservative. "He [Kolderup-Rosenvinge] had a strong conservative understanding of relationships both in matters of Church and State as a result of his birth, education, family connections, and occupation."[2] His conservatism is most clearly exemplified politically in his support for the bicamerical legislature with income and age restrictions limiting the eligible candidates for the upper house. There are also a number of subtle references to his political conservatism in his letters to Kierkegaard, the most explicit of which expresses his contempt for the 1848 French Revolution.[3] Personally, Kolderup-Rosenvinge was well liked, and he had a love for classical and contemporary literature. It is not clear when Kolderup-Rosenvinge first met Kierkegaard, but the first correspondence between them is in September 1847 when he wrote a thank-you note after receiving a copy of *Works of Love*.[4] It appears that the two men became friends just a few years before Kolderup-Rosenvinge died. He was a few years older than Kierkegaard and in poor health throughout much of their correspondence,[5] but their shared interests in literature and conservative politics, as well as their humor and wit, provide an explanation for why their relationship flourished during the last couple of years of Kolderup-Rosenvinge's life.

II. Kierkegaard's References to and Correspondence with Kolderup-Rosenvinge

Kierkegaard references Kolderup-Rosenvinge in two journal entries and in a series of letters where the two men corresponded from September 1847 until Kolderup-Rosenvinge's death in 1850.[6] In this section, I will briefly catalogue and describe the two references and the series of letters. The two journal references to Kolderup-Rosenvinge are on isolated topics recounted from prior conservations. In the first, he says that Kolderup-Rosenvinge told him that the Greek word δίκαιος (commonly

---

2 Matzen, "Kolderup-Rosenvinge," p. 351.

3 *B&A*, vol. 1, p. 210 / *LD*, Letter 187, p. 266. *B&A*, vol. 1, p. 240 / *LD*, Letter 216, p. 305.

4 *B&A*, vol. 1, p. 179 / *LD*, Letter 160, p. 226.

5 *B&A*, vol. 1, pp. 239–41 / *LD*, Letter 216, pp. 304–7.

6 The letters were first published in H.O. Lange, "Søren Kierkegaard's og Kolderup-Rosenvinge's Spadsereture i Breve," *Dansk Tidsskrift*, 1898, pp. 69–102. The article includes a three-page introduction as well as the letters themselves.

translated "righteous") actually means "equal." Kierkegaard proceeds to apply this notion of righteousness to monetary wealth and the story of the unfaithful steward (Luke 16:1–13).[7] The second journal reference recounts a conversation about how the medievals resolved the disagreement about the genetic separation necessary for blood-relations to permissibly marry.[8]

Both journal entries deal with topics that are not discussed in the exchanged letters and the content of the letters suggests that they were describing actual conversations rather than written correspondence. Furthermore, both entries deal with legal concepts—that is, the concept of equality in the first entry and the legal permissibility of marriage in the second.

The correspondence between Kolderup-Rosenvinge and Kierkegaard is somewhat unique in so far as we have what appears to be a complete collection of letters from Kierkegaard to Kolderup-Rosenvinge and vice versa. The letters are in most cases clearly dated, and they appear to form a narrative whole with each letter contributing to the overall development of two major themes (often discussed in jest) concerning walking and politics. Furthermore, almost without exception, each letter at some point discusses some element from the immediately prior letter; thus, one is able, with great accuracy, to pinpoint the immediate occasion for the letters, and in some cases we are even given clear explanations of why letters were not exchanged over a period of time (for example, Kierkegaard forgot to mail a previous letter, Kolderup-Rosenvinge was in poor health, etc.).[9]

There were two periods of time where Kierkegaard and Kolderup-Rosenvinge exchanged a number of letters in a relatively short period of time. In the first, there were seven letters exchanged from the end of July 1848 to August 1848. Kierkegaard begins this series of exchange after being repeatedly stood up for walks with Kolderup-Rosenvinge. Some of the first letters we have between the two men discuss their failure to coordinate a time to walk together[10] and it prompts Kierkegaard to "walk with [Kolderup-Rosenvinge] in writing."[11] Kierkegaard mentions the numerous times he has gone to Kolderup-Rosenvinge's house and been turned away. The two men playfully use the writing/walking metaphor throughout the first series of letters where Kierkegaard claims to understand walking rather than politics,[12] Kolderup-Rosenvinge refers to Kierkegaard as "a secret adherent of the movement party,"[13] which Kierkegaard confirms and expresses as "a little theory of 'motion.' "[14] Although much of the material is simply an expression of each man's wit and humor, some of the material—particularly Kierkegaard's "little theory of

---

7 *SKS* 21, 232, NB9:55 / *JP* 3, 2769.

8 *SKS* 21, 326–7, NB10:138 / *JP* 1, 762.

9 Some of the later letters are more personal in character though political topics are discussed briefly. As Kolderup-Rosenvinge's health declined, the narrative thread connecting the letters diminished as well.

10 *B&A*, vol. 1, p. 191 / *LD*, Letter 172, pp. 240–1. *B&A*, vol. 1, p. 191 / *LD*, Letter 173, p. 241.

11 *B&A*, vol. 1, p. 196 / *LD*, Letter 180, p. 247.

12 *B&A*, vol. 1, p. 202 / *LD*, Letter 184, p. 255.

13 *B&A*, vol. 1, p. 203 / *LD*, Letter 185, p. 255.

14 *B&A*, vol. 1, pp. 206–7 / *LD*, Letter 186, pp. 260–2.

motion" and its relation to religious and political movements—is interesting in its own right.

The first series of letters also briefly touches on a number of political topics including the 1848 political revolutions across Europe (particularly in France)[15] and the first Schleswig-Holstein war between Germany and Denmark, which resulted in a rise of anti-German sentiment in Denmark.[16] In the second series of letters (exchanged approximately a year after the first series in July and August 1849), the content was more personal in character concerning the death of Kolderup-Rosenvinge's granddaughter[17] and his declining health,[18] but they continued to discuss recent political developments concerning the recently adopted "Free Constitution"[19] and the problems associated with the 1848 French Revolution.[20] Kolderup-Rosenvinge's health was in sharp decline during this period, and it appears to have changed the content, tone, and quality of their correspondence.

Kierkegaard's journal entries that reference Kolderup-Rosenvinge and their correspondence show that the topics of law and politics were frequently discussed in their conversations and written correspondence. Although it is no surprise that Kolderup-Rosenvinge—a prominent lawyer and law professor—would discuss legal and political matters, it was not a topic that Kierkegaard often discussed. Thus, the letters provide a new perspective on Kierkegaard's relationship to the political developments in nineteenth-century Europe and Denmark. In the next section, I will discuss Kierkegaard's "little theory of 'motion'" and its relationship to his political polemics.

III. Walking Away From Politics

Kolderup-Rosenvinge and Kierkegaard's playful banter concerning walking culminates in a description of Kierkegaard's theory of motion. In an earlier letter, Kierkegaard had mentioned that "life is a path," and thus, Kierkegaard walks so that he can "walk away from everything," particularly politics.[21] Kolderup-Rosenvinge, who was well aware of Kierkegaard's disdain for political parties, quips that Kierkegaard is a "secret adherent to the movement party."[22] Kierkegaard pleads guilty to the charge and begins to develop his theory of motion which includes an account of how one "stops."

Up until this point in the letter, Kierkegaard was discussing an article he had read where a train is stopped by means of a brake [*Bremse*], but Kierkegaard says that it

---

15 *B&A*, vol. 1, 206 / *LD*, Letter 186, pp. 260–1. *B&A*, vol. 1, pp. 209–10 / *LD*, Letter 187, pp. 265–6. *B&A*, vol. 1, p. 213 / *LD*, Letter 188, p. 270.

16 *B&A*, vol. 1, p. 198 / *LD*, Letter 181, p. 249. *B&A*, vol. 1, p. 201 / *LD*, Letter 184, pp. 253–4.

17 *B&A*, vol. 1, p. 233 / *LD*, Letter 211, p. 296.

18 *B&A*, vol. 1, pp. 239–41 / *LD*, Letter 216, pp. 304–7.

19 *B&A*, vol. 1, p. 231 / *LD*, Letter 211, p. 293.

20 *B&A*, vol. 1, pp. 239–40 / *LD*, Letter 216, p. 305.

21 *B&A*, vol. 1, p. 202 / *LD*, Letter 184, p. 255.

22 *B&A*, vol. 1, p. 203 / *LD*, Letter 185, p. 255.

is silly to think that a gadfly [*Bremse*] will stop a train. "[T]he world has advanced so far in madness that it employs a gadfly [*Bremsen*] to stop...[which] cannot possibly live till Easter."[23] Kierkegaard continues to play on the two meanings of *Bremsen* throughout the article, and his theory of motion gives an account of how one changes or stops motion. According to Kierkegaard, his theory of motion and its attendant concept of stopping illustrate the problem with Europe's political revolutions. In order to fully describe the conception of revolution and politics contained in this letter, I will describe the central features of Kierkegaard's theory of motion and show how Kierkegaard relates the concept to his critique of the ongoing political revolutions across Europe.

Kierkegaard understands the political developments in Europe as a "vortex" [*Hvirvel*]. A vortex is a series of movements back and forth—like a typhoon—that lacks a fixed point. The calls for revolution and political change in Europe were, Kierkegaard thought, grounded in terms of competing teleological visions of how government should operate and function. Kierkegaard's criticism is that such a foundation for political change can only result in back and forth struggle between two (or more) competing visions of how society should be. While the current government is enacting its political agenda, the reformers overreact in their opposition to it. Eventually, the reformers will win out and enact their political agenda as an opposition party, and the old vanguard will overreact against the reformers and so on and so forth. The result is that the split in society grows ever larger encompassing a greater number of people and groups. These movements are in constant conflict with one another, and each one is unable to stop the other just as a gadfly [*Bremse*] is unable to stop a train.[24]

In light of this situation, what most people believe about political movements is mistaken. Kierkegaard explains:

> Most people believe that so long as one has a fixed point *to which* one wants to get, then motion is no vortex. But this is a misunderstanding. It all depends on having a fixed point *from which to set out*. Stopping is not possible at a point *ahead*, but at a point *behind*. That is, stopping is in the motion, consolidating the motion. And this is the difference between a political and a religious movement. Any purely political movement, which accordingly lacks the religious element...is a vortex, cannot be stopped, and is a prey to the illusion of wanting a fixed point ahead, which is wanting to stop by means of a gadfly [*Bremsen*]; for the fixed point, the only fixed point, lies behind.[25]

Kierkegaard's little theory of motion is an account of the proper source of political change. There is no *telos* that grounds social advances and revolutions. In fact, presenting and striving toward a teleological image of society contributes to the problem at hand. Political injustice and failure can only be remedied by means of a clear and fixed standard that unites those already engaged in the conflict. Kierkegaard characterizes this "fixed point" as "that single individual,"[26] and it

23 *B&A*, vol. 1, p. 205 / *LD*, Letter 186, p. 259. (Translation modified.)

24 *B&A*, vol. 1, pp. 206–7 / *LD*, Letter 186, pp. 260–1.

25 *B&A*, vol. 1, p. 207 / *LD*, Letter 186, p. 262.

26 *B&A*, vol. 1, p. 206 / *LD*, Letter 186, pp. 260–1.

is this type of individual—rather than the content of one's religious beliefs—that makes a movement religious rather than political.

Socrates who called himself a "gadfly" [*Bremse*] exemplifies this strategy of revolution. "[W]ith his gadfly's sting he drove them forward in such a way that they really moved backward, or in such a way that Sophistry perished and the single individual came to his senses at the fixed point behind."[27] Socrates showed how the *telos* toward which the Sophist aimed was not fixed at all. The only fixed point, on the contrary, is in the individual and in inwardness. The Sophist makes the same mistake that the nineteenth-century political reformers made—that is, they presented alternative visions of where they were going rather than coming from an ethically developed and secure foundation. Kierkegaard likewise walks away from politics because it asks the wrong question—it asks where "one should go instead of asking whence one should depart."[28]

Furthermore, just as Socrates was sacrificed for the truth, so the single individual "who is going to be used for stopping" must "accept the fact that he must be sacrificed….For [he] will be run over, but….he who accepted in advance the fact that he must be sacrificed has one more thought, his best thought, and as he is being run over, he conquers."[29] In death and in laying down one's life, one has provided the fixed point for stopping the whirlwind of political movements. This image of the martyr anticipates some of Kierkegaard's later characterizations of the Christian life.

Although the available evidence suggests that Kierkegaard and Kolderup-Rosenvinge only exchanged letters and closely interacted with one another for a relatively short period of time up until Kolderup-Rosenvinge's death, the two apparently were close acquaintances and friends during this period of time. They had significant personal discussions about family life and health, but they also discussed in some detail the ongoing political developments during this time period. Their discussions of, and characterization of, the political events of 1848–49 shed light on Kierkegaard's overall conception of the relationship between his conception of the individual and the political movements of his day. In one short letter, Kierkegaard has described the need for the single individual, the relationship between the religious and political, and the importance and place of the martyr who is willing to be sacrificed for the truth. Each of these themes are discussed in other places in the authorship, but their relationship is not as developed as it is in these letters.

27 *B&A*, vol. 1, p. 262 / *LD*, Letter 186, p. 262.

28 *B&A*, vol. 1, p. 208 / *LD*, Letter 186, p. 263.

29 Ibid.

Bibliography

I. Kolderup-Rosenvinge's Works in The Auction Catalogue *of Kierkegaard's Library*

(trans.), [Pedro Calderón de la Barca], *Dronning Zenobia. Oversat efter Calderons Drama: La gran Cenobia*, trans. by J.L.A. Kolderup-Rosenvinge, Copenhagen: Trykt hos E.C. Løser 1849 (*ASKB* 1934).

II. Works in The Auction Catalogue *of Kierkegaard's Library that Discuss Kolderup-Rosenvinge*

None.

III. Secondary Literature on Kierkegaard and Kolderup-Rosenvinge

Lange, H.O., "Søren Kierkegaard's og Kolderup-Rosenvinge's Spadsereture i Breve," *Dansk Tidsskrift*, 1898, pp. 69–102.

Tudvad, Peter, Kierkegaards Kobenhavn, Copenhagen: Politikens forlag 2004, p. 152; p. 157; p. 174; p. 185; pp. 191–2; p. 284; p. 304; pp. 323–4; p. 336; p. 477.

Orla Lehmann:
Kierkegaard's Political Alter-Ego?

Julie K. Allen

A common view in Kierkegaard scholarship holds that the nineteenth-century Danish politician Orla Lehmann represents the opposite ideological extreme from Søren Kierkegaard. After all, Lehmann was a firm believer in the democratic political process and one of the architects of Denmark's 1848 civil war in Schleswig-Holstein and transition to a constitutional monarchy. In his journals, Kierkegaard dismissed the former as incapable of truly resolving any problems, since "a decision through voting results in nothing," since "the matter is simply terminated."[1] He denounced the latter as a travesty resulting from the fact that "it is we ourselves who are internally disintegrating."[2] For most of Kierkegaard's adult life, Lehmann was one of the most prominent representatives of the Liberal party, which Kierkegaard derided as "the greatest cowards"[3] and compared to the "tailor in heaven" about whom he claims "in order to punish a single abuse which they notice from our Lord's usurped throne, they grab God's footstool and hurl it down to earth—yes, to punish it they would willingly destroy the whole world."[4] Such ringing denouncements of Lehmann's life's work make it seem obvious that these two men shared no common ground and were in fact working against each other in their respective crusades to change the condition and character of their countrymen.

Yet in his memoirs, while describing his tumultuous student days, in particular the torchlight procession across Copenhagen he organized in support of Professor Henrik Nicolai Clausen (1793–1877) in 1832, Lehmann makes the observation about his critics that "the fools did not know that the same is true of everything relating to the life of the spirit as Søren Kierkegaard says of Christendom: it sets things on fire."[5] This reference to Kierkegaard's attack on Christendom confirms not only that Lehmann was familiar with Kierkegaard's polemical articles against the Danish State Church, but also that he identified with them to a certain degree. It is significant that Lehmann links his own revolutionary efforts to change the course of Danish political history with Kierkegaard's incendiary struggle to reform Danish

1 *SKS* 24, 228, NB23:41 / *JP* 4, 4199.

2 *SKS* 23, 113, NB16:30 / *JP* 4, 4180.

3 *SKS* 20, 114, NB:189 / *JP* 4, 4115.

4 *SKS* 18, 37, EE:96.a / *KJN* 2, 32.

5 Orla Lehmann, *Efterladte Skrifter*, vols. 1–4, ed. by Hother Hage and Carl Ploug, Copenhagen: Thiele 1872–74, vol. 1, p. 70.

Christianity, because his comment suggests a fundamental similarity between them that has gone largely unnoticed in most scholarship. According to the standard interpretation, Lehmann appears as a fiery liberal, whose ideological excesses the arch-conservative Kierkegaard ridiculed, but in reality the relationship between their ideological positions and the outcomes they hoped to achieve is considerably more complex than such a simple dichotomy can convey, for both men sought the betterment of their homeland and countrymen, albeit by very different and often conflicting means.

The primary reason that Lehmann's name is linked with Kierkegaard's is because of their newspaper skirmish over the question of the freedom of the press in 1836. Although it functioned to a certain extent as Kierkegaard's public debut as a social critic, it was not particularly weighty in terms of either content or consequences. Kierkegaard himself did not even consider these early articles to be part of his authorship, at least not one worthy of mention in *The Point of View for My Work as an Author* (1859).[6] Given that their entire exchange of opinions encompassed only six newspaper articles, it is perhaps an overstatement to call it a feud, though Joakim Garff justifies this designation on the basis that the arguments became so convoluted that it "resembled more than anything else an account of a family feud in which, after a while, no one could remember who had said what, about what, or to whom—and certainly not why they had said it."[7] Yet despite the brevity of their encounter, it is very telling, both in terms of the issues they discuss and the manner in which they do so. The opposing ideological positions set forth in the articles serve to illuminate the nature of Lehmann and Kierkegaard's differences, as well as hinting at their underlying similarities of purpose. The ostensible issue was the freedom of the press, but the underlying issue was the potential for political reform to change social conditions.

However, their paths must have crossed many times prior to 1836. Just three years apart in age, Lehmann and Kierkegaard came from comparable backgrounds and followed very similar academic paths, such that they could not have escaped a casual acquaintance as they grew to adulthood. Both men emerged from Copenhagen's intellectual bourgeoisie, attended the prestigious *Borgerdydskolen*, and then went on to graduate from the University of Copenhagen, with time spent attending university lectures in Berlin. Yet despite these similarities, their intellectual paths diverged during their university years, directing each man toward the cause to which he would devote the rest of his life; in Lehmann's case, this was Danish national liberalism, particularly with regard to Schleswig-Holstein; in Kierkegaard's, it was the awakening of Danes from their spiritual sloth and ignorance.

Despite their public disagreements over specific issues and their generally dissimilar ideological positions, however, Kierkegaard and Lehmann shared certain fundamental goals that warrant a closer look at their relationship. Aside from the newspaper articles in 1836 and his unpublished comedy *The Battle between the Old and the New Soap-Cellars* (ca.1837), Kierkegaard did not write to or about

6 *SV1* XIII, 494, 517 / *PV*, 5–6, 23.

7 Joakim Garff, *Søren Kierkegaard: A Biography,* trans. by Bruce H. Kirmmse, Princeton and Oxford: Princeton University Press 2005, p. 65.

Lehmann, but his journals are filled with reflections on the issues that were central to Lehmann's career, confirming that Kierkegaard was aware of Lehmann's activities, even though he disagreed with them. Yet although they held differing views of how best to accomplish their goals, they both devoted their lives to improving living conditions in Denmark. While Lehmann worked to expand their political freedoms, Kierkegaard focused on the spiritual and intellectual awakening of the Danes. In an age when Danish society was dominated by a nearly obsessive interest in literature and art, when any interest in politics was considered to be in poor taste, both Lehmann and Kierkegaard stood out from the crowd by virtue of their outspokenness and willingness to brave public displeasure, censure, and even ridicule in the service of their beliefs.

I. Lehmann's Biography and Significance

The future politician and statesman Peter Martin Orla Lehmann was born in Copenhagen on May 19, 1810, the eldest child of Martin Christian Gottlieb Lehmann, a German-speaking court bureaucrat originally from Holstein, and Frederikke Louise Bech, the daughter of a former mayor of Copenhagen.[8] The competing national identities represented in his home came to play a central role in the development of Orla Lehmann's personal and professional life. Although his father held firmly to his German identity and insisted on a German-speaking home, none of the nine Lehmann children shared his pro-German orientation, for which Lehmann's Danish biographers give his mother full credit. On the contrary, Orla Lehmann became one of the most prominent spokesmen for the pro-Danish camp with regard to state policy toward the provinces of Schleswig and Holstein. During Orla's youth, the Lehmann family belonged to the leading intellectual circles in Copenhagen, rubbing shoulders with such luminaries as Hans Christian Ørsted (1777–1851) and Anders Sandøe Ørsted (1778–1860), their sister Sophie Ørsted (1782–1818), Adam Oehlenschläger (1779–1850), and later Jens Baggesen (1764–1826). His association with these Danish cultural icons may well have influenced his decision to identify with Danishness, but his fervor for the Danish national cause earned him the disapproval of his illustrious mentors, particularly H.C. Ørsted, with whose conservative political views Lehmann's radicality clashed.

Lehmann's choice of a Danish identity for himself guided his academic trajectory as well. After receiving instruction from his father in his earliest youth, he was enrolled at the age of nine at the recently established German *Realschule* for the St. Petri congregation, to which his father belonged. He distinguished himself there by his support of pan-Scandinavianism, publishing an article in the school newspaper *Germania* endorsing a plan to reestablish the Kalmar Union. In 1824, he transferred to the *Borgerdydskole* where Kierkegaard had been enrolled since 1821,

---

[8] There are no English biographies of Lehmann, but there are several in Danish. The most comprehensive Danish study of Lehmann is a two-volume set by Claus Friisberg; volume 1: *Orla Lehmann–Danmarks første moderne politiker. En politisk biografi*, Varde: Vestjysk Kulturforlag 2000; volume 2: *Kampen om Danmark 1850–70. Orla Lehmann og det nationale demokrati*, Varde: Vestjysk Kulturforlag 2002.

and where the two may have met for the first time. Lehmann entered the University of Copenhagen in 1827, along with Hans Lassen Martensen (1808–84) and Frederik Christian Bornemann (1810–61), initially as a student of literature, reading Heine together with Hans Christian Andersen (1805–75), and then as a student of law.

Inspired by the July Revolution of 1830, Lehmann became passionately interested in politics during his student days. He honed his impressive public speaking abilities at the Student Union, which Alastair Hannay identifies as a unique and important forum for public debate in Golden Age Copenhagen,[9] and which attracted many of the future leaders of Denmark's Liberal movement, such as Lehmann, as well as the young Kierkegaard. In 1832, Lehmann organized the above-mentioned torchlight procession in protest of H.N. Clausen's exclusion from the position of university rector and made a stirring speech in support of "the dauntless spokesman of intellectual freedom and truth," which brought him to the attention of the government censors, over whom he triumphantly prevailed.[10] He contributed his first political commentary to a Danish newspaper the same year and took active part in the legal debating society Astraea.

After completing his studies with distinction in 1833, Lehmann broadened his geographical horizons with a European grand tour, during which he made some acquaintances that would come to shape his political destiny. He spent the winter in Berlin, attending lectures by Schleiermacher and Savigny and developing a friendship with Anton Frederik Tscherning (1795–1874), a Danish liberal with whom he would later found the Society of the Friends of the Peasant, the forerunner of the Danish liberal party, and who served as Denmark's first minister of defense during the first Schleswig War (1848–50). Lehmann cut his tour short and returned to Copenhagen in May 1834 to attend on his mother's deathbed.

Instead of complying with his father's desire that he enter the civil service, Lehmann chose to pursue political journalism. Due to strict press censorship in Denmark, his determination to disseminate his liberal ideas among the Danish people was a dangerous undertaking that could lead to fines and imprisonment, but he soon became an influential spokesman for the forces of governmental reform that mounted in Denmark throughout the 1830s. Along with Jens Finsteen Giødwad (1811–91), Lehmann was one of the political editors of Andreas Peter Liunge's (1798–1879) *Kjøbenhavnsposten,* one of the country's leading liberal newspapers. In 1839, he became one of the editors of the daily national-liberal newspaper *Fædrelandet*, which served as the primary vehicle for the public dissemination of discourses of freedom and nationalism over the next decade.[11] Having gained public recognition and support through his journalistic work, Lehmann made the leap into politics by writing a petition on behalf of the Student Association to the newly crowned King Christian VIII (1786–1848) requesting a representative constitution in 1839.

---

9 Alastair Hannay, *Kierkegaard: A Biography*, Cambridge: Cambridge University Press 2001, p. 5.

10 C.St.A. Bille, "Lehmann, Peter Martin Orla" in *Dansk biografisk Lexikon*, vols. 1–19, ed. by C. F. Bricka, Copenhagen: Gyldendal 1887–1905, vol. 10, pp. 170–80. My translation.

11 Bille, "Lehmann," p. 173.

Over the course of the 1840s, largely as a result of his phenomenal public speaking abilities, Lehmann became an outspoken leader of the liberal reform movement that eventually brought about Denmark's transition from absolutism to a constitutional monarchy in 1848–49. In many cases, his main role was spurring his fellow liberals on. Bruce H. Kirmmse observes that Lehmann's "entire career (until 1848–49) consisted of goading the liberals into adopting increasingly more daring positions by pushing them further than they usually intended to go."[12] He attained sudden popularity in 1841 through his impromptu "Falster Address," a stirring declaration of the necessity of a constitution in order to secure the peasants' rights that earned him a three-month prison term and prompted his supporters to take to the streets of Copenhagen in protest. His *Skydebane* address of 1842 helped shape the idea of "national liberalism," while his emphatic endorsement of pan-Scandinavianism before an audience of visiting Swedish and Norwegian students in the Christiansborg *Ridehus* in 1845 earned him another trial, in which he was acquitted. He was one of the founders of the Society of the Friends of the Peasants, but broke with Tscherning over the question of retaining the provinces of Schleswig and Holstein. He was deeply engaged in the Schleswig question already from the early 1840s and has been credited with formulating the Eider position, with the slogan "Denmark to the Eider," which he prompted Carl Christian Hall (1812–88) to incorporate into the November constitution of 1863, thus provoking the invasion of Schleswig-Holstein by Prussia and Austria, which marked the beginning of the second Schleswig War and Denmark's eventual defeat.

Perhaps Lehmann's greatest claim to fame was as the author of the petition, on behalf of the liberal opposition, to King Frederik VII (1808–63, king from 1848) on March 21, 1848 for a democratic constitution. Lehmann was well-qualified to play such a prominent part in this drama. He had been in Paris during the revolutionary uproar a few weeks earlier and was the main speaker at the Casino meeting of the liberal opposition on March 20, where a resolution to demand a free constitution from the king was adopted. In response to the resolution's demand that the king "immediately surround the throne with men, whose insight, energy, and patriotism can give the government power and the nation trust," the king famously answered, "I am pleased that our views are so completely in harmony, for that which you desire, gentlemen, was already accomplished this morning. The old ministry has been dissolved."[13] In one day, almost two centuries of Danish absolutism came to an end, and Lehmann was deeply involved in the reconstruction of the Danish government, as well as in the ensuing civil war in Schleswig-Holstein. On March 24, he became part of Moltke's March ministry as a minister without portfolio and served as a diplomatic representative of the new Danish government in London and Berlin, where he encountered the aspiring Otto von Bismarck.[14] He left Moltke's government later that year over differences of opinion, but he was instrumental in editing Ditlev Gothard Monrad's (1811–87) draft constitution of 1849.

---

12 Bruce H. Kirmmse, *Kierkegaard in Golden Age Denmark*, Bloomington: Indiana University Press 1990, p. 49.

13 *Danskernes identitetshistorie*, ed. by Thorkild Borup Jensen, Copenhagen: C.A. Reitzel 1993, p. 190.

14 Bille, "Lehmann," p. 176.

Although he continued to be active in Danish politics until his death in Copenhagen on September 13, 1870, the events of 1848 marked the high point of Lehmann's influence, and his last decades were marked by disappointments and trials. Already in 1849, he lost much of his political power and personal motivation. After being defeated by a local peasant in a parliamentary election on the isolated island of Bornholm, he was appointed city counsellor of Vejle, but he was taken prisoner by the Germans after the battle of Kolding on April 23, 1849. He was given a brief leave to be with his wife on her deathbed in June, but remained a prisoner until August 1849. During the final two decades of his life, Lehmann served in the Danish government in a variety of capacities: as a city counsellor in Vejle from 1848 to 1861, as a member of the *Folketing* from 1851 to 1853, as a member of the *Landsting*, the upper house of parliament, from 1853 until his death, and as Minister of the Interior from 1861 to 1863 in Hall's second term as prime minister. Denmark's crushing defeat in the second Schleswig War in 1864 took a heavy toll on Lehmann, but he continued to crusade for the rights of ethnic Danes in the provinces claimed by Prussia. In his final decade, Lehmann produced most of his published works, including *The Matter of the Greek Succession*,[15] *On the Causes of Denmark's Misfortune*,[16] *The Icelandic Constitutional Dispute 1868–69*,[17] and his posthumously published memoirs.[18]

Lehmann was a firm believer in the principle of universal (male) suffrage, albeit within the limits of propriety and good sense. In an 1861 speech, he expresses his faith in a merit-based system (rather than a class-based one), but also some of his reservations about the actual practice of universal suffrage. He defended the June Constitution and praised the equality it created among citizens of Denmark:

> In Denmark not only are all equal before the law, but all have equal access to the goods of society and to participation in the governance of the state. I say "equal access," and I add, "everyone according to his ability"....The task of equality is not to drag down that which stands higher, but to lift up that which is low.[19]

In order to accomplish this goal, he suggests that a system be designed to enable "the talented, the cultured, and the well-to-do who in every civilized society have the dominant voice in the guidance of public affairs"[20] to "acquire culture and wealth, and thereby, respect and influence."[21] With this cultural and social power, the talented, cultured, and wealthy have the responsibility of winning the "devotion and confidence of the common peasant by showing a respectful and loving concern for

---

15 Orla Lehmann, *Den græske Thronfølgesag 1863*, ed. by Vejle Amts Historiske Samfund, Kolding: Konrad Jørgensens Bogtrykkeri 1970 (*Vejle Amts Aarbøgers Monografier*, vol. 7).

16 Orla Lehmann, *Om Aarsagerne til Danmarks Ulykke*, Copenhagen: Gad 1865.

17 Orla Lehmann, *Den islandske Forfatningssag i Landstinget 1868–69*, Copenhagen: Gad 1869.

18 Lehmann, *Efterladte Skrifter*.

19 Quoted from Kirmmse, *Kierkegaard in Golden Age Denmark*, p. 242.

20 Quoted from ibid., p. 243.

21 Ibid.

his well-being."[22] This paternalistic view toward the poor and uneducated does not differ terribly from the paternalistic notion of an absolutist king; it just substitutes the upper bourgeoisie for the monarch as the benevolent enforcer of "the noblest teachings of humanity and *Christianity*."[23] As Kirmmse points out, "the urban, elitist, Christian-humane notion of society put forth by Golden Age liberals was not really so very different from the Christian-humane 'conservative' vision espoused by the mainstream of the Golden Age."[24]

Nevertheless, Lehmann's most celebrated legacy is his tireless engagement on behalf of the development of a viable Danish democracy. His contemporaries praised him lavishly for his role in this process: Meïr Goldschmidt (1819–87) described him as "Freedom's bridegroom;"[25] Carl Ploug (1813–94) dubbed him "the Achilles of our Iliad,"[26] "the torchbearer of promises";[27] and Vilhelm Topsøe called him "a political Prometheus."[28] In his entry on Lehmann in the *Dansk Biografisk Lexikon* in 1887, Carl Steen Andersen Bille (1828–98) attributes Lehmann's political influence to the "warmth, enthusiasm, youthful energy and confident cheerfulness with which he lifted the new banner, to the compelling eloquence with which he argued his case, and to the magnetic force of his personality as a whole."[29] On the 100th anniversary of Lehmann's death, Johannes Lehmann proclaimed that "he will live as long as the Danish people remember their forefathers and their deeds. What Adam Oehlenschläger was for our literature and poetry, Orla Lehmann was for our political system."[30] Yet although few Lehmann scholars pay attention to his encounters with his most famous contemporary, Søren Kierkegaard, it should not be forgotten that Lehmann was in many ways Kierkegaard's political alter ego, providing contrast and stimulus to the development of Kierkegaard's views on the state, the media, and political freedom in Denmark.

II. Lehmann and Kierkegaard's Ideological Differences

Understanding Kierkegaard and Lehmann's antagonistic but productive relationship requires a brief examination of the social context of their exchange of opinions. Despite the establishment of four advisory legislative bodies, the Assemblies of Estates, in Denmark in 1830 as required by the Congress of Vienna, Danes did not enjoy particularly broad freedoms of expression or political activity during the first half of the nineteenth century. Since 1799, the Danish press had been subject to strict

---

22 Ibid.

23 Ibid.

24 Kirmmse, *Kierkegaard in Golden Age Denmark*, p. 243.

25 Bille, "Lehmann," p. 179.

26 Ibid.

27 Povl Engelstoft, "Lehmann, Peter Martin Orla," in *Dansk Biografisk Haandleksikon*, vols. 1–3, ed. by Svend Dahl and Povl Engelstoft, Copenhagen: Gyldendal 1920–6, vol. 2, p. 479. My translation.

28 Ibid.

29 Bille, "Lehmann," p. 179.

30 Johannes Lehmann, *Tværsnit*, Herning: Poul Kristensen 1975, p. 87.

governmental censorship with harsh penalties, including exile and the death penalty. Two of the most famous victims of this policy were the journalist Peter Andreas Heiberg (1758–1841) and the poet Malthe Conrad Bruun (1775–1826), who were sentenced to exile for life for transgressing these restrictions. A less prominent offender, Dr. Jacob Jacobsen Dampe (1790–1876), was condemned to death in 1820 for advocating a free constitution (his sentence was commuted to life imprisonment, of which he served more than 25 years).

Many Golden Age Danish intellectuals were content to overlook this repressive situation and focus instead on literary culture as a vehicle for the dissemination of ideas, which rendered Copenhagen society anemic in terms of political activity. Kierkegaard is often regarded as a part of this group, given his distaste for politics, his admiration for Danish Romanticism, and his association with Johan Ludvig Heiberg (1791–1860) at this point in his life. Lehmann, however, a disciple of H.N. Clausen, chafed against the restrictions on the press and made a point of voicing his opposition in public arenas, in particular in the liberal newspapers *Kjøbenhavnsposten* and *Fædrelandet*, despite the risks involved. An unsigned article written by Lehmann that appeared in *Fædrelandet* in December 1834, urging the Estates to push for popular government, earned *Fædrelandet*'s editor, Christian Nathan David (1793–1874), immediate retribution from the king, as well as a proposed law to withdraw the right of judicial appeal in censorship cases. Although Lehmann later served a brief jail sentence for his outspokenness against absolutism, Johannes Dam Hage (1800–37), the next editor of *Fædrelandet*, paid a higher price: being denied political expression and deprived of the editorship of *Fædrelandet* drove him to commit suicide in 1837.

The groundwork for Lehmann and Kierkegaard's newspaper feud was laid at the Student Association. In early November 1835, a philology student named Johannes Ostermann gave a speech congratulating the liberal press on its struggle against censorship. In his own speech the following week, Lehmann credited middle-class liberals with the rebirth of public life in Denmark. At the next meeting, on November 28, 1835, Kierkegaard made his debut as a public speaker, reading aloud a rebuttal, ostensibly to Ostermann but implicitly also to Lehmann, entitled, "Our Journalistic Literature: a Study from Nature in Noonday Light."[31] Rather than discussing press censorship *per se*, Kierkegaard critiques the liberal newspapers themselves. Citing facts that contradict Ostermann's glowing report on the liberal press, Kierkegaard contends that it had not in fact made the valiant effort Ostermann claimed, but had merely contented itself with "petty irritation" and "fitful fumbling" as "a substitute for genuine action."[32] Rather than realizing new freedoms, he charged, the liberal press had given "imagination free play and let a mighty tree spring forth from the factually given mustard seed."[33] Pointing out that surpassing the conservative papers which they despised was no great achievement, Kierkegaard accused the liberals of a "lack of genuine leadership and originality and merely 'aesthetic' posture,"[34] or, in other words, of cowardice.

31 *Pap.* I B 2 157–78 / *JP* 5, 5116.

32 Ibid.

33 Ibid.

34 Kirmmse, *Kierkegaard in Golden Age Denmark*, p. 50.

Both his contemporaries and later scholars have offered many possible explanations for why Kierkegaard chose to make his debut on this particular topic. Ostermann himself ascribed Kierkegaard's motivation to a sense of rivalry, while others believed he simply sought an opportunity to play his customary "witty dialectical game."[35] His well-received speech, which he recorded as having been a "hit,"[36] facilitated Kierkegaard's entry into Copenhagen's literary and journalistic circles, notably Heiberg's, which suggests that it was a strategic move on Kierkegaard's part to draw attention to himself and his talents. It has often been interpreted as an endorsement by Kierkegaard of the king's repressive attitude toward the press and therefore a confirmation of Kierkegaard's conservatism, but Garff argues that Kierkegaard regarded the whole incident as an experiment in "stirring up a tempest in a teapot" while avoiding a "somersault into the Siberia of freedom of the press."[37] According to Hannay, however, Kierkegaard's real target was not Ostermann himself, but rather Denmark's liberal elite, particularly Lehmann,[38] an interpretation that the subsequent newspaper feud seems to support.

In early 1836 Lehmann presented his case for greater freedom of the press in a five-part article entitled "Limitations on the Freedom of the Press" in *Kjøbenhavnsposten*.[39] In this article he restates many of Ostermann's points and answers the charges Kierkegaard made in his speech, though he does not explicitly admit that he is doing so. Although the article appeared anonymously, Lehmann acknowledged it as his own work, and it was included in his posthumously published papers, which were edited by his erstwhile clerk and fellow politician, the lawyer Edvard Philipp Hother Hage (1816–73).[40] In the fifth segment of the article, which appeared on February 12, 1836, Lehmann articulates the connection between a free press and healthy national self-esteem. He criticizes the Golden Age literary elite and denounces the artificial "sentimental-idyllic"[41] tendency of glorifying Danishness that it fostered: "the less satisfactory the state of the country, the more eager one became to impute to it falsely the lacking glory."[42] However, due to a recently awakening sense of citizenship, he argues, Denmark found itself in "the dawn of the life and the freedom of the people."[43] He attributes a major role in this bright future to the press, as an organ of self-critique: "We have now come so far that we have the courage to examine our condition because we feel the strength to improve it....If [a people] wishes to advance to a greater perfection, then it must first recognize its faults."[44] He rebukes the critics of the press for their contradictory

---

35 *Encounters with Kierkegaard: A Life as Seen by His Contemporaries*, trans. and ed. by Bruce H. Kirmmse, Princeton, New Jersey: Princeton University Press 1996, p. 64.

36 *SKS* 17, 37, AA:19 / *KJN* 1, 31.

37 Garff, *Søren Kierkegaard*, p. 62.

38 Hannay, *Kierkegaard*, p. 21.

39 Lehmann, *Efterladte Skrifter*, vol. 3, pp. 32–67 / *EPW*, Supplement, pp. 134–41.

40 Hage shared many of Lehmann's political opinions, but was an ardent admirer of Kierkegaard's early works.

41 *EPW*, Supplement, p. 136.

42 Ibid.

43 *EPW*, Supplement, p. 135.

44 *EPW*, Supplement, p. 137.

demands—"one wants it to be honest and sober and yet wishes to force it to flatter and be hypocritical"[45]—but he also admits, in an implicit concession to Kierkegaard, that the press also makes mistakes, due to its inexperience, ambiguous legal position, and desire for impartiality.

Kierkegaard responded to Lehmann's article with an alacrity that belies his supposed disinterest in political matters. On February 18, 1836, Kierkegaard's article "The Morning Observations in *Kjøbenhavnsposten*, no. 43" appeared under the pseudonym "B" in Heiberg's journal *Kjøbenhavns flyvende Post*, colloquially known as *Flyveposten*, the most influential aesthetic publication of the day but by this time also the organ of the conservative party. The title refers to Lehmann's expressed hope for the dawning of a new day in Danish politics, which Kierkegaard ridicules at the outset, setting the tone for the article's scathing wit and focus on incidental details rather than the substance of Lehmann's arguments. He rejects Lehmann's attempt to excuse the mistakes made by the press as a "naïve expression," "for when one says of *Kjøbenhavnsposten* that it is acrimonious and makes mistakes, one means that it is more acrimonious and makes more mistakes than one could wish."[46] Kierkegaard is particularly critical of Lehmann's oratorical flourishes, such as the "dawn" metaphor, and thus, as Julia Watkin points out, "deprives the oratory of power by drawing attention to such expressions,"[47] but his own text relies heavily on literary allusions and metaphors. Hannay explains that there is "no attempt here to introduce or defend a view, let alone to take up the issue of censorship—just plain polemics and an exercise in the art of scoring points."[48] In Garff's view, the result of the article's blend of "equal amounts of dialectical accuracy and ironic arbitrariness" is an "absurd, rollicking travesty that didn't care a fig about objectivity,"[49] but which effectively de-fangs Lehmann's critique by suggesting that it did not even exist. Kierkegaard's piece was so reminiscent of Heiberg's own style that the conservative journal *Statsvennen* gave Heiberg credit for it, which pleased Kierkegaard inordinately, but the opinions it expresses, in particular the defense of Danish Romantic literature, are Kierkegaard's own.

However, dismissing Kierkegaard's response to Lehmann as merely a vain exercise in wordplay, as many scholars do, ignores any clues it might provide to Kierkegaard's life work of awakening the minds and souls of his countrymen, or to connections between the national-political and the personal in his thinking. Watkin suggests that Kierkegaard's polemic against Lehmann contains the seeds of his "healthy contempt for political oratory and a suspicion of attempts to correct externals, as if such attempts could heal the natural human condition grounded in self-preservation and self-seeking.[50] Yet Kierkegaard does not suggest that the press should be muzzled or that it should not function as a social watchdog; instead, he criticizes the liberal press for its failure to go far enough in its supposedly radical

---

45 *EPW*, Supplement, p. 139.

46 *SV1* XIII, 10 / *EPW*, 7.

47 Julia Watkin, "Historical Introduction", in *EPW*, p. xx.

48 Hannay, *Kierkegaard*, p. 23.

49 Garff, *Søren Kierkegaard*, p. 64.

50 Watkin, "Historical Introduction," p. xxii.

reformism. He demands, "Where, then, is that energetic, that serious, reforming spirit?....Yes, certainly *Kjøbenhavnsposten* is reforming, but on closer examination it is rather a parody of the reforming endeavor."[51] He blames Lehmann and *Kjøbenhavnsposten* for having cried wolf in proclaiming a new dawn too often and without justification, but he does not discount the need for or the possibility of such a dawn. However, he did not believe that removing press censorship was the way to bring it about. In his journal he explained:

> Take away all constraint and let us flatter each other that we all, each one of us, are heroes. There is a clamoring for freedom of conscience, freedom of belief, etc. in these times when someone who really has a thought is already a great rarity. What does this clamoring mean; does it signify strength, heroism? Not quite. It signifies softness; it signifies that we are weaklings, coddled, who are eager to play the hero at bargain price.[52]

Although Lehmann has traditionally been seen as the progressive counterpart to Kierkegaard's conservatism, Kierkegaard's is no less interested in freedom than Lehmann, but the means he prescribes for reaching that end are far more radical.

The newspaper feud continued with another set of anonymous articles, which brought the dispute somewhat more into the personal realm. The first article, published on March 4 in *Fædrelandet*, defends Lehmann's position and charges "Mr. B" with having trivialized the debate by exercising his wit "at the cost of truth" and attempting "to bring down his opponent with mockery and witticisms."[53] The article was written by Johannes Hage, the editor of *Fædrelandet*, who objected in particular to Kierkegaard's disparagement of Liunge, the editor of *Kjøbenhavnsposten*, an attack that was likely designed to curry favor with Heiberg. He defends Liunge's qualifications as an editor and compares them negatively with Kierkegaard's "wit and dialectical skill when these are not matched by a love of truth but serve only to glorify one's own little self."[54]

Kierkegaard's rebuttal, a double-length article entitled "On the Polemic of *Fædrelandet*" that ran in *Flyveposten* on March 12 and 15, demonstrates his ongoing engagement with the issues raised by Lehmann. His tactics are similar to those he used in the first article, for example, the singling-out of particular expressions and phrases, but his target is once more the Danish Liberal movement, which *Kjøbenhavnsposten* and *Fædrelandet* represent. He admits that Liunge may be a fine editor, but insists that he is not equal to the task of the "reforming endeavor."[55] He refutes Lehmann's complaints about the "patriotic jingle of Danishness"[56] with a defense of Golden Age Denmark's "rich poetic abundance,"[57] its "fundamental stamp, its character, from which all its expressions of life must take their color," and its strength in enduring

---

51 *SV1* XIII, 14 / *EPW*, 11.

52 *SKS* 24, 110, NB22:8 / *JP* 2, 1264.

53 *Pap.* I B 3 / *EPW*, Supplement, p. 142.

54 *Pap.* I B 3 / *EPW*, Supplement, p. 144.

55 *SV1* XIII, 24 / *EPW*, 20.

56 *SV1* XIII, 21 / *EPW*, 17.

57 *SV1* XIII, 22 / *EPW*, 18.

the misfortunes of the early nineteenth century.[58] By contrast, he finds the liberal press sadly lacking in both wit and talent—"It is strange to see that a party that on the whole shouts so much about intelligence has so little of it"[59]—and hypocritical in its moralizing attitude.

As befitting a leader of the Liberals, Lehmann took up Kierkegaard's gauntlet with his "Reply to Mr. B. of *Flyveposten*," in *Kjøbenhavnsposten* on March 31, in which he seems to try to appease Kierkegaard while simultaneously upping the stakes by signing his own name to the article. He recounts the course of the polemic to that point and complains that while he and Hage had been attempting to improve the country's political and economic conditions, Kierkegaard's writing had focused on individual phrases "without ever coming forward with a policy of its own, new facts, or better information."[60] He clarifies that his negative assessment of conditions in early-nineteenth-century Denmark concerned itself exclusively with the "movements in political life,"[61] without regard to the cultural accomplishments of men such as Grundtvig, Oehlenschläger, Baggesen, and Ørsted. Employing a conciliatory tone, Lehmann compliments Kierkegaard on his "unmistakable talent in the use of powerful words and bold metaphors,"[62] but concludes that no serious content lies hidden behind the pretty veneer of Kierkegaard's words, noting with irony that "the kernel is hidden within a very thick shell"[63] and dismissing the essay as merely a "stylistic exercise in the humoristic manner."[64] Many scholars share Lehmann's opinion on this point, suggesting that Kierkegaard's early works provided him with the opportunity to experiment with a range of forms of expression before getting serious about making ideological statements, but Watkin emphasizes Kierkegaard's "ability to be very seriously engaged in discussion of an issue under the guise of not seeming to be so."[65]

Lehmann had signed his own name to his article "as a little courtesy toward him [Mr. B]"[66] and, despite Lehmann's protestation that this was not intended to pressure his opponent into abandoning his anonymity, "since it is totally immaterial to me what my opponent is called,"[67] Kierkegaard responded in kind, "for the sake of consistency,"[68] with the open letter "To Mr. Orla Lehmann," published in *Flyveposten* on April 10, 1836.[69] This was the first time Kierkegaard signed his own name to any piece, which fact alone would endow the article with some significance. In Lehmann's introduction to his own article in his memoirs, he explains his decision to include this particular selection in part "because the attack [to which he was responding] originated from

58 *SV1* XIII, 22–3 / *EPW*, 18.
59 *SV1* XIII, 25 / *EPW*, 21.
60 Lehmann, *Efterladte Skrifter*, vol. 3, p. 61 / *EPW*, Supplement, p. 152.
61 Lehmann, *Efterladte Skrifter*, vol. 3, p. 63 / *EPW*, Supplement, p. 155.
62 Lehmann, *Efterladte Skrifter*, vol. 3, p. 65 / *EPW*, Supplement, p. 157.
63 Lehmann, *Efterladte Skrifter*, vol. 3, p. 67 / *EPW*, Supplement, p. 158.
64 Ibid.
65 Watkin, "Historical Introduction," p. vii; p. xix.
66 Lehmann, *Efterladte Skrifter*, vol. 3, p. 67 / *EPW*, Supplement, p. 159.
67 Ibid.
68 *SV1* XIII, 39 / *EPW*, 34.
69 *SV1* XIII, 28–39 / *EPW*, 24–34.

a man, of whose later significance and fame no one then dreamed, but who marked his first path in literature here, namely Søren Kierkegaard."[70] Claiming authorship did not deter Kierkegaard from insisting on getting the last word in the debate; on the contrary, in defense of his own name, Kierkegaard's wit is sparkling and razor-sharp toward Lehmann and the entire Liberal party. He takes both *Kjøbenhavnsposten* and *Fædrelandet* to task for their "antiphonal chanting"[71] in support of each other and pretends confusion at the plethora of named and unnamed Liberal authors with whom he has done battle, noting wryly, "It seems, therefore, as if I had come to sit on the wonder stool and the Liberals sometimes danced round in a great crowd…and sometimes stepped forward individually in order to say what they wondered about."[72] In response to Lehmann's assessment of Kierkegaard's previous article as a "stylistic exercise in the humorous manner,"[73] he skewers Lehmann for wasting space in *Kjøbenhavnsposten* on a response to so inconsequential a text. He browbeats Lehmann on any number of points, not least his attempt as a "psychologist and searcher of hearts"[74] to explain Kierkegaard's motives in writing his previous article, in the course of which Lehmann had accused Kierkegaard of distorting the truth. He declines the "ambiguous praise that has been bestowed upon my personage"[75] and instead compares Lehmann to "the scholastic donkey of old,"[76] which cannot move in any direction. Hence, he concludes, "however willing I am, I cannot help him out, because he does not wish it himself, and consequently I must let him remain standing."[77]

Although Kierkegaard seemed to emerge the victor from this battle of wits and words, he was robbed of the satisfaction of having the last word by a belated attack from an unexpected corner. On May 4, 1836, another anti-Heibergian writer, presumably Peter Ludvig Møller (1814–65), jumped into the fray with three articles published as *Humoristiske Intelligensblade*.[78] The articles, whose author signs himself "X," are skillfully written enough to give rise to initial suspicions that they could have come from Kierkegaard's own pen, but devolve rapidly into cruel satire and crude allusions to Kierkegaard's "unique physiognomy."[79] Kierkegaard chose not to publish the reply he drafted to these attacks, perhaps because Heiberg and the Student Association thought poorly of the articles, as well as the fact that so much time had elapsed since the initial debate, but doubtless also because of the anonymous author's predilection for below-the-belt attacks.[80]

Yet despite Peter Rørdam's (1806–63) assessment that Kierkegaard had won the day and Lehmann had "fallen, totally beaten,"[81] Kierkegaard felt the need to express

---

70 Lehmann, *Efterladte Skrifter*, vol. 3, p. 61.

71 *SV1* XIII, 28 / *EPW*, 24.

72 Ibid.

73 *SV1* XIII, 30 / *EPW*, 25.

74 *SV1* XIII, 36 / *EPW*, 31.

75 Ibid.

76 *SV1* XIII, 38 / *EPW*, 33.

77 Ibid.

78 *EPW*, Supplement, pp. 160–88.

79 Garff, *Søren Kierkegaard*, p. 66.

80 Watkin, "Historical Introduction," p. xxiii.

81 Quoted from Hannay, *Kierkegaard*, p. 29.

his contempt for Lehmann's political views on one further occasion. In 1837, prompted in part by disagreement in the Student Association between rationalists and Hegelians, Kierkegaard wrote a "heroic-patriotic-cosmopolitan-philanthropic-fatalistic drama," *The Battle between the Old and the New Soap-Cellars*,[82] which features a parody of Lehmann. Although it was never published, the play was intended for performance for Copenhagen's intellectual elite; it relies heavily on allusions to places, persons, and issues that would have been familiar to students and professors of the time, most of which are obscure to modern readers. For example, the title refers to the row of booths and shops that lined *Gråbrødretorv* in the 1830s, including three soap cellars, where soap was made, shaped, and sold. The competition between these three soap cellars was fierce and the proprietors exploited the era's romantic fascination with the past and the mythical by attempting to outdo each other in naming their establishments, respectively, "The Old Soap Cellar," "The Truly Old Soap Cellar," and "This is the actual old soap cellar, where the old soap cellar people live." The underlying themes of the play are philosophy, politics, and religion, in particular the "problem of human existence and the need for an authentic philosophy of life by which to live,"[83] but the tone is highly satirical. Kierkegaard takes particularly sharp aim at Hegelianism, as indicated by the subtitle "The all-encompassing debate of everything against everything else—or: the crazier the better," but Lehmann and the Liberals are made ridiculous as well, by the portrayal of the inability of politics to resolve problems in the real lives of individuals.

The plot of the play is minimal, serving primarily as a framework for quasi-philosophical conversations between the many characters. The protagonist is an earnest but unhappy young man named Willibald, an existential Faustian doubter. Dissatisfied with his doubts about the world, he and his friend Echo flee reality for the realm of philosophical ideality, where they encounter a group of quarreling intellectuals, all supported at public expense, at the Prytaneum: the philosopher Mr. Merrythought, the provisional genius Holla Rushjob, the know-it-all journalist Mr. Phrase, and the acting judge Mr. Thomas Stuffing, a ventriloquist, a pedestrian, several grocers, a fly that sat on Hegel's nose during the writing of *The Phenomenology of Spirit*, and a horn that expresses the will and ideas of the people. Willibald hopes to be cured of his relativity but is plunged instead into the disagreements among the philosophers at the Prytaneum. By lying about the real world, he manages to bring about their reconciliation, and the group is renamed "The New-and-the-Old-Prytaneum." The play ends with a celebration of their reunification and the erection of a monument in commemoration of the event.

The character Holla Rushjob is modeled on Lehmann, as the phonetic similarity between "Holla" and "Orla" makes explicit, and Kierkegaard paints an unsympathetic picture of his one-time opponent, lacing the dialogue liberally with quotations from Lehmann's articles. When Holla first appears, Thomas Stuffing scolds him, "I am… most willing to acknowledge your immortal services to national affairs. But as far as style goes, and expression, there is always something that offends—your pen is not

[82] *SKS* 17, 280–97, DD:208 / *KJN* 1, 272–89.

[83] Watkin, "Historical Introduction," p. xxxv.

mild enough, if I may say so."[84] Holla makes long speeches about the importance of practical things, but he dislikes philosophy, which he calls "the old story of the past," and complains, "it was a state of idyllic innocence but now we are men; now we are to engage things in earnest."[85] In response to Willibald's question about why the sun in the Prytaneum stood still and the light always remained the same, Holla explains, "it is the light of dawn, it is the solemn breaking of the day, it is the sun's battle with the last exertions of the dark."[86] When the other philosophers disagree, Holla demands a vote or at least "that the question whether it should be put to a vote should itself be put to a vote."[87] Instead, they all agree to start afresh under their new name and all ends well. Kierkegaard's play seems to suggest that politics are a fool's errand and rejects Lehmann's confidence in the ability of the political system to effect change by turning away from the past and continually erecting new ideological structures, since such strategies perpetuate an illusory existence. By caricaturing Lehmann in this way, Kierkegaard is able to express his disagreement with Lehmann's belief in the political system and take revenge for the unpleasantness he experienced at Lehmann's hands during their feud, as evidenced by Stuffing's judgment of Holla, "Yes, he lacks form. Offensiveness is so evident in every one of his utterances."[88]

Yet although Kierkegaard apparently had little regard for Lehmann as a politician or journalist, from a modern perspective and with the benefit of hindsight, they do not appear to be as diametrically opposed in their views or dissimilar in the trajectories of their lives as many scholars and even they themselves believed themselves to be. Although he never shared Lehmann's passion for politics, toward the end of his life Kierkegaard came to espouse a more egalitarian view about the necessity of granting political power to the people that is quite similar to Lehmann's populist stance. Kirmmse argues that Kierkegaard "ultimately came to champion 'the common man' and to embrace the verdict of 1848–49 as a breath of 'fresh air' that would once and for all divest politics of the religious and metaphysical trappings with which the bankrupt traditional culture had attempted to support and justify itself."[89] Moreover, despite their talents and the public acclaim they received for their work at times, both Kierkegaard and Lehmann ultimately found themselves out of step with Danish society due to their single-minded determination to defend an unpopular cause. When all is said and done, what binds Kierkegaard and Lehmann together is their devotion to their fatherland and their untiring efforts on behalf of their countrymen. When a bust of Lehmann was placed in the Fredericia Town Hall on July 8, 1861, Lehmann expressed his hope that his life would be judged to have exemplified the motto, "He loved his neighbor as himself and his fatherland above all,"[90] a sentiment that might be applied just as fittingly to Kierkegaard as well.

---

84 *SKS* 17, 286, DD:208 / *KJN* 1, 278.

85 *SKS* 17, 287, DD:208 / *KJN* 1, 279.

86 *SKS* 17, 293, DD:208 / *KJN* 1, 285.

87 *SKS* 17, 295, DD:208 / *KJN* 1, 287.

88 *SKS* 17, 289, DD:208 / *KJN* 1, 280.

89 Kirmmse, *Kierkegaard in Golden Age Denmark*, p. 244.

90 Bille, "Lehmann," p. 180.

Bibliography

I. Lehmann's Works in The Auction Catalogue *of Kierkegaard's Library*

"Svar til Flyvepostens Hr. B.," *Kjøbenhavnsposten*, no. 96, March 31, 1836, pp. 383–5 (*ASKB* U 75).

II. Works in The Auction Catalogue *of Kierkegaard's Library that Discuss Lehmann*

[Hage, Johannes], "Om *Flyvepostens* Polemik," *Fædrelandet*, no. 77, March 4, 1836 (cf. *Pap.* I B 3) (*ASKB* U 39).

Sibbern, Frederik Christian, *Dikaiosyne: eller Bidrag til Politik og politisk Jurisprudents for Danske, i statsretlig, kirkelig og historisk Henseende*, vol. 1, Copenhagen 1843, pp. 222–30; p. 241, note; p. 268 (*ASKB* U 105).

III. Secondary Literature on Kierkegaard's Relation to Lehmann

Friisberg, Claus, *Orla Lehmann–Danmarks første moderne politiker: En politisk biografi*, Varde: Vestjysk Kulturforlag 2000, p. 89.

Garff, Joakim, *Søren Kierkegaard: A Biography,* trans. by Bruce H. Kirmmse, Princeton and Oxford: Princeton University Press 2005, p. 18; pp. 62–3; p. 65; p. 83; p. 493.

Hannay, Alastair, *Kierkegaard: A Biography*, Cambridge: Cambridge University Press 2001, pp. 21–8 passim; p. 67; p. 116; pp. 445–6.

Kirmmse, Bruce H., *Kierkegaard in Golden Age Denmark*, Bloomington: Indiana University Press 1990, pp. 49–51; p. 56; pp. 60–70 passim; p. 159; pp. 242–3.

Watkin, Julia, "Historical Introduction," *EPW*, see p. viii; p. xix-xxiii; p. xxxii; p. xxxvi.

Poul Martin Møller:

Kierkegaard and the Confidant of Socrates

Finn Gredal Jensen

According to one of the epithets in Søren Kierkegaard's dedication to *The Concept of Anxiety*, Poul Martin Møller was "the confidant of Socrates." With the title of the present article, I wish to imply not only that Møller, of course, knew Plato as well as other Socratic sources by heart—he even considered Plato's dialogues as a topic for a dissertation[1]—but more importantly that as a Socratic figure himself, by his very personality, he had a special maieutic impact on the young Kierkegaard; their relationship is, however, also surrounded by several undocumented assumptions or myths which I will try to sort out. The article is divided into three principal sections: (I) an overview of the life and works of Poul Martin Møller; (II) a discussion of the testimonies concerning Møller's and Søren Kierkegaard's personal relation; and (III) a discussion of the references and possible allusions to Møller's writings in the Kierkegaardian *corpus*. Finally, in a brief concluding section (IV), I will focus on some relevant aspects of Møller's portrait of Socrates.

I. An Overview of the Life and Works of P.M. Møller

Poul Martin Møller was born in Uldum vicarage near Vejle in Jutland on March 21, 1794 and died in Copenhagen on March 13, 1838, not yet 44 years of age.[2]

I would like to thank Jon Stewart for good suggestions and for helping me translate several of the quotations. I am also grateful to David D. Possen for his careful reading of the manuscript.

1 This is evident from a letter from Møller to his father from 1823 (*Poul Møller og hans Familie i Breve*, vols. 1–3, ed. by Morten Borup, Society for Danish Language and Literature, Copenhagen: C.A. Reitzel 1976, vol. 1, no. 52; below I will refer to this edition as "Borup" followed by the letter number). He planned to write the dissertation as soon as he had finished his Homer translations, but the following year, in another letter to his father, dated July 1, 1824 (Borup, Letter no. 56), he mentions the possibility of skipping over it: "I have myself often thought of skipping over the master's dissertation (not for the sake of indolence [*Mageliged*] but for the sake of my finances)."

2 Møller's first biographer was Frederik Christian Olsen (1802–74), whose *Poul Martin Møllers Levnet, med Breve fra hans Haand* was both published separately and included in Møller's *Efterladte Skrifter*, 1st ed., vol. 3, Copenhagen: C.A. Reitzel 1843 (separate pagination pp. 1–116). The major monograph on Møller remains Vilhelm Andersen, *Poul Møller. Hans*

His parents were Rasmus Møller (1763–1842) and Bodil Maria Thaulow (1765–1810). From 1802 Rasmus Møller was pastor in the village Købelev on the island of Lolland and, as an aged man, became bishop in Maribo in 1831. However, he was not only a theologian but also a keen philologist, who translated and published, among other things, Sallust, parts of Livy (Books 1–7), and a number of Cicero's speeches.[3] Poul together with his younger brother Hans Ulrik (in contrast to their four younger sisters) received tutoring from their father, and here his later thorough skills in classical languages and literature were founded. During the years 1807–09 he went to school in Nakskov and in 1810, together with his brother, was sent to the grammar school of Nykøbing Falster, where he met and became friends with his later stepbrother, the poet Christian Winther (1796–1876); after the death of his wife, Rasmus Møller remarried in 1811, and his new wife was Winther's mother Johanna Dorothea Borchsenius (1769–1830).

In 1812 Poul Martin Møller began his studies in theology at the University of Copenhagen, and in less than three-and-a-half years he completed them in January 1816 with the best grades, although while studying he was also teaching religion at the Borgerdyd School of Copenhagen and Latin at the other Borgerdyd School in Christianshavn.[4] Far more important than theology, however, was his participation in student life and founding of stimulating friendships with notable personalities

Liv og Skrifter efter trykte og utrykte Kilder i Hundredaaret for hans Fødsel, Copenhagen: G.E.C. Gad 1894 (2nd ed., vols. 1–2, 1904; 3rd ed., 1944). For further literature on Møller (and Kierkegaard), see the footnotes and the bibliography of the present article. In general, see also Henrik Denman, *Poul Martin Møller. En kommenteret bibliografi*, Roskilde: Denmans Forlag 1986.

3 Søren Kierkegaard owned Rasmus Møller's translations of Sallust, *Sallusts Catilinariske Krig oversat fra det Latinske. Et Forsøg*, Copenhagen: Fr. Brummer 1811 (two copies, *ASKB* 1273 and *ASKB* A I 184); *Sallusts Jugurthinske Krig oversat fra det Latinske. Et Forsøg*, Copenhagen: Fr. Brummer 1812 (*ASKB* A I 184), and his Latin edition of Livy, Books 1–10, based on editions by F.A. Stroth and F.W. Döring, *Titi Livii Operum omnium volumen I* [Books 1–5], Copenhagen: Gyldendal 1815 (*ASKB* A II 31), *Titi Livii Patavini Historiarum libri I–X...volumen II, libros VI–X continens*, Copenhagen: Gyldendal 1819 (*ASKB* A II 32), and the 2nd ed. of vol. 1, 1831, ed. by C.F. Ingerslev (*ASKB* 1256). Rasmus Møller also published a number of theological works; of these Kierkegaard owned his *Veiledning til en andægtig og forstandig Læsning af det Nye Testamente, især for ulærde Læsere*, 1st ed., Copenhagen: Andreas Seidelin 1820 (*ASKB* A I 18), and 2nd ed., 1824 (*ASKB* 83), cf. also the journal entry NB:123, *SKS* 20, 88 / *JP* 2, 1997; furthermore, his *Veiledning til en andægtig og forstandig Læsning af det Gamle Testamente, især for ulærde Læsere*, vols. 1–2, Copenhagen: Andreas Seidelin 1826 (*ASKB* 81–82), and his translations of the Prophets in *Det Gamle Testamentes poetiske og prophetiske Skrifter, efter Grundtexten paa ny oversatte og med Indholdsfortegnelse samt Anmærkninger forsynede*, published together with Jens Møller (who was not his brother, as stated in *SKS* K22, explanatory note to 179.8), Copenhagen: Andreas Seidelin 1828–30 (two copies, *ASKB* 86–88, 89–91).

4 Cf. Holger Lund, *Borgerdydsskolen i Kjøbenhavn 1787–1887. Et Mindeskrift i Anledning af Skolens Hundredaarsfest*, Copenhagen: Otto B. Wroblewskys Forlag 1887, p. 238; T.H. Erslew, *Almindeligt Forfatter-Lexicon for Kongeriget Danmark med tilhørende Bilande, fra 1814–1840*, vols. 1–3, Copenhagen: Forlagsforeningens Forlag 1843–53; vol. 2, 1847, p. 407.

such as Bernhard Severin Ingemann (1789–1862), Carsten Hauch (1790–1872), Johan Ludvig Heiberg (1791–1860), Niels Bygom Krarup (1792–1842), Peder Hjort (1793–1871), Just Mathias Thiele (1795–1874), Nicolai Christian Møhl (1798–1830), and of the older generation he saw, for instance, Heiberg's mother, Thomasine Gyllembourg-Ehrensvärd (1773–1856) and the Rahbeks at "Bakkehuset," Knud Lyne Rahbek (1760–1830) and Kamma Rahbek (1775–1829). In 1815 Møller published his first poem in a newspaper—in the following years he would publish several more poems, although he always wrote more than he published—and he proposed in vain to Margrethe Bloch, a daughter of his former headmaster from Nykøbing. Theology never interested him much, but philology did; his major publication in 1816 was a translation of the *Odyssey*, Book 9.[5] After an intermezzo as tutor of two young counts at the estate Espe near Korsør, he was back in Copenhagen where he participated in the literary controversy surrounding Jens Baggesen (1764–1826) in 1818; here he also composed a satire on Baggesen's supporter N.F.S. Grundtvig (1783–1872), "Draft of a Letter from Heaven."[6] At the same time he began serious studies in classical philology.

The following year, when the aforementioned Miliss Bloch got married, Møller, five months later, embarked as ship pastor on the frigate "Christianshavn" heading for China.[7] The ship raised anchor on November 1, 1819 and did not return until July 14, 1821. On this long voyage Møller hoped to study while on board. Among other things he seems to have read all of Cicero. He also wrote quite a lot, for instance, his famous poem "Joy over Denmark,"[8] but first and foremost he began collecting his ideas by means of aphorisms, the so-called "*Strøtanker*" (scattered thoughts). On his return to Copenhagen he resumed his participation in student life, but as a more mature person than before; he saw his old friends, and now also, among others, the philologist Christen Thaarup (1795–1849), one of the later editors of his posthumous writings. He took part in the Student Association ("Studenterforeningen"), where, in 1824, he recited parts of his unfinished novel *Adventures of a Danish Student*. His writings from these years include the poem "A Leaf from the Diary of Death" and an excellent translation into Danish of Lord Byron's "The Dream," and he published poems such as "April Song" ("Aprilsvise") and parts of "Scenes in Rosenborg Garden." He also continued his philological studies and now translated the *Odyssey*, Books 1–6, which would be published in 1825 as what, strange as it may sound, would turn out to be his

---

5 "Forsøg til en metrisk Oversættelse af Odysseus Eventyr i Kyklopens Hule, ved *P. M. Møller*, Candid. Theol.," published in the Christianshavn Borgerdyd School's *Indbydelses-skrift til den offentlige Examen i Borgerdydskolen i September 1816*, Copenhagen: Johan Frederik Schultz 1816, pp. 3–20.

6 On this see Section III, A below.

7 On this voyage see, for instance, Lone Klem, "Rejoicing over Denmark: Poul Martin Møller's Voyage to China on the Frigate 'Christianshavn' 1819–21," in *The Golden Age Revisited: Art and Culture in Denmark 1800–1850*, ed. by Bente Scavenius, Copenhagen: Gyldendal 1996, pp. 84–91.

8 The Kierkegaardian significance of this poem will be discussed below in Sections II (note 49) and III, B.

only book.[9] After his return from abroad in 1821, he had continued his work at the Borgerdyd School, now teaching Greek, the same year as Søren Kierkegaard started there;[10] but already from November 12 of the following year he was employed as adjunct at the Metropolitan School, teaching Greek and Latin.[11] One of Møller's pupils at this school was the later Bishop Hans Lassen Martensen (1808–84), who in his memoirs says, "Among the teachers, I will mention the genial, unforgettable Poul Møller, whom we pupils looked up to with admiration, and who, without trying, exerted such fruitful influence on us."[12] In the school's "*indbydelsesskrift*" or work of invitation, Møller in 1823 published a Latin treatise on Nemesis, "*De invidia diis ab Herodoto et æqualibus attributa pauca.*"[13] In 1826 he passed the written part of

---

9 *Homers Odyssees sex första Sange metrisk oversatte af Poul Möller, Adjunct ved Metropolitanskolen*, Copenhagen: Gyldendal 1825, 99 pages (an earlier version of the translation of the *Odyssey*, Book 5, he had published in 1822). In the above-mentioned letter, dated July 1, 1824 (Borup, Letter no. 56), from "Bakkehuset," where he sometimes stayed, Møller writes to his father that "in due course" ("*med Tiden*") he would like to translate all of the *Odyssey*, but he realizes how troublesome this would be—with the first six books he had much difficulty finishing the proofs, since he could never stop correcting the text—and adds, "When you know for how many years I have been engaged in translating Homer, then you will realize the truth that I cannot finish anything." This self-knowledge is even more evident in a letter from earlier that summer (Borup, Letter no. 55), also to his father, in which he says, "If one would conduct the matter properly, then a man could do nothing else for his whole lifetime than translate the *Odyssey*, but such a man I would not like to be."

10 Cf. Holger Lund, *Borgerdydsskolen*, p. 238. Søren Kierkegaard started at the school in 1821, but Per Krarup states that he "certainly could not have had him [Møller] as instructor at the school. Their acquaintance dates from his time as a university student." Per Krarup, *Søren Kierkegaard og Borgerdydskolen*, Copenhagen: Gyldendal 1977, pp. 61–2. There can be no doubt about this, since Møller was only teaching in the first form, i.e., the oldest pupils. Vilhelm Andersen's suggestion (*Poul Møller*, pp. 151–3) that the absentminded Latin teacher appearing in *Stages on Life's Way* (*SKS* 6, 191–2 / *SLW*, 204–5) might be a portrait of Møller was withdrawn in the second edition of his biography (the teacher Kierkegaard had in mind was Ernst Bojesen). At any rate, as a schoolboy Kierkegaard must have seen Møller on a daily basis at the school when he came there to teach. By the way, at this time Møller was a busy man also giving private tutoring, as usual due to financial reasons.

11 Cf. *Metropolitanskolen gennem 700 Aar*, ed. by C.A.S. Dalberg and P.M. Plum, Copenhagen: Gyldendal 1916, p. 116, and Appendix, "Hundrede Aars Metropolitanere," ed. by P.M. Plum, p. 11. Møller's first biographer and one of the editors of his posthumous writings, his friend Frederik Christian Olsen also taught Greek and Latin at the school, but not until 1828 after Møller had left (later, Olsen had an intermezzo teaching at the grammar school of Elsinore 1830–37, then again at the Metropolitan School, and in 1844 he moved to Jutland to become headmaster of the grammar school Viborg Katedralskole).

12 H.L. Martensen, *Af mit Levnet. Meddelelser*, vols. 1–3, Copenhagen: Gyldendal 1882–83, vol. 1, p. 16.

13 "De invidia diis ab Herodoto et æqualibus attributa pauca commentatus est *Paulus Möller*, Scholæ Adjunctus" ["On the Envy Attributed to the Gods by Herodotus and his Contemporaries: Some Considerations by Poul Møller, Adjunct at the School"], in *Examen publicum anniversarium in Schola Metropolitana X Calendarum Octobris A. MDCCCXXIII habendum indicit Rector Scholæ Nicolaus Lang Nissen, doctor philosophiæ et magister artium atque professor*, Havniae MDCCCXXIII: Typis Schultzianis, pp. 1–32. This treatise,

the university examination in philology, and the same year he proposed successfully to Betty Berg (1804–34).

"One should not attempt to seduce or persuade someone into philosophy," Friedrich Schlegel says in *Athenäums-Fragmente*, no. 417.[14] However, this is what Professor Frederik Christian Sibbern (1785–1872) seems to have done in relation to Møller. He persuaded him to become a professional philosopher, later always advising him, giving him lists of books to read, etc. But however hardworking and interested Møller was, he never became an original philosopher; in truth, as a "happy lover of Greek culture"—to use Kierkegaard's wording—he probably should have stuck to poetry and philology, where his great talents were. In the summer of 1826, Sibbern approached him as an intermediary with an offer of a professorship—first Møller was appointed lecturer, and then, in 1828 professor—in philosophy at the Frederiks-University of Christiania, today Oslo. Møller dropped his final, oral examination in philology and in October 1826 went to Norway. The next summer he got married in Denmark and brought his wife back north, and in 1828 and 1830 they had two sons (with two more to come later); but since he was busy during these years with philosophical reading and teaching, his literary production was modest. He and his family felt isolated and unsuited for life abroad, and undoubtedly Møller's job in Norway was always only intended as a springboard for a better post in Copenhagen.

Eventually, this became possible when on October 12, 1830 he was appointed professor in philosophy at the University of Copenhagen,[15] where his first lecture, in moral philosophy, took place on May 28, 1831.[16] In the years to come he would give lectures, in public or private, in several different disciplines; according to the course catalogues, the lectures announced were the following: moral philosophy (all summer semesters 1831–37); logic (summer semesters 1832, 1833, 1834); the history

---

which is the longest work extant in the Latin language from Møller's hand, was not included in the *Posthumous Writings*, but it was praised as "interesting" by J.L. Heiberg, who refers to it twice in his essay "Nemesis: A Popular-Philosophical Investigation" ("Nemesis. Et populair-philosophisk Forsøg"), in *Kjøbenhavns flyvende Post*, 1827, nos. 41, 43, 44, and 45; cf. *Heiberg's Contingency Regarded from the Point of View of Logic and Other Texts*, trans. and ed. by Jon Stewart, Copenhagen: Museum Tusculanum Press 2008 (*Texts from Golden Age Denmark*, vol. 4), pp. 101–25; p. 109 and p. 120.

14 "*Man soll niemanden zur Philosophie verführen oder bereden wollen.*" *Athenaeum. Eine Zeitschrift. Ersten Bandes Zweytes Stück*, ed. by A.W. Schlegel and F. Schlegel, Berlin: bey Friedrich Vieweg dem älteren 1798, p. 304; *Kritische Friedrich-Schlegel-Ausgabe*, ed. by E. Behler et al., vol. 2, *Charakteristiken und Kritiken I (1796–1801)*, ed. by H. Eichner, Munich, Paderborn, Vienna: Verlag Ferdinand Schöningh/Zürich: Thomas-Verlag 1967, p. 244.

15 Cf. *Akademiske Tidender*, vol. 1, ed. by H.P. Selmer, Copenhagen: Gyldendal 1833, p. 165.

16 This appears from a letter to Sibbern (Borup, Letter no. 122); in the course catalogue, *Index lectionum in Universitate Regia Hauniensi per semestre æstivum a Kalendis Maiis A. MDCCCXXXI habendarum*, Copenhagen: J.H. Schultz 1831, p. 7, one only reads the following: "*P. M. Möller, Philosophiæ P. P. E.* [Professor Publicus Extraordinarius], *quum advenerit, lectiones e valvis publicis indicabit.*"

of modern philosophy (winter semester 1831–32); metaphysics (winter semesters 1832–33, 1835–36, 1836–37); the history of ancient philosophy (winter semesters 1833–34, 1834–35); psychology (winter 1834–35, summer 1835, winter 1836–37, summer 1837); Aristotle's *De anima* (winter semester 1835–36); philosophical propaedeutics (summer 1836).[17] Due to illness, Møller in the winter semester 1837–38 was unable to give his announced lectures on "Ontology or the System of Categories"—on which he also began writing a textbook—and a planned *privatissime* course of lectures on ancient philosophy.[18] It would be difficult to imagine that the young Søren Kierkegaard participated in nothing of all this, but unfortunately, only in a few cases are the lists of auditors extant, and there are no other sources that could shed light on the matter. In just a single case Kierkegaard's name appears on an extant list for Møller's lectures, namely, the lectures in metaphysics, which were given in "three meetings a week," in the winter semester 1836–37.[19] In some cases we know the number of auditors, but not their identity.[20] To all appearances, Møller

[17] The winter semester ran from November 1 the one year until the end of March of the following year; summer semester ran from May 1 until the end of September.

[18] *Kjøbenhavns Universitets Aarbog for 1838*, ed. by H.P. Selmer, Copenhagen: Gyldendal 1839, p. 87; cf. *Kjøbenhavns Universitets Aarbog for 1837*, ed. by H.P. Selmer, Copenhagen: Gyldendal 1838, p. 86. It appears from a letter from Rasmus Møller to Bishop Mynster (Borup, Letter no. 179) that Møller before his death "had thrown a large amount of his manuscripts on the fire," including the textbook on *Ontologien eller Kategoriernes System* [*Ontology or the System of Categories*], which he was about to finish, but of which only an extant, minor part (Introduction and beginning of Chapter 1) was published in the *Posthumous Writings*, vol. 3, pp. 331–60 (the MS is at the Royal Library of Copenhagen, Collinske Samling 378, 4°; at the Royal Library, NKS 4000, 4°, there is also a larger MS, a fair copy not in Møller's hand, however, of the notes for the planned lectures). In a letter to F.C. Olsen (Borup, Letter no. 177), H.U. Møller quotes parts of a letter from his brother, before destroying it as he had been told to; P.M. Møller in that letter, from early 1837, writes that he is working on the last part, Sections VIII–XI, of his treatise on immortality, expecting to have it published in the April issue of the *Maanedsskrift for Litteratur*, but that later the same year he intends to publish a book on metaphysics (i.e., *Ontology or the System of Categories*), "which, while I am lecturing [on metaphysics 1836–37] I am revising, that is, rewriting completely for the third time….When I have published this strictly methodological work, which is so dry that not many people will read it (except for the young students, who without regard to the examinations, to my great surprise attend my lectures on this subject in large numbers), I believe that I have won the right to write aphoristically, desultorily and fragmentarily for a long time. Hereafter, namely, I will begin to write. Until now I have just been reading for so many years." With the expression "in large numbers" ("*i Mængde*") one should have in mind that for the lectures in metaphysics in the winter semester 1836–37 the number of auditors was 26, and the year before 24; cf. note 20.

[19] Peter Tudvad, *Kierkegaards København*, Copenhagen: Politikens Forlag 2004, p. 181. From Møller's years as professor at the philosophical faculty, the lists of participants exist only for the winter semester 1832–33, the summer semester 1833, the winter semester 1833–34, and then, some years later, for the winter semester 1836–37 and the summer semester 1837; see Tudvad, ibid., pp. 177–81, with references to Rigsarkivet, Copenhagen.

[20] According to H.P. Selmer, there were 160 auditors for Møller's lectures in moral philosophy and logic in the summer semester 1834, cf. *Akademiske Tidender*, vol. 2, ed. by H.P. Selmer, Copenhagen: Gyldendal 1834, p. 382; 21 auditors for the lectures in ancient

was a popular teacher; his friendly and natural disposition made an impression on his surroundings, but he was also known for his sudden spells of distraction.

In these years Møller did not have time for much more than reading and preparing himself for educational purposes. Furthermore, for financial reasons, since 1832 he was also teaching Greek and Danish composition at the other Borgerdyd School in Christianshavn, where his friend, the philologist N.B. Krarup was headmaster. His poetic veins had almost dried out; important, though, is his late masterpiece, "The Artist among the Rebels" ("Kunstneren mellem Oprørerne"), which appeared in December 1837 in H.P. Holst's and Christian Winther's *New Year's Gift from Danish Poets* (*Nytaarsgave fra danske Digtere*). He also wrote a number of reviews, most important his lengthy review of Thomasine Gyllembourg's *The Extremes*, published in 1836.[21] In the philosophical genre, except for a small review of a book by F.L.B. Zeuthen (1805–74) and his fine reviews of P.C. Kierkegaard's (1805–88) dissertation on the concept of the lie and Sibbern's *On Poetry and Art*, he only published the great treatise on immortality, "Thoughts on the Possibility of Proofs of Human Immortality,"[22] which appeared in 1837 in the prestigeous *Maanedsskrift for Litteratur*, of whose editorial board he was a member. He had many plans for projects that he wanted to do; for example, he had a preoccupation with the nihilistic figure of Ahasverus[23] and with the concept of affectation,[24] which he reflected upon for several years in his scattered thoughts, but eventually he was too ill to realize any of these plans. After the return from Norway, his wife had become still weaker and died in 1834, and this was a hard blow for him; earlier also one of their children had died. A few years later, in December 1836, he married his late wife's friend Eline von Bülow (1804–76), with whom he had a daughter. However, he soon became ill himself, apparently from liver cancer, and his condition worsened, accompanied by asthma. He died on March 13, 1838.

In 1839, the year after Møller's death, the first volume of his *Posthumous Writings* appeared, which were published in three volumes, 1839–43, edited by his stepbrother Christian Winther and his two friends Frederik Christian Olsen and Christen Thaarup.[25] Winther, to the best of his ability, took care of the poetical writings,

---

philosophy and 168 auditors in psychology in the winter semester 1834–35, cf. *Akademiske Tidender*, vol. 3, ed. by H.P. Selmer, Copenhagen: Gyldendal 1835, p. 151; 174 auditors for the lectures in moral philosophy and psychology in the summer semester 1835; 10 auditors in the lectures on *De anima* and 24 auditors in metaphysics in the winter semester 1835–36, and 111 auditors in moral philosophy in the summer semester 1836, cf. *Akademiske Tidender*, vol. 4, ed. by H.P. Selmer, Copenhagen: Gyldendal 1841, p. 420. For Møller's last two semesters as a lecturer, the lists of participants are extant, and according to these there were 26 auditors in metaphysics in the winter semester 1836–37 (one of which is proved to be Kierkegaard) and 143 in psychology in the summer semester 1837, cf. *Kjøbenhavns Universitets Aarbog for 1837*, ed. by H.P. Selmer, Copenhagen: Gyldendal 1838, p. 81.

21 This will be treated below, Section III, D.

22 Below, Section III, G.

23 Below, Section III, C.

24 Below, Section III, F.

25 *Efterladte Skrifter af Poul M. Møller*, vols. 1–3, ed. by C. Winther, F.C. Olsen, and C. Thaarup, 1st ed., Copenhagen: C.A. Reitzel 1839–43 (vol. 1, 1839; vol. 2, 1842; vol. 3, 1843)

including the Homer translations; Thaarup's main effort was his reconstruction of *Adventures of a Danish Student*; and Olsen first and foremost was the executor of the philosophical writings, and he also included a *vita*, the first biography of Møller, "Life of Poul Martin Møller, with Letters from his Hand."[26] The second edition in six volumes, 1848–50, included a number of additions (e.g., the *Batrachomyomachia* translation), whereas the third, published 1855–56, was almost identical to the second, except for the new editor L.V. Petersen's inclusion of the one-act drama "The Made-up Stories."[27]

What has been lacking in the Møller editions has especially been the philosophical lectures, of which only a minor part has ever been published.[28] Nevertheless, for the

(*ASKB* 1574–1576). In the following, in the notes, I will refer to the 1st ed. of the *Posthumous Writings* as *ES1*.

26 It was in accordance with Møller's wishes that Winther and Olsen edited his posthumous writings, cf. Winther's preface to *ES1*, vol. 1: "When my brother, *Poul Møller*, felt death approaching, he said to me: 'I can imagine that, as is usually the case, also after my death, someone is going to collect and publish what I have written. I therefore would like to confer upon you, in the present case, to attend to the publication of the aesthetical part [of the writings], and to leave out what you, with your knowledge of me, would presume that I myself would have omitted.—Ask *Olsen* to do the same with the philosophical part.' " According to F.C. Olsen's preface to *ES1*, vol. 2, Møller in his last days had also expressed the wish that Olsen, for the publication of the scholarly part of the writings, should seek advice and help from Professor Sibbern—and so Olsen did when deciding what to publish and what to leave out. The third editor Christen Thaarup got involved in the edition later, as it became clear that a third volume was necessary.

27 *Efterladte Skrifter af Poul M. Møller*, vols. 1–6, ed. by C. Winther, F.C. Olsen, C. Thaarup, and L.V. Petersen, 2nd ed. (*ES2*), Copenhagen: C.A. Reitzel 1848–50; *Efterladte Skrifter af Poul M. Møller*, vols. 1–6, ed. by L.V. Petersen, 3rd ed., (*ES3*), Copenhagen: C.A. Reitzel 1855–56. (The new editor, Lauritz Vilhelm Petersen (1817–79), theologian and an old pupil of Møller, is also known as the Danish translator of H.L. Martensen's dissertation, *De autonomia conscientiae sui humanae in theologiam dogmaticam nostri temporis introducta*, Copenhagen: J.D. Quist 1837 (*ASKB* 648); *Den menneskelige Selvbevidstheds Autonomie*, Copenhagen: C.A. Reitzel 1841 (*ASKB* 651)). The most important editions since then have been Christian Winther's selections of Møller's writings, *Poul M. Møllers Efterladte Skrifter*, vols. 1–2, Copenhagen: C.A. Reitzel 1873, and Vilhelm Andersen's edition, also selections, *Udvalgte Skrifter af Poul Møller*, vols. 1–2, Copenhagen: G.E.C. Gad 1895 (2nd ed., *Skrifter i Udvalg*, 1930); Johannes Brøndum-Nielsen in his *Poul Møller Studier*, Copenhagen: Gyldendal 1940, published some hitherto unknown poems (along with a facsimile of the satire *Smørialis's Digtervandringer* (1823), which he, in all probability wrongly, considered as genuine Møller). The letters of Møller have been edited and annotated by Morten Borup in *Poul Møller og hans Familie i Breve*. A modern annotated, historical-critical edition of P.M. Møller's collected writings, ed. by Finn Gredal Jensen, Kim Ravn, and Niels Stengaard, is being prepared at the Society for Danish Language and Literature, Copenhagen; the new edition will include material not published before.

28 In agreement with Sibbern's estimation, only the lecture manuscripts on the history of ancient philosophy (*ES1*, vol. 2, pp. 273–527, "Udkast til Forelæsninger over den ældre Philosophies Historie") and on moral philosophy (*ES1*, vol. 3, pp. 351–69, "Forelæsnings-Paragrapher over Moral-Philosophien") were published. Møller's notes for his lectures in formal logic had earlier been included in a textbook by Carl Berg, *Grundtrækkene af en*

public, who until then had only had access to a minimal part of Møller's authorship, with the first edition of the *Posthumous Writings* the full scope of his genius for the first time became visible. Møller was indeed highly creative, so when Carsten Hauch, with a reference to Jean Paul's *Aesthetics*, calls him a "passive" genius, he only seems to mean that by nature Møller was a fragmentist and that consequently he never published much (mainly because he had no special ambitions of doing so).[29] However, the claim is perhaps accurate in the sense that Møller conceived ideas and Kierkegaard could gather and realize them. His possible maieutic impact on Kierkegaard will be discussed in the following sections.

II. Kierkegaard—the Confidant of Møller?

It has often been stated that Søren Kierkegaard and Poul Martin Møller were "friends," but the sources supporting this supposition are very few. Nevertheless, it is obvious, even from the little we know, that in various respects Møller appeared as a *Socratic* figure, a mentor, for Kierkegaard, and that they were on a familiar footing. As will appear below from Section III, several traces of Møller's writings can be demonstrated in Kierkegaard's authorship. But for Kierkegaard, undoubtedly Møller's *personality* was more important than his thought, be it through his writings or through oral communication. Troels-Lund, who in his *Bakkehus og Solbjerg* not surprisingly underlines the importance of Møller's personality, has a good point in also emphasizing the major importance of his death: "In accordance with his [Kierkegaard's] characteristic nature, the death itself [of Møller], by which the relation was transformed into memory, brought them even closer together."[30] In the present section, I will treat Kierkegaard's remarks on Møller and the surviving testimonies concerning Kierkegaard's and Møller's relationship.

The best attestation of their personal relation is, of course, the printed dedication to *The Concept of Anxiety* (1844). This may well be seen as a précis of how Kierkegaard regarded Møller. It reads as follows: "To the late Professor Poul Martin Møller, the happy lover of Greek culture, the admirer of Homer, the confidant of Socrates, the interpreter of Aristotle—Denmark's joy in 'Joy over Denmark,' though

---

philosophisk Propædeutik eller Erkjendelseslære, tilligemed Poul Møllers kortfattede formelle Logik. Trykt som Manuskript til Brug for Elever af det kongl. Landcadetacademie, Copenhagen: C.A. Reitzel 1839 (*ASKB* 426, bought by Kierkegaard in 1844). As already mentioned, for the winter semester 1837–38 Møller had planned a series of lectures on "Ontology or the System of Categories," which was cancelled when he became ill, but parts of his manuscript for a planned book on the subject were published in *ES1*, vol. 3, pp. 331–60.

29 Carsten Hauch, *Minder fra min Barndom og min Ungdom*, Copenhagen: C.A. Reitzel 1867, pp. 297–8; cf. Jean Paul [Johann Paul Friedrich Richter], *Vorschule der Aesthetik, nebst einigen Vorlesungen in Leipzig über die Parteien der Zeit*, vols. 1–3, Hamburg: Friedrich Perthes 1804; 2nd ed., Stuttgart and Tübingen: Cotta 1813 (*ASKB* 1381–1383); see, in general, the 2nd Program, "Stufenfolge poetischer Kräfte," and 3rd Program, "Ueber das Genie." The passive (receptive, feminine) geniuses are treated in § 10.

30 Troels Frederik Troels-Lund, *Bakkehus og Solbjerg. Træk af et nyt Livssyns Udvikling i Norden*, vols. 1–3, Copenhagen: Gyldendal 1920–22, vol. 3, p. 200.

'widely traveled' always 'remembered in the Danish summer'—the object of my admiration, my profound loss, this work is dedicated."[31] A dedication of this kind is anything but formal; it is as personal as it can be in a public forum and in a public form. The universal genius of Møller is encircled with a number of epithets, not surprisingly with the primary focus being on his preoccupation with Hellenic culture, then on his poetry,[32] and concluding with the very personal statements, "the object of my admiration, my profound loss."

With some caution, a few things might be deduced from the dedication: Kierkegaard is well aware of Møller's Homer translations and acquainted with his familiarity with Plato's dialogues and other sources relating to Socrates;[33] the element "the interpreter of Aristotle" presumably refers to the treatment of Aristotle in Møller's lectures on ancient philosophy,[34] but undoubtedly in particular to his lectures regarding Aristotle's *On the Soul* (*De anima*).[35] As mentioned before, there is no evidence of Kierkegaard's participation in these or any other of Møller's lectures, with the sole exception of the lectures on metaphysics in the winter semester 1836–37, which is the only case where his name appears on one of the few extant lists of auditors in Møller's lectures.[36] Unfortunately, no such lists are extant for the five semesters from summer 1834 to summer 1836, and therefore we

---

31 *SKS* 4, 311 / *CA*, 5. The Danish wording is the following: "*Afdøde Professor Poul Martin Møller, Græcitetens lykkelige Elsker, Homers Beundrer, Socrates's Medvider, Aristoteles's Fortolker—Danmarks Glæde i Glæden over Danmark, skjøndt 'vidt forreist' altid 'mindet i den danske Sommer'—min Beundring, mit Savn, helliges dette Skrift.*"

32 See later below in Section III, B on "Joy over Denmark," which is the poem referred to in the dedication. See also note 49 in the present section on H.P. Rohde's theory of the influence of Hostrup's *The Opposite Neighbors*.

33 Møller treats Socrates in many different places in his writings, directly or indirectly, for instance in his scattered thoughts, but the first place to mention is his portrait of Socrates in the lecture notes on ancient philosophy—which is indeed personal, and more than just an excerpt of the sources he drew from when teaching, mainly Heinrich Ritter, *Geschichte der Philosophie alter Zeit*, vols. 1–4, Hamburg: Friedrich Perthes 1829–34 (of which Kierkegaard owned the 2nd ed. of vol. 1, Hamburg: Friedrich Perthes 1836 (*ASKB* 735) and the 1st ed. of vols. 2–4, Hamburg: Friedrich Perthes 1830–34 (*ASKB* 736–738)); this portrait of Socrates is found in *ES1*, vol. 2, pp. 357–75, and I will briefly discuss some central passages from it in the concluding Section IV of the present article.

34 In the lecture notes, printed in *ES1*, vol. 2, Aristotle is treated on pp. 455–505.

35 Unfortunately, the lecture notes on *De anima*, presumably very interesting, are lost. At the same time, Møller also translated *De anima*, however only Book 1, Chapters 1–3. This fragment, "Om Sjælen," was first published in *ES2*, vol. 3, 1848, pp. 213–28, and not in *ES1* owned by Kierkegaard.

36 On the lists of participants and in general on the extent of Møller's lectures see in detail above Section I. Søren Kierkegaard's name is not found on the extant lists for Møller's lectures in the winter semester 1832–33 (metaphysics), the summer semester 1833 (logic and moral philosophy), or the winter semester 1833–34 (the history of ancient philosophy); nor is it found on the lists for Møller's lectures in psychology in the winter semester 1836–37 or in moral philosophy and psychology in the summer semester 1837. However, on the basis of the extant lists we cannot necessarily deduce that Kierkegaard did not attend; he could have been present without being officially enrolled.

cannot be sure if Kierkegaard attended any of Møller's lectures in these years, but the natural presumption is that he did—even if he was a lazy student. There are no other sources to document this, and nowhere in Kierkegaard's writings is it possible to trace unambiguously identifiable elements of Møller's lectures.[37] Of course, we must assume that he read the selections of lecture notes which were published in the first edition of Møller's *Posthumous Writings*.[38]

The *draft* of the dedication, however, is more extensive and far more interesting since it contains some rather intimate personal elements that were left out in the book:

> To the late
> Professor *Poul Martin Møller*
> the happy lover of Greek culture, the admirer of Homer, the confidant of Socrates, the interpreter of Aristotle—Denmark's joy in "Joy over Denmark" though "widely traveled yet always remembered in the Danish summer"—the enthusiasm of my youth; the mighty trumpet of my awakening; the desired object of my feelings; the confidant of my beginnings; my lost friend; my sadly missed reader
> this work
> is dedicated.[39]

The elements "though 'widely…Danish summer' " and "the mighty trumpet…my feelings," are inserted later (in the English translation *CA* these are marked with asterisks). Another thing worth noticing is the detail that in front of "sadly missed" ("*savnede*") Kierkegaard deleted the intensifying "always" ("*altid*"). Then in the fair copy he deleted the whole passage "the enthusiasm of my youth…my sadly missed reader" and replaced it with the modest final wording, "the object of my admiration, my profound loss."[40]

---

37 When, for instance, Kierkegaard in NB4:29 (*SKS* 20, 301.18ff. / *JP* 3, 3352) refers to the conception that Socrates was a "practical" philosopher, this is not necessarily a reference to Møller calling Socrates "the founder of practical philosophy," *ES1*, vol. 2, p. 366, since this thought is not original. To take another example, not from the lectures, however, but from the fragment of Møller's *Ontology or the System of Categories*: when in *Pap.* VI C 1 / *JP* 5, 5798 Kierkegaard mentions a Hegelian confusion of τὸ ὄν and τὸ εἶναι, he credits Rasmus Nielsen, *Den propædeutiske Logik*, Copenhagen: P.G. Philipsen 1845 (*ASKB* 699), and not the relevant passage of Møller's work, cf. *ES1*, vol. 3, p. 350.

38 Kierkegaard also read Møller's notes on formal logic included in Berg's textbook, *Grundtrækkene af en philosophisk Propædeutik eller Erkjendelseslære*, which he bought in 1844. On the limited extent of publication of lecture notes in *ES1* see above in Section I.

39 *Pap.* V B 46 / *CA*, Supplement, p. 178. In Danish the draft reads thus: "*Afdøde Profs. Poul Martin Møller, Græcitetens lykkelige Elsker, Homers Beundrer, Socrates Medvider, Aristoteles*[s] *Fortolker—Danmarks Glæde i Glæden over Danmark, skjøndt 'vidt forreist, altid mindet i den danske Sommer'—min Ungdoms Begeistring; min Opvaagnens mægtige Basune; min Stemnings forønskede Gjenstand; min Begyndens Fortrolige; min tabte Ven; min savnede Læser helliges dette Skrift.*" Quoted from *SKS* K4, p. 344. The draft of the dedication is located in the Kierkegaard Archive, B, fasc. 15, quire 1, at the Royal Library of Copenhagen; MS 1.1, fol. 1v, in *SKS* K4, p. 310.

40 *Pap.* V B 72,3 / *SKS* K4, pp. 314–15, MS 3.1, fol. 2r. It is not certain when this correction took place; according to the editors of *SKS*, the dedication was changed in the last minute ("*ændret i sidste øjeblik*"), *SKS* K4, p. 323.

The translators of *The Concept of Anxiety*, Reidar Thomte and Albert B. Anderson, are right in assuming that "the dedication to Møller is in itself evidence that *The Concept of Anxiety* is not strictly pseudonymous. By means of the pseudonym and the abbreviations in the dedication, Kierkegaard concealed the privacy of his relationship to Møller."[41] The abbreviations they refer to, however, are not in the dedication; they are presumably thinking of the fact that, in the draft, the initials "*S. K.*" originally appeared under the epigraph or motto.[42] In the fair copy, the title page, too, was changed. The pseudonym "*Vigilius Haufniensis*" was inserted, but the lower part of the page was cut off; presumably, it contained Kierkegaard's name and—since the book is an "academic" work—his academic degree.[43] This is evident from the draft of the title, "*Concerning / The Concept of Anxiety* / A Plain and Simple Psychological Deliberation on the Dogmatic Issue of *Hereditary Sin* / by / S. Kierkegaard / M. A."[44] The fact that the pseudonym was introduced so late might explain the peculiarity that the book as a pseudonymous work contains a dedication.[45]

Regarding the question as to why among all his books Kierkegaard chose to dedicate *The Concept of Anxiety* to Møller there have been different theories of which I will briefly mention a few. Gregor Malantschuk suggests that this book is a realization of Møller's idea of a new world-view or "*Verdensanskuelse*" as developed in his treatise on the proofs of immortality.[46] There is also a strongly hypothetical explanation offered by Frithiof Brandt which has nothing to do with immortality in a strict sense, but rather with youth and the borders of mortality. In his *Den unge Søren Kierkegaard*, he develops a complex theory, based on ideas of P.A. Heiberg and Eduard Geismar, of a very personal background for *The Concept of Anxiety*: he argues that Møller helped Kierkegaard through his crisis in 1836. Brandt concludes: "The explanation for the dedication then becomes obvious. *The Concept of Anxiety* is

---

41 *CA*, Notes, p. 223.

42 *SKS* 4, 310 / *CA*, 3.

43 Cf. *SKS* K4, p. 323.

44 *Pap.* V B 42 / *CA*, Supplement, p. 177; cf. *SKS* K4, p. 310 (MS 1.1, fol. 1r): "*Om / Begrebet Angest.* / En slet og ret psychologisk Overveielse i Retning af / det dogmatiske Problem om *Arvesynden.* / af S. Kierkegaard / M: A:"

45 In a journal entry JJ:227, *SKS* 18, 213 / *KJN* 2, 196, Kierkegaard refers to the pseudonym in this way: "The sketch of an observer [Vigilius, i.e., watchman] that I dashed off in *The Concept of Anxiety* will probably upset some people. However, it does belong there and is a kind of watermark in the work. In general I always stand in a poetic relationship to my works, which is why I am a pseudonym. Simultaneously with the book's development of some theme, the corresponding individuality is drawn. Now Vigilius Hauf. draws several, but in the book I have dashed off a sketch of him in addition." This "sketch" is found in Caput II, cf. *SKS* 4, 359–60 / *CA*, 54–6.

46 On this, see further Gregor Malantschuk, "Søren Kierkegaard og Poul M. Møller," *Kierkegaardiana*, vol. 3, 1959, pp. 7–20 (reprinted in *Frihed og Eksistens. Studier i Søren Kierkegaards tænkning*, ed. by Niels Jørgen Cappelørn and Paul Müller, Copenhagen: C.A. Reitzel 1980, pp. 101–13). On the treatise on immortality see below Section III, G. Møller's concept of "alternating [*vexlende*] affectation" could have inspired Kierkegaard's concept of the demonic in *The Concept of Anxiety.* Generally, this book is what Møller would have called a "moral description of nature" which is the expression he uses of his theory of affectation; on this, see below Section III, F.

dedicated to the memory of the man who, with his powerful trumpet, tore Kierkegaard out of his reprobate period, and who in the subsequent difficult time was the desired object of his feelings."[47] This seems to be the upshot of Brandt's thorough analysis of the elements of the dedication. As a mighty apocalyptic father figure, a trumpet of awakening, Møller made the young Kierkegaard come to his senses, concentrate, and later reflect upon sin. Although there is no evidence whatsoever for how this awakening came about, there must be some truth to it. In the *Journal EE*, in an entry from July 28, 1839, Kierkegaard compares his "youthful excesses" with the sirens' song.[48] Møller, by contrast, led him in the right direction.[49]

Møller is described as "the enthusiasm of my youth." What does this mean? The other elements of the draft also indicate a very strong personal relation and confidentiality: "the desired object of my feelings; the confidant of my beginnings; my lost friend; my sadly missed reader." As to the last point, Møller as a reader of Kierkegaard, this must be rather limited. *From the Papers of One Still Living*, originally planned for J.L. Heiberg's *Perseus*, was published as a book on September 7, 1838, half a year after Møller's death on March 13, and Kierkegaard had possibly begun writing it in late April.[50] However, as regards the polemical articles published earlier in Heiberg's *Kjøbenhavns flyvende Post*, we can be certain that Møller read at least one of these, which is evident from the *Journal AA*:

> Something I can say which, when I noted this down, I would like to have added but omitted from a laughable vanity—since I was afraid of being regarded as vain by doing so—is what a hit the articles, as well as the address, made. I will simply refer to the fact that a paper (*Statsvennen* no. 3) came out which, under the impression that the first article (the one in no. 76) was by Heiberg, said: "that he had written many witty things but never anything as witty, and that old Rahbek, were he still alive, would have said it

---

47 Frithiof Brandt, *Den unge Søren Kierkegaard. En række nye bidrag*, Copenhagen: Levin & Munksgaard 1929, p. 415. (The chapter on Kierkegaard and Møller is on pp. 336–446.)

48 *SKS* 18, 52, EE:148 / *KJN* 2, 47.

49 To mention a more dubious theory, H.P. Rohde points to the fact that in the preface of *The Concept of Anxiety* (*SKS* 4, 314 / *CA*, 8) Vigilius Haufniensis says that he would gladly assume the name "Christen Madsen"; this figure appears as a character in J.C. Hostrup's (1818–92) play *Gjenboerne* [*The Opposite Neighbors*], which premiered at the Court Theater on February 20, 1844, in which both Kierkegaard and Møller are made the object of laughter, Kierkegaard as the caricature "Søren Kirk" (in the book version changed to Søren Torp), and Møller with the character Lieutenant Buddinge making rough fun of the poem "Joy over Denmark." To include this poem in the dedication to *The Concept of Anxiety* appearing in the same year would then be a natural way for Kierkegaard to show his reverence and make up for this sacrilege toward the late Møller. See H.P. Rohde, "Poul Møller," in *Kierkegaard's Teachers*, ed. by Niels Thulstrup and Marie Mikulová Thulstrup, Copenhagen: C.A. Reitzel 1982 (*Bibliotheca Kierkegaardiana*, vol. 10), pp. 89–109, especially pp. 102–8; cf. also H.P. Rohde, "Poul Møller og Søren Kierkegaard," in *Afhandlingerne på originalsproget i 'Søren Kierkegaard—Tænkning og sprogbrug i Danmark.' Festskrift i anledning af prof. dr. Masaru Otanis 70 års fødselsdag*, Copenhagen: privately printed [1983], pp. 1–22 (separate pagination; the original book appeared in Japanese in 1982).

50 Johnny Kondrup, "Tekstredegørelse til *Af en endnu Levendes Papirer*," *SKS* K1, p. 70.

> was priceless." Then that P. Møller, also thinking it was by Heiberg, ran off after him in the street to thank him for it, "since it was the best there had been since *Flyveposten* became political,"—but didn't catch up with him and met E. Boesen, who told him it was by me.[51]

Undoubtedly, this great recognition meant a lot to Kierkegaard, as is also clear from the beginning of the entry itself.[52] The "first article" referred to is "The Morning Observations in *Kjøbenhavnsposten* No. 43," in *Kjøbenhavns flyvende Post*, no. 76, on February 18, 1836, columns 1–6, signed with the pseudonym "B."[53] There is no evidence that Møller read the other articles, "On the Polemic of *Fædrelandet*" and "To Mr. Orla Lehmann,"[54] nor can we know whether he heard Kierkegaard's successful paper given to the Student Association on November 28, 1835, "Our Journalistic Literature: A Study from Nature in Noonday Light."[55]

What is essential here, however, is not whether Møller read one or more of these perhaps insignificant articles, but the fact that he was well acquainted with the young Kierkegaard's *polemical* nature, not only from reading him but primarily from speaking to him. An entry from January 20, 1847 in the *Journal NB* concludes with the observation,

> Humanly speaking, from now on I must be said not only to be running without a clear goal before me but going headlong toward certain ruin—trusting in God, precisely. This is the victory. This is how I understood life when I was ten years old, therefore, the prodigious polemic in my soul; this is how I understood it when I was twenty-five years old; so, too, now when I am thirty-four. This is why Poul Møller called me the most thoroughly polemical of men.[56]

---

51 *SKS* 17, 37.5–17, AA:19 / *KJN* 1, 31.

52 As would later be the case with his preferral of "how" for "what" in a more complex manner, the style at this point in Kierkegaard's early authorship seemed more important than, or at least veiled, the contents, and this *obscuritas* was quite "Latin" with an extremely intricate syntax, which is also obvious in his first books, *From the Papers of One Still Living* and *The Concept of Irony*. Møller's enthusiasm in regard to the undergraduate article in question might appear a bit strange, but he must have sensed the genius that was behind the form, and recognized that it was well-written and humorous. Kierkegaard's article was also recognized by Heiberg, the editor, who wrote to him: "Once more, my thanks for your essay! It pleased me even more on this new reading." *B&A*, vol. 1, p. 40 / *LD*, Letter 6, p. 51.

53 "Kjøbenhavnspostens Morgenbetragtninger i Nr. 43"; cf. *Bl.art.*, 3–8 / *EPW*, 6–11.

54 "Om Fædrelandets Polemik," in two parts, *Kjøbenhavns flyvende Post*, no. 82, columns 1–8, and no. 83, columns 1–4, March 12 and 15, 1836, was also signed with the pseudonym "B."; "Til Hr. Orla Lehmann," *Kjøbenhavns flyvende Post*, no. 87, columns 1–8, April 10, 1836, was signed "S. Kierkegaard." Cf. *Bl.art.*, 9–31 / *EPW*, 12–34. It is not documented whether Møller read Kierkegaard's earliest article, "Ogsaa et Forsvar for Qvindens høie Anlæg" ["Another Defense of Woman's Great Abilities"], signed "A.," in *Kjøbenhavns flyvende Post*, no. 34, December 17, 1834, columns 4–6; cf. *EPW*, 3–5.

55 "Vor Journal-Litteratur. Studium efter Naturen i Middagsbelysning"; *Pap.* I B 2 / *JP* 5, 5116; *EPW*, 35–52.

56 *SKS* 20, 83.17–23, NB:107 / *JP* 5, 5961.

This observation is repeated in an important entry from the summer of 1854 to be found in the *Journal NB30*, where one reads the following retrospective remark about Kierkegaard's life-long predisposition for opposition, a quality or vice which at this late point in his life is unfolded even more strongly in service of "the extraordinary." But he remembers well how originally this predisposition of his was often rebuked by Møller—and afterwards by Sibbern as Møller's "successor" in relation to the young man:

The Extraordinary

> In one sense it is dreadful, almost fatal, to be the extraordinary under the polemical conditions of the Christian extraordinary. Not merely that it is the greatest possible, an almost superhuman, strain, but this relation of opposition to others and the dimensions of that opposition are almost fatal to all merely human sympathy.
>
> That is why I have steadfastly—sympathy is my passion—desired only to point out the extraordinary.
>
> I recall the words of the dying Poul Møller, which he often said to me while he lived and which, if I remember correctly, he enjoined Sibbern to repeat to me (and in addition the words: Tell the little Kierkegaard that he should be careful not to lay out too big a plan of study, for that has been very detrimental to me): You are so thoroughly polemical that it is quite appalling.
>
> Although I am so thoroughly polemical and was so even in my youth, still Christianity is almost too polemical for me.[57]

Too big a plan of study, says Møller, has been very detrimental to himself, and he wanted young Kierkegaard to be spared that. Without doubt Møller is primarily thinking of his personal torments with reading Hegel and others, carefully instructed by his friend Sibbern, and the large amount of knowledge he had to obtain when becoming (and being) a professor of philosophy. That was hard work. As to young Kierkegaard, the word "study" rather refers to the very broad reading he undertook in those years: his preferred aesthetic studies of Romanticism, Faust, Don Juan, Ahasverus, and all kinds of things. For instance, in the journal entry BB:51 he uses the wording, "my studies" ("*mit Studium*") in reference to his grand project, and in Not3:16 "my project" ("*mit Forehavende*") refers to the same.[58] Henning Fenger says of this whole phenomenon: "There is no purpose in trying to enforce some plan or model upon such an incoherent body of material. It shows us Kierkegaard in his *Sturm und Drang* period, when his genius seeks to find itself in many different ways, via religion, philosophy, aesthetics, and, last but not least, literature."[59]

---

57 *SKS* 25, 459–61, NB30:93 (with facsimile of the journal page on p. 460) / *JP* 6, 6888.

58 Cf. Finn Gredal Jensen and Kim Ravn, "Tekstredegørelse til journalen BB," *SKS* K17, p. 139, note ("Critical Account of the Text," in *KJN* 1, p. 365, note 2), and Niels W. Bruun and Finn Gredal Jensen, "Tekstredegørelse til notesbog 3," *SKS* K19, pp. 145–6.

59 Henning Fenger, *Kierkegaard, the Myths and Their Origins: Studies in the Kierkegaardian Papers and Letters*, trans. by George C. Schoolfield, New Haven and London: Yale University Press 1980, p. 87 (in Danish, *Kierkegaard-Myter og Kierkegaard-Kilder. 9 kildekritiske studier i de Kierkegaardske papirer, breve og aktstykker*, Odense:

In the margin Kierkegaard added a short clarification. As far as his purported polemical nature is concerned, he is not sure exactly whether those were Møller's words to Sibbern to repeat to him—"You are so thoroughly polemical that it is quite appalling"—but he is certain that this is what Møller "always said to me while he was living," and it seems, from this and many other sources, that later Sibbern had taken over the role as intellectual counselor:

> I cannot remember exactly whether the dying P. M. enjoined Sibbern to say those words to me (You are so thoroughly polemical, etc.), and I am almost inclined to doubt it. But I remember very well the other words he asked S. to tell me the last time he spoke with him before his death. As for the first words (You are so thoroughly polemical), that is what he always said to me while he was living, and S., too, has used them against me several times afterward.[60]

In any case, an extremely talkative Kierkegaard is what Sibbern later experienced.[61] Sibbern's daughter, Augusta Sibbern Møller, wrote to Harald Høffding: "One of my childhood memories is of walking and holding my father's hand while S. Kierkegaard was on the other side of us, talking eagerly and stopping now and again in order to speak clearly about things that were important to him."[62] Sibbern himself writes that Kierkegaard "was continually preoccupied with himself...with what stirred inside him and with expressing it [*udgyde det*]."[63] Whether this was much different with the relationship to Møller is not easy to say. The fact that Kierkegaard might have talked most does not imply, however, that his genius was the greater of the two but, rather, that they were equal but their roles quite different: Møller as a Socratic deliverer of

---

Odense Universitetsforlag 1976 (*Odense University Studies in Scandinavian Languages and Literatures*, vol. 7), p. 75).

60 *SKS* 25, 461, NB30:93.a / *JP* 6, 6889. It is not known when was the last time Sibbern spoke to Møller. A short letter without date is preserved; it reads as follows: "Dear Sibbern! / Have the inconvenience of coming here to me if your affairs allow it, but stay here only five minutes. My blood is somewhat agitated: I cannot speak for very long at a time. / Your / P. Møller." Quoted from Sejer Kühle, *Søren Kierkegaard. Barndom og ungdom*, Copenhagen: Aschehoug 1950, p. 108, with a note referring to the MS at the Royal Library (Additamenta 274, 8°). The letter is found neither in Borup's edition nor in *Breve til og fra Sibbern*, vols. 1–2, ed. by C.L.N. Mynster, Copenhagen: Gyldendal 1866.

61 Cf. Kühle, *Søren Kierkegaard. Barndom og ungdom*, pp. 109–10.

62 Letter from Augusta Sibbern Møller to Harald Høffding, dated December 7, 1912, Royal Library, NKS 4620, 4°, translation from *Encounters with Kierkegaard*, p. 19; cf. Jens Himmelstrup, *Sibbern. En Monografi*, Copenhagen: J.H. Schultz 1934, p. 262.

63 Letter from Sibbern to H.P. Barfod, cf. *Encounters with Kierkegaard*, pp. 216–17. As to the role of Sibbern after Møller's death, one should also have in mind Kierkegaard's letter from Berlin to Sibbern from December 15, 1841. In this one reads: "Even now when I cannot personally ascertain it for myself every day, I have never doubted that you would maintain some of that interest with which you have always honored me, especially after Poul Møller's death." *B&A*, vol. 1, p. 83 / *LD*, Letter 55, p. 106; *Breve til og fra Sibbern*, vol. 1, p. 196. It appears from the same letter that Sibbern, in vain, had advised Kierkegaard to translate *The Concept of Irony* into German; at Kierkegaard's defense of his thesis a few months earlier, on September 29, 1841, Sibbern was *opponens ex officio.*

ideas that seemed perhaps to be there already, and Kierkegaard developing them further.

There is only a single testimony from Kierkegaard about a conversation he had with Møller, namely, an entry from July 6, 1837 found in the *Journal DD* (cited in full in Section III, C below). This "most interesting conversation," which took place on the evening of June 30, concerned irony and humor; according to Kierkegaard's account, Møller compared Christ's relation to his disciples to the love with which "Socrates encompassed his disciples."[64] For this reason, when speaking of Møller, "the desired object of my feelings," it seems natural to Kierkegaard in the next place to think of Socrates, the deliverer, and of the nature of the love for his "disciples."[65]

From Møller himself there are no traces left of his disciple Søren Kierkegaard. Nevertheless, a dialectical relation to a "Kierkegaard" is evidenced by a letter from 1837 to his younger brother Hans Ulrik Møller (1796–1862), with whom he discusses the treatise on immortality, which had just been published. In this letter one reads the following: "I especially enjoy debates in conversation when people can tolerate being refuted by the utmost ability and also in haste understand what the interlocutor means. Thus, I once last year carried on a long dispute with the Kierkegaard whom you know, and it interested me greatly."[66] The Kierkegaard referred to here, however, is most probably not Søren Kierkegaard, as assumed by some,[67] but his brother Peter Christian Kierkegaard, with whom Møller was also well acquainted.[68]

---

64 *SKS* 17, 225, DD:18 / *KJN* 1, 216.

65 One should also pay attention to the journal entry JJ:54 from 1843 with the heading "*My Judgment on* 'Either/Or' ": "There was a young man, happily gifted as an Alcibiades. He lost his way in the world. In his need he looked about for a Socrates but among his contemporaries found none. He then begged the gods to transform him himself into one. But look! He who had been so proud of being an Alcibiades became so humbled and mortified by the grace of the gods that when he received just what could make him proud, he felt humbler than all." *SKS* 18, 157, JJ:54 / *KJN* 2, 146. Take note of the wording, that "among his contemporaries [he] found none"—since Møller, his Socrates, was dead and therefore no longer among the contemporaries. Georg Brandes, Kierkegaard's first biographer, discusses this entry, however in a context where he does not mention Møller, cf. *Søren Kierkegaard. En kritisk Fremstilling i Grundrids*, Copenhagen: Gyldendal 1877, pp. 44–5.

66 Borup, Letter no. 151; first published by Morten Borup in "F.C. Olsens brevarkiv på Det kgl. Bibliotek," *Fund og Forskning i Det Kongelige Biblioteks Samlinger*, vol. 3, 1956, pp. 103–16; pp. 113–14.

67 Cf. Uffe Andreasen, *Poul Møller og romantismen – den filosofiske idealisme i Poul Møllers senere forfatterskab*, Copenhagen: Gyldendal 1973, p. 86; cf. pp. 67–8.

68 I agree with Morten Borup, who, in his explanatory note to the letter, says that "Poul Møller knew both Peter Christian and Søren K., but in all probability the person in question here is the elder of the two, P.C.K." *Poul Møller og hans Familie i Breve*, vol. 3, p. 120. In an earlier letter, in a very friendly tone, dated October 17, 1830, in which Møller answers P.C. Kierkegaard's inquiry about his position in Christiania (Oslo), which Peter Christian considered applying for (Borup, Letter no. 116), Møller thanks him for his doctoral dissertation on the concept of the lie (which Møller later reviewed thoroughly in the *Maanedsskrift for Litteratur*) and also "for the friendly disposition with which you have preserved the memory of our social life in Copenhagen."

From second-hand sources, however, it is obvious that Søren Kierkegaard and Møller spent much time together, and for a person like Kierkegaard, time is synonymous with words. In his Møller biography, Vilhelm Andersen writes that the two were often seen in the street together, and also in other public places.[69] We read in the poet Henrik Hertz's (1797/8–1870) diary of June 4, 1836, "Evening at Hb's [Heibergs] and said farewell before their trip to Paris. Kierkegaard, Poul Møller, etc., were there."[70] This does not say much, indicating only that they visited the same circles. Likewise, even the fact that in Møller's last years 1836–38 he lived at Nytorv, the same square where Kierkegaard lived in his paternal home until September 1, 1837, does not provide evidence that the two saw each other privately.[71]

More important is the testimony of Hans Brøchner (1820–75). In his "Recollections of Søren Kierkegaard," he tells of an episode that is very typical in the way it depicts Møller's personality. It took place on October 25, 1836 during the doctoral defence of F.O. Lange, at which occasion Møller and Madvig were the opponents.[72] Brøchner recalls what Kierkegaard told him:

---

69 Vilhelm Andersen, *Poul Møller*, p. 394. As is often the case, Andersen does not list any sources to support this statement.

70 *Encounters with Kierkegaard*, p. 218, with reference on p. 328 to the MS.

71 Møller lived at Nytorv no. 117, today no. 17; cf. Tudvad, *Kierkegaards København*, p. 29. Kierkegaard lived in his paternal home, Nytorv no. 2, apparently until September 1, 1837, when he moved to Løvstræde, cf. Tudvad, *Kierkegaards København*, p. 31.—For the sake of completeness I will mention a further testimony: in the summer of 1851 Kierkegaard received a letter from Petronella Ross, the former housekeeper of Rasmus Møller; she writes, "I know your brother in Sjælland, and in my youth I was a friend of his first wife, Marie B.; for many years I lived in the late Bishop Møller's house (you knew Poul Martin, his dear son). Bishop Boisen's wife placed me there." *B&A*, vol. 1, p. 304 / *LD*, Letter 280, p. 387. However, it is not very useful information that Kierkegaard "knew" Møller, since this can imply almost anything.

72 Frederik Olaus Lange (1798–1862) had been one of Kierkegaard's teachers at the Borgerdyd School, and Møller knew him personally. In his library Kierkegaard had Lange's dissertation, *De casuum universis causis et rationibus commentatio grammatica*, Copenhagen: Popp 1836 (*ASKB* 610), and Lange is obviously the Greek teacher portrayed in *Johannes Climacus, or De omnibus dubitandum est*, *Pap.* IV B 1, p. 107 / *JC*, 121. At an earlier time, Møller had reviewed Lange's Greek grammar, *Det græske Sprogs Grammatik til Skolernes Brug*, in *Dansk Litteratur-Tidende*, 1827, no. 5, pp. 65–74 (not reprinted in the *Posthumous Writings*). Møller and his wife saw the Langes until 1833 when they moved to Vordingborg where Lange taught at the grammar school, while working on his dissertation, and 1841 became its headmaster; when the school was closed in 1846 they moved back to Copenhagen, and he was employed at the university. From one of Lange's sons, the art historian Julius Lange (1838–96) we have the amusing evidence, in a letter to Vilhelm Andersen, dated December 27, 1894, that Møller reminded his mother, Louise Paludan-Müller (1803–62), of "a butcher" and that she did not approve of his perpetual habit of constantly giving a psychological analysis of his surroundings ("*hans idelige...Hang til psykologiske Iagttagelser over sine Omgivelser*"). Julius Lange presumes that her own nature possibly did not please Møller either, since "with her strong and bold ability of reflection she was occupied with everything in heaven and on earth and everything in between, and significantly surpassed the limits for femininity which he—somewhat narrow-minded [*bornert*]—had wanted to define….It is more provable that he must have hurt her somewhat with his critical statements about the first works of her younger

> S. K. often mentioned Poul Møller, and always with the most profound devotion. Far more than his writings, it was Poul Møller's character that had made an impression on him. He regretted that the time would soon come when—after the vivid memory of his personality had faded, and judgments of him would be based on his works—his significance would no longer be understood. He once told me of an amusing little episode regarding P. Møller. He [Møller] was to speak as an *ex officio* opponent at a doctoral defense and had jotted down his remarks on several loose sheets that were placed in the dissertation. He introduced each objection with the phrase *graviter vituperandum est* ["it must be seriously criticized (that)"], but as soon as *Præses* had given an answer to his objection, he said good-naturedly, *Concedo* ["I yield, I give way to (your argument, your words)"], and moved on to the next objection. After a rather short opposition he closed by expressing his sincere regrets that the time allotted him did not allow him to continue this interesting conversation. As he left he passed S. K., who was standing in the audience, and said in an undertone to him: "Shall we go down to Pleisch?" This was the tearoom he usually frequented. While he was acting as an opponent all his loose sheets of paper had fallen out of the book at once and had floated down onto the floor. Seeing the great man crawling around picking up the scattered sheets had contributed not a little to lifting the mood in the auditorium.[73]

As already mentioned, Møller's first biographer was his friend F.C. Olsen, the co-editor of the *Posthumous Writings*, who included his "Life of Poul Martin Møller" in the edition. Kierkegaard, of course, read this when it appeared in 1843, and this gave him something to complain about which he expresses at the end of a large footnote in the *Concluding Unscientific Postscript* in 1846. It has to do with Møller and Hegelianism—namely, that towards the end of his life he was moving away from it (or rather from Heiberg), on the threshold of something entirely new, and was only stopped by an early death—but towards the end of the note it also gives Kierkegaard the opportunity to deliver a very personal description of Møller's character. Characteristically, he writes earlier in the same note of Hegel, and of how Socrates, the master, might have had something to laugh at, just as Møller so often would do:

> Perhaps this note is an appropriate place for something I have to complain about. In *Poul Møllers Levnet* there is only a single reference that conveys any idea of how he in his last years viewed Hegel. In this restraint, the distinguished editor has presumably permitted himself to be guided by partiality and reverence for the deceased, by an uneasy regard for what certain people would say, what a speculative and almost Hegelian public might judge. Nevertheless, precisely when he thought he was acting out of partiality for the deceased, the editor perhaps damaged the impression of him. It is more noteworthy than many an aphorism included in the printed collection, and just as noteworthy as many a youthful episode preserved by the careful and tasteful biographer in his lovely and noble presentation, that P. M., when everything here at home was Hegelian, judged quite differently, that for some time he first spoke of Hegel almost with indignation, until his

---

and much beloved brother Frederik Paludan-Müller [1809–76]." *Breve fra Julius Lange,* ed. by P. Købke, Copenhagen: Det nordiske Forlag 1902, pp. 315–16.

73 *Encounters with Kierkegaard*, p. 241; Kirmmse's translation (slightly modified) is from the MS at the Royal Library, Copenhagen, Additamenta 415 d, 4°. Brøchner's memoirs were written in December 1871 and January 1872 and first published posthumously in 1877 (Brøchner died in 1875) in *Det nittende Aarhundrede*, vol. 5, pp. 337–74.

> wholesome, humorous nature made him smile, especially at Hegelianism, or, to recall P. M. even more clearly, made him laugh at it heartily. Who has been enamoured of P. M. and forgotten his humor; who has admired him and forgotten his wholesomeness; who has known him and forgotten his laughter, which did one good even when it was not entirely clear what he was laughing at, because his absentmindedness occasionally left one perplexed.[74]

The "single reference" that Kierkegaard mentions, but avoids spelling out, is found in a context where Olsen explains Møller's relation to Hegel with respect to metaphysics. Møller was moving away from Hegel, Olsen says, "and followed with lively interest the opposition against this philosopher and his followers; indeed he even became irritated, albeit only with the latter."[75] In a footnote he exemplifies the last point:

> Here is an example of one of these surprising, indeed, almost frightening judgments that one could now and then hear from him. A friend once asked him to try to see if he could give, in a brief sentence, the key point in the Hegelian philosophy. Poul Møller was silent for a moment, rubbing his chin as he lay on his sofa, and then said: "Yes—Hegel is really mad. He suffers from a monomania and believes that the Concept can extend itself like this"—here he made some wide motions with his hands and said no more.[76]

The verdict "mad" might have been too strong for Kierkegaard, after all, so he left it out, but nevertheless considered including it in another *Postscript* context. In Part Two, Section Two, Chapter 3, § 2, there is a passage that reads thus: "If the system otherwise lacks an ethics, it is in return completely moral with the aid of the category of the *spurious* infinity, and so exaggeratedly moral that it uses it even in logic."[77] This replaced the following reflection on skepticism and madness, which is found in the draft:

> Self-reflection was a skepticism; it is overcome in pure thinking. But pure thinking is a still more extreme skepticism. Despite all the inwardness of self-reflection, it nevertheless could not forget its relation to actuality in the sense of actuality, its relation to the *an sich* that pursues it. Pure thinking, however, is positive through having taken the whole matter imaginatively into a sphere where there is no relation to actuality at all. Pure thinking does not even dream that it is skepticism—but this itself is the most extreme skepticism. If, without pressing the comparison, one were to compare skepticism with insanity, a person who has a notion of being insane and whose life goes on amid this conflict is less mad, however, than one who jubilatingly triumphs as the cleverest of all.[78]

On a level with the word "insanity" Kierkegaard has inserted the following in the margin, "And Danish readers will not forget that Poul Møller regarded Hegel as

---

74 *SKS* 7, 40.31–36 and 41.6–18 / *CUP1*, 34, note.

75 F.C. Olsen (in *ES1*), p. 109.

76 Ibid., footnote. (Partly translated in *CUP2*, p. 189, note 40, but the Hongs render "*Begrebet kan udbrede sig saadan*" wrongly as "the concept as such can extend itself.")

77 *SKS* 7, 309.20–23 / *CUP1*, 338.

78 MS 10.1 in *SKS* K7, pp. 19–20, *Pap.* VI B 54,19 / *CUP2*, 75.

mad."[79] However, none of this was in the final edition of the *Postscript*, in which only the above-mentioned hint in the footnote appeared.

Poul Martin Møller died on March 13, 1838, not yet 44 years of age. In the month of April, Kierkegaard wrote in his journal, "*Poul Møller is dead.*"[80] The brevity of this report—although underlined in the manuscript—may be surprising, but before this he writes of his sorrow, "Again such a long time has passed in which I have been unable to collect myself for the least thing—I must now make another little shot at it."[81] Apparently, he lets his sad thoughts fly away and escape in a romantic and highly poetic marginal note, dated April 1: "This morning I saw half a score of wild geese fly away in the crisp cool air; they were right overhead at first and then farther and farther away, and at last they separated into two flocks, like two eyebrows over my eyes, which now gazed into the land of poetry."[82] The land of poetry is the land of departure from this world, the anticipation of eternal life, which is also reflected in another entry, possibly from the same day: "When the world grows dark for a real Christian in his hour of death, it is because the sunlight of eternal bliss shines too strongly in his eyes."[83] At least, the land of poetry was strongly unfolded when on the evening of April 1 the young Kierkegaard heard an actor recite Møller's poem "Joy over Denmark" and "was so strangely moved by the words: Do you remember the far-traveled man? yes, now he has traveled far—but I for one shall certainly remember him."[84]

III. References to the Writings of P.M. Møller

Søren Kierkegaard of course bought the first edition of Møller's *Posthumous Writings*, 1839–43 (*ASKB* 1574–1576). Strangely, he does not seem to refer or allude anywhere to Møller's main fictional prose work, the unfinished novel *Adventures of a Danish Student*, parts of which Møller read aloud in the Student Association in 1824; the fragments were first published in 1843 in volume 3 of the *Posthumous Writings*.[85] However, it goes without saying that he must have known the novel soon after its appearance, just as he knew all the other texts that became publicly accessible in this edition.[86] This is clear from his reaction when, for her 13th birthday, he gives his

79 Ibid. / *CUP2*, 76.

80 *SKS* 17, 252, DD:96 / *KJN* 1, 243.

81 Ibid.

82 *SKS* 17, 252, DD:96.a / *KJN* 1, 243.

83 *SKS* 17, 252, DD:99 / *KJN* 1, 243.

84 *SKS* 17, 253, DD:101 / *KJN* 1, 244. I will return to "Joy over Denmark" below in Section III, B.

85 A characteristic comparison of two important publications in 1843, volume 3 of Møller's *Posthumous Writings* and Kierkegaard's *Either/Or*, is found in a letter from Signe Læssøe to Hans Christian Andersen, dated April 7, 1843: "Another book has appeared here—you see, we are productive, even though it is not the literary season—which is just as lovable as *Either/Or* is unlovable, namely, the third part of Poul Møller's *Works*." Cf. *Encounters with Kierkegaard*, p. 58.

86 There is no evidence that Møller recited the novel in public any later than 1824. He might have done so privately, but in all probability Kierkegaard did not know it before its appearance in print in 1843.

niece Henriette Lund (1829–1909) a copy of Møller's writings and learns that she had already amused herself with the story of "the frizzy Frits."[87]

It is important to emphasize that, as noted, one can sense that Kierkegaard had read and was familiar with any text by Møller he had access to, but naturally he could not and did not find it worthwhile to mention or reflect upon each and every one of them. This should be remembered when in the following I will discuss the references and allusions to Møller's writings that are found in Kierkegaard. Note well that what is found in Møller's posthumous writings is sometimes treated by Kierkegaard at a point before they appeared, for example, irony, but in such cases one has to consider the possible influence from oral statements, that is, what Kierkegaard can remember from their conversations.

In the following treatment of Kierkegaard's use, or possible use, of Møller's writings, the order will as far as possible be chronological. I will begin with the early satire on Grundtvig, "Draft of a Letter from Heaven" (Section III, A). As an author, Møller's primary means of communication in his earlier years was poetry; I will discuss the two poems to which Kierkegaard pays special attention (Section III, B). Then I will turn to philosophy, first Møller's fragments on irony and nihilism, including his preoccupation with the figure of Ahasverus (Section III, C). The

---

[87] In her memoirs, issued after her death in 1909, one reads that "the trusty Anders [Kierkegaard's servant] returned with a new letter with quite different contents, accompanied by a package that on closer inspection turned out to be Poul Møller's posthumous works. Just a few days earlier, at my cousins', I had got hold of a book that quickly reduced me to the same state as the man of whom the Spanish king had remarked, 'Either he must be mad, or he is reading Don Quixote!' The story of 'the frizzy Frits' had sent me reeling with laughter and hilarity. Now that I had that treasure in my hands as my own rightful property, I was so overwhelmed with ecstasy that I could hardly find words with which to express this to Uncle Søren. Even so, he was somewhat disappointed that chance had placed a book by Poul Møller in my hands before he had managed to do so." Henriette Lund, *Erindringer fra Hjemmet*, Copenhagen: Gyldendal 1909, pp. 119–20; trans. by Kirmmse in *Encounters with Kierkegaard*, p. 166. When she reports that it was on her twelfth birthday (*Encounters*, p. 165), that is, 1842 (she was born in 1829), she must have been in error, since *Adventures of a Danish Student* was contained in volume 3 of *ES1* of 1843.—I will also mention a curiosity, of which Kierkegaard would not have known the existence: Henrik Hertz's planned but never completed satirical play, *The Fifth Monarchy*, in which Kierkegaard was meant to be a character, see *Encounters with Kierkegaard*, pp. 221–4. *Inter alia*, Kierkegaard would seduce a girl in a tent, "but under one of his assumed authorial pseudonyms," and would say "that he is not responsible for what has been done by that firm." (*Encounters*, p. 222). As far as Møller is concerned, the character Kierkegaard "can also refer to the scene in Poul Møller's *Adventures of a Danish Student*, in which thirteen-year-old Frits on his romantic escapade wants to earn his bread with his violin, and at a poor peasant farm is addressed prosaically and gruffly by a peasant woman. Now the latter would have been made even coarser by the author of *A Story of Everyday Life* and left at that. He would have sought an antithesis in *two* personalities: Frits with poetic, free tendencies—and the peasant woman, sunk *utterly* in the prose of life. But how different is the poetic, radiant clarity that P. Møller sheds upon the situation! The woman discovers that she was Frits' wet nurse, and now the full strength of the poetry of her existence (which every existence has) breaks through from beneath her hard crust. Frits is far from being *utterly* absorbed into the poetic" (*Encounters*, p. 224).

review of Thomasine Gyllembourg's novel *The Extremes* will then be regarded from Kierkegaard's point of view (Section III, D). The essay "On Telling Children Fairy Tales" will be compared to Kierkegaard's treatment of the subject (Section III, E). Møller's characteristic feature as a fragmentary writer is unfolded especially in his scattered thoughts, a few of which Kierkegaard refers to, including an aphorism on the concept of affectation, which was very central to Møller's philosophy (Section III, F). Eventually, I will discuss Kierkegaard's references to Møller's philosophical treatise of 1837, "Thoughts on the Possibility of Proofs of Human Immortality, with Regard to the Latest Literature on the Subject," considered in the light of the contemporary debate on the immortality of the soul (Section III, G).

A. "Draft of a Letter from Heaven"

The small satirical piece, "Draft of a Letter from Heaven, in Accordance with Grundtvig's New Historical Taste, Found by Poul Møller," was published in *Nyeste Skilderie af Kjøbenhavn* on December 19, 1818.[88] It is a parody of N.F.S. Grundtvig's peculiar style in his various contributions to the literary controversy between Adam Oehlenschläger (1779–1850) and Jens Baggesen, in which Møller participated as a member of "*Tylvten*" ("the twelve"), a group of admiring students who came to the support of the laureate poet Oehlenschläger when Baggesen attacked him.[89] The twelve students challenged Baggesen publicly by asking him to defend his criticism and comportment in Latin (several of the students, including Møller, were accomplished Latinists and debated in Latin at the reading club called "Lyceum").[90]

---

88 "Forsøg til et Himmelbrev i Grundtvigs nye, historiske Smag, fundet af Poul Møller," *Nyeste Skilderie af Kjøbenhavn,* vol. 15, ed. by S. Soldin, Copenhagen 1818, no. 101, columns 1696–9; reprinted in *ES1*, vol. 1, pp. 195–200.

89 On this controversy, see, for instance, in detail Kristian Arentzen, *Baggesen og Oehlenschläger. Literaturhistorisk Studie*, vols. 1–8, Copenhagen: Otto B. Wroblewsky 1870–78, especially vol. 7. The aesthetic dichotomy Grundtvig–Oehlenschläger is also touched upon by Møller later in his life when in one of his scattered thoughts he writes the following: "There is a way of producing ideas which is characteristic for the Christian age and which is completely in conflict with ancient taste. The author is not brooding over the idea for a classic work until it is ripe in him and does not constantly apply criticism and work for the production of the idea. By contrast, his entire life constitutes a continuous literary activity; his concepts are developed during the work so that his entire life as an author should only be regarded as a public course of thought, a kind of uninterrupted confession. One sees his striving in all the stages which he has run through, as a continuous stream, but one sees no finished products with independent organic life. Jean Paul's literary *Nachlass* is a fitting example of this unlimited productivity, which has its principle only in the author himself, and, to take an example which is closer to hand, Grundtvig. Goethe's and Oehlenschläger's works, by contrast, have value as classic art." *ES1*, vol. 3, p. 233.

90 The challenge to Baggesen was afterwards printed, of course in Latin, in the newspaper *Dagen*, no. 236, October 3, 1818, signed by "the twelve": A.G. Rudelbach, P.M. Møller, C. Hauch, C. Lütken, C. Flor, W.R. Dichman, N.B. Krarup, H. Brøchner (a theologian not identical with the philosopher, who was not born yet!), G.A. Dichman, L. Abrahams, N.C. Møhl, and L.C. Westergaard. More contributions, from both sides, to the controversy followed throughout the rest of the year in *Dagen*.

Møller played a leading role in this by bringing the challenge to Baggesen, and when Baggesen declined this, made the threat that three-quarters of the students living in the dormitory Regensen (where Møller also lived at times) would come and hiss off stage a piece which was written by one of Baggesen's friends, namely, Heiberg's *The Prophecy of Tycho Brahe*.[91] Møller wrote a splendid parody, "On the Smallness of Jens," of a Baggesen poem from 1786, "There was a Time when I was very Small."[92] And he wrote the "Draft of a Letter from Heaven," to which Kierkegaard presumably alludes when in the *Journal DD* in an entry dated July 13, 1837 he uses the formulation, "made in our study."[93] Similarly, he concludes a letter to Regine Olsen in the autumn of 1840 and mentions Møller: "In testimony whereof I permit my *eternalized* P. Møller to stand as witness. / Granted in *our* study."[94]

Although the equivalent Latin wording "*e museo meo/nostro (dabam/datum)*" is a common letter formula, it is obvious that here Kierkegaard had Møller's parody in mind, which he undoubtedly had enjoyed reading; as is well known, his own verdict of Grundtvig might be summarized in the closing words of the journal entry NB23:67 from 1851: "I think Grundtvig is nonsense."[95] It is in the same entry that Kierkegaard writes ironically of the mighty prophet Grundtvig stepping in and out of the State Church and defining it by his very presence along with his followers, "for as Poul Møller once pointed out that history and Grundtvig and Grundtvig and history are one, so also must Denmark and Grundtvig, and Grundtvig and Denmark be one—provided it is historical truth with the 'listening thousands.' "[96] This is also an allusion to Møller's "Draft of a Letter from Heaven," in which, for instance, the following closing words are ascribed to Grundtvig: "At the end I will cry out once more, Woe! indeed, three times, woe to the puppies who have opposed the chronicle and me, and me and the chronicle and the chronicle and me. Amen."[97]

In the *Concluding Unscientific Postscript*, Part One, Chapter 1, "The Historical Point of View," we read at the end of § 2, "The Church," a few statements about the

---

91 Cf. Hauch, *Minder om min Barndom og min Ungdom*, pp. 317–19. In his memoirs Hauch, who was one of "the twelve," does not say directly that the play in question was in fact J.L. Heiberg's *Tycho Brahes Spaadom* [*The Prophecy of Tycho Brahe*], which premiered on the King's birthday on January 28, 1819. His reasons for not mentioning this might be that as an old man he had forgotten it, or rather that the fact was perhaps somewhat too delicate or unflattering for an ideal portrait of Møller, since Heiberg was a close friend.

92 P.M. Møller, "Om Jenses Lidenhed," in *Hermes. Nytaarsgave for 1820*, ed. by Carsten Hauch et al., Copenhagen 1819, pp. 1–2; reprinted in *ES1*, vol. 1, pp. 17–18. In his memoirs Hauch writes of this poem: "The perfect execution and the virtuosity with which he turned Baggesen's own words against him have kept this poem above the river of oblivion, in which so much has sunk of what was written at the time with cleverness and power." Hauch, *Minder om min Barndom og min Ungdom*, p. 299.

93 "Resolution of July 13, 1837, made in our study [*givet paa vort Studerekammer*] at 6 o'clock in the evening." *SKS* 17, 229, DD:28.a / *KJN* 1, 221.

94 *B&A*, vol. 1, p. 50. / *LD*, Letter 17, p. 63.

95 "*Mig synes G. er et Vrøvl.*" *SKS* 24, 242.36, NB23:67.

96 *SKS* 24, 242.19–22, NB23:67.

97 *ES1*, vol. 1, p. 200. On Grundtvig's "chronicles" ("*Krøniker*"), see, for instance, the explanatory note to *SKS* 7, 52.4.

figures J.C. Lindberg and Grundtvig: the former "has a good head on his shoulders; however, what in truth all this is that is said about Grundtvig is highly dubious, that he is a seer, bard, skald, prophet, with an almost matchless [*mageløst*] outlook upon world history and with one eye for the profound."[98] This is quite modest when compared to the manuscripts, from which it appears that Kierkegaard planned to include a longer reflection on the whole Grundtvig phenomenon, in which he also touches upon his style and Møller's "Draft of a Letter from Heaven." This piece, however, was not included in the book. Among other things, we read in the draft that

> Grundtvig is his own caricature, so absolute is he. His absoluteness changes into parody just as does his style, which requires only a careful reproduction, be it polemical, as formerly by Poul Møller, or admiring, as by Siegfried Ley. Then it is parody, so that as a consequence friend and foe, by doing the same, produce the same effect. Indeed, even if these innocent and insignificant remarks should move Pastor Grundtvig and prompt him to put on his Asa-strength, I am certain that he will slay me so absolutely that I will come out of it completely unscathed....[99]

B. *"The Old Lover" and "Joy over Denmark"*

Kierkegaard only refers to Møller as a translator of the *Odyssey* very indirectly as "the admirer of Homer" in the dedication to *The Concept of Anxiety*.[100] As regards Møller's original poetry, we find several references in the writings, but only to some specific lines in two of his poems.[101]

---

98 *SKS* 7, 52.2–5 / *CUP1*, 46. Jacob Christian Lindberg (1797–1857) was an energetic supporter of Grundtvig.

99 *Pap.* VI B 29, p. 104 / *CUP2*, 18–19. The "Siegfried Ley" referred to here is Christian Sigfred Ley (1806–74), who never finished his studies in theology but worked as a tutor; he was a strong supporter of Grundtvig. Still in the fair copy we find the following version, which, however, was deleted: "His [i.e., Grundtvig's] life is so parodically patterned that one needs only to tell it quite simply and thereby write a satire, just as his style is so parodical that just a careful reproduction of it, for example, polemically by Møller in the past, or admiringly by Siegfried Ley, is a parody. This is a good demonstration that it is in itself parodical, that friend and foe by doing the same thing produce the same effect." *Pap.* VI B 98,17 / *CUP2*, 30–1.

100 Kierkegaard knew Møller's *Odyssey* translations at least after their reprint in 1839 in *ES1*, vol. 1. In the *Auctioneer's Sales Record* none of the original prints (1816, 1822, 1825) of the translations appear. There is no evidence that Kierkegaard knew of the existence of Møller's translation of the pseudo-Homeric *Batrachomyomachia*, "The Battle of Frogs and Mice," presumably written in the winter of 1816–17, but first printed in 1848 in *ES2* (not in *ASKB*), vol. 1, pp. 254–61, where Thaarup had completed the fragment; but that Kierkegaard has known the Greek poem, is clear from *Either/Or* in the passage where he compares Homer to Mozart's *Don Giovanni* and declares that Homer does not deserve immortality for the *Batrachomyomachia*; *SKS* 2, 58.13–20 / *EO1*, 50. On the "Odyssean" line of "Joy over Denmark," see below.

101 Apart from the two poems I will treat below, there is also an indirect reference to Møller's poem or small dramatic scene "Hans and Trine" (*ES1*, vol. 1, pp. 83–8, by the editors included in the suite of poems "Scenes in Rosenborg Garden"; originally, the poem, which was written on the journey to China, was published in *Gefion. Nytaarsgave for 1826*, ed. by Elisa

When visiting Constantin Constantius, the young man in love in *Repetition* (1843) despairingly keeps on repeating the sixth stanza of "The Old Lover" ("Den gamle Elsker"):

> Just as lovers frequently resort to the poet's words to let the sweet distress of love break forth in blissful joy, so also did he. As he paced back and forth, he repeated again and again a verse from Poul Møller:
>
> Then comes a dream from my youth
> To my easy-chair.
> A heartfelt longing comes over me for you,
> Thou sun of women![102]
>
> His eyes filled with tears, he threw himself down on a chair, he repeated the verse again and again. I was shaken by the scene.[103]

Beyer, Copenhagen: Forlagt af Udgiverinden 1825, pp. 154–9). However, this is only in the sense that J.L. Heiberg, in his vaudeville *Aprilsnarrene eller Intriguen i Skolen* [*April Fools, or Intrigue at School*], Copenhagen: F.A.C. Printzlau 1826 (which premiered on April 22, 1826), heavily refers to it, not only by using the same characters and names of the two young lovers, but also by letting Trine, in Scene 23, refer to Møller's work as a "*Pasquil*" about them that has recently appeared and has also been performed, with Hans' part recited by the actor C.N. Rosenkilde (1786–1861). It is this spoiled illusion Kierkegaard refers to when, in *Pap.* I A 23 / *JP* 2, 2241, he quotes Trine's words freely, "There is an old man, named Rosenkilde, who copies you." Heiberg's original wording here is, "Would you believe that the actor who played you [sc. Hans] is really an old geezer, named Rosenkilde; he was decked out in such a way that he looked like a schoolboy." Heiberg, *Aprilsnarrene*, p. 79 (*Poetiske Skrifter*, vols. 1–11, Copenhagen: C.A. Reitzel 1862, vol. 6, pp. 92–3). The declamation took place at the Court Theater in February 1826, and Rosenkilde, at the time, was an aged man, at least compared to Trine, who was performed by the 13-year-old Johanne Luise Pätges, the later Mrs. Heiberg (1812–90).

102 In Danish the quoted lines of the love poem read: "*Da kommer en Drøm fra min Ungdomsvaar / Til min Lænestol, / Efter dig jeg en inderlig Længsel faaer, / Du Qvindernes Sol.*" *ES1*, vol. 1, p. 12. The poem was originally published in *Iris. En Samling af Poesie og Prosa*, ed. by Carsten Hauch, Copenhagen: B. Brünnich 1819, pp. 112–5.

103 *SKS* 4, 13.21–31 / *R*, 135–6. (Translation of the stanza slightly modified.) Constantin Constantius was not able to forget this incident: "With the reader's permission, I shall once again consider the time he came to my room intoxicated with recollection, when his heart continuously *ging ihm über* in that verse by Poul Møller, when he confided that he had to deny himself lest he spend the whole day with the girl he loved. He repeated the same verse that evening when we parted. It will never be possible for me to forget that verse; indeed, I can more easily obliterate the recollection of his disappearance than the memory of that moment, just as the news of his disappearance disturbed me far less than his situation that first day." *SKS* 4, 23.2–11 / *R*, 146. Vilhelm Andersen, in his *Poul Møller*, p. 91, writes the following on the poem: "There are certainly many more young men than the young man in Kierkegaard's *Repetition* who have taken refuge in these verses by Poul Møller in order to let the sweet anxiety of love break out in blessed joy."

This poem, first published in 1819, but written in 1817 or early in 1818, when Møller was a private tutor at the estate Espe, seems to reflect his earlier, unhappy love for Margrethe Bloch. Since now the "old fixed idea" had "dissolved into a wholly pure elegy," as he wrote in a letter to his friend B.S. Ingemann,[104] he imagines himself as an old man who recalls his love of youth, but with a longing, so that once more he goes to seek her. In the present context, the unhappy old lover might well be regarded as Kierkegaard's own *alter ego*—although this is a somewhat strange identification—since a few years before, he had used the very same stanza in several letters to his fiancée, Regine Olsen. In one of these letters he compares her to the sun: "Whenever you catch a breath of that heliotrope at home, which is still fresh, please think of me, for truly my mind and my soul are turned toward this sun, and a heartfelt longing comes over me for you, thou sun of women."[105] Another letter begins with the wording, "My Regine! Am I dreaming, or 'comes a dream from my youth to my easy-chair?' "[106] Miss Olsen presumably knew the poem already and understood these quotations or allusions perfectly well.[107]

Also in *Notebook 7* from 1840–41, written in the same period as his engagement, Kierkegaard quoted the very same "dreamy" stanza and interpreted it in the following way:

> Dreaming rises to ever higher powers; thus a dream within a dream-existence (whereby it becomes transformed into a kind of actuality) has an infinitely volatilizing effect. With what infinite ardor a youth can read the words of P. Møller's poem: "The Old Lover":
>
> Then comes a dream from my youth
> To my easy-chair.
> A heartfelt longing comes over me for you,
> Thou sun of women!
>
> Here the dream is in the second power for the youth; he first of all dreams that he is old in order to suck in through the funnel of a whole life the most aromatic moment of his earliest youth.[108]

The second Møller poem that Kierkegaard refers to is "Joy over Denmark" ("Glæde over Danmark"), with the well-known opening line "*Rosen blusser alt i Danas Have*"

---

104 Borup, Letter no. 13.

105 *B&A*, vol. 1, pp. 51–2 / *LD*, Letter 19, p. 66. (Translation slightly modified.) See also Letter 18, in which he quotes the words "*fra min Ungdomsvaar.*"

106 *B&A*, vol. 1, p. 57 / *LD*, Letter 27, p. 72. (Translation slightly modified.)

107 Maybe Kierkegaard read it aloud to her, or she had read it herself. Niels Thulstrup claims in *B&A*, vol. 2, p. 33, commentary on p. 50.5, that Kierkegaard gave her the first volume (1839) of *ES1* ("S.K. gave Regine Olsen what had appeared of the first edition of P.M.'s *Posthumous Writings*"), but this has not been able to be verified; it seems that Thulstrup confused Regine Olsen with Henriette Lund, who tells that Uncle Søren gave her Møller's posthumous works (cf. *Encounters with Kierkegaard*, p. 166, and see the introduction to the present Section III); however, that took place not in 1839, but in 1843 after the appearance of *ES1*, vol. 3.

108 *SKS* 19, 208–9, Not7:9 / *JP* 1, 804. (Translation of the stanza slightly modified.)

("The rose already flushes in Dana's garden"). In the dedication to *The Concept of Anxiety*, the elements "Denmark's joy in 'Joy over Denmark,' though 'widely traveled' always 'remembered in the Danish summer' " allude to this poem.[109] It was written during the long voyage—or one might say Odyssey—to China (1819–21) and expresses the longing for Denmark and the friends at home.[110] The third stanza goes like this:

> Friends of mine in the Danish summer!
> Do you remember the widely traveled man
> Who, afar from Dana's fairest flowers,
> Where the southern wind beats the sail,
> Wanders from his dearest native land?[111]

The poem was first published back in 1823 and appeared in the first volume of the *Posthumous Writings* in 1839; but Kierkegaard knew it long before 1839 and had a very emotional relation to it, since its "Odyssean" line reminded him of Møller, who travelled in his youth—and had now left for good.[112] This is evident from the fact that he quotes this line in the *Journal DD* in the entry from April 2, 1838, written not long after Møller's death on March 13 of the same year. The actor N.P. Nielsen had recited the poem at the Royal Theater, which, as already mentioned, made a thorough impression.[113]

C. Fragments on Irony and Nihilism

Møller had a humorous nature, which Kierkegaard himself witnesses in the footnote quoted above from the *Postscript* where he says, "who has known him and forgotten his laughter, which did one good even when it was not entirely clear

---

[109] *SKS* 4, 311.4–6 / *CA*, 5. On the dedication see above in Section II.

[110] According to Vilhelm Andersen, it was written in Manila in July 1820; *Poul Møller*, p. 107.

[111] My translation. The Danish wording is the following: "*Mine Venner i den danske Sommer! / Mindes I den vidtforreiste Mand? / Som, saa langt fra Danas favre Blommer, / Her hvor Sydens Blæst paa Seilet trommer, / Flakker fra sit elskte Fødeland.*" *ES1*, vol. 1, p. 47. The poem was first published in K.L. Rahbek's *Tilskuerne. Et Ugeskrift*, no. 47, 1823, pp. 374–6.

[112] The allusion to the opening lines of Homer's *Odyssey* is obvious. However, Møller does not use the word "*vidtforreist*" (far-traveled, widely traveled) in his translation of Homer's *Odyssey*, where he renders the opening lines thus: "*Manden besynge du, Musa! den heel forslagne, der flakked' / Vidt om Land, da forstyrret han havde det hellige Troja.*"

[113] *SKS* 17, 253, DD:101 / *KJN* 1, 244. The actor Nicolai Peter Nielsen (1795–1860) recited the poem at the Royal Theater on the evening of April 1, 1838. It seems that it was part of his repertoire; he had recited it several times following a debut performance of it at the Theater on January 1, 1830. Kierkegaard later saw the actor couple N.P. Nielsen and Anna Nielsen (1803–56); cf. the extant draft of a letter from 1847, *B&A*, vol. 1, pp. 189–90 / *LD*, Letter 170, pp. 238–40.

what he was laughing at...."[114] Moreover, although in his writings he preferred direct communication—in the review of *The Extremes* he mentions the ideal that the author, "without tiring the reader with all too many pranks and beating around the bush [*Spilopper og Omsvøb*], should keep to the matter at hand and say straightforwardly what he has to say"[115]—Møller was himself an ironist in the Socratic sense (not in the romantic).[116] One might even say that his sparse or fragmented authorship is a negation, or in itself a manifestation of irony. In his writings, he treats the subject of irony non-ironically. If one wishes to explore this, one should pay special attention to the fragment "On the Concept of Irony," to a number of scattered thoughts, and to passages in the review of *The Extremes*.[117]

Møller's fragment "On the Concept of Irony," with the same title that Kierkegaard would later use for his dissertation, was meant for the *Maanedsskrift for Litteratur* as a response to Eggert Christopher Tryde's (1781–1860) review of Sibbern's book on aesthetics.[118] However, the study was never finished—what was completed, was an introduction concerning moral irony; Møller stopped short of treating poetical irony—and the fragment was not published until 1848 in the second edition of the *Posthumous Writings*, volume 3.[119] Tryde, in his review, had included some concluding remarks on irony in the context of German Romanticism. According to Tryde, the Romantics' *modus vivendi* points in the wrong direction away from God and toward the ideal in nature.[120]

---

114 *SKS* 7, 41 / *CUP1*, 34, note. Møller's humor is visible in many different contexts, and also on a smaller scale; as an example of this take the funny rhyme just quoted from "The Old Lover," *Lænestol/Sol* (easy-chair, sun); a more "serious" poet would hardly do this.

115 P.M. Møller, "Nye Fortællinger af Forfatteren til en Hverdagshistorie. Udgivne af *Johan Ludvig Heiberg*. Andet Bind: Extremerne. Kjøbenhavn. Paa Universitets-Boghandler *Reitzels* Forlag, trykt hos *J. D. Qvist*, Bog- og Nodetrykker. 1835. 223 S. 8," *Maanedsskrift for Litteratur*, vol. 15, Copenhagen: C.A. Reitzel 1836, pp. 135–63; p. 139; *ES1*, vol. 2, p. 131.

116 Cf. Vilhelm Andersen, *Poul Møller*, p. 396.

117 On this review see below Section III, D.

118 E.C. Tryde, "Om Poesie og Konst i Almindelighed, med Hensyn til alle Arter deraf, dog især Digte-, Maler-, Billedhugger- og Skuespiller-Konst; eller: Foredrag over almindelig Æsthetik og Poetik. Af *Dr. Frederik Christian Sibbern*, Professor i Philosophie. Første Deel. Kbhvn. 1834. 392 Sider. Forfatterens Forlag," *Maanedsskrift for Litteratur*, vol. 13, Copenhagen: C.A. Reitzel 1835, pp. 177–202; particularly pp. 200–2.

119 P.M. Møller, "Om Begrebet Ironie," in *ES2*, vol. 3, pp. 152–8.

120 Tryde, "Om Poesie og Konst i Almindelighed," pp. 200–1: "It seems characteristic in the more recent poetic products that one does not so much aim to emphasize that inward ideal, dwelling in the objects...in and for itself, as to know every form, every figure and shape of life, that is, the bad and the good, the base and the elevated, as a necessary condition for the ideal appearing and coming into existence." The negative, or immoral, character trait of such poetry is that it "seeks to detect something interesting even in what is the most mistaken, and that even when it feels happy about the objects, yet does not hold back a certain mockery about them, indeed, often openly mocks its own products as such." In a similar vein, Sibbern, in his *On Poetry and Art*, wrote of poetical irony "that in order to portray things with true objectivity, the poet must look to life and its figures, as to a game that he regards with a merely contemplative pleasure, without any mixture of sympathetic participation, indeed, with a contemplative smile, that is, with a mood like that which is found in real irony." F.C. Sibbern,

In his fragment, Møller never reaches a broader discussion of this profound nihilism of German romantic irony, but he only introduces the concept "such as it has formed itself in the aesthetic linguistic usage of the present."[121] As seen also in his review of *The Extremes*, his method is that of the licentiate in *Adventures of a Danish Student* (who studies mineralogy in order to identify the correct whetstone with which to sharpen his knife in order to get a good pen), beginning, so to speak, *ab ovo*, in this case with Greek morality, that is, the old dichotomy between desire and reason, and the question as to what should be the right means to moral good. Moral idealism was identical to subjectivity, as when later Fichte posited "the highest authority [*Fuldmagt*] in the individual's consciousness, so that he [the individual], according to his own moral conviction in the individual case, should decide what his duty was....The subjective conviction is then regarded as the highest since the will of the individual is identified with the moral law."[122] The necessary consequence of this autonomy is moral *nihilism*, Møller says, and then points out the universal danger this subjectivity implies, exemplified by Friedrich Schlegel's notorious novel *Lucinde* (1799), which was seen, also in Kierkegaard's dissertation, as a gospel of irony and in which one character says, "Nothing could be more insane...than the moralists reproaching you with being egoistic. They're completely wrong: for what god can possibly deserve a man's respect who isn't his own god?"[123] Pleasure and vegetation then become life proper and the true religion. Møller refers to Hegel who sees irony as identical with this empty attitude to life and defines it as "subjectivity which knows itself as the highest."[124] According to Hegel, it is one of "the moral forms of evil."[125] The romantic ironist distances himself from an empty world and

---

Om Poesie og Konst i Almindelighed, med Hensyn til alle Arter deraf, dog især Digte-, Maler-, Billedhugger- og Skuespillerkonst; eller: Foredrag over almindelig Æsthetik og Poetik, Part One, Copenhagen: Paa Forfatterens Forlag 1834, pp. 387–8; quoted by Tryde, p. 200.

121 *ES2*, vol. 3, p. 152.

122 Ibid., p. 154.

123 Trans. by Peter Firchow (*Friedrich Schlegel's* Lucinde *and the Fragments*, translated with an introduction by Peter Firchow, Minneapolis: University of Minneapolis Press 1971, p. 67). The passage, which is translated into Danish and quoted in *ES2*, vol. 3, p. 155, is found in the section "Idylle über den Müssiggang" ["An Idyll of Idleness"]. Schlegel's *Lucinde* is also treated in Møller's review of *The Extremes*, and of course in Kierkegaard's *The Concept of Irony*.

124 *ES2*, vol. 3, p. 155. In his *Elements of the Philosophy of Right,* § 140, Hegel uses this formulation in his account of Solger's use of irony in relation to that of Schlegel, who extended the meaning of the expression to include "that subjectivity which knows itself as supreme" (*"jene sich selbst als das Höchste wissende Subjektivität")*. G.W.F. Hegel, *Elements of the Philosophy of Right,* ed. by Allen W. Wood, trans. by H.B. Nisbet, Cambridge: Cambridge University Press 1991, p. 170, note; *Sämtliche Werke. Jubiläumsausgabe in 20 Bänden*, ed. by Hermann Glockner, Stuttgart: Friedrich Frommann Verlag 1928–41, vol. 7, p. 217, note.

125 *ES2*, vol. 3, p. 158. This view of romantic irony as moral evil and emptiness is developed by Hegel in *Elements of the Philosophy of Right*, § 140, *in fine*, where one reads: "In this shape, subjectivity is not only *empty* of all ethical *content* in the way of rights, duties, and laws, and is accordingly evil (evil, in fact, in an inherently wholly universal kind); in addition, its form is that of *subjective* emptiness, in that it knows itself as this emptiness of all

feels superior to it.[126] The concept of irony in the German romantic movement is an "aberration," which has only had a weak echo in Danish literature, but is met also in everyday conversation as a wish for a "thinking free from prejudice" and generally as a "mistrust of the concept of morality."[127] Not to be confused with irony, but akin to it, is sentimentality, which is a resignation towards outer life and a yielding to "an inward life, which is filled with longings and presentiments of what is to come, as the only things that are real."[128]

These thoughts were, of course, familiar to Kierkegaard, and were later treated thoroughly in his dissertation. Møller also treated irony and nihilism in a number of scattered thoughts and in his review of *The Extremes*, to which I will soon return. But as mentioned already, Møller's unfinished study on irony did not appear in the first edition of the *Posthumous Writings*, which Kierkegaard owned; so in any case he could not have read it prior to the publication of his own dissertation on irony. What is more important in regard to Kierkegaard is their personal relation and Møller's "ironic" or Socratic impact in their colloquies: the fact that the ideas sketched above and the contents of Møller's study were very probably imparted to Kierkegaard in one or more of their conversations. Unfortunately, there is not much evidence concerning this, but, as already pointed out above in Section II, we learn from the journal entry DD:18 of their "most interesting conversation" on the evening of June 30, 1837 concerning irony and humor. This journal entry is important evidence that they discussed the matter thoroughly (and presumably did so more than once). I will allow myself to quote the main text of the entry *in extenso*, since the distinctions made in it concerning irony and humor might be considered Kierkegaard's summary of their discussion and, of course, also his own further reflections on the subject:

> Irony can no doubt also produce a certain calm (which may then correspond to the peace that follows a humorous development), which, however, is a long way from being Christian reconciliation (brothers in Christ, where every other distinction vanishes

---

content and, in this knowledge, knows *itself* as the absolute." *Elements of the Philosophy of Right*, p. 182; *Jubiläumsausgabe*, vol. 7, p. 219.

126 Cf. K. Brian Soderquist, *The Isolated Self: Truth and Untruth in Søren Kierkegaard's* On the Concept of Irony, Copenhagen: C.A. Reitzel 2007 (*Danish Golden Age Studies*, vol. 1), p. 152. Soderquist writes, *inter alia*, "At first glance, Møller's characterization of romanticism seems to be in keeping with his own sensitivity to the rights of the subjective, inner life. But importantly, for Møller the kind of subjectivity celebrated by the romantics is closed off not only from bourgeois culture but also from a deeper moral order through which the self is formed and cultivated."

127 *ES2*, vol. 3, p. 156.

128 Ibid., p. 157. In his review of *The Extremes* (see below Section III, D), Møller has the following to say on the relationship between sentimental poetry and irony: "Irony was actually a natural continuation of this [of sentimental poetry], since sentimentality, when treated as art and driven to the extreme, is very closely related to heartlessness. A dim consciousness of this relation is presumably the reason for the fact that the sentimentalist who makes a career of his sympathy more than other people loathes an ironist. Since his [the ironist's] behavior appears to him as a parody of his own nature, he becomes agitated by the sight of it, just like a horse at the sight of a camel." *Maanedsskrift for Litteratur*, vol. 15, 1836, pp. 147–8; *ES1*, vol. 2, pp. 140–1.

absolutely, a nothing in proportion to being brothers in Christ—yet didn't Christ make distinctions? Didn't he love John more than the others (Poul Møller in a most interesting conversation on the evening of June 30)? It can produce a certain love, the kind which e.g. Socrates encompassed his disciples (spiritual pederasty, as Hamann says), but it is still egoistic, because he stood as their deliverer, expanded their anxious expressions and views in his higher consciousness, in his point of view [*Overskuen*]; yet the movement's diameter is not as great as the humorist (heaven—hell—the Christian must have scorned everything—the ironist's highest polemical movement is *nil admirari*). Irony is *egoistic* (it combats the bourgeois mentality yet persists with it, even though in the individual it ascends into the air like a songbird, jettisoning its ballast little by little, thus running the risk of ending with an "egoistic to-hell-with-it"; for irony has not yet slain itself by seeing itself, since the individual sees himself in irony's light). Humor is *lyrical* (it is the deepest earnestness about life—profound poetry, which cannot form itself as such and therefore crystallizes in the most baroque forms—it is the hemorrhoid *non fluens*—the *molimina* of the higher life).

The whole attitude in the Greek nature (Harmony—the beautiful) was such that, even if the individual disengaged himself and the battle began, the fight still bore the stamp of arising from this harmonious view of life, and so it soon came to an end without having gone full circle (Socrates). But then a view of life appeared which taught that all nature was corrupt (the deepest polemic, the widest stretch of wings); but nature took revenge—and now I get humor in the individual and irony in nature, and they meet, in that *humor* wants to be a fool in the world and the *irony* in the world assumes that is what they [men of humor] really are.

Some will say that irony and humor are basically the same, with only a difference of degree. I will answer with Paul, where he talks of the relationship of Christianity to Judaism: everything is new in Christ. [2 Cor 5:17]

The Christian humorist is like a plant only the root of which is visible, whose bloom unfolds to a loftier sun.[129]

That Kierkegaard returned to this entry later is evident from several marginal additions. One of these is dated October 30, 1837 and reads: "Socrates has a purely awakening effect—midwife that he was—not delivering except in an inauthentic sense."[130] In all of this it is impossible to say where Møller stops and Kierkegaard begins. Given these facts, all we can say is that Møller may well, Socratically, have delivered the subject for Kierkegaard's dissertation—but only the subject.[131] Therefore, it would not be completely fair to agree with Vilhelm Andersen that in Kierkegaard's treatment of romantic irony "one can certainly say without

---

129 *SKS* 17, 225–6, DD:18 / *KJN* 1, 216–17. On the reference to Hamann, see *SKS* K17, 396 / *KJN* 1, 503 (explanatory note to 216.35).

130 *SKS* 17, 225, DD:18.a / *KJN* 1, 216.

131 I will refrain here from discussing the contents of Kierkegaard's *The Concept of Irony*, since this has been done often enough. I refer especially to the thorough treatment by Soderquist, *The Isolated Self*. It is also worth noting that there seems to have been an ongoing debate about irony, which was discussed by many at the time, also in Copenhagen, cf. Soderquist, p. 151, note 3, with a reference to F.C. Olsen's footnote (*ES2*, vol. 3, p. 152), which, however, only says that Møller's essay "deserves publication more so because it makes a contribution to the history of the concept in question [irony] in our literature."

exaggeration that while the hand is Kierkegaard's, the spirit is Poul Møller's."[132] Møller was an inspiration; but he was no "ghostwriter." In the same context, Vilhelm Andersen pays attention to Møller's portrait of Socrates, including his irony, in the lectures on ancient philosophy (which were not published before 1842 in volume 2 of the *Posthumous Writings*, but which Kierkegaard might have followed), and he states that a possible inspiration from this source is not important, seeing that it was Kierkegaard's knowledge of Møller's personality that inspired him to his own somewhat peculiar understanding of Socrates' personality.[133]

A poet at heart, Møller did not limit himself to mere abstractions on the subject of nihilism; he went further than that in terms of fiction and used the figure of Ahasverus, the Wandering Jew (or, in German and Danish, "the Eternal Jew"). Such a personification or embodiment was indeed also a personal project, a way out of a crisis or mood of (aesthetic) despair that Møller himself had been stuck in; this involved the doubts about the values of human life, truth, science, and arts, presumably because of his liberating himself from Hegelianism.[134] This negation or nihilism was to be expressed and treated through the figure of Ahasverus, and the purpose would be to cure this negative or pessimistic view of life by exposing it and demonstrating its inadequacy—just as Kierkegaard would do later with the aesthete A in *Either/Or*.[135] Vilhelm Andersen suggests that if this great poetic plan

---

132 Vilhelm Andersen, *Poul Møller*, pp. 396–7.

133 Ibid., p. 396. Compare to this, for instance, H.P. Rohde's emphasis on a passage of Møller regarding the relation between Plato and Xenophon as sources to the historical Socrates: "Plato may be the main source, but he is not historically trustworthy in his description of Socrates' philosophy: he was himself a more speculative thinker and gives an idealized picture of him in his dialogues. Xenophon certainly is a far more reliable reporter, but his lack of philosophical talent may often have led him to misunderstand Socrates. They must therefore somehow be suited for correcting each other, and what they have in common may belong to the historical Socrates." (Rohde's trans. of *ES1*, vol. 2, p. 365, in H.P. Rohde, "Poul Møller," in *Kierkegaard's Teachers*, ed. by Niels Thulstrup and Marie Mikulová Thulstrup, Copenhagen: C.A. Reitzel 1982 (*Bibliotheca Kierkegaardiana*, vol. 10), pp. 89–109; p. 95). Rohde then compares this passage to the third Latin thesis of *The Concept of Irony*: "*Si quis comparationem inter Xenophontem et Platonem instituerit, inveniet, alterum nimium de Socrate detraxisse, alterum nimium eum evexisse, neutrum verum invenisse.*" *SKS* 1, 65.6–8. One cannot exclude that in such a case Møller's considerations might have been an inspiration, but the idea that the truth is in between, however, is not original.

134 Jørgen K. Bukdahl sees it as a general critical analysis of pantheism, cf. "Poul Martin Møllers opgør med 'nihilismen,' " *Dansk Udsyn*, vol. 45, ed. by Richard Andersen et al., Vejen: Askov Højskole 1965, pp. 266–90; p. 267. An apparent symptom of a personal crisis or spleen is the *Wanderlust* motif also present in Ahasverus, but clearer in the younger Møller: his Oriental travel, the presence of the motif in *Adventures of a Danish Student*, etc., cf. Vilhelm Andersen, *Poul Møller*, pp. 228ff.

135 The Kierkegaardian theme of seduction was another feature of Ahasverus; two of the fragments read: "His eyes look like a window-pane which is lightly bedewed by a young girl's sighs of love" (*ES1*, vol. 3, p. 329) and "His experiments with women whom he makes fall in love with him. He then surrounds himself with a lustre which stands at his service, since his cleverness is infinite, and he sees how true love can arise from it." (Not in *ES*, but in Vilhelm Andersen's selection, *Udvalgte Skrifter af Poul Møller*, vol. 2, p. 129).

from Møller's last years had ever been realized, it would probably have been of the same importance to his production as *Faust* had been to Goethe's.[136] It is not clear what form Møller's *Ahasverus* might have taken, maybe a diary, a monologue or dramatic scenes. Most of the small number of fragments or sketches that were meant for *Ahasverus* were first published in 1843 in volume 3 of the *Posthumous Writings*.[137] Here Kierkegaard read them when they appeared. It is not possible to say whether Møller had told Kierkegaard of his reflections on Ahasverus in one of their conversations, but Kierkegaard's own preoccupation with the subject is well documented in *Notebook 2* and *Journal BB*.[138] These entries date from 1835–37, that is, long before Møller's fragments were published posthumously. Yet, of course, the old legend of the Wandering Jew had earlier inspired numerous poets, especially in Romanticism, and this was also the case with the young Kierkegaard when, as a part of his personal project, he researched the three "representative" figures Don Juan, Faust, and the Wandering Jew. The subject of Ahasverus was also treated by other Danish poets at the time, for instance, by B.S. Ingemann in *Leaves from the Notebook of Jerusalem's Shoemaker* in 1833,[139] and later by J.C. Hostrup in *The Opposite Neighbors* in 1844,[140] and by Hans Christian Andersen in 1848.[141] Whereas Don Juan and Faust are discussed in various contexts by Kierkegaard, perhaps

136 Vilhelm Andersen, *Poul Møller*, p. 341. By the way, Kierkegaard notes in the entry BB:18, *SKS 17,* 107 / *KJN* 1, 100, that in Goethe's *Aus meinem Leben* (*Dichtung und Wahrheit*) "there is also his idea for an adaption of the Wandering Jew, in which, true to form, he tries to motivate the Wandering Jew's despair."

137 *ES1*, vol. 3, pp. 328–30. In the MS (Collinske Samling 365, 4°, Royal Library, Copenhagen) the sketches appear as two small series of scattered thoughts, but all marked with "*Ahasverus*."

138 *SKS* 19, 94–6, Not2:9–14 / *JP* 5, 5109–12; *JP* 5, 5087; *JP* 2, 2206, and BB:16–20, *SKS* 17, 107–9 / *KJN* 1, 100–2. On Kierkegaard's preoccupation with Ahasverus see, for instance, Knud Jensenius, *Nogle Kierkegaardstudier. "De tre store Ideer"*, Copenhagen: Nyt Nordisk Forlag Arnold Busck 1932, pp. 64ff. Troels-Lund, in *Bakkehus og Solbjerg*, vol. 3, p. 204, says, "There can hardly be any doubt that these different statements [by Møller on Ahasverus] were discussed orally by them and had an influence on Søren Kierkegaard."

139 B.S. Ingemann, *Blade af Jerusalems Skomagers Lommebog*, Copenhagen: Andreas Seidelin 1833 (*ASKB* 1571). This is one of the books listed by Kierkegaard in BB:16, *SKS* 17, 107.15–16 / *KJN* 1, 100.15–16.

140 J.C. Hostrup, *Gjenboerne. Vaudeville-Komedie*, Copenhagen: F. H. Eibe 1847 (the songs were published separately earlier, *Sange af Gjenboerne*, Copenhagen [1844]); first performed on February 20, 1844 at the Court Theater. In *The Opposite Neighbors* the Wandering Jew lends the student Klint the shoes of fortune which make him invisible. Another figure in this play is Søren Kirk, a caricature of Kierkegaard, see above Section II, note 49.

141 Hans Christian Andersen's dramatical poem *Ahasverus* (Copenhagen: C.A. Reitzel 1848) was published on December 16, 1847. Andersen had earlier used Ahasverus in his *Fodreise fra Holmens Canal til Østpynten af Amager i Aarene 1828 og 1829* (1829). The shoes of fortune, known from Hostrup's *The Opposite Neighbors*, also appear in Andersen's fairy tale "The Galoshes of Fortune" (1838), in which, by the way, we meet a parrot, probably alias Kierkegaard, insistingly repeating the words, "Come now, let us be men!" For a brief overview of Ahasverus and generally of Jewish elements in Danish literature, see Mogens Brøndsted's introduction to his anthology, *Ahasverus. Jødiske elementer i dansk litteratur*,

surprisingly he never developed to any larger extent the Wandering Jew, which was seen as the archetypal representative of the present age.[142] It is true that Ahasverus occurs now and then, but only in passing. A shorter passage in "The Unhappiest One" in *Either/Or* is especially worth noting:

> Indeed, if there were a human being who could not die, if what the legend tells of the Wandering Jew is true, why should we have scruples about pronouncing him the unhappiest one? Then why the grave was empty could be explained—namely, to indicate that the unhappiest one was the person who could not die, who could not slip down into a grave. That would settle the matter, the answer would be easy, for the unhappiest one of all would be the person who could not die, the happy one the person who could. Happy is the one who died in old age; happier is the one who died in youth; happiest is the one who died at birth; happiest of all the one who was never born. But this is not the way it is; death is the common fate of all human beings, and inasmuch as the unhappiest one has not been found, he must be sought within these confines.[143]

The idea of Frithiof Brandt is that the inspiration was the other way around, that is, from Kierkegaard to Møller, and that Møller's Ahasverus is a portrait of the young Kierkegaard.[144] This theory, however, is highly speculative. There is no evidence that young Kierkegaard is equivalent to Møller's description: "Ahasverus wants nothing. He regards himself as infinitely raised up above those people who want something," and, like Schopenhauer, Ahasverus does not recognize "an absolute difference between good and evil."[145] This kind of moral nihilism is identical with the moral irony which is found also in Fichte and in Schlegel's *Lucinde* and which is later criticized by Kierkegaard in *The Concept of Irony*.

Odense: Syddansk Universitetsforlag 2007 (*University of Southern Denmark Studies in Scandinavian Language and Literature*, vol. 78), pp. 9–54.

142 George Pattison suggests that Ahasverus is still present after all, "masked by the 'cosmopolitan face' of contemporary nihilism," George Pattison, *Kierkegaard, Religion and the Nineteenth-Century Crisis of Culture*, Cambridge: Cambridge University Press, 2002 p. 74; on Ahasverus see in general Chapter 4 (pp. 72–95). I do not agree that any "anti-Semitism" is to be found here, but, sad to say, this is definitely to be found in Kierkegaard elsewhere; in a scattered thought we read the following joke which is maybe not as amusing to a modern reader: "Those who write in the manner of Jews (Heine, Börne, Menzel) seem to be cheerful, but their gaiety recalls the apparent smile of newborn children which comes from them having a stomachache." *ES1*, vol. 3, p. 284. In his review of *The Extremes*, Møller speaks of the vain and tasteless schools of Young France and Young Germany; on this, see below, Section III, D. Kierkegaard's relation to the Jews of "Young Germany," that is, Heine, Börne, and others, is complex, but in a certain way respectful: for him they stand as exemplars of offense; in opposition to the titulary Christians, they have at least understood what true Christianity is and have said no thanks to it. It is not clear what he meant when in the *Journal NB32* Kierkegaard wrote of Møller that he "was well aware" that "Jews are especially suited to be publicists." *SKS* 26, 196, NB32:108 / *JP* 3, 2985. He cannot be thinking of *The Corsair*, which began in 1840 long after Møller's death.

143 *SKS* 2, 214.24–35 / *EO1*, 220–1.

144 See further Brandt, *Den unge Søren Kierkegaard*, pp. 336–446 and pp. 454–9.

145 *ES1*, vol. 2, p. 329.

D. The Review of The Extremes

In his travel diary Søren Kierkegaard's elder brother Peter Christian Kierkegaard notes on June 28, 1829 that he, in Berlin where he was staying at the time, has met Professor H.N. Clausen, with whom he has spoken, among other things, "about the new literary monthly, whose 14 members constitute a council, which judges all received reviews and writes most of them itself."[146] This characterization is quite fitting and gives a brief picture of how the *Maanedsskrift for Litteratur* functioned as an institution.[147] Møller became a member of the editorial board at the beginning of 1835 and published here in 1836 his lengthy review, written in December 1835, of Thomasine Gyllembourg's novel *The Extremes*.[148] As usual, she had used the pseudonym, "The Author of 'A Story from Everyday Life,' " but most people knew, and so also did Møller and Kierkegaard, that it was the mother of the editor, J.L. Heiberg—although the author is constantly referred to as "he." It can seem surprising that leading cultural figures such as Møller and Kierkegaard reviewed Gyllembourg so thoroughly (*The Extremes* and *Two Ages*, respectively), since her novels are by no means great literature.[149] However, as Klaus P. Mortensen points out, it was "a great art to be able to expand the ideal from the everyday," which was an until then uncovered area, although, despite their fascination with this art of reality, the reviewers did not have an eye for the feminine dimension.[150] The limits of the tolerance towards

---

146 P.C. Kierkegaard's diary for 1829–30, Royal Library, NKS 907, 8°, p. 64.

147 See, for instance, Vilhelm Andersen, *Poul Møller*, p. 327, on how the editorial board was organized and its work was carried out.

148 P.M. Møller, "Nye Fortællinger af Forfatteren til en Hverdagshistorie. Udgivne af *Johan Ludvig Heiberg*. Andet Bind: Extremerne. Kjøbenhavn. Paa Universitets-Boghandler *Reitzels* Forlag, trykt hos *J.D. Qvist*, Bog- og Nodetrykker. 1835. 223 S. 8," *Maanedsskrift for Litteratur*, vol. 15, Copenhagen: C.A. Reitzel 1836, pp. 135–63; reprinted in *ES1*, vol. 2, 1842, pp. 126–58. Earlier Møller had published two other reviews in the *Maanedsskrift for Litteratur*: of F.L.B. Zeuthen's *Noget om Philosophien og dens Dyrkelse, tildeels med Hensyn paa Danmark* (*Maanedsskrift*, vol. 6, 1831, pp. 266–70) and of P.C. Kierkegaard's doctoral dissertation, *De notione atque turpitudine mendacii commentatio* (*Maanedsskrift*, vol. 7, 1832, pp. 65–85). The review of Zeuthen gave rise to a small polemic; on this, see Jon Stewart, "Poul Martin Møller. Et nyt fund," *Fund og Forskning i Det Kongelige Biblioteks Samlinger*, vol. 44, 2005, pp. 415–23. Møller's other reviews were published in *Dansk Litteratur-Tidende*, the first one in 1824, and the last, of Sibbern's *On Poetry and Art*, in 1835.

149 They were not the first ones to review Gyllembourg, and two of the predecessors are mentioned by Møller, first, Carsten Hauch, "Noveller, gamle og nye, af Forfatteren til en Hverdags-Historie. Udgivet af *J. L. Heiberg*, to Bind. Kbhvn. 1833," *Prometheus. Maanedskrift for Poesie, Æsthetik og Kritik*, vol. 3, ed. by Adam Oehlenschläger, Copenhagen: Udgiverens Forlag 1833, pp. 289–329, and second, J.N. Madvig (using the pseudonym "Γ("), "Noveller, gamle og nye, af Forfatteren til 'En Hverdagshistorie.' Udgivne af *J. L. Heiberg*. 1ste, 2det og 3die Bind. Kjøbenhavn 1833–34. Reitzels Forlag," *Maanedsskrift for Litteratur*, vol. 11, Copenhagen: C.A. Reitzel 1834, pp. 363–92.

150 Klaus P. Mortensen, *Thomasines oprør – en familiehistorisk biografi om køn og kærlighed i forrige århundrede*, Copenhagen: G.E.C. Gad 1986, p. 151. Compare to this the following statement in Møller's review: "A few times one has seen the remark that in the author's poetical works [sc. novels] a one-sided emphasis was placed on a beautiful and cosy

women's aesthetic activities are obvious in, for example, Kierkegaard's draft of a sarcastic review of *Clara Raphael: Twelve Letters*,[151] or in Møller's sketches on "Femininity," in which one reads that "it is *unbecoming*, indeed, *detestable* that a woman be a poet by *profession*."[152] Their reviews of Gyllembourg might easily, on the surface, be seen as just a natural approach to, or a veneration for the Heibergian circle (Møller was a friend of Heiberg and Gyllembourg), but more importantly, they are points of departure for something that goes far beyond the mostly trivial contents of the novels, which in *The Extremes* is a somewhat banal love story, with the title referring to the conflicts or collisions arising on different levels, socially, politically, religiously, and in terms of age and sexes.[153] In the case of *The Extremes*, Møller takes the opportunity to develop his own view of art thoroughly in what might be seen as a critical discussion with both Hegelianism and with the romantic spleen practiced by himself in his earlier years. I will not develop this in detail here but only treat briefly what seems necessary in regard to Kierkegaard.

In a phenomenological introduction of massive proportions Møller reflects upon the art of reviewing and distinguishes three methods. The first type of review is a strictly scientific or systematic approach; he gives no examples of such "Hegelianism," but, as pointed out by Vilhelm Andersen, he might have in mind Heiberg's method as exercised in *On Vaudeville as a Dramatic Form of Poetry* (1826).[154] A second type of critique is what is named the ridiculing ("*persiflerende*") or new French review, where a random poetic work is used as "a motivation for a stream of witticisms" and sheer subjectivistic notions; this is found in "the vain and tasteless schools of Young France and Young Germany," particularly Heinrich Heine. The atomistic character causes "the thread of thought to be hidden almost wholly by the artificial pearls of the witticisms."[155] Møller employs a fine metaphor to describe such "conversational" or often political misuse of literary works of art: "The reviewer pregnant with witticisms

---

organization of the forms of social and domestic life. That he is also able to treat higher subject matter is seen from this novel in which religion and art are such essential moments in the harmony of the entire literary work." *Maanedsskrift for Litteratur*, vol. 15, p. 153; *ES1*, vol. 2, pp. 146–7.

151 *SKS* 24, 136–8, NB22:63 / *JP* 6, 6709. Mathilde Fibiger's (1830–72) anonymous work, *Clara Raphael. Tolv Breve*, Copenhagen: C.A. Reitzel 1851 (*ASKB* 1531), appeared in December 1850, edited by J.L. Heiberg, and shocked others in addition to Kierkegaard with its thoughts of emancipation. For an overview of the Clara Raphael Controversy, see, for instance, Katalin Nun, " 'A Passionflower Planted in a Cabbage Garden': Heiberg, Mathilde Fibiger and the Emancipation of Women," in *Johan Ludvig Heiberg: Philosopher, Littérateur, Dramaturge, and Political Thinker*, ed. by Jon Stewart, Copenhagen: Museum Tusculanum Press 2008 (*Danish Golden Age Studies*, vol. 5), pp. 493–516; see pp. 500–5.

152 P.M. Møller, "Qvindelighed," in *ES1*, vol. 3, pp. 314–21; see p. 318. The quotation is from the third study, by Vilhelm Andersen later entitled "Letter to a Lady," which is the draft of a letter to Vilhelmine Grüner (identical with Borup, Letter no. 50). In a letter to Heiberg, Møller says he is aware "that there is in your mother much that is unusual for women." Borup, Letter no. 113.

153 I will not here discuss the contents of the novel further.

154 *Udvalgte Skrifter af Poul Møller*, vol. 2, p. 163.

155 *Maanedsskrift for Litteratur*, vol. 15, pp. 135–7; *ES1*, vol. 2, pp. 127–9.

satisfies his own accidental drive with an unpleasant means, more or less as a cuckoo finds room for its egg in the nest of the robin."[156] Both of these approaches will easily be seen as nihilism, although this point is not expressed clearly in the review. To Møller, personal subjectivity or "personality" is the truth, and this is the third or middle path: as far as literary criticism is concerned, he calls it "the elementary review"; the reviewer's task is to weigh the poetic work with his own personality, "so that the reviewer from subjective reasons regards the relation of a poetic work to certain specific aesthetic demands, without being concerned with other respects."[157]

In *Either/Or*, among the papers of "A," we find the review of "*The First Love*: A Comedy in One Act by Scribe, translated by J.L. Heiberg," which is not a review, but rather a personal story of how a review was written. The author emphasizes his presentation's accidental character:

> Yet it was on the occasion of the occasion of this little review that I wanted to say something rather general about the occasion or about the occasion in general....He [the reader] might perhaps think that I ought to have thought the whole thing through before I started to write, and then I ought not to have begun to say something that later turned out to be nothing. Nevertheless, I do believe that he ought to give my method its due, insofar as he has convinced himself in a more satisfying manner that the occasion in general is something that is nothing....What is said here, then, must be regarded as a superfluity, like a superfluous title page that is not included when the work is bound. Therefore, I know no other way to conclude than in the incomparable laconic manner in which I see that Professor Poul Møller concluded the introduction of his excellent review of *The Extremes*: With this the introduction is concluded.[158]

With this concluding remark, Kierkegaard hardly thinks that Møller's long introduction to his review is superfluous; he only admires his manner of conclusion. But one cannot escape another observation in the passage quoted above: that the style itself is just what Møller, had he had the opportunity, might have considered indifferent and even "new French," much talk and little substance, as is so often the case with Kierkegaard, and maybe especially as a young person.

From another source it is clear that Kierkegaard read Møller's review of *The Extremes* as soon as it appeared in early 1836.[159] In *Notebook 3* we find a short excerpt of Schleiermacher's *Vertraute Briefe über die Lucinde*.[160] Kierkegaard had read the second edition of this book, which originally appeared anonymously in 1800 as *Vertraute Briefe über Friedrich Schlegels Lucinde* and was meant as a defense

156 Ibid., p. 136; *ES1*, vol. 2, p. 127.

157 Ibid., p. 144; *ES1*, vol. 2, p. 137.

158 *SKS* 2, 233.14–36 / *EO1*, 239–40.

159 *Maanedsskrift for Litteratur* does not appear explicitly in *The Auctioneer's Sales Record*, and Kierkegaard is not found on the list of subscribers, but he probably read it in a public library or reading society, for instance, the Athenæum or the Student Association.

160 *SKS* 19, 99, Not3:2 / *JP* 4, 3846. This entry is discussed by Richard E. Crouter, "Schleiermacher: Revisiting Kierkegaard's Relationship to Him," in *Kierkegaard and His German Contemporaries*, Tome II, *Theology*, ed. by Jon Stewart, Aldershot: Ashgate 2007 (*Kierkegaard Research: Sources, Reception and Resources*, vol. 6), pp. 197–231; see pp. 204–6.

for Schlegel's novel *Lucinde* (1799), which was only seen as immoral, a "gospel of the flesh," which piquantly advocated a most free physical relation between the sexes. In the second edition from 1835, the editor Karl Gutzkov in the preface sees the two writings by Schlegel and Schleiermacher generally as part of the social and political endeavors which are characteristic features of "Young Germany," and more specifically as a criticism of the age's bourgeois and religious surpression of love. In his notebook entry from October 1835 Kierkegaard praises Schleiermacher's book as "a true work of art," which "ought to be a model review and also an example of how such a thing can be most productive, in that he constructs a host of personalities out of the book itself and through them illuminates the work and also illuminates their individuality." This might well be one of Kierkegaard's inspirations for his use of pseudonyms. After the appearance of Møller's review of *The Extremes*, he added the following in the margin at the end of the entry: "See *Maanedsskrift for Litteratur*, eighth year, p. 140. An essay by P. Møller.—February 1836."[161] On p. 140 which is referred to—this is also in the review's introduction—Møller discusses whether a review can be a free art in the sense that the reviewer can choose any procedure he pleases, since in that case, according to Schlegel, a review of poems would be a new poem.[162]

It was important for Møller that poetry not give up its "connection with the rest of life."[163] Later in the review of *The Extremes* his points regarding the relationship between poetry and reality are unfolded further, that is, his concept of poetic realism. He says, for instance, "Poetry is a flower of social life, and what a people and its

---

161 *SKS* 19, 99, Not3:2.a / *JP* 4, 3847.

162 "Whether the series should be regarded as finished with such a poem to the second degree, which in this case would be a special kind of poetic work that could not be the object of any review, or whether the series could be continued indefinitely, he [Schlegel] has left undecided. In the latter case, poetry could wholly give up its connection with the rest of life; it would come to such an independence and autonomy that it could continually reproduce itself merely from itself, just as the snake, which is the symbol of eternity, maintains life by eating its own tail. German poetry presents an approach to this extreme in the many novels, novellas and lyric poems which are concerned almost solely with art and the works and endeavors of the artists. If one keeps to this extreme, the aesthetic review loses its scholarly character, and poetry swallows up aesthetics." *Maanedsskrift for Litteratur*, vol. 15, p. 140; *ES1*, vol. 2, p. 132.

163 Ibid. Much earlier, in his topographical satire, "Statistisk Skildring af Lægdsgaarden i Ølseby-Magle. Af en ung Geograph" (*ES1*, vol. 1, pp. 201–23), written on his journey to China, his point was the same. It says in the "*Prolegomena*" that "It is not without reason that in the more recent times people complain a lot about the disproportionately large number of students who occupy themselves with philosophy, art theory, total views, observations on the spirit of the age and such things which demand no small amount of learning. Let's assume that it is true that philosophy is the soul of the sciences, then a soul cannot, however, subsist on its own apart from the body. Already by now there is almost no body left. Soon the writers will have nothing else to make observations about than each other's observations; just like the German poets are already brought to the extreme that their poetry concerns virtually nothing but poetry. In the learned republic a strange inverted emanation prevails. All fields of study become every day more incorporeal, diluted and transfigured, so that one can highly fear that eventually they will dissolve completely into spirit and air." *ES1*, vol. 1, p. 203.

individuals have experienced provides in a certain sense the material for its higher life in poetry." Communicated by means of the *mimesis* of the genius, poetry should "with freshness and originality" proceed from actual life.[164] In German Romanticism, however, he sees the danger that art poetry has been regarded "as the sole form of revelation of the divine life in the human race."[165] To get to the core of this, the danger is of course romantic *irony* and its consequences: "indifference to the life conditions of other people, and as a result a consistent selfishness."[166] In Schlegel's *Lucinde*—which Kierkegaard was later to treat in *The Concept of Irony*—Møller sees the essence of this nihilistic philosophy of life in the maxim that "he has no god who is not himself his own god."[167] Møller concludes, "If the artist has come so far with such a complete irony that everything outside himself and his art, or his art and he himself are fully indifferent to him, then it is certainly all over with his art; the true poet must first and foremost be a true human being."[168] When it comes to this conflict between, on the one hand, idealism or poetic freedom of spirit and, on the other hand, poetic sympathy for the human condition, he sees Thomasine Gyllembourg's "genuine poetic disposition" as an expression of beautiful harmony between the two extremes: "Here is a warm and deep sympathy for the most heterogeneous directions of spirit [*Aandsretninger*], combined with a freedom of spirit which makes them all objects for a calming contemplation."[169] Unfortunately, such perfect harmony is seldom in contemporary poetry and can "be compared to the solitary fresh apples which can be seen here and there on the trees when the defoliation has begun."[170] I will not embark here on a comparison with Kierkegaard's review of *Two Ages* and what, later in his life, he had to say about Gyllembourg; but there is no doubt after all that both Møller and Kierkegaard admired the writer, even if she was a woman.[171]

---

164 *Maanedsskrift for Litteratur*, vol. 15, p. 145; *ES1*, vol. 2, p. 138.

165 Ibid., p. 146; *ES1*, vol. 2, p. 139. This had earlier led Peder Hjort to point to the fact that, in Møller's words, "art was not the absolute and eternal self, but one of its forms of revelation." Peder Hjort, "Om Digteren *Ingemann* og hans Værker," *Athene. Et Maanedsskrift*, vol. 5, ed. by Christian Molbech, Copenhagen: Gyldendal 1815, pp. 73–111 and pp. 388–428; the subject is treated in the theoretical introduction, pp. 74–90. (Hjort's review of Ingemann's *juvenilia* continued in *Athene*, vol. 6, 1816, pp. 158–98, pp. 366–83, and pp. 544–66.)

166 *Maanedsskrift for Litteratur*, vol. 15, p. 146; *ES1*, vol. 2, p. 139.

167 Ibid., p. 147; *ES1*, vol. 2, pp. 139–40; Møller here wrongly ascribes this maxim to the book's main character, and in Schlegel's work the true words are, "*welcher Gott kann dem Menschen ehrwürdig sein, der nicht sein eigner Gott ist?*" See also above, Section III, C, on Møller's "On the Concept of Irony."

168 Ibid., p. 147; *ES1*, vol. 2, p. 140.

169 Ibid., p. 149; *ES1*, vol. 2, p. 142. On this passage see also Elisabeth Hude, *Thomasine Gyllembourg og Hverdagshistorierne*, Copenhagen: Rosenkilde og Bagger 1951, p. 67.

170 *Maanedsskrift for Litteratur*, vol. 15, p. 157; *ES1*, vol. 2, p. 151.

171 In the review of *The Extremes*, Møller also anticipates what would be the theme of his great treatise on immortality the following year; on this, see below, Section III, G.

E. "On Telling Children Fairy Tales"

Among Møller's posthumous papers there is a short unfinished essay entitled "On Telling Children Fairy Tales."[172] Given that it was first published in 1843, Kierkegaard could not have read it when in 1837, in late January or early February, he wrote his rather similar long entry, BB:37, in the *Journal BB*.[173] However, since, according to the editor F.C. Olsen, the time of composition of Møller's essay is 1836 or 1837,[174] it is not unlikely that Møller's preoccupation with the subject was Kierkegaard's main inspiration and the occasion of his journal entry (which is actually a draft for a treatise). Probably, they had discussed this particular subject on the basis of the contemporary debate on children's literature and its effect upon the imagination of children.[175] In any case, there can be no doubt that childhood interested Kierkegaard a lot, since he recognized its fundamental importance for forming the personality, or, to use his language of favorite metaphors collected from grammar, in an entry from 1837, "Childhood is life's paradigmatic part; manhood its syntax."[176] Møller, too, himself a father, was of course well aware of the fact that "when one considers how firmly the sphere of imagination which is formed in a person's childhood remains during the entire rest of his life, it is then natural to be somewhat cautious in the choice of the fantasies with which one intentionally fills their [the children's] heads."[177]

What, then, are the points of similarity? In his essay, Møller expresses the opinion that it is damaging to fill children's minds with imaginary stories—which, by the way, is also evident from the way he generally regarded Hans Christian Andersen: he does not say so expressly, since he nowhere refers to Andersen's fairy tales, of which the first collection appeared in 1835, but in a letter to Sibbern, dated May 5, 1829 and written from Norway, Møller highly praises his old friend Hauch's tragedies *Bajazet* and *Tiberius*—he even says, "for my part, I place *Tiberius* above Shakespeare's *Julius Caesar* without hesitation"!—and he is terribly sorry that undeservedly *Tiberius* is not popular compared to the contemporary enthusiasm for young Andersen's fabulous, Hoffmannesque *Journey on Foot*. Møller, however, had read some excerpts of this novel in *Kjøbenhavns flyvende Post*: "I have read it on some loose pages, which have been brought near to dissolution due to people's zealous contrectation. I have been able to find nothing in them without strong reminiscences of light reading executed with a swift tongue or more correctly a self-indulgent chatter."[178] Although Andersen later changed his style, Møller would undoubtedly

172 P.M. Møller, "Om at fortælle Børn Eventyr," MS in Collinske Samling, 365, 4°, Royal Library, Copenhagen; first published in *ES1*, vol. 3, 1843, pp. 322–5.

173 *SKS* 17, 122–33, BB:37 / *KJN* 1, 116–25. Unfortunately, the MS is not extant, as far as this entry is concerned; the text source is *EP*, vol. 1, pp. 126–45.

174 *ES1*, vol. 3, p. 322, note.

175 On this debate, in which, among others, Christian Molbech participated, see the explanatory note to 122.23 in *SKS* K17, p. 241 / *KJN* 1, pp. 413–14.

176 *SKS* 17, 46.27–8, AA:30 / *KJN* 1, 40.

177 *ES1*, vol. 3, p. 323.

178 Borup, Letter no. 102. Møller wrote a review for the *Maanedsskrift for Litteratur* of Hauch's two tragedies *Bajazet* and *Tiberius*, but it was never published since he refused

have enjoyed Kierkegaard's similar critique in *From the Papers of One Still Living*, had he lived to read it. Later, long after he had returned from Norway in 1831 to the literary environment of Copenhagen, which apparently had now become more "artistic" than before, Møller expresses the same views in his review of Sibbern's book on aesthetics, *On Poetry and Art* (1834), in which one reads, *inter alia*:

> Another erring direction which the author [Sibbern] has occasion to discuss, he has also himself recently criticized zealously in one of our journals, namely, the rampant Epicureanism which brings both the artists as well as their public to regard art and poetry as merely a means to refined pleasure. This false taste, in several countries, leads even talented poets to avail themselves of coquette means, for example, metric rattles, in order to make their work quite ingratiating for the covetous reading world. But it is true here as in other spheres that the one-sided striving for pleasure prevents the true pleasure. The public will soon feel such a loathing toward the obsequious poetry that it will look back with regret to its fathers' masculine hardness.[179]

In like manner, Møller states in his essay on fairy tales as "a completely clear fact" that "an exaggerated reading of novels has given a number of our contemporaries a distorted mental disposition [*Aandsretning*], warped their emotions, placed them in an uninterrupted state of somnambulism, given them a distaste for hard work, and taught them a loathing of life's actual forms."[180] This aesthetic criticism is expressed *en miniature* in the essay on fairy tales. According to Vilhelm Andersen, Møller had, among others, Hans Christian Andersen in mind in a fragment of a poem, which is possibly from 1834, and which begins with the words: "A species will be born without a strength, / A race that nothing can and nothing will…."[181] This goes particularly for the new generation of poets, but similarly, Møller's essay on fairy tales is a work in practical pedagogy where he warns precisely against the mistaken upbringing of the new generation, understood as the children, and the harmful effect on their imagination.

---

the editorial board's demand that passages be changed, especially where he emphasized the realism of the plays. Apparently, the passage which had evoked criticism was the following: "As we make the claim about Hauch's poetic works that they are of equal psychological and aesthetic interest, and that it is more the idea of truth than of beauty that animates them, we believe that we have not thereby diminished their value, but have contributed to a correct picture of their quality....This kind of thoroughness in the representation of human spiritual life, especially in its extreme aberrations, is also found in our author, who in his works shows us that he is just as much a philosophical researcher of nature as a poet." (*ES1*, vol. 2, pp. 55–6). This refers to the fact that Hauch was also a natural scientist. The review, " '*Bajazet og Tiber.*' To Sørgespil af C. Hauch. Kjøbenhavn. Trykt paa C. A. Reitzels Forlag, i Fabritius de Tengnagels Officin. 1828," was first published in 1842 in *ES1*, vol. 2, pp. 54–68.

179 P.M. Møller, "Om Poesie og Konst i Almindelighed, med Hensyn til alle Arter deraf, dog især Digte-, Maler-, Billedhugger- og Skuespillerkonst; eller: Foredrag over almindelig Æsthetik og Poetik. Af *Dr.* Frederik Christian Sibbern, Professor i Philosophien. Første Deel. Kiøbenhavn. Paa Forfatterens Forlag, trykt hos Fabritius *de* Tengnagel. 1834," in *Dansk Litteratur-Tidende*, 1835, no. 12, pp. 181–92, and no. 13, pp. 205–9; see p. 209; reprinted in *ES1*, vol. 2, pp. 105–26; see pp. 125–6.

180 *ES1*, vol. 3, p. 322.

181 "*Der fødes skal en Art foruden Kræfter, / En Slægt, som Intet kan og Intet vil...*" The fragment is found in *ES1*, vol. 3, pp. 16–17. Cf. Vilhelm Andersen, *Poul Møller*, p. 352.

As a "new citizen of the world," Møller says, every child strives for knowledge when its consciousness awakens, that is, when the child "has a strong presentiment that his life is connected to the life of all of existence....One then commits a great injustice in interrupting his zealous striving to become familiar with the real world in order to entice him into a fairy world."[182] However, this does not entirely exclude the use of fantastic tales, but only to a modest extent; otherwise, "one then accustoms children to pursue the same occupation in smaller things as is pursued by the adults in larger things when they, as one says, pursue light reading as a pass-time."[183]

The approach of Kierkegaard, on the other hand, is not as negative. Initially, he underlines that the purpose of his treatise is only to inveigh about abuse.[184] Of the two ways of telling stories, he says, the method of nannies—the "nursery stories" that Møller also speaks of—is damaging, since when the child gets a clue of the narrator's insincerity, then a lack of confidence and a suspicion develops. The other kind of narrator is a person who is not like a child himself, but who basically knows what it is to be a child, "and from his higher standpoint offers the children a spiritual sustenance that suits them."[185] This is the frame of storytelling, and Kierkegaard then develops in detail how the storyteller ought to be: in short, a Socrates. Like the "Uncle Frands" he should engage the children and nurture "a constant mental mobility...a permanent attentiveness to whatever they hear and see."[186] However, like Møller, Kierkegaard gives some serious warnings about possible "false paths." Sentimentality might be one such path, and the idea that children only need entertainment another. In what Kierkegaard calls the "first stage," the narrator "fall[s] into 'being a child,' " tragi-comically speaks like children, etc. The alternative is to attempt to put play and

---

182 *ES1*, vol. 3, p. 323. In his treatise on immortality, which I will discuss below in Section III, G, Møller writes the following, "In the poetical works which nowadays present a fairy world for the imagination it is often the opinion of the infidel author and reader that temporarily one should be enchanted into a supersensuous world and yet keep the belief that no higher world exists. The consequence of this, however, is that the enchantment will be as might be expected. This attempted self-deception is more childish than that of a child for whom footstool and yardstick serve as throne and scepter, although the child is quite conscious that they actually are footstool and yardstick, since the child knows that footstools and scepters actually exist while the adult believes that what his fairy world means is altogether nothing. There is a level of art where the poet presents mythological traditions in which he himself believes; there is a second level where the poet's fantasies, even when borrowing motifs from such legends, are regarded by himself as a meaningless play; and a third level where the poet contemplates his artistic production as an image of a higher existence." *Maanedsskrift for Litteratur*, vol. 17, p. 56; *ES1*, vol. 2, pp. 219–20.

183 *ES1*, vol. 3, p. 324. In his introduction to "On Telling Children Fairy Tales," Vilhelm Andersen says that Møller wrote the essay on the basis of personal experiences and mentions that among his papers "there are excerpts of a treatise on the life of the Indians in North America, which he presumably familiarized himself with so that he could check it before exposing his sons to the cheap romanticism of the Indian stories." *Udvalgte Skrifter af Poul Møller*, vol. 2, p. 117. The MS containing these excerpts is found at the Royal Library, NKS 4783, 4°.

184 *SKS* 17, 122, BB:37 / *KJN* 1, 116.

185 *SKS* 17, 123 / *KJN* 1, 117.

186 *SKS* 17, 125 / *KJN* 1, 119.

stories to a useful purpose; this results in two paths: "*either* educating them, as one says, morally, *or* conveying to them some useful knowledge."[187] The practical output has been picture-books on natural history, but from all of this, Kierkegaard says, there developed only an atomistic knowledge "which did not enter into any deeper relation to children and their existence, and was *not appropriated* in their *souls* in any way."[188] In other words, the Socratic impact in such a case is absent. On the contrary, the children should ask questions, and as was stated earlier in the essay: "What matters is to bring *the poetic to bear on their lives in every way*, to exert a magical influence."[189]

Kierkegaard himself read fairy tales and folk tales[190] and was confident about their positive and refreshing nature: "What does the soul find so invigorating about *reading folk tales*? When I am tired of everything and 'full of days,' fairy-tales are for me always the revitalizing bath that proves so refreshing."[191] Møller, himself a poet, felt the same way. But they both warn that with children these means should be used with special care.

F. Scattered Thoughts and the Concept of Affectation

One of Møller's main characteristics was his inability to complete much of what he started, for which reason *aphorisms* were a perfect means of expression. On his journey to China 1819–21, in his intellectual solitude, he began writing down his thoughts in the form of aphorisms, or as he preferred to call them, "*Strøtanker*" (scattered thoughts). They covered a wide range of themes—from everyday life, aesthetics, psychology, religion, philology, philosophy, etc.—and he continued this practice for virtually the rest of his life.[192] Paul V. Rubow suggests as an inspiration the *Maximes* (1665) of François de La Rochefoucauld (1613–80), since in general these maxims treat affectation and cast light on the thought that human virtues are hidden vices.[193] However, Uffe Andreasen rightly points out that a French influence is not very likely, and that an acquaintance with La Rochefoucauld would only be indirect through Møller's reading of Arthur Schopenhauer's (1788–1860) *Die Welt als Wille und Vorstellung*, in which the Frenchman is quoted.[194] Moreover, according

187 *SKS* 17, 130 / *KJN* 1, 124.

188 Ibid.

189 *SKS* 17, 124 / *KJN* 1, 118.

190 Cf. *ASKB* 1407–1471.

191 *SKS* 17, 251.2–5, DD:94 / *KJN* 1, 241. Cf. Grethe Kjær, *Barndommens ulykkelige elsker. Kierkegaard om barnet og barndommen*, Copenhagen: C.A. Reitzel 1986, pp. 127ff.; in general, see her analysis on pp. 118ff.

192 Vilhelm Andersen suggests that he stopped in 1836: "As far as can be judged, no aphorisms are preserved from a time later than 1836." *Udvalgte Skrifter af Poul Møller*, vol. 2, p. 380.

193 Paul V. Rubow, *Kunsten at skrive—Kunsten at læse*, Copenhagen: Ejnar Munksgaard 1942, p. 45.

194 Uffe Andreasen, *Poul Møller og romantismen*, pp. 60–1. *Die Welt als Wille und Vorstellung* first appeared in 1819; Kierkegaard owned the 2nd ed. of 1844 (Leipzig: F.A. Brockhaus 1844; *ASKB* 773–773a).

to a letter to Sibbern, Møller read this work (whose overall pessimistic tendency he would later, in the treatise on immortality, describe as nihilistic) for the first time possibly in January 1828, which is several years after he began writing aphorisms on the journey to China.[195] As Rubow calls attention to elsewhere, a better candidate is possibly the German aphorist Georg Christoph Lichtenberg (1742–99).[196] The name of Friedrich Schlegel and his fragments might also be suggested in this context. However, nothing certain can be said about this, and maybe it is wiser only to note that Møller was simply a fragmentist by nature.

It would be natural to assume that Kierkegaard's "Diapsalmata" in *Either/Or* were inspired by Møller, but one must bear in mind that his scattered thoughts were not published until 1843 in volume 3 of the *Posthumous Writings*.[197] Apart from this, it is clear that several of the "Diapsalmata" date from much earlier since some of them are found as entries in his early journals (indeed, Kierkegaard's journal entries as such are often *obiter dicta* very similar to Møller's aphorisms, although with an aphorism one expects a certain finish and sharp point).[198] They are not necessarily identical with later "Diapsalmata," but the scheme is the same. To take an example, in the *Journal CC* there is an entry that reads "I prefer to talk with old ladies who retail family nonsense; next with the insane—and last of all with very reasonable people."[199] In *Either/Or* this has changed to the well-known "I prefer to talk with children, for one may still dare to hope that they may become rational beings; but those who have become that—good Lord!"[200] It is funny, then, when among Møller's scattered thoughts we find the following: "In a certain sense children are more rational than old people: the former regard those people who stand above them in terms of insight as the most insightful, the latter those who stand below them."[201] However, that a common thought like this is expressed by both thinkers, can be nothing but a coincidence. Nevertheless, there is no reason to doubt that Kierkegaard read all of Møller's scattered thoughts that were published—in the footnote earlier quoted from *Concluding Unscientific Postscript* he refers to them in general when speaking of Møller's anti-Hegelianism as "more noteworthy than many an aphorism

---

195 Borup, Letter no. 91, in which Møller says that he has just read two books of Schopenhauer, whom he had never heard of before; one of these books was *Die Welt als Wille und Vorstellung*.

196 Paul V. Rubow in a review of Olle Holmberg, *Tankar vid en kopp te*, Stockholm: Bonniers 1958, in *Berlingske Aftenavis*, November 25, 1958; cf. Andreasen, *Poul Møller og romantismen*, p. 61.

197 *ES1*, vol. 3, pp. 171–291 and pp. 303–13 (on affectation). Another thing is, of course, that "scattered thoughts" might have come to Kierkegaard orally from Møller himself, but this possibility does not concern the aphorisms as literary genre.

198 On Kierkegaard's use of earlier notes as "Diapsalmata," cf., for instance, Frithiof Brandt's introduction to *Kierkegaard-Manuskripter. Diapsalmata*, published by the Society for Danish Language and Literature (*Danske Digtere ved Arbejdet*, vol. 3), Copenhagen: Levin & Munksgaard 1935, and Brandes, *Søren Kierkegaard*, pp. 124–9.

199 *SKS* 17, 208, CC:24 / *KJN* 1, 199.

200 *SKS* 2, 27.23–4 / *EO1*, 19.

201 *ES1*, vol. 3, 275.

included in the printed edition"[202]—but only in a few cases it is possible to determine with absolute certainty that he was directly inspired by them.

In the *Concluding Unscientific Postscript* one reads, "Poul Møller has correctly pointed out that a court fool uses more wit in one year than many a witty author in his whole life."[203] This statement is typical for Møller, and indeed very Socratic. What matters is practical activity among people; what matters is existence. However, the aphorism in question is a bit more complex and reads like this *in extenso*:

> The humorous improvisor and the other oral poets have more genius than the poets who write, but less consciousness of it.[204] They are rich men, who amuse themselves by throwing gold out to the rabble, without themselves knowing its value. The poetic writers are not so often filled with inspiring thoughts as they are knowers of their genuineness. Every fortunate idea that they hit upon is noted and used in an appropriate manner. But even among the most voluminous comic authors there is not found as much wit as an outstanding court fool needs in one year.[205]

Kierkegaard uses this aphorism in the *Postscript*, Part 2, Section Two, Chapter 3, § 4, where Climacus treats the task and style of the subjective thinker. He explains the thought of Møller thus: "and why is that if it is not because the former [the court fool] is an existing person who every moment of the day must have wittiness at his disposal, whereas the other is witty only momentarily."[206]

In *The Book on Adler*, Chapter 4, "Psychological Conception of Adler as a Phenomenon, and as a Satire on the Hegelian Philosophy and the Present," Kierkegaard writes: "What Poul Møller says somewhere is so true and so mature, that one can certainly tolerate not doing anything, indeed, that it can even be entertaining for someone, when one is aware that there is something that one should do; the entertaining element lies in the consciousness that one has neglected something."[207] In a footnote to this he refers to the *Posthumous Writings*, volume 3, p. 217 *medio*, and then in the margin quotes one of Møller's scattered thoughts:

> During fairly complete idleness, one can still avoid boredom as long as an obligatory task is being neglected through the idleness, because one is then somewhat occupied by the continual struggle one is in with oneself. But as soon as the duty ceases, or one no longer feels any reminder of it at all, boredom sets in. The private tutor who from moment to moment postpones a working hour enjoys himself as long as he is on the point of going to his pupil, but when he has decided to skip the hour his enjoyment ceases. The reminder by conscience in that example was something unpleasant that served as a stimulation for something pleasant. A poet who is writing a tragedy, although it was part

202 *SKS* 7, 41.8 / *CUP1*, 34, note.

203 *SKS* 7, 321.30–2 / *CUP1*, 351.

204 Compare to this Jean Paul's "passive geniuses" touched upon in Section I, *in fine*.

205 *ESI*, vol. 3, pp. 176–7.

206 *SKS* 7, 321.32–4 / *CUP1*, 352.

207 *Pap*. VII–2 B 235, p. 214 / *BA*, 128; the Hongs have left out the passage "*at man godt kan holde ud...forsømmer Noget*," since they have published a later version of *The Book on Adler* in which this passage was deleted.

of his plan of life to study for a degree, will do it with greater enthusiasm than he will do it later if he gives up that plan.[208]

Kierkegaard uses this perhaps banal experience of postponing and pushing forward duties in his "psychological view" of Adler and in this case of the extent of his productivity: "In the same way it may also be the dim consciousness that instead of being productive he ought to be doing something else that makes Magister Adler so productive and makes his productivity so interesting to him, since he, rather than becoming clear to himself through his productivity, instead defends himself against what ethical simplicity would bid him to do."[209] It is not possible to say whether maybe at the same time Kierkegaard has also had in mind Møller's early, partly autobiographical essay on ingenious idlers, "Some Observations on the Development of Popular Ideas,"[210] which was originally given as a paper at the Student Association on February 19, 1825 under the title, "On the Influence of Idlers on their Contemporary Age."

In his last years Møller projected a treatise on the concept of *affectation*, a psychological and social theory of his own, developed over the years in numerous scattered thoughts on the subject and in a fragment that should be an introduction to the treatise. This fragment was begun in 1837, according to F.C. Olsen, who supplied it with the title "Introductory Observations for a Treatise on Affectation."[211] This "moral description of nature," as Møller calls it, might be considered his only original contribution to a philosophical anthropology, or one should perhaps say pathology. Earlier the concept of affectation was used in reference to function, to extraverted actions, but Møller uses it primarily of existence. For the same reason he had to give up a Hegelian concept of morality (*Sittlichkeit*), since for Hegel morality is reason's highest reality. But as Møller points out, a "previously formed speculative system" is useless for his purpose. He has in mind any deception of and falsehood to oneself, to one's individuality, and this cannot be defined in absolute terms, since truth in life is a personal matter, and it is more than morality.[212] Untruth is self-

208 *Pap.* VII–2 B 235, pp. 214–15 / *BA*, 128–9; *ESI*, vol. 3, p. 217.

209 *Pap.* VII–2 B 235, p. 215 / *BA*, 129.

210 P.M. Møller, "Nogle Betragtninger over populaire Ideers Udvikling," *Nyt Aftenblad*, no. 18, 1825, pp. 153–60; reprinted in *ESI*, vol. 2, pp. 3–19.

211 P.M. Møller, "Forberedelser til en Afhandling om Affectation," in *ESI*, vol. 3, pp. 291–302 and pp. 303–13 ("Strøtanker; om Affectation"); compare Olsen's footnote pp. 291–2. On this subject see, for instance, Peter Thielst, "Poul Martin Møller (1794–1838): Scattered Thoughts, Analysis of Affectation, Combat with Nihilism," *Danish Yearbook of Philosophy*, vol. 13, 1976, pp. 66–83; reprinted as "Poul Martin Møller: Scattered Thoughts, Analysis of Affectation, Struggle with Nihilism," in *Kierkegaard and His Contemporaries: The Culture of Golden Age Denmark*, ed. by Jon Stewart, Berlin and New York: Walter de Gruyter 2003 (*Kierkegaard Studies Monograph Series*, vol. 10), pp. 45–61.

212 The general, or Hegelian, understanding of truth Møller describes thus: "The life of the person who unfeignedly follows his natural desires has a kind of truth. There is a higher truth in the life of the person who has attained virtue (in the sense of the term employed by antiquity), so that even while still taking the content of his actions from his natural instincts, he has nonetheless achieved sufficient mastery over them to observe a certain moderation in satisfying them. A still higher level of personal truth is in the life of the person who determines

deception and lack of freedom. However, certain kinds of manifestations of life cannot be considered affectation, for instance, a lie or a conscious simulation, and this is neither the case with different types of abnormal behavior or "overwrought" conditions, also treated by Møller in his lectures on psychology.[213] In his introduction, Møller distinguishes between three degrees of affectation: momentary, permanent, and alternating. In short, the *momentary* deceit or corruption of the self is when a person's virtue has not become stable and strong, and when at times one is not true to one's own character, for instance, when socializing with others and becoming one with their "circle of consciousness"; however, paradoxically, often such affectation might prove necessary in existence. The *permanent* affectation is when a person has lost control of himself and "has taken up the habit of a determinate kind of false statements, in that he imagines that he has certain opinions, interests or inclinations, because he wishes to have them for one outward reason or another."[214] Finally, the worst affectation is the *alternating* one ("*vexlende Affectation*") where there is no longer a "permanent core in the person's thoughts and will, but at every moment of his life he creates a temporary personality which can be annulled in the following moment."[215] This seldom sort of culmination is total untruth in one's personal life.

Møller had collected material for many years on the concept of affectation, including all kinds of observations and reflections which are found especially among his scattered thoughts. Kierkegaard nowhere offers a sustained treatment of Møller's concept of affectation.[216] But at least in one case he refers to one of the scattered thoughts on affectation when in January 1847 he writes the following in the *Journal NB*:

> That even Poul Møller was tried in all sorts of doubt is at times apparent in some quite accidental expression. In an aphorism he speaks of fanatical pastors who speak glowingly and do not detect that all their religiosity is accelerated [*potenseret*] circulation of the blood. Alas, this is just where the knot binds. How many men live so transparently that they really know what's what? They think in entirely different categories from those in which they live. They speak in religious categories and live in categories of sensuousness, the categories of immediate well-being.[217]

---

all his intentions by means of pure rational autonomy....To the extent, then, that the human being's pure self-determination is the will that has been sanctified by religiosity, it acts in complete harmony with the entire world of Reason. The human being is what it is supposed to be, and its life cannot attain any higher truth. But this truth is nothing other than morality, and all deviation from it is immorality." *ES1*, vol. 3, pp. 293–4. Quoted from an unpublished translation by Bruce H. Kirmmse.

213 The MS with Møller's lecture notes on psychology is not published, but will be so in the new critical edition. It is found at the Royal Library in Copenhagen, Collinske Samling 379, 4°.

214 *ES1*, vol. 3, p. 298.

215 *ES1*, vol. 3, p. 299; trans. by Soderquist, *The Isolated Self*, p. 151.

216 Although the editors of *SKS* would apparently like him to do so, for instance, when he mentions "*affecterede Dyder*" in the journal entry JJ:313, cf. the extended explanatory note to *SKS* 18, 238.8 / *KJN* 2, 539, note to 219.4.

217 *SKS* 20, 80, NB:103 / *JP* 1, 1044. To this there is also a marginal addition reading, "If it is to become apparent that a sufferer has faith, then faith must appear simultaneously along

It appears from this journal entry that Kierkegaard was well aware of Møller's religious doubts over the years. The affectation of the servants of God, reflected upon in several scattered thoughts, had certainly not helped him to a stronger faith, if any, and, unlike Kierkegaard, he never seriously thought about becoming a pastor again after his journey to China. The aphorism referred to by Kierkegaard exemplifies momentary affectation and reads like this:

> The momentary exaltation is sometimes of a low sensual nature with dominant organic movement. The strong organic change necessarily awakens reflection (for every severe affection must do so), and the affect is preserved then as joy at its own activity and being lost in the idea. Such a half-mad delight over the raising of the functions of vegetative life, for example, of the circulation of the blood, often shines from the eyes of fanatical priests, who sometimes even clench their teeth and contort their face in their *rapture*. This is regarded by the lower part of the rabble, especially by uneducated women, as enthusiasm.[218]

As far as *immortality* is concerned, which will be treated in the next section, it seems—apart from intellectual reflections on the basis of a general debate on the subject at the time—to have been a personal experience that brought Møller to a religious clarification. After the death of his wife Betty in 1834, he wrote the following in a letter to his mother-in-law, Elisabeth Berg:

> The sorrowful divorce which we have experienced has made my thought of another and higher life much more alive and present than it has ever been before....I am wholly convinced that death and life on a larger scale are repetitions of the same alternation which lies in sleeping and awakening....I think, however, that an idea about whose validity one is assured can at certain times in one's life obtain an unusual clarity and strength, and present itself for one in such a light that it seems as if it were completely new.[219]

---

with the suffering. But what happens—as pain, misfortune, and opposition are gradually taken away, his life as interpreted by the secular mind becomes healthier and happier—and he thinks this is due to faith; whereas, on the contrary, it takes place through the restored vitality of immediacy." *SKS* 20, 80, NB:103.a / *JP* 1, 1045.

218 *ES1*, vol. 3, p. 241.

219 Borup, Letter no. 140. Just for the sake of comparison: in the treatise on immortality Møller says, "In general it is also the drive to know determinate human individuals as imperishable objects of their love which leads doubting or infidel thinkers back to the Christian world-view," and of certain natural scientists who have given up abstract pantheism it reads "that the death of individuals to whom they have been tied by strong sympathetic bonds has opened their eyes to the emptiness of their world-view." *Maanedskrift for Litteratur*, vol. 17, p. 52; *ES1*, vol. 2, p. 215. Kierkegaard might be thinking of this in a draft for Victor Eremita's speech in *Stages on Life's Way*, *Pap.* V B 178,8, p. 308 / *SLW*, Supplement, p. 548: "In olden days, one believed that immortality was proved by erotic love, somewhat like this: these two love each other for all eternity, ergo, there ought to be an eternity; nowadays one proves it by having loved very frequently, for is not a perfection such as this proof of an immortal spirit!"

G. The Treatise on Immortality

In Chapter 2 of Møller's unfinished novel *Adventures of a Danish Student*, the main character, the frizzy Frits, tells his friends how he reflected upon the serious consequences of hanging himself in a blooming apple tree as a result of his unhappy love for the miller's daughter: "But then I constantly realized that the imperishable part of me, at my departure from this temporal sphere, would perhaps move to such distant regions that I could neither hear nor see anything of the sensation which, in particular, I had intended with my despairing decision."[220] The question about the existence of "distant regions" was central in the contemporary debate about immortality which Møller also participated in and which is the theme of his most extensive philosophical work, the treatise "Thoughts on the Possibility of Proofs of Human Immortality, with Regard to the Latest Literature on the Subject," which was printed in two installments in the *Maanedsskrift for Litteratur* in 1837.[221] The complex content of this large treatise has been treated thoroughly before, and I will refer to such treatments for a more detailed discussion.[222] Apart from some general remarks, I will here confine myself to focusing on Kierkegaard's references or allusions to the treatise, particularly in the *Concluding Unscientific Postscript*.

Møller says in one of his scattered thoughts: "That faith in immortality is an essential moment in knowledge is first seen quite clearly when one decides to

220 *ES1*, vol. 3, p. 80.

221 P.M. Møller, "Tanker over Muligheden af Beviser for Menneskets Udødelighed, med Hensyn til den nyeste derhen hørende Literatur," *Maanedsskrift for Litteratur*, vol. 17, Copenhagen: C.A. Reitzel 1837, pp. 1–72 (January issue) and 422–53 (May issue); reprinted in *ES1*, vol. 2, 1842, pp. 158–272. The title might allude to Ludwig Feuerbach's anonymous work, *Gedanken über Tod und Unsterblichkeit, aus den Papieren eines Denkers, nebst einem Anhang theologisch-satyrischer Xenien, herausgegeben von einem seiner Freunde*, Nürnberg: J.A. Stein 1830. Møller's treatise has been translated into French, "Réflexions sur la possibilité de prouver l'immortalité de l'homme en rapport avec la littérature récent sur le sujet," in *Lectures philosophiques de Søren Kierkegaard. Kierkegaard chez ses contemporains danois*, ed. and trans. by Henri-Bernard Vergote, Paris: Presses Universitaires de France 1993, pp. 149–213. An English translation will later appear in the series *Texts from Golden Age Denmark*, vol. 9.

222 More recently, the subject has been discussed in Jon Stewart, *A History of Hegelianism in Golden Age Denmark*, Tome II, *The Martensen Period: 1837–1842*, Copenhagen: C.A. Reitzel 2007 (*Danish Golden Age Studies*, vol. 3), pp. 37–53, and in Lasse Horne Kjældgaard, *Sjælen efter døden. Guldalderens moderne gennembrud*, Copenhagen: Gyldendal 2007, especially pp. 83–112 on Møller; see also Kjældgaard's article, "What It Means to Be Immortal: Afterlife and Aesthetic Communication in Kierkegaard's *Concluding Unscientific Postscript*," *Kierkegaard Studies Yearbook*, 2005, pp. 90–112. For a general overview of the debate on immortality, see also, for instance, the two articles of István Czakó, "Unsterblichkeitsfurcht. Ein christlicher Beitrag zu einer zeitgenössischen Debatte in Søren Kierkegaards 'Gedanken, die hinterrücks verwunden—zur Erbauung,' " *Kierkegaard Studies Yearbook*, 2007, pp. 227–254, and "Heiberg and the Immortality Debate: A Historical Overview," in *Johan Ludvig Heiberg: Philosopher, Littérateur, Dramaturge, and Political Thinker*, ed. by Jon Stewart, Copenhagen: Museum Tusculanum Press 2008 (*Danish Golden Age Studies*, vol. 5), pp. 95–138.

completely eliminate this concept from one's system; only then it will become clear that it is an indispensable moment in a consistent and harmonious world-view."[223] So it appears, then, that in order to come to terms with the truth of immortality, one has to eliminate it altogether, and then consider the proofs of its possible reality. In a way this is once more a struggle with nihilism and now the negation of eternal life. "For it is quite possible that the negation has not as yet completed the full measure it must reach before it becomes entirely evident that the desolation to which it leads is not a sphere in which the human spirit is supposed to move," Møller states at the beginning of the treatise.[224] Furthermore, in his own age he saw the dying-out of a Goethe-like classicism, or maybe rather of a Greek idealistic approach—his late poem "The Artist among the Rebels" was a bitter protest against this development—only to be superseded by nihilism, conflict and disharmony in all aspects of human existence. The arts, an anticipation of eternal life, ought to lead the way.

After the death of Hegel (1831) there had been an ongoing debate on the immortality of the soul, initiated by Friedrich Richter's (1807–56) work *Die Lehre von den letzten Dingen* in 1833.[225] Hegel himself never treated the subject specifically; as Møller says, it is not evident anywhere that Hegel denies immortality, but nonetheless, "whoever is somewhat able to read between the lines in Hegel's writings will easily reach the inevitable conclusion that this philosopher holds the concept of personal immortality to be a notion with no reality at all."[226] In the first part of the treatise (Sections I–VII), which is the most important, Møller develops his own view of the matter, and in the second (Sections VIII–XI) gives a critical account of recent speculative literature on the proofs of immortality, especially Christian Hermann Weiße (1801–66),[227] the younger Fichte (1797–1879),[228] and Carl Friedrich Göschel (1781–1861).[229] But he is not satisfied with any of these, although generally he states—once more, as in the aphorism quoted above—that "it is true of every isolated proof of human immortality that it has the possibility of opening the prospect of a profound and exhaustive world-view."[230] However, this is not possible within the frames of a philosophical system, and indeed the treatise on immortality must be seen as Møller's definitive break with Hegelianism as such, and

223 This aphorism is not found in the *Posthumous Writings*, but was published by Vilhelm Andersen in *Udvalgte Skrifter af Poul Møller*, vol. 2, p. 397.

224 *Maanedsskrift for Litteratur*, vol. 17, p. 4; *ES1*, vol. 2, p. 162.

225 Friedrich Richter, *Die Lehre von den letzten Dingen*, vol. 1, *Eine wissenschaftliche Kritik, aus dem Standpunct der Religion unternommen*, Breslau: In Joh. Friedr. Korn des älteren Buchhandlung 1833; a second volume, *Die Lehre vom jüngsten Tage. Dogma und Kritik*, appeared in Berlin: Richter'sche Buchhandlung 1844.

226 *Maanedsskrift for Litteratur*, vol. 17, p. 25; *ES1*, vol. 2, p. 185.

227 C.H. Weiße, *Die philosophische Geheimlehre von der Unsterblichkeit des menschlichen Individuums*, Dresden: Ch.F. Grimmer'sche Buchhandlung 1834.

228 I.H. Fichte, *Die Idee der Persönlichkeit und der individuellen Fortdauer*, Elberfeld: Büschler'schen Verlagsbuchhandlung und Buchdruckerei 1834 (*ASKB* 505).

229 C.F. Göschel, *Von den Beweisen für die Unsterblichkeit der menschlichen Seele im Lichte der speculativen Philosophie*, Berlin: Duncker und Humblot 1835.

230 *Maanedsskrift for Litteratur*, vol. 17, p. 453; *ES1*, vol. 2, p. 271.

not only a critique of right Hegelians who, in his view, wrongly attribute a doctrine of immortality to Hegel.

Møller points to two different conceptions of the divine in modern philosophy: the theistic and the pantheistic, which derive from Leibniz and Spinoza, respectively. In recent times raw pantheism prevails (in theology apparent as "omnipresence," "omnipotence," etc.), and so it is obvious that "The doctrine of the souls as independent things or substances has disappeared for everyone who has even a little tinge of the age's philosophical culture; but thereby the doctrine of immortality has also lost its old foundation."[231] Most people asking for strict proofs of immortality have no conditions of doing so: "Only one who in passing moments is capable of feeling a true freedom from all mundane interests is receptive to the conviction of an actually existing supersensible world. I do not mean the freedom of irony, but the very freedom that leads to a true life in the world."[232] Møller then uses an anecdote of a bookkeeper and a theologian in order to illustrate the general self-deception. Afterwards he shows that immortality cannot be proved mathematically or ontologically (*a priori*). With the lack of any logical proof, what is necessary is a concrete, complete world-view ("*fuldstændig Verdensanskuelse*") that has to be accounted for *completely*, both empirically regarding the phenomena from the world of sense, and in terms of the Christian tradition of the supersensible. Hegelians who have tried to present a world-view without the doctrine of immortality have never succeeded with this, be it by means of logical pantheism or otherwise, and Hegelianism has outlived itself: "A life-view that outrages humanity's feeling of truth has refuted itself temporarily by its explicit and decisive statements, and thereby an endeavor is brought about to present the Christian tradition in a new scientific system that eventually succeeds the old in which the inadequacies are commonly felt."[233] Møller recognizes that he will not himself be able to supply a new true, universal world-view; that will be a task for the future to develop.[234]

All of this might seem very abstract, but at least one visible consequence of the negation of immortality, according to Møller, is a growing number of suicides, which is just a symptom of an overall nihilistic world-view consistent with the negation: "In accordance with the annihilation doctrine [*Tilintetgjørelseslæren*], the conduct of individuals toward one another will, for those who are aware of the brevity of life, be about as unimportant as a long dream. A life-view that leads to practical nihilism easily passes over to a positive striving for self-annihilation."[235] Also the love for

---

231 Ibid., p. 10; *ES1*, vol. 2, p. 168.

232 Ibid., p. 17; *ES1*, vol. 2, pp. 176–7.

233 Ibid., pp. 45–6; *ES1*, vol. 2, p. 208.

234 Carl Henrik Koch argues that Møller's treatise is an affiliation with I.H. Fichte's speculative theism, and that this was Møller's final philosophical position; for this, see further C.H. Koch, *Den danske idealisme 1800–1880*, Copenhagen: Gyldendal 2004 (*Den danske filosofis historie*, vol. 4, ed. by Sten Ebbesen and C.H. Koch), pp. 261–4.

235 *Maanedsskrift for Litteratur*, vol. 17, p. 51; *ES1*, vol. 2, p. 214. On what according to H.P. Barfod was a loose sheet of paper (*B-fort.* 405b, cf. *EP*, vol. 3, p. 317) Kierkegaard wrote: "A funeral speech?—The pattern which is interwoven should be Poul Møller." *Pap.* VII–1 B 224. It is not clear what he meant, but one of the other sheets it was found together with said, "At the grave of a suicide." *Pap.* VII–1 B 227.

one's fellow man becomes an illusion and loses its value: "The love that views its object as perishable is by necessity of a different nature than the love that knows its object to belong to what eternally exists."[236] Third, the ideal and contemplative drive loses its meaning, that is to say, science, art and religion lose their interest. As what one might call an "indirect proof," Møller argues that the creation of art necessarily implies a belief in immortality:

> In order that a human being may have enough centrifugal force to move in the regions of higher imagination, it must either, with a sort of reflection-free immortality, use life as an eternity, with no clear notion of its shortness, or it must be convinced of the reality of the concept of immortality. Here I set forth the claim without any hesitation that doubt of the immortality of individuals is the cancer of art, and the conviction of their destructibility is the grave of art....what I have to say here is meant literally: "True art is an anticipation of the blessed life."[237]

In his review in *Perseus* of V.H. Rothe's *Doctrine of the Trinity and Reconciliation*, Heiberg alluded bitterly to Møller as a deserter of Hegelianism.[238] Although Møller

---

236 *Maanedsskrift for Litteratur*, vol. 17, p. 52; *ES1*, vol. 2, p. 215. It seems strange, then, that many people appear happy, but this may easily be explained as self-deception: "That a great number of people who do not believe in immortality nevertheless display a great zest for life can generally be explained as a kind of thoughtlessness that accounts for their mediocre orientation in their own realm of ideas. But now the human race has acquired a melancholy direction that neither will allow its self-contradictions to remain unnoticed nor permit it to constantly forget itself in meaningless busyness." *Maanedsskrift for Litteratur*, vol. 17, p. 64; *ES1*, vol. 2, p. 228. The theme of busyness is also treated by Kierkegaard in many places, for instance, in the well-known diapsalma, *SKS* 2, 33 / *EO1*, 25.

237 *Maanedsskrift for Litteratur*, vol. 17, pp. 53–4; *ES1*, vol. 2, pp. 216–17. Møller's famous thesis that true art is an anticipation of the eternal or blessed life ("*Den sande Kunst er en Anticipation af det salige Liv*") might well be inspired by one of the works he discusses in his treatise, C.H. Weiße's *Die philosophische Geheimlehre*, in which one reads, *inter alia* (pp. 46–7): "*Daß in dem Schönen, in den Werken des Genius sich ein Ewiges und geistig Absolutes, daß in ihm sich der Weltgeist selbst nach einer der unendlich vielen Gestalten, in die er, der unerschöpfliche Proteus, sich zu verwandeln weiß, offenbart: dieß ist eine Wahrnehmung, eine Gewißheit, die man mit Recht die Grundlage aller höhern Geistesbildung unsers Zeitalters nennen kann.... Wir erwähnen dieß hier...nur, um in dem gemeinschaftlichen Boden eben derjenigen Bildungskreise unseres Zeitalters, von denen der Zweifel an persönlicher Unsterblichkeit vornehmlich auszugehen pflegt, die Stelle aufzuzeigen, von der eine wissenschaftliche Widerlegung dieses Zweifels zu beginnen hat.*" Cf. Jon Stewart, *A History of Hegelianism in Golden Age Denmark*, Tome II, p. 49, note 3.

238 Valdemar Henrik Rothe, *Læren om Treenighed og Forsoning. Et speculativt Forsøg i Anledning af Reformationsfesten*, Copenhagen: J.D. Quist 1836. In his review, "Recension over Hr. Dr. Rothes Treenigheds- og Forsoningslære," in *Perseus, Journal for den speculative Idee*, no. 1, ed. by J.L. Heiberg, Copenhagen: C.A. Reitzel 1837 (*ASKB* 569), p. 33, Heiberg asks if the attempts of certain philosophers "for progress beyond the present scope of philosophy, are not unwittingly a regress. It remains to be seen whether the system, which they just left, does not contain what they now are looking for outside it, in which case they would have gone over the stream after water [taken unnecessary trouble]. Yet it seems unlikely that these deserters will ever constitute their own corps, since their goal is too indeterminate. Even if

respected his old friend, at this time they had drifted away from each other, at least this was definitely true in Møller's last year when, in a letter to Hauch, after expressing his dissatisfaction with the idea that poetry could be "speculative" or philosophical—as was allegedly the case with Heiberg's play *Fata Morgana* (which premiered on January 29, 1838) and would later be the case with his "apocalyptic comedy," "A Soul after Death" (1841)—Møller wrote that he and Heiberg "had long since ceased to understand each other."[239] Sibbern, on the other hand, later warmly defended the then departed Møller in his review of the first issue of *Perseus* in the *Maanedsskrift* of 1838, and saw him as a thinker for whom Hegelianism could be nothing but a temporary stage: "He could not have avoided passing through Hegelianism as a phase. But a thinker like Poul Møller could not allow himself to remain in it forever. It does not belong to his character to let himself be recruited into a philosophy like Hegel's for a lifetime or let himself be made into a *Hegelianismo adscriptus*."[240] Sibbern was right: a free genius, Møller was now heading in another direction, however unfortunately stopped by an early death. Above in Section II, I have already treated the passages in Kierkegaard which also reflect this movement: for example, Møller's strong verdict on Hegelian madness—and his hearty laughter at it.

---

they could specify what it is that they are seeking, for example, a future world-view, they nevertheless could say nothing about the way which leads there, but this is exactly what is at issue in philosophy, which cannot be served by having its properties on the moon." Heiberg's strong reaction should be seen in the light that Møller's treatise was also a critical response to Heiberg's negative statements regarding religion in his analysis of the crisis of the age, *On the Significance of Philosophy for the Present Age* (in *Heiberg's On the Significance of Philosophy for the Present Age and Other Texts*, trans. and ed. by Jon Stewart, Copenhagen: C.A. Reitzel 2005 (*Texts from Golden Age Denmark*, vol. 1), pp. 83–121 (originally as *Om Philosophiens Betydning for den nuværende Tid. Et Indbydelses-Skrift til en Række af philosophiske Forelæsninger*, Copenhagen: C.A. Reitzel 1833)), cf. Kjældgaard, *Sjælen efter døden*, p. 86.

239 Borup, Letter no. 168. That this eventual lack of understanding was only on an intellectual level, is evidenced by the personal elements of Heiberg's beautiful, although also traditional, song for Møller's funeral, printed in *ES1* just after F.C. Olsen's *Poul Martin Møllers Levnet* (p. 116); cf. *Johan Ludvig Heibergs Poetiske Skrifter*, vols. 1–11, Copenhagen: C.A. Reitzel 1862; vol. 8, pp. 386–7.

240 F.C. Sibbern, "*Perseus, Journal for den speculative Idee*. Udgiven af Johan Ludvig Heiberg. Nr. 1, Juni 1837. Kjøbenhavn. Reitzels Forlag. XIV og 264 S. 8. Priis 1 Rbd. 84 Skill.—(Med stadigt Hensyn til Dr. Rothes: *Læren om Treenighed og Forsoning. Et speculativt Forsøg i Anledning af Reformationsfesten.*)," *Maanedsskrift for Litteratur*, vols. 19 and 20, 1838, a series of eight articles, of which the first three were also published separately as a book, *Bemærkninger og Undersøgelser, fornemmelig betreffende Hegels Philosophie, betragtet i Forhold til vor Tid*, Copenhagen: C.A. Reitzel 1838; the quotation is from Article I, "Angaaende det Hegelske Begreb om Philosophie med Hensyn til dens Udgangspunct og dens hele Grundlag," *Maanedsskrift for Litteratur*, vol. 19, pp. 315–60; see p. 336; *Bemærkninger og Undersøgelser*, p. 54. Trans. by Jon Stewart in his *A History of Hegelianism in Golden Age Denmark*, Tome II, p. 198.

The young Søren Kierkegaard had read the first part of Møller's treatise soon after its appearance in the January issue of *Maanedsskrift for Litteratur*, 1837.[241] This is evident from the *Journal BB*, in which he wrote the following entry on February 4, 1837. What struck him first and foremost at this time was the inserted story of the bookkeeper and the theologian:

> The episode Poul Møller has included in his treatise on the immortality of the soul in the latest issue of the *Maanedsskrift* is very interesting. Perhaps relieving the strict scholarly tone in this way with lighter passages, in which life nevertheless emerges much more fully, will become the usual thing, and will in scholarly domain compare somewhat to the chorus, to the comic parts of romantic dramas.[242]

With this "episode"—also Kierkegaard's Danish wording—or "*Fortælling*," to use Møller's own term, in which a bookkeeper, in vain, asks a theologian for quick, popular proofs of immortality while he is shaving and getting dressed (indirectly also a critique of Heiberg's popularizing philosophy), Møller livens up an otherwise heavy presentation in such an unusual manner that he even has to excuse himself to the reader for doing so. Kierkegaard compares it to the chorus of ancient dramas—not surprising, with Møller as a "happy lover of Greek culture"—or comic parts of romantic dramas. But one might also compare Møller's way of transcending to another method of communication to Plato's similes, or at least I believe that Møller's inspiration is clearly that of Socratic dialogues.[243] True, it is a "lighter passage" in most scholarly surroundings. Kierkegaard seems to have taken over this technique of anecdotal insertions from Møller, especially in the *Concluding*

---

241 *Maanedsskrift for Litteratur* does not appear in the *ASKB* and Kierkegaard is not found on the list of subscribers, but as already mentioned Kierkegaard possibly read it in a public library or reading society, e.g., the Athenæum. That he read the *Maanedsskrift* regularly is clear also, for instance, from his reference to Møller's review of *The Extremes* (cf. *SKS* 19, 99, Not3:2.a / *JP* 4, 3847), see above Section III, D, or from BB:32 (*SKS* 17, 121 / *KJN* 1, 115), in which he mentions Martensen's review of Heiberg's *Introductory Lecture to the Logic Course* (1835) in the *Maanedsskrift for Litteratur*, vol. 16, 1836, pp. 515–28.

242 *SKS* 17, 134, BB:41 / *KJN* 1, 127–8. There is a facsimile of the journal page 110 with the entry in *SKS* 17, 132 / *KJN* 1, 126.

243 The nature of the story has been explained differently; for instance, John Chr. Jørgensen calls it a "short story" ("*novelle*"); *Den sande kunst. Studier i dansk 1800-tals realisme. Poul Møller, Hans Egede Schack, Georg Brandes, Herman Bang*, Copenhagen: Borgen 1980, pp. 55–60. In the earlier-mentioned letter to his brother Hans Ulrik (Borup, Letter no. 151), Møller says the following, comparing the inserted story to his aphorisms: "I have deliberately written the piece which appears in the *Maanedsskrift* in a desultory style [*desultorisk Foredrag*] or in aphorisms, not just because I am proceeding so methodically in my lectures that, for a change, I feel the need to break free when I am my own master, but also because I believe that this kind of style will win a number of readers which the former style will miss out on; moreover, because I know that it is understood by many people who do not understand the more rigorous presentation. But the aphorisms are written haphazardly, just as hats are made for sale without any measurements being taken. It is only by chance if they happen to fit someone's head or not. They are more prone to both understanding and misunderstanding than the more rigorous presentation."

Unscientific Postscript with Johannes Climacus' scenes in Frederiksberg Garden and on the churchyard.[244] Kierkegaard also seizes upon a pregnant expression from Møller's story: "*À propos*, since we now have brought up the subject, could you not as a theologian briefly recount to me the best proofs of the immortality of the soul? Please do it while I sharpen my razor and take a shave."[245] He later uses this in the *Postscript* and replaces the bookkeeper with "a serious man" in search of the truth:

> But one of the gentlemen wishers, a "serious man" who really wants to do something for his eternal happiness, may say, "Is it not possible to find out for certain, clearly and briefly, what an eternal happiness is? Can't you describe it to me 'while I shave,' just as one describes the loveliness of a woman, the royal purple, or distant regions?"[246]

The thorough information that Kierkegaard received from Møller's treatise was undoubtedly useful to him, although, as a subscriber to the *Tidsskrift for udenlandsk*

---

244 *SKS* 7, 170–2 and 213–19 / *CUP1*, 185–8 and 234–40. Other examples of inserted pieces, although not in a strictly philosophical context, are the six episodes in " 'Guilty?'/ 'Not-Guilty?' " in *Stages on Life's Way*. Possibly inspired by Møller, Kierkegaard, in one of these pieces, entitled "A Possibility" ("En Mulighed"), also uses a bookkeeper (*SKS* 6, 257–68 / *SLW*, 276–88). Kierkegaard, or Frater Taciturnus, lets this bookkeeper talk "dirty" with an old sea captain (*SKS* 6, 267 / *SLW*, 287–8), exactly as Kierkegaard himself is reported to have done according to the journal entry JJ:113 about his conversations with an old "China sea captain," who tells him, among other things, "how in Manila everyone has a wench, or about the fun he had in his youth with wenches (it is his favorite expression) in London" (*SKS* 18, 176 / *KJN* 2, 163–4). In this entry, which Kierkegaard made use of in *Stages on Life's Way*, it is perhaps also worth noticing his special mention of the location Manila, capital of the Philippines, where Møller had been on his voyage to China. One of the texts Møller was working on, but did not complete, during his voyage, was a diary or description of the voyage, "Entries on the Voyage to China" ("Optegnelser paa Reisen til China"), *ES1*, vol. 3, pp. 131–68, in which we find another "naughty" incident, not from Manila, however, but from Anyer on Java, on June 9, 1820: "In their trading the Malayans would often afterwards cancel their transactions. I had bought some canes for a dress coat, but the savage came back and wanted to redo the deal. In another case a Malayan came to a sailor bringing back his payment saying: *Trada mau* (I don't want it), to which the sailor said K— my a—, and the Malayan had to leave again with unfinished business." *ES1*, vol. 3, p. 159. This episode Kierkegaard refers to in his small unpublished study from 1848, "Phister as Captain Scipio" (*Pap.* IX B 67–73 / *C*, Supplement, pp. 329–44): "To say, in regard to reflection and a reflective performance, neither more nor less than 'Bravo' or 'Bravissimo' is completely meaningless, is something that can only bore and weary the reflection that is the object of admiration and something that easily becomes a conversation like the one between a Japanese [*sic*] and a Danish sailor that Poul Møller has preserved. The Japanese said: *Tanko–Panko*, to which the sailor very appropriately responded: Kiss my a—." *Pap.* IX B 68, p. 386 / *C*, Supplement, p. 331.

245 *Maanedsskrift for Litteratur*, vol. 17, p. 20; *ES1*, vol. 2, p. 179.

246 *SKS* 7, 357.28–33 / *CUP1*, 392. It is also found in *The Book on Adler*: "Such things cannot be presented in a newspaper and be read 'while one shaves.' " *Pap.* VII–2 B 235, p. 83 / *BA*, 43. Apropos shaving, Kierkegaard is inspired by the picture of Caligula used by Møller in regard to suicide (*Maanedsskrift*, vol. 17, pp. 51–2; *ES1*, vol. 2, p. 214) when in the *Journal EE*, in an entry dated May 4, 1839, he writes, "Caligula's idea of wanting to have all heads put on one neck is nothing but an attempted, cowardly suicide." *SKS* 18, 24.32–3, EE:55 / *KJN* 2, 20.

theologisk Litteratur, that is, *Journal for Foreign Theological Literature*, he had earlier been able to follow the German debate on the subject, reported by the editors H.N. Clausen and M.H. Hohlenberg.[247] In his treatise, Møller also discusses the nihilism of Schopenhauer, who was apparently not very familiar to Danish readers, including Kierkegaard.[248] Regardless of what Kierkegaard read, there can be no doubt whatsoever that he truly believed in the immortality of the human soul. From all of the numerous places he discusses immortality, this is evident, for instance, from one of his *Christian Discourses* (1848), "There will be the Resurrection of the Dead, of the Righteous—and of the Unrighteous," Part IV of "Thoughts that Wound from Behind."[249] However, with the religious doubts he knew that Møller had had, he was also well aware how difficult his preoccupation with immortality must have been. He has his pseudonym write in the *Postscript*:

> I know that the late Professor Poul Møller, who certainly was familiar with the newest philosophy, did not until late in life become really aware of the infinite difficulty of the question of immortality when it is made simple, and when the question is not about a new demonstration and about the opinions, strung on a thread, of Tom, Dick, and Harry or about the best way of stringing opinions on a thread. I also know that in a treatise he tried to give an account and that this monograph clearly reflects his aversion to modern speculative thought. The difficulty in the question arises precisely when it is made simple, not in the way a well-trained assistant professor inquires about the immortality of human beings, abstractly understood as humankind in general, and thus about the immortality of human beings in general, fantastically understood as the race, and thus about the immortality of the human race.[250]

---

247 See, for instance, NB11:74, the commentary on *SKS* 22, 44.13. Later he also read, for instance, K.L. Michelet, *Vorlesungen über die Persönlichkeit Gottes und Unsterblichkeit der Seele oder die ewige Persönlichkeit des Geistes*, Berlin: Ferdinand Dümmler 1841 (*ASKB* 680), and D.F. Strauß, *Fremstilling af den christelige Troeslære i dens historiske Udvikling og i dens Kamp med den moderne Videnskab*, vols. 1–2, trans. by Hans Brøchner, Copenhagen: H.C. Klein 1842–43 (*ASKB* 803–804); vol. 2, pp. 582–601 (originally, *Die christliche Glaubenslehre in ihrer geschichtlichen Entwicklung und im Kampfe mit der modernen Wissenschaft dargestellt*, vols. 1–2, Tübingen and Stuttgart: Osiander 1840–41). One of the Diapsalmata in *Either/Or* refers to the writing of treatises on immortality, but we cannot be sure if he has also Møller in mind; cf. *SKS* 2, 43–4 / *EO1*, 34–5.

248 To all appearances, Kierkegaard did not read Schopenhauer before 1854; the first time he mentions him is in the journal entry NB29:26 (*SKS* 25, 314–15). See, in general, Simonella Davini, "Schopenhauer: Kierkegaard's Late Encounter with His Opposite," in *Kierkegaard and His German Contemporaries*, Tome I, *Philosophy*, ed. by Jon Stewart, Aldershot: Ashgate 2007 (*Kierkegaard Research: Sources, Reception and Resources*, vol. 6), pp. 277–91.

249 *SKS* 10, 211–21 / *CD*, 202–13. On this, see for instance, Kjældgaard, *Sjælen efter døden*, pp. 217–22, and István Czakó, "Unsterblichkeitsfurcht."

250 *SKS* 7, 159 / *CUP1*, 172. As regards "the opinions of Creti and Pleti," Kierkegaard makes fun of this for instance in a journal entry on "*The Faith of the Thousands and Millions*": "This is how it all hangs together. One impresses upon the child: You are immortal—and then says: Never pay attention to it any more; never think about it, now get on with the busy activity of life (which, frivolously, is called being earnest), get married, have children, make something of yourself, be active early and late, but for heaven's sake see to it that you never give immortality another thought, for you are immortal, this is absolutely certain—this is called

He seizes upon one of the main points of the treatise on immortality—and makes it even more difficult, as is the custom of Climacus: I am thinking of another pregnant, but more substantial expression, of course, than the one about the bookkeeper shaving, namely, Møller's statement that true art is an anticipation of the blessed life. This is repeated by Kierkegaard in a couple of places: in the very book he dedicated to Møller, *The Concept of Anxiety*, in which he also notes that "what Poul Møller said is true, that immortality must be present everywhere,"[251] and in the *Postscript*, where it is extended to the following emphasis of immortality presupposing that a

---

having faith." *SKS* 25, 442, NB30:70 / *JP* 4, 5045. On the "making-a-living demonstration" cf. the words of Judge William in *Either/Or*: "But if he makes a good living, then he has achieved his destiny, but the destiny of making a good living cannot be that he is supposed to die but, on the contrary, that he is supposed to live well on his good living—*ergo*, man is immortal. This demonstration could be called the popular demonstration or the making-a-living demonstration. If this demonstration is added to the previous demonstrations, then every reasonable doubt about immortality must be regarded as conquered. This demonstration lends itself splendidly to being placed in conjunction with the other demonstrations—indeed, it shows up here in its full glory since as a conclusion it implies the others and substantiates them." *SKS* 3, 265.28–266.1 / *EO2*, 279–80.

[251] *SKS* 4, 452.19 and 452.32–3 / *CA*, 153. In the draft, *Pap.* V B 66 / *CA*, Supplement, p. 210, the text reads, "Therefore, Poul Møller was right that immortality must be present throughout and not brought in as an appendix to the system." As regards the statement that "true art is an anticipation of the blessed life," the editors of *SKS* suggest (in the explanatory note to 452.19 in *SKS* K4, p. 520) that Kierkegaard, in this case, has H.L. Martensen in mind, since on the same page of the draft (*Pap.* V B 60, p. 137 / *CA*, Supplement, p. 207), where he added the statement on art in the margin, he also discusses Martensen. In the final text of *The Concept of Anxiety* one reads, "Art is an anticipation of eternal life, because poetry and art are the reconciliation only of the imagination, and they may well have the *Sinnigkeit* [thoughtfulness] of intuition but by no means the *Innigkeit* [inwardness] of earnestness. Some paint eternity elaborately with the tinsel of the imagination and yearn for it. Some envision eternity apocalyptically, pretend to be Dante, while Dante, no matter how much he conceded to the view of the imagination, did not suspend the effect of ethical judgment." *SKS* 4, 452.19–24 / *CA*, 153. In the draft, this reflection appears in the margin after the statement on the nature of art: "that art is an anticipation of eternal life. The apocalyptic, in which, not as in Dante, judgment ethically conceived is suspended. In every case merely a fantasy-view." *Pap.* V B 60, p. 127 / *CA*, Supplement, p. 207. With his remarks on the apocalyptic, Kierkegaard is alluding to Heiberg's "apocalyptic comedy," A Soul after Death (in *New Poems*, 1841), which Martensen reviewed—and compared to Dante's *Divine Comedy*—in the journal *Fædrelandet*, January 10, 11, and 12, 1841. Much earlier, in his essay, "Observations on the Idea of Faust with Reference to Lenau's *Faust*" ("Betragtninger over Ideen af *Faust*. Med Hensyn paa *Lenaus* Faust"), in *Perseus, Journal for den speculative Idee*, no. 1, ed. by J.L. Heiberg, Copenhagen: C.A. Reitzel 1837, pp. 91–164, Martensen had written about "apocalyptic poetry" as "an anticipation of the Day of Judgment" (p. 98). (In the forerunner, *Ueber Lenau's Faust*, Stuttgart: Verlag der J.G. Cotta'schen Buchhandlung 1836, there is no trace of anything resembling a treatment of apocalyptic poetry.) However, one should bear in mind that the first issue of *Perseus* appeared in June 1837, whereas the first part of Møller's treatise, in which he discusses art as an anticipation, was published earlier, in January 1837, and so Martensen, in his essay, might be thinking of Møller. In the present context, *The Concept of Anxiety*, I see no reason to doubt that Kierkegaard also had Møller in mind.

human becomes a self: "all idealizing passion is an anticipation of the eternal in existence in order for an existing person to exist."[252]

IV. Some Words of Conclusion

Poul Martin Møller's impact on Søren Kierkegaard was manifold, but personal more than philosophical. It has become something of a myth that they were close "friends" and that Møller was Kierkegaard's "teacher," but the sources of their relationship are very few and uncertain. What the sources show, however, notably the draft of the dedication to *The Concept of Anxiety*, is Kierkegaard's very special feelings towards Møller, and maybe even more so after his death. He admired Møller's strong personality and especially his humor. In his lectures on the history of ancient philosophy, Møller says the following of Socrates, and these words would probably fit himself from Kierkegaard's point of view: "Especially his constant good humor and fine wit, which was spread over his conversations, had to make interaction with him attractive for his young friends."[253] It is certain that they had deep conversations which were very inspiring to Kierkegaard, and undoubtedly also to Møller, who realized the genius of the young verbose man, even though he was "thoroughly polemical." Of the maieutic method Møller writes:

> But the point was actually that he would go into their individual circle of thought, for which he had a truly extraordinary gift. He assimilated himself for a moment completely with the other person's entire view and knew to the satisfaction of the other person how to develop his circle of thought so that he would have to completely ascribe to it....By going completely into the circle of thought of the other person, he obliged the other person to follow along since his own thoughts were developed to consequences which he had not dreamed of, and to completely unexpected results.[254]

If we assume an inspiration from Møller on Kierkegaard's thought—which, as shown, we have many reasons to do in the case of, for instance, mutual motifs such as Ahasverus, various thoughts on aesthetic despair, nihilism, irony and psychology, and the general focus on subjectivity—we will also have to assume an extensive degree of oral communication between the two, since many of Møller's ideas seem to show up in Kierkegaard's writings before the appearance of the *Posthumous Writings*. What counts will be quality rather than quantity, which might explain why Kierkegaard himself only recorded one single nightly conversation; it appears from other sources, however, that they spent much time together. I will quote another passage possibly more important for the understanding of Møller as a "confidant

252 *SKS* 7, 285.1–3 / *CUP1*, 312–13. In the footnote to this, *SKS* 7, 285 / *CUP1*, 313, it reads, "Poetry and art have been called an anticipation of the eternal. If one wants to call them that, one must nevertheless be aware that poetry and art are not essentially related to an existing person, since the contemplation of poetry and art, 'joy over the beautiful,' is disinterested, and the observer is contemplatively outside himself *qua* existing person."

253 *ES1*, vol. 2, p. 361.

254 *ES1*, vol. 2, pp. 363–4.

of Socrates" since it illustrates well his Socratic impact on Kierkegaard. Møller specifies Socrates' importance in the history of philosophy in the way that

> he strove to assert subjective reason and lead his fellow citizens out of their unconscious submission to objective reason; he brought his followers to go into themselves and form a subjective realm of thought which should be the norm for the determination of humanity. He certainly knew the good as the absolute, but when it was to be determined from the subjective standpoint, thinking, which was supposed to determine it, had to first turn in doubt against what counted as valid with divine authority.[255]

Likewise, Møller supplied Kierkegaard with the understanding that in human existence, knowledge of an individual *personal truth* is decisive, and Kierkegaard later developed and expanded this concept of subjectivity to the fullest especially in the *Concluding Unscientific Postscript*. This is Møller's most important area of influence, even if it is frequently overshadowed by Kierkegaard's polemical focus on religion. As Kierkegaard himself admitted, "Although I am so thoroughly polemical and was so even in my youth, still Christianity is almost too polemical for me."[256] In the broader contours of his thought, however, Kierkegaard was deeply inspired by Møller—though not so much by Møller's thought as by his being who and how he was, and by his showing the way to truth.

---

255 *ES1*, vol. 2, p. 374.

256 *SKS* 25, 461, NB30:93 / *JP* 6, 6888.

Bibliography

I. Møller's Works in The Auction Catalogue *of Kierkegaard's Library*

Efterladte Skrifter af Poul M. Møller, vols. 1–3, ed. by Christian Winther, F.C. Olsen, and Christen Thaarup, 1st ed., Copenhagen: C.A. Reitzel 1839–43 (*ASKB* 1574–1576).

II. Works in The Auction Catalogue *of Kierkegaard's Library that Discuss Møller*

Adler, Adolph Peter, *Theologiske Studier*, Copenhagen: Trykt paa Forfatterens Forlag hos Louis Klein i Commission hos Universitets-Boghandler C.A. Reitzel 1846, p. 27, note (*ASKB* U 12).

Berg, Carl, *Grundtrækkene af en philosophisk Propædeutik eller Erkjendelseslære, tilligemed Poul Møllers kortfattede formelle Logik. Trykt som Manuskript til Brug for Elever af det kongl. Landcadetacademie*, Copenhagen: C.A. Reitzel 1839 (*ASKB* 426).

Hebbel, Friedrich, *Mein Wort über das Drama! Eine Erwiderung an Professor Heiberg in Copenhagen*, Hamburg: Hoffmann und Campe 1843, p. 12 (*ASKB* U 54).

Heiberg, Johan Ludvig, "Om Malerkunsten i dens Forhold til de andre skjønne Kunster," in *Perseus, Journal for den speculative Idee*, vols. 1–2, ed. by J.L. Heiberg, Copenhagen: C.A. Reitzel 1837–38, vol. 2, pp. 101–81, see p. 121 (*ASKB* 569).

—— "Lyrisk Poesie," in *Intelligensblade*, nos. 25–6, 1843, ed. by J.L. Heiberg, Copenhagen: C.A. Reitzel 1843 [in *Intelligensblade*, vols. 1–4, nos. 1–48, ed. by Johan Ludvig Heiberg, Copenhagen: C.A. Reitzel 1842–44, vol. 3, pp. 25–72, see p. 57; p. 71] (*ASKB* U 56).

Martensen, Hans Lassen, *Den christelige Dogmatik*, Copenhagen: C.A. Reitzel 1849, p. 540, note (*ASKB* 653).

Nielsen, Rasmus, *Den propædeutiske Logik*, Copenhagen: P.G. Philipsen 1845, p. 41; p. 116; p. 279 (*ASKB* 699).

Olsen, Frederik Christian, *Poul Martin Møllers Levnet, med Breve fra hans Haand*, in *Efterladte Skrifter af Poul M. Møller*, 1st ed., vol. 3, Copenhagen: C.A. Reitzel 1843 (*ASKB* 1576). (Also published separately, Copenhagen: C.A. Reitzel 1843.)

Ørsted, Anders Sandøe, *Af mit Livs og min Tids Historie*, vols. 1–2, Copenhagen: Gyldendal 1851–52 [vols. 3–4, Copenhagen: Gyldendal 1855–57], vol. 1, p. 163 (*ASKB* 1959–1960).

III. Secondary Literature on Kierkegaard's Relation to Møller

Ammundsen, Valdemar, *Søren Kierkegaards Ungdom. Hans Slægt og hans religiøse Udvikling*, Copenhagen: J.H. Schultz 1912, p. 75, note; p. 79; p. 119; pp. 126–7.

Andersen, Vilhelm, *Poul Møller. Hans Liv og Skrifter efter trykte og utrykte Kilder i Hundredaaret for hans Fødsel*, 1st ed., Copenhagen: G.E.C. Gad 1894, p. 392; pp. 394–9 (2nd ed., 1904; 3rd ed., 1944).

—— *Tider og Typer af dansk Aands Historie. Første Række: Humanisme. Anden Del: Goethe. Anden Bog: Det nittende Aarhundredes sidste Halvdel*, Copenhagen: Gyldendal 1916, pp. 98–9; pp. 102–4; pp. 109–10.

Andreasen, Uffe, *Poul Møller og romantismen – den filosofiske idealisme i Poul Møllers senere forfatterskab*, Copenhagen: Gyldendal 1973, p. 16; p. 48; p. 59; p. 74; pp. 86–7.

Billeskov Jansen, F.J., *Studier i Søren Kierkegaards litterære Kunst*, Copenhagen: Rosenkilde & Bagger 1951, pp. 44–5. (Published in French as *L'art littéraire de Søren Kierkegaard*, trans. by Else-Marie Jacquet-Tisseau, Paris: Éditions de l'Orante 2000 (*Bibliothèque Kierkegaardienne*), pp. 43–4.)

—— "I grandi romanzi filosofici di Kierkegaard," in *Studi Kierkegaardiani*, ed. by Cornelio Fabro, Brescia: Morcelliana 1957, pp. 75–9.

—— "Den danske Idealisme eller Kjærlighedens Blomsterringe," *Meddelelser fra Dansklærerforeningen*, no. 3, 1968, pp. 177–80.

Brandes, Georg, *Søren Kierkegaard. En kritisk Fremstilling i Grundrids*, Copenhagen: Gyldendal 1877, p. 37; p. 56; pp. 65–6.

Brandt, Frithiof, *Den unge Søren Kierkegaard. En række nye bidrag*, Copenhagen: Levin & Munksgaard 1929, pp. 336–446; pp. 454–9.

Brøchner, Hans, "Erindringer om Søren Kierkegaard," *Det nittende Aarhundrede*, vol. 5, 1877, pp. 337–74, entry 36.

Brückner, Paul, *Lichtträger und Irrgeister*, Wuppertal-Elberfeld: Verlag Die Aue 1929, pp. 47–76.

Bukdahl, Jørgen K., "Poul Martin Møllers opgør med 'nihilismen,' " *Dansk Udsyn*, vol. 45, ed. by Richard Andersen et al., Vejen: Askov Højskole 1965, pp. 266–90.

Caron, Jacques, *Angoisse et Communication chez S. Kierkegaard*, Odense: Odense University Press 1992, pp. 25–37.

Czakó, István, "Unsterblichkeitsfurcht. Ein christlicher Beitrag zu einer zeitgenössischen Debatte in Søren Kierkegaards 'Gedanken, die hinterrücks verwunden—zur Erbauung,' " *Kierkegaard Studies Yearbook*, 2007, pp. 227–54.

—— "Heiberg and the Immortality Debate: A Historical Overview," in *Johan Ludvig Heiberg: Philosopher, Littérateur, Dramaturge, and Political Thinker*, ed. by Jon Stewart, Copenhagen: Museum Tusculanum Press 2008 (*Danish Golden Age Studies*, vol. 5), pp. 95–138.

Davini, Simonella, "Schopenhauer: Kierkegaard's Late Encounter with His Opposite," in *Kierkegaard and His German Contemporaries*, Tome I, *Philosophy*, ed. by Jon Stewart, Aldershot: Ashgate 2007 (*Kierkegaard Research: Sources, Reception and Resources*, vol. 6), pp. 277–91; see p. 278.

Egeløv, Arne, "Poul Martin Møller om Søren Kierkegaards Udseende," *Politiken*, May 12, 1842.

Fenger, Henning, "Kierkegaard: A Literary Approach," in *Kierkegaard and His Contemporaries: The Culture of Golden Age Denmark*, ed. by Jon Stewart, Berlin and New York: Walter de Gruyter 2003 (*Kierkegaard Studies Monograph Series*, vol. 10), pp. 301–18; see p. 304; p. 306. (Originally in *Scandinavica*, vol. 3, 1964, pp. 1–16.)

Fenves, Peter, *"Chatter": Language and History in Kierkegaard*, Stanford: Stanford University Press 1993, pp. 35–39.

Garff, Joakim, *Søren Kierkegaard: A Biography*, trans. by Bruce H. Kirmmse, Princeton: Princeton University Press 2004, p. 64; p. 69; pp. 86–9; pp. 90–5; p. 126; p. 144; p. 150; p. 179; p. 193; p. 320; p. 386; p. 421; p. 474; p. 707.

Geismar, Eduard, *Søren Kierkegaard. Hans Livsudvikling og Forfattervirksomhed*, vols. 1–6, Copenhagen: G.E.C. Gad 1926–28, vol. 1, pp. 60–5.

—— "Poul Martin Møllers Betydning for Søren Kierkegaard. I Hundredaaret for Poul Martin Møllers Død," *Berlingske Tidende*, October 9, 1938.

Glebe-Møller, Jens, " 'Udødeligheden er Dommen'—om sjælens udødelighed," *Dansk Teologisk Tidsskrift*, vol. 68, 2005, pp. 65–73; pp. 70–3.

Hansen, Valdemar, "Le principe de personnalité chez trois penseurs danois: Høffding, Kierkegaard, Poul Møller," *Storia della filosofia moderna e contemporanea*, vol. 12, Florence: Sansoni editore 1961 (*Atti del XII Congresso Internazionale di Filosofia*), pp. 205–10.

Heiberg, P.A., *Bidrag til et psykologisk Billede af Søren Kierkegaard i Barndom og Ungdom*, Copenhagen: Otto B. Wroblewski 1895, p. 108; pp. 132–3.

Henningsen, Bernd, *Poul Martin Møller oder Die dänische Erziehung des Søren Kierkegaard. Eine kritische Monographie mit einer ersten Übersetzung seiner Abhandlung über die "Affectation,"* Frankfurt am Main: Akademische Verlagsgesellschaft 1973.

Hermann, Jesper, "Forholdet mellem Poul Møller og Søren Kierkegaard, en dokumentation" (summary), in *Extracta. Resumeer af specialeopgaver fra det Filosofiske Fakultet ved Københavns Universitet 1967–1968*, ed. by Ivan Boserup et al., vol. 1, Copenhagen: Akademisk Forlag 1968, pp. 112–14.

Himmelstrup, Jens, *Søren Kierkegaards Opfattelse af Sokrates. En Studie i dansk Filosofis Historie*, Copenhagen: Arnold Busck 1924, pp. 175–6; pp. 318–19.

—— *Sibbern. En Monografi*, Copenhagen: J.H. Schultz 1934, pp. 170–1; pp. 262–3.

Høffding, Harald, *Søren Kierkegaard som Filosof*, Copenhagen: P.G. Philipsens Forlag 1892, pp. 24–7.

—— *Danske Filosofer*, Copenhagen: Gyldendalske Boghandel Nordisk Forlag 1909, p. 118; p. 123, note; p. 127; p. 148; pp. 150–1.

Jensenius, Knud, *Nogle Kierkegaardstudier. "De tre store Ideer,"* Copenhagen: Nyt Nordisk Forlag Arnold Busck 1932, pp. 125–53.

Jones, W. Glyn, "Sören Kierkegaard and Poul Martin Møller," *Modern Language Review*, vol. 60, 1965, pp. 73–82.

Jørgensen, Carl, *Søren Kierkegaard. En biografi med særligt henblik paa hans personlige etik*, vols. 1–5, Copenhagen: Nyt Nordisk Forlag Arnold Busck 1964, vol. 1, pp. 87–95.

Jørgensen, John Chr., *Den sande kunst. Studier i dansk 1800-tals realisme. Poul Møller, Hans Egede Schack, Georg Brandes, Herman Bang*, Copenhagen: Borgen 1980, p. 33; p. 54; p. 64; p. 148; p. 152; p. 164; p. 181.

Kabell, Aage, *Kierkegaardstudiet i Norden*, Copenhagen: H. Hagerup 1948, pp. 232–6.

Kirmmse, Bruce H., "Socrates in the Fast Lane: Kierkegaard's *The Concept of Irony* on the University's *Velocifère*: Documents, Context, Commentary, and Interpretation," in *The Concept of Irony*, ed. by Robert L. Perkins, Macon, Georgia: Mercer University Press 2001 (*International Kierkegaard Commentary*, vol. 2) pp. 17–99; see p. 51; pp. 61–2; pp. 66–7; pp. 87–93; pp. 95–8.

Kjældgaard, Lasse Horne, "What It Means to Be Immortal: Afterlife and Aesthetic Communication in Kierkegaard's *Concluding Unscientific Postscript*," *Kierkegaard Studies Yearbook*, 2005, pp. 90–112.

—— *Sjælen efter døden. Guldalderens moderne gennembrud*, Copenhagen: Gyldendal 2007, passim (on Møller especially pp. 83–112).

Kjær, Grethe, *Barndommens ulykkelige elsker. Kierkegaard om barnet og barndommen*, Copenhagen: C.A. Reitzel 1986, pp. 118–27.

Koch, Carl Henrik, *En flue på Hegels udødelige næse eller om Adolph Peter Adler og om Søren Kierkegaards forhold til ham*, Copenhagen: C.A. Reitzel 1990, pp. 24–6; p. 33; pp. 45–6; p. 57; pp. 75–6.

—— *Den danske idealisme 1800–1880*, Copenhagen: Gyldendal 2004 (*Den danske filosofis historie*, ed. by Sten Ebbesen and C.H. Koch, vol. 4), p. 249; p. 267; p. 269.

Kühle, Sejer, "Søren Kierkegaard og den Heibergske Kreds," *Personalhistorisk Tidsskrift*, vol. 48, 1947, pp. 1–13; pp. 3–7.

—— *Søren Kierkegaards barndom og ungdom*, Copenhagen: Aschehoug Dansk Forlag 1950, p. 25; p. 77; p. 80; pp. 101–14; pp. 122–9; p. 152; p. 158.

Lilhav, Preben, *Kierkegaards valg*, Risskov: Forlaget Sicana 2003, pp. 51–73.

Lübcke, Poul, "Det ontologiske program hos Poul Møller og Søren Kierkegaard," *Filosofiske Studier*, vol. 6, 1983, pp. 127–47.

—— "F.C. Sibbern: Epistemology as Ontology," in *Kierkegaard and His Contemporaries: The Culture of Golden Age Denmark*, ed. by Jon Stewart, Berlin and New York: Walter de Gruyter 2003 (*Kierkegaard Studies Monograph Series*, vol. 10), pp. 25–44; see pp. 28–9; p. 42. (Originally in *Danish Yearbook of Philosophy*, vol. 13, 1976, pp. 167–78).

Lund, Henriette, *Erindringer fra Hjemmet*, Copenhagen: Gyldendal 1909, pp. 119–20.

Madsen, Børge, "Poul Martin Møller og Kierkegaard," *Information*, August 6, 1963.

Magnussen, Rikard, *Søren Kierkegaard set udefra*, Copenhagen: Munksgaard 1942, pp. 120–3.

Malantschuk, Gregor, "Søren Kierkegaard og Poul M. Møller," *Kierkegaardiana*, vol. 3, 1959, pp. 7–20. (Reprinted in *Frihed og Eksistens. Studier i Søren Kierkegaards tænkning*, ed. by Niels Jørgen Cappelørn and Paul Müller, Copenhagen: C.A. Reitzel 1980, pp. 101–13.)

—— *Dialektik og Eksistens hos Søren Kierkegaard*, Copenhagen: C.A. Reitzel 1968, p. 29; pp. 141–2; p. 278.

Møller, A. Egelund, *Søren Kierkegaard om politik*, Copenhagen: Forlaget Strand 1975, pp. 30–5; pp. 155–6.

Mortensen, Klaus P., *Thomasines oprør – en familiehistorisk biografi om køn og kærlighed i forrige århundrede*, Copenhagen: G.E.C. Gad 1986, p. 151.

Nielsen, Svend Aage, *Kierkegaard og Regensen. Kierkegaards forhold til F.C. Petersen, Poul Martin Møller, D.G. Monrad, Magnus Eiriksson, Carl Ploug, P.L. Møller, Hans Brøchner og J.C. Hostrup*, Copenhagen: Graabrødre Torv's Forlag 1965, pp. 27–43.

Nordentoft, Kresten, *Kierkegaard's Psychology*, Pittsburgh: Duquesne University Press 1978, pp. 95–6; pp. 325–6; p. 394. (Originally *Kierkegaards psykologi*, Copenhagen: Hans Reitzels Forlag 1972, p. 113; p. 128; pp. 139–42; p. 199; p. 382; p. 419; p. 421.)

—— *"Hvad siger Brand-Majoren?" Kierkegaards opgør med sin samtid*, Copenhagen: G.E.C. Gad 1973, p. 27.

Nun, Katalin, "Thomasine Gyllembourg's *Two Ages* and her Portrayal of Everyday Life," in *Kierkegaard and His Contemporaries: The Culture of Golden Age Denmark*, ed. by Jon Stewart, Berlin and New York: Walter de Gruyter 2003 (*Kierkegaard Studies Monograph Series*, vol. 10), pp. 272–97; see p. 296.

Paludan-Müller, Martin, *Udlængsel og hjemve. Personlighedsopfattelse hos Poul Møller og hans forgængere*, Copenhagen: Museum Tusculanums Forlag 1987, pp. 7–8; pp. 14–15; p. 61; p. 88; pp. 92–3.

Pattison, George, *Kierkegaard's Theory and Critique of Art, Its Theological Significance*, Ph.D. Thesis, University of Durham 1983, pp. 89–102.

—— "Art in an Age of Reflection," in *The Cambridge Companion to Kierkegaard*, ed. by Alastair Hannay and Gordon D. Marino, Cambridge: Cambridge University Press 1998, pp. 76–100; see pp. 92–3, p. 96.

—— *Kierkegaard, Religion and the Nineteenth-Century Crisis of Culture*, Cambridge: Cambridge University Press 2002, p. 63; pp. 77–81; p. 90; p. 93; p. 98; pp. 228–9; p. 243.

—— "D.F. Strauss: Kierkegaard and Radical Demythologization," in *Kierkegaard and His German Contemporaries*, Tome II, *Theology*, ed. by Jon Stewart, Aldershot: Ashgate 2007 (*Kierkegaard Research: Sources, Reception and Resources*, vol. 6), pp. 233–57; see p. 250.

Politis, Hélène, "Kierkegaard: Documents philosophiques," in *Kierkegaard. Vingt-Cinq Études* (*Le Cahiers de Philosophie*, nos. 8–9), 1989, pp. 443–72.

Reuter, Hans, *S. Kierkegaards religionsphilosophische Gedanken im Verhältnis zu Hegels religionsphilosophischen System*, Leipzig: Verlag von Quelle & Meyer 1914 (*Abhandlungen zur Philosophie und ihrer Geschichte*, vol. 23), pp. 68–74.

Rohde, H.P., "Poul Møller," in *Kierkegaard's Teachers*, ed. by Niels Thulstrup and Marie Mikulová Thulstrup, Copenhagen: C.A. Reitzel 1982 (*Bibliotheca Kierkegaardiana*, vol. 10), pp. 89–109.

—— "Poul Møller og Søren Kierkegaard," in *Afhandlingerne på originalsproget i "Søren Kierkegaard – Tænkning og sprogbrug i Danmark." Festskrift i anledning af prof. dr. Masaru Otanis 70 års fødselsdag*, Copenhagen: privately printed [1983], pp. 1–22 (separate pagination).

Rosenau, Hartmut, "I.H. Fichte: Philosophy as the Most Cheerful Form of Service to God," in *Kierkegaard and His German Contemporaries*, Tome I, *Philosophy*, ed. by Jon Stewart, Aldershot: Ashgate 2007 (*Kierkegaard Research: Sources, Reception and Resources*, vol. 6), pp. 49–66; see p. 60.

Rubow, Paul V., *Kierkegaard og hans Samtidige*, Copenhagen: Gyldendal 1950, pp. 14–16.

Schäfer, Klaus, *Hermeneutische Ontologie in den Climacus-Schriften Sören Kierkegaards*, Munich: Kösel-Verlag 1968, pp. 117–20.

Scopetea, Sophia, *Kierkegaard og græciteten. En kamp med ironi*, Copenhagen: C.A. Reitzel 1995, p. 25; p. 57; p. 101, note 4; p. 156, note 31; p. 236, note 5.

Soderquist, K. Brian, "Kierkegaard's Contribution to the Danish Discussion of 'Irony,' " in *Kierkegaard and His Contemporaries: The Culture of Golden Age Denmark*, ed. by Jon Stewart, Berlin and New York: Walter de Gruyter 2003 (*Kierkegaard Studies Monograph Series*, vol. 10), pp. 78–105; see especially p. 79; p. 80; p. 88; pp. 90–8; pp. 101–5.

—— "The Closed Self: Kierkegaard and Poul Martin Møller on the Hubris of Romantic Irony," in *Kierkegaard and the Word(s): Essays on Hermeneutics and Communication*, ed. by Poul Houe and Gordon D. Marino, Copenhagen: C.A. Reitzel 2003, pp. 204–14.

—— *The Isolated Self: Truth and Untruth in Søren Kierkegaard's On the Concept of Irony*, Copenhagen: C.A. Reitzel 2007 (*Danish Golden Age Studies*, vol. 1), pp. 144–69.

Stewart, Jon, *Kierkegaard's Relations to Hegel Reconsidered*, Cambridge: Cambridge University Press 2003, pp. 74–7; pp. 81–2; p. 138; p. 453; p. 605; p. 630; p. 632.

—— "Introduction," in *Kierkegaard and His Contemporaries: The Culture of Golden Age Denmark*, ed. by Jon Stewart, Berlin and New York: Walter de Gruyter 2003 (*Kierkegaard Studies Monograph Series*, vol. 10), pp. 1–22; see pp. 8–9.

—— "Kierkegaard and Hegelianism in Golden Age Denmark," in *Kierkegaard and His Contemporaries: The Culture of Golden Age Denmark*, ed. by Jon Stewart, Berlin and New York: Walter de Gruyter 2003 (*Kierkegaard Studies Monograph Series*, vol. 10), pp. 106–45; see pp. 136–9; pp. 145–6.

—— *A History of Hegelianism in Golden Age Denmark*, Tome I, *The Heiberg Period: 1824–1836*, Copenhagen: C.A. Reitzel 2007 (*Danish Golden Age Studies*, vol. 3), pp. 63–4; pp. 202–3; p. 210; pp. 237–43; p. 462; pp. 506–7; p. 532.

—— *A History of Hegelianism in Golden Age Denmark,* Tome II, *The Martensen Period: 1837–1842,* Copenhagen: C.A. Reitzel 2007 (*Danish Golden Age Studies*, vol. 3), pp. 37–53; p. 163; p. 447; pp. 566–8; p. 614.

Summers, Richard M., "Aesthetics, Ethics, and Reality: A Study of *From the Papers of One Still Living*," in *Early Polemical Writings*, ed. by Robert L. Perkins, Macon, Georgia: Mercer University Press 1999 (*International Kierkegaard Commentary*, vol. 1), pp. 45–68.

Thielst, Peter, "Poul Martin Møller (1794–1838): Scattered Thoughts, Analysis of Affectation, Combat with Nihilism," *Danish Yearbook of Philosophy*, vol.

13, 1976, pp. 66–83. (Reprinted as "Poul Martin Møller: Scattered Thoughts, Analysis of Affectation, Struggle with Nihilism," in *Kierkegaard and His Contemporaries: The Culture of Golden Age Denmark*, ed. by Jon Stewart, Berlin and New York: Walter de Gruyter 2003 (*Kierkegaard Studies Monograph Series*, vol. 10), pp. 45–61.)

—— *Livet forstås baglæns, men må leves forlæns. Historier om Søren Kierkegaard*, Copenhagen: Gyldendal 1994, pp. 48–52.

Thulstrup, Niels, *Kierkegaard's Relation to Hegel*, trans. by George L. Stengren, Princeton: Princeton University Press 1980, p. 33; p. 51, note; p. 57; p. 105, note; p. 113; p. 115; p. 146; pp. 150–1; p. 154; pp. 174–5; p. 181, note; p. 192; p. 196; pp. 199–200; p. 212; p. 243, note; p. 351; p. 366. (Originally *Kierkegaards Forhold til Hegel og til den spekulative Idealisme indtil 1846*, Copenhagen: Gyldendal 1967; German translation, *Kierkegaards Verhältnis zu Hegel und zum spekulativen Idealismus 1835–1846*, Stuttgart: Verlag W. Kolhammer 1972.)

—— *Commentary on Kierkegaard's Concluding Unscientific Postscript*, trans. by Robert J. Widenmann, Princeton, New Jersey: Princeton University Press 1984, p. 75; pp. 83ff.; p. 172; p. 174; p. 179; p. 195; p. 223; p. 243; p. 246; pp. 316–17; p. 324; p. 341; p. 373. (Originally *Søren Kierkegaard. Afsluttende uvidenskabelige Efterskrift*, edited, introduced and annotated by Niels Thulstrup, vols. 1–2, Copenhagen: Gyldendal 1962.)

Troelsen, Bjarne, *Manden på Flydebroen. En fortælling om Søren Kierkegaard og det moderne menneskes tilblivelse*, Frederiksberg: Forlaget Anis 1997, pp. 48–52.

Troels-Lund, Troels Frederik, *Bakkehus og Solbjerg. Træk af et nyt Livssyns Udvikling i Norden*, vols. 1–3, Copenhagen: Gyldendal 1920–22, vol. 3, pp. 200–21.

Tudvad, Peter, *Kierkegaards København*, Copenhagen: Politikens Forlag 2004, p. 29; p. 73; p. 165; p. 176; pp. 179–82; p. 187; p. 202; p. 204; p. 236; p. 251.

Vergote, Henri-Bernard, "Poul Martin Moeller et Soeren Kierkegaard," *Revue de Métaphysique et de Morale*, vol. 75, 1970, pp. 452–76.

—— *Lectures philosophiques de Søren Kierkegaard. Kierkegaard chez ses contemporains danois. Textes de J.L. Heiberg, H.L. Martensen, P.M. Møller, F.C. Sibbern, F. Beck et S.A. Kierkegaard*, Paris: Presses Universitaires de France 1993.

Weltzer, Carl, *Peter og Søren Kierkegaard*, Copenhagen: G.E.C. Gad 1936, p. 98; pp. 120–3.

Ditlev Gothard Monrad:

Kierkegaard on Politics, the Liberal Movement, and the Danish Constitution

J. Michael Tilley

As is the case with a number of his other Danish contemporaries, Kierkegaard's arguments and claims often attack the person Ditlev Gothard Monrad rather than his arguments or positions. Kierkegaard's distaste for the liberal movement and his disdain for privileging the political over the religious regularly overshadowed any attempt on his part to do justice to Monrad's ideas. This sort of consideration may minimize some distance between the thought of Monrad and Kierkegaard, but ultimately, even when one attempts to reconstruct each of their respective views as fairly as possible, there are still fundamental disagreements between the two figures especially concerning the relationship between church and nation, religion and politics. In this article I argue that Kierkegaard's reaction to Monrad and to the concept of the People's Church of Denmark reveals an important component to his understanding of the relationship between Christianity and the political. The article is divided into three sections: (1) a brief overview of Monrad's life with emphasis on his religious, political, and literary achievements; (2) a description of Kierkegaard's direct references to Monrad in four journal entries; and (3) an account of Kierkegaard's views on the People's Church of Denmark as well as his conception of the political in light of the 1848–49 revolution in Denmark.

I. Short Overview of Monrad's Life and Main Works

Monrad is best known as the author of the Danish constitution, and he was also a prominent Danish politician and the Bishop of Lolland-Falster. He was born on November 24, 1811, and he died on March 28, 1887.[1] During their student years, Kierkegaard and Monrad attended the same schools. Like many other students

[1] The biographical and historical information contained in the first section, unless otherwise indicated, is from Povl Engelstoft's entry "Monrad, Ditlev Gothard," in *Dansk Biografisk Leksikon*, vols. 1–27, ed. by Povl Engelstoft, 2nd ed., Copenhagen: J.H. Schultz 1933–44, vol. 16, pp. 98–114.

during this time, Monrad studied theology, aesthetics, and philosophy.[2] He also took an interest in Semitic languages, ultimately defending his dissertation in the field.[3]

Monrad was also involved with the student meetings organized by Orla Lehmann (1810–70) after the death of Frederik VI on December 3, 1839,[4] and he shortly thereafter published five volumes of the *Political Leaflets* [*Politiske Flyveblade*]. Although Monrad was a member of a student organization that was very politically involved and he studied political science formally during a lengthy stay in Paris, he only became known as a political activist and thinker when he wrote his *Political Leaflets*. Monrad was also the editor of both *Fædrelandet* and the *Dansk Folkeblad* during the 1840s. In 1846, Monrad was appointed parish priest in Vester Ulslev in Lolland and thus became officially associated with the Church and State.[5] Upon Christian VIII's death in 1848 and the succession of his son Frederik VII, the people of Denmark demanded and received authorization for a new constitution. Monrad's experience as both a liberal political reformer and as a member of the State clergy made him an ideal candidate to promote and develop the new Danish constitution as a member of the March Ministry.[6] The March Ministry was a constitutional committee that was forged in order to develop a satisfactory constitution that would be sensitive to the demands of the reformers, the conservatives, the people of Denmark, and the established Church. The Danish Constitution was signed into law on June 5, 1849.

During and shortly after the political revolution, Monrad's life changed dramatically. He not only was ordained Bishop of Lolland-Falster (February 13, 1849), but he also was given a number of political positions within the new Danish government. His first office within the Danish government was as Cultural Minister responsible for Church, education, and culture, but he later became the Danish Prime Minister. As Prime Minister, Monrad was held responsible for the results of

2 Particularly during Monrad's student years and prior to leaving Denmark for New Zealand, he was known as a Hegelian. See Bruce Kirmmse, *Kierkegaard in Golden Age Denmark*, Bloomington, Indiana: Indiana University Press 1990, p. 491 and Jon Stewart, *Kierkegaard's Relations to Hegel Reconsidered*, Cambridge and New York: Cambridge University Press 2003, p. 69. Kirmmse even describes Monrad's concept of the People's Church (*den danske Folkekirke*) as a Hegelian concept. Nevertheless, later in life after he actually read Kierkegaard (*Stages on Life's Way*), Monrad was much more sympathetic to Kierkegaard. Cf. also Asger Nyholm, *Religion og Politik*, Copenhagen: Nyt Nordisk Forlag 1947, p. 300 and Svend Aage Nielsen, *Kierkegaard og Regensen*, Copenhagen: Graabrødre Torv's Forlag 1965, p. 68.

3 Monrad's degree was the same one Kierkegaard received, *Magistergraden*, which the latter received for *The Concept of Irony*. Like most of his contemporaries, Monrad's dissertation was written in Latin with the title *De formis quiescentibus linguarum Semiticarum* [*Concerning the Passive Forms in Semitic Languages*].

4 For an account of the relationship between Monrad and Kierkegaard during their early student years, see Nielsen, *Kierkegaard og Regensen*, pp. 45–69.

5 The Danish Church was a State Church [*statskirke*] during this time period, although it became the People's Church [*den danske Folkekirke*] in 1849.

6 The Danish historian Glædemark discusses Monrad's role in the March Ministry: H.J.H. Glædemark *Kirkeforfatningsspørgsmaalet i Danmark indtil 1874. En historisk-kirkeretlig studie*, Copenhagen: Munksgaard 1948, pp. 139–54. See also Nyholm, *Religion og Politik*, pp. 99–121.

the Second Schleswig War in which Denmark lost both Schleswig and Holstein. As a result, he left Denmark and moved with his family to New Zealand, where he lived from 1864 to 1869.

After returning to Denmark, he regained his position as Bishop of Lolland-Falster in 1871. He remained bishop there until his death in 1887. Although Monrad was the very embodiment of the union of religion and government in Denmark prior to 1864, he personally kept the two realms relatively separate after his return to Denmark.

II. Kierkegaard's References to Monrad

Kierkegaard makes reference to Monrad in four different journal entries. In three of the four references, Kierkegaard primarily identifies Monrad as a member of the liberal movement who is given religious and government appointments, such as his ordination as Bishop of Lolland-Falster[7] based on strategic political decisions by religious and political authorities. Two of these three entries express a general criticism of Jakob Peter Mynster (1775–1854) as the priest of Christendom in Denmark, and the third of these entries is critical both of the liberal movement and Mynster for giving the liberals too much authority. The fourth remaining reference is simply an offhanded comment in 1836 where Kierkegaard laments that his "situation" arose because he had borrowed money from Rasmus Kristian Rask (1787–1832) and Monrad.[8] The journal entry is only one sentence, and it is not clear why Kierkegaard needed to borrow the money, why he borrowed from Rask and Monrad, nor is it clear what his "situation" is. Because of the odd nature of this reference, and because the remaining references deal with similar subjects concerning Kierkegaard's view of the relationship between religion and politics, I will focus on these other three references.

The ordination of Monrad is unequivocally viewed by Kierkegaard as a political concession and is explicitly described as "worldly shrewdness" rather than Christian wisdom.[9] Kierkegaard interprets Monrad's ordination in this manner, even though Mynster and Monrad are relatively similar theologically,[10] because of Monrad's association with the liberal constitutional movement. Monrad's high-level religious

---

7 Lolland and Falster are two islands south of Zealand (where Copenhagen is located) that historically have constituted a relatively homogenous cultural and political entity. Lolland-Falster peasants were particularly active in the political arena just as the constitutional movement was gaining force.

8 *Pap.* I A 188 / *JP* 5, 5151.

9 *SKS* 22, 381–2, NB14:63.

10 Since Monrad was a parish priest on the island of Lolland, and since he was relatively similar to Mynster theologically, it is probably unfair of Kierkegaard to criticize the appointment of Monrad as Bishop of Lolland-Falster. There seem to be a number of very good theological and social reasons for the choice of Monrad as bishop, of which Kierkegaard is either ignorant or which he blatantly ignores. Still, we do not know the precise reason that Monrad was chosen for the position, and there is evidence that Hans Lassen Martensen made decisions about the position of bishop for Lolland-Falster based on pragmatic and political grounds. See *Biskop H. Martensens Breve*, ed. by Bjørn Kornerup, vols. 1–3, Copenhagen: Gads Forlag 1955–57, vol. 1, p. 120 and Kirmmse's translation of the quotation in *Kierkegaard*

appointment especially to a politically volatile region like Lolland-Falster appears from Kierkegaard's point of view as a sort of pragmatic political decision.

The apparent political character of Mynster's ordination of Monrad demonstrates that there is a radical difference between New Testament Christianity and Mynster's Christianity.[11] Furthermore, it shows that "Bishop Mynster's life, Christianity, is a lie" because Mynster maintains that Copenhagen, his entire diocese in Zealand, and all of Denmark are "in truth Christian."[12] Neither New Testament Christianity nor true Christianity is explicitly described in these journal entries, but it is evident that it involves some sort of commitment to the truth of Christianity even at the expense of one's wealth, cultural status, and reputation. The ordination of Monrad is evidence that Mynster is more concerned with maintaining the established Church and his position within it than with acting in accordance with the demands of New Testament Christianity.

Even though the primary thrust of these three entries is against Mynster, Kierkegaard is also critical of Monrad's political activity as a member of the March Ministry, the Danish constitutional committee. In one journal entry, Kierkegaard compares the political situation to the relationship between parents and children.[13] Although parents are able to submit themselves to their children, even more effectively than children could submit to their parents, it is still not the best state of affairs for the family, the parents, or the children. Likewise, the old vanguard, the religious establishment, the landowners, and the cultural elites are much more adept at submitting to the will of the new constitutional liberals than vice versa, but this, according to Kierkegaard, is not the best form of government. This comparison is applied specifically to Mynster's ordination of Monrad. Although Mynster is well-disciplined and can obey Monrad, "the young Monrad" is not able to do "his duty in obeying the old bishop."[14]

III. Kierkegaard's Reaction to Danish Political Movements and the Danish Constitution

Kierkegaard's criticism of Mynster, as well as his criticism of Monrad, because of Mynster's ordination of Monrad as Bishop of Lolland-Falster, reveals interesting facets of Kierkegaard's understanding of the relationship between Christianity and politics. It shows that he rejects any cooption of the democratic impulse for religious purposes. He interprets Mynster's decision to appoint Monrad as bishop as a political compromise that demonstrates how Mynster is all too willing to not only participate in the new political developments of 1849, but to use them to his own advantage. He reinscribes his own authority and position, and that of the Danish Church by appointing Monrad to a political region prone to revolt in the hope that Monrad's

---

in Golden Age Denmark, p. 194. Thus, it is not out of the realm of possibility that Mynster made the decision primarily for those sorts of reasons.

11 *Pap.* X–6 B 212.

12 *SKS* 22, 381–2, NB14:63.

13 *SKS* 20, 349–40, NB4:129 / *JP* 4, 4140.

14 *SKS* 20, 350, NB4:129 / *JP* 4, 4140.

position will quiet dissent. The flexibility of the established Church in capitulating to the demands of the time falsifies what Kierkegaard sees as genuine Christianity.

Implicit within this characterization is Kierkegaard's hope that the political events of 1848–49 would correct established Christianity in Denmark and allow one to reintroduce Christianity into Christendom. In *A Literary Review*, written just prior to the political developments of 1848–1849, Kierkegaard "prophesies" that the democratic tendencies and the leveling of the present age will make it possible for one to become a single individual capable of having a genuine relationship with God. The social demands of the public can make it such that one is satisfied with oneself and one's relation to God which in turn forces one to make up one's own mind rather than submitting to the will of the public.[15] The political revolution effectively would allow for the reintroduction of Christianity into Christendom. This claim, however, does not imply that Kierkegaard is in favor of democracy or the new political developments as such. Rather, he thinks they have the means for producing something which is virtually impossible in the cultural aristocracy of his times: that is to say, a person who is deeply sensitive to the importance of actually being a Christian in Christendom.

Mynster's cooption of Monrad demonstrates one way in which the established Church can preclude these sorts of religious developments. Another way that the established Church could relate to the new political developments is to use Christianity as a means to fight against the political changes. In such a situation, Christianity would serve as a cultural defense of the establishment. It would be a tool used to accomplish some other political, social, or cultural goal. Although such an approach is not discussed in the journal entries dealing explicitly with Monrad, it may be that such a criticism lurks behind Kierkegaard's identification of the State Church of Denmark (*Statskirke*) with the People's Church of Denmark (*den danske Folkekirke*).

Monrad is neither named in Kierkegaard's discussion of the People's Church nor is he the person who coined the term, but Monrad did author the Danish Constitution where the concept of the People's Church is employed in a unique way distinct from any previous uses.[16] Monrad found the concept to be appealing to a large, diverse group of people of influence, and he also thought the concept expressed theoretically the appropriate relationship between the people, the State, and the Church. I will first discuss the strategic political decision to use the concept, and then turn to the theoretical underpinnings of the concept.

The term "the People's Church" (*Folkekirke*), became very common among the Grundtvigians, and it escaped many of the critiques aimed at the State Church.

---

15 *SKS* 8, 88 / *TA*, 92.

16 Peter Christian Kierkegaard was the first to use the term "the People's Church." In 1841, P.C. Kierkegaard wrote, "Jesus Christ's Church in the People's Churches" ["*Jesu Christi Kirke i Folke-Kirkerne*"]. See *Peter Christian Kierkegaards Samlede Skrifter*, vols. 1–6, ed. by Poul Egede Glahn and Lavrids Nyegård, Copenhagen: Karl Schønbergs Forlag 1902–05, vol. 2, p. 1. The term was very popular among Grundtvigians because it expressed the idea of a national church, one formed by a nation of people rather than by a government or ruler.

Grundtvig (1783–1872) and his followers defended a free church formed by the people rather than the government or a ruler. The idea is that the communal life of the people, the nation, gives rise to a national or people's church rather than it being forced upon the people by religious authorities. Furthermore, Monrad's own liberal movement favored a Church constitution that would be ultimately responsive to the people, and the concept of the People's Church and an explicit provision guaranteeing religious freedom promises just this sort of responsiveness.[17] Lastly, Monrad identifies the Evangelical Lutheran Church as the People's Church, thereby satisfying the cultural and political conservatives in the Church who wanted to maintain this established Church relatively unchanged. Thus, Monrad's description of the Evangelical Lutheran Church as the People's Church of Denmark satisfied virtually all of the major political players in nineteenth-century Denmark. His use of the term, however, conceals a deep ambiguity.[18] It is unclear whether Monrad is emphasizing the fact that the People's Church is simply another name for the Evangelical Lutheran Church or asserting that the people have decided, in effect, that they are evangelical Lutherans and that this decision constitutes the authority of the Church for the people. The first view would be merely a change in semantics with very little, if any, change in the actual practices of the Church. The second view would constitute a fairly deep break with the traditional concept of the Danish Church.

Monrad, however, would not appreciate either of these two views. Although the term was agreeable to almost everyone of political influence for various reasons, Monrad had a distinctive Hegelian interpretation of the concept:

> Monrad's vision of the People's Church is Hegelian: the Church is necessary because "the spirit does not exhaust its whole being [*fylde*] in some single individuals [*enkelt individ*], but in [their] totality"; because to "feel the pulse of the spirit" the people must be organized as an organism; the Church should follow the spirit and be sovereign over the State, this organization will not deprive but give the single individuals [*de enkelte*] freedom and only by "pursuing its own higher purpose" does the Church promote "the State's interest."[19]

Monrad claims that the State interest is promoted by the existence of the Church since the Church organizes and structures the life of the people such that the people become good citizens and promote the good of the whole. Such a situation, it is

---

[17] The constitution itself embodies the idea that ecclesiastical and religious matters are governed by Danish law and subject to possible revision in the form of additional laws or constitutional changes. Paragraphs 81–4 in the 1849 Danish Constitution express the type of religious freedom in Denmark. The people have the following freedoms: freedom of worship, the freedom to refrain from giving personal financial (or other) contributions to a religion other than one's own, freedom to disagree with one's religious community, and it is also illegal to deprive a person of his or her civil or political rights because of a person's religion.

[18] Kirmmse discusses the "vague and elliptical language" of the Danish Constitution as it pertains to the People's Church. Kirmmse, *Kierkegaard and Golden Age of Denmark*, p. 75.

[19] See *Den Danske Kirkes Historie*, vols. 1–8, ed. by Hal Koch and Bjørn Kornerup, Copenhagen: Gyldendal 1950–66, vol. 7, p. 16. The translation from the Danish is my own.

asserted, does not deprive citizens of their freedom. Rather, the people voluntarily promote the betterment of all. It appears, therefore, that Monrad would simply deny the dilemma presented above, and he would claim that the Evangelical Lutheran Church and the people mutually presuppose and constitute the other. The Church builds the people, and the people have decided that they are Evangelical Lutherans.

Kierkegaard, however, does not seem to recognize any distinction between the People's Church and the State Church. Kierkegaard only uses the term "the People's Church" (*Folkekirke*), in a negative light and only in six journal entries, and in all but one of those entries there is an explicit identification of the State Church and the People's Church.[20] There are two ways to interpret this identification. On the one hand, one can take it as evidence that Kierkegaard simply did not understand the difference between the People's Church and the State Church. Just as there is a difference between a government of the people (e.g., the people's assembly (*Folketing*), which is the Danish parliament), and the State as such, so is there a difference between the People's Church and a State Church. A Church of the people would, ideally, be set up in such a way where there would be little or no conflict between the Danish people as a whole and the religious authorities. The people could demand, through the government, religious reformation if a situation arose where Christianity was undermined by the religious practices in the Church. According to this interpretation, not only does the Church function as the means for developing the people into a nation, but it is also the product or result of the collective will of the people. The evidence for this interpretation of Kierkegaard's equivocation is that Kierkegaard never distinguishes between the two concepts, and his criticisms of the People's Church are the very same ones directed at the State Church. There are certainly criticisms that would be applicable to the People's Church, even more so than the State Church (e.g., Kierkegaard's critique of determining religious truth by means of a vote), but Kierkegaard never directly presents this sort of argument as an explicit critique of the Danish constitution or the concept of the People's Church.

On the other hand, it may be that Kierkegaard is aware that some political and religious figures attempted to distinguish between the two concepts, but he thought such an attempt was doomed to fail. According to this interpretation, Kierkegaard recognized the political nature of Monrad's redescription of the State Church. The very same institution of the State Church is called People's Church as a political ploy designed to bring Grundtvigians, Monrad's own liberal movement, and the conservatives together, and ultimately the State Church as an institution would remain exactly the same as before. The only result would be that any form of criticism left to the people would be ideologically undermined since any criticism would be directed

---

20 *SKS* 24, 348, NB24:51 / *JP* 5, 6761. The following entry is the only reference to the People's Church in Kierkegaard's writings where it is not identified with the State Church, and it is a reference to Martensen's defense of the People's Church. Since Kierkegaard is referring to Martensen's use of the term and since he, earlier in the same entry, does equate the two terms, the use in this entry does not undermine the claim that Kierkegaard fails to make a distinction between the People's Church and the State Church: *Pap.* X–6 B 145, p. 213 / *JP* 5, 6786. *Pap.* X–6 B 212, p. 335. *SKS* 26, 381/2, NB35:18 / *JP* 5, 6932. *Pap.* XI–2 A 291 / *JP* 4, 4222. *Pap.* XI–2 A 373 / *JP* 4, 4503.

against one's own church, the People's Church. Perhaps Kierkegaard's greatest fear is that Christianity would become merely a cultural phenomenon used as a means to accomplish some other end rather than an expression of the truth, and the renaming of the State Church as the People's Church is a turn in that direction. It is not surprising, then, that Kierkegaard identifies both the State Church and the People's Church as a single object of his criticism. This view is a coherent reconstruction of a position that would explain many of Kierkegaard's criticisms of the State Church and his equivocation between the two terms. Nevertheless, there is no direct textual support for this interpretation and Kierkegaard, who regularly describes his own methods of attack, never explicitly articulates this strategy. But the latter view provides a much more elaborate and developed political theory that coincides well with Kierkegaard's criticism of cooption and his criticism and defense of the establishment.

Kierkegaard's relationship with Monrad is complicated by their personal relationship, but Kierkegaard's reaction to Mynster's ordination of Monrad as Bishop of Lolland-Falster and Kierkegaard's criticism of the People's Church, a term intimately related to Monrad, reveal two facets of Kierkegaard's political thought. First, it shows that Kierkegaard separates the religious from the political. The means of operation in the political arena, for example, voting, ballots, etc., are inappropriate for determining religious truth, and any attempt to popularize Christianity through political means falsifies the sanctity of that religious truth. Second, Kierkegaard's critique of political cooption is applicable to both Mynster's ordination of Monrad and Monrad's characterization of the Evangelical Lutheran Church, the State Church, as the People's Church. On the one hand, Kierkegaard thinks Mynster's ordination of Monrad exemplifies Mynster's commitment to his own religious authority and power rather than to God alone. On the other hand, clothing the State Church in a new name, the People's Church, ideologically insulates the religious establishment from criticism, and thereby coopts for itself critiques of the religious establishment. Since it is no longer the King's Church, the State Church, or Mynster's Church, but instead the Church of the people, any criticism of the Church is effectively undermined since it would also constitute a criticism of oneself.

Bibliography

I. Monrad's Works in The Auction Catalogue *of Kierkegaard's Library*

"Om Dandserinden, betragtet som reflecterende Poesie," *Kjöbenhavns flyvende Post, Interimsblade*, nos. 1–100, 1834–36, ed. by Johan Ludvig Heiberg, no. 2, 1834 (*ASKB* 1607).

Gjengangeren indeholdende Bidrag til den nyeste Tids Historie. Udgivet af Selskabet for Trykkefrihedens rette Brug, Copenhagen: J.C. Lund 1844 (*ASKB* A II 206).

The Minutes of speeches made by Monrad:

—— "Folketingets Forhandlinger om Religions- og Samvittighedsfrihed," *Dansk Kirketidende*, vols. 1–8, ed. by C.J. Brandt and R.Th. Fenger, Copenhagen: C.A. Reitzel 1845–53, vol. 5, no. 269, 1850 [for the minutes of Monrad's speech], see columns 1010–12 (*ASKB* 321–325).

II. Works in The Auction Catalogue *of Kierkegaard's Library that Discuss Monrad*

Fenger, P.A., "Mag. Monrads Udnævnelse til Biskop," *Dansk Kirketidende*, vol. 4, no. 180, 1899, columns 393–5.

III. Secondary Literature on Kierkegaard's Relation to Monrad

Kirmmse, Bruce, *Kierkegaard in Golden Age Denmark*, Bloomington, Indiana: Indiana University Press 1990, pp. 69–70; p. 75; 194; p. 355, p. 491, note 7.

Kühle, Sejer, *Søren Kierkegaards Barndom og Ungdom*, Copenhagen: Aschehoug Dansk Forlag 1950, p. 83; p. 103; p. 119; p. 122; p. 150; p. 169.

Nielsen, Svend Aage, *Kierkegaard og Regensen*, Copenhagen: Graabrødre Torv's Forlag 1965, p. 21; pp. 45–69; p. 76; p. 87; p. 132.

Rasmus Nielsen: From the Object of "Prodigious Concern" to a "Windbag"

Jon Stewart

The name Rasmus Nielsen (1809–84) is not well known to Kierkegaard scholars, even though he was an important figure in his own right; indeed, Nielsen was one of Denmark's greatest philosophers during a period that witnessed a blooming of Danish philosophy. Moreover, Nielsen played a role in most every phase of Kierkegaard's life. Kierkegaard owned several of Nielsen's works, and his journals are full of references to him. There also survives a fairly extensive correspondence of letters that passed between them.

In what follows, I wish to explore the significance of Nielsen for the development of Kierkegaard's thought. It is conventional to divide this relationship into three discernible phases. First, in his early years Kierkegaard was suspicious and perhaps even a bit envious of Nielsen. Second, in time, however, when Nielsen expressed an interest in Kierkegaard's writings, the two became friends. Third and finally, when Nielsen attempted to defend Kierkegaard's works in a way that displeased the latter, an irreparable break took place. In what follows I will trace each of these stages in turn; I wish to modify the general conception that the third stage ended in a clean break since there is clear evidence that they continued their relation for some time after thus. I will, however, begin by giving a brief overview of Nielsen's biography and writings. I wish to argue that despite the extensive degree to which Kierkegaard was exercised by Nielsen, there is very little that one can say about Nielsen as a source for Kierkegaard's thought. Most of Kierkegaard's reflections on Nielsen are of a rather personal nature, and although it is clear that he read Nielsen's works, only very rarely does he engage with them in a scholarly manner. In general, Kierkegaard seems to have maintained a rather dismissive stance with regard to Nielsen, and this prevented him from making use of Nielsen's writings in a more productive manner. By contrast, Nielsen actively made use of Kierkegaard's works both during the period of their friendship and even long after the latter's death.

I. Nielsen's Life and Work

Rasmus Nielsen was born on July 4, 1809 on the island of Funen in a small town called Rorslev.[1] Although he came from a family of uneducated farmers, his intellectual gifts were recognized early, and he was placed in the foster care of the pastor Erik Friisenberg Thorup, who gave him his earliest education. From 1829 he attended Viborg Cathedral School, where he received his first formal education. In a short period of time he caught up with the material that he had missed the previous years.

Nielsen completed his schooling and was admitted to the University of Copenhagen in 1832. He first studied philology, attending the lectures of Johan Nicolai Madvig (1804–86). Then he turned to both philosophy and theology; in the former field he was particularly inspired by the lectures of Frederik Christian Sibbern (1785–1872) and in the latter by those of Henrik Nicolai Clausen (1793–1877). He received his initial degree in theology in 1837. Three years later, in 1840, he defended his licentiate thesis with a work written in Latin under the title, *The Use of the Speculative Method in Sacred History*, a work that Kierkegaard owned.[2] This degree qualified Nielsen to give lectures at the university, which he did immediately thereafter in winter semester 1840–41, as *Privatdocent* in theology. He also received special permission to give lectures in the field of philosophy. In April 1841 he was finally awarded a permanent position, being named *professor extraordinarius* in Moral Philosophy, which was the position held by Poul Martin Møller (1794–1838) until his death.

During the initial period of his professorship, Nielsen was influenced by the philosophy of G.W.F. Hegel (1770–1831), which had been introduced into Denmark in the mid-1820s by the poet and critic Johan Ludvig Heiberg (1791–1860). More importantly, by this time Hegel's philosophy had become a popular trend among the students at the University of Copenhagen due to the lectures of Hans Lassen Martensen (1808–84).[3] Nielsen is reported to have asked the professors of philosophy

---

1 See V. Klein and P.A. Rosenberg, *Mindeskrift over Rasmus Nielsen*, Copenhagen: Schønberg 1909; Eduard Asmussen, *Entwicklungsgang und Grundprobleme der Philosophie Rasmus Nielsens*, Flensburg: Laban & Larsen 1911; P.A. Rosenberg, *Rasmus Nielsen. Nordens Filosof. En almenfattelig Fremstilling*, Copenhagen: Karl Schønberg 1903; V. Klein, *Oversigt over Rasmus Nielsens Skrifter*, Copenhagen: Nationale Forfatteres Forlag 1912; Frederik Algreen-Ussing, *Rasmus Nielsen, Professor i Philosophien. Et biographisk Forsøg*, Copenhagen: Thieles Bogtrykkeri 1864; Harald Høffding, "Rasmus Nielsen," in his *Danske Filosofer*, Copenhagen: Gyldendal 1909, pp. 184–95; Vilhelm Birkedal, "Rasmus Nielsen," in his *Personlige Oplevelser i et langt Liv*, vols. 1–3, Copenhagen: Karl Schønbergs Forlag 1890–91, vol. 2, pp. 239–53; Carl Henrik Koch, "Rasmus Nielsen," in his *Den danske idealisme 1800–1880*, Copenhagen: Gyldendal 2004, pp. 379–434; K. Kroman, "Rasmus Nielsen," in *K. Kroman. Træk af en dansk filosofs liv og tankeverden*, ed. by Valdemar Hansen, Copenhagen: Skandinavisk Bogforlag 1955, pp. 159–65.

2 Rasmus Nielsen, *De speculativa historiæ sacræ tractando metodo*, Copenhagen: Fabritius de Tengnagel 1840 (*ASKB* 697). (In Danish as *Om den spekulative Methodes Anvendelse paa den hellige Historie*, trans. by B.C. Bøggild, Copenhagen: H.C. Klein 1842.)

3 See Jon Stewart, *A History of Hegelianism in Golden Age Denmark*, Tome II, *The Martensen Period: 1837–1842*, Copenhagen: C.A. Reitzel 2007 (*Danish Golden Age Studies*, vol. 3), pp. 1–11.

at the university, Sibbern and Møller, for help with Hegel's philosophy, knowing that both of them were quite familiar with it.[4] In his memoirs Martensen recalls that when in July of 1837, he had the oral defense of his dissertation, *On the Autonomy of Human Self-Consciousness*,[5] he met Nielsen for the first time, when the latter, along with Heiberg, raised questions from the audience.[6] At the beginning of the 1840s Nielsen and Martensen were perceived as the two most important junior faculty members, who helped to promote Hegel's thought in the fields of philosophy and theology.

Nielsen was a profoundly productive author. In the same year as his appointment, he published a Bible commentary, entitled *Paul's Letter to the Romans*.[7] Also in 1841 he began the first installment of his *Speculative Logic in its Essentials*.[8] This work was the first unambiguous sign of Nielsen's Hegelian alignment since it represents a speculative logic following the model of Hegel's *Science of Logic*.[9] Nielsen's logic appeared in a series of installments until 1844. He continued his work on Hegelian logic in the following year with an extensive book entitled the *Propaedeutic Logic*.[10] This text covered the material not yet treated in his previous one. Kierkegaard owned a copy of this latter work and clearly read the former as well; indeed, he refers to the *Propaedeutic Logic* in a positive manner in his journals.[11] Both of Nielsen's books on logic were apparently outgrowths of lectures that he gave in the context of his usual teaching at the University of Copenhagen. In 1843 he published a work on church history,[12] and in 1849 a series of lectures on the life of Jesus.[13]

---

4 See P.A. Rosenberg, *Rasmus Nielsen. Nordens Filosof. En almenfattelig Fremstilling*, p. 28.

5 Hans Lassen Martensen, *De autonomia conscientiae sui humanae in theologiam dogmaticam nostri temporis introducta*, Copenhagen: I.D. Quist 1837 (*ASKB* 651).

6 See Hans Lassen Martensen, *Af mit Levnet*, vols. 1–3, Copenhagen: Gyldendal 1882–83, vol. 2, p. 2.

7 Rasmus Nielsen, *Pauli Brev til Romerne*, Copenhagen: [Forfatterens Forlag] 1841.

8 Rasmus Nielsen, *Den speculative Logik i dens Grundtræk*, Copenhagen: n.p. 1841–44; no. 1, 1841, pp. 1–64; no. 2, 1842, pp. 65–96; no. 3, 1843, pp. 97–144; no. 4, 1844, pp. 145–96.

9 G.W.F. Hegel, *Wissenschaft der Logik. Erster Band. Die objective Logik*, Nürnberg: Johann Leonard Schrag 1812; *Wissenschaft der Logik. Erster Band. Die objective Logik. Zweytes Buch. Die Lehre vom Wesen*, Nürnberg: Johann Leonard Schrag 1813; *Wissenschaft der Logik. Zweiter Band. Die subjective Logik oder Lehre vom Begriff*, Nürnberg: Johann Leonard Schrag 1816.

10 Rasmus Nielsen, *Den propædeutiske Logik*, Copenhagen: P.G. Philipsen 1845 (*ASKB* 699).

11 *Pap.* VI C 1 / *JP* 5, 5798: "The distinction between το ειναι—and το ον. The confusion in Hegelian philosophy; a fitting observation on this by R. Nielsen in his *Propaedeutic Logic*."

12 Rasmus Nielsen, *Forelæsningsparagrapher til Kirkehistoriens Philosophie. Et Schema for Tilhørere*, Copenhagen: P.G. Philipsen 1843 (*ASKB* 698).

13 Rasmus Nielsen, *Evangelietroen og den moderne Bevidsthed. Forelæsninger over Jesu Liv*, Copenhagen: C.A. Reitzel 1849 (*ASKB* 700). See also his *Evangelietroen og Theologien. Tolv Forelæsninger holdt ved Universitetet i Kjøbenhavn i Vinteren 1849–50*, Copenhagen: C.A. Reitzel 1850 (*ASKB* 702).

In the same year a controversy broke out when Martensen published his *Christian Dogmatics*.[14] This work was followed by a series of critical reviews.[15] In this context Nielsen, who had been sympathetic to Kierkegaard's views, wrote what purported to be a joint review of Martensen's new work and Kierkegaard's *Concluding Unscientific Postscript*, although only the former was really under critical consideration.[16] This review was one of the works that was the cause for Kierkegaard's dissatisfaction with Nielsen for reasons that we will explore below. Also in the context of this debate Nielsen published a short pamphlet, *A Few Words on Occasion of Prof. Scharling's Defense of Dr. Martensen's Dogmatics* and *Dr. H. Martensen's Dogmatic Elucidations Illuminated*.[17]

In 1850 Nielsen was named *professor ordinarius*, and his productivity continued unbroken. In 1853 he published *On Fate and Providence*,[18] a work that Meïr Goldschmidt (1819–87) compared with Kierkegaard's articles on the attack on the Church.[19] In the same year appeared Nielsen's only work of fiction, *A Life in the Underworld*, signed by the pseudonym Walther Paying.[20] In 1854 he published a work entitled *On Personal Truth and True Personality*, based on lectures that he gave at the University of Copenhagen.[21] At this time Nielsen reviewed Kierkegaard's *For Self-Examination* in *Fædrelandet*.[22] Here in the midst of Kierkegaard's attack on the Danish church, Nielsen under the cover of a book review indirectly defends his former friend and attempts to explain his motivations. However, he does not himself say much in this context since the review article consists primarily of quotations from Kierkegaard's text. Also in this context Nielsen published an article in 1855

---

14 Hans Lassen Martensen, *Den christelige Dogmatik*, Copenhagen: C.A. Reitzel 1849 (*ASKB* 653).

15 For an overview, see Niels Thulstrup, "Martensen's *Dogmatics* and its Reception," in *Kierkegaard and His Contemporaries: The Culture of Golden Age Denmark*, ed. by Jon Stewart, Berlin and New York: Walter de Gruyter 2003 (*Kierkegaard Studies Monograph Series*, vol. 10), pp. 181–202.

16 Rasmus Nielsen, *Mag. S. Kierkegaards "Johannes Climacus" og Dr. H. Martensens "Christelige Dogmatik." En undersøgende Anmeldelse*, Copenhagen: C.A. Reitzel 1849 (*ASKB* 701).

17 Rasmus Nielsen, *Et Par Ord i Anledning af Prof. Scharlings Apologie for Dr. Martensens Dogmatik*, Copenhagen: C.A. Reitzel 1850; *Dr. H. Martensens dogmatiske Oplysninger belyste*, Copenhagen: C.A. Reitzel 1850 (*ASKB* 703).

18 Rasmus Nielsen, *Om Skjæbne og Forsyn*, Copenhagen: Otto Schwartz 1853 (*ASKB* 704).

19 Meïr Goldschmidt, "Dagbog," entry from April 15, 1855, *Nord og Syd. Ny Række*, vol. 8, p. 42. (English translation in *Encounters with Kierkegaard: A Life as Seen By His Contemporaries*, trans. and ed. by Bruce H. Kirmmse, Princeton: Princeton University Press 1996, p. 108.)

20 [Walther Paying], *Et Levnetsløb i Underverdenen*, Copenhagen: Otto Schwartz 1853 (*ASKB* 716).

21 Rasmus Nielsen, *Om personlig Sandhed og sand Personlighed. Tolv Forelæsninger for dannede Tilhørere af begge Kjøn ved Universitetet i Vinteren 1854*, Copenhagen: Gyldendal 1854 (*ASKB* 705).

22 Rasmus Nielsen, "*Til Selvprøvelse, Samtiden anbefalet* af S. Kierkegaard; en uproductiv Anmeldelse," *Fædrelandet*, vol. 15, no. 303, December 29, 1854, p. 1215.

entitled "A Good Deed," in which he defends Kierkegaard.[23] This was followed by a work on the French philosopher Nicolas Malebranche (1638–1715).[24]

Nielsen is reported to have attended Kierkegaard's funeral on November 18, 1855, and to have been witness to the scandalous scene caused there by Kierkegaard's nephew Henrik Lund (1825–89).[25] After Kierkegaard's death in 1855, Nielsen continued to publish works on his person and thought. In 1857 Nielsen provided the service of editing the various articles that Kierkegaard had published in the different newspapers during his lifetime and printing them in a single volume.[26] In 1858 Nielsen published an article "On Kierkegaard's Mental Condition,"[27] in which he tries to show that there is a consistency in Kierkegaard's position that can be traced in his writings and that the criticism of the church was no mere *ad hominem* attack on Mynster. In 1860 he published a short collection entitled *On Kierkegaardian "Stages," A Picture of Life*, which featured extracts from Kierkegaard's texts.[28]

Nielsen had a long career at the university and continued to publish without pause virtually until the end, penning works on a number of different fields of philosophy.[29] As before, many of his publications during this late period were based on lectures that he had given in different contexts. Between the years 1869 and 1873 he was coeditor of *For Ide og Virkelighed*, an important philosophical journal of the

---

23 Rasmus Nielsen, "En god Gjerning," *Fædrelandet*, no. 8, January 10, 1855, pp. 29–30.

24 Rasmus Nielsen, *Om Theologiens Naturbegreb med særligt Hensyn til Malbranche: De la recherche de la vérité*, Copenhagen: Trykt i det Schultziske Officin 1855.

25 See *Encounters with Kierkegaard*, trans. and ed. by Bruce H. Kirmmse, p. 135; p. 191; p. 192.

26 Rasmus Nielsen, *S. Kierkegaard's Bladartikler, med Bilag samlede efter Forfatterens Død, udgivne som Supplement til hans øvrige Skrifter*, Copenhagen: C.A. Reitzel 1857.

27 Rasmus Nielsen, "Om S. Kierkegaards 'mentale Tilstand,' " *Nordisk Universitet-Tidskrift*, vol. 4, no. 1, 1858, pp. 1–29.

28 Rasmus Nielsen, *Paa Kierkegaardske "Stadier", et Livsbillede*, Copenhagen: Gyldendal 1860.

29 See for example, Rasmus Nielsen, *Philosophie og Mathematik. En propædeutisk Afhandling*, Copenhagen: Gyldendal 1857; *Philosophisk Propædeutik i Grundtræk*, Copenhagen: Gyldendal 1857; *Mathematik og Dialektik. En philosophisk Afhandling*, Copenhagen: Gyldendal 1859; *Forelæsninger over "Philosophisk Propædeutik" fra Universitetsaaret 1860–61*, Copenhagen: Gyldendal 1862; *Forelæsninger over "Philosophisk Propædeutik" fra Universitetsaaret 1861–62*, Copenhagen: Gyldendal 1863; *Grundideernes Logik*, vols. 1–2, Copenhagen: Gyldendal 1864–66; *Propædeutik og Psychologie. Cursus for Universitetsaaret 1866–67*, Copenhagen: Gyldendal 1866; *Propædeutik og Logik. Cursus for Universitetsaaret 1868–69*, Copenhagen: Gyldendal 1868; *Om Hindringer og Betingelser for det aandelig Liv i Nutiden. Sexten Forelæsninger holdte ved Universitet i Christiania September–Oktober 1867*, Copenhagen: Gyldendal 1868; *Religionsphilosophie*, Copenhagen: Gyldendal 1869; *Logik og Psychologie. Cursus for Universitetsaaret 1871–72*, Copenhagen: J.H. Schubothes Boghandel 1871; *Natur og Aand. Bidrag til en med Physiken stemmende Naturphilosophie*, Copenhagen: J.H. Schubothes Boghandel 1873; *Om Liv og Haab. Sex Forelæsninger*, Copenhagen: Gyldendal 1875; *Almindelig Videnskabslære i Grundtræk*, Copenhagen: Gyldendal 1880.

day.[30] He ultimately retired in 1883 and died in Copenhagen on September 30 the following year.

II. Kierkegaard and Nielsen until 1848: The Initial Period of Alienation

Kierkegaard's references to Nielsen in the period corresponding to the first part of the authorship are fairly sparse. In a marginal note in his *Journal EE* from the year 1839, Kierkegaard makes a satirical reference to Nielsen. On August 29, 1839 Nielsen published an advertisement in *Kjøbenhavnsposten* in which he announced that he was going to be publishing a book with the title *Basic Elements of Christian Morality*.[31] With this advertisement he invites interested parties to subscribe to buy a copy of the work when it appears. Apparently in reaction to this, Kierkegaard writes somewhat enigmatically in his journal: "Rasmus Nielsen's sure and trusty Morality found in Mads Madsen's Chest or The World Seen from a Cellar Steps."[32] Nielsen's book never appeared.

Kierkegaard presumably knew Nielsen from the period when they were both students at the University of Copenhagen. As was noted above, Nielsen received his degree in 1840, with Kierkegaard receiving his master's degree for *The Concept of Irony* the following year. At some point after Nielsen received his appointment in April 1841, Sibbern spoke with Kierkegaard in order to encourage him to apply for a vacant post at the University of Copenhagen. The conversation, recorded by Hans Brøchner (1820–75), is said to have run as follows:

> Once he [Kierkegaard] told me that Sibbern had suggested he apply for a position as a lecturer in philosophy. Kierkegaard had replied that in that case he would have to insist on a couple of years in which to prepare himself. "Oh! How can you imagine that they would hire you under such conditions?" asked Sibbern. "Yes, of course, I could do like Rasmus Nielsen and let them hire me unprepared." Sibbern became cross and said: "You always have to pick on Nielsen!"[33]

This comment clearly evidences the young Kierkegaard's lack of respect for Nielsen at this time. He straightforwardly implies that Nielsen is not qualified for his new position. The academic world then as now was small, and Nielsen learned of Kierkegaard's remark. When Sibbern was looking among his colleagues for committee members for Kierkegaard's dissertation, he asked Nielsen, who declined the offer, although he would have been a natural choice.[34]

---

30 *For Ide og Virkelighed: et Tidsskrift*, vols. 1–8, ed. by Rasmus Nielsen, Bjørnsterne Bjørnson and Rudolf Schmidt, Copenhagen: Christian Steen 1869–73.

31 *Kjøbenhavnsposten*, no. 229, August 21, 1839, p. 920.

32 *SKS* 18, 58, EE:167.a / *KJN* 2, 53.

33 Hans Brøchner, "Erindringer om Søren Kierkegaard," in *Det Nittende Aarhundrede, Maanedsskrift for Literatur og Kritik*, March, 1876–77, § 21. (English translation cited from *Encounters with Kierkegaard*, trans. and ed. by Bruce H. Kirmmse, p. 235.)

34 See Carl Weltzer, "Omkring Søren Kierkegaards Disputats," in *Kirkehistoriske Samlinger*, Sjette Række, ed. by J. Oskar Andersen and Bjørn Kornerup, Copenhagen: G.E.C. Gads Forlag 1948–50, p. 286.

Despite this personal animosity, there are elements in Nielsen's early works that must have appealed to Kierkegaard. Although Nielsen was interested in Hegel's philosophy and particularly the dialectical method, he was in fact critical of some of Hegel's Danish followers, as was Kierkegaard. In *The Use of the Speculative Method in Sacred History*, he explicitly criticizes Heiberg and Martensen.[35] He argues against the application of speculative philosophy or, as he writes, "panlogism" to dogmatics. He argues that the Concept cannot take the place of the Christian God. Since speculative philosophy regards the Concept as the highest and thus in effect holds it in veneration, it "has a false god."[36] Nielsen argues that the truth of the situation is the other way around. The Concept does not ground God, but God grounds the Concept: "it is a positive power of God which grounds the whole of real existence and thus puts the ontological forms immanently in all things."[37] Already here one can hear echoes of Kierkegaard's well-known criticisms.

Nielsen argues that speculative philosophy is unsuccessful in bringing about the reconciliation that it desires. Speculation offers only an apparent reconciliation since the terms of its opposition are not genuine, but rather are merely terms of thought. By contrast, Christian dogmatics posits a genuine and real contrast between God and the world, which Nielsen refers to the "absolute opposition."[38] Here again we can discern the faint outlines of Kierkegaard's doctrine of absolute difference in *Philosophical Fragments* and the *Postscript*.[39] Moreover, Nielsen is, like Kierkegaard, aware of the dangers of reducing or eliminating the individual in a speculative system of thought. He claims that the natural result of panlogism is that it "must sacrifice individual self-consciousness."[40] Here he refers explicitly to the controversial matter of the absence of a doctrine of immortality in Hegel's philosophy. Christian dogmatics, he argues, provides just such a doctrine and thus preserves the integrity of the individual.

Although Kierkegaard might have had reason to be sympathetic to parts of this work, he was presumably alienated by claims made about it two years later when it was translated from Latin into Danish.[41] The translation was the work of one Balthasar Christopher Bøggild (1816–92), who was quite zealous in his statements about Nielsen's book and the impact it had had on intellectual life in Denmark. He claims that Nielsen has "labored for the speculative development of theology" and has been "the organ for an almost wholly new consciousness in our fatherland."[42]

---

35 Nielsen, *De speculativa historiæ sacræ tractando metodo*, p. 138, note.

36 Ibid., p. 136.

37 Ibid., p. 137.

38 Ibid., p. 139.

39 See *SKS* 4, 249 / *PF*, 44–5. See also *SKS* 7, 374–5 / *CUP1*, 412: "But between God and a human being (let speculative thought just keep humankind to perform tricks with) there is an absolute difference; therefore a person's absolute relationship with God must specifically express the absolute difference, and the direct likeness becomes impudence, conceited pretense, presumption, and the like."

40 Nielsen, *De speculativa historiæ sacræ tractando metodo*, p. 139.

41 Rasmus Nielsen, *Om den spekulative Methodes Anvendelse paa den hellige Historie*, trans. by B.C. Bøggild. Copenhagen: H.C. Klein 1842.

42 Nielsen, *Om den spekulative Methodes Anvendelse paa den hellige Historie*, [p. i] (the preface consists of two unnumbered pages).

This tone sounds suspiciously like the kind of ambitious statements that were being made about Martensen's work five years earlier,[43] and the parallel does not go unnoticed here. Bøggild states explicitly that Nielsen is in effect working alongside Martensen and continuing the latter's project from *On the Autonomy of Human Self-Consciousness in Modern Dogmatic Theology*. Both are portrayed as criticizing various forms of rationalism: while Martensen criticizes Kant and Schleiermacher, Nielsen criticizes D.F. Strauss as well as right Hegelianism.

One of Nielsen's works that clearly caught Kierkegaard's eye was his *Speculative Logic in its Essentials*, which appeared in a series of four installments, beginning in 1841.[44] This work was based on lectures that Nielsen gave, and he seems to have added new installments as he worked through the material in the course. Due to the fact that the text was printed in arks, that is, 16 pages at a time, the individual installments were not cleanly divided into discrete chapters or sections but rather simply ended when the ark ended; as a result each installment stopped, as it were, *in medias res*, right in the middle of a sentence that would only be continued with the next installment.

As before Nielsen offered a subscription scheme for interested readers. At the beginning of the very first installment he writes, in a kind of preface:

> This outline is to be regarded as a fragment of a philosophical methodology, the first part of which will contain the logic with a preliminary introduction. The necessity of having a printed guide for the oral lecture has hastened the publication. The remaining installments will follow eventually as the lecture announced in the catalogue of courses approaches.
>
> Copenhagen, the 10th of November 1841.
>
> R. Nielsen.[45]

This work was never completed, and the fourth installment ends right in the middle of an unfinished sentence. Kierkegaard seizes upon this and satirizes it in a couple of different places. The absurdity, he believes, lies in the contradiction between Nielsen's pretension of creating a complete system of logic along the lines of Hegel but yet leaving the system incomplete by failing to follow up on all the promised installments of the work.[46]

In his article "Public Confession" from *Fædrelandet* on June 12, 1842, Kierkegaard refers satirically to Nielsen's text.[47] Alluding specifically to the passage quoted above, he writes:

---

43 See Stewart, *A History of Hegelianism in Golden Age Denmark*, Tome II, *The Martensen Period: 1837–1842*, pp. 1–11.

44 Nielsen, *Den speculative Logik i dens Grundtræk*; see Koch, "Rasmus Nielsen," in his *Den danske idealisme 1800–1880*, pp. 379–434.

45 Nielsen *Den speculative Logik i dens Grundtræk*, overleaf to the first volume, 1841.

46 Kierkegaard returns to this again and again, criticizing Nielsen for promising a philosophical system that he never delivers on. *SKS* 7, 118 / *CUP1*, 122. *SKS* 7, 103 / *CUP1*, 106. *SKS* 7, 104 / *CUP1*, 107. *SKS* 7, 198 / *CUP1*, 216. *SV1* XIII, 399f. / *COR*, 5–6. *Pap.* III B 192 / *JP* 3, 3288. *Pap.* VII–1 B 88, p. 294 / *CUP2*, Supplement, p. 134. *SKS* 20, 417, NB5:115. *Pap.* X–6 B 88, p. 94. *Pap.* X–6 B 89, p. 98.

47 *SV1* XIII, 397–406 / *COR*, 3–12.

Prof. R. Nielsen already has published twenty-one logical §§ that constitute the first part of a logic that in turn constitutes the first part of an all-encompassing encyclopaedia, as intimated on the jacket, although its size is not more explicitly given, presumably not to intimidate....It has often been encouraging to me to think that Professor R. Nielsen is writing such a book. He has already written twenty-one §§ and several years ago he published a subscription prospectus for a systematic ethics that will amount to at least twenty-four printed sheets when it is finished.[48]

This same criticism is taken up again a few years later in the *Concluding Unscientific Postscript* in 1846.[49] In one passage, for example, Kierkegaard has Johannes Climacus write: "When someone goes on continually writing or dictating sections of a work, with promises that everything will become clear at the end, it becomes more and more difficult to discover where the beginning of the confusion lies and to acquire a firm point of departure."[50] Kierkegaard constantly harps on the promises to complete the system at some indeterminate point in the future: "When I for the last time very innocently said to one of the initiates, 'Now tell me honestly, is it [sc. the system] indeed completely finished, because if that is the case, I will prostrate myself, even if I should ruin a pair of trousers'...I would invariably receive the answer, 'No, it is not entirely finished yet.' "[51] In the printed text itself Kierkegaard conceals the specific target of this satire, but in earlier drafts Nielsen's name does in fact appear.[52]

Nielsen's work somewhat enigmatically begins on page 1 with § 11 and has no introduction as such. The reason for this is unclear, but it might be that since the entire work was being printed incrementally in installments, Nielsen simply intended to go back and add §§ 1–10 at some later point. Indeed, in the passage quoted above, where Nielsen mentions his subscription scheme, he refers to "a preliminary introduction" which was to be added to the text later.[53] In "Public Confession" Kierkegaard also makes sport of this unfortunate element of Nielsen's text. He refers to the fact that Nielsen has written the first 21 paragraphs of a system, but then in a footnote, he qualifies this claim as follows: "Well, not actually twenty-one paragraphs in all, since the first ten are missing, but in recompense he has dramatically hurled us headlong into the system."[54]

Despite these satirical remarks, there were elements in Nielsen's text that would have appealed to Kierkegaard. For example, Nielsen anticipates Kierkegaard's juxtaposition of Hegelian mediation with the problem of motion in the Eleatics.[55] Nielsen also speaks of a qualitative leap in connection with his account of Hegel's

---

48 *SV1* XIII, 399–400 / *COR*, 5–6.

49 *SKS* 7, 114 / *CUP1*, 117. *SKS* 7, 304 / *CUP1*, 333.

50 *SKS* 7, 299 / *CUP1*, 327.

51 *SKS* 7, 104 / *CUP1*, 107. *SKS* 7, 103 / *CUP1*, 106. Cf. "Similarly, a professor publishes the outline of a system, assuming that the work, by being reviewed and debated, will come out sooner or later in a new and totally revised form" (*SKS* 7, 198 / *CUP1*, 216). See also *SKS* 4, 305–6 / *PF*, 109–10.

52 *Pap.* VI B 40:7 / *CUP2*, Supplement, pp. 42–3.

53 Nielsen, *Den speculative Logik i dens Grundtræk*, no. 1, overleaf.

54 *SV1* XIII, 400, note / *COR*, 5, note.

55 Nielsen, *Den speculative Logik i dens Grundtræk*, no. 1, § 14, pp. 28ff.

analysis of this idea.[56] It is quite possible that the inspiration for some of Kierkegaard's criticisms of speculative logic is to be found in this text.

Given these scattered remarks, it seems clear that up to the publication of the *Postscript* in 1846 Kierkegaard did not take Nielsen seriously as a thinker. Nielsen is ridiculed along the same lines as the other Danish Hegelians, Heiberg and Martensen. This raises the question of why Kierkegaard later was amenable to entering into such a close relation to Nielsen and even staking his hopes on Nielsen helping him to advance the campaign that the Kierkegaardian authorship represented. The reason for this, I believe, is that, despite his satirical comments, Kierkegaard in fact found things in Nielsen's work (as he did in Heiberg's and Martensen's) that he was receptive to and could even make use of. One often sees that open animosity in fact hides a deeper sympathy. In any case, it is probably safe to assume that Kierkegaard's disposition towards Nielsen was somewhat mixed up until this point.

III. The Initial Period of Friendship: July 1848–May 1849

Despite Kierkegaard's veiled and open attacks on him, Nielsen nonetheless became interested in his thought. He seems particularly to have read the *Concluding Unscientific Postscript* with great interest. Kierkegaard's ideas about Christianity and the nature of faith vis-à-vis knowing made a deep impression, which enjoined Nielsen to pause and rethink his own views in a fundamental manner. With this new inspiration, he approached Kierkegaard, and the two developed a relationship that might even be designated as "friendship" during this time.[57] They took regular walks together, which gave them the opportunity to discuss key philosophical and theological issues of mutual interest. This rapprochement seems to have taken place at some point prior to July 1848, which is the time from which the first letters date that testify to the fact of their friendship. It is clear right from the start that Kierkegaard regarded his relation with Nielsen as a very special one. He was constantly evaluating it in the privacy of his own mind as is evidenced in his journals. There can be no doubt that Nielsen was a highly significant figure in his life during these few years.

Kierkegaard was positively disposed towards Nielsen once the latter had expressed his agreement with his views. Brøchner describes the relationship at this time as follows: "At a later point, when Nielsen had allied himself with Kierkegaard, he [Kierkegaard] spoke of him with more interest and acknowledged his talents. Once he said: 'Nielsen is the only one of our younger authors of this general tendency who may amount to something.' "[58]

---

56 Ibid., no. 1, § 18, p. 62.

57 For an account of this period of the relation between Kierkegaard and Nielsen, see Koch, "Rasmus Nielsen," in his *Den danske idealisme 1800–1880*, pp. 392–5; Asmussen, *Entwicklungsgang und Grundprobleme der Philosophie Rasmus Nielsens*, pp. 16–28.

58 Brøchner, "Erindringer om Søren Kierkegaard", § 21. English translation cited from *Encounters with Kierkegaard*, trans. and ed. by Bruce H. Kirmmse, p. 235.

While he was spending the summer away from Copenhagen in Taarbæk in north Zealand, Nielsen wrote a letter to Kierkegaard on July 21, 1848.[59] This letter evinces a degree of familiarity; Nielsen recounts how he was enjoying the fresh air of the country and renewing his energies by reading Hebrew. In response to this, Kierkegaard apparently wrote a letter in order to invite Nielsen for a visit upon his return to Copenhagen. This letter is not extant; however, Nielsen's response to it, from August 1848, is.[60] Here Nielsen comments in a jocular way on Kierkegaard's address: on the corner of Tornebuskegade, that is, Thornbush Street, and Rosengaard that is, Rose Court, where Kierkegaard had lived since April of that year.[61] In this letter Nielsen refers to his "frequent writing,"[62] which seems to imply that there were other letters from this correspondence that are no longer extant. In any case there is a draft of a letter to Nielsen from August of 1848, in which Kierkegaard confirms his invitation from his earlier letter: "Do let me know as soon as you come to Copenhagen so that I may send for you. I place emphasis on this invitation."[63] The tone of this letter is quite friendly. Moreover, Kierkegaard even goes so far as to paste Nielsen's humble and thankful response to the invitation into his *Journal NB6*: "Let me thank you, oh, let me thank you for wanting to call for me. I will come soon—in silence; for I notice that with you one must be very quiet in order to hear correctly what you are saying. Your R. Nielsen."[64] Although this entry is not dated, this was presumably in August of 1848.[65]

During this period Kierkegaard believed that he saw his health starting to fail, and he feared that he would soon die. At the time he had just published his article about the actress Johanne Luise Heiberg (1812–90), "The Crisis and a Crisis in the Life of an Actress."[66] In this context he writes in his *Journal NB6* presumably from August 1848:[67]

> The thought that I would soon die, the thought in which I have rested, has now been disturbed by the publication of that little article; it would disturb me if this were to be the last thing I publish. But, on the other hand, the thought of dying now was only a

59 *B&A*, vol. 1, p. 195 / *LD*, Letter 179, pp. 245–6; see also *B&A*, vol. 1, pp. 193–4 / *LD*, Letter 177, p. 244.

60 *B&A*, vol. 1, pp. 198–9 / *LD*, Letter 182, pp. 249–50.

61 *LD*, Notes, p. 478.

62 *B&A*, vol. 1, p. 199 / *LD*, Letter 182, p. 250.

63 *B&A*, vol. 1, p. 200 / *LD*, Letter 183, p. 252.

64 *SKS* 21, 11, NB6:2. See *SKS* K21, 53.

65 *SKS* K21, 15.

66 Kierkegaard, "Krisen og en Krise i en Skuespillerindes Liv, af Inter et Inter. En Artikel i Anledning af 'Romeo og Julies' Gjenoptagelse paa Repertoiret ved Nytaarstid 1847," *Fædrelandet*, vol. 9, no. 188, July 24, 1848, columns 1485–90; no. 189, July 25, 1848, columns 1493–1500; no. 190, July 26, 1848, columns 1501–6; no. 191, July 27, 1848, columns 1509–16.

67 Kierkegaard used the *Journal NB6* from July 16 to August 21, 1848. (See Niels W. Bruun et al., "Tekstredegørelse" to *Journal NB6* in *SKS* K21, p. 10.) His invitation to Nielsen was also presumably in August.

> depressive notion—how good then that I published that little article. This very thing had to be probed—and the publication of the article served to do this.[68]

Then in the margin to this he adds somewhat enigmatically, "But in my case there is R. Nielsen as one who can provide explanation."[69] The idea seems to be that if Kierkegaard were to die and "The Crisis and a Crisis in the Life of an Actress" proved to be his last published work, Rasmus Nielsen would be there to explain its role with respect to the authorship as a whole.

A few entries later Kierkegaard writes at length in a retrospective manner about his authorship, referring to the importance of governance in his development. He fears that his poor health will not allow him to finish and publish the books that he is currently working on:

> My energies, that is, my physical energies, are declining; the state of my health varies terribly. I hardly see my way even to publishing the essentially decisive works I have ready ("A Cycle of Essays," "The Sickness unto Death," "Come All You Who Labor and Are Heavy Laden," "Blessed Is He Who Is Not Offended").[70]

Given his concern for his health and his new friendship with Nielsen, Kierkegaard wished to designate the latter as the posthumous editor of his *Nachlass*.[71] He refers positively to Nielsen as someone who might be entrusted with the task of the publication of these works: "I live in the faith that God will place the accent of governance on the life of an extremely unhappy, humanly understood, man who nevertheless by the help of God has felt indescribably blessed—but my wish is that now R. Nielsen might be relied on."[72] While this statement is admittedly somewhat cryptic, this is a key entry. Kierkegaard brings Nielsen into relation with the concept of governance. As we know from *The Point of View*, Kierkegaard believed that divine governance was steering his life and his authorship. Thus, his authorship was conceived as a form of service for God. With his health failing, Kierkegaard was concerned with what would happen to his authorship if he should die. Thus now Nielsen enters the picture. Nielsen can now be relied upon to take care for the proper understanding of the authorship after Kierkegaard's death. This also seems to mean that Nielsen is to be given the responsibility for the publication of Kierkegaard's posthumous works.

In the next entry Kierkegaard states even more directly what he means by this: "Now add the thought of death to the publication of that little article! If I were to die without that: indeed, anyone could publish my posthumous papers, and in any case

---

68 *SKS* 21, 50, NB6:67 / *JP* 6, 6232.

69 *SKS* 21, 50, NB6:67.a / *JP* 6, 6233.

70 *SKS* 21, 56, NB6:74 / *JP* 6, 6238.

71 See Niels Jørgen Cappelørn, Joakim Garff, and Johnny Kondrup, *Written Images. Søren Kierkegaard's Journals, Notebooks, Booklets, Sheets, Scraps and Slips of Paper*, trans. by Bruce H. Kirmmse, Princeton and Oxford: Princeton University Press 2003, pp. 30–42; pp. 64–5; p. 69. This is clear from a note found later where Kierkegaard designates Nielsen as the one responsible for the publication of this material. See the picture of this note in *Written Images*, pp. 22–3.

72 *SKS* 21, 57, NB6:74 / *JP* 6, 6238.

R. Nielsen would be there."[73] Most clearly, he writes, "It is my wish that after my death *Prof. Nielsen* do whatever is necessary with respect to the publication of the entirety of my literary remains, manuscripts, journals, etc., which are to be turned over to him."[74] This statement seemed to have the tone of a kind of last will and testament, and for this reason it caused great vexation when it was discovered by Hans Peter Barfod (1834–92), the first editor of Kierkegaard's posthumous works.[75]

In a long journal entry Kierkegaard discusses in detail his relation to Nielsen. He clearly shows some reservations about Nielsen's understanding of his works. Kierkegaard originally intended to finish the aesthetic authorship with the *Postscript* and *A Literary Review*, and now, in the midst of the religious authorship, a new aesthetic work appears, "The Crisis and a Crisis in the Life of an Actress." He ponders how Nielsen will understand this:

> The relationship to R. Nielsen in this matter has made me very uneasy in fear and trembling. I had given R. N. a direct communication. But on the other hand, to what extent R. N. had really understood me, to what extent he was capable of venturing something for the truth, is not at all clear to me. Here was the opportunity to make a test, and I felt that I owed it to the cause, to him, and to myself. Fortunately he was staying in the country. He has maintained constantly that he had understood the aesthetic to have been used as an enticement and an incognito. He has also maintained that he understood that it always depended entirely upon involvement. But whether that is entirely true, he never did really put to the test. He scarcely understood the significance of *Either/Or* and of the two upbuilding discourses. Not until much later, especially when I became an exclusively religious author, and when I drew him to me did he understand it. Well, fine, that means he did not understand it in the form of reduplication; he understood it as a direct communication, that I explained to him that it was done that way. We must now find out; the question of what he thinks of this seemingly suddenly aesthetic article about an actress must be put to him.[76]

One way in which Kierkegaard wishes to test Nielsen is to see if he is attentive to a critical remark about Martensen. Given Nielsen's previous association with Martensen, Kierkegaard was naturally apprehensive about their current relation. Thus, it is understandable that Kierkegaard would wish to confirm that Nielsen is now critical of his colleague:

> Furthermore, the article contains a little allusion to Martensen. If R. Nielsen in some way wants to avoid holding a judgment in common with the persons concerned, that is up to him. In brief, for a moment he must stand entirely alone so that I can see where we are. It is something entirely different to talk afterwards about this reduplication, consequently in direct form, than to have to pass judgment at the moment oneself.[77]

---

73 *SKS* 21, 57, NB6:75 / *C*, Supplement, p. 421.

74 H. Gottsched (ed.), *Af Søren Kierkegaards Efterladte Papirer. 1849*, Copenhagen: C.A. Reitzels Forlag 1880, p. 637. Note that this entry does not appear in the *Papirer* edition.

75 See Cappelørn, Garff, and Kondrup, *Written Images. Søren Kierkegaard's Journals, Notebooks, Booklets, Sheets, Scraps and Slips of Paper*, pp. 30–42.

76 *SKS* 21, 58, NB6:76 / *JP* 6, 6239.

77 Ibid.

Here it seems that "The Crisis and a Crisis in the Life of an Actress" and not the *Postscript* is the key piece of writing that was the occasion for Nielsen and Kierkegaard to come together. Moreover, it should be noted that Kierkegaard, quite coy in this relation, takes the credit for the relationship, saying that he drew Nielsen to himself. In any case, Kierkegaard is particularly interested in whether or not Nielsen is able to independently appropriate what he has learned in his own concrete lived existence as a form of "reduplication."

Kierkegaard continues the entry, noting how much he appreciated the fact that Nielsen had understood him:

> Oh, it is very strenuous to serve the truth in self-denial. I had given many people in many ways the impression that I was a devotional author—and then to disturb this impression myself. I did cherish R. Nielsen's having understood me as much as he did—and then to have to lose all this.
>
> Yes, it is very strenuous to serve the truth in this way, constantly exposing oneself to misunderstanding—in order if possible to keep men awake, in order that the religious may not again become an indolent habit, and it might be like that for R. N. I must in fear and trembling let God judge between him and me, so that he does not attach himself too much to me but to God. But, humanly speaking, it is hard for me to work against myself in this way simply in order to serve the truth....
>
> Oh, R. N. scarcely dreams of how he has occupied me on this occasion, and why? Because he has become involved in my God-relation. That is infinitely crucial. In this way I am strong and weak. Actually there is not a man living with whom I would not dare to take this up, relying on my superiority over him—and any man, whoever he is, who comes in touch with my God relationship, becomes a prodigious concern to me.[78]

Of profound interest is Kierkegaard's claim that he took Nielsen into his own "God-relation." This is particularly perplexing since Kierkegaard is well known for his insistent claims that one's God-relation is always deeply personal and individual. What could it mean that Nielsen plays a role in his God-relation? In order to understand this one must recall that Kierkegaard believed that his authorship was a part of his God-relation since it was steered by governance. Nielsen is brought into this relation since Kierkegaard chooses him to be responsible for carrying on this work of the authorship after his death, either by publishing it or giving the correct interpretation of it. Thus, just as Kierkegaard believes that he is directed by governance, since he has chosen Nielsen for this special role, Nielsen is also directed by governance to a second degree, so to speak. Occupying this special relation like few other people in Kierkegaard's life, Nielsen thus becomes "a prodigious concern" for him.

Kierkegaard continues his considerations of Nielsen in a couple of entries in *NB7*, which Kierkegaard used from August 21 to November 26, 1848.[79] Here he worries that his friendship with Nielsen might turn into a faction or "coterie." This seems to echo Brøchner's formulation, quoted above, about how Nielsen "allied" himself with Kierkegaard, as if the goal were to launch a common campaign. Kierkegaard writes:

---

78 *SKS* 21, 58–9, NB6:76 / *JP* 6, 6239.

79 See Garff et al., "Tekstredegørelse" to *Journal NB7* in *SKS* K21, p. 64.

R. Nielsen is a curious fellow. We had an agreement or understanding that there should be a relationship between us but that it by no means may become a coterie. But what is a coterie? It implies an advance agreement among the persons concerned about future action and a mutual judgment about what has been done, which is then broadcast. Consequently that must not be done. So I write a note to him, an altogether proper one, and yet—and this certainly was not unfortunate—yet done in such a way that it was sufficient to maintain the relationship while it became an alienating factor with respect to that little thing I wrote, something of such great importance to my whole authorship that I scarcely dared communicate anything about it directly right away. Had I done so, I would have lost myself, become saddled with an inconsistency which I perhaps never would have lived down. But R. N. was offended—and then chooses not to answer at all, so I actually had to believe that he had not received the letter.[80]

Here Kierkegaard attributes great significance to the relation and is profoundly exercised by it. He is clearly troubled by the lack of response by Nielsen and is afraid that he has alienated him. In the next entry he is relieved since Nielsen has returned and Kierkegaard has discussed the matter with him in person: "Finally he has come to town, and I have spoken with him and assured myself of the situation. There was hardly much danger here. But the *summa summarum* is, as I understood it from the beginning, it is me who should be brought up to learn something. For this a person is always used whom I take into my God-relation."[81] Thus Nielsen is to be used by Kierkegaard as a tool to some purpose in Kierkegaard's God-relation. The purpose clearly has to do with Nielsen's role in promoting the authorship.

Seeing Nielsen in person seems only to have given Kierkegaard a temporary reprieve. He is still vexed since he feels that he still does not know exactly where Nielsen stands. The situation is made particularly acute given Kierkegaard's conviction that he will soon die. In an entry not without a somewhat melodramatic tone, Kierkegaard writes:

How I have suffered because of this relation to R. N. To have him out there in suspense, perhaps even offended, and then to have my responsibility and my fear and trembling—and yet unable to have acted or to act otherwise! And then not to be able to get to see the actual situation because he was out in the country. And then to know that the danger was probably not so great, humanly speaking, but yet before God to have to hold out alone all that time with the most dreadful possibilities! Frightful! And a dying man like me, who was so quiet and calm and reconciled to the thought of death—and now suddenly to suffer and endure so long the torture of not being able to die because I must first see his situation and my responsibility. Frightful!

...God be praised that I published that article, God be praised that I kept R. N. in suspense and did not weaken and give him direct communication; but above all God be praised that God is to me what he has always been: love. Now I can die tomorrow and I can go on living—everything is in order.[82]

Here Kierkegaard is quite vexed by the idea that he is dying and that certain things between him and Nielsen have not yet been cleared up. Kierkegaard seems proud

80 *SKS* 21, 78–9, NB7:6 / *JP* 6, 6246.

81 *SKS* 21, 79, NB7:7.

82 *SKS* 21, 80, NB7:9 / *C*, Supplement, pp. 423–4.

of the fact that despite his own sufferings, he has kept Nielsen guessing and has not revealed his true intentions with direct communication. In the next entry he mentions that he has prayed for Nielsen and taken him up into his God-relation again.[83]

At the beginning of the next year, Kierkegaard continues his deliberations about his relation to Nielsen in his *Journal NB9*, which he wrote in from January 2 to February 9, 1849.[84] In one entry he considers the unenviable prospect of his death and Nielsen carrying on in his name. He is deeply concerned that Nielsen is not well suited to this and would fail to carry on the Kierkegaardian campaign correctly since he does not understand the concept of reduplication.[85] In the next entry he writes, clearly referring to Nielsen:

> The true is really always defenseless in this world, where there very rarely are even ten who have the capability, the time, the diligence, and the moral character to follow through in pursuing the truth—but here in the world the mob of contemporaries is the judge, and they are far too confused to understand the truth but understand untruth very easily. I have regarded it as my religious duty to draw a person to me in order not to leave out the human tribunal completely. He now gets communications from me which he otherwise would never get—and gets them privately. Here again is the possibility that I may become completely defenseless. If vanity and a secular mentality run away with him, he will publish this in a confused form as his own and will create an enormous furor. My efforts at reclamation would be useless. Alas, and a person who is already married, a professor, a knight—what real hope is there of his competence to serve the truth, in a more profound sense what fondness can he have for an undertaking in which all these qualifications are just so many N.B.'s, while at any moment he can turn to the other side, where these are substantiations.[86]

Kierkegaard regards Nielsen as a kind of student to whom he gives information as he wishes. Again he is vexed by the prospect of Nielsen publishing works in which he claims to present Kierkegaard's position. Kierkegaard seems quite convinced that Nielsen would only present his views in a confused manner. This reflection is prophetic since this is precisely what happens and what causes the conflict between the two men later the same year.

In the next entry Kierkegaard again clearly has Nielsen in mind, without mentioning him explicitly:

> If that which one has to communicate is, for example, a conception of something historical or the like, it may be a good thing for someone else to arrive at the same conception, and all one has to do is simply to work to get this idea acknowledged. But if the point of a person's activity is to do what is true: then one additional assistant professor is just a new calamity, and not least when he gets assistance privately and confidentially.[87]

---

83 *SKS* 21, 80–1, NB7:10 / *JP* 6, 6247.

84 See Garff et al., "Tekstredegørelse" to *Journal NB9* in *SKS* K21, p. 170.

85 *SKS* 21, 205, NB9:13.

86 *SKS* 21, 206, NB9:14 / *JP* 6, 6301.

87 *SKS* 21, 206, NB9:15 / *JP* 6, 6302.

Here Kierkegaard is clearly worried about the possibility that Nielsen, an assistant professor, will present his views about the private inward nature of religious faith by means of direct communication.

He continues his reflections in the *Journal NB10*, which Kierkegaard used from February 9 to May 2, 1849.[88] At the beginning of one entry Kierkegaard states that he has "not collided with the established order" and indeed that he is "suited to preserving the established order."[89] This is striking to read when one considers his violent attack on the Church some five years later. In this connection, he writes:

> Now I see it more clearly—that, rightly understood, I am or ought to be the movement, the awakening, only in a soft and dormant period (for I am the more ideal established order), but in rebellious times I am quite clearly conservative. What R. Nielsen said is quite true—that in a way Bishop Mynster regards me as an exaggeration—in peace-time; but now he thinks that I am more suitable.[90]

Nielsen's role in this entry seems at first glance to be fairly minimal, but upon closer inspection one can see that it is clear that Nielsen has helped Kierkegaard to understand his mission better. His goal with his writings is that of "awakening." The reference to Nielsen's account of what Mynster has said seems to imply that the two men had discussed such things privately, perhaps on their walks together. This is again clear indication that Nielsen is, at this point in time, involved in Kierkegaard's authorship in the sense that it is intended as a part of a wider campaign for religious reform.

For some unknown reason, Kierkegaard seems to have come to question his planned role for Nielsen. Somewhat later in the same journal he writes:

> I have become involved with R. Nielsen because I considered it my religious duty to have at least one man, so that it could not be said that I bypassed completely this claim.
>
> Of course he can be of no benefit to me ultimately: he is too heavy, too thick-skinned, too spoiled by the age of Christian VIII. Were I to become secular-minded, he naturally would be of advantage to me.
>
> I have been obliged to be a little distant with him, for otherwise he prattles pleasantly about my cause, my cause which either should be intensified unconditionally or hidden in deepest silence.[91]

Here Kierkegaard speaks very strategically about his relation to Nielsen. He seems clearly to want to use Nielsen in the service of his general religious endeavor, but he realizes that this will not work. However, he does not seem overly irritated by the situation yet. In the next entry, Kierkegaard writes, "R. Nielsen can understand me up to a point, but he cannot resist himself, is fascinated by all this profundity, hurries home, jots it down, and communicates it—instead of first acting upon it himself. His communication of the truth will never in all eternity become action."[92]

---

88 See Niels W. Bruun et al., "Tekstredegørelse" to *Journal NB10* in *SKS* K21, p. 224.

89 *SKS* 21, 262, NB10:14 / *JP* 6, 6335.

90 Ibid.

91 *SKS* 21, 273, NB10:32 / *JP* 6, 6341.

92 *SKS* 21, 273, NB10:33 / *JP* 6, 6342.

From these passages it is evident that even at this early period of their relationship, Kierkegaard cannot be said to have a carefree, open and amicable relation to Nielsen. He is constantly worried about offending Nielsen or about Nielsen misunderstanding or misrepresenting him. This somewhat unstable relation was merely a foreboding of things to come.

IV. The First Test of the Friendship:
Nielsen's The Faith of the Gospels *(May–September 1849)*

It was during this period that Nielsen, under Kierkegaard's influence, published his lectures *The Faith of the Gospels and Modern Consciousness. Lectures on the Life of Jesus*.[93] This work appeared on May 19, 1849.[94] Kierkegaard might have been aware of these lectures prior to their publication.[95] Instead of being flattered that he had inspired Nielsen, Kierkegaard was offended since he believed Nielsen to have stolen his ideas and presented them as his own. This was for Kierkegaard a warning shot in their relationship. In his *Journal NB11*, Kierkegaard reacts to this as follows:

> R. Nielsen's book is out. Realizing the wrong I have suffered in the interest of truth, realizing my mastery of the circumstances, he still thought, as I suspected, that if he only enlisted my support and I stayed by him somewhat—that it could be done, that he could even gain importance, perhaps be a success.
>
> That was the enthusiasm for the rightness of my cause.
>
> In fact, he did come to the right one.
>
> The writings are plundered in many ways, the pseudonyms most of all, which he never cites, perhaps with deliberate shrewdness, as the least read.
>
> And then my conversations![96]

Kierkegaard clearly feels that Nielsen has betrayed the relationship of familiarity. Nielsen has stolen ideas both from Kierkegaard's works and from private conversations. Kierkegaard seems to believe that Nielsen's motivation for doing so was to gain success by making use of his ideas.

In a letter dated May 25, 1849, Nielsen writes to Kierkegaard, begging his pardon for an unnamed mistake.[97] This can be taken as a response to Kierkegaard's criticism of him, which he communicated either in writing or personally. In a letter with the same date, Nielsen indicates that he has something serious to discuss with Kierkegaard, but that it is of such a character that he would prefer not to discuss it on their usual walk. (They already apparently had a rendezvous for a walk.) In any case, it is clear that he is waiting for the latter to respond and feels somewhat rebuffed: "you may conclude that it is unlikely that we shall meet again until you find the time at some point and the opportunity 'to call upon me' once more. Whether this will

---

93 Nielsen, *Evangelietroen og den moderne Bevidsthed. Forelæsninger over Jesu Liv.*

94 See *Pap.* X–6, p. 224, note 343. *LD*, Notes, p. 483.

95 *SKS* 21, 262, NB10:13. Already here Kierkegaard complains that Nielsen "in his production apparently makes use of what he gets from me."

96 *SKS* 22, 32, NB11:46 / *JP* 6, 6415.

97 *B&A*, vol. 1, pp. 228–9 / *LD*, Letter 208, p. 290.

ever happen, whether it happens this year or in future years, must of course depend on you: I have the time to wait."[98] From an extant draft, one can see Kierkegaard's response, in which, with a tone of being offended, he indicates that he went in vain to their designated meeting place for their walk and Nielsen did not come. He accuses Nielsen of being "somewhat artificial" by not simply showing up and saying that he had something he wanted to discuss with him that was of such a nature that he would prefer not to discuss it on their walk.[99]

Kierkegaard seems to refer to Nielsen indirectly in an entry later in *NB11*, where he discusses the desire to have a "single adherent." Here he talks about how the truth gets lost in the conveying of it from one person to another. Thus, he must realize that there is a certain inevitability in Nielsen's confused presentation of his ideas. He reasons as follows:

> Take the supreme example: if Christ, who was truth, had insisted absolutely upon not exposing truth to any misinterpretation, refused to become involved in any accommodation: then his whole life would have been one single monologue.
>
> The point is that I have too profoundly understood that truth does not win by means of adherents but constantly suffers loss the more it acquires. My life's thought was the extreme consequence of that.[100]

Here Kierkegaard seems to regret the fact that Nielsen has become his adherent since the inevitable result is that his ideas are misrepresented and communicated in a confused manner.

Nielsen's close relation to Kierkegaard meant at the same time an alienation from Martensen. Nielsen thus in effect allied himself with Kierkegaard against Martensen, to whom he had once stood so close. It was this common enemy that brought Nielsen and Kierkegaard back together again after this initial tension regarding Nielsen's *The Faith of the Gospels and Modern Consciousness*. On July 19, 1849, Martensen published his *Christian Dogmatics*. On the next day Nielsen writes the following two-sentence letter to Kierkegaard: " 'The System' has arrived. It got here the day before yesterday with 'the Omnibus.' "[101] In response to this Kierkegaard notes the association of Nielsen's reference to "the Omnibus" and one of Kierkegaard's own favorite phrase, which he associates with Martensen, "*de omnibus dubitandum est*."[102] With this letter Kierkegaard sends to Nielsen a copy of *The Sickness unto Death*, which had just appeared. Nielsen responds to this graciously with a note of thanks dated July 28, 1849.[103] Kierkegaard responds very positively to Nielsen's comments in a letter from August 4 of the same year.[104] From the tone of these letters it is clear that their relationship, while having experienced a few bumps in the road, had not been entirely destroyed by this point. The publication

98 *B&A*, vol. 1, p. 229 / *LD*, Letter 209, p. 291.

99 *B&A*, vol. 1, pp. 229–30 / *LD*, Letter 210, p. 292.

100 *SKS* 22, 60–1, NB11:107 / *JP* 6, 6402.

101 *B&A*, vol. 1, pp. 234–5 / *LD*, Letter 212, p. 298.

102 *B&A*, vol. 1, p. 235 / *LD*, Letter 213, pp. 298–9.

103 *B&A*, vol. 1, p. 238 / *LD*, Letter 215, p. 303.

104 *B&A*, vol. 1, pp. 243–4 / *LD*, Letter 219, p. 310.

of Martensen's book seems to have reenergized the friendship, and there follows an intensive correspondence during the months of August and September since Nielsen was staying in Lyngby at the end of the summer, and his stay had to be prolonged due to illness.[105] Nielsen takes special pleasure in relating to Kierkegaard how he saw both Mynster and Martensen at a dinner party where he was staying.[106] The tone of this letter clearly bespeaks a degree of intimacy and a sense that Nielsen and Kierkegaard are working in tandem for a specific cause. In any case they both agree to get together in person once Nielsen returns to the city. In a letter dated September 20, 1849, Nielsen announces that he is back in Copenhagen.[107]

With their agreement on their criticism of Martensen, Nielsen and Kierkegaard seem to have put their friendship back on the right track. However, the strain in their relation was to reemerge soon thereafter. This probably gave Nielsen the mistaken impression that he would have Kierkegaard's full approbation if he were to criticize Martensen publicly. He was, however, sadly mistaken on this point.

V. The Second Test of the Friendship: Nielsen's Joint Review (September 1849–April 1850)

As has just been seen, Nielsen and Kierkegaard had discussed critically Martensen's *Christian Dogmatics* on their walks. Nielsen decided to make public his criticisms with a review of Martensen's work, which was being discussed with great animation at the time. He decided to do this with the aforementioned dual book review in which he juxtaposed Kierkegaard's *Postscript* to Martensen's *Christian Dogmatics*. This work appeared as a monograph, entitled *Mag. S. Kierkegaard's "Johannes Climacus" and Dr. H. Martensen's "Christian Dogmatics." An Investigative Review*.[108] It is dated September 18, 1849, and the work was presumably published in the October of that year. This monograph represented a second major blow to Nielsen's and Kierkegaard's relationship. Once again Kierkegaard felt that Nielsen had misused his ideas in the polemic against Martensen. Moreover, Nielsen failed to understand the concept of indirect communication and the use of the pseudonyms by attacking Martensen so directly.

---

105 *B&A*, vol. 1, pp. 243–4 / *LD*, Letter 219, pp. 310–11. *B&A*, vol. 1, pp. 244–5 / *LD*, Letter 220, pp. 311–12. *B&A*, vol. 1, p. 245 / *LD*, Letter 221, pp. 312–13. *B&A*, vol. 1, p. 246 / *LD*, Letter 222, p. 313. *B&A*, vol. 1, p. 246 / *LD*, Letter 223, pp. 313–14. *B&A*, vol. 1, p. 247 / *LD*, Letter 224, pp. 314–15. *B&A*, vol. 1, pp. 247–8 / *LD*, Letter 225, pp. 315–16. *B&A*, vol. 1, p. 248 / *LD*, Letter 226, pp. 316–17. *B&A*, vol. 1, p. 249 / *LD*, Letter 227, p. 317. *B&A*, vol. 1, pp. 249–50 / *LD*, Letter 228, pp. 317–18. *B&A*, vol. 1, pp. 250–1 / *LD*, Letter 229, pp. 319–20. *B&A*, vol. 1, p. 251 / *LD*, Letter 230, p. 320. *B&A*, vol. 1, pp. 251–2 / *LD*, Letter 231, pp. 320–1.

106 *B&A*, vol. 1, pp. 247–8 / *LD*, Letter 225, pp. 315–16.

107 *B&A*, vol. 1, p. 251 / *LD*, Letter 230, p. 320.

108 Nielsen, *Magister S. Kierkegaards "Johannes Climacus" og Dr. H. Martensens "Christelige Dogmatik." En undersøgende Anmeldelse*. For an account of this work, see Niels Thulstrup, "Martensen's Dogmatics and its Reception," in *Kierkegaard and His Contemporaries: The Culture of Golden Age Denmark*, ed. by Jon Stewart, pp. 187–92.

In the *Journal NB14* from 1849, which Kierkegaard wrote in from November 9, 1849 until January 6, 1850,[109] he makes the following comment about Nielsen's alienation from Martensen:

> The day before yesterday I took a walk with Nielsen. It was the last time this year. The conversation turned in such a way that he himself acknowledged that there was some personal reason, at least in part, for his changing his course. "He felt himself to be left out in the cold compared with Martensen; for several years now Martensen had been occupying the place in The Royal Society which belonged to him," and so on. Well, it is good that he himself says this. I am hoping both that actuality will properly shape him up and that through his relationship to me he will come to a completely different view of life, and then something good might come out of it. The fact that he himself now acknowledges it indicates that some change has already taken place in him.[110]

This remark clearly reflects the fact that Martensen and his *Christian Dogmatics* were the central object of discussion during these months. In their conversations, Nielsen and Kierkegaard clearly found consolation and pleasure in criticizing him.

From their correspondence from the first months of 1850 one can again sense a degree of tension in the relationship. In letters dated January 17, 1850 Nielsen writes to tell Kierkegaard that he cannot come on their usual walk since he has caught a cold.[111] This letter is followed by another one on February 22, in which he cancels again, this time giving no explanation.[112]

In his *Journal NB15* from 1850 (which he used between January 6 and February 15, 1850), Kierkegaard writes the following about Nielsen, whom he compares with P.M. Stilling (1812–69):

> It is sad to have an eye such as mine. I saw R. Nielsen's ideal possibility—but do not dare say it to him directly, nor can it help to do so, for then it will turn into something else entirely and in the strictest sense not be the ideal. He did not see it. I see the possibility in Stilling, and here it is the same. So also with a number of others. I yearningly anticipate the moment when an existential ideality will appear in our setting. Now if this were something reserved for only the exceptionally talented—but this is a possibility for anyone—and yet it is so rare![113]

In the entry immediately prior to this he discusses the importance of avoiding forming a coterie in religious matters. Despite this, Kierkegaard is apparently on the look out for likeminded writers, who might be interested in joining forces with him. His disappointment in Nielsen has led him to consider Stilling as another possible candidate.

---

109 See Finn Gredal Jensen and Steen Tullberg, "Tekstredegørelse" to *Journal NB14* in *SKS* K22, p. 425.

110 *SKS* 22, 414, NB14:120 / *JP* 6, 6563.

111 *B&A*, vol. 1, pp. 268–9. / *LD*, Letter 247, pp. 342–3.

112 *B&A*, vol. 1, p. 270 / *LD*, Letter 249, p. 344.

113 *SKS* 23, 22, NB15:23 / *JP* 6, 6573.

Kierkegaard wrote in his *Journal NB17* from March 6, 1850 to May 15 of the same year.[114] Here he complains that Nielsen, the academic philosopher, is not able to shake off his role in this capacity. This leads him to misrepresent Kierkegaard's views since he is always inclined to lecture and to give a straightforward account of his views instead of using strategies such as indirect communication. In his journal Kierkegaard writes:

> R.N.'s misfortune is actually that he is warped by scholarliness and does not yet have an idea of what it is to be a person who calmly rests in his assurance of the correctness of the matter but also acts as a person....He had begun with a quite simple and straightforward explanation, in which he, speaking not without a certain decorous sense of self about the studies in philosophy that he is conscious of having made, explained that these writings had changed him in his view.[115]

In the same entry he goes on to express his disappoint at how things have developed with Nielsen. Here he gives an insightful sketch of the kind of relation he wished he could have had with him:

> With all this vacillation and these errors almost two years have now passed. How much has been lost! How beautiful the whole thing could have been, how purely transparent the relationship, so wholly free, neither disciple nor the like, no, a respectable person, who in agreement with me about having found a decision in these writings, decides to work for the cause.
>
> However, perhaps such a metamorphosis is too much to ask of a former speculative professor, at least in the first instance. And how clear has the difference from Martensen become, while now similarity is so close.
>
> I have learned so much in the trial of patience.[116]

It is interesting that Kierkegaard states here that he was not interested in having a student or a disciple but rather another "respectable" person who could work for the cause in his own way. Thus Nielsen's ideal role is not that of a subordinate. The idea seems to be that they would have been independent partners working for a common goal. The last part of the passage is also interesting, since here Kierkegaard indirectly reproaches himself for believing that Nielsen could so radically transform himself to take up Kierkegaard's cause.

VI. The Third Test of the Friendship: *Nielsen's* The Faith of the Gospels and Theology *(April–September 1850)*

One would think that by now Nielsen would realize the danger of publishing material that included Kierkegaard's thoughts or passages from his works. Nonetheless on April 6, 1850, he published his *The Faith of the Gospels and Theology*, which

114 See Bruun et al., "Tekstredegørelse" to *Journal NB17* in *SKS* K23, p. 257.

115 *SKS* 23, 169, NB17:7.

116 *SKS* 23, 170, NB17:7.

was also based on a series of lectures that he gave.[117] This is a very extensive work that Kierkegaard constantly refers to simply as "the big book." Once again, in Kierkegaard's eyes, Nielsen makes himself guilty of misunderstanding and misrepresentation, and once again his efforts for "the cause" seem to be wholly misdirected and ill advised.

In his *Journal NB17* from 1850, Kierkegaard writes a long entry entitled "Concerning R. Nielsen." Here he explains in detail his initial reaction to Nielsen's latest publication:

> Last Thursday I took a walk with him and then finally managed to get said a little bit about the fact that I regarded his entire change of direction from the big book with the 12 lectures as an attempt by a clever person who was perhaps the most clever in a matter, and who wanted to advance the cause thus instead of serving it in a simple manner; further I said that the entire affair with Martensen was a mistake and had nothing to do with my cause but was personal animosity, moreover, that he changed it into a doctrine, and finally that he plagiarized all too much even from our conversations.[118]

Kierkegaard believes that Nielsen has departed from the correct path by allowing his personal animosity for Martensen to blind him. Instead of working for the Kierkegaardian campaign, Nielsen has engaged in needless polemics with his colleague. This kind of polemic has, in Kierkegaard's view, nothing to do with his cause. This is somewhat odd given the later attack on the Church, in which Kierkegaard quite directly criticizes precisely Martensen.

In the same entry Kierkegaard recounts how, after his critical comments, he attempted to make a reconciliation with Nielsen. He continues:

> He became somewhat angry or, more correctly, testy. However, I turned away from this, led the conversation over to other things, and we walked home *in bona caritate*.
>
> I now thought that this coming Thursday I would take up the matter again, and if he was willing to listen to reason and accept what is the truth, then perhaps I would succeed in making him feel obliged to do something for the cause in a simple manner as reviewer or the like.
>
> But no, today I received a letter in which he renounces wanting to take a walk with me on Thursday.[119]

Kierkegaard presumably refers here to the letter from Nielsen that he received on April 18, 1850.[120] In this letter Nielsen writes to cancel their usual walk. He does so in a somewhat terse manner that leaves it an open question of what exactly his motivations are: "Under the circumstances I must now for the time being renounce going for walks

---

117 Nielsen, *Evangelietroen og Theologien. Tolv Forelæsninger holdt ved Universitetet i Kjøbenhavn i Vinteren 1849–50.*

118 *SKS* 23, 215–16, NB17:71.

119 Ibid.

120 *B&A*, vol. 1, p. 273 / *LD*, Letter 252, p. 348. This letter is dated "Thursday, March 19, 1850," which commentators believe must be an error due to the fact that March 19, 1850 was a Tuesday and not a Thursday. Moreover, Kierkegaard received this letter on April 18, 1850. See *SKS* K23, p. 308.

with you on Thursdays, and accordingly I must ask you not to expect me today."[121] Nielsen presumably felt somewhat offended by Kierkegaard's rebuke and tried tactfully, albeit inauthentically, to withdraw gradually from the relationship. For Nielsen, Kierkegaard's negative reaction must have come as a surprise since the former had been led to believe that they two were in agreement in their criticism of Martensen.

In any case, Kierkegaard clearly sensed that something was amiss. In a couple of drafts to a letter, he voices his suspicions and invites Nielsen to elaborate on what he means by "under the circumstances."[122] In draft to a letter, Kierkegaard indicates his irritation with Nielsen and announces that he must end their relationship:

> During the years I have conversed with you, our relationship has been approximately this: with regard to every single one of your public performances (your writings), I have most firmly told you that from my point of view I could not approve of them. Furthermore, I have explained why not, and you yourself have also spoken in such a manner that I must consider myself as having been understood. Moreover, in private you have always expressed yourself very differently from the way you have in public. But you always said that I would find that your next book would be different. Therefore I have continued to wait.
>
> But now this will have to come to an end. I must hereby—completely without anger—break off a relationship that was indeed begun with a certain hope and that I do not give up as hopeless at this moment either.[123]

However, Kierkegaard apparently reconsidered the matter, and this draft was discarded. Instead, in the letter that was sent, he was much more reconciliatory.[124] Here Kierkegaard expresses his fear that a misunderstanding has arisen and proposes that they meet the next day in order to sort things out. Nielsen willingly accepts the offer.[125]

The meeting apparently resulted in a kind of small-scale reconciliation, which Kierkegaard records as follows in an entry with the heading "R. Nielsen":

> I wrote N. a note (so that in no way I would be the one who had done him an injustice, even the slightest). We talked together Wednesday, April 30. I told him that I wanted a freer relationship.
>
> To hope is my element, especially when it has a touch of implausibility. I hope for him. It is still possible that he will finish properly even though he began in a wrong way. Would that he had never written the big book. His conduct after what happened between us, the way he has behaved for a year—Oh, that forced me to keep a detective's eye on him, something so alien to me, something I never desired, even though I always have this penetrating eye but never use it. Yes, if the relationship were such that the problem was whether to do something very contrived and that he perhaps was not sufficiently ingenious—Oh, something like that does not prompt me to use this penetrating eye. But the nub was that what he should have done was very simple and uncomplicated

---

121 *B&A*, vol. 1, p. 273 / *LD*, Letter 252, p. 348.

122 *B&A*, vol. 1, pp. 273–4 / *LD*, Letter 253, pp. 348–9. *B&A*, vol. 1, p. 274 / *LD*, Letter 254, pp. 349–50.

123 *B&A*, vol. 1, pp. 275–6 / *LD*, Letter 257, pp. 351–2.

124 *B&A*, vol. 1, pp. 277–8. / *LD*, Letter 259, pp. 353–4.

125 *B&A*, vol. 1, p. 278 / *LD*, Letter 260, p. 354.

> (something he himself frequently admitted he understood) and that he nevertheless continues to do something contrived instead.[126]

From this account it seems that the two agreed to have a more relaxed and less intensive relationship. This seems to be the natural culmination of what Kierkegaard regarded as the repetition of mistakes in Nielsen's various publications. While Kierkegaard continued to hope that Nielsen would grasp the nature of the cause and the proper means of its communication, he was again and again disappointed with each of Nielsen's new publications, which demonstrated clearly that Nielsen had failed to understand the key points.

There follow a handful of journal entries in the *Journal NB18*, which Kierkegaard kept from May 15 until June 9, 1850,[127] which concern his relation to Nielsen or Nielsen's role in the attack on Martensen.[128] In one of these he contrasts his relation to Nielsen to that of Socrates to his student Plato:

> I certainly am no Socrates and Nielsen no Plato, but the relation may still be analogous.
>
> Take Plato, now! Indubitably Plato had a great preponderance of ideas that were his own, but he, in order to keep the point of departure clear, never hesitated to attribute everything to Socrates, he never wearied of what the people perhaps got tired of—that it was always Socrates, Socrates.
>
> But Nielsen took the ideas and concealed where they came from; finally he gave his source but concealed the extent of his borrowing, also that I had gone out of my way to initiate him into my cause.
>
> I have done nothing but have put everything into the hands of Governance.[129]

Kierkegaard had long used Socrates as his model. Here he hits upon the comparison of Socrates and Plato with respect to his relation as a Socratic teacher of Nielsen.

On September 25, 1850 Kierkegaard's pseudonymous *Practice in Christianity* was published. He then sent a copy to Nielsen with the dedication: "To Prof. R. Nielsen, Knight of the Dannebrog, Cordially from the Editor."[130] This demonstrates that the two were still on fairly good terms. But there is another dimension to this story. According to Cappelørn, Kierkegaard had originally planned to have Nielsen be the editor of both *The Sickness unto Death* and *Practice in Christianity*.[131] When Kierkegaard realized that Nielsen was incapable of playing the role that Kierkegaard had planned for him and the relation became strained, he ultimately was forced to

---

126 *SKS* 23, 227, NB17:78 / *JP* 6, 6610.

127 See Bruun et al., "Tekstredegørelse" to *Journal NB18* in *SKS* K23, p. 335.

128 *SKS* 23, 264–5, NB18:23. *SKS* 23, 266–7, NB18:26. *SKS* 23, 270, NB18:30. *SKS* 23, 282–3, NB18:49. *SKS* 23, 308–9, NB18:82.

129 *SKS* 23, 319, NB18:93 / *JP* 6, 6630.

130 See Niels Jørgen Cappelørn, "Fire 'nye' Kierkegaard-dedikationer. Lidt til belysning af Kierkegaards forhold til R. Nielsen og J.P. Mynster," *Kierkegaardiana*, vol. 9, 1974, pp. 248–66.

131 Cappelørn argues for this based on an interpretation of *SKS* 21, 57, NB6:75 / *C*, Supplement, p. 421.

make a decision and to go ahead with the publications with himself as editor. This, according to Cappelørn, marked the decisive point in the relationship.[132]

After this the references to Nielsen diminish substantially.[133] Somewhat astonishingly, the two apparently continued to take their regular walks together as is attested by a letter that Nielsen writes to Kierkegaard on February 4, 1852, in which he writes to cancel their walk due to ill health.[134] Given this, it is probably more accurate to say that, instead of breaking down in a single major conflict, the friendship simply gradually faded away over time.

VII. Drafts of Potential Polemical Works Against Nielsen

One result of the break with Nielsen was that, starting already in 1849, Kierkegaard wrote a series of drafts for polemical articles against him.[135] While none of these was ever published, by their sheer number and volume, they demonstrate how important the relationship was to him. Since they are so numerous, it would be impossible to explore all of these in this context. I will instead simply attempt to provide a general sense of their tone and content by focusing on a couple of the most insightful of these.

The first of these dates presumably already from the fall of 1849. Kierkegaard writes the following heading for his drafts:

> Polemika
> R. Nielsen
> by
> Johannes Climacus
> Writing exercises in character that are not to be used.[136]

From this, one might infer that Kierkegaard never intended to publish these drafts but that they were all conceived merely as "writing exercises." In any case, it seems clear that already at this early point in their relationship Kierkegaard had intended to write several different critical statements about Nielsen's person and work.

One long sketch is entitled "On Prof. Nielsen's Relationship to My Pseudonym Johannes Climacus." This is a useful sketch since in it Kierkegaard attempts to enumerate systematically his objections to Nielsen. It is doubly useful since by contrasting his writings with those of Nielsen, Kierkegaard makes clear some of his own main goals with the authorship generally. Here he begins by writing:

---

132 Cappelørn, "Fire 'nye' Kierkegaard-dedikationer," p. 258.

133 See *SKS* 23, 341ff., NB19:20. *SKS* 23, 350–1, NB19:29. *SKS* 23, 356–7, NB19:36. *SKS* 23, 357–8, NB19:39. *SKS* 23, 412, NB20:36. *SKS* 23, 457, NB20:120. *SKS* 24, 70, NB21:116. *SKS* 24, 140, NB22:66. *SKS* 24, 147, NB22:85. *SKS* 24, 283, NB23:160. *SKS* 24, 392–3, NB24:114. *SKS* 24, 399ff., NB24:125. *SKS* 24, 525–6, NB25:112.

134 *B&A*, vol. 1, p. 315 / *LD*, Letter 291, p. 400.

135 *Pap.* X–6 B 83–102, pp. 91–125.

136 *Pap.* X–6 B 83 / *JP* 6, 6403.

> A.
> What I Cannot Approve
>
> 1. "There must be no direct teaching"—in the pseudonymous writers this has found adequate expression in the abeyance of direct teaching. A μεταβασις εις αλλο γενος is made in relation to teaching directly; the idea is reduplicated in the form—everything is changed into a poet-communication by a poor individual human being like most people, an experimental humorist—everything is situated in existence.
>
> It is different with Prof. Nielsen. His presentation, his address, are more or less direct teaching, especially if compared with the pseudonym's. The numerous scholarly allusions recalled by the professor are reminiscent of "the professor," and it becomes more or less a kind of doctrine that there must be no direct teaching.
>
> From the standpoint of the idea, the cause has retrogressed, because it has acquired a less consistent form.[137]

The point here seems quite straightforward. In order for the cause to be advanced, indirect communication must be applied. Nielsen, by contrast, engages in direct communication. His works attempt to be scholarly in the way that Kierkegaard's pseudonymous works do not. Therefore, the cause has suffered instead of moving forward.

The second objection that Kierkegaard raises against Nielsen concerns not the form but the content of his writings. Kierkegaard continues:

> 2. In the pseudonymous writings the content of Christianity has been compressed to its least possible minimum simply in order to give all the more powerful momentum toward becoming a Christian and to keep the nervous energy all the more intensively concentrated so as to be able to master the confusion and prevent the intrusion of "the parenthetical."
>
> It is different with Prof. N. With him the contents expand. He goes into an investigation of each particular miracle etc. etc.—in short, he goes into details. At the same time it is made difficult to provide momentum and to maintain the qualitative tension, because doubt and reflection are essentially related to this dispersive trend, to the details, and they get the upper hand as soon as one gets involved in them.
>
> From the standpoint of the idea there has been a loss, and the tension of the issue has been weakened—and yet no doubt many have now become aware of the cause.[138]

Here Kierkegaard indicates that he has made a conscious effort to avoid detailed scholarly discussions about key points of Christian dogma. Instead, he has put all the emphasis on the formal nature of belief itself. By contrast, Nielsen cannot resist the need to fill out the Christian belief with a determinate content. By so doing, he, however, departs from Kierkegaard's intention and puts the emphasis in a different place. Thus, instead of working for the Kierkegaardian cause, Nielsen engages in a more traditional form of Christian dogmatics.

Kierkegaard emphasizes that the goal of the pseudonyms was not to create an abstract theory but instead to produce a lived form of Christianity in each individual. Again this constitutes a point of contrast to Nielsen's works:

---

137 *Pap.* X–6 B 121 / *JP* 6, 6574.

138 *Pap.* X–6 B 121 / *JP* 6, 6574.

> 3. The new direction must be away from science and scholarship, away from theory. The pseudonym does not concentrate upon this thought; the pseudonym himself is continuously this new direction; the entire work is repulsion and the new direction is into existential inwardness.
>
> It is quite different with Prof. N. Here this thought is dwelt upon, details are gone into, the same thought is followed through in relation to the particular theological disciplines—sheer lingering. But in the very second there is one second of lingering, science and scholarship are on the way to becoming the stronger, for science and scholarship are and consist in lingering, whereas faith is itself the impetus of the existential away from that from which one is to move. But in the very second of lingering, theory thrusts itself forward and begins to take shape, for theory is and consists in lingering. And with Prof. N. the new direction is not taken; it does not find its expression qualitatively different from all theorizing. A kind of concluding paragraph is formulated so one can always remember that a new direction is to be taken. N. is much too professionally serious to be able to take a new direction as that jesting Joh. Climacus can in all consistency, because "to turn," "to turn away," so one always takes himself back, is impossible without the unity of jest and earnestness.
>
> From the standpoint of the idea, there is a loss—although no doubt more have now become aware of the cause.[139]

Nielsen is accused again of being too academic. He cannot resist the temptation to develop a theory or to make a theoretical point out of each individual insight. The focus of "the cause" should rather be to lead the reader away from such theoretical reflections and towards an inward consideration of one's own life and faith relation. From Nielsen's perspective, many of Kierkegaard's statements are in need of explanation and clarification. In his works, he thus attempts to provide just this. But in Kierkegaard's eyes, this is precisely what one is to refrain from doing.

In his fourth objection to Nielsen, Kierkegaard explains the function of the pseudonyms, which he believes Nielsen has overlooked. He writes:

> 4. The significance of the pseudonym, as of all the pseudonyms, is: the communication of interiority. In the infinite distance of the idea from actuality, yet in another sense so close to it, interiority becomes audible. But there is no finite relation to actuality, no one is attacked, no name is named; no one is under obligation to appropriate this communication, no one is constrained, although it does not follow thereby that no one by himself has a truth-duty toward this communication.
>
> In this context, Prof. N.'s attack on Prof. Martensen is not a forward step, especially the way it was done. Some individual theses were drawn out of the pseudonym and were transferred into subjects of dispute: whether Prof. M. is right or the pseudonym. In this way "that poor individual human being, a human being like most people," the pseudonym (as represented by these few propositions), is changed into a kind of assistant professor who is brought into a learned dispute with the eminent Professor M. The qualitative difference is thereby lost: that it is a communication of interiority which, as the pseudonym has done it, "without authority" must be made audible at the distance of the idea or be appealed to with authority. But it is not the subject of any discussion or dispute. To want to debate about interiority means that one does not really

139 *Pap.* X–6 B 121 / *JP* 6, 6574.

> have interiority or has it only to a certain degree, i.e., not inwardly—which one can learn from Joh. Climacus.
>
> The no less speculative Prof. N. cannot be in the right as opposed to Prof. Martensen, but in terms of the idea, there has been a loss for the pseudonym.[140]

Kierkegaard claims here that the pseudonyms help to take the polemical tone out of the works. Instead, they invite the readers to turn inwardly and examine themselves. Grandstanding polemics simply distract attention from this goal. For this reason Nielsen's overt criticisms of Martensen are entirely misguided. This is somewhat striking given the fact that Kierkegaard is known for being a profoundly polemical author and he does not shirk from direct polemics in his later attack on the Church.

The fifth point seems to concern Nielsen's "plundering" of Kierkegaard's pseudonymous works. Here we read:

> 5. If I were to speak of Prof. N.'s relation to my entire work as an author or to the pseudonym on the whole, or if I were to go into the details of the professor's writings, I would have very many objections. But then this matter, which is already prolix enough, would become even more prolix. But there is, I think, one single observation that ought to be made. Even if Prof. N. himself was not immediately aware of his use of the pseudonyms, he gradually became aware of it; but to what extent will an ordinary reader of his works be able to see it, and I am probably the best reader. Essentially it is a matter of indifference. I mention it simply so it may not seem, if someone else raises the point, as if there were a definite solidarity between Prof. N. and me, inasmuch as I, who must have seen it very readily, had said nothing about it.
>
> From the standpoint of the idea something has been lost; the matter is no longer at a point of intensity as with the pseudonym, the issue not in such qualitative tension, but instead Prof. Martensen has been attacked and a dispute about faith has been sought. But so it goes in the world. A view is always truest the first time; the next time it has already become less true, but then it extends itself, gains more and more attention and acceptability.[141]

The idea here seems to be that due to Nielsen's use of the pseudonymous writings, the naïve reader could well get the impression that Nielsen and Kierkegaard are working in league with one another in order, for example, to criticize Martensen. This is, of course, a mistaken impression that could well be damaging to the cause.

With each of these points Kierkegaard concludes by indicating that Nielsen's misunderstanding has somehow diminished the campaign and set back the cause. As he goes on to say, his hope was that Nielsen would work for the cause in a simple manner, but instead he has turned it into an academic exercise and thus undermined it.

VIII. The Final Period

In the last period of Kierkegaard's life from 1854 to 1855, he returns to Nielsen. He seems to have considered writing an article in which he officially distances himself

140 *Pap*. X–6 B 121 / *JP* 6, 6574.

141 *Pap*. X–6 B 121 / *JP* 6, 6574.

from Nielsen's works. Under the title "Just a Word about Prof. R. Nielsen's Books after 1848," Kierkegaard writes the following rather detailed account:

> Lest my silence be misinterpreted as consent, just a word: from my point of view I not only cannot give approval but must categorically take exception to Prof. Nielsen's books. Indeed, although I have had various experiences as an author which cannot rightly be called pleasant, still Prof. Nielsen's conduct is the only thing that has distressed me, even deeply distressed me.—This, then, to prevent if possible the misinterpretation of my silence as approval. Incidentally, it will readily be seen that this implies no judgment whatsoever on Prof. Nielsen's books from any other standpoint whatsoever.
>
> Why I must categorically take exception to Prof. Nielsen's books, why Prof. Nielsen's conduct has distressed me, even deeply distressed me, I shall not elaborate. Space does not permit. Moreover, very few have the background that would enable them to understand me regarding this matter. The one best qualified is Prof. Nielsen himself, and this I have repeatedly said to him privately and may do it again.
>
> I can, however, explain briefly why I have been silent until now. In the first place I was always personally prompted to wait and see if the "next book" would be such that from my standpoint I might be able to approve of it. In the second place, Prof. Nielsen is a man of such knowledge and talents that he bears waiting for a while. In the third place, I knew that Prof. N. had enthusiastically spent time studying my writings, by which, linguistically and stylistically, he is as if possessed. In the fourth place, Prof. Nielsen's conduct had brought him unpleasantness from a quite different quarter, and therefore I was unwilling (especially as long as the actual leader of the coterie, the old bishop, was living) to express my judgment when it could not be positive. In the fifth place, on my own account I had to give careful consideration to this step since my own experiences had taught me that to a large extent I would get the blame for it in the city where I live, where I, laughed to scorn—eyes up!—have had the honor to serve Christianity.[142]

From this it is clear that Nielsen is far from forgotten. Kierkegaard seems to have felt the need to set the record straight at this point. His desire not to get drawn into the polemics between Nielsen and Martensen is perfectly understandable.

Despite this critical assessment, one could argue that Nielsen and Kierkegaard were well on their way to a reconciliation during the attack on the Church. At this time, when Kierkegaard had few friends left, Nielsen stood by him, first with the aforementioned review of *For Self-Examination*,[143] and then with an article more directly in his support. This latter piece appeared on January 10, 1855 in *Fædrelandet* under the title, "A Good Deed."[144] Kierkegaard touches on this article briefly in his article "On Bishop Martensen's Silence" published in *Fædrelandet* on May 26, 1855.[145] There Nielsen's use of the *Concluding Unscientific Postscript* to attack Martensen is also mentioned critically.[146] Nielsen's article is likewise mentioned in a draft dated June 1, 1855:

---

142 *Pap.* XI–3 B 13 / *JP* 6, 6869.

143 Rasmus Nielsen, "*Til Selvprøvelse, Samtiden anbefalet* af S. Kierkegaard; en uproductiv Anmeldelse," *Fædrelandet*, no. 303, vol. 15, December 29, 1854, p. 1215.

144 Rasmus Nielsen, "En god Gjerning," *Fædrelandet*, no. 8, January 10, 1855, pp. 29–30.

145 *SV1* XIV, 99 / *M*, 84.

146 *SV1* XIV, 96–7 / *M*, 81–2.

> That, seen in the idea, I have been victorious over the "truth-witnesses" is something anyone who can see must admit if he wants to see. Nor did it at any moment ever occur to me to doubt that, understood in their way, I would be victorious, because what Prof. Nielsen said about me in *Fædrelandet*, that I have the idea, is true; I know that on a scale completely different from that on which Prof. Nielsen knows it.[147]

Kierkegaard mentions this article on a loose paper,[148] and even drafted a response to it entitled "On Occasion of Prof. Nielsen's Appearance on this Occasion."[149]

In a draft to *The Moment*, number 10, which Kierkegaard did not manage to publish before he died, he writes, somewhat surprisingly, "The only one who on occasion has said more or less true words about my significance is R. Nielsen; but this truth he has heard from me in private conversations."[150] This is the last statement about Nielsen from Kierkegaard's hand, and it is strikingly positive. Perhaps Nielsen's recent article in the immediate context of the attack on the Church helped to mollify Kierkegaard somewhat.

Given all his efforts, it is quite plausible that Nielsen still believed himself to be working for the cause at this point in time, even after all the conflicts the two men had had. It is not out of the question that with his later publications, both of Kierkegaard's own works and in defense of him, that Nielsen saw himself as continuing the joint campaign that he began with Kierkegaard in 1848.

Nielsen seems to have run through the entire spectrum of Kierkegaard's emotions. On the one hand, he was for Kierkegaard "a prodigious concern,"[151] whom Kierkegaard thought to entrust with the publication of his posthumous writings; but then, on the other hand, he was mocked as a "windbag."[152] Nielsen was considered to be a partner in the cause that Kierkegaard's authorship represented, yet he is reproached for not understanding certain fundamental aspects of that cause. There was clearly something very special about this relationship that both attracted and repulsed Kierkegaard. This ambiguity is reflected in a part of the description that Brøchner gives of the relation:

> However, it was more N.'s intellectual talents than his character that K. appreciated. From the period in which K. struggled with himself over whether or not he should enter into polemics with the clerical establishment, there is an entry in his diary where he reflects on whether he ought to acquaint anyone with his thoughts. He mentions N., who at that time had attached himself very closely to him, and whom K. saw daily. But he rejects the thought again with these unflattering words about N.: "No! Nielsen is a windbag!"[153]

---

147 *Pap.* XI–3 B 136, p. 215 / *M*, Supplement, p. 552.

148 *Pap.* XI–2 A 413.

149 *Pap.* XI–3 B 101, pp. 162–4.

150 *SVI* XIV, 354 / *M*, 343. This draft is dated September 1, 1855.

151 *SKS* 21, 58–9, NB6:76 / *JP* 6, 6239.

152 Hans Brøchner, "Erindringer om Søren Kierkegaard" in *Det Nittende Aarhundrede, Maanedsskrift for Literatur og Kritik*, March, 1876–77, § 21. English translation cited from *Encounters with Kierkegaard*, trans. and ed. by Bruce H. Kirmmse, p. 235.

153 Ibid.

Despite the large amount of material that we have from Kierkegaard's hand about his relation to Nielsen, very little of it is actually insightful from a philosophical or theological perspective. By far the vast majority of pages can be characterized as purely personal or autobiographical. To be sure, these journal entries and letters offer ample material for a psychologizing biographer, but it remains to be seen how much this material helps us to a better insight into Kierkegaard's writings or thought. The fact that he was so entirely dismissive of Nielsen's works results in the fact that we are left with few principled positions or criticisms that can be evaluated. Instead, there is an abundance of material relevant for moral evaluation if one wishes to engage in this kind of thing. At best one can say that the negative example of Nielsen shows by the sharpness of his contours some of the important elements about Kierkegaard's thought and writings that are often forgotten in the academic world of today, where his authorship has been pushed and pulled in different ways in order to fit into the specific disciplinary requirements of philosophy, theology, or literature. Perhaps by studying Kierkegaard's criticisms of Nielsen, we can take a step towards returning to his own goals and intentions with his writings.

Bibliography

I. Nielsen's Works in The Auction Catalogue *of Kierkegaard's Library*

De speculativa historiae sacrae tractandae metodo commentatio, Copenhagen: Tengnagel 1840 (*ASKB* 697).

Forelæsningsparagrapher til Kirkehistoriens Philosophie. Et Schema for Tilhørere, Copenhagen: P.G. Philipsens Forlag 1843 (*ASKB* 698).

Den propædeutiske Logik, Copenhagen: P.G. Philipsens Forlag 1845 (*ASKB* 699).

Evangelietroen og den moderne Bevidsthed. Forelæsninger over Jesu Liv, Copenhagen: C.A. Reitzel 1849 (*ASKB* 700).

Mag. S. Kierkegaards "Johannes Climacus" og Dr. H. Martensens "Christelige Dogmatik." En undersøgende Anmeldelse, Copenhagen: C.A. Reitzel 1849 (*ASKB* 701).

Evangelietroen og Theologien. Tolv Forelæsninger holdt ved Universitetet i Kjøbenhavn i Vinteren 1849–50, Copenhagen: C.A. Reitzel 1850 (*ASKB* 702).

Dr. H. Martensens dogmatiske Oplysninger belyste, Copenhagen: C.A. Reitzel 1850 (*ASKB* 703).

Om Skjæbne og Forsyn, Copenhagen: Otto Schwartz 1853 (*ASKB* 704).

Om personlig Sandhed og sand Personlighed. Tolv Forelæsninger for dannede Tilhørere af begge Kjøn ved Universitetet i Vinteren 1854, Copenhagen: Gyldendal 1854 (*ASKB* 705).

[Walther Paying], *Et Levnetsløb i Underverdenen*, Copenhagen: Otto Schwartz 1853 (*ASKB* 716).

II. Works in The Auction Catalogue *of Kierkegaard's Library that Discuss Nielsen*

Beck, Frederik, *Begrebet Mythus eller den religiøse Aands Form*, Copenhagen: P.G. Philipsen 1842, p. 107, note (*ASKB* 424).

Martensen, H.[ans], *Dogmatiske Oplysninger. Et Leilighedsskrift*, Copenhagen: C.A. Reitzel 1850 (*ASKB* 654).

Stilling, Peter Michael, *Den moderne Atheisme eller den saakaldte Neohegelianismes Conseqvenser af den hegelske Philosophie*, Copenhagen: C.A. Reitzel 1844, p. 37; p. 42, note (*ASKB* 801).

Zeuthen, Ludvig, *Om Ydmyghed. En Afhandling*, Copenhagen: Gyldendal 1852, p. 129, note; p. 142, note (*ASKB* 916).

III. Secondary Literature on Kierkegaard's Relation to Nielsen

Algreen-Ussing, Frederik, *Rasmus Nielsen, Professor i Philosophien. Et biographisk Forsøg*, Copenhagen: Thieles Bogtrykkeri 1864, p. 10.

Arildsen, Skat, "Striden om Tro og Viden," in his *Biskop Hans Lassen Martensen. Hans Liv, Udvikling og Arbejde*, Copenhagen: G.E.C. Gads Forlag 1932, pp. 325–406; especially, p. 325, p. 336, p. 338, pp. 340–1, p. 348, pp. 352–4, p. 390.

Asmussen, Eduard, "Sören Kierkegaard und Rasmus Nielsen," in his *Entwicklungsgang und Grundprobleme der Philosophie Rasmus Nielsens*, Flensburg: Laban & Larsen 1911, pp. 16–25.

Birkedal, Vilhelm, "Rasmus Nielsen," in his *Personlige Oplevelser i et langt Liv*, vols. 1–3, Copenhagen: Karl Schønbergs Forlag 1890–91, vol. 2, pp. 239–53.

Cappelørn, Niels Jørgen, "Fire 'nye' Kierkegaard-dedikationer. Lidt til belysning af Kierkegaards forhold til R. Nielsen og J.P. Mynster," *Kierkegaardiana*, vol. 9, 1974, pp. 248–66.

Cappelørn, Niels Jørgen, Joakim Garff, and Johnny Kondrup, *Written Images: Søren Kierkegaard's Journals, Notebooks, Booklets, Sheets, Scraps and Slips of Paper*, trans. by Bruce H. Kirmmse, Princeton and Oxford: Princeton University Press 2003, pp. 30–42; pp. 64–5; p. 69.

Fabro, Cornelio, "Ragione e fede in Rasmus Nielsen," in *Nuovi Studi Kierkegaardiani*, Bollettino del Centro Italiano di Studi Kierkegaardiani, Supplemento semestrale di *Velia. Rivista di Filosofia Teoretica*, vol. 1, 1993, pp. 11–24.

Fich, A.G., "Over Kierkegaard, Grundtvig og Nielsen," *Theologisk Tidsskrift*, 1875, pp. 201–40; pp. 304–45.

Hansen, Knud Lundbek, "Rasmus Nielsen og Søren Kierkegaard," *Tidehverv*, no. 58, 1984, pp. 60–6.

Høffding, Harald, "Rasmus Nielsen," in his *Danske Filosofer*, Copenhagen: Gyldendal 1909, pp. 184–95, see especially, pp. 186–8 and pp. 191–5.

Hohlenberg, Johannes, "Kierkegaard seeks an Associate," in his *Sören Kierkegaard*, trans. by T.H. Croxall, New York: Pantheon Books 1954, pp. 210–11 (in Danish as "Kierkegaard søger en kampfælle," in his *Søren Kierkegaard*, Copenhagen: H. Hagerup 1940, pp. 241–60).

Hultberg, Helge, "Kierkegaard og Rasmus Nielsen," *Kierkegaardiana*, vol. 12, 1982, pp. 9–21.

Jørgensen, Carl, "Skuffelsen med Rs. Nielsen," in his *Søren Kierkegaards Skuffelser*, Copenhagen: Nyt Nordisk Forlag Arnold Busck 1967, pp. 35–40.

Jungersen, Frederik, *Dansk Protestantisme ved S. Kjerkegård, N. F. S. Grundtvig og R. Nielsen. Ti Foredrag holdt på Borchs Kollegium i Foråret 1873*, Copenhagen: Karl Schønberg 1873.

Klein, V. and P.A. Rosenberg, *Mindeskrift over Rasmus Nielsen*, Copenhagen: Det Schønbergske Forlag 1909, pp. 74–7.

Koch, Carl Henrik, "Rasmus Nielsen," in his *Den danske idealisme 1800–1880*, Copenhagen: Gyldendal 2004, pp. 379–434; especially pp. 392–5; p. 410.

Malik, Habib C., *Receiving Søren Kierkegaard. The Early Impact and Transmission of His Thought*, Washington, D.C.: Catholic University of America Press 1997, see p. 18; p. 21; p. 62; pp. 93–7; p. 111; p. 120; p. 129; p. 130; p. 147; p. 157; p. 174; pp. 178–215; pp. 226–7; pp. 234–6; p. 239; p. 243; p. 253; p. 261; p. 270; pp. 275–6; p. 294; pp. 306–7; p. 310; pp. 320–1; p. 326; p. 395.

Nielsen, Svend Aage, *Kierkegaard og Regensen.* Copenhagen: Graabrødre Torv's Forlag 1965, see pp. 109–29.

Rosenberg, P.A., *Rasmus Nielsen. Nordens Filosof. En almenfattelig Fremstilling*, Copenhagen: Karl Schønbergs Forlag 1903, especially pp. 41–57.

Rubow, Paul V., *Kierkegaard og hans Samtidige*, Copenhagen: Gyldendal 1950, pp. 18–19; p. 29.

Scopetea, Sophia, *Kierkegaard og græciteten. En kamp med ironi*, Copenhagen: C.A. Reitzel 1995, see p. 51; p. 90, note 61; p. 92, note 74; p. 423; p. 445, note 106.

Selmer, Ludvig, *Professor Frederik Petersen og hans samtid*, Oslo: Land og Kirke 1948, see pp. 41–82 passim.

Stewart, Jon, "Kierkegaard and Hegelianism in Golden Age Denmark," *Kierkegaard and His Contemporaries: The Culture of Golden Age Denmark*, ed. by Jon Stewart, Berlin and New York: Walter de Gruyter 2003 (*Kierkegaard Studies Monograph Series*, vol. 10), pp. 106–45.

—— *Kierkegaard's Relations to Hegel Reconsidered*, Cambridge and New York: Cambridge University Press 2003, p. 11, note; pp. 68–9; p. 138; p. 208; p. 233; p. 280; p. 307; pp. 309–10; p. 381; pp. 384–5; pp. 440–1; p. 446; p. 455; pp. 461–3; p. 465; pp. 520–1; p. 522; p. 626; p. 645.

Thielst, Peter, "Rasmus Nielsen og biskop Mynster," in his *Livet forstås baglæns, men må leves forlæns. Historier om Søren Kierkegaard*, Copenhagen: Gyldendal 1994, pp. 255–60.

Thulstrup, Niels, *Commentary on Kierkegaard's* Concluding Unscientific Postscript, trans. by Robert J. Widenmann, Princeton, New Jersey: Princeton University Press 1984, see p. 79; pp. 117–18; p. 133; pp. 154–5; p. 240 (in Danish as *Søren Kierkegaard. Afsluttende uvidenskabelige Efterskrift udgivet med Indledning og Kommentar af Niels Thulstrup*, vols. 1–2, Copenhagen: Gyldendal 1962).

—— "Martensen's *Dogmatics* and its Reception," in *Kierkegaard and His Contemporaries: The Culture of Golden Age Denmark*, ed. by Jon Stewart, Berlin and New York: Walter de Gruyter 2003 (*Kierkegaard Studies Monograph Series*, vol. 10), pp. 181–202; see pp. 187–91; p. 195; pp. 200–1.

Hans Christian Ørsted:

Søren Kierkegaard and *The Spirit in Nature*

Bjarne Troelsen

I.

The natural scientist Hans Christian Ørsted (1777–1851) was one of the most significant and influential personalities of his age and together with the sculptor Bertel Thorvaldsen (1768–1844), the poet Hans Christian Andersen (1805–75), and the thinker Søren Kierkegaard, constituted the small handful of figures from the "Danish Golden Age" who achieved international and even world fame.

Ørsted's fame is connected to his discovery in 1820 of electro-magnetism, which was the occasion for extensive research, which led to new theories and discoveries, including Michael Faraday's (1791–1867) discovery in 1831 of electric induction, which constituted the foundation of all later electro-technology.

Danish culture in the first half of the nineteenth century was, however, primarily dominated by the human sciences, especially theology and philosophy, and the disciplines of aesthetics such as literature, theater, painting, music, and ballet along with a significant aesthetic reflection and debate, which were discussed in the age's many literary, aesthetic, and philosophical journals.

At the beginning of the period the natural sciences were extremely weak: when H.C. Ørsted, in 1794, traveled to Copenhagen due to an interest in chemistry which had been awakened in him through the work in his father's pharmacy in Rudkøbing, one of the few possibilities was an education in pharmacology, which like the other natural scientific field, served as an auxiliary discipline for the study of medicine.

Ørsted passed his examination in pharmacology with the highest grade in 1797, but his interests reached far beyond the narrow realm of the natural sciences. In 1796 he had won the gold medal for his response to the University of Copenhagen's prize essay question in aesthetics. In his youth he formed a lifelong friendship with the most important poet of Danish Romanticism, Adam Oehlenschläger (1779–1850). Over a series of years he served as an industrious literary reviewer for the journal, the *Maanedsskrift for Litteratur*. In various ways he supported H.C. Andersen in his first difficult years. In fact Ørsted is named by Andersen as one of the first people to have grasped the genius in the way that the latter exploited the genre of the fairy tale, and the only person who foresaw that it was fairy tales that would "make him immortal."[1]

Ørsted was, moreover, profoundly interested in the Danish language and suggested, in agreement with a moderate purism, a long series of linguistic neologisms both inside and outside the scientific disciplines and fields he was occupied with, and in the everyday language. More than 2,000 of Ørsted's neologisms thus entered into ordinary Danish linguistic usage.

Moreover, he made an invaluable effort to develop the natural scientific curriculum and integrate a basic knowledge of the natural sciences into the general *Bildung*, which, as noted, was oriented in a wholly one-sided manner towards theology, aesthetics, and philosophy. From 1815 until his death he was the secretary of the Royal Danish Academy of Sciences, and in 1824 he took the initiative in the creation of the Society for the Promotion of the Natural Sciences. He played a decisive role in the creation of The Polytechnic Institute in 1829 (today Denmark's Technical University) and was its director from its foundation until his death. Moreover, he was a member of the Academic Council of the University of Copenhagen and at various periods the rector of the University.

The common point for these wide-ranging interests and activities has more the character of the philosophy of nature than practical or applied science. Ørsted was not blind to the practical and technological application of the theory he helped to develop, but what interested him was the insight into the innermost essence of existence, which he believed rigorous studies of nature could provide an essential contribution to. It is characteristic of Ørsted that he left it to others to develop further his great discovery in the direction of practical applicability. Something entirely different was decisive for him, namely, that the discovery of the unity of electricity and magnetism could be conceived as the final confirmation of the idea which had been his guiding thread throughout his entire scientific works until then: that all forces which appear in nature are manifestations of a single fundamental force, the *spirit in nature* or *God*.

It was Immanuel Kant's (1724–1804) scientific treatise, *Metaphysische Anfangsgründe der Naturwissenschaft* from 1786, which in a decisive way came to shape Ørsted's scientific thinking and research. His *Habilitationsschrift* from 1799, *Dissertatio de forma mataphysices elementaris naturae externae*, is in the main a defense of and further development of Kant's metaphysics of nature, which for its part was a critical examination of atomism and an adoption of the idea that matter is a continuum, whose essence is force, which appears to empirical observation as attraction and repulsion. All forces of nature must be understood as different forms of appearance of these two basic forces, modified by the conditions under which they appear. This basic view was further developed and enforced during Ørsted's first great journey abroad from 1801 to 1804 to Germany, France, and Holland, where he, in Jena, among other places, met the main figures of German idealism: Friedrich Wilhelm Joseph Schelling (1775–1854), Johann Gottlieb Fichte (1762–1814), the brothers August Wilhelm (1767–1845) and Friedrich von Schlegel (1772–1829)

[1] Cf. H.C. Andersen's letter to Henriette Wulff on March 16, 1835, in *Breve fra H.C. Andersen*, ed. by C.St.A. Bille and Nicolaj Bøgh, Copenhagen: Aschehoug 2000, p. 215.

as well as the natural scientist Johann Wilhelm Ritter (1776–1810), with whom he formed a lifelong friendship. Ørsted regarded it as his task, through empirical research and experiments, to investigate and, if possible, support German idealism's speculative idea about the unity of spirit and nature, as it was formulated, for example, by Schelling: "Nature is the visible spirit, and spirit the invisible nature."[2]

This is the basic idea which also lies behind Ørsted's first serious work in experimental physics, a series of investigations, in the years 1805–07, of the so-called acoustic figures, which the German physicist Ernst Chladni (1756–1827) had discovered: when one places a metal plate, covered with fine sand or powder, into musical oscillations by rubbing the edge with a violin bow, so that a sound is produced, the powder organizes itself on the plate in special patterns. Ørsted showed, among other things, that a special clear and pleasant sound produced mathematically perfect hyperboles.[3]

In addition to the scientific treatises, which were published internationally in Latin or one of the other main European languages, Ørsted wrote in Danish a long series of philosophical articles, speeches, dialogues, and treatises, where he made his contemporary readers participants in the insight into the divine unity of existence, which his studies of nature had taught him. The most important of these he collected toward the end of his life under the title *The Spirit in Nature*, which constituted the first two volumes of his *Collected Works*.[4] The titles of the individual treatises in this, his philosophical *magnum opus*, are telling: "The Spiritual in the Material," "All of Existence a Dominion of Reason," "The Cultivation of Science Considered as an Exercise of Religion," "The Relation of Natural Science and Poetry," "On the Formative Influence Exercised by Natural Science in its Practical Application," etc.

It is not difficult to find passages in this work which, in an abbreviated form, illustrate Ørsted's basic philosophical idea. Thus, in, for example, "The Cultivation of Science Considered as an Exercise of Religion," he writes about the person who seeks to penetrate the world "with the eye of experience" and discovers that the physical things "about whose reality many believe to be the most certain," are merely transitory and are always only on "a path from birth to destruction":

> If he then asks himself where the *Constant* is, reason and experience answer in one voice, that it is only in the powers which produce things, and in the laws by which they work; the powers resolve themselves into one fundamental power which expresses itself

---

2 Cf. Friedrich Wilhelm Joseph Schelling, *Ideen zu einer Philosophie der Natur* (1797) in his *Ausgewählte Werke. Schriften von 1794–1798*, Darmstadt: Wissenschaftliche Buchgesellschaft, 1980, p. 380. (In English as *Ideas for a Philosophy of Nature as Introduction to the Study of This Science*, trans. by Errol E. Harris and Peter Heath, Cambridge: Cambridge University Press 1995 [1988].)

3 In 1808 Ørsted received the silver medal from the Academy of the Sciences for the treatise *Forsøg over Klangfigurerne* published in *Det Kongelige Danske Videnskabernes Selskabs Skrifter for Aar 1807 og 1808.*

4 H.C. Ørsted, *Aanden i Naturen*, vols. 1–2 in *H.C. Ørsted: Samlede og efterladte Skrifter*, vols. 1–9, Copenhagen: A.F. Høst 1851–52. (In English as *The Soul in Nature*, trans. from German by Leonora and Joanna B. Horner, London: Dawsons of Pall Mall 1966 [London: H.G. Bohn 1852].)

> in two opposite ways, and, on a closer investigation the laws appear as the one reason which pervades and governs all Nature. If he now properly comprehends the whole harmony of Nature, he perceives that it is not merely an idea, or an abstract notion, as it is called, but that reason and the power to which everything is indebted for its essential nature is only the revelation of a self-sustaining, living Omniscience. The Constant in nature is derived, therefore, from the eternal, self-sustaining Being; the indications of life, from that which possesses life; the connection and harmony of the whole, from the only perfect wisdom. How can he, when he sees this, be otherwise animated than by the deepest feelings of humility, of devotion, and of love? If anyone has learnt a different lesson from his observation of nature, it could only be because he had lost his way amidst the dispersion and variety of creation, and had not looked upwards to the eternal unity of truth.[5]

II.

There is nothing to indicate that Søren Kierkegaard and H.C. Ørsted had any particularly close relation to one another. In Kierkegaard's published works there are only a few references to *The Spirit in Nature*, and in the journals and notebooks Ørsted is mentioned some odd five or six times. This is hardly surprising: they belonged to two different generations, and Ørsted's decisive scholarly efforts lay only in the periphery of Kierkegaard's field of interest.

Nevertheless, from the few references Kierkegaard does make to him, it is clear that their paths crossed on various occasions: they belonged to the same academic world and the same cultural elite, and Ørsted, generally speaking, had such a central position in society that a man like Kierkegaard could hardly have avoided having some relation to him.

Ørsted was the rector of the university when Kierkegaard in 1841 submitted his master's thesis, *The Concept of Irony with Constant Reference to Socrates*. Kierkegaard sought a dispensation to submit the treatise in Danish instead of Latin, as was customary, and on this occasion the work was sent around to a series of the university's experts for their judgment. It was returned to Ørsted with various remarks about the Kierkegaardian style's disharmony with normal academic standards, but, in spite of this, it was recommended that the work be accepted and that the dispensation be granted. Ørsted read the treatise and wished to have statements from a few more experts before he allowed it to pass, and in a private letter to Professor Frederik Christian Sibbern (1785–1872) he says that the treatise "makes a generally unpleasant impression on me, particularly because of two things both of which I detest: verbosity and affectation."[6] There can be no doubt that Kierkegaard's manner of expression lies far from the linguistic and stylistic ideas that Ørsted praised and practiced. The treatise was, however, accepted and defended, and rector Ørsted's name stands together with that of Professor Sibbern on the magister diploma.[7]

---

5 Ørsted, *The Soul in Nature*, pp. 136–7 (originally *H.C. Ørsted: Samlede og efterladte Skrifter af H.C. Ørsted*, vol. 1, p. 182).

6 See *Encounters with Kierkegaard: A Life as Seen by His Contempraries*, ed. by Bruce H. Kirmmse, Princeton, New Jersey: Princeton University Press 1996, p. 32.

7 See *B&A*, vol. 1, pp. 18–19 / *LD*, Document XVII, pp. 25–6.

One, perhaps two, entries from Kierkegaard's posthumous papers give evidence of chance meetings and conversations between the two: one entry from 1849 runs as follows:

> The saying that Councilor H.C. Ørsted told me is a good one: When a lark wants to fart like an elephant, it has to blow up.
>
> And in the same way all scholarly theology must blow up, because it has wanted to be the supreme wisdom instead of remaining what it is, an unassuming triviality.[8]

The entry implies nothing about on what occasion or in what connection Ørsted had made the reported statement, but Kierkegaard's formulation does not seem to imply that the conversation was about learned theology, which he now applies the saying to.

A second entry from 1850 with the heading "What and—How" treats a central Kierkegaardian theme, speech as existential action:

> the distinction is whether one speaks or whether one acts by speaking, whether one uses the voice, facial expression, arm-gestures, a single word thrice, perhaps ten times underscored, etc., for emphasis, in order to make an impression on whether one uses his life, his existence, every hour of his day, sacrifices, etc. for emphasis. This emphasis is the elevated emphasis which transforms what is spoken into something entirely different, even though a speaker says literally the same thing.
>
> There is, as I said today to His Excellency Ørsted, there is an infinite difference in ways of putting one's thoughts into the world, between being issued as a one-dollar, a ten-dollar, or a hundred-dollar note. Two men may say the same thing, perhaps word for word, but which one says it—this is not the same—no, this is the infinite distinction.[9]

It is hardly possible to determine with any certainty whether the Ørsted who appears in this quotation is in fact H.C. Ørsted or his younger brother the jurist, philosopher of law, and government minister Anders Sandøe Ørsted (1778–1860). After H.C. Ørsted's being named, in 1850, a Privy Councilor, he moved up into the first class of rank on equal footing with his brother the government minister, and both hereafter bore the title of "His Excellency." But we can conclude from this that Kierkegaard had dealings with the Ørsted brothers in the same way that he did with many other nobles of the age, and exchanged opinions and thoughts with them, possibly on his legendary walks through the streets of Copenhagen.

A passage from a letter to J.L.A. Kolderup-Rosenvinge (1798–1850) from August 1848 can, moreover, be taken to imply that Kierkegaard was present at some of Ørsted's lectures on physics:

> We have not been at war for a long time, but it has never impressed me as a real war. To me the whole thing seems more like a lecture (such as Ørsted's on physics) during which experiments are conducted, or during which the presentation is illustrated with experiments.[10]

8 *SKS* 22, 56, NB11:98 / *JP* 4, 4780.

9 *SKS* 23, 91–2, NB15:128 / *JP* 1, 678.

10 *B&A*, vol. 1, p. 201 / *LD*, Letter 184, p. 253.

However, it could easily be the case that one could know this much about Ørsted's lectures without personally being present.

III.

More important are, of course, those entries where Kierkegaard directly takes a position on H.C. Ørsted as a person or thinker. One of the earliest entries from Kierkegaard's hand is entry number 12 from the *Journal AA* from 1835, which has the appearance of a letter to Kierkegaard's relative, the paleontologist Peter Wilhelm Lund (1801–80), who at that time had begun a stay in Brazil, where he would remain for the rest of his life. He had stayed in Copenhagen in the summer of 1831, where Kierkegaard apparently met him for the first time. It is not known whether the letter was sent, but much evidence indicates that the text was perhaps begun as a letter but then developed into a series of far-reaching considerations about how one finds one's place in life; it was then put in among the reflections, notes, aphorisms, and literary essays which constitute this, the first of Kierkegaard's journals.

In this relatively long text, the young Kierkegaard makes a series of considerations about what field of studies he should throw himself into: "It is perhaps precisely a misfortune of my life that I am interested in far too much and not decisively in any one thing; my interests are not all subordinated to one thing but stand on an equal footing,"[11] he writes immediately before he—perhaps out of respect for the letter's prominent addressee—takes first of all a study of the natural sciences under consideration. He divides the natural scientists into two classes, the primarily empirical ones, who collect data and classify them without giving a more general point of view aimed as a unitary picture, and

> ...the kind of investigators into nature who through their speculation have found, or tried to find, that Archimedean point which is nowhere in the world and from which they have surveyed the whole and seen the details in their proper light. And as far as they are concerned, I won't deny they have made an extremely salutary impression upon me. The peace, harmony, and joy one finds in them is seldom found elsewhere. We have here in town 3 worthy representatives: an Ørsted, whose face to me has always resembled a Chladni figure that nature has touched in the right way.[12]

After this he mentions two botanists, Joachim Frederik Schouw (1789–1852) and Jens Wilken Hornemann (1770–1841), names which are accompanied by a similarly rhetorically sharp characterization.

The passage clearly expresses what is in focus for Kierkegaard at this early period of time. What he pays attention to is the formative effect that science and studies can have on the personality, if one's studies lead one beyond the finite and in the direction of the "Archimedean point which is nature in the world." Ørsted's face is seen as a "Chladni figure," which reveals how the spirit in nature, the eternal in the finite, stamps the scientist, who lets himself "be sounded" by nature through studies

---

11 *SKS* 17, 20–1, AA:12 / *KJN* 1, 15.

12 *SKS* 17, 20–1, AA:12 / *KJN* 1, 16.

and "speculation." The 22-year-old Kierkegaard is still here in complete agreement with the notion of *Bildung* which was central to the Danish Golden Age in poetry, art, philosophy, and religion, and with which he would later come decisively into conflict.

IV.

Kierkegaard's respect for Ørsted as a natural scientist and human being remained intact throughout his life, but when Ørsted moved into Kierkegaard's own area—the philosophical and religious—his assessment looks rather different. In no. 58 of the journal, *Den Frisindede*, from May 1846, a reader had given expression to the view that Kierkegaard was one of the most misunderstood authors in recent times. This view is commented upon by the editor of the paper, Claudius C. Rosenhoff (1804–69), who in part agrees with the contributor but at the same time blames Kierkegaard's "ironic vanity" for the fact that he is not always understood, and he adds that one can well expect of the greatest philosopher, "however high the regions are that he floats in," that he expresses his opinion "so clearly that common sense can grasp it without commentary or exegesis."[13] Rosenhoff continues: "There is now, for example, Hans Christian Ørsted—he is also a philosopher; but whether he now appears as such, or as a natural scientist or as a poet, he lets us get a hint of his philosophy, then 'the mass' knows just as certainly as the select few 'what it actually is he means.' "[14]

The comparison did not please Kierkegaard. In the *Journal NB* he complains about the "obtrusiveness and levelling" which is developed in "a little country such as Denmark," where there is only room for a single "genuinely outstanding person" in any given field, "but this person must live in continual contact and association, also in continual literary skirmishes among those of reputation, with various nonentities—who also are somewhat alike."[15] Kierkegaard mentions the poet Christian Winther (1796–1876), "who would be outstanding in Germany as well," vis-à-vis insignificant figures such as Hans Peter Holst (1811–93) and Povl Frederik Barfod (1811–96), who are also counted as poets: "perhaps each one of the three writes a poem for a festive occasion: ergo all three are poets. The one who loses out in this situation is Christian Winther." After several examples of the same injustice, Kierkegaard brings up the issue that rankles: "In somewhat the same way *Den Frisindede* (Mr. Rosenhaab) informed me that I ought to be just as popular as such a profound philosopher as H.C. Ørsted. *Pro dii immortales*—only 'on the mountain' is it possible for one to say anything like that in earnest."

With the publication in 1849 of the first volume of *The Spirit in Nature*, the judgment is given with no beating around the bush:

> The *Berlingske Tidende* trumpets Ørsted's book (*The Spirit in Nature*) as a work which will clear up the relations between faith and science, a work which "even when it is

13 Quoted from *SKS* K20, p. 38.

14 Ibid.

15 *SKS* 20, 34, NB:32 / *JP* 5, 5909.

> polemical always uses the finest phrases of the cultured urbanite." One is tempted to answer: The whole book from first to last is scientifically—that is, philosophically-scientifically—insignificant, and even when it tries to be most significant it always moves in the direction of the most insignificant phrases of triviality.[16]

Kierkegaard nowhere comments directly on Ørsted's philosophical and religious views; nevertheless it is perhaps possible against the background of some indirect allusions to gain an impression of what lies behind this negative judgment.

When Ørsted, in 1849, published the first part of *The Spirit in Nature*, he came—presumably contrary to his intention—to fan the controversy about science and religious faith, which until that point had only smouldered, but which elsewhere, for example, in Germany, had been ablaze for many years. In Denmark there was a huge consensus about the view that Christianity and philosophy, faith and thought did not stand in opposition to one another, and Ørsted had, through his many presentations for a generally educated audience, from his special natural scientific world-view, shown that natural science, when seen correctly, could not come into conflict with the Christian religion. When his most important articles and dialogues appeared collected, it was, however, clear for many people that if the religiosity which was present as a bearing element in Ørsted's conception of nature was supposed to be able to be unified with Christianity, then a series of essential Christian dogmas and ideas of faith would either have to be abandoned or revised and reinterpreted in a substantial way. His friend of youth, then Copenhagen's bishop, Jakob Peter Mynster (1775–1854), set forth this view with a critical article in *Nyt theologisk Tidsskrift*, which Ørsted responded to in the second volume of *The Spirit in Nature*, which appeared in 1850. Mynster responded to this, and the entire debate between the two was described and critically commented upon by the journalist Rudolph Peter Christian Varberg (1828–69) in the piece, *The Conflict between Ørsted and Mynster, or Science and the Official Theology*, which he published anonymously under the pseudonym "H-t" in 1851.[17] Rudolph Varberg was friends with, and influenced by, one of Denmark's first socialist (or perhaps rather anarchist) thinkers and agitators, Frederik Dreier (1827–53), and was familiar with David Friedrich Strauss' (1808–74) and Ludwig Feuerbach's (1804–72) critique of religion, and in his account of the controversy between Ørsted and Mynster he makes clear with a certain malevolently joyous triumph the latent criticism of Christianity in Ørsted's works, which Ørsted himself did everything to underplay. Varberg was vocally pleased about the more and more pressed situation of official theology, now that the attackers came both from the side of science and from the side of religion. In the piece Ørsted is made into the unintended flagbearer for the scientific attack, while the attack from the religious side is led by some people whom he calls "the knights of faith," who find inspiration in "the writings of the unnamed but well-known,"[18] a clear allusion to the often pseudonymous writings of Kierkegaard.

---

16 *SKS* 22, 415–16, NB14:124 / *JP* 6, 6564.

17 See Rudolph Peter Christian Varberg, *Striden mellem Ørsted og Mynster, eller Videnskaben og den officielle Theologi*, Copenhagen: P.G. Philipsen 1851, p. 30.

18 Ibid., p. 4

Kierkegaard did not himself interfere in the conflict or directly comment upon it. But that he read Varberg's piece is evident from an entry from 1851 with the heading "To be a Christian." Here he speaks about the fact that the ideality of being a Christian has wholly been lost, so that it is conceived as something which anyone can easily be:

> In order to stop here I have brought in ideality. At least one will receive respect for what it is to be a Christian, so anyone can attempt or choose if he wants to be one or not.
>
> One ridicules prayer (as now in the little piece, "The Conflict between Ørsted and Mynster" by H-t). If I were to act here, what would I do? I would so idealize prayer in its entire infinity that it would be evident that perhaps there was not a single person who was competent to pray.[19]

In the piece Varberg had quite aptly defined Ørsted's religiosity as "a somewhat theologizing pantheism" and sums up:

> In Ørsted, the so-called God is the point of unity for the laws of nature, the forces of the world, the center for the order of the world: what happens is not a consequence of his arbitrary decisions but arises with necessity from the individual things and the nature of all of existence; it is thus and cannot be otherwise. Whether it is thus something minor like a shower on a certain day, then it also has its ground in the necessity of nature, likewise there is no room here for the divine arbitrariness (however unfitting it is subsequently in a long drought to order a church prayer for rain!).[20]

Since in Ørsted's world-view there was no room for an arbitrary and free acting divinity, a phenomenon such as prayer becomes, according to Varberg, meaningless. But, for Kierkegaard, prayer is something wholly different from a childishly naïve appeal to a sovereign and freely acting divinity for help in one or another precarious situation. The correct form of prayer is to "let the one who prays see to it that the form of the prayer is proper, a yielding of himself in the inner being,"[21] and for the one correctly praying it must be such that "the prayer's inwardness in God becomes the most important to him and not a means for the attainment of an end,"[22] as Kierkegaard writes in one of the *Four Upbuilding Discourses* from 1844 with the characteristic title "One Who Prays Aright Struggles in Prayers and Is Victorious—in That God Is Victorious." The making inward in prayer only leads to its end, when the wish or desire which evoked the prayer is completely dissolved in submission to God's will.

Six months after Ørsted's death, in September 1851, Kierkegaard published a short work, *For Self-Examination Recommended to the Present Age*. Here we find Kierkegaard's only direct allusion to this entire discussion. The second main section of the work is a kind of edifying discourse on the theme of the imitation of Christ with the heading, "Christ is the Way" from the account of the ascension in the first

19 *SKS* 24, 339, NB24:38.

20 Varberg, *Striden mellem Ørsted og Mynster*, p. 30.

21 *SKS* 5, 366 / *EUD*, 383.

22 *SKS* 5, 374 / *EUD*, 392.

chapter of the Acts of the Apostles. Toward the end of this discourse we find the following passage: "You may even, if you ever think about it, doubt and say: An Ascension—that goes against all the laws of nature, against the spirit in nature—but only the nature spirit!"[23] Christianity's answer to all doubt about the ascension, as well as about every other problem of dogmatics, is, according to Kierkegaard, that doubt can only be regarded as a symptom of the fact "that I have coddled myself with respect to *imitation*, that my life is not exerted enough in this direction....But above all do not become self-important by doubting; there is, I assure you, no basis for it either, since all such doubt is actually a self-indictment."[24]

The odd insertion "but only the nature spirit" in the quotation above points to the fact that Kierkegaard's concept *spirit* is something fundamentally different from that of Romanticism—and of Ørsted—in the title "the spirit in nature." This is clear from another place in Kierkegaard's published authorship, where there is a reference to Ørsted's philosophical *magnum opus*. This appears in the work immediately following the one previously mentioned, *Judge for Yourself! For Self-Examination Recommended to the Present Age. Second Series* written in 1851–52, but only sent to the publishers in 1876 by his brother Peter Christian Kierkegaard (1805–88). The second main section of this work is likewise an edifying discourse, this time on his favorite text Matthew 6:24–34 with the parable of the lilies of the field and the birds of the air. Here he writes:

> So pay attention to the lily and the bird! Surely there is spirit [*Aand*] in nature—especially when the Gospel inspirits [*beaander*] it, because then nature is pure symbol and pure instruction for man; it too is inspired [*indblæst*] by God and is "profitable for instruction, for reproof, for correction."[25]

Nature is, for Kierkegaard, only inspirited when God's spirit makes it the symbol for the human being, whom spirit has made receptive to the edification which lies in the observation of the lilies and the birds.

"A human being is spirit," according to the famous introductory words of *The Sickness unto Death* from 1849. "But what is spirit? Spirit is the self. But what is the self? The self is the relation that relates itself to itself or is the relation's relating itself to itself in the relation."[26] In Kierkegaard, spirit is a determination of inwardness: it is the "place" of, the very condition for, the self-relation and the God-relation, and only through the subject, struck by the spirit of God, can nature "be enspirited," and become the symbol of edification and instruction. In itself nature is *spiritless*, and the fact that the ascension is at odds with "the spirit in nature" is not any problem for the true Christian, who has understood that Christianity is not a doctrine or a metaphysical theory about the world, but a making-inward in an effort to imitate Christ and nothing else. Thus, Kierkegaard rejects the entire controversy as irrelevant from the Christian standpoint.

---

23 *SV1*, XII, p. 354 / *JFY*, 70.

24 *SV1*, XII, p. 353 / *JFY*, 69.

25 *SV1* XII, p. 452 / *JFY*, 182.

26 *SKS* 11, 129 / *SUD*, 13.

It is against this background that one must also understand a reference to H.C. Ørsted in Kierkegaard's papers, namely, an entry from 1850: one of several drafts[27] in response to the theologian Magnús Eiríksson (1806–81), who had recently published a work with the cumbersome title, *Is Faith a Paradox "on the Strength of the Absurd"? A Question Occasioned by Fear and Trembling by Johannes de Silentio, Answered with the Help of a Knight of Faith's Secret Communications, for the Common Edification of Jews, Christians and Followers of Islam by the Said Knight of Faith's Brother Theophilus Nicolaus.*[28] In one of the preliminary drafts to his response (which was never completed for publication) Kierkegaard makes the suggestion that a formulation in the work, "one, which possibly out of sheer religiosity rejects all of the characteristic doctrines of Christianity," should be understood as a reference to the author himself, after which he continues: "but what you certainly do not have the right to, is to obscurely imply that the world-famous physicist, Conf. Ørsted in his innermost being should be a Christian in this case; possibly out of sheer religiosity to reject all of the characteristic doctrines of Christianity."[29]

Varberg had drawn attention to the fact that H.C. Ørsted, as the unpolemical person he was, had shrunk from drawing the necessary consequences of his own metaphysics of nature in relation to Christianity. Varberg then took it upon himself to do so on Ørsted's behalf. Magnús Eiríksson is apparently of the same opinion: that a natural-philosophical religiosity like Ørsted's must lead to a rejection of Christianity's "characteristic doctrines." Kierkegaard rejects the idea of regarding Ørsted's metaphysics of nature, as it is formulated in *The Spirit in Nature*, as an essential expression of Ørsted's personal religiosity. The two things, for Kierkegaard, have nothing in principle to do with one another.

H.C. Ørsted's significance for Kierkegaard as a thinker is, as will have been evident, quite limited. But, by contrast, one can see the few entries about Ørsted and the allusions in his works to *The Spirit in Nature* as a mirror for Kierkegaard's "lack of contemporaneity" with the dominant cultural movements in the Danish Golden Age. From Kierkegaard's virtual silence about Ørsted's metaphysics of nature, which was so highly appreciated at the time, one can venture a summation of his position on this in something like the following direction: religiously it does not even come into consideration, since it falls outside the category of the religious, and philosophically it is "a triviality."

Translated by Jon Stewart

---

27 *Pap.* X–6 B 68–82 / *JP* 6, 6598–6601; *JP* 1, 11–12.

28 *Er Troen et Paradox og "i Kraft af det Absurde"? Et Spørgsmaal foranlediget ved "Frygt og Bæven, af Johannes de Silentio," besvaret ved Hjælp af en Troes-Ridders fortrolige Meddelelser, til fælles Opbyggelse for Jøder, Christne og Muhamedanere, af bemeldte Troes-Ridders Broder Theophilus Nicolaus*, Copenhagen: Chr. Stehen & Søn 1850.

29 *Pap.* X–6 B 72. A formulation with almost the same wording is found at *Pap.* X–6 B 68 / *JP* 6, 6598.

Bibliography

I. Ørsted's Works in The Auction Catalogue *of Kierkegaard's Library*

Videnskaben om Naturens almindelige Love, vol. 1, Copenhagen: Fr. Brummer 1809 (*ASKB* 292) [only one volume was published].

"De religione Christiana litterarum fautrice et universæ ingenii culturæ adjutrice," *Nyt theologisk Bibliothek*, vols. 1–20, ed. by Jens Møller, Copenhagen: Andreas Seidelin 1821–32, vol. 10, 1826, pp. 86–104 (*ASKB* 336–345).

Aanden i Naturen, vols. 1–2, Copenhagen: Høst 1850 (*ASKB* 945).

"Bernstofferne," *Kjöbenhavns flyvende Post, Interimsblade*, nos. 1–100, 1834–36, ed. by Johan Ludvig Heiberg, no. 61, 1835 (*ASKB* 1607).

The Minutes of speeches made by H.C. Ørsted:

——"Om Religionsfriheden udenfor den danske Folkekirke. Et Uddrag af Rigsdagsforhandlingerne den 12. Apr. samt 3. og 5. Mai," *Dansk Kirketidende*, vols. 1–8, ed. by C.J. Brandt and R.Th. Fenger, Copenhagen: C.A. Reitzel 1845–53, vol. 4, no. 192, 1849 [for the minutes of H.C. Ørsted's speech], see columns 591–3 (*ASKB* 321–325).

II. Works in The Auction Catalogue *of Kierkegaard's Library that Discuss Ørsted*

Frauenstädt, Julius, *Die Naturwissenschaft in ihrem Einfluß auf Poesie, Religion, Moral und Philosophie*, Leipzig: F.A. Brockhaus 1855, p. 13; pp. 37–8; p. 83 (*ASKB* 516).

Jürgens, H., *Nogle Bemærkninger, sigtende til at belyse L. Wengels Piece: Om academiske Anliggender*, Copenhagen: C.A. Reitzel 1844, p. 3; pp. 12–16 (*ASKB* U 73).

Mynster, Jakob Peter, *Blandede Skrivter*, vols. 1–3, Copenhagen: Gyldendal 1852–53 [vols. 4–6, Copenhagen: Gyldendal 1855–57], vol. 2, pp. 216–17; pp. 218–43; pp. 244–59 (*ASKB* 358–363).

Sibbern, Frederik Christian, *Logik som Tænkelære fra en intelligent Iagttagelses Standpunct og i analytisk-genetisk Fremstilling*, 2nd enlarged and revised ed., Copenhagen: Paa Forfatterens Forlag trykt hos Fabritius de Tengnagel 1835, p. 94 (*ASKB* 777).

Steffens, Henrich, *Anthropologie*, vols.1–2, Breslau: Josef Max 1822, vol. 1, p. 80; p. 120; p. 124; p. 468; p. 471; p. 474; vol. 2, pp. 46–8; p. 79 (*ASKB* 795–796).

—— *Was ich erlebte. Aus der Erinnerung niedergeschrieben*, vols. 1–10, Breslau: Josef Max und Comp. 1840–44, vol. 4, p. 432; vol. 5, p. 30; vol. 9, p. 265; p. 269; vol. 10, p. 401; p. 404 (*ASKB* 1834–1843).

Theophilus, Nicolaus [Magnus Eiriksson], *Er Troen et Paradox og "i Kraft af det Absurde"? Et Spørgsmaal foranlediget ved "Frygt og Bæven, af Johannes de Silentio," besvaret ved hjælp af en Troes-Ridders fortrolige Meddelelser, til fælles Opbyggelse for Jøder, Christne og Muhamedanere, af bemeldte Troes-Ridders Broder Theophilus Nicolaus*, Copenhagen: Chr. Stehen & Søn 1850, pp. 182–215 (*ASKB* 831).

Thortsen, Carl Adolph, *Historisk Udsigt over den danske Litteratur indtil Aar 1814*, Copenhagen: C.A. Reitzel 1839, p. 139 (*ASKB* 970).

Waitz, Theodor, *Lehrbuch der Psychologie als Naturwissenschaft*, Braunschweig: Friedrich Vieweg und Sohn 1849, p. 346, note (*ASKB* 852).

Wengel, L., *Om academiske Anliggender*, Copenhagen: I Commission hos H.C. Klein 1844, pp. 16–19 (*ASKB* U 109).

Zeuthen, Ludvig, *Om Ydmyghed. En Afhandling*, Copenhagen: Gyldendal 1852, pp. 1–9 passim; p. 13; p. 18; p. 22; p. 24; p. 32; p. 35; p. 76; pp. 89–90; pp. 91–102 passim (*ASKB* 916).

III. Secondary Literature on Kierkegaard's Relation to Ørsted

Fenger, Henning, *Kierkegaard, the Myths and Their Origins. Studies in the Kierkegaardian Papers and Letters*, trans. by George C. Schoolfield, New Haven and London: Yale University Press 1980, p. 84; p. 92. (Originally as *Kierkegaard-Myter og Kierkegaard-Kilder. 9 kildekritiske studier i de Kierkegaardske papirer, breve og aktstykker*, Odense: Odense Universitetsforlag 1976.)

Lilhav, Preben, "H.C. Ørsted," in his *Kierkegaards valg*, Risskov: Forlaget Sicana 2003, pp. 47–51.

Malik, Habib C., "Kierkegaard and Some Contemporaries (i): The 'Non-Reception' by Andersen and Ørsted," in his *Receiving Søren Kierkegaard. The Early Impact and Transmission of His Thought*, Washington, D.C.: Catholic University of America Press 1997, pp. 1–42.

Thulstrup, Marie Mikulová, "Kierkegaard og naturvidenskaben," *Kierkegaardiana*, vol. 8, 1971, pp. 53–63.

Frederik Christian Sibbern:
"the lovable, remarkable thinker, Councilor Sibbern" and "the political Simple-Peter Sibbern"[1]

Carl Henrik Koch

I.

It has been said of Søren Kierkegaard and the professor of philosophy F.C. Sibbern that "It is wrong if one, due to the genius and passion of the apprentice, forgets the soberness of the master."[2] The painful reflection, which characterized Kierkegaard, was foreign to Sibbern, who often seems childish in his immediacy and naiveté, and the irony, which the master of irony industriously availed himself of, was not in Sibbern's nature. He was a sober, staid personality in a fragmented age.

In addition to the characterization of the two people mentioned in the statement, which has never been challenged, there is also a claim that between Denmark's greatest non-academic philosopher and contemporary critic and the nineteenth century's most important Danish academic philosopher and one of the main cultural figures of the Danish Golden Age, there existed a student–teacher relation. However, this is a truth in need of some qualification. The notion that Sibbern in a very concrete sense was one of Kierkegaard's teachers comes from the fact that it was one of Sibbern's professional duties to give instruction and examinations in a series of philosophical disciplines, which were a requirement for the second part of the so-called Second Examination, which Kierkegaard passed on October 27, 1831.[3] Whether Kierkegaard was inspired by Sibbern's philosophical views is, however, an entirely different question, which I will return to below.

---

1 *Pap.* IX A 493, p. 284 / *JP* 6, 6196.

2 Vilhelm Andersen, *Den danske Litteratur i det nittende Aarhundredes første Halvdel* (vol. 3 in Carl S. Petersen and Vilhelm Andersen, *Illustreret dansk Litteraturhistorie*), Copenhagen: Gyldendal 1924, p. 320.

3 See *B&A*, vol. 1, pp. 7–8 / *LD*, Document 10, p. 9. The Second Examination had two parts. The first part included the fields Latin, Greek, Hebrew, history, and elementary mathematics, the second part, theoretical philosophy (that is, metaphysics and epistemology), practical philosophy (that is, moral philosophy and psychology), physics, and advanced mathematics.

At the age of 16 Kierkegaard enrolled at the University of Copenhagen in October 1830, and in the same month he took the General Certificate (*Examen Artium*), which, in accordance with the procedures of the time, was taken at the University. According to the catalogue of courses, in the winter semester 1830–31, which lasted from November l, 1830 to March 31, 1831, lectures were offered in the fields which were the subject matter of the Second Examination; these included Christian ethics, by the professor of theology Jens Møller (1779–1833),[4] and "basic philosophy," that is, metaphysics and epistemology, by Sibbern, who also gave a course in the foundations of psychology. After the end of the winter semester, the student was supposed to pass the first part of the Second Examination. The courses in Christian ethics and psychology continued in the summer semester of 1831, which lasted from April 1 to September 30: in addition to this, Sibbern also offered a course on logic. The catalogue of courses gives no information about what discipline Poul Møller (1794–1838), who had been appointed *Professor philosophiae* at the University of Copenhagen on April 1, 1831, was teaching this semester.[5]

It cannot be determined which lectures in philosophy Søren Kierkegaard attended in his first year at the University.[6] It is possible that he merely availed himself of the student notes to these lectures, which were in circulation, or that he was given private tutorials. In any case, he must have met Sibbern at the examination table. Perhaps this meeting was the occasion for a closer personal relation between the two. Many years later Sibbern told Hans Peter Barfod (1834–92), the first editor of Kierkegaard's posthumous papers, that Kierkegaard had been a regular visitor at his home from the beginning of the 1830s and that he was especially close to him during the period of Kierkegaard's engagement. He adds that they did not see each other during the last years of Kierkegaard's life.[7] Sibbern's daughter Augusta, who

4 Jens Møller probably based his instruction on P.E. Müller's *Christeligt Moralsystem til Brug ved Academiske Forelæsninger*, 2nd ed., Copenhagen: Brummer 1827. (On Müller's moral philosophy, see Carl Henrik Koch, *Den danske idealisme*, Copenhagen: Gyldendal 2004, pp. 283–4.) The instruction in moral philosophy for the Second Examination had, from 1804 to 1830, been given by the professor of theology P.E. Müller. Jens Møller seems to have taken over this instruction after P.E. Müller in 1830 was named bishop. P.E. Müller's book is the only one of the textbooks, which constituted the basis for the instruction in the philosophical disciplines for the Second Examination, which appears in the *Auction Catalogue* of Kierkegaard's library (*ASKB* 691).

5 Vilhelm Andersen states in his book, *Poul Møller. Hans Liv og Skrifter efter trykte og utrykte Kilder* (3rd ed., Copenhagen: Gyldendal 1944, p. 303), without giving any source, that Poul Møller in the first four summer semesters from 1831 to 1834 gave lecture courses on logic and moral philosophy. However, it sounds improbable that he would have given a course in logic already in summer semester 1831, when Sibbern—as noted—was giving a course in this discipline.

6 The information which Valdemar Ammundsen gives in *Søren Kierkegaards Ungdom. Hans Slægt og hans religiøse Udvikling* (Copenhagen: Schultz 1912, pp. 78–9) could not be verified. Cf. Peter Tudvad, *Kierkegaards København*, Copenhagen: Politiken 2004, pp. 175–7.

7 Bruce H. Kirmmse (ed.), *Søren Kierkegaard truffet. Et liv set af hans samtidige*, Copenhagen: C.A. Reitzel 1996, pp. 295–6. *Encounters with Kierkegaard: A Life as Seen by His Contemporaries*, Princeton: Princeton University Press 1996, p. 215.

was born in 1838, could, in 1912 as a 74-year-old, tell the professor of philosophy Harald Høffding about Kierkegaard's frequent visits to her childhood home and about how she as a child had walked alongside him, holding her father's hand.[8] When Kierkegaard's father died in 1838, Sibbern said to him, "Now you will never get your theological degree."[9]

Sibbern himself does not recall having carried out philosophical discussions with Kierkegaard, "because he was one of those people who was continually preoccupied with himself. That is, he was preoccupied with what stirred inside him and with expressing it."[10] However, Kierkegaard during his "Hegelian period," that is, at the end of the 1830s and possibly before 1838, when Sibbern's criticism of Hegel appeared,[11] asked him in what relation philosophy stands to life—a question which, Sibbern writes, "astonished me, because the gist of the whole of my philosophy was the study of life and reality. But subsequently I of course realized that the question was a natural one for a Hegelianized thinker, because the Hegelians did not study philosophy existentially—to cite the expression used by Welhaven when I once spoke with him about philosophy."[12]

Philosophy's point of departure was, for Sibbern, existence, as it appears in experience and in natural science, in morality, in faith, and in the experience of

---

8 Kirmmse, *Søren Kierkegaard truffet*, p. 40. (*Encounters*, p. 19.)

9 *SKS* 18, 234, JJ:297 / *KJN* 2, 214.

10 Kirmmse, *Søren Kierkegaard truffet*, p. 295. (*Encounters*, pp. 216–17.)

11 F.C. Sibbern, review of "Perseus, *Journal for den speculative Idee*. Udgiven af Johan Ludvig Heiberg. Nr. 1, Juni 1837. Copenhagen. Reitzels Forlag. XIV og 264 S. 8. Priis 1 Rbd. 84 Skill.—(Med stadigt Hensyn til Dr. Rothes: *Læren om Treenighed og Forsoning. Et speculativt Forsøg i Anledning af Reformationsfesten*)," in *Maanedsskrift for Litteratur*, vol. 19, Article I, pp. 283–360; Article II, pp. 424–60; Article III, pp. 546–82; vol. 20, 1838, Article IV, pp. 20–60; Article V, pp. 103–36; Article VI, pp. 193–244; Article VII, pp. 293–308; Article VIII, pp. 405–49. A part of Sibbern's review also appeared as a monograph under the title, *Bemærkninger og Undersøgelser, fornemmelig betreffende Hegels Philosophie, betragtet i Forhold til vor Tid, Særtryk af en i Maanedsskrift for Litteratur 10. Aargang indrykket Recension over Professor Heibergs Perseus No. 1*, Copenhagen: C.A. Reitzel 1838.

12 Kirmmse, *Søren Kierkegaard truffet*, pp. 295–6 (*Encounters*, p. 217). Sibbern first mentioned this episode—albeit without mentioning names—in his review of a work by the Swedish philosopher Axel Nyblæus in *Fædrelandet*, no. 155, July 7, 1855. See also F.C. Sibbern's *Om Philosophiens Begreb, Natur og Væsen. En Fremstilling af Philosophiens Propædeutik* (Copenhagen: Schultz 1843, p. 77), where he writes, "And here two questions can be answered for us. The one is—oddly enough—the question posed in our age: *in what relation does philosophy stand to life and actuality*. The other is that which concerns the claim, which appears in our age, that *philosophy should begin without presuppositions*." In connection with the latter question Sibbern refers to his criticism of Hegel. The poet Johan Sebastian Welhaven (1807–73) was from 1840 to 1868 employed, first as lecturer, and from 1846 as professor in philosophy at the University of Kristiania (Oslo). His only known philosophical work is a lecture manuscript from 1841. See J.S. Welhaven, *Metaphysik i 100§§*, ed. by Egil A. Wyller and Asbjørn Aarnes with a study by A.H. Winsnes, *Welhaven og filosofien*, Oslo: Johan Grundt Tanum 1965. From Welhaven's manuscript it emerges that he, like Sibbern, was a child of the Romantic philosophy of nature in the form that it appeared in Schelling and his Danish student, Henrich Steffens.

beauty. Through reflection on the given, one seeks the fundamental unity which lies behind everything, that is, the absolute or the Idea—or with the almost untranslatable terms that Sibbern used in his philosophical *magnum opus*, *Speculative Cosmology*, the "Al-Gyldige" (the Universal Valid), the "Al-Virksomme" (the Universal Active) and the "Al-Ideelle" (the Universal Perfect).[13] Every knowledge is knowledge from causes, and only when the primal cause of existence is known can a systematic and *a priori* knowledge of the manifold of existence be developed. In his criticism of the Hegelian school, Sibbern accordingly distinguished between an explicative and a speculative philosophy. Sibbern wrote here:

> First an explicative philosophy enters the scene. When explicated, empirical things, faith, moral feeling, the feeling of beauty, etc. will display their main moments to the thinking observer, to which explicative ontology and logic are then added. The result is made subject to interaction and discussion during which the speculative Idea is established. Finally, the speculative knowledge thus gained must present itself as such in the philosophical system, in essential unity with that explicated knowledge.[14]

For Sibbern, philosophy was therefore a return to the primal cause of everything from a given world-view and life-view, which is the result of life's activity in the observer. With this the whole is determined, from which everything particular should be understood, in agreement with the holism of the Romantic philosophy of nature, which Sibbern ascribed to. This was the aim of his "existential" philosophy. Philosophy should proceed from life and cast the light of elucidation over human existence as a whole and thus, like all other knowledge, contribute to the development and consolidation of the subject's personality. Therefore, there was nothing strange in the fact that Sibbern was astonished at the young Søren Kierkegaard's question.

II.

Frederik Christian Sibbern was born in 1785 in Copenhagen.[15] His parents came from Holsten, which was a duchy under the Danish crown. In 1802 he entered the

---

13 F.C. Sibbern, *Speculativ Kosmologie med Grundlag til en speculativ Theologie*, Copenhagen: Schultz 1846.

14 *Maanedsskrift for Litteratur*, vol. 19, no. 4, pp. 347–8. Sibbern's concept of philosophy is also explicated in his *Om Erkjendelse og Granskning. Til Indledning i det akademiske Studium*, Copenhagen: Fr. Brummer 1822 and in his *Om Philosophiens Begreb, Natur og Væsen*. A more compact account is found in a series of letters, which Sibbern wrote in 1824 to a relative (Susanne Perbøl), see *Breve til og fra F.C. Sibbern. Udgivet af C.L.N. Mynster*, vols. 1–2, Copenhagen: Gyldendal 1866, vol. 2, pp. 118–34, and in a letter from 1828 to Poul Møller, see *Poul Møller og hans Familie i Breve*, ed. by Morten Borup, vols. 1–3, Copenhagen: C.A. Reitzel 1976, vol. 1, pp. 178–89. See also Jens Himmelstrup, *Sibbern. En Monografi*, Copenhagen: Schultz 1934, pp. 75–106 and Koch, *Den danske idealisme*, pp. 108–14.

15 On Sibbern's life and works, see Otto Borchsenius, *Fra Fyrrerne. Literære Skizzer*, vol. 1, series 1–2, Copenhagen: C.A. Reitzel & Otto. B. Wroblewsky 1878–80, series 1, pp. 309–71; Harald Høffding, *Mindre Arbejder*, vols. 1–3, Copenhagen: Det Nordiske Forlag 1899–1913, vol. 1, pp. 61–112, Harald Høffding, *Danske Filosofer*, Copenhagen: Gyldendal

University of Copenhagen, where he chose law as his field of study. During his time as a student he responded to three philosophical prize questions, for all of which he received the prize. In 1810 he passed his examination in law and one year later defended for his degree a treatise on the relation between morality and jurisprudence.[16] After this he departed on an extended *Bildungsreise*, where he visited, among others, Henrich Steffens (1773–1845) in Halle and Schelling (1775–1854) in Munich—the two Romantic philosophers of nature who had decisive influence on him.[17] But already in the summer of 1813 he was called home to take up the professorship in philosophy at the University of Copenhagen. Only in 1870, after 57 years in the position, did he reluctantly retire due to old age. He died two years later.

Sibbern's numerous works encompass the whole of the period's systematic philosophy, from logic and epistemology to psychology and political and moral philosophy and aesthetics. In addition to this, he penned two literary works, which are counted among the classics of Danish Golden Age literature, and in which he in the form of an epistolary novella, portrays a young man's experience of the after-pains of an unhappy love.[18] Moreover, Sibbern published a long series of articles and polemical pieces on current political issues stemming from political developments in Denmark from the 1830s to the 1860s.[19]

Sibbern's philosophical thinking was, like that of Schelling and Steffens, wholly dominated and in a Spinozistic spirit stamped by a search for unity and harmony and can in this sense be characterized as a philosophy of unity. The manifold of existence is a form of appearance of what he, in agreement with Schelling and Steffens, called "life," which, in opposition to Spinoza's substance but in agreement with the Romantic philosophy of nature, he conceived as dynamic and self-developing. Life is the overarching unity behind everything, or, as, for example, Schelling wrote, life is the principle which binds organic and inorganic matter together, which is individualized in the individual living beings, but which nevertheless is the same everywhere.[20] The development which constitutes life itself has a *telos*, which is the

---

1909, pp. 97–117, Jens Himmelstrup: *Sibbern. En Monografi*, Copenhagen: Schultz 1934, Carl Henrik Koch, *Strejftog i den danske filosofis historie*, Copenhagen: C.A. Reitzel 2000, pp. 54–72 and Koch, *Den danske idealisme*, pp. 87–160.

16 F.C. Sibbern, *De principiis philosophicis disciplinae juris*, Copenhagen: Andreas Seidelin 1811.

17 On Henrich Steffens, see F. Paul: *Henrich Steffens. Naturphilosophie und Universalromantik*, Munich: Wilhelm Fink 1973 and Koch, *Den danske idealisme*, pp. 31–56.

18 F.C. Sibbern, *Efterladte Breve af Gabrielis. Samlede og udgivne af Frederik Christian Sibbern*, Copenhagen: C. Græbe 1826 and *Ud af Gabrielis's Breve til og fra Hjemmet. Samlet og udgivet af Frederik Christian Sibbern*, Copenhagen: C.A. Reitzel 1850.

19 See the bibliography in Jens Himmelstrup's *Sibbern*, pp. 307–10 and T.H. Erslev's *Almindeligt Forfatter-Lexicon...fra 1814–1840*, vols. 1–3, Copenhagen: Forlagsforeningens Forlag 1843–53, vol. 3, pp. 161–8 along with the same author's *Supplement til Almindeligt Forfatter-Lexicon*, vols. 1–3, Copenhagen: Forlagsforeningens Forlag 1858–68, vol. 3, pp. 162–5.

20 *Schellings Werke. Nach der Originalausgabe in neuer Anordnung*, vols. 1–13, ed. by Manfred Schröter, Munich: C.H. Beck & R. Oldenbourg 1927–59 (*Münchner Jubiläumsdruck*), vol. 1, p. 418; p. 571.

realization of the determination of the human being. As a unity, the geological, the biological, and the cultural development move forward towards the realization of the human being as a free and independent individual. Here Sibbern's philosophy becomes both personalism and a humane *Bildungsphilosophie*. The person should be developed and made firm concurrently with the individual human being energetically and actively attaining knowledge of his environment in the natural scientific, social, and cultural environment.

Sibbern regarded life as being subject to a constant dialectical development, that is, a constant split and unification at ever high levels. Families, nations, and the international community are all examples of this kind of higher unity.[21] The final goal is the full and complete development of the human being as a moral and spiritual being, that is, as a person. In and by the fact that the human being's essence is realized, then also is what Sibbern—and, earlier, Kant[22]—called "the realm of God" realized. Therefore, his philosophy is intended to end in a philosophy of Christianity or, to use the fashionable word of the age, in a speculative theology.

In Sibbern's philosophy of Christianity, Christianity and philosophy are united, without either thought, revelation or faith suffering any harm. For faith Jesus is the promised Messiah, that is, Christ, and the philosophy of Christianity is supposed to show, for example, what it means that Jesus is Christ, and what it means that the threefold God appears as a human being. Faith is therefore a presupposition for the philosophy of Christianity; but this philosophy should also for its part strengthen faith. Hans Lassen Martensen (1808–84), who, as a young man, had attended Sibbern's lectures on the philosophy of Christianity, and whose theological thinking bears traces of the influence of Sibbern, writes in his memoirs about the teacher from his youth:

> He claimed that when Christianity is the truth, then the gospel may not be merely assumed because it is written not only because it has been handed down by the Church, indeed not merely because it speaks to our conscience and our heart, but also because its truth is recognized in thought as truth, in its objective reality and validity in itself.[23]

Although the speculative approach to Christianity was not possible for everyone, it was Sibbern's view that the speculative treatment of it "was a demand of the age that Christianity also had to be preached speculatively not only for the few, and in this demand he was supported by powerful streams of the age."[24]

For many years Sibbern gave lectures on his philosophy of Christianity, but he never managed to make a final presentation of it, which is presumably due to

---

21 F.C. Sibbern, *Psychologie, indledet ved almindelig Biologie, i sammentrængt Fremstilling*, 4th ed., Copenhagen: Schultz 1862, pp. 81ff.

22 Kant, *Critik der praktischen Vernunft*, Riga: Hartknoch 1788, p. 230.

23 Hans Lassen Martensen, *Af mit Levnet*, vols. 1–3, Copenhagen: Gyldendal 1882–83, vol. 1, p. 62.

24 Ibid., p. 62. The main lines of Sibbern's philosophy of Christianity and its significance for Martensen are described by Skat Arildsen in his *Biskop Hans Lassen Martensen. Hans Liv, Udvikling og Arbejde*, vol. 1 (this was the only volume to appear): *Studier i det 19. Aarhundredes Danske Aandsliv*, Copenhagen: Gad 1932, pp. 42–51.

the fact that his religious view changed such that the Bible's letter in time dropped entirely into the background to the advantage of what he conceived as the moral essence of Christianity, namely, the demands of neighbor love and brotherly love. While the age's leading Danish theologians, Jakob Peter Mynster (1775–1854) and his successor to the bishop's chair Hans Lassen Martensen, in their attempt to unite Christianity and the bourgeois culture of the Golden Age, were proponents of a dogmatically stamped Christian humanism, Sibbern's mature life-view was a Christian humanism without a trace of literal faith and completely emancipated from the traditional dogmas of Christianity.

The purpose of the formation of the person, Sibbern wrote in his philosophical testament, the final chapter of the fourth edition of his textbook on psychology, is "to constitute the organ, in which and through which the Universal-Valid's realm shall live in its Universal-Validity."[25] "The Universal-Valid" is the unifying primal ground of existence, the unity of the objective and the subjective or life as such, and the organ which Sibbern speaks of is the person. Only personally obtained knowledge is true knowledge, that is, truth should be reached by means of subjective work and interest, and must thereby be seen in connection with the life that one lives. This is what one can call Sibbern's principle of subjectivity. This principle comes to expression literarily in Sibbern's epistolary novel from 1850:

> I have never asked myself whether this philosophy [that is, the newest] is the correct, final philosophy to which one can adhere. I have nourished and refreshed myself with it, and it was enough for me. For me, it was only a matter of vital concern what I could and should adhere to, and what could help me through life.[26]

In 1846, in a work on Christian freedom of expression, he stated that in an age where it is the gospel of philosophy to preach objectivity—here he is thinking of Hegelianism—he took the path of subjectivity, the path which everything spiritual which is supposed to gain a foothold in existence must go; for only through the heart, that is, via a personal engagement, is the truth realized in us.[27] Sibbern's emphasis on the subjective, that is, the personal acquisition of the objective, is therefore not an expression of subjectivism or relativism but an emphasis on the fact that the person should be formed by means of the objective, that is, theoretical and practical knowledge, religion and culture in general, which is acquired by means of a personal effort. As an immanent and goal-oriented process, the entire development of the world has the person as its final goal at the inorganic, the organic, and the cultural level. This is the central, guiding thought in Sibbern's philosophy of the personality.

---

25 F.C. Sibbern, *Psychologie, indledet ved almindelig Biologie, i sammentrængt Fremstilling*, 4th ed., p. 543.

26 F.C. Sibbern, *Efterladte Breve af Gabrielis*, pp. 15–16.

27 F.C. Sibbern, *Om den christelige Yttringsfrihed i kirkelig Henseende* (*Indbydelsesskrift til Kjøbenhavns Universitets Fest i Anledning af Hans Majestæt Kongens Fødselsdag den 18de September 1846*), Copenhagen: Schultz 1846, pp. 21–5.

III.

Sibbern's philosophical authorship was introduced in 1819 with a short book with the charming title *On Passion and Love between Man and Woman*.[28] Already in this little work Sibbern's search for unity comes to expression since he conceives love between the sexes as both a physical and a spiritual striving for unity and unification. Love has a natural drive as its basis, but in the authentic, complete love, spirit and sensuality are united.

In the same year as his book on love appeared, Sibbern published the first part of a textbook on psychology for use in the instruction for the Second Examination. In this work he describes, in agreement with Johan Nicolai Tetens (1738–1807) and Kant (1724–1804), cognition, feeling and will as three co-existing and cooperative expressions of consciousness, that is, three ways in which life expresses itself in and for consciousness. Sibbern writes:

> Life cannot be thought as expressing itself in the one manner, without it also immediately expressing itself in two other manners. In all conscious life, in every concrete expression of life (also in every individual act of knowing for itself, and also in each and every feeling or expression of the will), there arises a conceiving and a representing, a self-determining and finally a sense of the personal condition.[29]

Every phenomenon of consciousness contains an element of cognition, that is, a representation of something, and is shaped by emotions and requires concentration or mental energy to be able to maintain itself. It is the latter that the word "self-determination" refers to. With an expression, which Sibbern later used in connection with his critique of Hegel's philosophy, cognition, feeling, and will are "collateral" (parallel). By one-sidedly emphasizing reason, Hegel "forgets the most important considerations with respect to what, in a *collateral* manner and in a *collateral* respect, is of importance in life and existence."[30] Sibbern's conception of the connection between cognition, feeling, and will—that they belong together and are collateral or parallel—and his emphasis on the fact that the equal value of these expressions of life in the mental constitution of the human being, constitute the psychological basis for his principle of subjectivity. The human being is not merely a being of reason but also, as a being of reason, is both feeling and willing. And a truth is only a personal truth for the individual, when it has been acquired by means of subjective work, which involves reason, feeling, and will.

The second part of Sibbern's psychology appeared in 1828 and treats human emotions and drives.[31] It can be claimed here to a larger degree than in the first part that this is an original work based on a deep insight into his own and fellow humans'

---

28 F.C. Sibbern, *Om Elskov eller Kjerlighed imellem Mand og Qvinde*, Copenhagen: Gyldendal 1819.

29 F.C. Sibbern, *Menneskets aandelige Natur og Væsen. Et Udkast til en Psychologie*, vol. 1, Copenhagen: Gyldendal 1819, p. 120.

30 *Maanedsskrift for Litteratur*, vol. 19, 1838, p. 294.

31 F.C. Sibbern, *Menneskets aandelige Natur og Væsen. Et Udkast til en Psychologie*, vol. 2, Copenhagen: Tengnagel 1828.

mental life. Based in large part on introspection, the work is, to a far greater extent than other contemporary textbooks in psychology, based on experience. Sibbern's penetrating botanizing into emotional life can still be read profitably today. Later Danish psychologists have been especially attentive to Sibbern's discovery of a further group of feelings alongside the feelings of pleasure and pain, namely, what he called mixed feelings. These consist not in shifting experiences of pleasure and pain, attraction and repulsion, but in these two basic feelings together going into a total feeling, which is the case, for example, with the experience of melancholy and longing. Concerning the feeling of gratitude, Sibbern writes as follows: "there is something mixed because a certain feeling of depression and dependence is overwhelmed by the feeling of affection, which, like love, is always pleasant."[32]

In 1822 Sibbern published a propaedeutic, that is, an introduction to academic studies with the title *On Knowledge and Enquiry*, which in 1843 was succeeded by *On the Concept, Nature and Essence of Philosophy*.[33] Here he can portray how human cognition and the human person are developed by means of an interaction between the individual life and the Idea, that is, the primal ground of existence, the principle of life, the universal or God, later called by Sibbern "Al-Livet" (Universal Life). The more general knowledge a human being manages to acquire and maintain, the stronger his personality. The thought is the same in Hegel: increasing universality runs parallel to increasing individuality; the more we become conscious of the biological and cultural whole, which has brought us to be the individuals we are, the more individuality and the more personality we possess. By means of personal effort and engagement, the individual acquires the universal, by which his personality is formed. In the same year that *On Knowledge and Enquiry* appeared, Sibbern also published a textbook on logic, which, in a revised and expanded form, appeared in a further six editions, which were all slightly different; the last of these appeared in 1866.

Alongside these many textbooks stand three systematic works, which must be designated as main works: namely, an aesthetics in three volumes,[34] the aforementioned *Speculative Cosmology* and a long work on the psycho-physical problem, which is one of the most extensive treatments of this problem from the perspective of a Spinozist-Schellingian philosophy of identity.[35] To this large opus is added—in addition to a series of shorter writings and articles, of which his aforementioned criticism of Hegel should be especially emphasized—an odd work from his old age, a futuristic novel or utopia, in which Sibbern's anarchistic criticism of his age and

---

32 Ibid., vol. 1, p. 288.

33 F.C. Sibbern, *Om Erkjendelse og Granskning. Til Indledning i det akademiske Studium*, Copenhagen: Fr. Brummers Forlag 1822; *Om Philosophiens Begreb, Natur og Væsen*, Copenhagen: Schultz 1843.

34 F.C. Sibbern, *Om Poesie og Konst i Almindelighed, med Hensyn til alle Arter deraf, dog især Digte-, Maler-, Billedhugger og Skuespillerkonst; eller: Foredrag over almindelig Æsthetik og Poetik*, vol. 1, Copenhagen: Tengnagel 1834, vol. 2, Copenhagen: Schultz 1853, vol. 3, Copenhagen: Schultz 1869.

35 F.C. Sibbern, *Om Forholdet imellem Sjæl og Legeme, saavel i Almindelighed som i phrenologisk, pathognomonisk, physiognomonisk og ethisk Henseende i Særdeleshed*, Copenhagen: Schultz 1849.

his criticism of religion are expressed. The work appeared in two volumes, both of which are incomplete and end in mid-sentence,[36] and will be mentioned again in connection with the account of Sibbern's religious development and the criticism of religion and the age connected with it. But first I will give a more detailed account of Sibbern's criticism of Hegel.

IV.

In Kierkegaard's draft of an unused foreword to *The Concept of Anxiety* (which was later, with only minor modifications, included in *Prefaces* from 1844) he praises in his usual ironical manner the "philosophical optimism, [that is, the age's Danish Hegelianism] in which for several years now we have already been inordinately comfortable, indeed blissful unless Professor Sibbern every now and then disturbingly intervenes to produce something."[37] The occasion for the remark was presumably Sibbern's criticism of Hegelian philosophy from 1838.

In 1837 the leading Hegelian on the Danish Parnassus, Johan Ludvig Heiberg (1791–1860), had published the first volume of his journal *Perseus, Journal for den speculative Idee*, which Sibbern—as noted above—reviewed in the leading literary journal of the day. As a kind of introduction to the actual critical treatment of the content of *Perseus*, Sibbern directed a violent attack against Hegelian philosophy.

Sibbern had studied Hegel in detail and had previously referred to him several times, for example, in his first propaedeutic, where he refers to "the profound and penetrating *Logic* of Hegel."[38] But in the review of Heiberg's journal the tone was very different; although Sibbern also here speaks respectfully of some parts of Hegel's philosophy, other parts, by contrast, especially Hegel's philosophy of nature, are virtually ridiculed. Sibbern was well oriented in the various natural sciences and concluded that Hegel did not philosophize about nature but rather sought to subordinate it to philosophy:

> a true philosophy of nature can only come about by a thorough philosophical (not merely empirical) study of nature. Hegel, whose philosophy of nature constitutes the *partie honteuse* of his philosophy, although in no way its *partie modeste*, can serve as a warning in this respect, not against an immanent philosophy of nature *per se* but against one schematized according to the whims and caprices of an ontology foreign to it.[39]

When Sibbern criticizes Hegel for not having developed an immanent philosophy of nature, this is a part of his general criticism of Hegel for not casting any philosophical light either on nature, religion or morality from within, since Hegel did not allow the speculative idea, that is, the Idea in Sibbern's sense, to penetrate the researched field, but subordinated it to foreign concepts coming from the outside.

---

36 F.C. Sibbern, *Meddelelser af Indholdet af et Skrivt fra Aaret 2135*, vols. 1–2, Copenhagen: C.A. Reitzel 1858–72.

37 *Pap.* V B 47.5. See *P*, Supplement, 119.

38 Sibbern, *Om Erkjendelse og Granskning*, p. 82.

39 *Maanedsskrift for Litteratur*, vol. 19, p. 310.

The two most significant criticisms which Sibbern brings forth against Hegel build in part on his thought that when the explicative philosophy has analyzed a field of study, speculative philosophy should explain and understand the individual analyzed moments in their internal connections, and in part on his doctrine of the interrelations between cognition, feeling, and will and the concomitant principle of subjectivity. Sibbern developed this latter criticism into an objection in principle to the Hegelian dialectic. I will give an account of this criticism in the last section in connection with Kierkegaard's use of the expression "the collateral," which he took from Sibbern's works.

Sibbern's distinction between explicative and speculative philosophy shows that he regarded it as the task of philosophy to explain "*everything—everything given*—the entire *actual content of* life,"[40] which includes both the world of the senses, which is the concern of the senses and reason, and what Sibbern called the superrational, that is, everything that lies beyond the sphere of reason, such as faith in immortality, the aesthetic experience, conscience, etc. This does not mean that speculative philosophy is able to prove, for example, the immortality of the soul. At this point in time Sibbern believed that faith in immortality belonged to the life-view and world-view, which is the point of departure and object of explicative philosophy. Therefore, the immortality of the soul is one of philosophy's presuppositions, and this is why its task is to understand and explain the immortality of the soul from the Idea.

The task of speculative philosophy is thus to explain and elucidate everything immediately given, that is, the whole of existence, as it immediately appears to us. Its task is not, as in Hegel, to overcome the immediate. The given must still be kept in mind as the touchstone of speculative thought. In this manner the given as the sphere of existence (and not of thought) becomes both the point of departure of philosophy and its limit. Sibbern writes:

> It is here a matter of intellectually appropriating the environment in which one already exists and lives, but at the same time expanding one's horizon therein so that one can more fully and in greater scope move about in those regions in which one already exists, whereby also many a point in them can only now be discovered and many views beyond them be opened up.[41]

As previously mentioned, Sibbern also criticized Hegel for placing emphasis on reason in a one-sided manner and therefore not taking into account that the human being is more than a mere rational being:

> What above all gives human existence its higher significance is the fact that human beings not only outwardly stand in relation to their environment but also inwardly stand in relation to what constitutes their lives and to the inner source of life [sc. the Universal Life], and, moreover, to their outward senses, and have a sense, which is directed to what

---

40 Ibid., p. 350.

41 Ibid., p. 338.

> is perceived inwardly, and which, from the beginning, appears in the form of emotion, in and for which the content of life coming from this source asserts itself.[42]

The will is then added to reason and feeling, and these three expressions of life constitute the foundation for the human being's mental existence, since the synthesis of them is a presupposition for the human being's "full existence." But Sibbern believed that Hegel failed to pay "attention to the collateral elements in existence and to the actual idea of organization or to the kind of organization [sc. the human being] to which the collateral elements essentially belong."[43] Hegel had thus overlooked the fact that the truth forces its way like an external power, but what is cognized should, with the intervention of the will, be obtained by means of personal sympathetic insight and affection. Only when this happens "does the universal [that is, the truth] come to be incarnated actually and correctly in the individuality."[44] With this Sibbern can formulate his principle of subjectivity:

> In all cognition we possess actually only the cognized in the full, complete manner, in so far as we therein possess the true, as having been made personal in us, as something, in which we willingly and gladly move ourselves, in which we have and enjoy our own personal existence. The more this pathos is lost, the more cognition stands as a shadow picture in us, a reminiscence....[45]

From his holism, Sibbern must also criticize Hegel for what he calls its "inverse course" in the *Phenomenology* and the *Logic*. According to Sibbern, everything must be seen from the idea of the totality, and Hegel must also have done this in order to be able to write his works. But his philosophy aimed to be presuppositionless:

> There is no question in Hegel of beginning *a constitutore* [from the founder, i.e., from God]. The entire inverse course, which Hegel takes—in that he does not presuppose the idea of the originary, the actual all-constituting, but in his entire philosophy goes downwards from above, in order to reach there and end up where the level is reached, from which, according to his own entire doctrine, everything first is supposed to be shown in its truth—implies that he totally lacks the actual basis for a true deduction and the true explanation.[46]

The capstone in the Hegelian logic was the absolute Idea, about which Hegel wrote: "*Alles Übrige ist Irrthum, Trübheit, Meinung, Streben, Willkür und Vergänglichkeit*; *die absolute Idee allein ist* Seyn, *unvergängliches* Leben, sich wissende Wahrheit, *und ist* alle Wahrheit."[47] But if this Idea is to explain everything, everything must be taken up in it. Sibbern says polemically, this should rather read: "*Erst in dieser*

---

42 Ibid., pp. 439–40.

43 Ibid., p. 440.

44 Ibid., p. 443.

45 Ibid., p. 455.

46 Ibid., p. 320.

47 G.W.F. Hegel, *Wissenschaft der Logik* in *Sämtliche Werke. Jubiläumsausgabe*, vols. 1–20, ed. by Hermann Glockner, Stuttgart: Friedrich Frommann Verlag 1928–41, vol. 5, p. 328.

Idee findet alles Uebrige seine Wahrheit, Klarheit, Bedeutung o.s.v."[48] He thereby underscores that Hegel in his "inverse course" has discarded "life's actual content." To recall the young Søren Kierkegaard's question to Sibbern concerning the relation of philosophy to life, in his criticism of Hegel, Sibbern claimed that there was no connection between life and Hegel's abstract philosophy. Some years later the author of the *Concluding Unscientific Postscript* was in agreement with him.

V.

Already in the *Speculative Cosmology* from 1846 Sibbern showed himself, on the one hand, to be a man who was inspired by what he conceived as the spirit of Christianity, namely, that the goal of existence is a life in God, but, on the other hand, also as a thinker, who with respect to dogmatics was hardly orthodox. In the year after the publication of the cosmology, he wrote in the University of Copenhagen's *Festschrift* for 1847, that it could be shown from the Holy Writ that one "can completely belong to the society and realm of God's only begotten Son without being a Christian, indeed, without knowing the name of Christ or speaking or having knowledge of his words and deeds."[49] In a *Festschrift* from the year 1846 he had pointed to the fact that the Bible was not handed down to the people of today in an indisputable manner. From this one can learn

> that as Spirit's free activity is that upon which everything depends, so also precisely here should it ultimately alone become our alpha and omega.
>
> Both this Spirit's free activity and even the Holy Writ's free and spiritual activity must win here. Since we enter into a freer relation to this and let the internal, true, general edification be the main thing and the one and all of our striving, this Holy Writ itself arises in a freer relation to us and now, in agreement with its entire nature, can express itself with a free movement, which it to such a high degree bears the stamp of.[50]

Sibbern now believes that one must freely relate to the Bible as the source of faith. The human spirit, in its free development, should not be compelled by the letter. The Lutheran principle of the text and theological dogmatics must yield to an undogmatic humanism, animated by the spirit of Christianity.

But Sibbern was aware that the true human life, as he imagined it, was an ideal and not reality. In his *Speculative Cosmology* he had written that "About humanity we must in a spiritual sense recognize that here on earth it only exists in its first childhood and that at bottom it has still not emerged from the embryonic stage...."[51]

---

48 *Maanedsskrift for Litteratur*, vol. 19, p. 324.

49 F.C. Sibbern, *Bidrag til at opklare den christelige og kirkelige Frihed saavel i Almindelighed som med Hensyn til Danmark i Særdeleshed* (*Indbydelsesskrift til Kjøbenhavns Universitets Fest i Anledning af Hans Majestæts Kongens Fødselsdag den 18de September 1847*), Copenhagen: Schultz 1847, p. 1.

50 Sibbern, *Om den christelige Yttringsfrihed i kirkelig Henseende*, p. 55.

51 Sibbern, *Speculativ Kosmologie*, p. 57.

In an entirely Kierkegaardian manner *Communications of the Content of a Work from the Year 2135* pretends to be edited by Sibbern but written by one of his friends, who has now left, based on the recollections of a manuscript which the friend by accident had acquired, but which later was lost in a fire. At the same time Sibbern writes in his preface to the work that it undeniably has the appearance of being made up by him himself as an essential part of the presentation of his entire life-view and world-view, and that it occupies a place in his universe of thought like the role which the *Republic* plays in Plato's authorship.[52]

Sibbern's utopia had no resonance at the time. In the work he turned against a money-based economy and the right to own private property, which he regarded as being among the most important sources of Europe's malaise. Not least of all the degeneration of the love relation between men and women and between parents and children to something close to a property relation was such a thorn in the side that he almost became a proponent of free love and for the right of children to choose their own parents.[53] Another cause of the age's corruption was the stiffened and divided Christianity, which had resulted in the dogmas of hereditary sin, infernal punishment, and the trinity of the divinity of Christ. The spirit of Christianity, Sibbern thought, is nourished not by a dogmatic or a literal orthodoxy, but by "the basic source of inner all-life...and it is here with us and in us."[54] Human beings should find the divine in their inwardness and not in books.

In Sibbern's *Communications* he tells of how the last half of the nineteenth century was stamped by "selfishness, ambition, resentment, confusion, bitterness and whatever else they are called, these spiritual masters and false gods of the nineteenth century."[55] Civil freedom has made good progress under "the government of the absolute monarchy," that is, under absolutism, but with the introduction of "the free constitution," that is, democracy, there emerged an increased demand for equality, which set into motion a negative development. Denmark had been the land of freedom under the absolute monarchy, whereas freedom was in a bad state under the constitutional system.[56] The educated class was in the 1890s reduced to inactivity and "bore in its hearts a deeper bitterness and resentment about the entire existing condition of society, grounded and rooted more in an insight into the deep validity and justice of their demands."[57] It was not only the men who nourished these feelings, but also the women, who had received equal rights, nourished a deep anger. Equality had led to the fact that "the struggle of everyone with each other to earn a livelihood [had become]...even more acute because the number of those seeking favor and struggling with each other had become larger."[58] Also the private property rights had contributed to a struggle of everyone against everyone.[59] The trouble came

52 *Meddelelser af Indholdet af et Skrivt fra Aaret 2135*, vol. 1, pp. 6–7.
53 Ibid., pp. 433ff.
54 Ibid., p. 451.
55 Ibid., p. 52.
56 Ibid., pp. 639–40 and p. 648.
57 Ibid., p. 31.
58 Ibid.
59 Ibid., p. 136.

first to the well-to-do, and spiritual fatigue and paralysis increased. Then a sleep spread over Europe, people died younger and younger, cities and countries became less and less populated, and society fell apart:

> The great all-encompassing dissolution had included everything. The state Constitution, the legislation of laws, the churches, the schools, finances, trade and business, property and property rights, criminal and punitive laws, the division of labor, human differences and human inequalities, master and servant relations: everything had disappeared, everything dissolved, never to return again.[60]

All of the institutions which had perverted human society were gone.

In the course of the twentieth century the situation gradually changed; the sleep gradually wore off and life-expectancy increased. From around the middle of the century a childishness and peacefulness were dominant everywhere in Europe, and the last half of the century was a time of reconstruction. People agreed that they did not want to have a return to a society like the former one.

The society which Sibbern imagines could arise from the ruins of the nineteenth century, has great similarities with the thoughts which the Englishman William Godwin (1756–1836) in the eighteenth century and especially the Frenchman Pierre-Joseph Proudhon (1809–65) in the nineteenth century had about the just society. The ideology which Sibbern's work builds on was, like theirs, anarchistic. Everyone in the future society should live a equal, healthy, and natural life and

> everything that in the previous century had been called the uneducated could not arise any longer. People should all become educated, indeed not only to become noble-minded but also to become sophisticated, if they have the inner gifts to become so as well as the desire and inclination to do so, or out of attentiveness for what is better, would do their best to be educated. In all fields one would first and primarily cultivate the field of the souls.[61]

Sibbern found one essential cause of the evils which plagued society in the way in which Christianity was practiced. The struggle for the correct understanding of the doctrine of Christ, "the many Church conflicts and arrogance" have led to "a terrible sense of mine and yours arising,"[62] and Christianity was constantly "going to work as if it had to be concerned with something other than promoting human justice and human welfare."[63] In the nineteenth century Christians went to court against each other, engaged in quarrels instead of making peace among people, which—if it was correctly understood—was Christianity's real concern. Perhaps we hear here a distancing from Kierkegaard's criticism of the Danish Church and its pastors. In the future, literal faith would belong to a distant past. According to Sibbern, one of the people of the twenty-second century says, "Should we not praise ourselves as happy since we are free from all dependence on the word of the Christian Holy Writ, as dear

60 Ibid., p. 65.
61 Ibid., p. 112.
62 Ibid., p. 145.
63 Ibid., p. 181.

as it otherwise is to us?"[64] Even a dogma so important for traditional Christianity as that of immortality must be abandoned. The information that the Bible gave about immortality

> was, on the one hand, of such a kind that one could not accept but must turn away from, and, on the other hand, of such a kind that, like so much else, kept one in uncertainty. Therefore, one must feel oneself thrown to the great mundane book of the fullness of life which appears both in the corporeal and the spiritual world....No matter whether immortality was or was not for individuals, one wanted to live in Europe as one lived.[65]

By contrast, "the great book of the fullness of life" seems, in opposition to the Bible, to teach people to believe in immortality.

The contemporary disposition both to Sibbern's utopia, with its critique of religion, and to its author is clearly expressed in the funeral sermon that Hans Lassen Martensen gave at his bier in 1872. When Sibbern, he said in perhaps a somewhat condescending and overbearing tone, but also with great respect for the person,

> in his great, perhaps sometimes, too great mental movement tread the ways of thought where we could not follow him, indeed, even when we could not help but find that he on these ways was distancing himself from the truth, we knew, however, that he himself was true; we knew that love of God and men was and remained in his heart.[66]

That the latter claim had been the case had never been doubted by anyone.

VI.

As is clear from the above, Søren Kierkegaard from his years of youth had a close personal relation to Sibbern, who was almost 30 years his elder. Although Sibbern does not recall having had any philosophical conversations with Kierkegaard, he appeared in 1841 as an official opponent at the oral defense of Kierkegaard's master's thesis, *The Concept of Irony with Constant Reference to Socrates*. In connection with the acceptance of the treatise for defense, Sibbern had expressed the wish that "a few things that are appropriate to a lower sort of genre could be trimmed away as luxuriant growths...."[67] At some point Sibbern recommended to Kierkegaard that the treatise appear in a German translation.[68] It is not known what remarks the two exchanged during the defense, but two passages in *On Poetry and Art* where Kierkegaard is mentioned are perhaps reminiscences of Sibbern's opposition at the defense. In the one passage, he states that Kierkegaard along with Jean Paul can be accused of sensationalism, and that Jean Paul's somewhat

64 Ibid., vol. 2, p. 227.

65 Ibid.

66 Hans Lassen Martensen, *Ved Frederik Christian Sibberns Jordefærd i Frue Kirke den 21de December 1872*, Copenhagen: Gyldendal 1872, p. 13.

67 Kirmmse, *Søren Kierkegaard truffet*, p. 52. (*Encounters*, p. 29.)

68 *B&A*, vol. 1, p. 84 / *LD*, Letter 55, p. 108.

sauntering style can be found in Kierkegaard's works;[69] in the other passage Sibbern expresses his astonishment that Kierkegaard who, like Hegel, found that Fichte's philosophy, by confusing the empirical and the finite I with the eternal and confuses metaphysical actuality, which the I, according to Fichte, posits, with real actuality, has ended in irony; here irony is understood in the sense that when the I believes that it is occupied with the world, it really is occupied with itself, and thus there is a misrelation between what is expressed (the world as such) and its content (the world which the I posits), which is the basic form of irony.[70] In Fichte's idealism everything is (in conflict with Joseph Butler's famous statement: "Everything is what it is, and not another thing")[71] in actuality something wholly different. But in spite of these critical remarks, Sibbern seems to have had respect for Kierkegaard as a philosopher. Hans Brøchner (1820–75) in his memoirs about Kierkegaard tells that Sibbern once at the beginning of the 1840s had encouraged Kierkegaard to apply for a position as lecturer in philosophy at the University of Copenhagen. To this Kierkegaard is said to have answered:

> in that case he would have to insist on a couple of years in which to prepare himself. "Oh! How can you imagine that they would hire you under such conditions?" asked Sibbern. "Yes, of course, I could do like Rasmus Nielsen and let them hire me unprepared." Sibbern became cross and said: "You always have to pick on Nielsen!"[72]

Perhaps this was one of the occasions where Sibbern used Poul Møller's reply to the young Kierkegaard: "You are so thoroughly polemical that it is quite appalling."[73]

Hans Brøchner also tells in his memoirs of Kierkegaard that the latter for his part had greatly appreciated Sibbern

> even though he was not blind to his weaknesses. Among these he once emphasized Sibbern's complete lack of irony, and, from a psychological point of view, his lack of an awareness of the disguised passions, the reduplication by which the one passion assumes the form of another. In his opinion, this was why Sibbern was often taken in when many people, ladies, in particular, turned to him to consult him as a sort of psychological and spiritual advisor.[74]

In general Kierkegaard seems, however, to have had great respect for Sibbern as a spiritual advisor. Andreas Ferdinand Schiødte (1816–87), who was some years younger than Kierkegaard, tells that once as a young man in a depressed state of mind he had met Kierkegaard, who had recommended that he visit Sibbern: "I ought

---

69 Sibbern, *Om Poesie og Konst*, vol. 2, pp. 102–3.

70 Ibid., vol. 3, p. 257. Sibbern refers to the section "Irony after Fichte," *SKS* 1, 308ff. / *CI*, 272ff.

71 *The Works of Bishop Butler*, vols. 1–2, ed. by W.E. Gladstone, vol. 2, Oxford: Clarendon Press 1896, p. 25.

72 Kirmmse, *Søren Kierkegaard truffet*, p. 323. (*Encounters*, p. 235.)

73 *SKS* 25, 461, NB30:93/ *JP*, 6, 6888.

74 Kirmmse, *Søren Kierkegaard truffet*, pp. 331–2 (*Encounters*, p. 241.)

to see him; he was a whole person, the very soul of kindness; there was something calming in associating with him."[75]

Kierkegaard's remark about Sibbern's shortcomings as a spiritual advisor for women is possibly related to the fact that Sibbern had been a kind of spiritual advisor for Regine Olsen after Kierkegaard had broken off the engagement with her. Sibbern visited the home of Regine Olsen, and after the break with Kierkegaard, he was the one whom she looked to, and who also later seems to have been a point of connection between the two formerly engaged people.[76] Thus in 1843 Regine Olsen through Sibbern—it seems—received a copy of Kierkegaard's *Two Edifying Discourses*, and Sibbern reported back to Kierkegaard that she had read them.[77]

From Berlin Kierkegaard wrote on October 31 to Emil Boesen (1812–79) that the day before his departure from Copenhagen (that is, October 24, 1841) Sibbern came looking for him to in order to give him a thorough dressing down; but when he could only find Kierkegaard's brother, Peter Christian Kierkegaard (1805–88), he bore the brunt of it. Kierkegaard's brother became angry and said that the matter did not concern Sibbern.[78] On November 18, 1841 Kierkegaard wrote to the somewhat older theologian Peter Johannes Spang (1796–1846) and asked:

> What is Sibbern doing? For I do assume that the sane and lofty in him have prevailed once more, or has he really placed himself at the head of the gossipmongers at tea parties? If so, what danger is there in that? I am no longer in town, and if I were, Sibbern would be man enough to prevent my approaching any girl, at least according to his own conceited idea of himself.[79]

In the same letter Kierkegaard amuses himself with the thought that Sibbern for a fee could be placed on the back of a horse to watch over the safety of young girls, and when he for this reason takes leave of his position as professor, then Kierkegaard could take over his post. For Sibbern knew that a professor in philosophy would never behave in matters of love as Kierkegaard had done towards Regine Olsen.

In December 1841 the good relation between Sibbern and Kierkegaard seems to be reestablished. On December 15 Kierkegaard wrote a long letter to Sibbern and told him about the lectures he was attending in Berlin.[80]

As Sibbern's religious disposition changed in a more liberal direction and Kierkegaard's became more extreme, Sibbern increasingly turned away from him. In a letter to Petronella Ross (1805–75) from March 26, 1855 Sibbern sharply distanced himself from Kierkegaard's attack on the memory of Mynster and charged him with religious narrow-mindedness, although he also knew that Kierkegaard's religious works had had significance for many people.[81] In Sibbern's utopian work this

---

75 Kirmmse, *Søren Kierkegaard truffet*, p. 270. (*Encounters*, p. 194.)

76 Kirmmse, *Søren Kierkegaard truffet*, p. 62; pp. 292–3. (*Encounters*, p. 37; pp. 213ff.)

77 *SKS* 24, 521-3, NB25:109 / *JP* 6, 6800.

78 *B&A*, vol. 1, p. 71 / *LD*, Letter 49, p. 90.

79 *B&A*, vol. 1, p. 76 / *LD*, Letter 51, p. 96.

80 *B&A*, vol. 1, pp. 83–5 / *LD*, Letter 55, pp. 106–8.

81 Kirmmse, *Søren Kierkegaard truffet*, pp. 151–3. (*Encounters*, pp. 103–5.)

criticism is repeated. One passage is aimed at the zeal to condemn, which had set off Kierkegaard's attack on Mynster's memory;[82] in another passage he speaks directly but with full recognition of Kierkegaard's pseudonymous and Christian authorship, about his criticism of Mynster and the attack on Martensen; here the criticism of the Church and its officials is described as a result of "a physical derangement or whatever one now would call such an illness which has brought the spirit into disorder and derangement."[83]

For his part Kierkegaard in his journals criticized Sibbern as a political author. He speaks here of Sibbern who is like a "low-comedy character who fools around in dance halls and other such places," when he "fools around as an author in a certain class of newspapers that belong in the basement of literature. As far as S. is concerned, one is certainly obliged to yield to grief."[84] The occasion for this remark was an article in the newspaper *Nyt Aftenblad*, where Sibbern from February 29, 1848 to September 6 of the same year had published 53 articles under the common title "Occasioned Observations on Politics,"[85] in which he had commented upon political events in the Denmark of the day and especially the war against the rebels in Schleswig-Holstein. In a letter to the jurist J.L.A. Kolderup-Rosenvinge (1792–1850) from the summer of 1848, Kierkegaard is sarcastic about the fact that it apparently always occurs to Sibbern that people expected that he constantly make his opinions known.[86] *Nyt Aftenblad* was a conservative newspaper, which was critical of the age's liberal tendencies and was supported financially by King Christian VIII. With the death of the king, the economic foundation of the newspaper disappeared.[87] The last number appeared on October 7, 1848.

It seems, however, not to have been Sibbern's general political disposition which was the occasion for Kierkegaard's criticism. Sibbern was the Danish defender of absolute monarchy, an advocate of the advisory Assembly of the Estates of the Realm and critically disposed toward the age's ideas about democracy and constitutional monarchy. On these points Kierkegaard was generally in agreement with him. It was rather the fact that Sibbern regarded Meïr Aron Goldschmidt (1819–87)—the object of Kierkegaard's animosity and until 1846 the editor of the political-satirical weekly *The Corsair*, in which he had been subjected to ridicule and derision—as an ally.

On March 8, 1848 *Nyt Aftenblad* published Sibbern's third article "Concerning the Monthly *North and South*."[88] *North and South* was a literary-political journal which Goldschmidt had started publishing. In the program statement in the first issue of the journal from December 1847 he had praised the Danish absolute monarchy and its reform policy with, among other things, the introduction of the advisory

---

82 Sibbern, *Meddelelser af Indholdet af et Skrivt fra Aaret 2135*, vol. 1, p. 453.

83 Ibid., pp. 720–1.

84 *Pap.* IX A 493, p. 284 / *JP* 6, 6196.

85 F.C. Sibbern, "Foranledigede Betragtninger i politisk Hensigt," *Nyt Aftenblad*, February 29–September 6, 1848.

86 *B&A*, vol. 1, p. 205 / *LD*, Letter 186, p. 259.

87 Klaus Bruhn Jensen (ed.), *Dansk Mediehistorie*, vols. 1–4, [Copenhagen]: Samleren 1996–2003, vol. 1 (*Mediernes forhistorie* 1840–80), p. 101.

88 F.C. Sibbern, "Angaaende Maanedsskriftet 'Nord og Syd,' " *Nyt Aftenblad*, March 8, 1848, on the front page.

Assembly of the Estates of the Realm and had criticized the liberal opposition, which "had exclusively fought against the government and tried to make it unpopular in order to come to power, and while it was supposed to function as a representative for the idea of freedom, it has led the struggle without respect to any idea."[89]

According to Goldschmidt, freedom in general is a realization of the human being's free will together with his reason and conscience, and political freedom should result in the citizens of society having equal opportunity to achieve "equal happiness, each according to his own abilities and merits."[90] Freedom in this sense was wholly compatible, Goldschmidt believed, with a monarchical government. Goldschmidt also mentions examples of the liberal opposition standing in "line on one side with the government and with freedom on the other side." [91] That no great political progress has happened under absolutism is due, Goldschmidt claims, not to any shortcoming of absolutism. The reason is rather the indolence and laziness of the people. "The political misfortune does not consist in having a despotic government, but in being a lazy people."[92]

Occasioned by this program statement, Sibbern wrote that it had been a true joy for him "that the editor of *North and South* in a similar direction [as Sibbern himself] defends with resoluteness the true but little known cause of freedom against power-seeking, while he also shows that the so-called aspiration towards freedom only aims to give us a mass of most gracious masters instead of one."[93] This last bit is not something that Goldschmidt had written.

It was probably, among other things, with this passage in mind that in 1849, occasioned by the fact that Bishop J.P. Mynster in the legislative national assembly on April 12 had spoken of "the talented editor of *North and South*,"[94] Kierkegaard had noted in his journal that one could have expected this from "from a simpleton such as Sibbern has become in recent years...but not from Mynster."[95]

It was a later article by Sibbern that was the occasion for Kierkegaard's irritation with Sibbern's activity as a political writer to reach an absolute high point. On July 15, 1848 Sibbern, under the title "Another Word about the Unrest and yet another about the Reaction"[96] had spoken about the reaction to liberal tendencies—a reaction loved by him and from his view already present; these tendencies asserted themselves due, among other things, to the natural enthusiasm resulting from the war against the rebels in Schleswig-Holstein.

On 22 March 1848 the king had appointed the so-called March Ministry, which consisted of individual representatives of the old absolutist administration along with a series of liberal opposition leaders. Its program was, among other things, to produce suggestions for a new, liberal constitution. It was a reaction against this

89 *Nord og Syd*, vol. 1, 1848, pp. 9–10.

90 Ibid., p. 16.

91 Ibid., p. 11.

92 Ibid., p. 25.

93 *Nyt Aftenblad*, no. 57, March 8, 1848, on the front page.

94 *Beretninger om Forhandlingerne paa Rigsdagen*, no. 322, 1849, column 2544.

95 *SKS* 22, 85, NB11:146.

96 F.C. Sibbern, "Ogsaa et Ord om Uroen og atter eet om Reactionen," *Nyt Aftenblad*, July 15, 1848, on the front page.

ministry that Sibbern discussed in the article from 15 July. "They [that is, the liberal press] speak of a reaction, which haunts," Sibbern writes:

> Certainly it haunts. But what does this mean? It gets ready for rising from the grave in order to hold Judgment Day on those who sit high according to their own imagination. And it wants to come from all four corners of the world. From the side of the old competence it will come, and I wish that we now would receive the thorough and extensive criticism of the course of the entire opposition from 1840 onward, which we hope to receive from the hand of this competence [Sibbern is here presumably thinking of the Danish monarchy's leading official, the jurist A.S. Ørsted]. From the side of youthful genius, it will come or stand there as large as life under the figure of *North and South*, and will certainly take care that it does not spoil itself [here he is thinking of Goldschmidt]. From an already long-formed hotbed of the great social tasks of the future, it will come or certainly is already present long since [here Sibbern is perhaps thinking of himself]. From the side of the Christian, religious and ethical fullness, it will come, and here I think also that we already have it.[97]

With the reaction from the Christian side, Sibbern is possibly thinking of Kierkegaard, whose irritation at Sibbern can therefore be due to the fact that Sibbern had lumped him together with Goldschmidt. Thus it could hardly have been Sibbern's political views which were the cause of Kierkegaard's anger, but rather that it was not only implied that he was a part of a movement, which would be bad enough, but also that he was for the same cause as Goldschmidt.

It was in this context that Kierkegaard used the expression "the political Simple-Peter Sibbern." He compared Sibbern with the garrulous barber Gert Westphaler from Ludvig Holberg's comedy *Mester Gert Westphaler*, who by chance comes to drink "dus" with the executioner from Schleswig, that is, takes wine with him as a token of discarding the formal "*De*" form of address in exchange for the informal "*du*." And Sibbern is similar to Gert Westphaler both with respect to his garrulousness and his "dus" brothership, for he is

> drinking "Dus" with the executioner—the wretched discarded tool of literary despicableness and envy—or as Sibbern calls his Dus-brother, student Goldschmidt, the youthful genius. These two understand each other—of course, not the lovable, remarkable thinker, Councilor Sibbern, but the political Simple-Peter Sibbern—and the naughty boy of literature Goldschmidt—who both make a practice of handing each other compliments....[98]

Kierkegaard has hardly expressed his irritation with the "loveable, remarkable thinker, Councillor Sibbern," and the relation between them apparently did not change in character. In any case in 1850 Kierkegaard mentions a meeting with Sibbern, where the latter, laughing, told him that a reader of *Practice in Christianity* had understood the inserted lines in the first part as an attempt to make Christianity the object of laughter and that the same reader had regarded the matter as being so serious that the clergy would have to take up the affair. Kierkegaard's reaction was

---

97 *Nyt Aftenblad*, no. 164, July 15, 1848, on the front page.

98 *Pap*. IX A 493, p. 284 / *JP* 6, 6196.

"It would in fact be a splendid satire on the present-day clergy, however little my desire for such troubles."[99]

From Sibbern's statements to one of his two daughters and to H.P. Barfod one can discern the manner in which he regarded Kierkegaard. He knew nothing about the melancholy which Kierkegaard himself talks about several times in his journals.[100] For example, Kierkegaard wrote in 1850: "I am a severe melancholic who has the good fortune and the virtuosity to be able to conceal it, and for that I have struggled."[101] He was apparently also successful in maintaining this concealment vis-à-vis the psychologically insightful Sibbern. Since the body and the soul constituted, for Sibbern, a unity, he could describe Kierkegaard as a type in the following manner:

> He had a witty, somewhat sarcastic face and a brisk way of walking. He was thin and not large of build, with a crookedness that seemed just on the verge of hunchback, and he also took pleasure in sarcasm, but it was coupled with wit and humor, as sarcasm generally seems to be.[102]

Sibbern also briefly characterized the authorship as a whole: "I must say that K. was a thoroughgoing egocentrist, and with respect to his writings—which contain much that is excellent, so that I would certainly like to see a chrestomathy excerpted from them—I must nonetheless say that in general, *In vielen Worten wenige Klarheit*."[103] All in all, Sibbern would probably have regarded our present admiration of the philosopher Kierkegaard with astonishment. And on this point he would be generally in harmony with his and Kierkegaard's contemporaries.

VII.

There is no doubt about the fact that Kierkegaard as a student for the Second Examination was in a sense Sibbern's pupil and that for several years there had been a close personal relation between them, but this was also weakened in the latter years of Kierkegaard's life. It is, however, considerably more difficult to determine whether—and to what extent—Kierkegaard was inspired by Sibbern's thought. The published works give no answer. Here Sibbern's name is absent.

It is a known fact in Kierkegaard research that the sources of Kierkegaard's thought can only be determined with great caution and always only in the form of a hypothesis. As an author, Kierkegaard was careful to conceal his hand.

Since Kierkegaard and Sibbern, according to the latter, did not discuss philosophical themes, one possible effect of the older on the younger either came about by means of Sibbern's lectures or by means of Kierkegaard's reading of his works—under the presupposition that Sibbern recalls this correctly.

---

99 *SKS* 24, 83, NB21:133 / *JP* 6, 6696.

100 Kirmmse, *Søren Kierkegaard truffet*, p. 296. (*Encounters*, p. 217.)

101 *SKS* 23, 420, NB20:53 / *JP* 6, 6659.

102 Kirmmse, *Søren Kierkegaard truffet*, p. 295. (*Encounters*, p. 216.)

103 Kirmmse, *Søren Kierkegaard truffet*, p. 293. (*Encounters*, p. 215.)

As mentioned above, we do not know whether Kierkegaard attended Sibbern's lectures in those disciplines which were to be tested at the Second Examination. By contrast, we do know that he in any case attended some of the lectures on "the philosophy of Christianity" that Sibbern gave in winter semester 1838–39. From the lecture from December 17, 1838 Kierkegaard notes in his journal:

> It was an excellent observation Sibbern made today in his lectures: how one must assume a genuinely ideal being, which had in itself a being prior to its expression in actual being, as one could also see from the fact that one would not say of eternal truths that they now come into being, but that they are now revealed, i.e., in the fullness of time.[104]

Earlier Sibbern had treated the same issue in more detail in the first section of his review of Heiberg's *Perseus*,[105] which Kierkegaard may be presumed not to have read at this point. As will be clear, Kierkegaard read Sibbern's criticism of Hegel's philosophy at a later time. He himself did not have a subscription to the *Maanedsskrift for Litteratur*; but the Athenæum reading society, which he was a member of, did, and he could easily have borrowed the journal from there. In all probability he first read Sibbern's criticism when it appeared as an independent monograph toward the end of the year.[106]

It is immediately obvious that Sibbern's point that eternal truths are discovered and do not come into being, has an affinity with Johannes Climacus' discussion of coming-into-being in *Philosophical Fragments* and his rejection of the view that necessity comes into being.[107] Time and coming-into-being belong together, the eternal and necessary have no coming-into-being; it does not belong to the category of time, or, to use an expression from Johannes Climacus, the eternal and the necessary are not "dialectical with respect to time."[108] Immediately Sibbern's statement concerns only what was generally known within the Platonic tradition and therefore also in Kant, and immediately there is nothing to indicate that the Interlude in *Philosophical Fragments* is inspired by Sibbern.

Kierkegaard was a creative reader. What he got out of books was for the most part himself.[109] Or as Quidam writes in "Guilty/Not Guilty": "Take a book, the poorest one written, but read it with the passion that it is the only book you will read—ultimately you will read everything out of it, that is, as much as there was in yourself, and you could never get more out of reading, even if you read the best of books."[110] Anyone who seeks Kierkegaard's sources in the literature that was accessible to him ought to keep this passage in mind.

It is evident from Kierkegaard's journals that he read Sibbern's *Posthumous Letters of Gabrielis* from 1826. In an entry from 1835 he problematizes one of the

104 *SKS* 17, 271, DD:179 / *KJN* 1, 262.

105 *Maanedsskrift for Litteratur*, vol. 19, 1838, pp. 356–7.

106 The monograph is found in Kierkegaard's book collection, *ASKB* 778.

107 *SKS* 4, 274 / *PF*, 74.

108 The expression is used about nature in *Philosophical Fragments*, *SKS* 4, 276 / *PF*, 76.

109 See Carl Roos, *Kierkegaard og Goethe*, Copenhagen: Gad 1955, pp. 7–18.

110 *SKS* 6, 338 / *SLW*, 364.

significant differences between Goethe's Werther and Gabrielis, namely, that the latter, even in his love pains, wishes to preserve life. Life was such a central concept in Sibbern's philosophical world-view that it is impossible to imagine that in despair his hero would, like Werther, choose death. Gabrielis writes:

> I would preserve only life. To die in this state would be terrible. No, even here something must remain of me; or I would wish to bear this burden of existence through all countries and all centuries until the return of the Lord.[111]

But the young Kierkegaard asks in connection with some reflections on the theme of "the Wandering Jew," is not Gabrielis' wish to wander around the world like the wandering Jew rather than to take his own life, in contradiction with his character?[112] Immediately one must agree with Kierkegaard. It does not seem to lie in such a soft and sensitive character like that of Gabrielis to say "yes" to life out of sheer bravado.

In addition to Sibbern's first Gabrielis book—which does not appear in the *Auction Catalogue of Kierkegaard's Library*—there is from Kierkegaard's journal entries only evidence to claim that among the books by Sibbern which were a part of his library at the time of his death, he had read only Sibbern's criticism of Hegel's philosophy.[113] It must be regarded as probable that the reason why of all of Sibbern's books Kierkegaard read just this one is that he became attentive to Sibbern's use of the expression "the collateral."[114]

In an entry from 1839 Kierkegaard wrote in relation to the fact that I.H. Fichte (1797–1879) in an article had rejected—in Kierkegaard's own words—"the current method of regarding the one [sc. Judaism] as proceeding from the other [sc. paganism] in a dialectical process," and that "this vindicates the significance of what Sibbern calls the collateral."[115]

---

111 *Efterladte Breve af Gabrielis*, p. 32.

112 *SKS* 19, 95–6, Not2:14 / *JP* 2, 2206.

113 See *SKS* 18, 52, EE:147b / *KJN* 2, 47 and *SKS* 19, 414, Not13:49 / *JP* 3, 3657.

114 Gregor Malantschuk has, in *Dialektik og Eksistens hos Søren Kierkegaard*, (Copenhagen: Hans Reitzel 1968, pp. 123–7) and in "Søren Kierkegaard og den kollaterale Tænkning," (in his *Frihed og Eksistens. Studier i Søren Kierkegaards Tænkning*, Copenhagen: C.A. Reitzel 1980, pp. 162–76) argued that Kierkegaard received important impulses from Sibbern's pointing out that existence contains many collateral elements and that Kierkegaardian thought can be characterized as "collateral thinking."

115 *SKS* 18, 52, EE:147b / *KJN* 2, 47, see also *SKS* K18, p. 76, cf. I.H. Fichte, "Aphorismen über die Zukunft der Theologie, in ihrem Verhältnisse zur Spekulation und Mythologie," *Zeitschrift für Philosophie und spekulative Theologie*, vol. 3, Bonn 1839, pp. 199–286, especially p. 252, where Fichte writes the following about the relation between paganism and Judaism: "*Möchte nun hierin das Princip fast der gesammten ethnischen Religionen begriffen sein, so läßt sich auch ein durchgreifender Gegensatz zwischen ihnen und der mosaischen Religion kaum in Abrede stellen, wobei jedoch beide Principe nicht gerade bloß wie das Wahre und Falsche, oder das Höhere und Niedere, sondern mehr wie sich gegenseitig ausschliessende, aber entsprechende Hälften zu einander sich verhalten. Nur in Eine Reihe, in ein dialektisches Verhältniss von auseinander hervorgehende Stufen, wie dies versucht worden, lassen beide sich nicht bringen.*"

That Fichte has "vindicated" Sibbern's concept of the collateral may mean that he, by pointing out that paganism and Judaism are not dialectically connected but are parallel, has justified the concept by showing that in the world of actuality there are collateral phenomena.

It is the very main nerve of the Hegelian dialectic that is at issue here for the young Kierkegaard. If the categories of thought, which, in agreement with philosophical idealism, are at the same time also ontological categories, can be developed from the categories "being" and "nothing," which—although opposites—are identical, and the entire cultural process which has led to the present can be portrayed as a collective universal history, where the one phase arises from and can be understood by the previous one, then no member in these processes is parallel or collateral with anything else, but each of them is either subordinated to or superior to every other. With the concept of "the collateral" Sibbern had challenged the Hegelian dialectic or what he called "Hegel's trilogistic course" or his "linear course."[116]

In his criticism of Hegel, Sibbern had drawn attention to the fact that in many of the triads, which can be posited, where, according to a dialectical analysis, the second member should be both the opposite of the first and something that arises from it, the first two members are parallel and mutually independent and come together only in order to form the third. This is the case, Sibbern writes,

> when faith and speculation, each coming from its side—the former from the side of feeling, sympathy, emotion, submission, the latter from the side of thought, pure reason, insight, the actual penetrating cognition—go up in a higher unity without that the one here can be said to have in the other its mediating element, or its phenomenal aspect, or its particular, or its objective, or what one now further wants, through which it merely itself came to its own fuller appearance, and thereby attached itself together with itself.[117]

Although Sibbern does not mention it, he may well mean that his philosophy of Christianity is a higher unity of faith and speculative philosophy.

In 1843 Kierkegaard returned again to Sibbern's concept of the collateral:

> If the understanding, feeling, and will are essential qualifications in a man, belong essentially to human nature, then all this chaff that the world-development now occupies a higher level vanishes into thin air....
>
> Therefore, however much the understanding advances, religion still can never be abolished, not only for those without authority, who probably would continue, but also for those with authority.
>
> The great individual is great simply because he has everything at once.
>
> Any other view overlooks the significance of the individuals in the race and reflects only on the history of the race, from which it would follow that essentially different men would be produced at different times and the universal unity in being a human being would be abrogated.[118]

---

116 *Maanedsskrift for Litteratur*, vol. 19, 1838, p. 560.

117 Ibid., pp. 560–1.

118 *SKS* 19, 414, Not13:49 / *JP* 3, 3657.

After this Kierkegaard discusses the idea that "the great individual" only in a quantitative sense and not a qualitative sense differs from the most insignificant. He ends the entry with the words "*the collateral.*"

While in connection with the previous discussion of the collateral the Hegelian dialectic was attacked, now it is the Hegelian philosophy of history which is under fire. By speaking of the idea that historical development generally goes in the direction of a consolidation of the supremacy of reason at the cost of other mental faculties, one overlooks the human difference—not with respect to the mental faculties, for everyone has the same ones, but with respect to the different kinds of strengths of the individual abilities. And this difference, Kierkegaard believes, has an influence on the course of history. Further, if an epoch's people are seen, for example, exclusively as being determined by their feelings, but a later epoch's people are exclusively rational beings, all talk of any common humanity would be meaningless, and this would render existential thinking impossible. For example, it would be meaningless to speak, as Vigilius Haufniensis does in *The Concept of Anxiety*, about anxiety about the Fall, that is, the dread that the flesh could win over spirit as something common for humanity.

In his criticism of Hegel, Sibbern had complained of "the one-sided overemphasis that he has given to *thought*, as if it were the highest and really true element of human existence."[119] Kierkegaard's entry expresses the same criticism, and not least of all in Johannes Climacus' *Concluding Unscientific Postscript*, "thought's supremacy in Hegel"—to use Sibbern's expression—is rejected. For the existing subjectivity is the highest truth: "*An objective uncertainty, held fast through appropriation with the most passionate inwardness*."[120] In this definition the elements of feeling and will are prominent, whereas the domain of thought, the objective certainty, is not represented in any other way than that thinking is required to reach it. And this thinking can well be characterized as "collateral thinking," since thinking, feeling, and will are all present as mutually irreducible mental faculties. Malantschuk writes:

> It was especially through his teacher Frederik Christian Sibbern that Kierkegaard became aware of this form of thinking about human existence....Kierkegaard thereafter in his own special way went more thoroughly into Sibbern's view of the collateral, and this further study became an essential part of his dialectical thinking. One can therefore with some justice characterize this thinking as a collateral thinking, that is, a thinking which constantly respects the many parallel elements and series of concepts.[121]

It can be remarked with respect to Malantschuk's treatment of "the collateral" that in Sibbern and in Kierkegaard it is first and foremost existence, that is, the sphere of existence that contains collateral elements. And since this is the case, the relation between a series of concepts can also be characterized as collateral. Therefore, the word designates first and foremost an ontological relation and only in a derived sense a conceptual one.

---

119 *Maanedsskrift for Litteratur*, vol. 19, 1838, p. 438.

120 *SKS* 7, 186 / *CUP1*, 203.

121 Malantschuk, *Frihed og Eksistens*, pp. 162–3.

It cannot be dismissed that Sibbern with his talk of the collateral inspired Kierkegaard on an essential point. However, by the same token it cannot be proved. The reflections about the collateral in Sibbern are methodological and respond to the question: "How should one, when taking into account the essential features of human existence, think about this?" Kierkegaard's—or in any case Johannes Climacus'—thinking about existence generally takes into account Sibbern's response to the question. However, by far the most empirically-minded philosophers implicitly presupposed the existence of something collateral. In modern times the "supremacy" of thinking has only been claimed by the philosophical rationalists Spinoza and Leibniz, by Wolff and his followers, and by Fichte and Hegel and their followers. Not least of all, Kant's philosophy is stamped by collateral thinking. And it lies in Tetens' very tripartite division of the expression of consciousness, which had turned against the Leibniz-Wolffian doctrine of a single faculty, that thinking, feeling, and will are collateral. Kierkegaard's inspiration could thus have come from many places: but it could very possibly, as Malantschuk claims, have come from Sibbern. The statement that I.H. Fichte has "vindicated" Sibbern's concept of the collateral points in this direction, although it cannot be regarded as proven that Kierkegaard and his pseudonyms also on this point were in agreement with the points of view maintained before the then contemporary Danish philosophy.

Finally, I will briefly discuss two features of Sibbern's thought which—although there is no textual evidence to support the claim—could have inspired Kierkegaard. The first is Sibbern's emphasis on the idea that every speculative philosophy must presuppose an explicative philosophy which issues from a concrete life-view and world-view, that is, that the sphere of existence and the condition of existence precede and are a presupposition, which cannot be avoided, for all thought. The second is whether the psychological powers of observation and the ability, connected to it according to Sibbern, to determine and describe mental phenomena has had significance for Kierkegaard. With respect to the first claim, one can point to Poul Møller, who also seems to have inspired Sibbern in the latter's criticism of Hegel. Poul Møller had originally been disposed—however, not uncritically—towards Hegelianism, but in a treatise on the possible proofs for the immortality of the soul from 1837 had claimed that philosophical reflection presupposes a concrete view of life and that "a scientific presentation of the basic tenets of philosophy...and every principal point is predetermined in the world-view that successively unfolds during the presentation and which in its totality constitutes its own defense."[122] Since thinking thus presupposes and is limited by the sphere of existence, this sphere, as Johannes Climacus thinks too, cannot be identical with that of thought. We know that Kierkegaard read this treatise.[123] But it cannot be determined whether this is a case of an influence. As before, one can only conclude that there is a certain agreement

---

122 Poul Martin Møller, "Tanker over Muligheden af Beviser for Menneskets Udødelighed, med Hensyn til den nyeste derhen hørende Literatur," *Maanedsskrift for Litteratur*, vol. 17, 1837, pp. 1–72 and pp. 422–53; pp. 38–9. For an account of Poul Møller's treatise, see also Koch, *Den danske idealisme*, pp. 258–64.

123 *SKS* 17, 134, BB:41 / *KJN* 1, 127–8.

between Kierkegaard and his pseudonyms on the one side and Hegel's critics in then contemporary Danish philosophy on the other.

Although Kierkegaard in connection with the taking of the Second Examination must have attained an, albeit rudimentary, knowledge of Sibbern's psychology, it can be demonstrated neither that Kierkegaard read Sibbern's textbook on psychology from 1819 to 1828 nor that the conceptual determinations in it can be found in Kierkegaard's authorship. By contrast, the difference between Sibbern and Kierkegaard is underscored as follows in the most extensive investigation of Kierkegaard's psychology:

> It is the interest in the *function* of emotional states which differentiates Kierkegaard from more introspectionism. Kierkegaard has said of one of his contemporaries, the philosopher and psychologist F.C. Sibbern, that he is satisfied with describing the individual emotions, and therefore lacks "an eye for the disguised passions, for the reduplication by which one passion takes the form of another." [124]

Here it is stated that while Sibbern kept to a phenomenological description of the human life of consciousness, the psychology of the pseudonyms was in its disposition a dynamic psychology. One can also point to the fact that while Sibbern in his psychology strived to make his psychological observations scientific, this endeavor was foreign to Kierkegaard. In the preface to *The Sickness unto Death. A Christian Psychological Exposition for Upbuilding and Awakening* the author writes, "this little book is such that a college student could write it, in another sense, perhaps such that not every professor could write it."[125] This last bit could be a little dig at Sibbern.

Translated by Jon Stewart

---

124 Kresten Nordentoft, *Kierkegaards psykologi*, Copenhagen: Hans Reitzel 1972, p. 24. (*Kierkegaard's Psychology*, trans. by Bruce H. Kirmmse, Pittsburgh: Duquesne University Press 1972, p. 4.) The quotation contained in this comes from Hans Brøchner's memoirs of Kierkegaard, see Kirmmse, *Søren Kierkegaard truffet*, pp. 331–2. (*Encounters*, p. 241.)

125 *SKS* 11, 118 / *SUD*, 6.

Bibliography

I. Sibbern's Works in The Auction Catalogue *of Kierkegaard's Library*

"Magnos viros magna et præclara non factis suis tantum dictisve, sed qvoqve tota sua personalitate efficere posse, idqve in Luthero imprimis spectari," *Nyt theologisk Bibliothek*, vols. 1–20, ed. by Jens Møller, Copenhagen: Andreas Seidelin 1821–32, vol. 6, 1824, pp. 172–99 (*ASKB* 336–345).

"Sendebrev om Frihedslæren," *Nyt theologisk Bibliothek*, vol. 17, 1830, pp. 222–8 (*ASKB* 336–345).

Logik som Tænkelære, 2nd ed., Copenhagen: Schultz 1835 (*ASKB* 777).

Bemærkninger og Undersøgelser, fornemmelige betreffende Hegels Philosophie, betragtet i forhold til vor Tid, Copenhagen: C.A. Reitzel 1838 (*ASKB* 778).

Om Philosophiens Begreb, Natur og Væsen. En Fremstilling af Philosophiens Propædeutik, Copenhagen: Schultz 1843 (*ASKB* 779).

Speculativ Kosmologie med Grundlag til en speculativ Theologie, Copenhagen: Schultz 1846 (*ASKB* 780).

Om Forholdet imellem Sjæl og Legeme, saavel i Almindelighed som i phrenologisk, pathognomonisk, physiognomonisk og ethisk Henseende i Særdeleshed, Copenhagen: Schultz 1849 (*ASKB* 781).

Nogle Betragtninger over Stat og Kirke, Copenhagen: Schultz 1849 (*ASKB* 782).

Bidrag til at oplyse nogle ontologiske Udtryk i Aristoteles's Metaphysik, Copenhagen: Schultz 1848 (*ASKB* 1848).

Dikaiosyne eller Bidrag til Politik og politisk Jurisprudents for Danske, i statsretlig, kirkelig og historisk Henseende, I, Copenhagen: J.D. Qvist 1843 (*ASKB* U 105).

II. Works in The Auction Catalogue *of Kierkegaard's Library that Discuss Sibbern*

Heiberg, Johan Ludvig, *Prosaiske Skrifter*, vol. 3, Copenhagen: J.H. Schubothe 1843 (vol. 3, in Johan Ludvig Heiberg, *Prosaiske Skrifter*, vols. 1–3, Copenhagen: J.H. Schubothe 1841–43, which is part of *Johan Ludvig Heiberg's Samlede Skrifter* consisting of *Skuespil*, vols. 1–7, Copenhagen: J.H. Schubothe 1833–41 and *Digte og Fortællinger*, vols. 1–2, Copenhagen: J.H. Schubothe 1834–35), p. 301; pp. 311–20 passim; p. 350; p. 368 (*ASKB* 1560).

Helweg, Fr., [Review of] "Fr. Chr. Sibbern. *Om den christelige Yttringsfrihed i kirkelig Henseende*," *Dansk Kirketidende*, vols. 1–8, ed. by C.J. Brandt and R.Th. Fenger, Copenhagen: C.A. Reitzel 1845–53, vol. 2, no. 55, 1846, columns 45–8 (*ASKB* 321–325).

Martensen, Hans Lassen, *De Autonomia conscientiæ sui humanæ in theologiam dogmaticam nostri temporis introducta*, Copenhagen: I.D. Quist 1837, p. 18, note; p. 94, note (*ASKB* 648).

—— *Den menneskelige Selvbevidstheds Autonomie i vor Tids dogmatiske Theologie*, Copenhagen: C.A. Reitzel 1841, p. 15, note; p. 77, note (*ASKB* 651, translation of *ASKB* 648, cf. also *ASKB* A I 41).

—— *Den christelige Dogmatik*, Copenhagen: C.A. Reitzel 1849, p. 80, note; p. 150, note; p. 182, note; p. 322 note; p. 428, note; p. 545, note (*ASKB* 653).

Møller, Poul Martin, "*Logik som Tænkelære*, af Dr. F.C. Sibbern, Professor i Philosophien ved Kjøbenhavns Universitet. Ny Udarbeidelse endnu som foreløbigt Aftryk for Tilhørere. Kbhavn. Trykt hos Directeur Jens Hostrup Schultz. 1827. (Hidtil utrykt Anmeldelse, ufuldendt)," in *Efterladte Skrifter af Poul M. Møller*, vols. 1–3, ed. by Christian Winther, F.C. Olsen, and Christen Thaarup Copenhagen: C.A. Reitzel 1839–43, vol. 2, pp. 105–26 (*ASKB* 1574–1576).

—— "Recension af Bogen: *Om Poesie og Kunst i Almindelighed, med Hensyn til alle Arter deraf, dog især Digte-, Maler-, Billedhugger- og Skuespillerkunst; eller: Foredrag over almindelig Æsthetik og Poetik*, af Dr. F.C. Sibbern, Første Deel. Kbhavn 1834 (Trykt i *Dansk Litteraturtidende*, 1835, No. 12 og 13)," in *Efterladte Skrifter af Poul M. Møller*, vols. 1–3, ed. by Christian Winther, F.C. Olsen, and Christen Thaarup, Copenhagen: C.A. Reitzel 1839–43, vol. 2, pp. 105–26 (*ASKB* 1574–1576).

—— *Efterladte Skrifter af Poul M. Møller*, vols. 1–3, ed. by Christian Winther, F.C. Olsen, and Christen Thaarup, Copenhagen: C.A. Reitzel 1839–43, vol. 3, p. 195 (*ASKB* 1574–1576).

Mynster, Jakob Peter, *Om Hukommelsen. En psychologisk Undersögelse*, Copenhagen: Jens Hostrup Schultz 1849, p. 28, note (*ASKB* 692).

—— "Recension af Efterladte Breve af Gabrielis" in his *Blandede Skrivter*, vols. 1–3, Copenhagen: Gyldendal 1852–53 [vols. 4–6, Copenhagen: Gyldendal 1855–57], vol. 2, 1853, pp. 349–56; see also, vol. 1, p. 28; p. 31, note; p. 225, note; p. 234, note; p. 263; vol. 2, p. 79; p. 116; p. 118; p. 120; p. 124; p. 210; p. 347 (*ASKB* 358–363).

Nielsen, Rasmus, *De speculativa historiæ sacræ tractandæ methodo commentatio*, Copenhagen: Tengnagel 1840, p. 45, note; p. 138, note (*ASKB* 697).

—— *Den propædeutiske Logik*, Copenhagen: P.G. Philipsen 1845, p. 14; p. 18; p. 21; p. 29; p. 36; p. 96; p. 131; p. 256 (*ASKB* 699).

Thomsen, Grimur, *Om den nyfranske Poesi, et Forsøg til Besvarelse af Universitetets æsthetiske Priisspørgsmaal for 1841: "Har Smag og Sands for Poesi gjort Frem- eller Tilbageskridt i Frankrig i de sidste Tider og hvilken er Aarsagen?,"* Copenhagen: Wahlske Boghandlings Forlag 1843, p. 80 (*ASKB* 1390).

Zeuthen, Ludvig, *Humanitet betragtet fra et christeligt Standpunkt, med stadigt Hensyn til den nærværende Tid*, Copenhagen: Gyldendalske Boghandling 1846, p. 11; p. 46 (*ASKB* 915).

—— *Om Ydmyghed. En Afhandling*, Copenhagen: Gyldendal 1852, p. 80, note (*ASKB* 916).

III. Secondary Literature on Kierkegaard's Relation to Sibbern

Borchsenius, Otto, *Fra Fyrrerne. Literære Skizzer*, 1st series, Copenhagen: C.A. Reitzel and Otto B. Wroblewsky 1878, pp. 287–301.

Fenger, Henning, *Kierkegaard, the Myths and Their Origins. Studies in the Kierkegaardian Papers and Letters*, trans. by George C. Schoolfield, New Haven and London: Yale University Press 1980, p. 28; p. 42; p. 64; p. 84; pp. 88–9; p. 113; pp. 120–2; p. 135; p. 137; pp. 146–8; p. 177. (Originally as *Kierkegaard-Myter og Kierkegaard-Kilder. 9 kildekritiske studier i de Kierkegaardske papirer, breve og aktstykker*, Odense: Odense Universitetsforlag 1976.)

Furtak, Rick Anthony, *Wisdom in Love: Kierkegaard and the Ancient Quest for Emotional Integrity*, Notre Dame: University of Notre Dame Press 2005, p. 42; p. 48.

Himmelstrup, Jens, *Søren Kierkegaards Opfattelse af Sokrates. En studie i dansk filosofis historie*, Copenhagen: Arnold Busck 1924, see pp. 317–18.

—— "Sibbern og Kierkegaard," *Nordisk tidskrift för videnskap, konst och industri*, 1926, pp. 185–96.

—— "Sibbern og Kierkegaard," in his *Sibbern. En Monografi*, Copenhagen: J.H. Schultz 1934, pp. 258–87.

Høffding, Harald, *Søren Kierkegaard som filosof*, Copenhagen, P.G. Philipsens Forlag 1892, pp. 21–4.

—— "Sibbern og Kierkegaard," in his *Religiøse Tanketyper*, Copenhagen 1927, pp. 98–111.

Kühle, Sejer, *Søren Kierkegaards Barndom og Ungdom*, Copenhagen: Aschehoug Dansk Forlag 1950, p. 15; p. 18; p. 77; p. 104; pp. 108ff.; pp. 112–17 passim; p. 167; p. 177; p. 196; p. 203; p. 206.

Lilhav, Preben, "Filosofi (Sibbern og Poul Møller)," in his *Kierkegaards valg*, Risskov: Forlaget Sicana 2003, pp. 51–73.

Lübcke, Poul, "F.C. Sibbern: Epistemologi as Ontology," in *Kierkegaard and His Contemporaries. The Culture of Golden Age Denmark*, ed. by Jon Stewart, New York and Berlin: Walter de Gruyter 2003 (*Kierkegaard Studies Monograph Series*, vol. 10), pp. 25–44.

Magnussen, Rikard, "F.C. Sibbern og Søren Kierkegaard," in his *Søren Kierkegaard set udefra*, Copenhagen: Ejnar Munksgaard 1942, pp. 113–27.

Malantschuk, Gregor, *Dialektik og Eksistens hos Søren Kierkegaard*, Copenhagen: Hans Reitzel 1968, pp. 123–7.

—— *Frihed og Eksistens. Studier i Søren Kierkegaards Tænkning*, Copenhagen: C.A. Reitzel 1980, pp. 162–76.

Malik, Habib C., *Receiving Søren Kierkegaard. The Early Impact and Transmission of His Thought*. Washington, D.C.: Catholic University Press of America 1997, pp. 43–9.

Møller, A. Egelund, "Søren Kierkegaard og professor Sibbern," in his *Søren Kierkegaard om politik*, Copenhagen: Forlaget Strand 1975, pp. 36–9.

Reuter, Hans, *S. Kierkegaards religionsphilosophische Gedanken im Verhältnis zu Hegels religionsphilosophischem Systems*, Leipzig: Verlag von Quelle & Meyer 1914 (*Abhandlungen zur Philosophie und ihrer Geschichte*, no. 23), pp. 68–74.

Rubow, Paul V., *Kierkegaard og hans Samtidige*, Copenhagen: Gyldendal 1950, pp. 16–18.

Söderquist, K. Brian, "Kierkegaard's Contribution to the Danish Discussion of 'Irony,'" in *Kierkegaard and His Contemporaries: The Culture of Golden Age Denmark*, ed. by Jon Stewart, Berlin and New York: Walter de Gruyter, 2003 (*Kierkegaard Studies Monograph Series*, vol. 10), pp. 78–105.

Stewart, Jon, *Kierkegaard's Relations to Hegel Reconsidered*, Cambridge and New York: Cambridge University Press 2003.

Thielst, Peter, "Frederik Christian Sibbern," in his *5 danske filosoffer fra det 19. århundrede*, Frederiksberg: Det lille forlag 1998, pp. 15–22.

—— "Sibbern and Møller," in his *Livet forstås baglæns, men må leves forlæns. Historier om Søren Kierkegaard*, Copenhagen: Gyldendal 1994, pp. 48–52.

Thulstrup, Niels, *Kierkegaard's Relation to Hegel*, trans. by George L. Stengren, Princeton, New Jersey: Princeton University Press 1980, see p. 22, note; p. 33 passim; p. 43; p. 51, note; p. 57; p. 115; p. 150; p. 176; p. 178; p. 184; p. 202; p. 204; p. 207; p. 212; p. 264; p. 275; p. 295; p. 314; p. 380 (in Danish as *Kierkegaards forhold til Hegel*, Copenhagen: Gyldendal 1967).

—— *Commentary on Kierkegaard's* Concluding Unscientific Postscript, trans. by Robert J. Widenmann, Princeton, New Jersey: Princeton University Press 1984, see p. 75; p. 77; pp. 80ff.; p. 99; p. 126; p. 220; p. 228; p. 245; p. 306; p. 345 (in Danish as *Søren Kierkegaard. Afsluttende uvidenskabelige Efterskrift udgivet med Indledning og Kommentar af Niels Thulstrup*, vols. 1–2, Copenhagen: Gyldendal 1962).

Tjønneland, Eivind, *Ironie als Symptom. Eine kritische Auseinandersetzung mit Søren Kierkegaards Über den Begriff der Ironie*, Frankfurt am Main: Peter Lang 2004 (*Texte und Untersuchungen zur Germanistik und Skandinavistik*, vol. 54), see pp. 117–19; pp. 270–80.

Vergote, Henri-Bernard, *Lectures philosophiques de Søren Kierkegaard. Kierkegaard chez ses contemporains danois. Textes de J.L. Heiberg, H.L. Martensen, P.M. Møller, F.C. Sibbern, F. Beck et S.A. Kierkegaard*, Paris: Presses Universitaires de France 1993 (*Philosophique D'ajourd'hui*).

Widenmann, Robert J., "Sibbern," in *Kierkegaard's Teachers*, ed. by Niels Thulstrup and Marie Mikulová Thulstrup, Copenhagen: C.A. Reitzel 1982 (*Bibliotheca Kierkegaardiana*, vol. 10), pp. 70–88.

Henrich Steffens:
Combining Danish Romanticism with Christian Orthodoxy

Andrew J. Burgess

The relationship between Henrich (sometimes "Henrik") Steffens (1773–1845)[1] and Søren Kierkegaard is a good example of the substantial revisions regularly called for in the writing of the history of philosophy. A century ago the question to be discussed

[1] Kierkegaard scholarship is fortunate that the fullest and most up-to-date treatment of Henrich Steffens' philosophy of religion has been compiled by a student of Kierkegaard, Helge Hultberg, in three works: *Den unge Henrich Steffens, 1773–1811*, Copenhagen: Bianco Luno 1973; *Den ældre Henrich Steffens, 1811–1845*, Copenhagen: C.A. Reitzel 1981; and "Steffens und Kierkegaard," *Kierkegaardiana*, vol. 10, 1977, pp. 190–9. More recent scholarship is represented in *Henrik Steffens—Vermittler zwischen Natur und Geist*, ed. by Otto Lorenz and Bernd Henningsen, Berlin: Arno Spitz 1999. Other important resources on Steffens' philosophy include Jørgen Bukdahl, "Vejen til myten og eventyret," in *Søren Kierkegaard og den menige mand*, 2nd ed., Copenhagen: C.A. Reitzel 1996 [1970] (*Søren Kierkegaard Selskabets Populære Skrifter*, vols. 9–10), pp. 11–21 (English translation: "Henrich Steffens: The Way to Myth and Fairy Tale," in *Søren Kierkegaard and the Common Man*, Grand Rapids, Michigan: Eerdmans 2001, pp. 7–18); Dietrich von Engelhardt, "Henrik Steffens im Spektrum der Naturwissenschaft und Naturphilosophie in der Epoche der Romantik," in *Henrik Steffens-Vermittler zwischen Natur und Geist*, ed. by Lorenz and Henningsen, pp. 89–112; Trond Berg Eriksen, "Philosophiebegriff und Wissensvermittlung in Steffens' Kopenhagener Vorlesungen," in *Henrik Steffens-Vermittler zwischen Natur und Geist*, ed. by Lorenz and Henningsen, pp. 11–26; Harald Høffding, "Henrik Steffens," in *Danske Filosofer*, Copenhagen: Gyldendal 1909, pp. 40–48; Friedrich Jung, *Henrik Steffens und das Problem des Einheit von Vernunft und Offenbarung*, Ph.D. Thesis, University of Marburg 1961; Carl Henrik Koch, "Henrich Steffens," in *Den danske idealisme, 1800–1880*, Copenhagen: Gyldendal 2004, pp. 31–56; Johnny Kondrup, "Efterskrift," in *Indledning til philosophiske Forelæsninger*, Copenhagen: C.A.Reitzel 1996, pp. 59–22; Ingetraut Ludolphy, *Henrich Steffens. Sein Verhältnis zu den Lutheranern und sein Anteil an Entstehung und Schicksal der altlutherischen Gemeinde in Breslau*, Berlin: Evangelische Verlagsanstalt 1962; Tonny Aagaard Olesen, "Kierkegaards Schelling: Eine historische Einführung," in *Kierkegaard und Schelling: Freiheit, Angst und Wirklichkeit*, ed. by Jochem Hennigfeld and Jon Stewart, Berlin: Walter de Gruyter 2003 (*Kierkegaard Studies Monograph Series*, vol. 8), pp. 1–102, see especially pp. 8–13; pp. 33–43; and Fritz Paul, *Henrich Steffens: Naturphilosophie und Universalromantik*, Munich: Wilhelm Fink 1973. For a bibliography until 1977 consult Aage Jørgensen, "Litteraturen om Henrich Steffens 1845–1977," in *Henrich Steffens-en mosaik*, Aarhus: Akademisk Forlag 1977, pp. 146–160. Some references after 1977 are included

might have been the significance of Kierkegaard for the understanding of Steffens. The classic 1911 edition of the English language *Encyclopedia Britannica*, for example, offered a longer entry for Steffens than for Kierkegaard, and it described Kierkegaard's philosophical stance as "a reaction against the speculative thinkers," whom it listed as Steffens, Niels Treschow (1751–1833), and Frederik Christian Sibbern (1785–1872).[2]

Today that estimate of the relative importance of these men would need to be exactly reversed. Like Treschow and Sibbern, Steffens is remembered mostly for his role in the development of nineteenth-century Danish philosophy.[3] Kierkegaard, on the other hand, is a world figure, so that the current challenge is to account for his persistent fascination with Steffens' writings. The duration of time during which Kierkegaard drew ideas from Steffens' works is unusually long, compared to his engagement with many other thinkers, lasting all the way from Kierkegaard's student days up to the late 1840s. Kierkegaard owned several of Steffens' most important writings and may have read from others he did not own,[4] and he often referred positively to Steffens in both his notebooks and published works.

Part of the difficulty for defining the relationship between Kierkegaard and Steffens is that some of Steffens' influence on Kierkegaard was indirect or, when direct, specific and incidental. In fact, an important part of Steffens' influence would have come indirectly through the impact of Steffens' 1802–04 Copenhagen lectures upon some intellectual leaders of the early Danish Golden Age. At one time or other, several key Danish thinkers with significant relations to Kierkegaard—including Jakob Peter (later Bishop) Mynster (1775–1854), Adam Oehlenschläger (1779–

---

following the individual essays in *Henrik Steffens—Vermittler zwischen Natur und Geist*, ed. by Lorenz and Henningsen.

2 "Kierkegaard, Sören Aaby," *Encyclopedia Britannica*, 11th ed., New York: Encyclopedia Britannica 1911, vol. 15, p. 788.

3 Although Steffens spent most of his academic career in Germany and became deeply involved in the cultural and political life there, even serving briefly as a Prussian military officer in the war against Napoleon, he kept active contact throughout his life with the intellectual leaders of Copenhagen, where he had largely grown up, and he exercised most of his influence through Danish philosophy and literature. Recently Steffens has received special recognition from Norway, on the basis of his birth in Stavanger (then part of Denmark) and because of the way in which the Norwegian poet Henrik Wergeland, in the 1830 poem "Skabelsen, Mennesket, og Messias," described him with the phrase "Norges bortblæste Laurblad"; Henrik Wergeland, *Samlede Skrifter*, vols. 1–23, ed. by Herman Jæger and Didrik Arup Seip, Kristiania: Steen 1918–40, vol. 2 (1919), pp. 2–7; cited in Paul, *Naturphilosophie und Universalromantik*, p. 216. Wergeland's description of Steffens as Norway's "laurel leaf" provided the title for Ingeborg Møller's *Henrik Steffens. "Norges bortblæste Laurbærblad,"* Oslo: Gyldendal 1948 and also for the second Henrik-Steffens Symposium, held in Oslo on May 2, 1998. The 1998 symposium's papers were published in *Henrik Steffens–Vermittler zwischen Natur und Geist*, ed. by Lorenz and Henningsen, in 1999.

4 For example, in a draft for a passage that did not get included in *Concluding Unscientific Postscript*, Kierkegaard contrasts the style of a particular passage from Steffens' 1802 lectures (*Indledning til philosophiske Forelæsninger*, ed. by Johnny Kondrup, Copenhagen: C.A. Reitzel 1996, p. 128) with that of Grundtvig (*Pap*. VI B 29, p. 106 / *CUP2*, Supplement, p. 20).

1854), Nikolai Frederik Severin Grundtvig (1783–1872), and Sibbern—were drawn to Steffens' teachings, at least briefly. Steffens' family ties were an important factor that affected his involvement with some of these men. After his mother died in 1788, he went to live with his mother's brother, Frederik Ludvig Bang (1747–1820), who was a professor of medicine in Copenhagen and who was the step-father to J.P. Mynster[5] and his older brother, Ole Hieronymus Mynster (1772–1818). Another sister of F.L. Bang was the mother of Grundtvig.[6] Later Kierkegaard was also directly indebted to Steffens' works, and Kierkegaard regularly noted down particular passages from Steffens he might later adapt for use in his own writings.

In order to allow for both the possibilities of indirect and direct influences of Steffens upon Kierkegaard, therefore, this article will first survey the place Steffens held within Danish and German intellectual life during the first half of the nineteenth century, especially as part of the Danish "Golden Age," then examine the various references to Steffens in Kierkegaard's published and unpublished writings, and finally comment on the significance Steffens may have had for Kierkegaard's intellectual development.

I. The Indirect Influences: Romanticism and Christian Orthodoxy

Steffens' philosophy of religion moves between two poles, each of which was particularly important during a period of his life.[7] Starting in 1797, when he left Copenhagen to study at Jena with the others of the early Romantic circle, Steffens was a committed Romantic and follower of Schelling, both in his scientific and in his religious views. Beginning in 1811, however, he turned sharply against that position, and in 1823 he published his change of views in *On the False Theology and the True Religion*: *A Voice from the Congregation*.[8]

Distinguishing the two poles is complicated by several factors. (1) Steffens' fame rests largely upon his Romantic credentials, and particularly upon his 1802–04 Copenhagen lectures, which are popularly credited with introducing Romanticism to Denmark. Much of the available literature on Steffens, therefore, treats this period as definitive for his work and virtually ignores his later writing. (2) In 1831 Steffens apparently renounced his change with the book *How I Became a Lutheran Again*,

5 The relationship between Henrich Steffens and J.P. Mynster is discussed in Ørsted's 694-page study, *J.P. Mynster og Henrich Steffens*.

6 Ibid., p. 26.

7 Accordingly, Helge Hultberg finds he needs to write two books, one on young Steffens and one on the old (see Hultberg, *Den unge Henrich Steffens* and *Den ældre Henrich Steffens*). In this respect he follows the other main authority on this area of Steffens, see Jung, *Henrik Steffens und das Problem des Einheit von Vernunft und Offenbarung*. The two differ on the date for the break, since Hultberg places the date at the beginning of Steffens' change of heart (1811), and Jung places it at the time when Steffens published his new views (1823).

8 Henrik Steffens, *Von der falschen Theologie und dem wahren Glauben. Eine Stimme aus der Gemeinde*, Breslau: Josef Max 1823.

and What Lutheranism Is to Me. A Confession by Henrich Steffens,[9] but in practice continued on much as before. (3) Despite a perceptible movement in his writings from the Romantic to the orthodox Christian pole, Steffens continued until the end to insist on the validity of both poles, even when doing so involved him in apparent inconsistencies, to the consternation of his friends and foes alike. Nonetheless, because Kierkegaard's writings show influences from both Romanticism and his later, more traditional, views, both will be presented here.

II. Steffens and Early Danish Romanticism

Steffens and Danish Romanticism are inextricably bound up together, because his 1802–04 lectures are commonly credited with introducing Romanticism to Denmark. Philosophy, however, whether Romantic or not, was not his first area of study. Perhaps under the influence of his uncle F.L. Bang, Steffens' academic career began in various natural sciences, especially mineralogy,[10] and in 1797 he received a doctoral degree in that field. During this period Schelling's speculative philosophy of nature drew him more and more away from strictly empirical research, so that in 1798, when he received a two-year stipend for study in Germany, he took the opportunity to leave for the university at Jena, where members of the early Romantic circle were gathering. Besides Schelling (1775–1854), who had just come to Jena, that university then hosted Ludwig Tieck (1773–1853), Friedrich von Hardenberg (Novalis) (1772–1801), Friedrich von Schlegel (1772–1829), and August Wilhelm Schlegel (1767–1845). The Jena circle was also in contact with Johann Wolfgang von Goethe (1849–1832) in Weimar and Friedrich Schleiermacher (768–1834) in Berlin.[11] Johann Gottlieb Fichte (1762–1814), too, was still at Jena that year, and Steffens listened to his lectures,[12] but Georg Wilhelm Friedrich Hegel (1770–1831) did not arrive until 1800, after Steffens had left.

Steffens' main role in the group's discussions was as a resident expert in natural science, a fact which would have aligned him more with Schelling than with the more literary Schlegel brothers.[13] After a year in the stimulating company of this early Romantic circle, Steffens left for two years to study under the renowned mineralogist Abraham Gottlob Werner (1749–1817) at Freiberg in Saxony. There he published his first important scientific study, *Contributions to the Inner Natural History of the Earth* (1801),[14] in which he drew upon his broad background in the natural sciences

---

9 Henrik Steffens, *Wie ich wieder Lutheraner wurde und was mir das Luthertum ist. Eine Confession*, Breslau: Josef Max 1831.

10 Henrik Steffens, *Was ich erlebte: Aus der Erinnerung niedergeschrieben*, vols. 1–10, Breslau: Josef Max 1841–44, vol. 2, pp. 192–3 (*ASKB* 1834–1843).

11 Kondrup, "Efterskrift," pp. 169–73.

12 Ørsted, *J.P. Mynster og Henrich Steffens*, p. 40; *Was ich erlebte*, vol. 4, pp. 157–8.

13 Kondrup, "Efterskrift," p. 173. As Fritz Paul points out, however, Steffens also found some positive aspects in the Schlegel brothers' attitude toward experimental science, see Paul, *Naturphilosophie und Universalromantik*, p. 127.

14 Henrik Steffens, *Beyträge zur innern Naturgeschichte der Erde*, Freyberg: Crazischen Buchhandlung 1801.

to portray a Romantic, speculative interpretation of the organic unity of spirit and nature.[15] The following year he left for Dresden and the surrounding area, where he began preparing a set of public lectures for delivery in Copenhagen.[16]

Steffens' 1802–04 lectures in Copenhagen set out to bring Jena Romanticism to Denmark and also, from a personal standpoint, to open up a possible academic position for himself in his native country.[17] In the first respect he was brilliantly successful, creating a public sensation and drawing an enthusiastic reception from a wide range of young intellectuals. One of the reasons for the immediate impact of the lectures was the close-knit network of family and friends of which Steffens was a part. Thus in 1802 it was his cousin O.H. Mynster who introduced Steffens to the promising young poet Oehlenschläger.[18] O.H. Mynster's younger brother, J.P. Mynster, was later recruited to provide a theological defense for Oehlenschläger's poem "The Golden Horn," which had become a manifesto for the emerging Danish Romantic movement.[19] With others the impact of the lectures was delayed. For Steffens' cousin Grundtvig, for example, the force of the lectures did not strike home until several years later, in 1805.[20] F.C. Sibbern, who heard only part of the lectures, was initially unimpressed and did not become enthusiastic about the new philosophy until later, after he had spoken with Steffens.[21] The physicist Hans Christian Ørsted (1777–1851), who might otherwise have been a receptive audience for Steffens' scientific teachings, was not at the lectures at all, because he was already in Germany as Steffens' successor in the travelling science fellowship, and the two had little chance during this period to exchange views.[22] After Steffens left Copenhagen for Halle, Ørsted became the chief representative for the natural sciences among the Copenhagen Romantics, and, as time went on, he came to be critical of what he took to be Steffens' lack of experimental rigor.[23]

Although for Steffens the public reception to the radical lectures was all he could have hoped, their success only marked him as a radical by the authorities and made his job search harder than it might otherwise have been, and the philosophy position then open in Copenhagen was given to Treschow instead.[24]Accordingly, in

15 See, for example, Paul, *Naturphilosophie und Universalromantik*, pp. 140–1.

16 Steffens, *Was ich erlebte*, vol. 4, pp. 380–436.

17 On Steffens' 1803 Copenhagen lectures, see especially Kondrup, "Efterskrift," pp. 59–221.

18 Steffens, *Was ich erlebte*, vol. 5, pp. 25–6; cf. Kondrup, "Efterskrift," *Indledning*, p. 184.

19 Bruce H. Kirmmse, *Kierkegaard in Golden Age Denmark*, Bloomington: Indiana University Press 1990, pp. 108–17.

20 Flemming Lundgreen-Nielsen, "Grundtvig and Romanticism," in *Kierkegaard and His Contemporaries: The Culture of Golden Age Denmark*, ed. by Jon Stewart, Berlin: Walter de Gruyter 2003 (*Kierkegaard Studies Monograph Series*, vol. 10), p. 205.

21 Paul Kallmoes, *Frederik Christian Sibbern: Træk af en dansk filosofs liv og tænkning*, Copenhagen: Munksgaard 1946, p. 24.

22 Kondrup,"Efterskrift," p. 186.

23 John L. Greenway, "Ørsted's Acoustics and Andersen's 'The Bell,' " in *Kierkegaard and His Contemporaries: The Culture of Golden Age Denmark*, ed. by Jon Stewart, p. 269.

24 Steffens, *Was ich erlebte*, vol. 5, p. 61.

1804, Steffens, unable to find any other university position in Denmark, left for a professorship in mineralogy at the university in Halle.[25] Schleiermacher also moved to Halle about this time, and the two men found they shared many ideas. Again, in 1807, when Steffens had to leave Halle for a while because Napoleon's forces had occupied the city, he tried and failed to get a teaching post in Denmark.[26] When Schleiermacher became a professor at Berlin in 1811, he tried, unsuccessfully, to get Steffens a position there as well.[27] Finally, in 1811, Steffens was offered a professorship in physics and philosophy at the new university in Breslau,[28] where he remained for many years, until 1832.

Over the years each of the Copenhagen Romantics drifted off in a separate direction, as, one by one, they declared their independence from Steffens' lectures. Perhaps there was something implicit in the Romantic attitude that drove them apart, since the Jena circle also broke up in a similar way. Still, for all those in the Copenhagen group, the speculative dream with which they had been inspired, directly or indirectly, through Steffens' lectures had left a deep imprint upon their later thinking.[29]

III. Transition to Christian Orthodoxy

True Romantic that he was, Steffens himself was forever moving off in new directions too. Early in his teaching career he had taken up German political and academic causes unpopular among conservatives. After the restoration of the old regimes in 1815, when conservatism became the standard, he adopted a mediating role with his *Caricatures of the Most Holy* (1819–21),[30] which balanced both sides of a whole range of issues, but his attempt to hold the middle ground only alienated his former allies, including even Schleiermacher.[31] The actions that aroused the greatest confusion among the Romantics, however, were his shifts in religious positions. Since his first years in Jena he had been a close associate of Schleiermacher, and those ties had strengthened during their time together in Halle. During Steffens' professorship in Breslau, however, he became an adherent of the so-called "old Lutheran" movement at the university led by Professor Johann Gottfried Scheibel

---

25 Ibid., pp. 102–18.

26 Ibid., pp. 242–63.

27 Richard B. Brandt, *The Philosophy of Schleiermacher: The Development of His Theory of Scientific and Religious Knowledge*, New York: Harper and Brothers 1941, p. 148.

28 Steffens, *Was ich erlebte*, vol. 6, pp. 237–9.

29 Kathryn Shailer-Hanson, however, has shown that even Oehlenschläger, the early standard bearer for Romantic poetry in Denmark, had already embarked upon a "thoroughly romantic" path a year before he heard Steffens' lectures, see Kathryn Shailer-Hanson, "Adam Oehlenschläger's *Erik and Roller* and Danish Romanticism," in *Kierkegaard and His Contemporaries: The Culture of Golden Age Denmark*, ed. by Jon Stewart, pp. 234–5.

30 Henrik Steffens, *Caricaturen des Heiligsten, aus der Erinnerung niedergeschrieben*, vols. 1–2, Leipzig: F.A. Brockhaus 1919–21 (*ASKB* 793–794).

31 Hultberg, *Den ældre Henrich Steffens*, pp. 38–45.

(1783–1843),[32] who was fighting against the union of Lutheran and Reformed congregations then being imposed by the Prussian king. In keeping with his new religious convictions, Steffens, published in 1823 a sharp attack upon his own earlier theological views, under the title *On the False Theology and the True Religion.*[33] Unfortunately, the publisher advertised the book as an attack on Schleiermacher, although Steffens had not specifically identified the theology in that way.[34]

Meanwhile, Steffens' new ideas were beginning to alarm some of his former associates in Copenhagen as well. In the fall of 1824 Steffens announced that he planned to visit there, prompting Poul Martin Møller (1794–1838) to write that "all the world" is delighted at the news that Steffens is about to make a visit to Copenhagen and especially Sibbern is "entirely crazy with joy" over Steffens.[35] As the report of Steffens' new book filtered up to Denmark, however, the little circle of Copenhagen Romantics were all, in one way or another, bemused or dismayed. Only Steffens' cousin Grundtvig looked for understanding from the new Steffens. Since 1819 Grundtvig had been carrying on with Steffens a correspondence through which, among other things, he hoped to interest Steffens in his own writings about Nordic literature. When Steffens did visit Copenhagen in 1824, however, the little circle of Romantics that hosted Steffens pointedly excluded Grundtvig, and later, when the family held its own celebration, to which Grundtvig was of course invited, Steffens immediately began to criticize Grundtvig's writings about literature.[36] After that Grundtvig continued to send Steffens his Nordic, rather than his Christian works, even though Steffens preferred the latter, and the once cordial communications between the two cousins faded into mere politeness.[37]

Some years later, in the middle of 1830, the "old Lutheran" congregation in Breslau to which Steffens belonged came under increased pressure from the Prussian government over the long promised union of Lutheran and Reformed churches. From that point on, the existence of such a specifically Lutheran congregation was a direct challenge to the authority of the state. As had happened before, Steffens found himself caught in the middle. Unlike most others in the congregation he felt that his allegiance to the Lutheran, as opposed to the Reformed, confession was not decisive; his obedience to the Prussian king was. The result was that, through

---

32 See Ludolphy, *Henrich Steffens*, pp. 97–107. Through a detailed examination of original government sources Ludolphy demonstrates the inadequacy of the earlier interpretation of Steffens' actions put forward by Georg Froböß (*Drei Lutheraner an der Universität Breslau. Die Professoren Scheibel, Steffens, Huschke in ihrer religiösen Entwicklung bis zu ihrem Eintritt in die Kämpfe der lutherischen Kirche im Jahre 1830*, Breslau: Kaufmann 1911), which questioned Steffens' integrity in the bitter dispute.

33 Steffens, *Von der falschen Theologie und dem wahren Glauben.*

34 Hultberg, *Den ældre Henrich Steffens*, pp. 56–7.

35 Ibid., p. 66. See also P.M. Møller's 1824 poem in honor of Steffens, "Hilsen til Henrik Steffens," *Efterladte Skrifter af Poul M. Møller*, vols. 1–3, 1st ed., Copenhagen: C.A. Reitzel 1839–43, vol. 3, pp. 14–5

36 Flemming Lundgreen-Nielsen, "Grundtvig und Steffens," in *Henrik Steffens—Vermittler zwischen Natur und Geist*, ed. by Lorenz and Henningsen, pp. 78–81; Cf. also Hultberg, *Den ældre Henrich Steffens*, pp. 73–9.

37 Hultberg, *Den ældre Henrich Steffens*, p. 79.

the personal support of the Prussian crown princess, the state began negotiations with Steffens, and he was offered a chair in philosophy at the university of Berlin, which had been his lifelong dream.[38] For his part, Steffens published in 1831 a book formally declaring his departure from the "old Lutheran" congregation: *How I Became a Lutheran Again, and What Lutheranism Is To Me: A Confession by Henrich Steffens*.[39] It is a strange book, the first half full of rambling reminiscences of his childhood and of the struggles of his pious and hard-working parents, and the second half a replay of themes he had explored in his early Romantic theology. What it lacks is either any firm confession that he had ever been mistaken or any substantive rationale for the step he was about to take. Still, the wording did not really matter, since state authority had been upheld. Steffens was not one to become a martyr. In temperament and conviction, he was a born mediator nonetheless, and during the following years, as one congregation member after another was arrested and Scheibel himself was repeatedly banished, Steffens quietly but effectively used the relationship he had established with the Prussian crown princess to negotiate better treatment for them in their distress.[40]

Freed from the economic and social pressures that had troubled most of his adult life, Steffens now basked in recognition from the academic and political authorities. In Denmark, for example, professors such as Sibbern, while not necessarily agreeing with Steffens' ideas, were glad to recognize the Berlin professor as one of their own. As a young man, Martensen, too, had become excited about Steffens' book *On the False Theology and the True Religion*, but his impression changed completely when he heard Steffens lecture in Berlin in 1834,[41] and by the late 1830s Martensen's strong preference was for Hegel. Still, Martensen did bring out occasional points from Steffens in his 1838–39 lectures on speculative dogmatics, to which Kierkegaard listened.[42] At the end of the decade Steffens even received an invitation from the Danish crown prince, whom Steffens had known in Berlin, to attend that prince's coronation as Christian VIII, an event that marked the peak of Steffens' Danish fame.[43]

---

38 Ludolphy, *Henrich Steffens*, pp. 86–96, especially p. 91 and p. 96.

39 Steffens, *Wie ich wieder Lutheraner wurde*.

40 Ludolphy, *Henrich Steffens*, pp. 136–45.

41 Skat Arildsen, *H.L. Martensen: Hans liv, udvikling, og arbejde*, Copenhagen: Gad 1932, p. 21, pp. 82–3.

42 One such Steffens idea is "What human being is for nature, Christ is for the human race" (*Pap*. II C 27 in *Pap*. XIII C 27, p. 31). This remark in Martensen's lectures is not, however, recorded in the notes Kierkegaard himself took (see *Pap*. II C 26–7 in *Pap*. XIII, p. 3). In Kierkegaard's own notes on those lectures this remark would have come in *SKS* 18, 393, KK:11 / *KJN* 2, 349.

43 In his memoirs Steffens dwelt at length on the many honors he received at the coronation (Steffens, *Was ich erlebte*, vol. 10, pp. 343–58). Steffens' prolixity may be part of the reason Kierkegaard selected this occasion as the basis for his parody of the "memoir style" in the fragmentary "Writing Sampler," some years later: "The latest assembly of the Estates or something similar from the present day, narrated by an old person under the delusion that it is fifty years ago. —I can remember Sager well; he was red in the face. —First and foremost

In spite of the many twists and turns in Steffens' positions, there remains an underlying unity, grounded ultimately in his appropriation of the early Schelling, synthesizing natural science on one side with religion on the other. What changes is that over the course of his academic career the weight shifts from a stress on science to one on religion. By the end of his life the shift is obvious, especially in the two-volume work he titled *Christian Philosophy of Religion* (1839),[44] which is organized into two volumes, one stressing nature philosophy and the other dogmatics, but for which the overall topic is philosophy of religion, not science. Apart from this one book, Steffens was better known in Berlin for his hospitality, vigorous lecturing style, and genial personality than for his academic productivity. The thin volume that included his scholarly writings of the period, called *Posthumous Writings*,[45] was dwarfed by his semi-popular, ten-volume memoirs *What I Experienced* (1841–44).[46] From a philosophical point of view, Steffens had already said what he had to say.

IV. Direct References to Steffens in Kierkegaard's Unpublished Writings

Kierkegaard had in his library, and took some notes from, several of Steffens' major works. At the time of his death, however, he did not own Steffens' 1802–04 Copenhagen lectures, and he made only one incidental reference to them in a draft for the *Concluding Unscientific Postscript*.[47] His reading of Steffens was either from the period when Steffens was in transition from his earlier affiliation with the Jena Romantics to a more orthodox Christian position, that is, the above-mentioned *Caricatures of the Most Holy* (1819 and 1821), *Anthropology* (1822),[48] and the novel *The Four Norwegians*,[49] or else from the last works Steffens published just before he

---

I saw Prof. Sibbern there (in the Estates) (just as Steffens saw Thorvaldsen at the coronation where he was not present.)" (*Pap.* VI B 201 / *P*, Supplement, p. 131).

44 Henrik Steffens, *Christliche Religionsphilosophie*, vols. 1–2, Breslau: Josef Max 1839 (*ASKB* 797–798).

45 Henrik Steffens, *Nachgelassene Schriften. Mit einem Vorworte von Schelling*, Berlin: E.H. Schroeder 1846 (*ASKB* 799).

46 Steffens, *Was ich erlebte*, Although Kierkegaard cites the German edition from his personal library, a Danish translation was already available at the time: *Hvad jeg oplevede: Nedskrevet efter hukommelsen*, vols. 1–10, Copenhagen: C. Steen 1840–45. There has since also been a much abridged, one-volume English translation made of *Was ich erlebte*, called *The Story of My Career, as a Student at Freiberg and Jena, and as Professor at Halle, Breslau and Berlin, With Personal Reminiscences of Goethe, Schiller, Schelling, Schleiermacher, Fichte, Novalis, Schlegel, Neander, and others*, trans. by William L. Gage, Boston: Gould & Lincoln 1863.

47 *Pap.* VI B 29, p. 106 / *CUP2*, 20.

48 Henrik Steffens, *Anthropologie*, vols. 1–2, Breslau: Josef Max 1822 (*ASKB* 795–796). Although it is impossible to be certain, Kierkegaard's mistaken reference to Steffens' *Anthropologie* (see *SKS* 20, 424, NB5:137a / *JP* 3, 2641) and perhaps also his letter to Sibbern in 1841 (*B&A*, vol. 1, pp. 83–4 / *LD*, Letter 55, pp. 106–7) give some support to the view that Kierkegaard did read at least part of the *Anthropologie*.

49 Originally in German as Henrik Steffens, *Die vier Norweger: Ein Cyklus von Novellen*, vols. 1–6, Breslau: Josef Max 1828 (Danish translation: *De fire Nordmænd. En Cyclus af*

died: that is, *Christian Philosophy of Religion* and *What I Experienced.* Kierkegaard does not cite, and may not have read, Steffens' posthumous writings.[50] Apart from Steffens' works in natural science, his novels, and of course his Copenhagen lectures, these books constitute the most important, and certainly the lengthiest, part of Steffens' scholarly writing. Kierkegaard's references to these works in unpublished writings (notebooks, loose papers, and drafts) fall into three periods: 1835–38, during Kierkegaard's student days; 1841–46, as he was writing his early pseudonymous works; and 1847–48, as he was writing mainly religious works. The two cases in which Kierkegaard made explicit reference to Steffens in the published writings (*Concept of Irony* and *Either/Or I*) will be discussed in the third section of this essay.

A. 1835–38

The decade in Berlin during which Steffens achieved international fame was also the period during which Kierkegaard pursued his studies and, in the middle of which, Kierkegaard came upon Steffens' writings in Copenhagen. During the period 1836–37 Kierkegaard took notes on two of these long works, the two-volume *Caricatures of the Most Holy* and the three-volume novel *The Four Norwegians*, from both of which he later incorporated ideas into his own writings. In both works Kierkegaard found stimulating resources for reflection, particularly regarding topics such as mythology, the origins of language, and the importance of intuition, that had been popular among Romantic philosophers.

Kierkegaard's first reference to Steffens' writings came in a letter written to a classmate, Peter Engel Lind (1814–1903), on July 6, 1835, during the summer at Gilleleje when Kierkegaard was pondering the direction for his own life. In the letter he writes that the task of focusing the "mirror" of reflection upon his inner self "pleases me because I see that I am able to do it, because I feel I have strength enough to hold the mirror, whether it shows me my ideal or my caricature, those two extremes between which life constantly moves, as H. Steffens says."[51] Just six months later (January 13, 1836) he purchased *Caricatures of the Most Holy* at Reitzels, and by the following fall he had worked through the nearly 1,200 pages of that work and begun taking notes on various passages that fit in with his own reflections.

Accordingly, on September 28, 1836, Kierkegaard copied out a passage from near the end of volume, one that describes European languages as "having meaning only for the ear," and which states that a language in which the accentuation matches the inner changes of mood "is truly called a *Christian* language and points to the

---

Noveller ved Heinrich Steffens, vols. 1–3 (vols. 4–6 in *Henrich Steffens's samlede Fortællinger*, vols. 1–21, trans. by J.R. Reiersen, ed. by Carl Frederik Güntelberg, Copenhagen: C. Steens Forlag 1834–45), Copenhagen: C. Steens Forlag 1835 (*ASKB* 1586–1588)).

50 Kierkegaard does, however, quote a saying from Schelling's preface to the volume in his notebooks (see *SKS*, 18, 297, JJ:471 / *KJN* 2, 274) and in his draft for the "Moral" of his unfinished work "Writing Sampler" (see *Pap.* VII-2 B 274:24, p. 335 / *WS*, p. 90).

51 *B&A*, vol. 1, p. 38 / *LD*, Letter 5, p. 49.

victory of love over the law."[52] Kierkegaard, however, applied Steffens' words to make a different point from that which Steffens made in the original text. He distinguished between, on the one hand, Greek and Latin poetry, which depends upon the "quantity" (length) of the vowels in a syllable, and, on the other hand, poetry in modern languages, which depends upon a syllabic accent. Steffens had been contrasting non-European and the European languages, but the distinction Kierkegaard drew was between the classical and the Romantic.

In another notebook entry relating to language, Kierkegaard pointed to Steffens' whole philosophy as an especially bold form of metaphor. "There could be some very interesting investigations of the various uses of metaphor in various languages and at various levels of development,"[53] Kierkegaard writes. "In living language we use images more casually; there is a certain fragrance which is shed over the style but which generally does not actually displace the essential expression."[54] He then contrasts this modern approach with the classical practice of separating the metaphor from the development of the story, before he goes on to put Steffens into a third category: "It should also be noted that the nature philosophers who see in all nature a metaphor of human life (for example, *Karikaturen des Heiligsten* II, Introduction) constitute a special mode."[55] Kierkegaard also recopied a series of loose pieces of paper telling about the musical in language, and he added a passage in German from the second volume of Steffens' work, remarking: "Likewise, Steffens speaks about how music can approach a human being 'in the self-seeking of wildly agitated tones' (cf. *Caricatures of the Most Holy*, second part, p. 103). Oct. 9, 1836."[56]

At the start of 1837 Kierkegaard began commenting on Steffens' three-volume novel *The Four Norwegians*. Within this long narrative Kierkegaard found many examples of that "self-seeking" he had so admired in Steffens before. In one notebook entry, for example, Kierkegaard complimented Steffens for his skill in telling stories to children, treating the children as "self-seeking" individuals. "Regarding the *way* in which I think it necessary, in all teaching and all up-bringing of children, to allow the child *to bring forth life in himself in all stillness*, I now find a good comment in Steffens' *4 Norwegians*, which I have been reading these days."[57] Not all references were as closely assimilated into Kierkegaard's reflections as that one, however. In another entry Kierkegaard merely copied down from Steffens' novel a passage about Roland, as an example of a man of heroic excellence.[58]

During this period Kierkegaard was reading widely in Romantic authors, and Steffens was neither his sole nor even necessarily his most helpful source. At one

---

52 *Pap.* I A 250 / *JP* 3, 2304. The passage Kierkegaard refers to in the note is Steffens, *Caricaturen des Heiligsten*, vol. 1, p. 350.

53 *Pap.* I A 251 / *JP* 3, 2305.

54 Ibid.

55 Ibid.

56 *Pap.* I A 260. Kierkegaard quotes the Steffens passage and its reference in German.

57 *SKS* 17, 131, BB:37 / *KJN* 1, 125. In the passage referred to in Steffens' novel, a mother tells how her half-grown daughter, Dorothea, by tenderly caring for her dolls, remains in the realm of healthy childhood, which hovers between fairy tales and real life (*SKS* K17, 248–9).

58 *SKS* 17, 138, BB:48 / *KJN* 1, 131–2.

point, for example, Kierkegaard remarked that he had a greater debt to Clemens Brentano (1778–1842) than he did to Steffens, with respect to the concept of presentiment. After praising Brentano's story *Little Ane* for its masterful treatment of the presentiment of evil, Kierkegaard went on to commend Steffens much less enthusiastically than he had Brentano:

> Regarding presentiment, there is also quite a lot in Steffens' *The 4 Norwegians*, not scholarly research, that is, but elements of it, except that, with him, it has become rather monotonous, in that each of his heroes begins practically every one of his more important and, in the novel, more gripping lines by talking about the Norwegian mountains, so that besides the vagueness it must needs have, their presentiment also has something abstract about it. Their consciousness contains too few other factors that might at least let such things be intimated.[59]

Steffens simply had not developed the characterization of his heroes sufficiently that they could exemplify such a profound concept of presentiment.

B. 1841–46

Once Kierkegaard began writing his own books, Steffens references turned up in them, or in their drafts, or in comments about them, for example, in his 1841 dissertation, *The Concept of Irony*, *Either/Or I* (1843), *The Concept of Anxiety* (1844), *Stages on Life's Way* (1845), and the *Concluding Unscientific Postscript* (1846). With the first two of these books Kierkegaard used Steffens as a significant part of the argument and mentioned his name explicitly in the text, so that they deserve separate treatment in the third section of this article. In the other three books the references to Steffens are either in the draft, in one case for *The Concept of Anxiety* and in another for the *Concluding Unscientific Postscript*; or, in a third case, the reference serves as a separate comment on the text of "In vino veritas," in *Stages on Life's Way*. The most important of these references comes in a 1844 draft for *The Concept of Anxiety*, which mentions Steffens as a source for his treatment of "objective anxiety," that is to say, the anxiousness that one may ascribe to nature itself, not because it was created anxious, but because it "is placed in an entirely different light because of Adam's sin."[60] Physical nature itself is different as a result of human sin, and the "nature philosophers" are just the ones to emphasize this fact: "Some men of Schelling's school have been especially aware of the alteration that has taken place in nature because of sin," the pseudonym Vigilius Haufniensis

---

59 *SKS* 17, 43–4, AA:23 / *KJN* 1, 37. The commentary in *SKS* K17, 109, illustrates this stylistic feature with a passage from *De fire Normænd*, 3:314–15. In an undated loose paper Kierkegaard elaborates on the difference between the kind of presentiment of evil found in Clemens Brentano and the kind in Steffens' novel: "On the whole *The Norwegian* is remarkable with regard to presentiment—the oppressive presentiment which is here developed almost to monotony—is not presentiment usually found in connection with evil, original sin." (*Pap.* II A 588 / *JP* 3, 3555)

60 *SKS* 4, 363 / *CA* 58.

remarks,[61] leaving unspecified who these men might be. The draft specifies them: "Some men, particularly of the Schelling school, like Schubert, Eschenmayer, Görres, Steffens."[62] According to Haufniensis, however, when such followers of Schelling go on and ascribe anxiety to inanimate nature, they are simply confusing the two subject areas of dogmatics and natural philosophy.[63] *Stages on Life's Way*, too, has its tie to Steffens, as it interprets the first part of the book as a whole in terms of one of Steffens' favorite terms, "caricature." In an undated loose paper Kierkegaard reflected that all of the characters from the "In vino veritas" section of the book are, in one way or another, "caricatures of the most holy," because of the way each of the five speakers distort the nature of women.[64] In fact, however, the reference to Steffens' book here is misleading, since the way Kierkegaard is using the term "caricature" does not conform to Steffens' technical terminology. Steffens' approach in his book is to start from two opposite caricatures and to analyze each of them, with the goal of identifying the ideal type that lies between them,[65] while all Kierkegaard needs for his comment about the characters in "In vino veritas" is for the term "caricature" to be used in a non-technical sense.[66] The reference in the *Concluding Unscientific Postscript* is again only in a draft, part of a long outburst against Grundtvig in which the pseudonym Johannes Climacus compares Steffens' literary style to Grundtvig's. The outcome of the comparison is easy to predict. Steffens' remark in his 1802 lectures that "Nero, not Brutus, was the last Roman," is "unjustified," Climacus writes, but at least it is "short, ingeniously expressed, provocative," compared to Grundtvig's "italicized, yard long annually recurring lecture" on that sort of topic.[67]

In addition to the above citations, Kierkegaard also read and took notes on at least some of the 10 volumes of the memoirs, *What I Experienced*, that Steffens wrote toward the end of his life, but none of the references later turned up in Kierkegaard's published works. In 1843, for example, Kierkegaard jotted down in his notebook an entertaining story about a man who wore a wig and could not function unless he wore it and who finally became insane.[68] Another time, in the margin of a draft for "Nebuchadnezzar's Dream" in *Stages on Life's Way*, Kierkegaard gave an amusing twist to the title of Steffens' memoirs, by calling it "*Was ich erlebte* [What I experienced] when I was an ox."[69] The closest Kierkegaard came to including any of

61 *SKS* 4, 363–4 / *CA*, 59–60.

62 *Pap.* V B 53:18 / *CA*, Supplement, p. 187; Cf. also *SKS* K4, 423.

63 *SKS* 4, 364 / *CA*, 60.

64 *Pap.* V A 110 / *JP* 5, 5755.

65 See Steffens, *Caricaturen des Heiligsten*, vol. 2, pp. 211–15.

66 Andrew J. Burgess, "Caricatures and the Comic in the Early Journals," *Kierkegaard Studies Yearbook*, 2003, pp. 125–42, especially p. 141.

67 *Pap.* VI B 29, p. 106 / *CUP2*, Supplement, p. 20. Kierkegaard misquotes Steffens here, since in his Copenhagen lectures Steffens actually writes "Cato, not Brutus"; Henrik Steffens, *Indledning til phlosophiske Forelæsninger*, ed. by Johnny Kondrup, Copenhagen: C.A. Reitzel 1996, p. 128.

68 *SKS* 18, 192, JJ:161 / *KJN* 2, 178. The story is found in Steffens, *Was ich erlebte*, vol. 7, pp. 215–16.

69 *Pap.* V B 132 / *SLW*, Supplement, p. 608.

these references in his publications was in his draft for "Writing Sampler," where he parenthetically brought up Steffens' claim that he "saw Thorvaldsen at the coronation where he was not present,"[70] but the "Writing Sampler" was never completed.

The only comment of any substance that Kierkegaard made about a passage in Steffens' memoirs was on the topic of the "leap," and on that topic Kierkegaard found Steffens to be badly mixed up. In the passage Steffens had argued against the possibility of spontaneous generation, discussing efforts to bring in religious considerations.[71] Kierkegaard responds with puzzlement to Steffens' claim: "One cannot see whether it is a reflection on nature, a bold expression of wonder, or whether the objection against a *generatio aequivoca* or spontaneous transition is drawn from ethics, from which it should be drawn. The dialectical point is completely lacking."[72] Kierkegaard's criticism of Steffens here is similar to the one he made earlier in *The Concept of Anxiety* about the "nature philosophers" generally, that they tended to blur the distinctions between dogmatics and natural philosophy.[73]

C. 1847–48

Finally, during 1847, as Kierkegaard was engaged, for the most part, in his own explicitly religiously authorship, he entered comments about Steffens' *Christian Philosophy of Religion* into his notebooks. The first of the comments is the most important, and it is not flattering: "Henrich Steffens is a good example of a well-meaning orthodoxy which does not hesitate to assert that if there is in Christianity only the slightest thing which is to be subjected to the corrective of thinking in the sense that thinking is supposed to decide anything, then everything is lost—and which nevertheless itself *am Ende* remains in confusion."[74] Nonetheless, despite this dismissal of Steffens' project, Kierkegaard still continued to pick out selections from *Christian Philosophy of Religion* and record them in his notebooks. Only a few entries later in the same notebook comes a dated entry (October 3, 1847) containing two short quotations, in the original German, carefully noted so that he will be able to find them again: "Henrich Steffens, *Religions-Philosophie*, II, p. 260, *medio*: thus the frightful certainty expresses itself, that also inwardly, in history, evil = the standard. P. 262, the Savior has died for the whole world, but is only risen for Christians."[75] That same month Kierkegaard cited approvingly a remark by Steffens praising Kant for his honesty, even where Steffens did not agree with Kant: "Let us rather say it straightforwardly with honest Kant, who declares the relationship to God to be a kind of mental weakness, a hallucination. To be involved with something unseen is this, too. Steffens quite properly quotes this somewhere in

70 *Pap.* VI B 201 / *WS*, 131, and see note 14, p. 193. Steffens' statement is in his *Was ich erlebte*, vol. 10, p. 369.

71 Steffens, *Was ich erlebte*, vol. 10, pp. 118–20, especially p. 118.

72 *Pap.* V C 9 / *JP* 3, 2351.

73 *SKS* 4, 364 / *CA*, 60.

74 *SKS* 20, 222, NB2:209 / *JP* 3, 3049.

75 *SKS* 20, 224, NB2:215 / *JP* 5, 6059. *SKS* K20, 218, notes that the second quotation is actually a shortened form of Steffens' text: "*Der Heiland, äußerte eine mir innig befreundete Person, sei für die ganze Welt gestorben, aber nur für die wahren Christen auferstanden.*"

his philosophy of religion."[76] Kierkegaard did not even lose his interest in Steffens' scientific observations, and a month later he wrote: "What remarkable things are told about the stork—that when the water is so low that it cannot drink, it throws in stones until the water is deep enough. I read this in several authors from antiquity, then in Montaigne, and now finally in Steffens' *Religions-Philosophie*."[77] The last citation from Steffens appeared during 1848, and it is simply a marginal reference[78] back to the Steffens remark Kierkegaard copied down a year earlier, about the frightful certainty of evil's power,[79] as Kierkegaard was pondering why there needed to be martyrs within a sinful world. In this way Steffens, who had inspired Kierkegaard during the period of the early pseudonymous writings, here draws Kierkegaard's attention even when he is putting together his most profound religious writings, such as *Practice in Christianity*. The irony is that Steffens, who had struggled all his life to get ahead and, after publicly changing his theological position, finally landed a position at the university of Berlin, still helped occasion this reflection by Kierkegaard on the topic of martyrdom.

IV. Steffens and Kierkegaard: On the Project of Combining Danish Romanticism and Christian Orthodoxy

The foregoing Steffens notebook entries and book references tell a story more complex than at first appears. Today Steffens is known for his 1802–04 Copenhagen lectures, and little attention is usually paid to his later career. When Kierkegaard, fresh from finishing his dissertation, journeyed to Berlin in 1841, however, the Steffens he went to hear was not the brash speculative mineralogist recently arrived from Jena, nor was Danish Romanticism what it once had been. During the intervening years Steffens had become an established professor whose just-published philosophy of religion consisted largely of traditional Christian dogmatics. Meanwhile, the aesthetics from Oehlenschläger, the man who with H.C. Ørsted had helped lead Danish Romanticism after Steffens left Denmark, had long ago been eclipsed by that of the Hegelian Johan Ludvig Heiberg (1791–1860),[80] for whose journal Kierkegaard had written some of his first essays.

---

76 *SKS* 20, 229, NB2:235 / *JP* 2, 2236. (See Steffens, *Christliche Religionsphilosophie*, vol. 2, pp. 212–13; *Kants gesammelte Schriften*, vols. 1–29, Abtheilungen 1–4, ed. by the Königlich-Preußischen Akademie der Wissenschaften, Berlin et al.: de Gruyter 1900–, Abtheilung 1 (*Werke*), vol. 6 (*Religion innerhalb der Grenzen der bloßen Vernunft* (1907)), p. 195. (English translation: *Religion Within the Boundaries of Mere Reason*, in *Religion and Rational Theology*, trans. and ed. by Allen W. Wood and George di Giovanni, Cambridge: Cambridge University Press 1996 (*The Cambridge Edition of the Works of Immanuel Kant*) see p. 210.)

77 *SKS* 20, 249, NB3:12 / *JP* 3, 2848. See Steffens, *Christian Philosophy of Religion*, vol. 1, p. 29; see also *SKS* K20, 246.

78 *SKS* 20, 424, NB5:137a / *JP* 3, 2641.

79 *SKS* 20, 224, NB2:215 / *JP* 5, 6059.

80 Paul, *Naturphilosophie und Frühromantik*, p. 211.

Among all that Kierkegaard wrote regarding Steffens, one document sums up the questions surrounding the relationship between the two men: the 1841 letter to Sibbern after he quit attending Steffens' lectures at the University of Berlin. Since his early student days Kierkegaard had been enthusiastic about Steffens. The first chance he had, he traveled to Berlin, hoping, among other things to hear Steffens. Instead, he quit going to the lectures and declined to have anything to do with Steffens or the other students from Denmark. From that time on, however, he continued to study works of Steffens and to make reading notes about him, more consistently, more positively, and for a longer period, than almost any other figure we know of the time. Instead of one question, there are really two: first, why should Kierkegaard be enthusiastic about Steffens in the first place?; and, second, why, without apparently changing the opinion of Steffens that he had formed in Berlin, did he keep reading him in such a positive way? The first question revolves around his appreciation for Danish Romanticism, but the second, and more difficult, question has to do with Kierkegaard and Steffens' attitude toward philosophy of religion and the possibilities for Christian dogmatics.

A. The Legacy of Danish Romanticism

The story of Kierkegaard's first and only encounter with Steffens in person is a familiar part of Kierkegaard lore. After successfully defending his doctoral dissertation in the summer of 1841, Kierkegaard left for Berlin on October 25, partly, at least, in order to attend lectures by Steffens. Surprisingly, however, Kierkegaard stopped attending Steffens' lectures after only a short while. Nonetheless, Kierkegaard continued for many years taking notes on each of Steffens' new, multi-volume works and incorporating some of their ideas into his own publications.

Kierkegaard mentioned his reasons for quitting Steffens' lectures in a pair of letters, one to Peter Johannes Spang (1796–1846), pastor of Holy Spirit Church in Copenhagen, and the other, a month later, to Sibbern. The letter to Spang strikes the flippant note of a Berlin tourist: "The streets are too broad for my liking and so are Steffens' lectures. One cannot see from one side to the other nor keep track of the passersby, just as with Steffens' lectures; but of course the passers-by are exceedingly interesting, just as Steffens' lectures are. I think Steffens resembles Reitzel. Have you seen him?—I do not mean Reitzel, but Steffens."[81] To Sibbern, on the other hand, Kierkegaard goes into much more detail than he does with Spang:

> So here I am in Berlin going to lectures. I am attending lectures by Marheineke, Werder, and Schelling. I have heard Steffens a few times and have also paid my fee to hear him, but oddly enough, he does not appeal to me at all. And I, who have read with such great enthusiasm much of what he has written, *Karrikaturen des Heiligsten*, to mention just one example, I, who had really looked forward to hearing him in order to ascertain for myself what is usually said about him, that he is matchless when it comes to monologue—I am utterly disappointed. His delivery seems so uncertain and hesitant that one begins to question what progress one is making, and when a flash of genius transfigures him, I miss that artistic awareness, that oratorical brilliance I

[81] *B&A*, vol. 1, p. 77 / *LD*, Letter 51, p. 97.

> have so often admired in his writings. He lectures on anthropology, but the material is essentially the same as that contained in his published book. So I prefer to read him. But his *Anthropologie* will always make fairly heavy reading for anybody not well versed in the natural sciences. — I am, by the way, sorry to find myself disappointed in this respect. That's why I have not called on him either. On the whole I live as isolated as possible and I am withdrawing more and more into myself.[82]

The explanation is puzzling. Kierkegaard says that he is "utterly disappointed" in Steffens' lectures because they are not as brilliant and inspiring as everyone else reported them to be. As a result, he does not even call on Steffens, as any student might be expected to do with such a genial host, who is also a compatriot, but instead withdraws into himself, keeping apart both from Steffens and from the other Danish students in Berlin.[83]

Still, this does not mean that Kierkegaard is rejecting Steffens and the Romantic philosophy he popularly represented. This can be seen by looking at the two books Kierkegaard published that explicitly mention Steffens' name and deal with his philosophy: his dissertation, *The Concept of Irony, With Continual Reference to Socrates*, which was written during two of the three years before this event in 1841; and the first part of *Either/Or*, which was published two years later, in 1843.

The discussion of Steffens in *The Concept of Irony* provides, on the whole, a positive role for Steffens' philosophy. The passage comes at a key point in the dissertation, in a section dealing with Socrates' use of myth. Unexpectedly Kierkegaard launches into an extended discussion about how a metaphor gains a wider and wider scope until it becomes a full-scale myth:

> When the metaphor finally acquires such dimensions that all existence becomes visible in it, this is the retrograde movement toward the mythical. Nature philosophy frequently provides examples of this. For example, H. Steffens' preface to *Karrikaturen des Heiligsten* is that kind of grand and ambitious metaphor in which nature-existence becomes a myth about the existence of spirit. Thus the metaphor overwhelms the individual—he loses his freedom, or rather he sinks into a state in which he does not have reality, because the metaphor now is not a free production and an artistic creation, and however busily thought inspects the particulars, however ingenious it is in making associations, however cosily it adapts its existence to them, it is still unable to separate the whole from the itself and make it appear light and fleeting in the sphere of pure poetry.[84]

---

82 *B&A*, vol. 1, pp. 83–4 / *LD*, Letter 55, pp. 106–7.

83 A letter from one of those Danish students (Caspar Wilhelm Smith) in Berlin reported that the Danish contingent then at the university, 15 strong, shared copies of the Danish newspapers *Fædrelandet* and *Corsaren* and also borrowed *Dagen* from Steffens. See Aagaard Olesen, "Kierkegaards Schelling," p. 40.

84 *SKS* 1, 157 / *CI*, 104. (See Steffens, *Caricaturen des Heiligsten*, vol. 2, pp. 1–215; see also *SKS* K1, p. 237.) Kierkegaard is plainly drawing on the entry in his notes where Steffens is identified as one of "the nature philosophers who see in all nature a metaphor of human life." (*Pap.* I A 251 / *JP* 3, 2305) Cf. Bukdahl, "Vejen til myten og eventyret," p. 17. (English translation: "Henrich Steffens: The Way to Myth and Fairy Tale," p. 14.)

After this statement Kierkegaard then develops the theme in the lines that follow. The problem he finds is that, as soon as Steffens posits a metaphor, "the metaphor overwhelms the individual," and "he loses his freedom."[85] Although the context here is a discussion of Plato's myths, the description of how myths or metaphors function fits Steffens much better than it does Plato.

It is significant that in this passage, and also in the draft for *The Concept of Anxiety*,[86] Kierkegaard identifies Steffens as a specialist in "nature philosophy" or "natural philosophy," rather than as a "Romantic," but that in the second part of the dissertation he criticizes the so-called "Romantic ironists," particularly through Friedrich Schlegel's novel *Lucinde*.[87] The reason for the terminology goes back to a division years before in Jena, between Schelling and Steffens, on the one hand, and Friedrich and August Schlegel, on the other.[88] Starting from Schelling, Steffens (along with Ørsted) and their "nature philosophy" helped lead early Danish Romanticism along a different path from that followed by the early Romanticism in Germany associated with the Schlegel brothers. The cosmic metaphors Kierkegaard's dissertation ascribes to Steffens are especially characteristic of the Danish tradition.

Nonetheless, the overlap between the early German and the early Danish Romanticisms is sufficient that Steffens' all-encompassing metaphors can still be pressed into service to make a point in a work representing the other, Schlegel tradition, and that is just what happens in Kierkegaard's next book, *Either/Or*. In his essay, "The Immediate Erotic Stages or the Musical-Erotic," Mr. A, the pseudonymous author of the first part of *Either/Or*, draws from some ideas deriving from Steffens and which Kierkegaard had taken down in his notebooks, and at one point Mr. A explicitly acknowledges the debt:

> Language addresses itself to the ear. No other medium does this. The ear, in turn, is the most spiritually qualified sense. Most people, I believe, will agree with me on this point if anyone wishes more information about this, I refer him to the preface to Steffens' *Karrikaturen des Heiligsten*. Apart from language, music is the only medium that is addressed to the ear. Here again is an analogy and a testimony to the sense in which music is a language.[89]

Of the presupposition he needs, that music is a language, Mr. A feels secure, since he has no less an authority than Steffens on his side.

Unlike the passage in the dissertation, this reference from Steffens in "The Immediate Erotic Stages or the Musical-Erotic" is an integral step in the argument of the whole essay. Without the testimony from Steffens the case the pseudonym Mr. A is making, that Mozart's opera *Don Giovanni* is the supreme example of human art, could not get off the ground. The argument closely follows the pattern used by the

---

85 Ibid.

86 *SKS* 4, 363–4 / *CA*, 59–60.

87 *SKS* 1, 321–34 / *CI*, 286–301.

88 Paul, *Naturphilosophie und Universalromantik*, p. 202.

89 *SKS* 2, 74 / *EO1*, 68. The section of the introduction to Steffens' second volume that deals with language comes on pages 82–120 of *Caricatures of the Most Holy* (*SKS* K2–3, 118 / *EO1*, Notes, p. 617, note 23).

prominent Danish Hegel aesthete Johan Ludvig Heiberg in his *Introductory Lecture for the Logic Course at the Royal Military College*.[90] Heiberg adopts a Hegelian style of dialectic in order to demonstrate, first that poetry is the highest form of art, and then, that the Spanish poet Calderón is the supreme master of "lyric drama," which is the "highest peak of poetry."[91] Mr. A, for his part, follows a quite similar set of steps to show that Mozart's *Don Giovanni* is the supreme example of art. The most obvious difference between the two arguments is the new premise Mr. A draws from Steffens, that music is a language, so that the supreme form of art will have to include a musical element. Mr. A modifies and does not simply take over Steffens' description of the relationship of music and language—fortunately, since Steffens' account abounds in overextended and imprecise metaphors and fanciful scientific analogies—but he does insist on the analogy between language and music, and that is mainly what he needs for his argument.

The respect for, and at the same time, critical and limited appropriation of parts of Steffens' *Caricatures* and of his novel *The Four Norwegians*, that Kierkegaard shows here in the first part of *Either/Or*, were already in evidence in his 1836–38 notes and notebook entries.[92] The specific section of *Caricatures* he drew on from Steffens here was particularly important for him.[93] In these pages Steffens had stretched to the limit a biological concept, *Selbstsucht* (roughly translatable, in varying contexts, as "self-seeking," "egoism," or "self-orientation") until it became a metaphor that covered a basic drive in all living things, even, indeed especially, at the intellectual and spiritual level. One snippet that attracted Kierkegaard's attention was Steffens' remark that music can approach a human being "in the self-seeking of wildly agitated tones."[94] Kierkegaard himself very rarely employed the German word *Selbstsucht*, but about three months later, as he was beginning to read Steffens'

---

90 Johan Ludvig Heiberg, *Indlednings-Foredrag til det i November 1834 begyndte logiske Cursus paa den kongelige militaire Høiskole*, Copenhagen: J.H. Schubothe 1835, see pp. 14–17. Reprinted in *Prosaiske Skrifter*, vols. 1–11, Copenhagen: C.A. Reitzel 1861, vol. 1, see pp. 478–81; English translation: *Introductory Lecture to the Logic Course at the Royal Military College that Began in November 1834*, in *Heiberg's Introductory Lecture to the Logic Course and Other Texts*, trans. and ed. by Jon Stewart, Copenhagen: C.A. Reitzel 2007 (*Texts from Golden Age Denmark*, vol. 3), see pp. 51–6. Cf. also Jon Stewart, *Kierkegaard's Relations to Hegel Reconsidered*, Cambridge: Cambridge University Press 2003, pp. 210–11.

91 Heiberg, *Introductory Lecture to the Logic Course*, p. 56.

92 Kierkegaard also corrects Steffens at some points. One example of such correction comes in the margin of *Pap.* I A 250 / *JP* 3, 2304. In this passage Steffens had written that a language with accentuation (that is, a European language) "is truly called a Christian language and points to the victory of love over the law." In the margin Kierkegaard changes this, replacing the word "Christian" with "what I would call: romantic."

93 Steffens, *Caricaturen des Heiligsten*, vol. 2, pp. 93–7.

94 *Pap.* I A 260. The significance of the remark is underlined by the fact that, whereas all the other six remarks from that date had been recopied from several months earlier, back in August; only the Steffens reference had to be added here. This recopying is indicated by another entry, *Pap.* I A 263, also dated October 9, 1836, which says (presumably concerning *Pap.* I A 256–62): "NB: All these remarks are found on some pieces of paper and seem all to stem from the month of August. The remark about H. Steffens and its relation to the main remark is quoted from a later kind and date."

novel *The Four Norwegians*, he used that word again, without any explicit reference to Stephens, but this time following up the analogy between language and music by writing about "the *Selbstsucht* of "words" rather than of "tones":

> There are people who speak by associating ideas, but far beneath this there is a standpoint I would call "the *Selbstsucht* of words," where one word carries another along with it, where words which are often in each other's company seek one another out—something like what would happen if the words in a dictionary came alive and wanted to position themselves in the order to which they had become accustomed.[95]

Just as each musical tone is to find its own place in a composition, so each word is to find its own place in a text without being forced into sentences and paragraphs.

Kierkegaard's application of the term *Selbstsucht* here is typical of his highly personal, selective appropriation of Steffens' terminology. From out of a confusing tangle of interlocking metaphors Kierkegaard plucks a single phrase, "the *Selbstsucht* of tones," and then puts it to work for his own purposes. Steffens' cosmic metaphors he simply ignores. When the book *Caricatures of the Most Holy* was published, it was primarily a political document, trying to overcome the divide between reactionary and liberal movements in the aftermath of the Napoleonic wars. Coming to that text many years later and in a different historical context, Kierkegaard found Steffens' remarks about language to be the book's main attraction, and instead of reading Steffens' notion of caricature as political and social critique, he emphasized the contrast between the ideals, and the caricatures of those ideals, within a person's own life. This does not mean that Kierkegaard was ignoring what Steffens' book had said, only that he was focusing upon a different target than the book had once had, so that language and its relation to a person's life, rather than politics, became the center of interest.

The answer to the question posed at the start of this section is clear. Did Kierkegaard turn away from Steffens' ideas after his disappointing 1841 encounter in Berlin? Clearly the answer is no. The first Kierkegaard book after that event, *Either/Or*, paid at least as much attention to Steffens as did the dissertation, which had come before. In the years that followed, moreover, Kierkegaard continued to refer to Steffens in his notes and notebooks with remarkable regularity, even though he never again referred to Steffens by name in his published works.

B. The Possibility of an Orthodox Christian Dogmatics

One of the most puzzling features of the relationship between Steffens and Kierkegaard is the disproportion between the attention Kierkegaard gives to Steffens and what he gives to other, much better known figures, even after Kierkegaard had been disappointed with Steffens' Berlin lectures. Strangely, it is often easier to document from Kierkegaard's notebooks his reading of one of the main works of Steffens than it is of a philosopher such as Schelling, for example, or even Kant. Hardly a year went by in Kierkegaard's drafts or notebooks without a quotation, comment, or other reference relating to Steffens.

---

[95] *SKS* 18, 82, FF:34 / *KJN* 2, 75.

There are indeed good reasons why Kierkegaard might have wanted to read Steffens. For one thing, Kierkegaard simply enjoyed reading him. The "great enthusiasm" with which Kierkegaard's 1841 letter to Sibbern says he had read Steffens' books, and the appreciation for "that artistic awareness, that oratorical brilliance" he had found there,[96] remained, even after he became disappointed with Steffens otherwise.

Another possible reason was that Kierkegaard knew that Steffens, in addition to being a well-known scholar who had exerted influence on some of the leading Danish scholars of Kierkegaard's time, was also a writer of popular and semi-popular literature available in Danish. In addition to the translation of *The False Theology and the True Religion* in 1825, not long after it was written, 21 of his books had been translated into Danish by the mid-1840s, including 11 historical novels and the 10-volume memoirs,[97] and the memoirs were already being published in a second edition, part of which Kierkegaard owned. If Kierkegaard needed some figure to represent a movement such as "nature philosophy" to a Danish readership, Steffens would be just the person to choose.

In addition, there is also another reason to be considered, more important yet much more likely to be overlooked than the others, and that is Kierkegaard's interest in Steffens' work on philosophy of religion. Early in his career Steffens had been forced to make his living in mineralogy, rather than the other side of his research interests, but after he took the position at Berlin in 1832, he had the opportunity to redress the balance, and in 1839 he published in two big volumes of what might be considered to be the culmination of his efforts in this area, the *Christian Philosophy of Religion*.[98] The publication of this work, just as Kierkegaard was writing his dissertation, may help to explain part of the disappointment Kierkegaard expressed to Sibbern about Steffens' lectures in 1841. "He lectures on anthropology," Kierkegaard writes in his letter, "but the material is essentially the same as in the published book. So I prefer to read him."[99] A letter that same month from another Danish student to Sibbern helps to explain the background of the situation: "Steffens has canceled his lecture on philosophy of religion, because Schelling is lecturing about 'Philosophy of Revelation.' Therefore I am merely listening to him on the topic of anthropology."[100] Steffens, ever deferential to his younger colleague, had turned over the spotlight to Schelling. Kierkegaard, who would surely have preferred to hear lectures on Christian philosophy of religion rather than anthropology, started listening to Steffens' lectures for a while but soon dropped out.

If the reason Kierkegaard continued reading Steffens was in order to study his philosophy of religion, however, little evidence of that research shows up in Kierkegaard's notebooks for the following period, and no references at all to Steffens' book on the subject until six years later. Even then, in 1847, Kierkegaard's

---

96 *B&A*, vol. 1, pp. 83–4 / *LD*, Letter 55, pp. 106–7.

97 *Henrich Steffens's Samlede Fortællinger*.

98 Steffens, *Christliche Religionsphilosophie*.

99 *B&A*, vol. 1, pp. 83–4 / *LD*, Letter 55, pp. 106–7.

100 Letter from J.A. Bornemann to Sibbern, December 15, 1841, see Aagaard Olesen, "Kierkegaards Schelling," p. 43.

evaluation of the book seems uncompromisingly negative. "Steffens," he writes, "is a good example of a well-meaning orthodoxy," but his thinking is badly confused. The example Kierkegaard picks is the concept of miracle, but it could have been any of several others in the book. Steffens wants to use philosophy—to defend the concept of miracles against philosophy. Steffens sets out to show "that miracles are an obstacle to thought," but to do that he "provides a theory which, *thinking*, finds the inclusion of miracles to be entirely in order. Is this not the primacy of thought if it decides that I may very well believe in miracles."[101]

Even Steffens himself may have suspected that he could not carry off this kind of argument. As he was working on the manuscript for the book, he found himself unsure whether he could write it, and he tried to renew his relationship with Schelling in order to receive some advice before he put the book into print.[102] After that appeal had been ignored and the book was about to appear in print, he wrote to Schelling again and confessed that it would be appearing "too soon."[103] Later Schelling complained to a friend, confidentially, that, if Steffens knew the book was bad, "why did he let it be published?"[104] Why indeed?

The irony in the situation is that some of Kierkegaard's profoundest thoughts may have been inspired from Steffens' *Christian Philosophy of Religion*, and from the least likely part of the book at that. As one might expect even from a follower of Schelling, the topics for the two volumes are apportioned to two separate volumes, the first dealing with nature's "teleology," and the second with "ethics," which includes religion. The two parts differ not only in content but also in methodology. The goal of the first volume, as Steffens remarks at the very beginning of the book, is to "reconcile" natural philosophy and Christianity,[105] and this is the part that faces Kierkegaard's unsparing critique. The goal of the second volume, on the other hand, is to show how traditional Christian doctrines fit into the possibilities opened up by volume one. The list of doctrines is, in order: the origin of sin, the nature of evil, grace and human freedom, prayer, damnation, the situation after death, the church, holy scripture, sacraments, song, and the sermon. This kind of list would seem to be the last place to look for insights into philosophy of religion.

Nonetheless, in 1925 Torsten Bohlin published the discovery that the chapter on "Evil in Nature," in the second volume of Steffens' *Christian Philosophy of Religion*, is a source—and, as far as he could tell, the distinctive source—for *The Concept of Anxiety*'s key teaching about the "alteration" that takes place in human beings when sin enters the world. In his draft of *The Concept of Anxiety* Kierkegaard had identified Steffens as one of the "Schelling school" dealing with "objective anxiety,"[106] but to show that Stephens was also the source for Kierkegaard's distinctive views about

101 *SKS* 20, 222, NB2:209 / *JP* 3, 3049.

102 Hultberg, *Den ældre Henrich Steffens*, pp. 102–7.

103 Quoted from ibid., p. 106.

104 Ibid., p. 107.

105 Steffens, *Christliche Religionsphilosophie*, vol. 1, p. ii.

106 *Pap.* V B 53, 18 / *CA*, Supplement, p. 187. Cf. *SKS* K4, 423.

how the sin that is found in nature impacts human consciousness as well was something new.[107]

If Bohlin is right,[108] the implications of his discovery extend, beyond the interpretation of that particular section of *The Concept of Anxiety*, to the whole book, and to all the other early pseudonymous works besides, since it shows that Kierkegaard's reading of *Christian Philosophy of Religion* did not begin in 1847, when he began making entries about that book in his notebooks, but at least as early as 1844. Such an assumption is plausible in any case. Otherwise it would seem strange that, after Kierkegaard had set his heart on hearing Steffens on this topic back in 1841, he never got around to looking into the book until so many years later.

That implication, in turn, presents a daunting challenge to Kierkegaard scholarship. Kierkegaard's usual approach to Steffens is to isolate particular passages that attract him and then to appropriate them within very different contexts than they had occupied in the original text. Anyone looking to discover some fingerprints from the second volume of *Christian Philosophy of Religion* in Kierkegaard's writings might therefore need to pore over a vast number of unpromising-looking pages in Steffens, without any assurance that there ever was such influence or, even if there was, that any traces of it still remained in Kierkegaard's formulations. Yet the possibility that Kierkegaard might have been partially indebted to Steffens for some of his analyses of Christian doctrines cannot be discounted, because there are reasons to think that Kierkegaard would find Steffens' discussion of Christian doctrines attractive. For example, two of the objections that Grundtvig raised against Steffens during 1824 in a letter to J.P. Mynster—Steffens' use of historical-critical methods in approaching the Bible, and his praise of the Moravians[109]—might well, for Kierkegaard, have counted in Steffens' favor. Moreover, the dogmatic formulations employed by some other potential sources from which Kierkegaard might have borrowed (and in fact did borrow)—for example, from traditionalists such as Karl Gottlieb Bretschneider (1776–1848) or Karl Hase (1800–90), or from right-wing Hegelian theologians—came pre-packaged in various schematisms. Of course, Steffens held strong philosophical commitments too, but the logical structures within which Steffens worked were looser and less confining than those of many of the other philosophers and theologians of the time, making it easier than otherwise for Kierkegaard to push aside the packaging and extract particular ideas he could integrate into his own thinking.

In his definitive treatment of the relationship between Steffens and Kierkegaard, Helge Hultberg concluded that Steffens might be called Kierkegaard's predecessor

---

107 Torsten Bohlin, *Kierkegaards dogmatiska åskådning i dess historiska sammanhang*, Stockholm: Svenska kyrkans diakonistyrelses bokförlag 1925, pp. 155–7; Bohlin, *Kierkegaards dogmatische Anschauung in ihrem geschichtlichen Zusammenhang*, trans. into German by Ilse Meyer-Lüne, Gütersloh: C. Bertelsmann 1927, pp. 188–90.

108 Bohlin's interpretation is acknowledged by Paul, *Naturphilosophie und Universalromantik*, p. 213, and Bukdahl, "Vejen til myten og eventyret," p. 20. (English translation: "Henrich Steffens: The Way to Myth and Fairy Tale," p. 17.)

109 Hultberg, *Den ældre Henrich Steffens*, p. 76.

better than any other person. "Although Kierkegaard could not see it," he notes, "Steffens is in a certain sense his preparation—but, note well, not because Steffens was an individualist, 'existentialist,' but, on the contrary, because he tried not to be one. He is the missing link between German (and Danish) idealism and Kierkegaard."[110] Like Kierkegaard, Steffens wanted to clarify philosophically some major Christian doctrines, but after writing *Christian Philosophy of Religion*, even Steffens seems to have realized the task was beyond him. Kierkegaard must have recognized Steffens' shortcomings by 1841, if not before. Although after that time Kierkegaard still kept checking all the Steffens sources he owned and recording passages from them in his notebooks, he does not give any indication he thought Steffens was up to the job. If the task were to be accomplished, Kierkegaard would have to take it on himself.

[110] Hultberg, "Steffens und Kierkegaard," *Kierkegaardiana*, vol. 10, 1977, p. 199. Hultberg is responding to the old misunderstanding of Kierkegaard as a radical individualist, as claimed by such writers as Harald Høffding in *Danske Filosofer*, Copenhagen: Gyldendal 1905, p. 47, and Vilhelm Andersen, in *Illustreret dansk Litteraturhistorie*, vols. 1–6, Copenhagen: Gyldendal 1916–34, vol. 3 (1921), p. 19.

Bibliography

I. Steffens' Works in The Auction Catalogue *of Kierkegaard's Library*

Caricaturen des Heiligsten: in zwei Theilen, vols. 1–2, Leipzig: F.A. Brockhaus 1919–21 (*ASKB* 793–794).

Anthropologie, vols. 1–2, Breslau: Josef Max 1822 (*ASKB* 795–796).

Christliche Religionsphilosophie, vols. 1–2, Breslau: Josef Max 1839 (*ASKB* 797–798).

Nachgelassene Schriften. Mit einem Vorworte von Schelling, Berlin: E.H. Schroeder 1846 (*ASKB* 799).

De fire Nordmænd. En Cyclus af Noveller ved Heinrich Steffens, vols. 1–3 (vols. 4–6 in *Henrich Steffens's samlede Fortællinger*, vols. 1–21, trans. by J.R. Reiersen, ed. by Carl Frederik Güntelberg, Copenhagen: C. Steens Forlag 1834–45), Copenhagen: C. Steens Forlag 1835 (*ASKB* 1586–1588).

Was ich erlebte. Aus der Erinnerung niedergeschrieben, vols. 1–10, Breslau: Joseph Max 1841–44 (*ASKB* 1834–1843).

II. Works in The Auction Catalogue *of Kierkegaard's Library that Discuss Steffens*

Baader, Franz von, *Fermenta Cognitionis*, vols. 1–5, Berlin: Reimer 1822–24, vol. 4, 1823, pp. 22–3; p. 26 (*ASKB* 394).

—— *Philosophische Schriften und Aufsätze*, vols. 1–2, Münster: Theissing 1831–32, vol. 2, p. 58, note; p. 65, note (*ASKB* 400–401).

—— *Revision der Philosopheme der Hegel'schen Schule bezüglich auf das Christenthum. Nebst zehn Thesen aus einer religiösen Philosophie*, Stuttgart: S.G. Liesching 1839, p. 162, note (*ASKB* 416).

Bruch, Johann Friedrich, *Die Lehre von den göttlichen Eigenschaften*, Hamburg: Friedrich Perthes 1842, p. 122, note (*ASKB* 439).

Erdmann, Johann Eduard, *Vorlesungen über Glauben und Wissen als Einleitung in die Dogmatik und Religionsphilosophie*, Berlin: Duncker und Humblot 1837, p. 111 (*ASKB* 479).

Fichte, Immanuel Hermann, *Sätze zur Vorschule der Theologie*, Stuttgart and Tübingen: J.G. Cotta 1826, p. 174; p. 176; p. 182; p. 193 (*ASKB* 501).

—— *Grundzüge zum Systeme der Philosophie*, vols. 1–2, Heidelberg: I.C.B. Mohr 1833–36, vol. 1, p. 215, note (*ASKB* 502–503).

—— *Die speculative Theologie oder allgemeine Religionslehre*, Heidelberg: Akademische Buchhandlung von J.C.B. Mohr 1846 (vol. 3, in *Grundzüge zum Systeme der Philosophie*), p. 570 (*ASKB* 509; for vols. 1–2, see *ASKB* 502–503).

—— *System der Ethik*, vols. 1–2.1, Leipzig: Dyk 1850–51, vol. 1, *Die philosophischen Lehren von Recht, Staat und Sitte in Deutschland, Frankreich und England von der Mitte des Achtzehnten Jahrhunderts bis zur Gegenwart*, 1850, pp. 452–65 (*ASKB* 510–511) (for vol. 2.2, Leipzig: Dyk 1853, see *ASKB* 504).

Heine, Heinrich, *Die romantische Schule*, Hamburg: Hoffmann und Campe 1836, pp. 178–9 (*ASKB* U 63).

Martensen, Hans Lassen, *Den christelige Dogmatik*, Copenhagen: C.A. Reitzel 1849, p. 250; p. 387; p. 547, note (*ASKB* 653).

Michelet, Karl Ludwig, "Steffens," in his *Geschichte der letzten Systeme der Philosophie in Deutschland von Kant bis Hegel*, vols. 1–2, Berlin: Duncker und Humblot 1837–38, vol. 2, pp. 505–60 (*ASKB* 678–679).

[Møller, Jens], "H. Steffens om Religiøsitet og Videnskabelighed i de Nordamerikanske Fristater," *Nyt theologisk Bibliothek*, vols. 1–20, ed. by Jens Møller, Copenhagen: Andreas Seidelin 1821–32, vol. 3, 1823, pp. 138–9 (*ASKB* 336–345).

[Møller, Poul Martin], *Efterladte Skrifter af Poul M. Møller*, vols. 1–3, ed. by Christian Winther, F.C. Olsen, and Christen Thaarup, Copenhagen: C.A. Reitzel 1839–43, vol. 3, pp. 14–15; p. 206 (*ASKB* 1574–1576).

Mynster, Jakob Peter, *Blandede Skrivter*, vols. 1–3, Copenhagen: Gyldendal 1852–53 [vols. 4–6, Copenhagen: Gyldendal 1855–57], vol. 3, p. 163 (*ASKB* 358–363).

Ørsted, Anders Sandøe, *Af mit Livs og min Tids Historie*, vols. 1–2, Copenhagen: Gyldendal 1851–52 (vols. 3–4, Copenhagen: Gyldendal 1855–57), vol. 1, p. 95 (*ASKB* 1959–1960).

Rosenkranz, Karl, *Erinnerungen an Karl Daub*, Berlin: Duncker und Humblot 1837, p. 22 (*ASKB* 743).

—— *Psychologie oder die Wissenschaft vom subjectiven Geist*, Königsberg: Bornträger 1837, p. 22; p. 36; p. 42; p. 134 (*ASKB* 744).

—— *Schelling. Vorlesungen, gehalten im Sommer 1842 an der Universität zu Königsberg*, Danzig: Fr. Sam. Gerhard 1843, p. XIV; p. 41; p. 77; p. 85; p. 92; p. 109; p. 138; p. 149; p. 169; p. 207; p. 319 (*ASKB* 766).

Rudelbach, Andreas, *De ethices principiis hucusque vulgo traditis, disquisito historico-philosophica, quœ systematum ethicorum secundum primas causas amplioris criseos introductionem continet*, Copenhagen: Hartv. Frid. Popp 1822, p. 110, note; p. 159, note (*ASKB* 750).

—— *Om Psalme-Literaturen og Psalmebogs-Sagen, Historisk-kritiske Undersøgelser*, vol. 1, Copenhagen: C.G. Iversen 1854, p. 379; pp. 393–4 (vol. 2, 1856) (*ASKB* 193).

Schelling, Friedrich Wilhelm Joseph von, "Aus einem öffentlichen Vortrag zu H. Steffens Andenken, gehalten am 24. April 1845. (Mit einigen Erweiterungen.)," in *Nachgelassene Schriften. Mit einem Vorworte von Schelling*, Berlin: E.H. Schroeder 1839, pp. iii–lxiii (*ASKB* 799).

Sibbern, Frederik Christian, *Om Philosophiens Begreb, Natur og Væsen. En Fremstilling af Philosophiens Propædeutik*, Copenhagen: Forfatterens eget Forlag 1843, p. 54; p. 58; p. 69 (*ASKB* 779).

—— *Speculativ Kosmologie med Grundlag til en speculativ Theologie*, Copenhagen: Forfatterens eget Forlag 1846, p. 7; p. 10 (*ASKB* 780).

Thortsen, Carl Adolph, *Historisk Udsigt over den danske Litteratur indtil Aar 1814*, Copenhagen: C.A. Reitzel 1839, p. 137 (*ASKB* 970).

Weiße, Christian Hermann, "Die philosophische Literatur der Gegenwart. Erster Artikel. Schleiermacher. Hegel. Steffens," *Zeitschrift für Philosophie und spekulative Theologie*, vols. 1–16, ed. by I.H. Fichte and Christian Hermann Weiße, Bonn et al.: Eduard Weber 1837–46, vol. 6, 1840, pp. 267–309 (*ASKB* 877–911).

Zeuthen, Ludvig, *Humanitet betragtet fra et christeligt Standpunkt, med stadigt Hensyn til den nærværende Tid*, Copenhagen: Gyldendal 1846, p. 30; p. 34; p. 62, note; p. 97 (*ASKB* 915).

—— *Om Ydmyghed. En Afhandling*, Copenhagen: Gyldendal 1852, p. 81 (*ASKB* 916).

III. Secondary Literature on Kierkegaard's Relation to Steffens

Bohlin, Torsten, *Kierkegaards dogmatiske åndskådning, dess historiska sammanhang*, Stockholm: Svenska kyrkans diakonistyrelses bokförlag 1925, pp. 155–7. (German translation: *Kierkegaards dogmatische Anschauung in ihrem geschichtlichen Zusammenhang*, Gütersloh: C. Bertelsmann, 1927, pp. 188–90.)

Bukdahl, Jørgen, "Vejen til myten og eventyret," *Søren Kierkegaard og den menige mand*, Copenhagen: C.A. Reitzel 1970 (*Søren Kierkegaard Selskabets Populære Skrifter*, vols. 9–10), pp. 11–21. (English translation: "Henrich Stephens: The Way to Myth and Fairy Tale," in *Søren Kierkegaard and the Common Man*, Grand Rapids, Michigan: Eerdmans 2001, pp. 7–18.)

Burgess, Andrew John, "Caricatures and the Comic in the Early Journals," *Kierkegaard Studies Yearbook*, 2003, pp. 125–42.

Høffding, Harald, *Danske Filosofer*, Copenhagen: Gyldendal 1909, p. 47.

Hultberg, Helge, *Den ældre Henrich Steffens. 1811–1845*, Copenhagen: C.A. Reitzel 1977, pp. 114–20.

— *Den unge Henrich Steffens. 1773–1811*, Copenhagen: Bianco Luno 1973, p. 106; p. 110.

— "Steffens und Kierkegaard," *Kierkegaardiana*, vol. 10, 1977, pp. 190–9.

Jung, Friedrich, *Henrik Steffens und das Problem des Einheit von Vernunft und Offenbarung*, Marburg 1961, pp. 70–1.

Kirmmse, Bruce H., *Kierkegaard in Golden Age Denmark*, Bloomington: Indiana University Press 1990; pp. 80–1.

Olesen, Tonny Aagaard, "Kierkegaards Schelling," *Kierkegaard und Schelling: Freiheit, Angst und Wirklichkeit*, ed. by Jochem Hennigfeld and Jon Stewart, Berlin: Walter de Gruyter, 2003 (*Kierkegaard Studies Monograph Series*, vol. 8), pp. 1–102, see especially pp. 33–43.

Paul, Fritz, *Henrich Steffens: Naturphilosophie und Universalromantik*, Munich: Wilhelm Fink 1973, pp. 202–14.

Vergote, Henri-Bernard, "L'esprit comme pressentiment selon H. Steffens," in his *Sens et répétition. Essai sur l'ironie kierkegaardienne*, vols. 1–2, Paris: Cerf/Orante 1982, vol. 2, pp. 321–6.

Peter Michael Stilling:
As Successor? "Undeniably a Possibility"[1]

Carl Henrik Koch

Peter Michael Stilling (1812–69) belonged to Søren Kierkegaard's generation. He was, like Adolph Peter Adler (1812–69), one of the Danish right Hegelians of the same generation, who, after first having been a follower of Hans Lassen Martensen (1808–84), then of Rasmus Nielsen (1809–84), ultimately followed the latter into the Kierkegaardian camp. Kierkegaard had a greater personal sympathy for Stilling than what he nourished for Rasmus Nielsen, whom he stood in a closer relation with than he ever did with Stilling. Even in 1849–50 Kierkegaard indicated that Nielsen, if he had changed his course, could be his successor, and continued: "Which, by the way, also Mag. Stilling seems to look promising for; he is undeniably a possibility, under whom there is already a fire, or who is skating on such a thin ice that he has an idea of the 'current.' "[2] To have an idea of "the current" meant, for Kierkegaard, to know that in Christianity God demands sacrifice and suffering from the human being, that is, the imitation of Christ.[3]

But Stilling never made it further than being a possibility. The meeting with Kierkegaard's thought and his personal circumstances caused him to be led away from faith. He was an omen of the development which leading figures in the generation after Kierkegaard, for example, Georg Brandes (1842–1927) and Harald Høffding (1843–1931), ran through: after having been through the Kierkegaardian acid bath, both found peace in a humanistic life-view, which granted life its rights. Or, as the young Georg Brandes wrote in his diary late one night in 1868: "The Christian and the human have for a long time desired a divorce. Now it is complete."[4] A few years before the young Høffding had pushed away Kierkegaard's books because he "could not reconcile their harmony with what life now taught me."[5] Life had conquered the church stormer's life-denying Christianity. But where Brandes and Høffding, on the strength of their comprehensive authorships, became leading cultural personalities,

---

1 See *Pap.* X–6 B 123, p. 164.

2 Ibid.

3 Cf. *SKS* 20, 192, NB2:129. *SKS* 20, 239, NB2:262.

4 Georg Brandes, *Levned*, vols. 1–3, Copenhagen: Gyldendal 1905–08, vol. 1, *Barndom og første Ungdom*, p. 235.

5 Harald Høffding, "Forord and Efterskrift til min Religionsfilosofi," *Mindre Arbejder*, vols. 1–3, Copenhagen: Gyldendal 1899–1913, vol. 2, p. 48.

Stilling, after his encounter with the Kierkegaardian conception of Christianity, for the most part gave up all further literary activity.

I.

P.M. Stilling was born in Viborg and, after completing his studies at the town's Cathedral school, was enrolled in 1832 at the University of Copenhagen where he embarked on the study of theology. But philosophy also attracted him. He attended Poul Martin Møller's (1794–1838) lectures on metaphysics and Frederik Christian Sibbern's on the philosophy of Christianity, which was Sibbern's variant of the age's speculative theology. In particular, Hans Lassen Martensen's lectures in 1837–38 on speculative dogmatics with their combination of philosophy and theology seem to have captivated him and encouraged him to make a closer study of the more recent philosophy and especially Hegel. He does not seem to have been in any hurry to take his qualifying examination in theology. He became a student of Rasmus Nielsen, and while he never took the examination,[6] nevertheless in 1844 received special permission to defend a thesis for the degree of magister—the later doctoral degree—without first having taken the usual qualifying examination.[7] From 1846 to 1850 he lectured at the university as *privatdocent*.

In 1847 rumor had it that Sibbern and presumably also Rasmus Nielsen were working to get Stilling appointed at the university as extraordinary instructor, but it proved to be in vain.[8] Stilling had in 1846 married a rich woman. Only a year later his wife died, which threw him into a religious-existential crisis, which seems to have arisen from a perceived contradiction between Christianity and conjugal life.[9] At the beginning of the 1850s he publicly and definitively distanced himself from speculative theology and aligned himself with Kierkegaard's conception of the impossibility of unifying faith and scholarly theology; but at the same time he hinted that he rejected faith. Then he married again in 1854 and initially bought an estate and later two others in North Jutland. He published nothing more after 1853.

Stilling's philosophical development falls into three sharply distinct periods. He entered the literary scene as an orthodox right Hegelian, then was seized by the Kierkegaardian conception of Christianity and stood on Rasmus Nielsen's side in the controversy about the relation between faith and knowledge, which was played out after Martensen had published his *Christian Dogmatics* in 1849. Then he seems to have rejected Rasmus Nielsen's attempt to delimit religion's field from that of

---

6 As late as 1840 Stilling seems to be preparing to complete the theological degree. See Brøchner's memories about Kierkegaard in *Encounters with Kierkegaard*, ed. by Bruce H. Kirmmse, Princeton, New Jersey: Princeton University Press 1996, p. 228.

7 See Stilling's autobiography in *Indbydelsesskrift til Københauns Universitets Aarsfest 1844*, Copenhagen: Schultz 1844.

8 See *Hans Brøchners rejsedagbøger fra årene 1847 og 1852–53*, ed. by Carl Henrik Koch and Vibeke Koch, Copenhagen: Society for Danish Language and Literature, C.A. Reitzel 1996, pp. 108–10.

9 *SKS* 22, 411, NB14:112. *SKS* 23, 132–3, NB16:56 / *JP* 6, 6590.

science in such a way that there cannot arise a split between faith and knowledge. Stilling wrote in 1853:

> The more I think about religion and try to grasp it, the more I experience that, taken in the old Christian sense, it is contrary to the understanding, and the more I am pressed to choose one of two alternatives: either to preserve faith with the loss of understanding, or to preserve my understanding with the loss of faith.[10]

In this final period he seems to have chosen the understanding and rejected faith—but also to have given up philosophy.

In 1841–42 the first issues of Rasmus Nielsen's unfinished *Speculative Logic in its Essentials* appeared,[11] which moved Stilling, in 1842, to publish a brief account of the significance of Hegel's logic for science.[12] In logic thought or the "I" is occupied with itself; but since every determination of the other-being, that is, what stands opposite thought as its object, happens with the help of the determinations of thought, the categories of logic, the "I" thus finds itself again

> in everything, and finds everything in itself, and only for the sight of thought does the sanctuary of existence open its holy of the holies. The logical "I" [sc. subjective reason] feels at home everywhere in its environment; its relation to it is free since it everywhere finds itself again and affirms itself.[13]

Hegel's philosophy is conceived as panlogism since the domination of reason is limited not only to the subjective sphere of the "I," thought or subjective being, but also encompasses objective being. Therefore, in Hegel's speculative logic

> the opposition between subjective reason and objective reason...is sublated, and in this one side of that Hegelian identity of thought and being shows itself, namely, that what is a necessary determination of reason (thought determination), is also a necessary determination with the objective universe so that everything is subordinated to the power of thought.[14]

The Hegelian dialectic is therefore not only a formal dialectic, which plays itself out in the world of thought, but also a real dialectic:

> In general, to the extent that panlogism is true [sc. thought and being are one] the dialectic must be able to be proven in all areas, both in the world of nature and in the world of spirit. It is the principle for all life and movement, and is the soul in all processes in the

---

10 Peter Michael Stilling, *Er Religionsforskerens Forhold til den saakaldte Aabenbaring det samme som Naturforskerens Forhold til Naturen?*, Copenhagen: C.A. Reitzel 1853, pp. 3–4.

11 Rasmus Nielsen, *Den speculative Logik i dens Grundtræk*, nos. 1–4, Copenhagen 1841–44.

12 Peter Michael Stilling, *Philosophiske Betragtninger over den speculative Logiks Betydning for Videnskaben, i Anledning af Professor R. Nielsens: "den speculative Logik i dens Grundtræk,"* Copenhagen: C.A. Reitzel 1842.

13 Ibid., p. 16.

14 Ibid., p. 13.

> objective world of nature, which likewise prevents the fossilization of nature since it drives it beyond itself and into the world of spirit.[15]

With the help of the dialectic, human beings are raised up into the realm of eternity and infinity, that is, up to the absolute knowledge of the absolute, which means the divine. Speculative logic is therefore "an essential moment in an all-encompassing *knowledge of the Self, the Universe and God.*"[16] With this, the significance of speculative logic is determined as a tool to obtain knowledge—and not least of all to attain a theological knowledge—and thereby as a tool for the education of the person.

In the same year that Stilling's *Philosophical Observations* appeared, Søren Kierkegaard, in *Fædrelandet*, poked fun at the fact that the Hegelian system's, or just "the system's," appearance was conceived as a sign of the significance of the age, and that philosophy and theology would reach their finite and complete stage. He writes ironically:

> We cannot go backward; Hegel's *Logic* has stood the test of Prof. Nielsen's thought. The moment approaches; for the last time Stilling has undertaken to administer extreme unction to us, to establish us in the proper point of view, and if we will only stay there, it will come, it will surely come. But when it comes, what is the future going to undertake? There is nothing for it to do; we have done it all. It can blissfully rest in the system, it can read at leisure the twenty-eight volumes, which were no easy matter to write.[17]

Kierkegaard's satirical remarks did not, however, knock Stilling off course. His next literary work was a highly positive review from 1843 of H.L. Martensen's *Outline to a System of Moral Philosophy*, which had appeared in 1841.[18] In the review Stilling declared himself to be in agreement with Martensen in the fact that Hegel had placed too little emphasis on "the moment of the individual and the person," and that "the ethical perfection of the person...is mediated not only by the family and the state [as in Hegel] but also by art, science and religion."[19] By contrast, he disagreed with Martensen in the latter's attempt to establish a moral philosophy as an independent science in relation to the philosophy of law and the philosophy of religion.

Stilling announced his full affiliation with right Hegelianism with its reconciliation of faith and knowledge, that is, theological knowledge, in his master's thesis from 1844.[20] Here he refuted atheism, that is, the denial of the existence of a personal divinity, which he found was a consequence of the new or left Hegelians' impoverished understanding of the Hegelian system. He also took aim at the left Hegelians' naturalism. When they rejected the divine's transcendence, they also had to deny the teleology of the world, that is, that the free human being, made

---

15 Ibid., p. 30.

16 Ibid., p. 62.

17 *SV1* XIII, p. 402 / *COR*, p. 8.

18 Hans Lassen Martensen, *Grundrids til Moralphilosophiens System. Udgivet til Brug ved academiske Forelæsninger*, Copenhagen: C.A. Reitzel 1841.

19 *Theologisk Tidskrift*, ed. by C.E. Scharling and C.T. Engelstoft, vol. 7, 1843, p. 91.

20 Peter Michael Stilling, *Den moderne Atheisme eller den saakaldte Neohegelianismes Conseqvenser af den hegelske Philosophie*, Copenhagen: C.A. Reitzel 1844.

spirit, was the end goal of historical development, and therefore had to deny the eschatological thought which the right Hegelians ascribed to the Hegelian system. By demonstrating the self-contradictions in the left Hegelians' view that the divine is merely an unconscious product of the human fantasy and power of the imagination (the "autotheistic tendency" of left Hegelianism),[21] and by demonstrating the untenability of naturalism, Stilling wanted to "set into motion the self-dissolution of atheism" and optimistically attempted "to carry the dissolution to the point that the Christian world-view's dawn will rise above the conflicting forces...."[22]

The target of Stilling's attack on left Hegelianism was partly David Friedrich Strauss, whose *Die christliche Glaubenslehre* had appeared in 1840–41 and was published in Danish translation in 1842–43, partly Ludwig Feuerbach's *Das Wesen des Christenthums* from 1841 and, finally, Carl Ludwig Michelet (1801–93), who, with his *Vorlesungen über die Persönlichkeit Gottes und Unsterblichkeit der Seele* from the same year, had consistently carried further the Hegelian philosophy of immanence. That Stilling—incorrectly—categorized Michelet among the left Hegelians is due especially to the fact that Michelet had maintained that the immortality which great personalities could participate in was to be preserved in the memories of the generations to come. Michelet, who had been the editor of several of Hegel's posthumous lectures, was neither right nor left Hegelian, but, by contrast, an orthodox Hegelian. Since Stilling, however, regarded right Hegelianism with its theistic interpretation of Hegel's system as being the correct Hegelianism, he had to reckon Michelet to the left Hegelians' party.

Christianity can, Stilling thought, be characterized as a religion which claims the existence of a personal deity, of a personal god-man (Christ), and which assumes personal immortality. The burning question at the time—and a question whose response after Hegel's death constituted a split between left and right Hegelians—was whether the Hegelian system was in agreement with the basic premises of Christianity. Stilling sought to show that this was the case in an extensive and sometimes very technical analysis. Although he was forced to admit that a certain indeterminacy prevailed in Hegel in connection with the fundamental dogmas, Hegel's system could nonetheless be correctly designated as theistic. For example, in a criticism of Spinozism, Hegel said that Spinoza had not attained the Christian consciousness' true concept of God as "the absolute *Person*."[23]

Like other right Hegelians, Stilling found again the personal deity in the Hegelian concept of the Absolute. According to this concept, the Absolute is the dialectical unity of subjectivity and objectivity. Or, as Hegel put it in the *Phenomenology of Spirit*: The truth is not only substance but also subject.[24] The right Hegelians—and

---

21 Ibid., p. 3.

22 Ibid., p. iii.

23 Cf. the addition to § 151 in G.W.F. Hegel, *Enzyklopädie der philosophischen Wissenschaften*, in *Sämtliche Werke. Jubiläumsausgabe*, vols. 1–20, ed. by Hermann Glockner, Stuttgart: Friedrich Frommann Verlag 1928–41, vol. 8, pp. 338–41.

24 Hegel, *Phänomenologie des Geistes*, in *Sämtliche Werke. Jubiläumsausgabe*, vol. 2, p. 22.

also Stilling—found in the double character of the Absolute a foundation of the personality and transcendence of God:

> After its pure logical concept, the absolute Idea shall just as much be taken subjectively as objectively, that is, in the sense of the original source of the universe. Posited as objective, or in the form of *theos*, it steps forth from the indeterminate logical universality and "is applied" to a *determinate* content, God. In this determinate form, it comes to develop as original self-consciousness, as original will and original knowledge in the system of its own ideas, as divine personality in its inner Trinitarian movements in the depths of mystery....[25]

The indeterminacy on this point in Hegel is due to the fact, Stilling thought, that Hegel had not clearly integrated the doctrine of logic about the Absolute with the doctrine of the philosophy of religion about the divine personality. The Absolute realizes itself in the development toward freedom, that is, the divine is revealed in the world. But if the distinction between God and the world is not emphasized, this identity between God and the world is understood as pantheism. According to Stilling, Hegel neglects this in his logic, even if "the Hegelian logic...no less than the Hegelian philosophy of religion, *wants* to maintain the Christian concept of God, since it declares the absolute personality, the absolute idea, as the category in which God must be thought."[26]

By contrast, in the Hegelian philosophy, there are far fewer difficulties associated with Christology than with the doctrine of a personal God. This is due to the fact that the historical development is always a mediation between opposites and here also a mediation between the human and the divine, an opposition which is mediated in and by the fact that the Absolute, that is, God enters into "the need and pain of finitude."[27] Finally, there is the question of personal immortality. In connection with this Stilling admits that the Hegelian system does not immediately contain a proof for personal immortality; but he thinks, however, without giving reasons for it, that one can claim that immortality is a presupposition of the system. Therefore, his conclusion is that Hegel's "philosophy has the tendency to preserve the object of faith according to its essential core; its relation to faith is not a revolutionary or polemical one, but an irenic one."[28] In the Hegelian system, faith and knowledge are united. In the works of the left Hegelians, who claimed to be Hegel's true descendants, faith and knowledge or religion and philosophy stood in a polemical relation to one another.

With his master's thesis Stilling concluded his speculative authorship. About a dozen years later he wrote, not without a certain pride, about this period in his life:

> None of my generation—I dare say it freely—has in his time placed greater youthful trust in speculative theology than I; none of those my age has dedicated to it his youth and his best energies with greater love of the truth and zeal than I; none of those my

---

25 Stilling, *Den moderne Atheisme eller den saakaldte Neohegelianismes Conseqvenser af den hegelske Philosophie*, p. 33.

26 Ibid., p. 38.

27 Ibid., p. 43.

28 Ibid., p. 51.

> age—for I also dare say this—has felt a deeper suffering and pain with the struggle between faith and thought than I.[29]

With the final words Stilling refers to his participation in the first conflict about faith and knowledge, which marked his acceptance of Kierkegaard's and Rasmus Nielsen's rejection of any form of science of faith. Scholarly theology and Christian faith are entities which cannot be united, or as Rasmus Nielsen repeated again and again in *Evangelical Faith and Theology* from 1850: "Christianity is higher than science, and the faith of the gospels is different in kind from theology."[30]

In the preface to *Christian Dogmatics* from 1849,[31] H.L. Martensen had attacked people "who did not feel the urge to continuous thinking, but could be satisfied with thinking scattered thoughts and aphorisms and flashes of wit," and who regard "the concept of a science of faith as a self-contradiction, which eliminated true Christianity."[32] Although Kierkegaard was not mentioned by name, it was clear whom Martensen was aiming at, and Rasmus Nielsen, who at that time stood in a relation to Kierkegaard as a kind of disciple, immediately went on a counteroffensive.[33] Nielsen was also the main actor in the controversy about the relation between faith and knowledge which followed.[34] His debate with Martensen is stamped with great zeal; the polemical tone is not without humor, but he cannot be said to be free from the charge of being somewhat superficial. Also in his journals Kierkegaard repeatedly distanced himself from Rasmus Nielsen's attack on Martensen, since he regarded it more as a result of a personal relation of opposition than as an undertaking in the name of an idea. Understandably enough, Kierkegaard did not appreciate that someone else took up his affairs and, virtually using Kierkegaard's own words, presented his views, as if they were his own. Kierkegaard's ultimate judgment on Rasmus Nielsen was that he was a mediocre talent, who had plagiarized the pseudonymous authorship and misused the confidence that Kierkegaard had shown him.

Stilling followed Rasmus Nielsen in the attack on Martensen, but his contribution to the controversy from 1850 is written with far more discipline than that of Nielsen. It was in its precision a far harsher attack on Martensen's scholarliness than Nielsen's often humorous, but just as often superficial, criticism. The sharpness in Stilling's contribution seems to be what lies behind Jakob Peter Mynster's (1775–1854) criticism of the tone which he used towards Martensen.[35]

The basic view in Stilling's attack on Martensen, which has the title *On the Imagined Reconciliation of Faith and Knowledge particularly with Respect to Prof.*

---

29 Stilling, *Er Religionsforskerens Forhold til den saakaldte Aabenbaring det samme som Naturforskerens Forhold til Naturen?*, p. 3.

30 Rasmus Nielsen, *Evangelietroen og Theologien*, Copenhagen: C.A. Reitzel 1850, see, for example, p. 37.

31 Martensen, *Den christelige Dogmatik*, Copenhagen: C.A. Reitzel 1849.

32 Ibid., p. III.

33 Rasmus Nielsen, *Mag. S. Kierkegaards "Johannes Climacus" og Dr. H. Martensens "Christelige Dogmatik." En undersøgende Anmeldelse*, Copenhagen: C.A. Reitzel 1849.

34 Concerning this controversy, see C.H. Koch: *Den danske idealisme 1800–1880*, Copenhagen: Gyldendal 2004, pp. 361–78.

35 *SKS* 23, 346, NB19:27.

Martensen's "Christian Dogmatics,"[36] is Kierkegaardian. Speculation, *in casu* Martensen's right-Hegelian theology is a human affair since it is the human being's attempt to appropriate—that is, to subjectivize—the objective, namely, the truths of faith, which causes the subject to be objectified. Thus, the distance between the subject and the object is overcome: the two are united, and the result is, in the Hegelian jargon of the age, a subject-object. But, for the believer, theoretical speculation is an all too violent and indeed even irrelevant moment in the maelstrom of life:

> And from this comes the fact that all attempts to digest and appropriate the Christian solid food in the speculative-theoretical process are sometimes revealed and unveiled as an "attack," against which the divine, so to speak, protests with the words: "No! you are not *here*, human being, but I am, the Lord, the overreaching one, who goes beyond *your* concept, a cross for *your* thought, a cross which can only be endured by the head, by taking all thoughts prisoner under faith's unconditioned obedience, which is more acceptable to me than the fatness of rams."[37]

Three possibilities seem to be available concerning the relation between subject and object. First, the independence of the object, that is, the truths of faith, can be asserted vis-à-vis the subject. But in this case, the task of thought is only to bow to the dogmas, which is not a genuine unity of subject and object, but an attack on the subject. Then the subject's independence can be asserted, and the dogmas must bow to thought, whereby they are distorted, which implies that some dogmas—for example, about evil as a person—must be rejected. In this situation the question is "whether the independent subject is able, with the process of knowing, to appropriate the undistorted Christian object, or not."[38] But from the point of view of existence, from the uncertainty, doubt and insecurity which characterize the acting human being in contradiction to the thinking one, thought cannot overcome the opposition between subject and object. Only faith is able to do this:

> But while thought is light as a feather, and the logical dialectic like a game, where it plays badminton with thought, then, by contrast, the burden of existence and actuality on the beleaguered one is heavy as a mountain, and the dialectical virtue of faith is a virtue which *changes* the heavy mountain of suffering into the light feather of the joy of faith, a dialectical force, which only—as is well known—became promised to faith, and not to thought; a dialectical force which is only awakened to the extent that the force does not continue to slumber, under the potencies of the innermost life forces in the struggles of tribulations.[39]

Speculation is not the way forth to faith. Rather, thought dissolves the immediate certainty of faith by nourishing doubt.

---

36 Peter Michael Stilling, *Om den indbildte Forsoning af Tro og–Viden med særligt Hensyn til Prof. Martensens "christelige Dogmatik,"* Copenhagen: C.A. Reitzel 1850.

37 Ibid., pp. 12–13.

38 Ibid., pp. 20–1.

39 Ibid., pp. 31–2.

Stilling then raises the concrete question of whether Martensen in his dogmatics was successful in the rational understanding of the dogmas. Did he reach certainty of thought, that is, a speculative understanding the dogmas?

As examples of dogmas which Stilling regards as so essentially Christian are doctrines such as the dogma of the Trinity, the dogma of the Incarnation, the dogma of ubiquity (the doctrine that the divine is all-present), and the dogma of immortality. According to Stilling, these are and continue to be "the cross for thought," that is, they are in their paradoxicality incomprehensible. For example, the divine is a personality, an absolute "I," but it does not follow from this as from the dogma of the Trinity that he is three "I's" and yet one and the same. If one speculates about this, then one becomes dizzy from theorizing:

> If there are three "I's" in one "I," then it can actually be more precisely analyzed, 1) the Father as "I," 2) the Son as "I," 3) the Spirit as "I," and thus 4) the "I," which montheistically in the flight of continuity and in pure identity with itself, has in an encircling and overlapping manner, Father, Son and Spirit as *disappearing* differences in itself, that is—a quadrad of "I's."[40]

Speculation only creates confusion and doubt about the content of the dogma. Speculative theology is therefore not able to comprehend the dogmas, for they are incomprehensible.

Martensen had one goal, namely, with the help of speculation and on a biblical basis, to reach a scholarly theology to the advantage of the church. But, Stilling thinks, he was not successful in dogmatics at mediating, in a speculative and Hegelian manner, the believing subject and its object. For polemical reasons Stilling grants that it is true that Martensen's dogmatics is at the same time biblical, ecclesiastical, and speculative, but it can be dissolved into

> 1) a biblical, 2) an ecclesiastical, and 3) a speculative part, more or less as in the inorganic world a piece of granite is an aggregate of and can be separated into the 3 constitutent parts, 1) quartz, 2) feldspar and 3) mica; the constituent parts, which are mutually *indifferent* to the *external* connection and prove their indifference to this connection by the fact that the connection can be *decomposed.* The actual category of our thoroughly criticized *Christian Dogmatics* thus becomes the category of "the *aggregate*," the category of eclecticism, which wants to have the advantage of being everything and precisely for this reason, as is natural, is prevented in a *decisive*, that is, qualitative manner, from becoming something.[41]

Both for Rasmus Nielsen and for Stilling, the criticism of Martensen aimed more or less at the same thing. On the one hand, Martensen had not carried out his speculative program, and if he had done so, he would have made faith superfluous. On the other hand, he likewise did not hold onto faith as a principle, and if he had done so, he would have realized the impotency of speculation vis-à-vis the Christian dogmas. Since he had tried to unite speculation and faith, and each leads to the sublation of the other, he had tried to do something impossible. Martensen never responded to

---

40 Ibid., p. 78.

41 Ibid., p. 94.

Stilling, but dismissed him briefly with the arrogant words that "serious matters do not suffer being touched with unwashed hands."[42]

Just as Kierkegaard did not publicly express himself about Rasmus Nielsen's fight for his views against Martensen, so also he remained silent about Stilling's. But on occasion of the conflict, he wrote, among other things, in his journal: "For my part I have many things to object against the turn my cause has taken—but I do not wish to say a word about this as long as it can in some way here in Denmark be used to blame someone with the charge that they have dared to study my writings and acknowledge it."[43]

However, Kierkegaard considered publicly distancing himself from Rasmus Nielsen.[44] Years later during the attack on the Church in 1855, Kierkegaard noted in *Fædrelandet* Martensen's silence towards one of his attackers, namely Stilling, who in his attempt to make him aware of the fact that Kierkegaard's pseudonym Johannes Climacus had refuted him, had long been the most dangerous for him.[45]

Stilling concluded his authorship in 1853 with yet another attack on Martensen.[46] The attack was a delayed response to Martensen's polemical work, *Dogmatic Elucidations* from 1850, in which he refuted and corrected Rasmus Nielsen. In the work Martensen had somewhat boldly compared the contents of dogmatics to the revelation with the natural scientist's relation to nature. But, Stilling answered him, while the natural scientist relates to nature and not to the handed-down opinions about nature, dogmatics relates to the handed-down reports about the revelations, that is, the Bible, and not to personally experienced revelations. Therefore, to draw a parallel between these two relations is a misunderstanding. For

> the Bible is not, like the object of the natural scientist, nature, the fact *itself* in its irrefutable facticity and authority. It is only the biblical author's report and idea about something, which seems to make a demand to be regarded as a fact and will not be satisfied with partially counting as myth, as a product of the myth-making, imagining consciousness.[47]

With these last words he seems to have affiliated himself with D.F. Strauss' doctrine that the Christian stories are a myth, a conception of the figure of Christ, which he distanced himself from in the sharpest terms in his master's thesis. He seems to have taken leave not only of speculative theology, to which he had devoted himself in his youth, but also of Kierkegaard and biblical faith. After this he was silent.

---

42 Martensen, *Dogmatiske Oplysninger. Et Leilighedsskrift*, Copenhagen: C.A. Reitzel 1850, p. 7.

43 *Pap.* X–6 B 109, pp. 136f.

44 *Pap.* X–6, B 110–127.

45 *SV1* XIV, 94 / *M*, 79.

46 Stilling, *Er Religionsforskerens Forhold til den saakaldte Aabenbaring det samme som Naturforskerens Forhold til Naturen?*

47 Ibid., p. 43.

II.

In numerous journal entries and drafts to articles, Kierkegaard during the years from 1848 to 1850 was occupied with his relation to Rasmus Nielsen. "I saw," he writes somewhere, "R. Nielsen's ideal possibility—but I do not dare say it to him directly, and it would not help anyway; for then it would become something wholly different and not ideality in the strictest sense."[48] With "ideality" one should understand in this context a passionately held acceptance of Christianity's demand to the individual, or as was written in *Stages on Life's Way*, "to be out on 70,000 fathoms of water and yet be joyful."[49] This kind of ideality should come from within; only indirectly can there be a communication of the possibility for this, that is, the possibility—as Kierkegaard demands—for living and struggling for the realization of Christianity. Kierkegaard's life and authorship was an indirect communication of this kind to his contemporaries. Nielsen did not understand this communication and failed.

In the same breath as Kierkegaard here speaks about Nielsen's possibility, he also mentions Stilling as a possibility. The background for this was that Stilling had lost his wife and had decided, it seems, to live his life in fidelity with the deceased, which had brought Kierkegaard to become interested in his "existential condition."

On occasion of the fact that Stilling had sent Kierkegaard his polemical piece against Martensen, Kierkegaard had considered writing to him. He did not want to express his joy over the fact that Stilling had become his follower, but rather that Stilling was a follower of his deceased wife. Somewhat surprisingly, given his view of the possibility of direct communication, he wanted to continue:

> And understood thus—let me tell you—you are a possibility; I know how to evaluate this, no expert in precious jewels has a sharper eye for refractions than I for the existential possibility's noble preciousness. By being wholly devoted to someone deceased, one is rather assured against wasting one's time on trivialities or of frittering away one's life in "serious vanity."[50]

The letter was never sent.[51] The question for Kierkegaard seems to have been whether Stilling had been able to raise his erotically conditioned despair above his wife's death, and the decision borne from this about being true to her, into the sphere of ethics. If this were not the case, then a designation of him as "a possibility" would merely be "an incitement which tempts fantasy"; if Stilling, by contrast, had understood fidelity toward the deceased as an ethical matter, he would be in a development, which, for Kierkegaard, pointed in the direction of the religious.

Either by means of direct conversation with Stilling or in some other way having obtained more precise information about his situation, Kierkegaard seems, some time later, to have realized that Stilling was not so far along in his development as

---

48 *SKS* 23, 22, NB15:23 / *JP* 6, 6573.

49 *SKS* 6, 440 / *SLW*, 477.

50 *SKS* 22, 411, NB14:112.

51 There is also a draft of a letter in which Kierkegaard thanks Stilling for the treatise against Martensen and in which he also discusses the grief which Stilling experienced with the death of his wife in 1847, see *B&A*, vol. 1, p. 265 / *LD*, Letter 241, pp. 338–9.

one could have hoped. The decisive thing for Stilling's condition was more the pride with which he maintained his endeavor than an ethical understanding of life. In addition, Stilling had apparently grounded his decision religiously without, however, in a Kierkegaardian sense, having been right-minded in relation to the religious. Kierkegaard, however, still regarded him as a possibility, but also saw clearly the result that Stilling remarried and became "a despaired attacker of the religious' 'inhuman strictness.' "[52] But the possibility which is now at issue is significantly less comprehensive that the previous one. In Kierkegaard's eyes, Stilling now had only one possibility for being an author who could passionately express a religious need, which speculative theology could not satisfy.

A later entry shows that Kierkegaard directly spoke with Stilling about his situation. Stilling had apparently expressed how difficult it was for him to remain unmarried. By having made his decision to be faithful to his deceased wife, which included sexual abstinence, he had imposed on himself great sufferings, and—as Stilling expressed—it was Christianity which imposed these torments on him. But Christianity, thought Kierkegaard, had nothing to do with Stilling's dilemma which had torn him between being faithful to the deceased and his need to get remarried. For Christianity allows him to marry as many times as he wishes.

But even against this background, Kierkegaard regards Stilling more positively than Rasmus Nielsen, about whom the conclusion was that he was a mediocre talent. Regarding Stilling, he writes by way of conclusion: "If the man really would, what potential he has! But he demonstrates precisely what it means that a human being is not disciplined in Christianity any more, and just he demonstrates the need for, if not the monastery, something similar to it. A Church institute would help him."[53] Stilling's "existential condition" was thus, for Kierkegaard, an example of the obstacles which the age's Christianity, made bourgeois, had set up against the actualization of his undertaking.

Kierkegaard's interest in Stilling's existential condition was hardly caused only by his wish to receive a few collaborators to realize his grand project, namely, to correct an age gone astray. He was not only "a secret agent in the highest service."[54] But he was also a researcher of the human. The fundamental dilemma for Stilling, namely, the choice between the erotic and the religious was something that Kierkegaard himself had struggled with in his engagement with Regine Olsen.

Translated by Jon Stewart

---

52 *SKS* 23, 38, NB15:56.

53 *SKS* 23, 133, NB16:56 / *JP* 6, 6590.

54 *SKS* 20, 424–5, NB5:138 / *JP* 6, 6192.

Bibliography

I. Stilling's Works in The Auction Catalogue *of Kierkegaard's Library*

Den moderne Atheisme eller den saakaldte Neohegelianismes Conseqvenser af den hegelske Philosophie, Copenhagen: C.A. Reitzel 1844 (*ASKB* 801).

Om den indbildte Forsoning af Tro og–Viden med særligt Hensyn til Prof. Martensens "christelige Dogmatik." Kritisk-Polemisk Afhandling, Copenhagen: C.A. Reitzel 1850 (*ASKB* 802).

II. Works in The Auction Catalogue *of Kierkegaard's Library that Discuss Stilling*

Adler, Adolph Peter, *Populaire Foredrag over Hegels objective Logik*, Copenhagen: C.A. Reitzel 1842, p. 18, note; p. 25, note; p. 34, note (*ASKB* 383).

Anonymous [review of three works, including Stilling's], "Et Par Spørgsmaal til Professor C.E. Scharling i Anledning af hans saakaldte Anmeldelse af Dr. Martensens christelige Dogmatik (1850)," *Dansk Kirketidende*, vol. 5, 1850, columns 598–600, see column 600 (*ASKB* 321–325).

Jürgens, H., *Nogle Bemærkninger, sigtende til at belyse L. Wengels Piece: Om academiske Anliggender*, Copenhagen: C.A. Reitzel 1844, p. 3; p. 12 (*ASKB* U 73).

Martensen, Hans Lassen, *Dogmatiske Oplysninger. Et Leilighedsskrift*, Copenhagen: C.A. Reitzel 1850, pp. 7–8 (*ASKB* 654).

Nielsen, Rasmus, *Den propædeutiske Logik*, Copenhagen: P.G. Philipsen 1845, p. 279 (*ASKB* 699).

Wengel, L., *Om academiske Anliggender*, Copenhagen: I Commission hos H.C. Klein 1844, pp. 19–20 (*ASKB* U 109).

Zeuthen, Ludvig, *Om Ydmyghed. En Afhandling*, Copenhagen: Gyldendalske Boghandel 1852, p. 18; p. 27; pp. 87–8; pp. 105–7; p. 147, note (*ASKB* 916).

III. Secondary Literature on Kierkegaards's Relation to Stilling

Koch, Carl Henrik: *Den danske idealisme 1800–1880*, Copenhagen: Gyldendal 2004, pp. 370–3 and 473–85.

Rubow, Paul V., *Kierkegaard og hans Samtidige*, Copenhagen: Gyldendal 1950, pp. 20–1.

Frederik Ludvig Zeuthen:

"I struck a light, lit a fire—now it is burning. And this 'fire' Dr. Zeuthen wants to extinguish—with an 'enema syringe.'"[1]

Carl Henrik Koch

Frederik Ludvig Zeuthen (1805–74) and Søren Kierkegaard collided during the latter's attack on the Church in 1854–55. Zeuthen, a pastor in the Danish church, swung the sword over the church stormer with a certain unctuousness, and although Kierkegaard considered an extended response, it ended only with a brief piece against the attacker. Zeuthen was a warrior for the Lord. In the history of the Danish church he is remembered as an energetic critic of Grundtvig's and his followers' view of the origin of the creed. Not least of all Kierkegaard's elder brother, Peter Christian Kierkegaard (1805–88) bore the brunt of his critique,[2] although responded at length and sharply[3]—it was not without reason that during his journey abroad from 1828 to 1830 he was given the nickname, "*Der Disputierteufel aus Norden*."[4] Jakob Peter Mynster (1775–1854), the bishop of Zealand, seems to have appreciated Zeuthen—although he had noted a characteristic unctuous element in his preaching style.[5] Zeuthen was also a warm follower of the bishop's and his successor's, Hans Lassen Martensen's (1808–84) theology of mediation, according to which Christianity and bourgeois culture constitute a unity. It was this unity that Søren Kierkegaard designated mockingly as "Christendom." But whereas Søren Kierkegaard, according to Zeuthen's view, had to say "either Christianity or culture," the relation between bourgeois culture and Christianity was, for Zeuthen, a "both/and." They have, he claims, "stood together in history, and it is to Christianity's merit that it has furthered

---

1 *Pap.* XI–3 B 142, p. 227 / *M*, Supplement, p. 533.

2 Cf. Frederik Ludvig Zeuthen, *Om den saakaldte "Kirkelige Anskuelse,"* Copenhagen: Andr. Fr. Høst 1858, *Nogle Ord om Troesbekjendelsen og Daaben*, Copenhagen: G.E.C. Gad 1873.

3 "Oplysninger og Bemærkninger til Forsvar for Læren om Kirke-Ordet og dens Venner," in *Nordisk Tidsskrift for christelig Theologi*, vol. 2, 1840, pp. 58–96; pp. 218–28, republished in P.C. Kierkegaard, *Samlede Skrifter*, vols. 1–6, 1902–06, Copenhagen: K. Schönberg, vol. 1, pp. 356–405.

4 Carl Weltzer, *Peter og Søren Kierkegaard*, Copenhagen: G.E.C. Gad 1936, p. 25.

5 *J.P. Mynsters Visitatsdagbøger*, vols. 1–2, ed. by B. Kornerup, Copenhagen: Munksgaard 1937, vol. 2, p. 26.

culture. They have even stood in such a direct relation to each other that new life in Christianity, by returning to the New Testament's doctrine, has been accompanied by a new life in culture (as with the Reformation)."[6] If anyone was, Zeuthen was an adherent of the *status quo*.

Søren Kierkegaard seems always to have regarded Zeuthen as a mediocre spirit.[7] A preserved correspondence between them illuminates the relationship. As a young man, Zeuthen had lived under oppressive conditions and had to go into debt in order to make ends meet, which moved him to write to Kierkegaard, who in the first section of *Christian Discourses* from 1848 had spoken of "The Care of Poverty" as a worry for the day today and for the day tomorrow. Neither the bird nor the Christian, only the heathen has this worry. But, Zeuthen thinks, the worry of poverty for the day yesterday is a worry not for "what one will eat, but for what one *has* eaten and—*not paid for*...this worry of poverty is the most difficult kind...."[8] The remark can seem somewhat irrelevant. Johan Ludvig Heiberg was not entirely wrong when he in a polemic with Zeuthen from 1833 remarked that it does not seem so much to be the issue that occupied Zeuthen but rather "to make the world attentive to his own light."[9] Kierkegaard's response to Zeuthen's somewhat long-winded letter was then also in all his friendly jocularity only quite brief. He thanks Zeuthen for the remark about worry for yesterday, which he will remember tomorrow: "So, you see, you have provided me with a worry about the day tomorrow!"[10] A few days later Kierkegaard, however, wrote in his journal that in some planned "New Discourses on the Lilies and the Birds," "consideration could also be given to Zeuthen's comment (which in a casual allusion in my answer I hinted at wanting to consider) in a letter a week ago: 'that there also is a worry about yesterday.' "[11] It is also clear from Kierkegaard's response that he and his correspondent occasionally met when Zeuthen was in the city, and that Zeuthen did not want to participate in Kierkegaard's walks—his daily bath in humanity—but wanted to be received in his home, where only few were granted entry.[12] In 1854–55 the tone between them was sharpened not a little. They no longer exchanged unobliging pleasantries.

The professor of philosophy Rasmus Nielsen (1809–84) had, after a brief Kierkegaardian period, sought to define a religious life-view against the onrushing natural sciences. In a little philosophical textbook, which appeared in 1857, he briefly gives an account of his view of the relation between faith and knowledge. Whereas faith, according to Nielsen (and Kierkegaard) declares subjectivity to be the truth, science declares objectivity to be the truth. But in and with these declarations,

---

6 *Ugeskrift for den evangeliske Kirke i Danmark,* vol. 5, 1855, p. 351.

7 Cf. *Pap*. XI–3 B 142, p. 225.

8 *B&A*, p. 192 / *LD*, Letter 175, p. 243.

9 Johan Ludvig Heiberg, *Prosaiske Skrifter*, vols. 1–11, Copenhagen: C.A. Reitzel 1861–62, vol. 1, p. 453. (English translation in *Heiberg's On the Significance of Philosophy for the Present Age and Other Texts*, trans. and ed. by Jon Stewart, Copenhagen: C.A. Reitzel 2005, p. 133.)

10 *B&A*, vol. 1, p. 193 / *LD*, Letter 175, p. 243.

11 *SKS* 20, 358, NB4:154b / *WA*, Supplement, p. 198.

12 Cf. Frederik Ludvig Zeuthen, *Et Par Aar af mit Liv*, Copenhagen: G.E.C. Gad 1869, p. 23.

faith has renounced having any influence on science, and vice versa science has renounced having any influence on faith. The spheres of science and faith are thus different. From this it follows that:

> Faith and knowledge can then be united without contradiction in one consciousness; their mutual conflict does not originate from a matter of principle. The conflict is psychological; it is the human frailty which neither has enough resignation to reconcile itself with science's objective view or enough inwardness to hold firmly to faith.[13]

In the middle of the 1860s Rasmus Nielsen's attempt to ensure faith against an attack from the natural scientific side unleashed one of the most comprehensive controversies in nineteenth-century Danish history of ideas. It lasted more than five years and called forth more then 25 monographs and books and almost 100 articles in newspapers and journals.[14] Zeuthen also participated in the controversy, waging a veritable war in publications against Rasmus Nielsen.[15] Based on the attempt at unity, which characterized Schelling's idealism, a division of existence into a sphere of faith, which is the object of religious knowing, and a sphere of science, which is the object sphere of theoretical knowing, must lead to a rejection of philosophy, "whose goal is a *continuous* conception of knowledge of *the whole.*"[16] Zeuthen was not able to, and did not want to, give up the idea of the unifiability of a scientific and religious world-view, which Schelling and the Romantic philosophy of nature stood for, and which in Denmark had been represented not least of all by Hans Christian Ørsted.

I.

Ludvig Zeuthen came from an old family of pastors.[17] His mother was a sister of Heinrich Steffens, and this close relationship with one of the main figures of the Romantic philosophy of nature had a decisive significance for his philosophical views. All through his life, Schelling and Steffens were his philosophical models. After completing his theological examination in 1826—the study of theology had for him resulted in a certain religious coolness—he worked for a time as a private

---

13 Rasmus Nielsen, *Philosophisk Propædeutik i Grundtræk*, Copenhagen: Gyldendal 1857, p. 77.

14 Cf. Carl Henrik Koch, *Den danske idealisme 1800–1880*, Copenhagen: Gyldendal 2004 (*Den danske Filosofis historie*, vol. 3), pp. 435–61.

15 Frederik Ludvig Zeuthen, *Om Tro og Viden. Sendebrev til Rasmus Nielsen*, Copenhagen: G.E.C. Gad 1866; *Om Tro og Viden. Andet Sendebrev til Rasmus Nielsen*, Copenhagen: G.E.C. Gad 1866; Rasmus Nielsen, *Svar til Hr. Dr. Phil. Pastor Zeuthen i Anledning af hans Sendebrev om Tro og Viden*, Copenhagen: Gyldendal 1866; and Zeuthen, *Tolv Sætninger. Mit tredie Indlæg i Forhandlingen om Tro og Viden*, Copenhagen: G.E.C. Gad 1867.

16 Frederik Ludvig Zeuthen, *Mine første 25 Aar (1805–1830)*, Copenhagen: G.E.C. Gad 1866, p. 35, note.

17 Zeuthen himself describes his childhood and youth and his philosophical and theological development in *Mine første 25 Aar*; *Et Par Aar af mit Liv*; and *Min Udenlandsreise i Aarene 1833–1834*, Copenhagen: G.E.C. Gad 1875.

tutor in a Jutland vicarage, where most of his free time was used for philosophical studies, not least of all of Kant's philosophy. The local peasants called him "the wild man."[18] In 1827 Zeuthen journeyed to visit Steffens in Breslau. The trip took him first to Berlin where he heard the lectures of Schleiermacher and his antagonist Marheineke, Hegel, and the church historian Neander. About Schleiermacher and Hegel he later wrote:

> Hegel and Schleiermacher were, as is well known, the antipodes of the scholarly world, but here in the halls of the University one saw them meet, and, after having heard Schleiermacher talk about the *feeling* of absolute dependence as the true essence of religiosity, one could then learn from Hegel that it is by virtue of thought (and not feeling) that human beings are distinguished from animals, and that the truth in religion rests in thought alone. Hegel was in no way pleasing to me, neither his lectures nor his appearance.[19]

Some years after his personal meeting with Hegel, he was one of the first in Denmark to write against Hegelian philosophy.

During the years 1833–34 Zeuthen was underway again. This time he went to Munich where he heard Schelling's lectures and was captivated by his late philosophy, Schelling's so-called positive philosophy, which in opposition to the Hegelian, negative philosophy, that had its point of departure in conceptual relations, that is, the possible, made its point of departure the actual, concrete existence. In Munich he attended Schelling's lectures on the history of philosophical systems and studied notes of his lectures on the philosophy of mythology.

After his return home from his first journey abroad, Zeuthen published a series of short philosophical treatises and in 1833 a *Habilitationsschrift* in philosophy, in which he criticized Hegel. He hoped in vain to obtain an appointment at the University of Copenhagen as instructor in moral philosophy;[20] but as he later wrote, "My philosophical efforts aimed essentially at winning a view of the world in which I, with respect to my living, my practical life, my conditions, could find rest."[21] He found rest in positive Christianity and became a pastor in South Jutland, and in 1842 transferred to Zealand, and from 1860 until his death acted as parish pastor in the old garrison town of Fredericia. Here since the French Revolution there had been a large Catholic community, which caused the ever-polemical man to write against the Roman Church.[22]

Zeuthen only arrived at a genuinely complete philosophical world-view with the study of Schelling's posthumously published *Philosophie der Offenbarung* (1854). He presented the result of his philosophical enlightenment in a series of shorter treatises and in the book *Philosophical Treatises for an Orientation in the Schellingian World-*

---

18 Fr. Hammerich, *Et Levnetsløb*, Copenhagen: Forlagsbureauet i København (O.H. Delbanco. G.E.C. Gad. F. Hegel) 1882, p. 153.

19 Zeuthen, *Mine første 25 Aar*, pp. 99–100.

20 Ibid., p. 133.

21 Zeuthen, *Et Par Aar af mit Liv*, p. 60.

22 Zeuthen, *Om Romerkirken. Nogle Oplysninger og Betragtninger*, Fredericia: L.W. Riemenschneider 1863.

View from 1860,[23] which is one of the last fruits of Danish Schellingianism. In this work he attempts to unify the natural sciences and theology based on a Schellingian foundation. "Neither the doctrine of nature nor theology," writes Zeuthen, "are able to give the correct concept of nature. Each of these sciences regards nature from its side, but *philosophy's* goal is, if possible, to grasp nature itself according to its own essence, thus also to understand *the possibility of these different sides*."[24]

The unity between theology and natural science should be won again. But in order to realize this program, theology must be grounded philosophically or scientifically, for a conception "which *only* recognizes the supersensible's existence based on a divine revelation as an *external fact*, stands in a *scientific* sense on equal footing with materialism."[25] It is not sufficient to claim that both the revealed and the material appear as inexplicable facts: both must, to use an expression from Schelling, be given an *a priori* construction.

Zeuthen was neither an original nor a clear thinker, but he is an interesting figure in nineteenth-century Danish history of ideas because he, as a young person at a very early period distanced himself from Hegelianism, and, when he became older, based on Schelling's theistically colored positive philosophy, attempted to build bridges between the emerging natural sciences, on the one hand, and theology, on the other, that is, to unite faith and knowledge, which, among other things, came to expression in his polemic with Rasmus Nielsen. He was a late exponent of the attempts within nineteenth-century Danish theology to develop a scientific theology or—to use the age's designation—a speculative theology based on German idealism. Zeuthen could have made his own the words which served as introduction to a Danish translation of some sections of Schelling's *Philosophie der Offenbarung*: "What gives this main work in speculative theology significance for Christian theology is the definite recognition of Christianity as a given historical reality, the definite recognition of the task of speculation; to bring to understanding the object of Christianity as it appears."[26] No mediation was possible between Kierkegaard's view of Christianity and Zeuthen's and—as will be clear later—not even the possibility of an objective negotiation between them.

II.

In 1831 Zeuthen published a short work with the title *Something about Philosophy and its Cultivation partly with Respect to Denmark*,[27] in which he defended philosophy against the charge of being unscholarly due to the fact that there were so many different philosophical systems and they were often so difficult to

[23] Frederik Ludvig Zeuthen, *Philosophiske Afhandlinger til Orientering i den schellingske Verdensbetragtning*, Copenhagen: Fr. Wöldike 1860.

[24] Ibid., pp. V–VI.

[25] Ibid., p. 10, note.

[26] "Aabenbaringens Philosophi. Af F.W.J.v, Schelling," *Nyt Tidsskrift for udenlandsk theologisk Litteratur*, ed. by H.N. Clausen, vol. 7, 1859, p. 417.

[27] Frederik Ludvig Zeuthen, *Noget om Philosophien og dens Dyrkelse, tildeels med Hensyn paa Danmark*, Copenhagen: J.D. Quist 1831.

understand. He answered the first criticism by pointing out that the subject matter of philosophy is the inner essence of things and the supersensible actuality, which one can approach in numerous ways. Philosophy only achieves its completion when all possible views have been taken into account. Every philosophical system thus has its relative justification and validity, and the "more important philosophical systems" may therefore be regarded as

> moments in the development of the human spirit....Thus it is the duty of every later philosophical system to take into account the previous ones so that one sees them in their validity, which must be granted to them, although the absolute validity is denied them.... Therefore a complete philosophical system can only be regarded as the ideal goal of the *efforts* of philosophers through all ages.[28]

Zeuthen must also reject the second criticism about the incomprehensibility of philosophy. To occupy oneself with philosophy presupposes a "philosophical spirit," "acuity of the understanding and strength over the vague abilities of representation," a marked "philosophical talent" and a special education, and is not something for the common man.[29] This almost sounds like an attempt at a self-characterization! What appears as the incomprehensibility of philosophy is due to the person's lack of background and is therefore, above all, a subjective matter. The common man approaches the supersensible actuality through religion, whereas the scholarly occupation with the highest things is the office of philosophy. Throughout his entire authorship, Zeuthen maintains the idea of theology being founded in philosophy.

Although some of Zeuthen's viewpoints sound Hegelian, here as everywhere in his works it is Schelling and Steffens and their doctrine of life as something overarching, which are his true sources of inspiration: "If the philosopher is to fathom life's meaning, the riddle of existence, then he must known life and existence in their fullness; hence he has experienced what life is and what life gives; but such experience is essentially in feeling."[30] The riddle of existence can only be solved by someone who fully knows life as it is: "But just as (according to Schelling) nature is like a humble and quiet beauty, which does not parade her charms, so also in life what is most significant and for thought most attractive is not to be found on the surface with accidental attention and with a fleeting glance."[31] The task of philosophy is to penetrate down into the first ground of things and to reach what is highest and what is most primary, namely, the divine.

The constellation of problems that Zeuthen treats in his next short book, *On the Moral Independence of Man. A Philosophical Enquiry* from 1832,[32] was a variant of Schelling's in *Philosophische Untersuchungen über das Wesen der menschlichen Freiheit* (1809), namely, the question of how the human being's moral independence, that is, his freedom, is compatible with the view that his actions as

---

28 Ibid., pp. 8–9.

29 Ibid., pp. 17–18.

30 Ibid., p. 18.

31 Ibid., p. 31.

32 Frederik Ludvig Zeuthen, *Menneskets moralske Selvstændighed. Et philosophisk Forsøg*, Copenhagen: C.A. Reitzel 1832.

a moral being are determined by the wish to realize what is morally good, that is, with his dependence on this. On the one hand, morality presupposes that man is free and acts independently, but, on the other hand, in his actions he is subordinate to the commands of the almighty, that is, the divine. To act morally man must act freely, but at the same time act with a view toward realizing the universal. Zeuthen solved the problem in the same way that Kant, Schelling and Hegel had done, that is, by uniting the opposites, independence (freedom) and dependence (necessity):

> Moral independence is opposed to moral dependence, but the two relations must, for just this reason, be united. Since one essentially, with respect to oneself, is independent, so that the good which one has chosen intentionally, penetrates without pushing out other goods, so that man is morally dependent, desiring these.[33]

Later in the work the theological overtones come out more sharply. To be morally independent, that is, to be subordinate to oneself and not to outside forces and inner sensible impulses, "is a condition in man or a relation between that by which man is moved and driven such that the life of man thereby possesses a firmness, unity and peace, and this can only be possible by means of an *absolute submission to the almighty*,"[34] that is, in a destruction of selfishness. To subordinate oneself to the almighty or God is an expression of trust, and moral independence, Zeuthen can conclude, "is grounded in the absolute trust in God." Thus founded, it appears as a "continued objectifying of the manifold (that is, a destruction of egoism) [and] implies or, more correctly, *is* in itself the true inner *peace*. The absolute self [sc. the independent self or person] has founded the absolute."[35] The person is, as Schelling said in his *Freiheitsschrift*, a spiritualization of selfishness, that is, of sensuality and the instincts.

In 1833 Zeuthen defended a treatise with the title *On the Concept of Humility and Especially the Philosophical Kind* for the degree of Magister in philosophy (which was later regarded as a doctoral degree).[36] In this work he accused Hegelianism of philosophical immodesty because it did not take its point of departure in Christianity or in what he calls "the religious tradition" but, by constrast, lets thinking alone be philosophy's presuppositionless tool. The task of philosophy is, according to Zeuthen, to investigate the religious concepts and truths of faith and give an account of their agreement with other concepts and with knowledge achieved in other ways.[37] Philosophy is therefore not presuppositionless but must take its point of departure in the religious tradition. Zeuthen's attack on Hegel was first and foremost occasioned by Johan Ludvig Heiberg's *On the Significance of Philosophy for the Present Age* and evoked a sharp and dismissive response from Heiberg, who in satirical terms

---

33 Ibid., p. 23.

34 Ibid., p. 43.

35 Ibid., p. 101.

36 Frederik Ludvig Zeuthen, *De notione modestiae inprimis philosophicae*, Copenhagen: J.D. Quist 1833.

37 Ibid., p. 75.

denies that his young attacker has any ability for philosophical thinking or any adequate philosophical insight.[38]

As mentioned above, it was only after the publication of Schelling's lectures on the philosophy of revelation (*Philosophie der Offenbarung*, 1854), that Zeuthen attained a philosophical clarification. The result was his aforementioned *Philosophical Treatises for an Orientation in the Schellingian World-View* (1860), which contains a series of often very difficult treatises, in which Zeuthen, usually without any explanation, treats a series of Schellingian themes such as the criticism of Hegel for failing to provide a transition between thought and being, and the positive philosophy's point of departure in what is or what exists and not—as in Hegel—in the concept of "being" (*Sein*). Zeuthen's general goal was to show that in both philosophy and the natural sciences it is, as he called it, "the first thinkable thing," which is equivalent with God, which is thus the point of departure in both philosophy and natural science. He wrote:

> Many outstanding men of science, for example, the natural scientist, belong to the most noble-minded human beings, but he does not recognize the revelation. He can seem to be Christian according to his heart, but according to his confession or his conscious faith he is not. And why not? Because according to the ideas he has of Christianity and what he must otherwise know to be the eternal truth, there exists a real contradiction between the two.[39]

But the contradiction is only apparent. In order to show that not only the theologian but also the natural scientist must presuppose something divine, Zeuthen does not posit the propositions and principles of science vis-à-vis those of theology, but is satisfied to regard what must be the *a priori* presupposition for making any statement at all, that is, for thought in its coming into existence. His further analysis is a summary of one of the main thoughts in Schelling's *Philosophie der Offenbarung*, namely, that the existing (*das Seiende*) as source of its existence presupposes a will to produce, which, on the one hand, is pure potentiality, and on the other, is also itself an existing (*ein Seiend*). Schelling called this first principle "pure being" or "God."[40]

In order that something can be determined as existing (*seiend*), a number of possible predicates must be present, which can be ascribed to it and which delimit what it can be. When the knowing subject makes a judgment, he gives a possible predicate reality at the same time as he himself receives content. The subject is thus the first, that is, a presupposition for any thought at all; but it is also what in a dialectical manner appears in the process of knowing. Accordingly, nature is limited

---

38 Heiberg, *Prosaiske Skrifter*, vol. 1, pp. 453–60. Heiberg's response originally appeared in the newspaper *Dagen*, no. 100, 1833. (English translation: "On Occasion of Magister Zeuthen's so-called Elucidations," in *Heiberg's On the Significance of Philosophy for the Present Age and Other Texts*, pp. 133–83.)

39 Frederik Ludvig Zeuthen, *Philosophiske Afhandlinger til Orientering i den schellingske Verdensbetragtning*, p. 37.

40 See lecture 10 in *Philosophie der Offenbarung*, in *Schellings Werke, nach der Originalen Ausgabe in neuer Anordnung*, vols. 1–13, ed. by Manfred Schröter, Munich: Beck 1954–66, supplemental volume 6, pp. 198–222.

by what can be nature, that is, by the sum total of the possible characteristics of objects of nature. Zeuthen calls the sum total of these possibilities, in agreement with Schelling, "the pure capability" or "the subject." "We cannot make nature as a whole the object of thought, of concept, without claiming the existence of a mediating thought, namely, the subject, which *can be* nature and, for thought, is thus *prius naturae* [a presupposition of nature]."[41] This presupposition of nature or of the existing (*das Seiende*) is what Schelling had called the "pure This" or the necessarily existing "impossibility" and the necessarily existing "Original Subject," that is, God.[42] It follows from this that natural science, in its conceiving of nature, must presuppose the divine. Against the background of this conception, Zeuthen must of course reject Rasmus Nielsen's solution to the problem of the relation between faith and knowledge.

III.

In 1855—during Kierkegaard's attack on the Danish Church and its officials—Zeuthen published a treatise with the title "Spirit and Letter,"[43] in which he found occasion in a few places to attack Kierkegaard. Here he charges him with clinging "to the scripture's individuals letters." Referring to Kierkegaard's statement in *For Self-Examination. Recommended to the Present Age* (1851) that it is, for example, easy to understand the scriptural passages in which it is said that one must give one's property to the poor (Matthew 19:21),[44] for this should be taken literally, Zeuthen writes:

> He [sc. Kierkegaard] has, above all in his most recent publication, distorted Christianity by making primary what in any case can only be the secondary, the consequential, by giving *sufferings* the place which can only be ascribed to *faith*. A justice of sufferings is like a justice of deeds.[45]

With the final words here he refers to the Roman Church's doctrine of the significance of good deeds for redemption.

Zeuthen does not deny that it could be justified that Kierkegaard attacked the church's officials for worldliness, but he could of course not agree with Kierkegaard that, from a Christian point of view, only he who "casts the world from himself and lets himself stand as cast away by the world," is a true Christian. Just like "the masses," Kierkegaard looks at what is striking and outer and not at what is inner. Zeuthen continues:

41 Zeuthen, *Philosophiske Afhandlinger*, p. 54.

42 Ibid., pp. 65–6.

43 Frederik Ludvig Zeuthen, "Aand og Bogstav," in *Ugeskrift for den evangeliske Kirke i Danmark*, vol. 5, 1855, [1] pp. 7–14 (January 5, 1855); "Indledning," [2] pp. 89–108 (January 26, 1855); "Om Bogstavtroen og den levende Tro," [3] pp. 169–83 (February 16, 1855); "Om Bogstavet som Betingelse for Indsigt i Christendommens Aand," [4] pp. 329–52 (April 20, 1855); "Forholdet mellem Loven (το γραμμα) og Evangelium (Aanden, som levendegjør)."

44 *SV1* XII, 323 / *JFY*, 34–5.

45 Zeuthen, "Aand og Bogstav," p. 90.

> But what is terribly unreasonable in K.'s attack is that he allows himself to do what only Our Lord can do since he demands of a witness to the truth that he *really* should give away his earthly possessions. If I could make myself a witness to the truth, in accordance with K.'s demand, then I could not in good conscience do so since God's creation is not to be despised. This must *be demanded* by God if it should happen.[46]

Zeuthen thus criticizes Kierkegaard for speaking on behalf of God, although he seems to want to make the appearance of walking the path of humility. But this is only appearance since Kierkegaard confuses humility and physical mortification—in which there can be not just a little arrogance—with true Christian humility.[47] For this reason, Kierkegaard has become "an unusual proof of how it is not the spirit which makes one spiritual, but only what makes one humble and righteous and sober, which understands how to use the letter of the scriptures in order, through it, to find or show the spirit of Christianity and its demands."[48]

Kierkegaard responded to Zeuthen briefly and harshly in *Fædrelandet* on May 15, 1855. It is, in Kierkegaard's view, inane to believe that he does not know what can be said in defense of the existing order and its Christianity. In the *Concluding Unscientific Postscript* Johannes Climacus said what can be said in defense of this, and he looked to see "whether any of my contemporaries here in the country can do it better."[49] And he is not really in the mood to repeat the lesson for someone who wants to condescendingly teach him about what he himself has treated and put behind himself.

Throughout the summer of 1855 Zeuthen published three short pieces aimed against Kierkegaard. The title was *Polemical Papers against Dr. Søren Kierkegaard*.[50] Zeuthen never received a response to his indictment, but in Kierkegaard's posthumous papers there is a draft of a response.[51] In the autumn Kierkegaard also seems to have considered publishing a few pieces in which he intended to give Zeuthen a harsh treatment.[52]

Zeuthen published his polemical papers with the motto, "We cannot do anything against the truth, but only for the truth. 2 Cor. 13:8." In spite of their polemical nature, the pieces contain some remarks worth noting.

Against Kierkegaard's demand that one take the command to "abandon *everything* and follow Jesus" wholly literally, Zeuthen remarks in the first piece that it is wholly

---

46 Ibid., p. 179.

47 Ibid., p. 342.

48 Ibid., p. 183.

49 *SV1*, XIV, 76 / *M*, 66.

50 Frederik Ludvig Zeuthen, *Polemiske Blade imod Dr. Søren Kierkegaard*, nos. 1–3, Copenhagen: Gyldendalske Forlag 1855. (This entry is given as follows in the Rohde catalogue: "Et Bundt Smaaskifter og Blade indeholdende Artikler og Polemik imod Dr. S. Kierkegaard, af [J.] V[ictor]. Bloch, [F.L.B.] Zeuthen, [H.L.] Martensen, [J.] Paludan-Müller, [C.H.] Thura[h], m. Flere." Cf. *ASKB* 2190.)

51 *Pap.* XI–3 B 142 / *M*, Supplement, pp. 530–5.

52 *Pap.* XI–3 B 168, pp. 280–1 / *M*, Supplement, pp. 596–8. *Pap.* XI–3 B 179, p. 298 / *M*, Supplement, p. 563. *Pap.* XI–3 B 192 / *M*, Supplement, pp. 576–7.

insufficient to demand the imitation of Christ only as an outward abandoning of the world. "As far as I know," writes Zeuthen,

> even if all priests would abandon everything, but were tortured by longing for everything, then they would not have abandoned everything as a Christian should do. Therefore, as long as one cannot bring about a change from *within* by evoking a new desire and a new love, then one will accomplish nothing Christian in this direction.[53]

According to Zeuthen, Kierkegaard in his struggle against the official Christendom had thrown out to the public his "either/or": either Christian or human being. But the mistake is that Kierkegaard

> *without further ado* wants to have the abstract, that which is true and correct in the idea, applied to actuality, as if there were not with our life in the world, as human beings, a both/and, given and determined ahead of time by God, if one will, a divine "also"..., that is, a respect for the world and its given condition with governance to bring forth the idea.[54]

The task for the Christian is to unite the idea, which here must be understood as the ideal, with actuality. Kierkegaard wants just the opposite. Either, as Zeuthen later writes, the consequence of Kierkegaard's conception of Christianity is absurd, namely, that "Christ became a human being in order that we should cease to be human beings in order to reveal how it would be to live in even the most profitable activity without seeking suffering, the goal of which is death and to be lost."[55]

In his second piece Zeuthen points out that with Kierkegaard's emphasis on the Christian as the individual, he fails to appreciate the life of the religious community. Expressed polemically, he says, "Our Father," is reduced in Kierkegaard, to "my Father."[56] Zeuthen also emphasizes that Kierkegaard's Christianity is a polemical Christianity, which is only characterized negatively as standing in opposition to the official Christianity.

In the third piece, Zeuthen makes the historically correct observation or rather prediction that Kierkegaard, with his criticism of the official Christianity, does a service for the impious by

> strengthening the souls with a proclivity to infidelity in their Christian infidelity, in their rejection of *all Christianity*. "Yes," they say, "that is what we have thought all along, as Dr. K. has clearly presented it by emphasizing the demands of self-hatred and suffering, etc. as the main demand, something so unnatural and inhuman that no reasonable person can accept it."[57]

This is precisely what happened. With his energetic criticism of the official Christianity, Kierkegaard, ironically, played a role in leading Danish intellectual life

---

53 Zeuthen, *Polemiske Blade imod Dr. Søren Kierkegaard*, no. 1, pp. 14–15.

54 Ibid., p. 16.

55 Zeuthen, *Polemiske Blade imod Dr. Søren Kierkegaard*, no. 3, p. 11.

56 Zeuthen, *Polemiske Blade imod Dr. Søren Kierkegaard*, no. 2, p. 4.

57 Zeuthen, *Polemiske Blade imod Dr. Søren Kierkegaard*, no. 3, p. 3.

into the age of positivism. Two of the leading cultural personalities in the following epoch, the literary critic Georg Brandes and the professor of philosophy Harald Høffding had both, as young men, sought to live up to the Kierkegaardian demands, but had been forced to reject them, as inhuman and as a failure to appreciate life and its demands.

The main content of the third piece is the juxtaposition of the gospel of suffering, which Zeuthen thinks Kierkegaard is the spokesman for, and the gospel of love, which Zeuthen regards as being the true Christian gospel. Zeuthen thinks it cannot be suffering which is the essential thing but, by contrast, the truth for the sake of which suffering can come upon one. And perhaps this truth can be promoted by other means than by suffering. In addition to this, "love of truth seeks the promotion of truth, the craving for suffering for the truth seeks egoistically its own and not the truth or what belongs to truth or what serves it best."[58] On the whole, it is true that death is the highest suffering but not the highest truth.

Zeuthen concludes his treatise against Kierkegaard by again underscoring that he, with this gospel of suffering, approaches the Roman Church's doctrine of good works: "In his writings [sc. Kierkegaard's] we are referred to sufferings with which the human being also wants to achieve his *own* justification, which does not give to God what is God's, and does not recognize God's compassionate love."[59] To want suffering is egoistically to want one's own and not humbly to receive God's love and mercy.

Kierkegaard's draft of a response to Zeuthen's criticism was exclusively polemical and is especially an expression of his irritation at an insisting, insignificant and mediocre person who persists and only waits for "the opportunity to do something."[60] He is especially sarcastic about the motto, Zeuthen had chosen:

> Dr. Z's motto is: "We can do nothing against the truth, but for the truth"—quite as could be expected; indeed, could mediocrity ever write a polemical religious article without this motto, which very likely is supposed to conceal the truth that mediocrity can do nothing either for or against the truth.[61]

The whole thing in Kierkegaard ends in a joke:

> If only he does not go ahead and change the motto, then I ask no more. That is, I regard it as appropriate that it be practiced continually, and therefore that "we can do nothing" be printed each time on the title page, to which one can then reply as Frederik VI is supposed to have replied to someone who, kneeling before him, received the ennobling shoulder-strike and recited the formula, "I am unworthy, your Majesty": "Yes, to be sure, we know that."[62]

Thus ended the polemic between Kierkegaard and Zeuthen.

---

58 Ibid., p. 9.

59 Ibid., p. 20.

60 *Pap*. XI–3 B 142, p. 224 / *M*, Supplement, p. 531.

61 *Pap*. XI–3 B 142, p. 225 / *M*, Supplement, p. 532.

62 *Pap*. XI–3 B 192 / *M*, Supplement, pp. 576–7; and *Pap*. XI–3 B 168, p. 281 / *M*, Supplement, p. 598.

At the auction of Kierkegaard's library in April 1856, Zeuthen bought around 30 volumes and was thus one of the largest of the registered private buyers. His purchases covered a large disciplinary spectrum from Kierkegaard's Hebrew Bible (*ASKB* 1), to hymn books (*ASKB* 204–207) and Mynster's sermons (*ASKB* 228), to a five-volume work on the history of the female sex (*ASKB* 664–667) and a German edition in seven volumes of Montaigne's *Essais* (*ASKB* 681–687). His interests were many-sided.

In one of his memoirs Zeuthen writes that the correspondence with Kierkegaard from 1848—from which Zeuthen quotes Kierkegaard's letter—shows that the relation between them had not always been as it was then:

> ...there was a one-sidedness which in the middle of the richness of thought and richness of spirit always more and more appeared in his works; when this one-sidedness took control and became absolute toward the end of his life (in *The Moment*), and became a truly, albeit constant spiritual disease, then *every* pastor, for him, "wore a long garment and shrouded the essence of nonsense." Then I wrote against him, among other things, *Polemiske Blade* in 3 issues.[63]

This was Zeuthen's last word about Kierkegaard. In spite of everything, it shows a greater generosity than what Kierkegaard had been able to show for his opponent.

Translated by Jon Stewart

63 Zeuthen, *Et Par Aar af mit Liv*, p. 22, note.

Bibliography

I. Zeuthen's Works in The Auction Catalogue *of Kierkegaard's Library*

Om den christelige Tro i dens Betydning for Verdenshistorien. Et Forsøg, Copenhagen: Gyldendal 1838 (*ASKB* 259).

"Berigtigelse," *Dansk Kirketidende*, vols. 1–8, ed. by C. J. Brandt and R.Th. Fenger, Copenhagen: C.A. Reitzel 1845–53, vol. 2, no. 103, columns 809–10 (*ASKB* 321–325).

"Et Par Ord i Anledning af Conventstriden," *Dansk Kirketidende*, vol. 3, no. 141, 1848, columns 602–4 (*ASKB* 321-325).

Humanitet betragtet fra et christeligt Standpunkt, med stadigt Hensyn til den nærværende Tid, Copenhagen: Gyldendal 1846 (*ASKB* 915).

Om Ydmyghed. En Afhandling, Copenhagen: Gyldendal 1852 (*ASKB* 916).

Polemiske Blade imod Dr. Søren Kierkegaard, nos. 1–3, Copenhagen: Gyldendalske Forlag 1855 (Cf. *ASKB* 2190).

The Minutes of speeches made by Zeuthen:

—— "Roskilde Præstecovent. Mødet i Ringsted d. 20de Octbr. 1847" [the minutes of the pastoral meeting on October 20, 1847], *Dansk Kirketidende*, vol. 3, nos. 114–15, 1847 [for the minutes of Zeuthen's speech], see columns 145–69.

II. Works in The Auction Catalogue *of Kierkegaard's Library that Discuss Zeuthen*

Anonymous, [Review of] "*Betragtninger over Statens Forhold til Kirken*," *Dansk Kirketidende*, vol. 4, no. 175, 1849, columns 293–5 (*ASKB* 321–325).

Birkedal, Vilhelm, "Mag. Zeuthens Foredrag ved Roeskilde Konvent," *Dansk Kirketidende*, vol. 3, no. 129, 1848, columns 393–408 and vol. 3, no. 130, 1848, columns 409–24 (*ASKB* 321–325).

Brandt, C., [Review of] "Mag. L. Zeuthen. *Humanitet, betragtet fra et christeligt Standpunkt, med stadigt Hensyn til den nærværende Tid*," *Dansk Kirketidende*, vol. 2, no. 58, 1846, columns 94–6 (*ASKB* 321–325).

Martensen, Hans Lassen, *Den christelige Dogmatik*, Copenhagen: C.A. Reitzel 1849, p. 166, note (*ASKB* 653).

[Møller, Poul Martin], "Recension af: *Noget om Philosophien og dens Dyrkelse, tildeels med Hensyn paa Danmark*. Af L. Zeuthen, Candidat i Theologien og Alumnus paa Borchs Collegium. Kbhavn 1831," in *Efterladte Skrifter af Poul M. Møller*, vols. 1–3, ed. by Christian Winther, F.C. Olsen, and Christen Thaarup, Copenhagen: C.A. Reitzel 1839–43, vol. 2, pp. 69–73 (*ASKB* 1574–1576).

Fenger, J.F., "Om Roeskilde Convent i Aaret 1847," *Dansk Kirketidende*, vol. 3, no. 134, 1848, pp. 483–8 (*ASKB* 321–325).

Fenger, R. Th. and C.J. Brandt, "Erklæring fra Udgiverne," *Dansk Kirketidende*, vol. 3, no. 131, 1848, pp. 439–40 (*ASKB* 321–325).

III. Secondary Literature on Kierkegaard's Relation to Zeuthen

Carl Henrik Koch, *Den danske idealisme 1800–1880*, Copenhagen: Gyldendal 2004, pp. 161–73.

Magnussen, Rikard, "F.L.B. Zeuthen og Søren Kierkegaard," in his *Søren Kierkegaard set udefra*, Copenhagen: Ejnar Munksgaard 1942, pp. 105–7.

Index of Persons

Index of Subjects